AUDIENCES and INTENTIONS

A Book of Arguments

THIRD EDITION

Nancy Mason Bradbury

Smith College

Arthur Quinn

University of California, Berkeley

Allyn and Bacon

Boston   London   Toronto   Sydney   Tokyo   Singapore

Vice President: Eben W. Ludlow
Editorial Assistant: Liz Egan
Marketing Manager: Lisa Kimball
Production Administrator: Rowena Dores
Editorial-Production Service: Lauren Green Shafer
Cover Administrator: Linda Knowles
Composition Buyer: Linda Cox
Manufacturing Buyer: Megan Cochran

Library of Congress Cataloging-in-Publication Data

Audiences and intentions : a book of arguments / [edited by] Nancy
    Mason Bradbury, Arthur Quinn. — 3rd ed.
        p.   cm.
    Includes bibliographical references (p.) and index.
    ISBN 0-205-26174-4
    1. College readers.   2. Persuasion (Rhetoric)   3. English
language—Rhetoric.   I. Bradbury, Nancy M.   II. Quinn, Arthur.
PE1417.A84   1997
808'.0427—dc21   96–48203
                                                                          CIP

Credits

EDWARD ABBEY, "The Damnation of a Canyon." From *Beyond the Wall* by Edward Abbey. Copyright © 1971, 1976, 1977, 1979, 1984 by Edward Abbey. Reprinted by permission of Henry Holt and Co., Inc.
GORDON ALLPORT, *The Nature of Prejudice, 25th Anniversary Edition,* © 1979 by Addison-Wesley Publishing Company, Inc. Reprinted by permission of Addison-Wesley Publishing Company, Inc.

Credits continued on page 600, which constitutes an extension of the copyright page.

Printed in the United States of America

10 9 8 7 6 5 4 3 2 1   99 98 97 96

Contents

Preaching to the Converted: A Common Intention   96

Reacting and Writing   109

Additional Readings   110

Three Essays on Education

Six Essays on the Arts   132

4 ARGUMENT'S ETHICAL DIMENSION 280

Reacting and Writing 545

IV. Politics, Principles, and Practicalities 546

Preface

CHANGES IN THE THIRD EDITION

In preparing the new edition of *Audiences and Intentions: A Book of Arguments,* we have followed the advice of *our* audience. Over the past few years, we have talked to numerous teachers and students who have used this book. Many had perceptive suggestions for improving it, and this new edition benefits from their collective wisdom.

As requested, we have added more commentary on the selections. We have added new readings to extend the book's usefulness in critical thinking courses. In response to suggestions by readers, we reworked the section on *ethos* in Chapter 3. While this edition includes more contemporary and cross-cultural selections, it retains the wealth of classical arguments that sets our reader apart from those devoted almost exclusively to recent writings. Each of the symposia in Chapter 5 has been updated. In short, we think we have made this a better work by attending to what our readers had to say about it, thus making them our collaborators.

THE APPROACH

We wrote this book because we needed it ourselves. Over the years we had become convinced that training in argument offers student writers help where they most need it: in developing a clear sense of audience and purpose. What we needed for our own courses was a collection of compact and challenging arguments that our students could analyze and write about. We also needed an emphasis different from that of the best readers available to us. While many composition texts present argument as a variation on exposition, we prefer to treat exposition and narration as kinds of arguments. Finally, we wanted a book that would introduce students to the basic concepts of argument but would not restrict its users to any particular pedagogical method.

Studying argument has taught us a healthy respect for intellectual pluralism. There are many ways to skin a cat and many ways to fish in troubled waters. Most teachers of argument we know—ourselves included—are emphatically eclectic and given to improvisation. The last thing we wanted was a reader that tied our hands. We hope that this book will help teachers like our-selves without getting in their way. These readings can be used either with another textbook that suits the teacher's pedagogical preferences or as a depar-ture point for an approach of the teacher's own. We designed the collection to be compatible with any rhetorical method for teaching writing—that is, any method that regards a piece of writing as a communication whereby the author attempts to bring about some change in the audience's ideas or attitudes.

We do not see argument as a form of gladiatorial combat in which the object is to silence the opponent by means of a symbolic beheading. Argument for us is not a blood sport. But neither is it an entirely bloodless activity, one in which nothing human is at stake. We do not think of argument as the dreary task of striking a posture toward some issue by filling empty paragraphs with musty pros and cons. From our point of view, the first method errs by charac-terizing the audience as the arguer's prey; the second errs by addressing an audience so abstract as to be meaningless. Thus we should perhaps say that the book is compatible with any rhetorical approach that takes seriously the idea that the audience should play a positive and essential role in shaping the argument.

The audiences that interest us most exist somewhere between the angelic choirs and the survival of the fittest. A thoughtfully defined audience can play an invigorating role by becoming a partner in the investigation, a participant in a developing dialogue. As an author can be more persuasive by tailoring an argument to a particular audience, so the very process of adjusting to the right audience can help writers discover where their real convictions lie. Taking alternative viewpoints seriously will always improve the presentation of an argument, but it can also transform the very points the arguer makes. Writing can then become a process of discovery, a way of generating knowledge about the world and about ourselves.

THE READINGS

The selections include arguments that fail disastrously as well as those that suc-ceed and arguments that were swindles or seductions in disguise as well as those of noble intent. If we have realized *our* intention, readers should find little to support the deadening notion that the argument is over when the requisite number of pros and cons (or the minimum page limit) has been reached. While some of the readings are familiar from the "Argument and Persuasion" sections of the best known readers, many have never before been anthologized for writ-ing students. In particular, we have found some of the most interesting and use-ful arguments within plays, novels, and histories. Arguments in these selections are often addressed to an audience within the text. In these cases, the dialogue has already begun when the reader arrives.

Instead of simply including Lincoln's Gettysburg Address, for instance, we give a sampling of the many and conflicting contemporary reactions to the speech as compiled by Carl Sandburg in his biography of Lincoln. These reactions ranged from those who proclaimed it "the right thing in the right place, and a perfect thing in every respect" to those who thought it an embarrassment, a permanent blemish on Lincoln's record. (Lincoln himself seemed inclined toward the latter view.)

When set in context, even the most venerated classical texts need not silence students (whether by awe or by apathy). Instead, these works should encourage students to add their own voices to the ongoing conversation. One of the reasons for our including classical texts is their compelling relevance to the present. What does Thucydides have to contribute to a discussion of American politics? What do *Medea* and *Pride and Prejudice* have to add to a discussion of contemporary society? The answers are far from obvious, and that is what makes them so interesting. In addition, these answers should broaden the range of possible responses to the many very recent works also included here.

THE ORGANIZATION

The readings in this book are intended to serve a dual function in helping students to master argument. All the readings can themselves serve as subjects for analysis: students can argue orally or in writing about the selection's audience, intention, rhetorical tools employed, and the ethical problems raised by the means of persuasion. Many selections also introduce issues on which the students can take positions. In our own writing courses, we first concentrate on analyzing (orally and in writing) the arguments of others and then move to constructing independent arguments on issues raised by the readings. Thus the first four chapters of *Audiences and Intentions* stress critical reading, thinking, and writing. Each one introduces a fundamental concept and asks the students to analyze the chapter's readings with that concept in mind. We include additional readings at the end of Chapters 1–3, introduced with a minimum of commentary so that students can work on fresh materials without our biases. Then, in the last chapter, we invite the student writer to take part in four dialogues about issues of long-standing concern.

We should emphasize, however, that opportunities for both analysis and independent argument are present throughout the book, and our questions try to stimulate both. A teacher may prefer to integrate the two activities throughout or to reorder the selections. For example, students can take independent positions on arguments such as Gould's or King's in Chapter 1, and they can analyze or detail the workings of any of the arguments in the later chapters.

The four symposia in Chapter 5 show how a central issue can generate a variety of viewpoints. In addition to the usual tactic of setting one opinion against another in direct debate, we have combined readings that engage one another in more complicated ways—by starting from different assumptions and by using different techniques or even different forms of discourse to try to solve the same problems. Because we use arguments from widely different time periods, we hope that our readers will discover both continuity and change in the conventions of argument in Western culture. We also hope that our readers will notice how tenacious certain problems are, and how the same issues engage the old voices of classic texts as well as the new voices of emerging groups.

Throughout the book, we have included questions for thought, discussion, and writing, both woven into our introductions and separately in sections labeled "Reacting and Writing." Rather than giving formal assignments, we try to help students to develop topics of their own. Thus we phrase our ideas as suggestions: "You might do this; you could try that." Teachers who want to offer more specific guidance can select an appropriate question or topic and add whatever additional instructions suit their needs. The *Instructor's Manual* also provides suggestions for how to use the readings and offers ideas for syllabus design.

ACKNOWLEDGMENTS

We wish to thank the staff at Allyn and Bacon for their help in putting together this book. We are very grateful to Barbara Heinssen at Macmillan for her support and enthusiasm through two editions and to Eben Ludlow, Liz Egan, and Lauren Green Shafer of Allyn and Bacon for guidance through the third. We thank Rebecca Kidd for her work with the permissions and for being an invaluable ally. Many reviewers have offered useful suggestions through the long history of the project—particularly memorable to us was the anonymous early reader self-identified as from the Corn Belt who understood what we were trying to do before it was entirely clear to us. We would also like to acknowledge the valuable comments, criticisms, and suggestions of Frederick J. Antczak, University of Iowa; Grant Boswell, Brigham Young University; Eric Caine, Kings River Community College; Marvin Diogenes, University of Arizona; Laird Durley, Kings River Community College; Theresa Enos, University of Arizona; John T. Gage, University of Oregon; George Gopen, Duke University; Patricia Graves, Georgia State University; Christine Hult, Utah State University; Linda B. Knoblock, Paradise Valley Community College; Nancy Lowe, Pennsylvania State University; Jeanette P. Morgan, University of Houston; Patricia Roberts, University of North Carolina; Tim J. Saben, Portland Community College; Richard Tracz, Oakton Community College; J. Randall Woodland, University of Michigan; Linda Woodson, University of Texas, San Antonio; Richard J. Zbaracki, Iowa State University; and Brett Averett and her Honors English students at Westfield State College.

N.M.B.
A.Q.

A Note to the Reader

We designed *Audiences and Intentions* to provide teachers and students with some compact and challenging arguments. Our understanding of *argument* is very simple and very broad: we use this term to mean "any speech or piece of writing in which the author attempts to bring about some change in the listener's or reader's ideas or attitudes." If this definition seems to you to include nearly all the speech and writing you can think of—short of a dry cleaning bill or a baseball schedule—we won't argue. If you or your teacher develops a stricter definition, you will want to ask yourself which of the readings in this book fit that definition of argument.

You will quickly see that our readings are not model essays for you to imitate directly in your own writing. Some of our selections are in verse, some are old-fashioned in style and language, and many do not resemble in outward form the sort of essay that you are likely to produce in a classroom. What, then, do we envision as their role in your writing process? They are meant, first of all, to encourage the kind of active, critical reading that ultimately enriches your ability to write. In particular, gauging your own responses to arguments made by others will help you develop a subtle awareness of how audiences are likely to respond to you. And although many of the readings do not provide models for the form of your arguments, they do provide applications of the skills and techniques involved in creating them. You will need to grasp the underlying concepts in these arguments and apply them to an argument of your own created for an audience of your own, rather than trying to imitate in detail the form of some highly sophisticated piece of professional writing. As a final connection to your writing process, our questions frequently ask you for written responses. Your reactions to these questions might take the form of a writer's notebook entries, short exercises, or longer essays, depending on your instructor's plan for the course. Naturally the readings are also meant to provoke discussion—to allow you to compare argumentative strategies, to express your own opinions about the success or failure of a given piece, to agree or disagree with our analyses and those of your classmates—in short, to get you arguing.

We urge you to take up this book with a good, full-sized dictionary in the other hand. How do you pronounce "Thucydides"? Where is Peoria? What exactly do frequently used words like *text* or *context* or *concept* mean? What were the dates of the U.S. Civil War? A dictionary cannot inform you in depth about complex questions, but it can give you the small pieces of information that you need to read serious works with fuller understanding. We could have done this work for you, at least up to a point, but the arguments you will encounter in life (and in most other college courses) will generally not come with their people, places, events, and hard words identified in notes. We want you to prepare to meet those arguments.

Finally, it may be well to mention our choice to use a substantial number of arguments extracted from longer works. You may feel that you are at a disadvantage when you have not read the entire piece from which a selection is taken. There is no question that reading wholes is better than reading parts. If you are trying to learn something about the play *Julius Caesar* or about Shakespeare or drama or the Elizabethan period, you won't want to read our excerpt from the play, but the work in its entirety. If, however, you want to learn about how to construct an argument, then the advantages of taking rich, complex, and compact examples from longer works are many, as we hope you will discover. The brevity of our selections allows us to present a wide variety of arguments in a small space. We also encourage you to read more of those works that interest, anger, delight, or puzzle you. At the end of the book, you can find a list of further readings.

CHAPTER 1

The Concept of Audience

You already know how to argue. When you make and evaluate arguments, you don't need to start from scratch. Life has already taught you the elementary course.

This fact used to be brought home to us when we taught together a course on argumentative writing and critical thinking. Such courses were a scarce resource on our campus, and, whenever one was offered, the instructors could expect at least twice as many students as they could admit. On the first day, we would ask our prospective students for a brief sample of their writing. Most of them saw this as an opportunity to argue for a place in the course. Among the hundred or so paragraphs we would receive, we could find virtually every form of argument we would be teaching throughout the semester. Why, then, teach people things they already know?

We all do know how to argue but often only within a narrow range. For instance, we all know how to be persuasive, at least sometimes, with family and friends. But this knack for arguing usually works better in person than on paper and is difficult to apply to new situations.

Even people who have a natural gift for argument can profit from training. Some people do have this gift, just as some are natural athletes. A National Football League defensive back was once asked what he thought about while he was trying to cover a receiver with world-class speed zigzagging down the field. "If you have to think," he responded, "you don't belong in the NFL." Of course, he was right in a sense, but his answer was still misleading. That defensive back had spent much of the preceding week studying game films of the various receivers he was going to have to cover—and he had spent much of his life learning how to zigzag backward with his hands up. Moreover, at some point in his development, he probably came under the care of a good coach who perfected his natural technique and then drilled him mercilessly so he would not have to think in the clutch. An Olympic swimmer, to take another example,

1

may not be consciously thinking of anything at all as she paces herself in a competition. But chances are, when she first began to train, she was thinking something like "stroke, kick, breathe."

The purpose of studying argument systematically is to perfect natural technique and then to practice it until the right arguments for each situation spring to mind almost spontaneously. The way to do this is not to learn some grand theory, any more than every athlete needs to understand human physiology in order to run or to swim. An effective way to train is to analyze the argumentative practice of others, to understand it, and then to adapt it to your own circumstances. This book is designed to provide opportunities for such analyses and adaptations.

Like the Olympics, the study of argument by Western thinkers began with the ancient Greeks. According to legend, persuasive techniques were first formally taught in the Greek city-state of Syracuse in ancient Sicily. When the citizens of Syracuse overthrew the wealthy tyrants in power and established a democracy, this political and economic upheaval caused legal disputes to arise everywhere. Rather than hiring advocates as we do, the early Greeks pleaded their own cases in court. Citizens suddenly found themselves strongly motivated to improve their persuasive skills; the ability to construct articulate and compelling speeches could help them to defend their interests. The story is that two enterprising teachers named Corax and Tisias began to offer training in argumentation and thereby invented rhetoric, the systematic study of effective communication. Thus, rhetoric as a formal art allegedly began in a context that required direct, oral confrontation and immediate judgment.

Entranced with the power of the well-constructed argument, the ancient Greeks and later the Romans compiled a great body of practical advice on this topic, much of which is still found in writing textbooks today. The author of the most theoretical and sophisticated of these ancient works, Aristotle, thought of communication as involving three elements: the subject, the character of the speaker, and the nature of the audience. Greek and Roman teachers could rely on their pupils to regard all three elements as crucial. Because they generally delivered their arguments orally, speakers most often engaged their audiences in highly charged, face-to-face encounters. In the Roman Senate, for example, members of a particular faction frequently sat together, and sitting near an individual could indicate support for him. The greatest Roman orator, Cicero, once delivered a series of thundering speeches against his political enemy, Catiline. He mentions in one speech that the senators have taken his side in a literal, physical sense, leaving Catiline sitting entirely alone. The story dramatizes the point that an ancient speaker could scarcely fail to consider his audience.

YOUR PARTICULAR AUDIENCE

In the old, largely oral world of the Greeks and Romans, "consider your audience" generally meant "think about the preferences, beliefs, and preconceptions of the particular people listening to you and then adapt your speech accordingly." We can call this targeted group of real people the speaker's or writer's *particular audience.* The ancient philosopher Plato had such an understanding of audience in mind when he spoke of addressing complex speeches to complicated souls and simple speeches to simple souls. Aristotle acted on the same understanding of audience when he compiled information meant to help the orator decide how to address old people, young people, hot-headed people, and so on. Conducting a survey is one modern method of learning about the attitudes and beliefs of a particular audience.

In ordinary life, you consider your audience when you speak gently to someone who looks frightened, when you speak distinctly to someone not fluent in English, or when you speak forcefully to someone determined to ignore you. You abbreviate your arguments when your listener looks convinced; you elaborate on them when your listener looks skeptical. Up to a point, a writer can think of his or her audience in the same way that a speaker does. If you write to your family for help in meeting unexpected expenses, you say very much what you might say in person; you know, for example, that stressing the high cost of books will carry you much further than stressing the high cost of dinners at elegant restaurants. In this case, your family members are your particular audience, and you consider what you know of their values and priorities.

The audience problem in the following paragraph would be the same whether the author was speaking or writing:

> Banning "immoral" books is useless. Anyone can see that reading a story doesn't affect the way you actually act. How could anyone believe that you might somehow turn into an evil character that you read about? Plato's ridiculous argument makes about as much sense as saying that reading a cookbook can make you fat.

Because the writer argues against Plato's claim that literature has the power to affect our morals, it seems likely that he hopes to persuade those particular individuals who take the other side (those inclined to agree with Plato) and those not yet committed. But how can the members of an audience take seriously a writer who speaks so scornfully not only of their opinions but also of them as holders of those opinions? Even uncommitted readers are likely to be put off by the tone. Quite possibly the writer would not have made the same mistake if he had been speaking rather than writing. Face to face with an intelligent person who believed deeply in the argument under attack, he would be less likely to write off that argument as "ridiculous." Writing introduces new problems for the arguer at the same time that it opens up new opportunities.

YOUR IMPLIED AUDIENCE

The notion of a *particular audience,* of audience as a specific, targeted group in the real world, works for some written communications but not for all. If you have been urged to consider your audience for a piece of written work and found that advice puzzling, your uncertainty is well justified. The writer's audience is a complex idea, one that intrigues philosophers, literary critics, linguists, and psychologists. (It may occur to you that the audience for a spontaneous speech isn't all that simple a concept either, but our subject is the writer's audience.) To account for what goes on in the process of writing an argument, we need to distinguish a second type of audience, the audience suggested by the finished written argument—what we will call the *implied audience.*

The spread of writing alarmed many inhabitants of the old oral world because of the ease with which it could detach itself from the writer. No matter what particular audience a writer might have intended to address, almost anyone who can read can pick up a piece of writing. In his philosophical dialogue, *The Phaedrus,* Plato worried that "once a thing is put in writing, it rolls about all over the place, falling into the hands of those who have no concern with it just as easily as it falls into the hands of those who can truly understand it; it doesn't have any idea whom to address and whom to avoid." Writing "rolled about" in the ancient world because writers used scrolls instead of books, but the problem remains the same—the writer's text goes off on its own, with no one to supervise the reader's use of it.

Creating Your Audience

We are sometimes told that Shakespeare punctuated his serious plays with broadly comic scenes because he wished to appeal to rowdy theatergoers who might otherwise get bored and cause trouble. If there is any truth to this, it is another example of considering one's particular audience. By this theory, Shakespeare analyzed the interests of one segment of the people he assumed would attend his plays, and he adapted his work to accommodate those interests. But Shakespeare's work still speaks powerfully to modern reading and playgoing audiences, and we certainly cannot argue that he analyzed us specifically or adapted his work to accommodate our particular preconceptions. If we are not part of Shakespeare's particular audience, how then does his work continue to draw us in?

We can't fully answer this question, at least for geniuses whose works endure through the ages. But for most writers the process of considering one's particular audience might go something like this. You sit down to write out an idea that you first explored in a discussion. All through that discussion, an intelligent, thoughtful friend had disagreed with your position. She was open-minded, despite her firm views, and she listened intently to your points. She took you very seriously, but she did not agree with what you said. Thinking back over the discussion, you begin to see why she thinks so differently: she starts from different preconceptions; her underlying assumptions are not the same as yours. With this new understanding, you begin to think of points that would make your position clearer and more acceptable to someone with her assumptions and beliefs. You take her as your particular audience and begin to compose your written argument.

You find that writing to this classmate makes the paper easier to compose. But then a change occurs in your focus, almost without your realizing it. You find that as you get more absorbed in finding out what you really think, you are concentrating less on this individual classmate and more on her assumptions and beliefs. You broaden your notion of the audience to include others who think as this classmate does. In your written essay, especially after revision, your audience becomes even more open-minded, even better informed, even more thought provoking than the individual who disagreed with you in discussion. In your mind, you have moved from contemplating your particular audience to creating your implied one.

With practice, you will also find that taking the opposing viewpoints so seriously begins to affect the very point that you are making. Taking an audience seriously leads to more than simple acknowledgments such as "Some people might disagree with me because...." When your audience becomes a genuine part of your essay, a sort of partner in investigation, you will find that your essays are not only more persuasive but fuller and more thoughtful as well. If you discover that you have changed your mind quite radically in the process of considering the alternatives, so much the better. Argument is inquiry, not war. In an inquiry, changing your mind is learning, not surrender or retreat.

"Consider your audience" can thus mean something more than analyzing and assessing a particular audience—a target group in the real world—and then adapting your work to accommodate it. In fact, it might be more accurate to speak of "inventing," "defining," or "creating" your audience, rather than simply considering it, since the process bears some relation to the way that fiction writers create characters. They may draw inspiration from real people, but they don't hesitate to reshape those people to suit the needs of their written work. As you compose, you are creating an implicit portrait of the audience for your piece of writing. Anyone looking for such information in your paper should be able to draw some conclusions about the attitudes and beliefs of this audience. The portrait you create of your implied audience will not contain everything you know about the particular audience you originally intended to reach. This will allow your essay to "roll about" and attract readers from beyond your immediate experience.

Thus, whether you realize it or not, you are always creating a portrait of your audience within your text—not an explicit portrait, but one that a reader can detect by analyzing the assumptions you make without providing evidence, the opinions you believe that you must defend, the way that you present yourself, the authorities you use to support your points. If, for example, you argue that a political candidate should be elected simply because she will work to make abortion illegal, we have learned something about your implied audience—it must be opposed to abortion. If you argue that the candidate should be elected because she worked her own way through college and law school, we learn something about the qualities your implied audience values.

Learning about Audiences from Other Writers

What if you have never experienced anything remotely resembling this process we have described? What if you've tried writing to a real person but couldn't begin to incorporate that person into an essay? How can you introduce into your writing a rich and subtle awareness of audience?

You can learn more about audience in the same way that you have gained the persuasive abilities you already have: by experience and observation. But in addition to learning from the scattered, uneven examples gathered from daily life, you can learn from writers who have shrewdly considered their particular audiences and skillfully recreated them as implied audiences. You can also learn from examples of how the process can go wrong. Much of what writers know about how to present themselves to their audiences they learn from other writers. In working through the selections in this book, you will encounter a wide variety of arguments. You will gain most from them if you ask yourself in each case, "What is my response to this text?" and "What exactly in this text is causing me to respond in this way?" "Does this text seem to be written to someone with my knowledge, attitudes, and beliefs?" "If not, how would it have to be changed to include me in its audience? Or how would I have to change to be in its audience?" "How might one alter this text to appeal to different audiences?"

Our experience is that most subtle writers began as subtle readers. Of course, a reader is not necessarily the same as an implied audience. With writing out there rolling about on its own, readers can read anything they choose, even if they are not part of the implied audience. To grasp this distinction, imagine yourself thumbing through a magazine and glancing idly down the children's page. You see a piece on wolves, written simply enough for a six-year-old to understand. But you've always been interested in wolves and you read through the little article. You are a reader of the piece even though you are not part of its implied audience.

As a reader, what do you do about this problem? Probably one of three things. You might do your best to ignore the simple language, shutting out the inappropriateness of the presentation in order to extract the information the piece contains. Or you might do the opposite and concentrate on the presentation. You could think about the differences between yourself and the implied audience, about how the author has made the information accessible to an audience with a small vocabulary and little reading experience. Or, if the piece is vividly written, you might manage to enter imaginatively into the world of the essay, discovering wolves as a child might discover them.

Although the child's essay is a particularly dramatic example, such adjustments by readers are almost unavoidable. Your readers will frequently face choices similar to those that you made when you imagined reading the piece on wolves. They might find themselves doggedly ignoring an inappropriate presentation to get to the ideas or information in your piece. Or they might be fascinated by the inappropriateness of the presentation and spend their time noticing that they are decidedly not in the audience for this piece. Or, if you have succeeded in creating an appealing new role for the members of your implied audience, they might be willing to make any adjustments required to fit smoothly into that role. Becoming part of the implied audience for a work isn't necessarily a matter of pretending that you are simpler or less informed than you actually are. A written work can ask you to be more perceptive, more intuitive, or more broad-minded than you usually are. Often the best works create for themselves the most appealing audiences.

Some works, however, purposely imply very narrow audiences. How long, for instance, does it take to decide whether you are part of the audience for the book, *Parametric Integer Programming,* by Robert M. Nauss (Columbia, MO, 1979)? It begins

I. Introduction

   A parametric integer linear program (PILP) may be defined as a family of closely related integer linear programs (ILP). Parametric linear programming (PLP) theory is firmly entrenched, and a parametric capability is provided in most commercial linear programming (LP) packages. PILP, on the other hand, is a virgin field. This is natural since until recently methods for solving ILPs were not efficient. However, in the past few years the state of the art for ILP has developed to such an extent that research on PILP solution techniques may be undertaken with some optimism.

   PLP is traditionally thought of as varying a scalar parameter continuously over a specified range, resulting in a continuum of objective functions or of right-hand sides (resources allocations).

Some of you may well be within Nauss's implied audience, but Nancy Bradbury and Arthur Quinn are certainly not. Nauss's definition of a "parametric integer linear program" as "a family of closely related integer linear programs" is not adequate for our needs. (Are these *computer* programs? In the last sentence, "right-hand sides" of what?)

Nauss has taken others in his field as his implied audience. Thomas B. Sheridan, a professor of engineering and applied psychology, chooses to write to nonexperts in his article, "Computer Control and Human Alienation" (*Technology Review,* October 1980), which begins

What computers are good at and what people are good at tend to be different. Computers have good memories and are fast, consistent, and reliable but as yet are not creative or readily able to adapt to novel situations. People have poor memories, are slow, seldom do things the same way twice, and are unreliable, but they are adaptable and creative. Computers are a different race from people. It is a wonderful ideal to design systems wherein these two can complement and wed their talents.

For those persons who program computers and design them into control systems, this interaction can be fulfilling. For others, however, dealing with computers on computer terms is intimidating. What is the difference between the two groups of people in their relation to the computer? And what makes control by computers so alienating?

1. A first factor is that some people compare themselves with computers and worry about their inferiority and threatened obsolescence. . . . But rather than worry about this, we should celebrate those ways in which people are not computers, and let computers take over the jobs where they clearly outperform us.

The nonspecialists in Sheridan's implied audience may share the computer phobia that he describes. Notice his use of ordinary language and his reassuring description of us as "adaptable and creative" in ways that a computer cannot be, at least for now. Sheridan can, of course, write technical material like Nauss's when his audience is his technical peers, and Nauss would surely write differently if his implied audience included those of us who have never heard of integer linear programs or scalar parameters. Our understanding of audience continually shapes our decisions about how to make an argument.

EXAMPLES OF THE ARGUER–AUDIENCE RELATIONSHIP

As a fuller example of the writer–audience relationship, here are two letters from a mother to her college-aged daughter. Because they were written more than fifty years ago, you will be able to "try on" the role of audience, noting where the letters seem amusingly outdated and where you find it easy to put yourself into the audience.

Margaret Banning

TWO LETTERS TO SUSAN

Banning has considered her particular audience and, in the process of writing, created an implied audience. She is not addressing a crowd of strangers but a person she knows as well as she knows anyone. In these letters a clear portrait of the daughter emerges, even though the mother is writing to her daughter and thus has no need to describe Susan's character traits explicitly. When we speak of creating your implied audience, we mean shaping an implicit portrait, like the one we get of Susan. *Naturally, we don't have in mind your adding a paragraph to your essay announcing your audience's traits. Writing "my audience is open-minded and concerned about social justice" would make no sense. First of all, you are writing to your audience, and it would thus be more logical to write, "you are open-minded and believe in social justice." When it appears in this form, you can see how inappropriate such an explicit discussion of audience usually is. Let your sense of audience show itself in the arguments you choose, in how you present them, and in how you present yourself.*

In these letters, notice how the writer creates an implicit portrait of Susan and how she creates an implicit portrait of herself. Watch the way that Banning uses aspects of her own personality—her humor, for instance—to assist in the persuasive process.

I

November 15, 1934

Dear Susan:

1   No, you can't drive to Detroit for Thanksgiving with the two boys and Ann. I thought that I'd better put that simple, declarative sentence at the beginning of this letter so that you wouldn't be kept in suspense even if you are put in a bad temper. I'm sorry to have to be so definite and final. I would like to leave the decision to your own judgment, but this is one of the few times when I can't do that. For the judgment of so many people, young and old, is a little askew about just such propositions as four young people motoring together for most of two days and a night without any stops except for breath and coffee.

2   I do agree with much of what you wrote me. It would be delightful to be there for that Thanksgiving dance and it wouldn't be expensive to carry out your plan. I quite understand that you can manage the complicated schedules all around by leaving Wednesday afternoon, driving all that night and most of Thursday, and I don't doubt that you would have a grand time until Saturday noon and all be back in college by Sunday night. Also I know that Mark is probably the best driver of all your friends and that he behaves well. His father was like that too. He was also—though this bit of history may not interest you—rather dashing in his ways, like Mark. I don't know the other boy, David, or is it Daniel? (your handwriting certainly doesn't get any better) but I'll take your word for all the sterling qualities you say he has. Nobody need argue with me about Ann, after the way she measured up to family troubles and kept gay all last summer. Even you are all that I sometimes say you are, but it doesn't affect the situation.

3   In fact, I think it aggravates it. Such young people as you four have no right to do things that confuse you with people who are quite different in habits and ideas of control. You write, quote, please don't say that I can't go

because of the looks of the thing because that's such rubbish and not like you, unquote. You're wrong on both counts. It is not rubbish and it is like me. I get a little angry about this high-handed scrapping of the looks of things. What else have we to go by? How else can the average person form an opinion of a girl's sense of values or even of her chastity except by the looks of her conduct? If looks are so unimportant, why do you yourself spend so much time on your physical looks before you go out with strangers? In your own crowd you will go around all day wearing shorts and a sweat shirt and that eternal and dreadful red checked scarf that should be burned. But if you are going to be with people you don't know or who don't know who you are, it is different. Then you are careful to make yourself look as if you were decently bred, as if you could read and write, and as if you had good taste in clothes and cosmetics. You wouldn't be caught wearing cheap perfume, would you? Then why do you want to wear cheap perfume on your conduct?

4   Looks do matter and I do not mean just hair and skin and teeth and clothes. Looks are also your social contact with the world. Suppose you take this drive. How would it look to strangers? Two young men (of marriageable age) take two young women (also of marriageable age) on a forty-hour drive. Everyone knows that many girls go on forty-hour drives with men with extremely bad results, such as over-excited emotions, reckless conduct, and road accidents. How is anyone to make a special case of you? Why should anyone? It looks as if you deliberately assumed the pathetic privileges of girls who want to be with men at any cost to their reputations.

5   You wrote also that you think that it is nobody's business except your own what you do, but you are wrong. This is the kind of world—and there doesn't seem to be any other—in which conduct is social as well as individual. The main point of your education, from kindergarten up, has been to make you understand that, and I don't want you to break down at this small test. Your conduct is not entirely your own business, though it begins there. Afterwards it affects other people's conduct. Other girls, seeing you go off on an unchaperoned motor jaunt, think it's all right to do the same thing. Parents doubt and wonder. Men, and even boys, grow skeptical and more careless. You confuse things by such conduct.

6   I must also point out, even in the face of your cool young rage, that you ask a great deal more than gasoline and company of Mark and David—who may be Daniel. An unchaperoned girl, for whom a young man is responsible to parents whom he knows and respects, is a great burden to a young man. You are—so you said yourself—decent. Mark would have you on his hands in situations when people would not know whether you are decent or not. Suppose you all had an accident. Suppose, for example, that you couldn't make this trip without a long stop, speed being so eminently respectable but stops always so questionable. If you trail into some hotel after midnight, though a tourist camp should be all any of you can afford this year, it

wouldn't be so easy for either of those boys. Did it ever occur to you that there's something almost crooked in the way decent girls nowadays use the shelter of their established respectability to make things awkward for men?

7   There's another thing in my mind which is only partly relevant. You make no mention of it, assuming the coolest of friendly relations between the four of you. But suppose that David-Daniel (I'm beginning to love that name) found himself more excited than you anticipate by the proximity—and what proximity!—of you two good-looking girls. That happens. I seem to remember having mentioned it before. It might happen to one of those two boys. And how about you and Ann? Are you quite frank with me or yourselves? Isn't part of the lure of this trip the fact that you yourself do like Mark very much? Your plan really is to drive a car full of high explosives for forty hours, from dark to dawn, and enjoy your own daring no matter who blows up.

8   You wrote me that it would be such fun that you hope I'll see it your way. That's always a very disarming argument, but I think it's on my side this time. You see, if there were any necessity for this trip I would feel differently about it. If you were compelled for some real reason to travel that way, if there were a war or a siege to make it necessary, or if it were the only way you could see Mark for years, I would say that you could do it. But fun—that so-transient fun—of just missing being hit by a bus or finding the best hamburgers in the world at a roadside inn, or being cut in on twenty times at that Thanksgiving dance—isn't a good enough reason.

9   It is no fun for me either, to disappoint you like this. It isn't easy to be the person who sometimes has to try to preserve your happiness at the expense of your fun. After Thanksgiving—I know you probably can't do it until then—will you please believe that's true?

With love to you, Ann, Mark and David-Daniel,

Mother

II

February 5, 1935

Dear Susan:

1   Your very full explanations about the new evening coat, the overdraft in your bank account and the general state of your finances are all here, kindness of air mail. There is a bill for you from the dry-cleaners here too. I suppose it has something to do with the cleaning of your clothes at Christmas time. I'm forwarding it to you and I hope it hasn't the bad taste to arrive on Valentine's Day.

2   That was a very plausible letter. Good bargains like that do turn up in February and I know how well gold lamé with a fur collar would set off the head and shoulders of a blond young person with a good skin. In fact I got to

thinking of that picture with so much interest that I had to remind myself callously that the fact at issue is that you are in debt, overdrawn and have no money rightfully coming to you for about eighteen days.

3   Of course you have the coat! Technically it belongs to you, though full title still must rest with the shop that hasn't been entirely paid for it, and the bank may have some claim on a few gold threads. You say that they were glad to give you credit at the shop. I wonder. They probably trust the fact that you are in a good, respectable college. Or they believe your parents will stand back of a purchase even if you shouldn't have made it.

4   As I remember, you and I spent a long time considering what your allowance ought to be. You said it was large enough. You knew that it was much less than many of your friends have to spend. But you were sure that it would take care of all your personal expenses if we paid college fees and railway fares. Anyway, it was all we could afford to give you and you were satisfied. But here we are already with a condition of failure on our hands.

5   Yes, I know that you don't consider it that. By the end of April this elegant garment will be paid for in full, and you now have juggled your original budget until you think that you can get along on less than you estimated for other expenses. Perhaps you can, unless something else turns up that you think must be bought because it is so becoming or such a good bargain.

6   Those two arguments have led more women to lead dishonest lives than any others in the world. I was thinking of it the other day, before I had your letter, in connection with the Davis Wades.

7   Did you know that they are going to get a divorce? I'm very sorry about it. They were so much in love. But apparently Kitty was just too expensive for poor Davis. They got to the point where they quarrelled incessantly about money, and one day Davis called up every shop in town and cut off her credit. It was a horrid business but I don't think he knew what else to do. Kitty couldn't resist buying what she wanted or what someone told her she wanted. But it was bitterly humiliating for her, and she left him and went home to her family and started suit for divorce.

8   I don't want to make moral lessons out of your friends' tragedies, but it seems to me that case makes one thing very clear. Spending power is almost as important as earning power. A person who can spend money well is a very useful citizen. One reason this country is in such a bad state of nerves today is that so many people were like Kitty Wade, spending money according to their desires instead of according to their resources.

9   When you went back to college, and until you saw this particular evening wrap, you didn't think you needed one. You had the black velvet for warmish weather, and your winter coat seemed to be all right for both day and night wear. It was also on the theory that you didn't need any more expensive things until spring that you bought that brown plaid wool dress. You wanted it and it looked well on you and you were prepared to do with-

out other things in order to have it. Now you feel the same way about this coat. That can't go on indefinitely.

10   I know why you want it. It would be fun to have a golden wrap when you go to that prom with Mark next month, and it would make you feel very grand and important passing doormen. Mark's eyes would probably stick out at the sight of you. But it isn't very fair to him, if he should happen to be the man you marry. You aren't making a very good preparation for happiness with a man if you go into debt and are overdrawn at the bank in order to delight his eyes. You don't delight them long by those methods.

11   Susan dear, if you can't keep your desires within your allowance now, the chances are that you couldn't keep them within the limits of a fortune. It isn't a question of how much money you have, but how you handle it. I've known plenty of rich women who were always in money difficulties. This isn't a question of forty-five dollars—thirty-nine dollars and fifty cents, I mean. It's a question of whether you can control your desires or whether you are going to spend a good part of your life making excuses for the trouble you get into because of them.

12   The world is full of beautiful and becoming things and they'll be constantly pressed on your attention. But don't begin to cheat. The minute you take an article from a shop that you can not pay for, it's just a form of shoplifting, no matter if you still have credit. And if you draw checks on a bank for more money than you have in it, it's an ugly business.

13   The point at which I almost break down is that I would so like to see you in that coat. I would like to do a little personal cheating, and help you buy it. But I am not going to indulge myself. I shall cover the overdraft and I shall have to take that much from your allowance next month. It makes a big hole in it, doesn't it? What are you going to do about new shoes and this impatient cleaning bill?

14   You know—or at least I do—that the evening coat may not be as gratifying as you think. I doubt if Mark needs to be dazzled into greater affection for you. And doormen simply don't remember. If there is time and you've not had it altered, why don't you send it back to the shop with a frank note? If you can't do that, regard it as your big dissipation in clothes and try to get enough pleasure out of being dashing to make up for wearing your old evening dress in the Easter vacation.

15   I know just how it is. Once I bought one of those coats myself. Mine was trimmed with silver fox.

Love, *Mother*

◆ ◆ ◆

From the point of view of audience, these letters are more complicated than they seem. We didn't find them in a trunk in an attic; Banning published them with others in a book. Because she would hardly need to publish her letters in order to reach her daughter, she must have had a wider audience in mind. What audience might she want to "overhear" her advice to her daughter? The letters deal with various problems that arise between parents and their college-aged children: conflicts over drinking, money, reckless driving, and so on. Because each letter is devoted largely to advice on one particular issue, we may suspect that Banning didn't really write these letters to her daughter in the same form that they appear in the published collection. Thus, although we might at first have assumed that Banning simply considered her daughter as her very particular audience, we now see more clearly that she has created an implied audience as well. Unless we research her life story, we can't even be sure that Banning had a daughter of her own: she could be a school teacher without children, for example, who wrote her *Letters to Susan* because she objected to the way that her pupils were being raised.

Or take another possibility: all the letters are connected by the presence of the impetuous but good-hearted Susan. Whole novels have been written under the pretense that they are simply a collection of real letters that happened to come into the author's hands. *Letters to Susan* could be a novel posing as advice to the young or as a work on child-rearing. Notice how each hypothesis about the author's relationship to her audience transforms our understanding of the letters.

F. Scott Fitzgerald

LETTER TO SCOTTIE

This letter is also from a parent, this time a father, to his child, written at about the same time as Letters to Susan. *The father is not just a parent but someone who had once been one of the most celebrated writers of his time. The novels of F. Scott Fitzgerald virtually defined the loose life-style of the "Roaring Twenties," the world of speakeasies, flappers, and apparently never-ending parties. This was a life Fitzgerald both wrote about and lived, and this living contributed to the mental breakdowns of his wife and his own premature death in 1940 at the age of forty-four, a then largely forgotten figure trying to work in Hollywood. So, to say the least, Fitzgerald had not been a model parent nor had his personal life been one he would wish his daughter to emulate or even admire. How does he draw upon all this to try to get his daughter to listen to him? What kind of portrait do we get of Scottie? Why does he insist that she read the letter over again?*

July 7, 1938

Dearest Scottie:

[1]   I don't think I will be writing letters many more years and I wish you would read this letter twice—bitter as it may seem.[1] You will reject it now, but at a later period some of it may come back to you as truth. When I'm talking to you, you think of me as an older person, an "authority," and when I speak of my own youth what I say becomes unreal to you—for the young can't believe in the youth of their fathers. But perhaps this little bit will be understandable if I put it in writing.

[2]   When I was your age I lived with a great dream. The dream grew and I learned how to speak of it and make people listen. Then the dream divided one day when I decided to marry your mother after all, even though I knew she was spoiled and meant no good to me. I was sorry immediately I had married her but, being patient in those days, made the best of it and got to love her in another way. You came along and for a long time we made quite a lot of happiness out of our lives. But I was a man divided—she wanted me to work too much for *her* and not enough for my dream. She realized too late that work was dignity, and the only dignity, and tried to atone for it by working herself, but it was too late and she broke and is broken forever.

[3]   It was too late also for me to recoup the damage—I had spent most of my resources, spiritual and material, on her, but I struggled on for five years till my health collapsed, and all I cared about was drink and forgetting.

[4]   The mistake I made was in marrying her. We belonged to different worlds—she might have been happy with a kind simple man in a southern garden. She didn't have the strength for the big stage—sometimes she pretended, and pretended beautifully, but she didn't have it. She was soft when she should have been hard, and hard when she should have been yielding. She never knew how to use her energy—she's passed that failing on to you.

[5]   For a long time I hated *her* mother for giving her nothing in the line of good habit—nothing but "getting by" and conceit. I never wanted to see again in this world women who were brought up as idlers. And one of my chief desires in life was to keep you from being that kind of person, one who brings ruin to themselves and others. When you began to show disturbing signs at about fourteen, I comforted myself with the idea that you were too precocious socially and a strict school would fix things. But sometimes I think that idlers seem to be a special class for whom nothing can be planned, plead as one will with them—their only contribution to the human family is to warm a seat at the common table.

---

[1]After graduation, while studying for college boards at Ethel Walker's, Scottie had broken bounds and been asked to leave the school. Fitzgerald's fear that it might prevent her from getting into Vassar occasioned this letter.

6 My reforming days are over, and if you are that way I don't want to change you. But I don't want to be upset by idlers inside my family or out. I want my energies and my earnings for people who talk my language.

7 I have begun to fear that you don't. You don't realize that what I am doing here is the last tired effort of a man who once did something finer and better. There is not enough energy, or call it money, to carry anyone who is dead weight and I am angry and resentful in my soul when I feel that I am doing this. People like _____ and _____ and your mother must be carried because their illness makes them useless. But it is a different story that *you* have spent two years doing no useful work at all, improving neither your body nor your mind, but only writing reams and reams of dreary letters to dreary people, with no possible object except obtaining invitations which you could not accept. Those letters go on, even in your sleep, so that I know your whole trip now is one long waiting for the post. It is like an old gossip who cannot still her tongue.

8 You have reached the age when one is of interest to an adult only insofar as one seems to have a future. The mind of a little child is fascinating, for it looks on old things with new eyes—but at about twelve this changes. The adolescent offers nothing, can do nothing, say nothing that the adult cannot do better. Living with you in Baltimore (and you have told Harold that I alternated between strictness and neglect, by which I suppose you mean the times I was so inconsiderate as to have T. B., or to retire into myself to write, for I had little social life apart from you) represented a rather too domestic duty forced on me by your mother's illness. But I endured your Top Hats and Telephones until the day you snubbed me at dancing school, less willingly after that. . . .

9 To sum up: What you have done to please me or make me proud is practically negligible since the time you made yourself a good diver at camp (and now you are softer than you have ever been). In your career as a "wild society girl," vintage of 1925, I'm not interested. I don't want any of it—it would bore me, like dining with the Ritz Brothers. When I do not feel you are "going somewhere," your company tends to depress me for the silly waste and triviality involved. On the other hand, when occasionally I see signs of life and intention in you, there is no company in the world I prefer. For there is no doubt that you have something in your belly, some real gusto for life—a real dream of your own—and my idea was to wed it to something solid before it was too late—as it was too late for your mother to learn anything when she got around to it. Once when you spoke French as a child it was enchanting with your odd bits of knowledge—now your conversation is as commonplace as if you'd spent the last two years in the Corn Hollow High School— what you saw in *Life* and read in *Sexy Romances.*

10 I shall come East in September to meet your boat—but this letter is a declaration that I am no longer interested in your promissory notes but only in

what I see. I love you always but I am only interested by people who think and work as I do and it isn't likely that *I* shall change at my age. Whether you will—or want to—remains to be seen.

Daddy

P. S. If you keep the diary, please don't let it be the dry stuff I could buy in a ten-franc guide book. I'm not interested in dates and places, even the Battle of New Orleans, unless you have some unusual reaction to them. Don't try to be witty in the writing, unless it's natural—just true and real.

P. P. S. Will you please read this letter a second time? I wrote it over twice.

◆   ◆   ◆

Scottie Fitzgerald Lanahan published her father's letters after his death with no significant alterations. We know on the other hand that Banning herself prepared *Letters to Susan* for publication. Do the letters reflect this difference, or does Fitzgerald, too, seem to anticipate a wider audience for his letters?

Scottie Fitzgerald Lanahan

MY FATHER'S LETTERS

Here is an excerpt from Lanahan's comments on her father's letters. Is her reaction what you would have predicted? Note her comments on the image her father creates of his implied audience: "an imaginary daughter," "far more popular and glamorous than I was," "more wicked and hell-bent on pleasure than I could possibly have been." We don't know which characterization of Scottie is more accurate, but her comments about the differences between herself and the daughter addressed in the letter help to illustrate our point about the way that a writer recreates an audience within a written work.

[1]   So these gorgeous letters, these absolute pearls of wisdom and literary style, would arrive at Vassar and I'd simply examine them for checks and news, then stick them in my lower right-hand drawer. I'm proud of myself for saving them; I knew they were great letters, and my motives were certainly not acquisitive, because Daddy was an impecunious and obscure author then, with no prospect in sight of *The Great Gatsby* being translated

into twenty-seven languages. I saved them the way you save *War and Peace* to read, or Florence to spend some time in later.

2   But at the time I didn't want to be told what to read, how to read it, what courses to take, whether to try out for the college paper, what girls to room with, what football games to go to, how to feel about the Spanish Civil War, whether or not to drink, whether or not to "throw myself away" (if only Daddy had had a daughter at Vassar *now*, what glorious prose he could have composed on this subject!), not to write music for our campus productions, not to put a peroxide streak in my hair, not to go to a debutante party in New York, whether or not to try my hand at social work, and so on and on until I half expected, at the age of eighteen, to be lectured to on when to take a bath....

3   Malcolm Cowley said in a review in *The New York Times* once that "Fitzgerald wasn't writing those letters to his daughter at Vassar; he was writing them to himself at Princeton." This is the point, really. I was an imaginary daughter, as fictional as one of his early heroines. He made me sound far more popular and glamorous than I was—I was actually only vaguely pretty, and only danced with by friends, of which fortunately I had a number—but he wanted me so desperately to be so that in these letters, I sound like my contemporary glamor queen, Brenda Frazier. He also made me sound more wicked and hell-bent on pleasure than I could possibly have been. It's true that I preferred boys, Fred Astaire, and fun to the sheer hard labor of working. I *still* prefer boys, Fred Astaire, and fun to the sheer hard labor of working. Doesn't almost everybody?

4   There's a moral to all this, and I'm about to get it off my chest:

To college students (including my own two): "Don't ignore any good advice, unless it comes from your own parents. Somebody else's parents might very well be right."

To parents (poor struggling creatures): "Don't drop your pearls before swine, at least without making sure the swine are going to put them in the lower right-hand drawer."

5   Listen carefully to my father, now. Because what he offers is good advice, and I'm sure if he hadn't been my own father that I loved and "hated" simultaneously, I would have profited by it and be the best educated, most attractive, most successful, most faultless woman on earth today.

1963

◆ ◆ ◆

Giving advice to young people about such matters as their social lives and their devotion to their studies puts the giver in a challenging rhetorical situation. Young people are often sensitive to infringements on their freedom and can be particularly unreceptive to anything that sounds like preaching or nagging. If you are under twenty-two, you are in a better position than your teacher to evaluate Banning's and Fitzgerald's efforts to reach their audiences. If you are a parent, you will sympathize with their difficulties.

Samuel Clemens

ADVICE TO YOUTH

Here is another example of an older person advising young people about how to conduct their lives. This time the situation is a public speech presented to a particular audience in the real world. If it is difficult to make our advice palatable to our own children, whose interests and inclinations are known to us, imagine how much more difficult it is to offer effective words of wisdom to an assortment of unknown young people.

Listen to the way that Samuel Clemens addresses such a group. Clemens (who, under his pen name Mark Twain, wrote Huckleberry Finn *and* Tom Sawyer*) was famous for using humor to make serious points. In general, what would be the advantages of offering advice with humor? How might that technique overcome anticipated resistance in a particular audience? Is Clemens here trying to persuade his audience of something serious or only trying to amuse them? Note how he plays with our expectations to make us laugh, in paragraph 6 for instance. You might go through this piece and indicate the places where you think Clemens himself expected his audience to laugh, and how these expectations would have influenced his timing when he delivered the speech. How much of his text would you have to change if you were giving this speech to a group of your fellow students?*

1   Being told I would be expected to talk here, I inquired what sort of a talk I ought to make. They said it should be something suitable to youth—something didactic, instructive, or something in the nature of good advice. Very well. I have a few things in my mind which I have often longed to say for the instruction of the young; for it is in one's tender early years that such things will best take root and be most enduring and most valuable. First, then, I will say to you, my young friends—and I say it beseechingly, urgingly—

2   Always obey your parents, when they are present. This is the best policy in the long run, because if you don't they will make you. Most parents think they know better than you do, and you can generally make more by humoring that superstition than you can by acting on your own better judgment.

3   Be respectful to your superiors, if you have any, also to strangers, and sometimes to others. If a person offends you, and you are in doubt as to whether it was intentional or not, do not resort to extreme measures; simply watch your chance and hit him with a brick. That will be sufficient. If you shall find that he had not intended any offense, come out frankly and confess yourself in the wrong when you struck him; acknowledge it like a man and say you didn't mean to. Yes, always avoid violence; in this age of charity and kindliness, the time has gone by for such things. Leave dynamite to the low and unrefined.

4   Go to bed early, get up early—this is wise. Some authorities say get up with the sun; some others say get up with one thing, some with another. But a lark is really the best thing to get up with. It gives you a splendid reputation with everybody to know that you get up with the lark; and if you get the right kind of a lark, and work at him right, you can easily train him to get up at half past nine, every time—it is no trick at all.

5   Now as to the matter of lying. You want to be very careful about lying; otherwise you are nearly sure to get caught. Once caught, you can never again be, in the eyes of the good and the pure, what you were before. Many a young person has injured himself permanently through a single clumsy and illfinished lie, the result of carelessness born of incomplete training. Some authorities hold that the young ought not to lie at all. That, of course, is putting it rather stronger than necessary; still, while I cannot go quite so far as that, I do maintain, and I believe I am right, that the young ought to be temperate in the use of this great art until practice and experience shall give them that confidence, elegance, and precision which alone can make the accomplishment graceful and profitable. Patience, diligence, painstaking attention to detail—these are the requirements; these, in time, will make the student perfect; upon these, and upon these only, may he rely as the sure foundation for future eminence. Think what tedious years of study, thought, practice, experience, went to the equipment of that peerless old master who was able to impose upon the whole world the lofty and sounding maxim that "truth is mighty and will prevail"—the most majestic compound fracture of fact which any of woman born has yet achieved. For the history of our race, and each individual's experience, are sown thick with evidence that a truth is not hard to kill and that a lie told well is immortal. There is in Boston a monument of the man who discovered anaesthesia; many people are aware, in these latter days, that that man didn't discover it at all, but stole the discovery from another man. Is this truth mighty, and will it prevail? Ah no, my hearers, the monument is made of hardy material, but the lie it tells will outlast it a

million years. An awkward, feeble, leaky lie is a thing which you ought to make it your unceasing study to avoid; such a lie as that has no more real permanence than an average truth. Why, you might as well tell the truth at once and be done with it. A feeble, stupid, preposterous lie will not live two years—except it be a slander upon somebody. It is indestructible, then, of course, but that is no merit of yours. A final word: begin your practice of this gracious and beautiful art early—begin now. If I had begun earlier, I could have learned how.

6   Never handle firearms carelessly. The sorrow and suffering that have been caused through the innocent but heedless handling of firearms by the young! Only four days ago, right in the next farmhouse to the one where I am spending the summer, a grandmother, old and gray and sweet, one of the loveliest spirits in the land, was sitting at her work, when her young grandson crept in and got down an old, battered, rusty gun which had not been touched for many years and was supposed not to be loaded, and pointed it at her, laughing and threatening to shoot. In her fright she ran screaming and pleading toward the door on the other side of the room; but as she passed him he placed the gun almost against her very breast and pulled the trigger! He had supposed it was not loaded. And he was right—it wasn't. So there wasn't any harm done. It is the only case of that kind I ever heard of. Therefore, just the same, don't you meddle with old unloaded firearms; they are the most deadly and unerring things that have ever been created by man. You don't have to take any pains at all with them; you don't have to have a rest, you don't have to have any sights on the gun, you don't have to take aim, even. No, you just pick out a relative and bang away, and you are sure to get him. A youth who can't hit a cathedral at thirty yards with a Gatling gun in three-quarters of an hour, can take up an old empty musket and bag his grandmother every time, at a hundred. Think what Waterloo would have been if one of the armies had been boys armed with old muskets supposed not to be loaded, and the other army had been composed of their female relations. The very thought of it makes one shudder.

7   There are many sorts of books; but good ones are the sort for the young to read. Remember that. They are a great, an inestimable, an unspeakable means of improvement. Therefore be careful in your selection, my young friends; be very careful; confine yourselves exclusively to Robertson's Sermons, Baxter's *Saint's Rest, The Innocents Abroad,* and works of that kind.

8   But I have said enough. I hope you will treasure up the instructions which I have given you, and make them a guide to your feet and a light to your understanding. Build your character thoughtfully and painstakingly upon these precepts, and by and by, when you have got it built, you will be surprised and gratified to see how nicely and sharply it resembles everybody else's.

1882

Imamu Amiri Baraka (LeRoi Jones)

YOUNG SOUL

A final example of "advice to youth" is this poem by Imamu Amiri Baraka (LeRoi Jones), written in the 1960s and collected in a volume called Black Magic. As a poet and dramatist, Baraka was one of the most eloquent African-American voices of protest during the 1960s. He wrote, "To understand that you are black in a society where black is an extreme liability is one thing, but to understand that it is the society that is lacking and impossibly deformed, and not yourself, isolates you even more." This extreme sense of alienation (which would lead to Baraka's conversion to Islam) does limit the kinds of advice he might offer youth. If a society is impossibly deformed, then there is no sense in trying to improve it. Is this pessimism about society consistent with the advice offered by the poem? Do you think Baraka's poem is primarily addressed to an African-American audience? Or is it addressed to any young audience that has suffered some "liability"? Or is this poem just a serious version of Clemens's advice to do what you want?

```
     First, feel, then feel, then
     read, or read, then feel, then
     fall, or stand, where you
     already are. Think
5    of your self, and the other
     selves . . . think
     of your parents, your mothers
     and sisters, your bentslick
     father, then feel, or
10   fall, on your knees
     if nothing else will move you,
                         then read
                         and look deeply
                         into all matters
15                       come close to you
                         city boys—
                         country men

20                       Make some muscle
                         in your head, but
                         use the muscle
                         in yr heart
```

1964

We hope that we've shown how important an audience can be to an argument. To see how a poorly conceived sense of audience can devastate an argument, we can look at a passage from Jane Austen's early nineteenth-century novel *Pride and Prejudice*.

Jane Austen

MR. COLLINS PROPOSES

In this reading, the clergyman Mr. Collins attempts to win the hand of the novel's heroine, Elizabeth Bennet. Mr. Collins also happens to be the heir to Elizabeth's father's estate; Mr. Bennet is not free to leave his property to Elizabeth and his other daughters.

One aspect of this situation is distinctly in Collins's favor: He is addressing a single person. Thus he can count on one relatively coherent set of values and beliefs in his audience. The author makes clear, however, that Collins's audience doesn't much relish the idea of becoming his wife. His case is endangered from the beginning, when he makes his listener want to laugh at the contrast between his composed manner and his claim to be carried away by emotion. He can hardly please Elizabeth by anticipating the deaths of both her parents—perfectly healthy people of middle age—and in the course of his speech, the remainder of her father's life span dwindles from "many years" to "several years." Does his insistence on regarding her frankly stated refusal as feminine coyness help his case? Hardly. In creating his implied audience, Collins transforms attractive, intelligent, and popular young Elizabeth into an impoverished spinster with little to recommend her beyond her humility and "usefulness." Not only is he a stupid and greedy man, he assumes that his audience is equally stupid and greedy. But notice also how complex fictional arguments can be: at the same time that Mr. Collins creates an offensive role for his audience, Jane Austen creates a positive, perceptive image for her own audience by trusting her readers to laugh at Mr. Collins's blunders.

1 The next day opened a new scene at Longbourn. Mr. Collins made his declaration in form. Having resolved to do it without loss of time, as his leave of absence extended only to the following Saturday, and having no feelings of diffidence to make it distressing to himself even at the moment, he set about it in a very orderly manner, with all the observances, which he supposed a regular part of the business. On finding Mrs. Bennet, Elizabeth, and

one of the younger girls together, soon after breakfast, he addressed the mother in these words: "May I hope, madam, for your interest with your fair daughter Elizabeth, when I solicit for the honour of a private audience with her in the course of this morning?"

2   Before Elizabeth had time for anything but a blush of surprise, Mrs. Bennet instantly answered, "Oh dear!—yes—certainly. I am sure Lizzy will be very happy—I am sure she can have no objection. Come, Kitty, I want you upstairs." And, gathering her work together, she was hastening away, when Elizabeth called out:

3   "Dear madam, do not go. I beg you will not go. Mr. Collins must excuse me. He can have nothing to say to me that anybody need not hear. I am going away myself."

4   "No, no, nonsense, Lizzy. I desire you will stay where you are." And upon Elizabeth's seeming really, with vexed and embarrassed looks, about to escape, she added: "Lizzy, I *insist* upon you staying and hearing Mr. Collins."

5   Elizabeth would not oppose such an injunction—and a moment's consideration making her also sensible that it would be wisest to get it over as soon and as quietly as possible, she sat down again, and tried to conceal, by incessant employment, the feelings which were divided between distress and diversion. Mrs. Bennet and Kitty walked off, and as soon as they were gone Mr. Collins began.

6   "Believe me, my dear Miss Elizabeth, that your modesty, so far from doing you any disservice, rather adds to your other perfections. You would have been less amiable in my eyes had there *not* been this little unwillingness; but allow me to assure you, that I have your respected mother's permission for this address. You can hardly doubt the purport of my discourse, however your natural delicacy may lead you to dissemble; my attentions have been too marked to be mistaken. Almost as soon as I entered the house, I singled you out as the companion of my future life. But before I am run away with my feelings on this subject, perhaps it would be advisable for me to state my reasons for marrying—and, moreover, for coming into Hertfordshire with the design of selecting a wife, as I certainly did."

7   The idea of Mr. Collins, with all his solemn composure, being run away with by his feelings, made Elizabeth so near laughing, that she could not use the short pause he allowed in any attempt to stop him farther, and he continued:

8   "My reasons for marrying are, first, that I think it a right thing for every clergyman in easy circumstances (like myself) to set the example of matrimony in his parish; secondly, that I am convinced it will add very greatly to my happiness; and thirdly—which perhaps I ought to have mentioned earlier, that it is the particular advice and recommendation of the very noble lady whom I have the honour of calling patroness. Twice has she condescended to give me her opinion (unasked too!) on this subject; and it was but

the very Saturday night before I left Hunsford—between our pools at quadrille, while Mrs. Jenkinson was arranging Miss de Bourgh's footstool, that she said, 'Mr. Collins, you must marry. A clergyman like you must marry. Choose properly, choose a gentlewoman for *my* sake; and for your *own*, let her be an active, useful sort of person, not brought up high, but able to make a small income go a good way. This is my advice. Find such a woman as soon as you can, bring her to Hunsford, and I will visit her.' Allow me, by the way, to observe, my fair cousin, that I do not reckon the notice and kindness of Lady Catherine de Bourgh as among the least of the advantages in my power to offer. You will find her manners beyond anything I can describe; and your wit and vivacity, I think, must be acceptable to her, especially when tempered with the silence and respect which her rank will inevitably excite. Thus much for my general intention in favour of matrimony; it remains to be told why my views were directed to Longbourn instead of my own neighborhood, where I assure you there are many amiable young women. But the fact is, that being, as I am, to inherit this estate after the death of your honoured father (who, however, may live many years longer), I could not satisfy myself without resolving to choose a wife from among his daughters, that the loss to them might be as little as possible, when the melancholy event takes place— which, however, as I have already said, may not be for several years. This has been my motive, my fair cousin, and I flatter myself it will not sink me in your esteem. And now nothing remains for me but to assure you in the most animated language of the violence of my affection. To fortune I am perfectly indifferent, and shall make no demand of that nature on your father, since I am well aware that it could not be complied with; and that one thousand pounds in the four per cents, which will not be yours till after your mother's decease, is all that you may ever be entitled to. On that head, therefore, I shall be uniformly silent; and you may assure yourself that no ungenerous reproach shall ever pass my lips when we are married."

9 It was absolutely necessary to interrupt him now.

10 "You are too hasty, sir," she cried. "You forget that I have made no answer. Let me do it without further loss of time. Accept my thanks for the compliment you are paying me. I am very sensible of the honour of your proposals, but it is impossible for me to do otherwise than decline them."

11 "I am not now to learn," replied Mr. Collins, with a formal wave of the hand, "that it is usual with young ladies to reject the addresses of the man whom they secretly mean to accept, when he first applies for their favour; and that sometimes the refusal is repeated a second or even a third time. I am therefore by no means discouraged by what you have just said, and shall hope to lead you to the altar ere long."

12 "Upon my word, sir," cried Elizabeth, "your hope is rather an extraordinary one after my declaration. I do assure you that I am not one of those young ladies (if such young ladies there are) who are so daring as to risk their

happiness on the chance of being asked a second time. I am perfectly serious in my refusal. You could not make *me* happy, and I am convinced that I am the last woman in the world who would make you so. Nay, were your friend Lady Catherine to know me, I am persuaded she would find me in every respect ill qualified for the situation."

13   "Were it certain that Lady Catherine would think so," said Mr. Collins very gravely—"but I cannot imagine that her ladyship would at all disapprove of you. And you may be certain that when I have the honour of seeing her again, I shall speak in the highest terms of your modesty, economy, and other amiable qualifications."

14   "Indeed, Mr. Collins, all praise of me will be unnecessary. You must give me leave to judge for myself, and pay me the compliment of believing what I say. I wish you very happy and very rich, and by refusing your hand, do all in my power to prevent your being otherwise. In making me the offer, you must have satisfied the delicacy of your feelings with regard to my family, and may take possession of Longbourn estate whenever it falls without any self-reproach. This matter may be considered therefore, as finally settled." And rising as she thus spoke, she would have quitted the room, had not Mr. Collins thus addressed her:

15   "When I do myself the honour of speaking to you next on the subject, I shall hope to receive a more favourable answer than you have now given me; though I am far from accusing you of cruelty at present, because I know it to be the established custom of your sex to reject a man on the first application, and perhaps you have even now said as much to encourage my suit as would be consistent with the true delicacy of the female character."

16   "Really, Mr. Collins," cried Elizabeth with some warmth, "you puzzle me exceedingly. If what I have hitherto said can appear to you in the form of encouragement, I know not how to express my refusal in such a way as may convince you of its being one."

17   "You must give me leave to flatter myself, my dear cousin, that your refusal of my addresses is merely words of course. My reason for believing it are briefly these: It does not appear to me that my hand is unworthy of your acceptance, or that the establishment I can offer would be any other than highly desirable. My situation in life, my connections with the family of de Bourgh, and my relationship to your own, are circumstances highly in my favour; and you should take it into further consideration, that in spite of your manifold attractions, it is by no means certain that another offer of marriage may ever be made you. Your portion is unhappily so small that it will in all likelihood undo the effects of your loveliness and amiable qualifications. As I must therefore conclude that you are not serious in your rejection of me, I shall choose to attribute it to your wish of increasing my love by suspense, according to the usual practice of elegant females."

18   "I do assure you, sir, that I have no pretensions whatever to that kind of elegance which consists in tormenting a respectable man. I would rather be

paid the compliment of being believed sincere. I thank you again and again for the honour you have done me in your proposals, but to accept them is absolutely impossible. My feelings in every respect forbid it. Can I speak plainer? Do not consider me now as an elegant female, intending to plague you, but as a rational creature, speaking the truth from her heart."

19   "You are uniformly charming!" cried he, with an air of awkward gallantry; "and I am persuaded that when sanctioned by the express authority of both your excellent parents, my proposals will not fail of being acceptable."

20   To such perseverance in wilful self-deception Elizabeth would make no reply, and immediately and in silence withdrew; determined, that if he persisted in considering her repeated refusals as flattering encouragement, to apply to her father, whose negative might be uttered in such a manner as must be decisive, and whose behaviour at least could not be mistaken for the affectation and coquetry of an elegant female.

◆ ◆ ◆

You might think that such a proposal could never work, but arguments do not fail "in general"; they fail in relation to particular audiences. It seems that an audience exists for Mr. Collins's persuasive techniques after all. Mr. Collins soon redirects his suit to Elizabeth's friend Charlotte Lucas.

21   Miss Lucas perceived him from an upper window as he walked towards the house, and instantly set out to meet him accidentally in the lane. But little had she dared to hope that so much love and eloquence awaited her there.

22   In as short a time as Mr. Collins's long speeches would allow, everything was settled between them to the satisfaction of both; and as they entered the house, he earnestly entreated her to name the day that was to make him the happiest of men; and though such a solicitation must be waived for the present, the lady felt no inclination to trifle with his happiness. The stupidity with which he was favoured by nature must guard his courtship from any charm that could make a woman wish for its continuance; and Miss Lucas, who accepted him solely from the pure and disinterested desire of an establishment, cared not how soon that establishment were gained.

23   Sir William and Lady Lucas were speedily applied to for their consent; and it was bestowed with a most joyful alacrity. Mr. Collins's present circumstances made it a most eligible match for their daughter, to whom they could give little fortune; and his prospects of future wealth were exceedingly fair. Lady Lucas began directly to calculate with more interest than the matter had ever excited before how many years longer Mr. Bennet was likely to live; and Sir William gave it as his decided opinion that whenever Mr. Collins should be in possession of the Longbourn estate, it would be highly expedient that both he and his wife should make their appearance at St. James's. The whole

family in short were properly overjoyed on the occasion. The younger girls formed hopes of *coming out* a year or two sooner than they might otherwise have done; and the boys were relieved from their apprehension of Charlotte's dying an old maid. Charlotte herself was tolerably composed. She had gained her point, and had time to consider of it. Her reflections were in general satisfactory. Mr. Collins to be sure was neither sensible nor agreeable; his society was irksome, and his attachment to her must be imaginary. But still he would be her husband. Without thinking highly either of men or of matrimony, marriage had always been her object; it was the only honourable provision for well-educated young women of small fortune, and however uncertain of giving happiness, must be their pleasantest preservative from want. This preservative she had now obtained; and at the age of twenty-seven, without having ever been handsome, she felt all the good luck of it. . . .

24   . . . Miss Lucas called soon after breakfast, and in a private conference with Elizabeth related the event of the day before.

25   The possibility of Mr. Collins's fancying himself in love with her friend had once occurred to Elizabeth within the last day or two; but that Charlotte could encourage him seemed almost as far from possibility as that she could encourage him herself, and her astonishment was consequently so great as to overcome at first the bounds of decorum, and she could not help crying out,

26   "Engaged to Mr. Collins! my dear Charlotte—impossible!"

27   The steady countenance which Miss Lucas had commanded in telling her story gave way to a momentary confusion here on receiving so direct a reproach; though, as it was no more than she expected, she soon regained her composure, and calmly replied.

28   "Why should you be surprised, my dear Eliza? Do you think it incredible that Mr. Collins should be able to procure any woman's good opinion, because he was not so happy as to succeed with you?"

29   But Elizabeth had now recollected herself, and making a strong effort for it was able to assure her with tolerable firmness that the prospect of their relationship was highly grateful to her, and that she wished her all imaginable happiness.

30   "I see what you are feeling," replied Charlotte, "you must be surprised, very much surprised—so lately as Mr. Collins was wishing to marry you. But when you have had time to think it over, I hope you will be satisfied with what I have done. I am not romantic, you know. I never was. I ask only a comfortable home; and considering Mr. Collins's character, connections, and situation in life, I am convinced that my chance of happiness with him is as fair as most people can boast on entering the marriage state."

31   Elizabeth quietly answered, "Undoubtedly"—and after an awkward pause, they returned to the rest of the family. . . .

1813

◆ ◆ ◆

Notice that Elizabeth's friend has few illusions about Collins's character. Nevertheless, the friend has lower expectations about marriage, and hence for this audience Mr. Collins's offer of financial security outweighs his obnoxious qualities.

AUDIENCES ALL AROUND

Nothing will help you more as a writer and critical thinker than getting in the habit of looking for audience in every piece of discourse you find. We are daily inundated with messages for which we may or may not be the audience. Even if we are not, they offer the opportunity to practice thinking rhetorically, to seek a portrait of an audience where we might not have thought to look for one before.

Advertisements

Advertisements are a good place to start to practice this. A cigarette advertisement showing a stylish woman and the slogan, "You've come a long way, baby," is not directed to men, to women deeply committed to traditional values, or to women who do not like being called "baby." What's left might seem to you a pretty narrow audience, but the persistence of this slogan shows it is not. (As P. T. Barnum is supposed to have said, "No one ever went broke underestimating the American public.") Look at the text of the following advertisement, also for cigarettes, but this one showing a man of fashionably casual appearance.

> WHAT I'M DOING ABOUT SMOKING. I am smoking Vantage. I took up smoking more than 15 years ago in the Marine Corps. I started smoking then because I wanted to. And I intend to keep smoking as long as I want to. But that doesn't make me bury my head in the sand and ignore the stuff in the papers about smoking. My attitude is, OK, if high tar and nicotine cigarettes are a concern to me, I'd better do something about it. So I did. I started to smoke Vantage.

Apparently you can be a no-nonsense guy who won't be bullied and still change cigarette brands because of health worries. An ad for cigars that appeared in 1918 featured another military veteran. Its text began, "Did I bayonet my first Hun? Sure! How did it feel? It doesn't feel! There he is! There you are! One of us has got to go. I preferred to stay." Of course, even to understand this ad you have to know that "Hun" was a common derogatory term for Germans during the recently ended war. More important, you cannot be squeamish about bayonet fights or doubtful about the war. Buy a White Owl cigar to feel more manly—as well as patriotic, for the advertisement later informs us that this doughboy "first met the dependable Owl Cigar while boosting that dependable investment—the Liberty bond."

This last advertisement might seem remote from the kind that might work on you or your contemporaries, but the following lead-in to an appeal for a famous soft drink should not, as college students are its obvious audience. "Three hours to sunrise. The time for classes is past. Now you have to put it all together. And it isn't easy. But you have the head for it. And the heart. And a Pepsi Cola handy to give you a lift. Pepsi gives you more than just a big taste. It gives you energy to keep going. And you're going a long way." Provided, of course, you tank up on enough sugar and caffeine.

Signs

We always have our students on the lookout for interesting signs. Take, for instance, something as simple as the "No Trespassing" sign. The persons or institutions posting such signs all have essentially the same end in mind, but their perceptions of their audiences may vary—hence different signs. "Private property." "Keep out. This means you." "Beware of dog." "Please do not intrude." "Don't even think about coming in here." "Thank you for not walking on the lawn." "No pasar." "This area is temporarily off-limits. The blue herons are nesting." "Trespassers will be prosecuted to the full extent of the law. County Ord. 37j 4.05." "These premises protected by Ace Security Systems." Our favorite such sign was put up by librarians to try to cajole faculty not to pass through their working area as a shortcut. After a variety of other signs were tried without success, someone finally put up (in elaborate Gothic script), "Abandon all hope, ye who enter here." This allusion to Dante's *Inferno,* where such a sign marked the entrance to hell, worked where all else had failed; reading the sign, most faculty would smile, and then take another route.

Form Letters

Form letters are another commonplace item on which to practice looking for audience. Here are the first paragraphs of form letters that used to be sent to applicants for graduate programs at the University of California, Berkeley.

> I am happy to inform you that your application for admission to graduate standing at the University of California, Berkeley, has been approved for the quarter and program indicated below. Our decision has been based on careful consideration of your qualifications and intentions in comparison with those of many other applicants. For this reason, I wish to stress that our approval is a specific one for the quarter and program mentioned.

> I have carefully reviewed your application and have obtained the advice of the departmental faculty with whom you wished to be associated. I regret to inform you on the basis of our review, your admission to the Graduate Division of the University of California, Berkeley, has been denied.

Note that the order of the first two sentences has been reversed. In the first letter, the dean gives the accepted applicant the good news, then he describes the procedures. In the second, the dean describes the procedures, and only then drops the bomb of rejection. (Presumably, he wanted to get the bit about procedures in before the disappointed applicant stopped reading.) The dean can afford to be stern with conditions for the accepted applicant, but is kindly and full of regret for the rejected. If you think that the regret may not be altogether sincere, look again at the first sentence of the rejection letter. The dean of the whole graduate division of the University of California claims to have reviewed the rejected application carefully. A moment's reflection would allow you to realize that the dean himself would never have had time to look at even a small fraction of the applications; in fact, probably the closest he has come to these applications, both accepted and rejected, is working in the same building to which they were sent. Why then tell this fib? Consider the audience. If he had first said that the department has rejected the application and had then offered his own condolences, a small percentage of the applicants would have appealed to him directly because he sounded concerned. That would have meant hundreds of appeals, which in practice had no chance for success—in other words, just more work for the university and more disappointment for the applicants. The fib is an effective way to communicate to a disappointed audience a simple message: "Don't appeal to me." You might ask at this point whether in this instance the end justifies the means. An effective fib like this does start to raise the complicated ethical questions on which we will concentrate in Chapter 4.

Presenting Yourself to Your Audience

These ethical questions are also raised when we realize that the way people present themselves is itself often influenced by their perception of audience. They will tend to emphasize aspects of themselves that they think the audience will admire or at least find pleasing. Politicians are the past masters of this technique. One of our favorites was a congressman named W. R. Poage who rose to considerable prominence in the U.S. House of Representatives. Here is Poage addressing a meeting of the National Wool Growers. Being a career politician was not the least of the problems Poage thought he had with this particular audience, as the beginning of his speech shows.

> Twelve years ago it was my privilege to speak to your annual convention over in Fort Worth. At that time I explained that I was rather poorly qualified to discuss the problems of the sheepman because, although my maternal grandfather was a sheepman, my father was an old time cowman who never did appreciate the characteristics of the lamb or its mammy—in spite of the recognition granted it in poetry, art, and even the Good Book, he just would not have a sheep on his ranch—not even the pet I so much wanted. In spite of all this background, I grew up to know that there are not, and never have been, any finer people than those who grow the sheep, the goats, and the cattle—in short, the ranchmen of America. Among this group I am happy to number many of the finest friends I have anywhere, and among them America can count many of her very best citizens.

Here is a humble person who—unlike his father—has always appreciated sheep. Note how even his choice of down-home phrases like "mammy," "Good Book," and even "over in" (instead of the simpler "at") contribute to an image he thinks his audience will find attractive. He certainly thinks they will agree with him that they are fine friends and good citizens.

Poage clearly was trying to tell his audience what he thought they wanted to hear—and judging from his electoral success, we must conclude that he was probably correct in his assessment of his particular audience, on this and many other occasions. Needless to say, a writer or speaker might decide to do other-wise, and to suffer the attendant risks. Many of the most enduring leaders or teachers have told their audiences exactly what they were not prepared to hear, did not want to hear. Herman Melville, for instance, while he was writing his greatest novel *Moby Dick*, became convinced that no audience for his novel actually existed. As he put it, "In a world of lies, Truth is forced to fly like a scared white doe in the woodlands; and only by cunning glimpses will she reveal herself." But he knew that his readers would be expecting from his book thrilling adventures interlaced with exotic information (a pretty good formula for a best-seller today, come to think of it). He praised his contemporary, Hawthorne, for writing works "directly calculated to deceive—egregiously deceive—the superficial skimmer of pages." Melville had his own main char-acter tell a whaling story within the novel to a group of listeners whose inter-ruptions and questions show that they are obviously missing the whole point, exactly as Melville expected that his readers would. Melville's pessimistic assessment of his audience was correct, and his novel had to wait seventy years before being recognized as one of the classics of American literature. Some of his admirers simply say that Melville was ahead of his time; others, that he was addressing only a persistent cultural elite—the fit but few who take the time to recognize genius. Still others say that *Moby Dick* called its own audience into existence, and seventy years was a short time in which to achieve such a feat. All we can say for sure is that Melville knew his particular audience well but disdained it and addressed instead an implied audience that was capable of cunning glimpses at fleeting truth.

The Gospel of Mark

THE PARABLE OF THE SOWER

The following is one of the most familiar passages from the New Testament of the Bible. It directly addresses the problem of the audience for Jesus's teach-ings, not just in his own time but in subsequent ages as well. Note that there are two divisions of the audience. There is the division suggested by the parable itself, the listeners representing different kinds of ground for the seed. But there is also the division between those to whom Jesus will explain the parable and those to whom he will not. Note that simply being a disciple does not automatically make him or her fertile ground for teaching; among those to whom Jesus explained the parable were many who abandoned him rather than suffer persecution, one who denied him three times, and one who is alleged to have betrayed him.

1   Again he [Jesus] began to teach beside the sea. And a very large crowd gathered about him, so that he got into a boat and sat in it on the sea; and the whole crowd was beside the sea on the land. And he taught them many things in parables, and in his teaching he said to them: "Listen! A sower went out to sow. And as he sowed, some seed fell along the path, and the birds came and devoured it. Other seed fell on rocky ground, where it had not much soil, and immediately it sprang up, since it had no depth of soil; and when the sun rose it was scorched, and since it had no root it withered away. Other seed fell among thorns and the thorns grew up and choked it, and it yielded no grain. And other seeds fell into good soil and brought forth grain, growing up and increasing and yielding thirtyfold and sixtyfold and a hundredfold." And he said, "He who has ears to hear, let him hear."

2   And when he was alone, those who were about him with the twelve asked him concerning the parables. And he said to them, "To you has been given the secret of the kingdom of God, but for those outside everything is in parables; so that they may indeed see but not perceive, and may indeed hear but not understand; lest they should turn again, and be forgiven." And he said to them, "Do you not understand this parable? How then will you understand all the parables? The sower sows the word. And these are the ones along the path, where the word is sown; when they hear, Satan immediately comes and takes away the word which is sown in them. And these in like manner are the ones sown upon rocky ground, who, when they hear the word, immediately receive it with joy; and they have no root in themselves, but endure for a while; then, when tribulation or persecution arises on account of the word, immediately they fall away. And others are the ones sown among thorns; they are those who hear the word, but the cares of the world, and the delight in riches, and the desire for other things, enter in and choke the word, and it proves unfruitful. But those that were sown upon the good soil are the ones who hear the word and accept it and bear fruit, thirtyfold and sixtyfold and a hundredfold."

3   And he said to them, "Is a lamp brought in to be put under a bushel, or under a bed, and not on a stand? For there is nothing hid, except to be made manifest; nor is anything secret, except to come to light. If any man has ears to hear, let him hear." And he said to them, "Take heed what you hear; the

measure you give will be the measure you get, and still more will be given you. For to him who has will more be given; and from him who has not, even what he has will be taken away."

4   And he said, "The kingdom of God is as if a man should scatter seed upon the ground, and should sleep and rise night and day, and the seed should sprout and grow, he knows not how. The earth produces of itself, first the blade, then the ear, then the full grain in the ear. But when the grain is ripe, at once he puts in the sickle, because the harvest has come."

5   And he said, "With what can we compare the kingdom of God, or what parable shall we use for it? It is like a grain of mustard seed, which, when sown upon the ground, is the smallest of all the seeds on earth; yet when it is sown it grows up and becomes the greatest of all shrubs, and puts forth large branches, so that the birds of the air can make nests in its shade."

6   With many such parables he spoke the word to them, as they were able to hear it; he did not speak to them without a parable, but privately to his own disciples he explained everything.

1st century, A.D.

Reacting and Writing

◆   **"Two Letters to Susan"**

Do you find the majority of the mother's arguments persuasive? What do you know about Susan from reading the letters? Do you think she will take her mother's advice? Can you describe the techniques the mother uses to get her points across to Susan? You might try writing a modern version of one of the letters. What exactly would be involved in bringing the letter up-to-date? Would the issue itself have to change? Can you write a deliberately unpersuasive "letter to Susan" in which the mother reveals her lack of trust and her desire for control in a way that is guaranteed to alienate the daughter? (The selection "Mr. Collins Proposes" is full of ideas for how to alienate an audience.)

◆   **"Letter to Scottie" and "My Father's Letters"**

Does Fitzgerald's opening paragraph help to put his reader in a receptive frame of mind? Does it warn her to expect a lecture? When he says in paragraph 6 that he doesn't want to change Scottie, does that seem to you to be true? Can you write an up-to-date version of this letter that would create a positive portrait of a modern college student while urging him or her to make some changes? How does the "Scottie" implied by F. Scott Fitzgerald's letter differ from the "Susan" implied by Banning's? Compare Fitzgerald's attempts to persuade his daughter Scottie with Banning's attempts to persuade Susan. Which parent seems more likely to persuade, Banning or Fitzgerald? Why?

◆   **"Advice to Youth"**

Does Clemens create an appealing role for his audience? How do you respond to his advice? Do you think that he has simply given up on the idea of seriously advising these young people and chosen to entertain them instead? Is he genuinely worried about all the issues he raises, such as the handling of firearms? Why does he raise these issues? If you think that he is trying to persuade his audience of something, what is it, and how is he trying to do it? Try writing a speech to a graduating high school or college class that pretends to advise one thing and in reality advises another.

◆   **"Young Soul"**

Because it is a poem, Baraka's "advice to youth" comes in a very compressed form. Decide what you think Baraka's advice is, and see if you can put it in the form of a commencement speech to a high school or college class, bringing in examples and stories to make the advice persuasive to your audience. Or you could put it in the form of a letter from a parent to a child. Baraka is an African-American man: Do you think that his advice is directed more particularly to an African-American audience, or is race irrelevant to the point he is making? Do you find yourself in the audience for his argument? Is it persuasive to you? Why or why not?

◆   **"Mr. Collins Proposes"**

Mr. Collins's blunders may help you to see more clearly our point about how a work implies its audience. Try writing a deliberately unpersuasive commencement speech that talks down to the members of its audience and makes them resist the message. This exercise may be more effective if you try to ruin what is really a worthwhile message by creating an unappealing portrait of the audience. Or try a welcoming speech to the students from a representative of a college or university— one that gives perfectly good advice and yet makes the students want to withdraw before classes start.

◆   **"The Parable of the Sower"**

Take one of your essays (or letters) and try an experiment. Describe some audiences for which you would not attempt to adapt it. Describe a situation in which you would address your essay not to the particular audience at hand but to an imagined audience in the indefinite future. Adapt your essay to a complex audience that has many divergent tendencies. (Teachers, by the way, have to do this all the time when they find themselves with students of diverse backgrounds, interests, and abilities.) Finally, think about those aspects of yourself that you would be prepared to downplay or even to deny in order to influence an audience important to you—and those aspects you would not change. Such imaginative explorations of your own rhetorical limits can be voyages of discovery.

Additional Readings

Arthur Quinn

SCIENCE, LITERATURE AND RHETORIC

We thought it would be useful to show you how this chapter's argument would have to be adapted to reach an audience quite different from you. The following is a piece written by one of us for the Society for the Study of Science and Literature, a group of scholars interested in the relationship between science and the humanities. The point of the following essay, intended for these professional academics, is exactly the same as the one made in this chapter: start by considering audience.

1   Rhetoric's most important contribution to the study of science and literature is a method to determine common ground between scientific discourse and literary, a method that does not prejudge in favor of either side. First I have to define what I mean by rhetoric and to distinguish its approach to discourse from those commonly employed in the evaluation of scientific and literary discourse, respectively. The most convenient way to do this is through the scheme that M. H. Abrams uses at the beginning of *The Mirror and the Lamp* (1953) to distinguish the four chief ways in which human discourse has been analyzed and evaluated within the Western tradition.

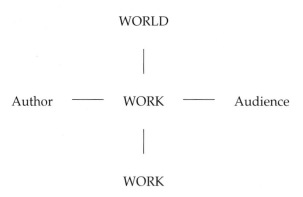

2   We can, like the scientist, attend to the relationship between the discourse and the world at large. Is the discourse true? Does it accurately represent or mirror the world? Second, we can attend to the relationship between the discourse and its author. Is it an adequate expression of the author's personality

or feelings? Is it authentic, spontaneous, sincere? Third, we can evaluate the discourse in relation to itself. Then we are seeking the beauty of the discourse, intrinsically if possible, separate from the author or the world. We are treating it as an aesthetic object. Fourth, we can take a pragmatic, or rhetorical, approach to discourse.

3   Rhetoric focuses upon the relationship between the discourse and its audience. This relationship gives rise to characteristic questions: What is the intended audience? What response from that audience does the author hope to get? How does the author's presentation of himself, his *ethos,* assist him in this task? How does the arrangement of the piece, as well as its style, shape the audience's response? The list of questions is hardly exhaustive. While the mimetic approach has dominated our understanding of scientific discourse, and the expressive and aesthetic approaches have, at least since the Romantics, dominated our understanding of literature, rhetoric, with its emphasis on audience, has been traditionally associated with oratory in general, and with political and legal discourse in particular. In oratory both the author and audience are physically present to one another, and their interaction is palpable. In politics and law the primary aim is power and influence—not beauty, or self-expression, or even truth.

4   The exemplary work of literary critics such as Wayne Booth in *The Rhetoric of Fiction* (1961), to give just one example, has demonstrated just how fruitful the application of rhetorical analysis to literary texts can be. Historians and philosophers of science have been moving in exactly the same direction, although less self-consciously, and with less recognition of the fact. Historians took the lead by showing that science is not as isomorphic, as methodologically homogeneous, as once was thought. Thomas Kuhn, in *The Structure of Scientific Revolutions* (2nd ed., 1970), calls the plurality of scientific methods "paradigms." Paul Feyerabend, in his *Against Method* (1975), argues simply that we should no longer seek *The* Scientific Method, but rather be satisfied with distinct rhetorics of science. Thus, following Feyerabend's line, when we deal with a great scientific work such as Darwin's *Origin of Species,* we should not try to reduce it to some method that philosophers of science in our own time happen to prefer. We should rather treat it as a great piece of deliberative rhetoric that did in fact convince many of the best young biologists of Darwin's time to use his theory as the basis for their own future research—this despite the many and fundamental objections to his theory that he himself could not answer. Let us look at his skill in a little more detail.

5   Darwin consistently seeks to soften his readers' opposition to his theory by showing that he sympathizes with their difficulties. A master of tactical concession, Darwin time and again places himself with his objecting readers, sympathizing with them, showing them he understands, and thereby mollifying them. Some of the difficulties facing his theory are, he says, "so grave that to this day I can never reflect on them without being staggered." Any

attempt to explain the eye by natural selection seems, "I freely confess, absurd in the highest possible degree." And when Darwin must admonish his readers, he is careful always to do it at least partly at his own expense. The truth of the continual struggle for existence is difficult to bear constantly in mind—"at least I have found it so." The natural grouping of organisms into groups subordinate to groups is a fact "the wonder of which we are apt to overlook."

6   Darwin also seems to have been sensitive to the irrational resistance that his theory would provoke, particularly in its destruction of much of his readers' comforting sense of nature's harmony and beauty. Most of his figurative language is clustered in passages where he tries to retain the appearance of this beauty and harmony for his readers, partly at least by showing them that he still sees it. Adaptations are not just adaptations for Darwin—they are "beautiful adaptations." Nature at times becomes a personified "she" mothering over her children. The whole organic world becomes a lovely Tree of Life which "fills with its dead and broken branches the crust of the earth and covers the surface with its ever branching and beautiful ramifications." Darwin can even occasionally try to reassure his readers directly. "When we reflect on this struggle, we may console ourselves with the full belief that the war of nature is not incessant, that no fear is felt, that death is generally prompt, and that the vigorous, the healthy, and the happy survive and multiply." His readers may never again be able to believe rationally that this is the best of all possible worlds; Darwin will, nonetheless, for the time being, permit them to feel it may be so. Literary critics such as Stanley Edgar Hyman, writing in *The Tangled Bank* (1962), have understood the aesthetics of Darwin's style, but it has remained for rhetoric to make the connection between aesthetic effect and overall plausibility and persuasiveness.

7   What the Darwin example shows is that in the study of scientific discourse, as much as in the study of literature, rhetorical analysis is proving fruitful. The question remains one of how rhetorical analysis can help bring science and literature together. Rather than speaking in abstractions, I want, once again, to show how in one instance, the author-audience relationship in a great work of literature bears remarkable resemblance to the author-audience relationship implicit in a roughly contemporaneous great work of science. I want to point to a rhetorical similarity between Milton's *Paradise Lost* and Newton's *Principia*. (Newton is supposed to have "discovered" gravity in 1665–6; Milton published the first edition of his epic poem in 1667.)

8   One of the classic interpretive questions about *Paradise Lost* is, why does the snake have all the good lines? Or, to put it somewhat more elegantly, why are the virtuous characters so dull and the evil ones so interesting? Of course, there have been any number of attempted answers, Blake for one thinking that Milton was of the Devil's party whether he knew it or not. Stanley Fish, himself a prominent participant in the revival of rhetoric within literary studies, has suggested a rhetorical answer. In *Surprised by Sin* (1967), Fish argues

that—*mirabile dictu*—Milton knew what he was doing, that he intended these effects.

9   Why would Milton have done such a thing? Fish believes the answer is clear once we consider Milton's view of his audience. Milton believed his audience to be composed of fallen men—men, indeed, who because of their fallen nature were not inclined to admit their own fundamental depravity, unless of course they were illuminated by grace. In *Paradise Lost* Milton was recounting for this audience the epic of how they became depraved. An important part of this recounting was for Milton's audience to realize, to realize fully, that they were indeed the sons and daughters of Adam and Eve, that they were fallen creatures, weak to the temptations of the Arch-Tempter. So Milton gave his Lucifer the tools of his trade, fully expecting his audience to fall again and again to Lucifer's charms, to fall only to be reminded again and again that they have listened in admiration to the embodiment of all evil. The saved in Milton's audience would be chastened by these reminders, the damned only perplexed.

10   No one might seem farther from this religious exchange between Milton and his audience than Isaac Newton, who was virtually deified by his eighteenth-century readers for his cold rationalism and objectivity. However, much of the most important work on Newton over the past twenty-five years has shown this Newton to be a figment of eighteenth-century scientific ideology. The real Newton was much closer to Milton than Voltaire would have liked to admit. But first let us look at Newton's idiosyncrasies as a writer.

11   Newton was extremely reluctant to make public his natural philosophy. As published, some of the most important parts of the *Principia* (1687) are tucked away in structurally unimportant sections. The discussion of absolute space and time, for instance, is included in a scholium. For a time he considered suppressing the whole third book of the *Principia,* the very book in which his mathematics is finally applied to the physical world. In short, his attitude to his own writing at times seems so secretive as to be almost pathological, leading at least one historian—Frank Manuel—to seek a psychoanalytic explanation. A different explanation is suggested by Newton's efforts at biblical exegesis.

12   Newton believed that he was living in the last days, the time prophesied in Daniel and the Apocalypse. The forces of the anti-Christ were on the march, and the people of God were being sorely tested. It was also a time when the people of God were recovering the revelation of God in its pristine form. No longer would this revelation be obscured in myth and allegory; now it could be rationally demonstrated, at least to those who were not wicked at heart.

13   The rhetorical implications of Newton's view of his own situation are striking. Newton faced a particularly acute form of the standard problem of the author forced to address a composite audience containing diverse and

even opposed elements. It is the same audience problem that Milton had, but in a more extreme form.

14   In such a rhetorical context, Newton's reluctance to publish is understandable. His writing, once published, would be not just for Cambridge, but for the entire learned (Latin-literate) world. It was work that was going to be read by the wicked as well as the wise. With his work, the wise might be purified; but with it the wicked might just as easily try to do wickedly. Newton might decide to speak to this mixed audience, but he need not decide to speak to it candidly. He would write so that the good would understand, and the rest would be vexed. This decision is reflected, as I have tried to show in detail in my *Confidence of British Philosophers* (1977)—not just in Newton's general attitude toward his writing, but in the details of his presentation, or rather half-presentation, of his theories.

15   I think the kind of rhetorical affinity which I have sketched here between Milton and Newton should be found between other poets and scientists of other times and places—between, say, Victorian poets (and novelists) and Darwin. Noting these is one important way to create a bridge between the sciences and the humanities.

16   What I have been trying to suggest through my examples (at once so fragmentary and superficial in themselves) is that the rhetorical perspective on discourse, with its emphasis on audience, has a decisive contribution to make to our understanding of the relation between science and literature. The traditional philosophies of science have emphasized the difference between science and nonscience, emphasized what sets science apart, even above, other disciplines. So, too, traditional literary theory has emphasized the peculiarly aesthetic use of language, what sets literature apart, even above. Rhetoric simply offers a complementary perspective, one that emphasizes the common ground of all discourse by which one person endeavors to influence others. The great scientist and the great literary artist may be something more than skillful rhetors, but they are at least that—and this may be exactly what they share.

1986

Stephen Jay Gould

GENESIS VS. GEOLOGY

Stephen Jay Gould is a paleontologist who has written a series of popular works on scientific topics. His works have been widely praised for making technical subjects interesting to those who do not share his specialized knowledge.

In this essay, originally published in The Atlantic Monthly *in 1982, he argues that evolution should be taught in American public schools because it is science, and that creationism should not be taught because it is religion. As you read the essay, try to decide where Gould's audience stands when he begins and where he hopes they will stand when he ends. Read the opening paragraphs carefully and see if you think that he includes creationists or religious people generally in his audience. (For instance, does he attempt to convince creationists themselves that their views are religion, not science, and thus do not belong in public schools?) What examples can you find of Gould's making his points accessible to general audiences? How would someone who believes that alternatives to evolution should be given equal time in schools respond to Gould's specific points?*

1   G. K. Chesterton once mused over Noah's dinnertime conversations during those long nights on a vast and tempestuous sea:

> And Noah he often said to his wife
>   when he sat down to dine,
> "I don't care where the water goes if
>   it doesn't get into the wine."

2   Noah's insouciance has not been matched by defenders of his famous flood. For centuries, fundamentalists have tried very hard to find a place for the subsiding torrents. They have struggled even more valiantly to devise a source for all that water. Our modern oceans, extensive as they are, will not override Mt. Everest. One seventeenth-century searcher said: "I can as soon believe that a man would be drowned in his own spittle as that the world should be deluged by the water in it."

3   With the advent of creationism, a solution to this old dilemma has been put forward. In *The Genesis Flood* (1961), the founding document of the creationist movement, John Whitcomb and Henry Morris seek guidance from Genesis 1:6–7, which states that God created the firmament and then slid it into place amidst the waters, thus dividing "the waters which were under the firmament from the waters which were above the firmament: and it was so." The waters under the firmament include seas and interior fluid that may rise in volcanic eruptions. But what are the waters above the firmament? Whitcomb and Morris reason that Moses cannot refer here to transient rain clouds, because he also tells us (Genesis 2:5) that "the Lord God had not caused it to rain upon the earth." The authors therefore imagine that the earth, in those palmy days, was surrounded by a gigantic canopy of water vapor (which, being invisible, did not obscure the light of Genesis 1:3). "These upper waters," Whitcomb and Morris write, "were therefore placed in that position by divine creativity, not by the normal processes of the hydrological cycle of the present day." Upwelling from the depths together with the liquefaction, puncturing, and descent of the celestial canopy produced more than enough water for Noah's worldwide flood.

4   Fanciful solutions often generate a cascade of additional difficulties. In this case, Morris, a hydraulic engineer by training, and Whitcomb invoke a divine assist to gather the waters into their canopy, but then can't find a natural way to get them down. So they invoke a miracle: God put the water there in the first place; let him then release it.

> The simple fact of the matter is that one cannot have *any* kind of a Genesis Flood without acknowledging the presence of supernatural elements.... It is obvious that the opening of the "windows of heaven" in order to allow "the waters which were above the firmament" to fall upon the earth, and the breaking up of "all the fountains of the great deep" were supernatural acts of God.

5   Since we usually define science, at least in part, as a system of explanation that relies upon invariant natural laws, this charmingly direct invocation of miracles (suspensions of natural law) would seem to negate the central claims of the modern creationist movement—that creationism is not religion but a scientific alternative to evolution; that creationism has been disregarded by scientists because they are a fanatical and dogmatic lot who cannot appreciate new advances; and that creationists must therefore seek legislative redress in their attempts to force a "balanced treatment" for both creationism and evolution in the science classrooms of our public schools.

6   Legislative history has driven creationists to this strategy of claiming scientific status for their religious view. The older laws, which banned the teaching of evolution outright and led to John Scopes's conviction in 1925, were overturned by the Supreme Court in 1968, but not before they had exerted a chilling effect upon teaching for forty years. (Evolution is the indispensable organizing principle of the life sciences, but I did not hear the word in my 1956 high school biology class. New York City, to be sure, suffered no restrictive ordinances, but publishers, following the principle of the "least common denominator" as a sales strategy, tailored the national editions of their textbooks to the few states that considered it criminal to place an ape on the family escutcheon.) A second attempt to mandate equal time for frankly religious views of life's history passed the Tennessee state legislature in the 1970s but failed a constitutional challenge in the court. This judicial blocking left only one legislative path open—the claim that creationism is a science.

7   The third strategy had some initial success, and "balanced treatment" acts to equate "evolution science" and "creation science" in classrooms passed the Arkansas and Louisiana legislatures in 1981. The ACLU has sued for a federal-court ruling on the Louisiana law's constitutionality, and a trial is likely this year. The Arkansas law was challenged by the ACLU in 1981, on behalf of local plaintiffs (including twelve practicing theologians who felt more threatened by the bill than many scientists did). Federal Judge William R. Overton heard the Arkansas case in Little Rock last December. I spent the better part of

a day on the stand, a witness for the prosecution, testifying primarily about how the fossil record refutes "flood geology" and supports evolution.

8   On January 5, Judge Overton delivered his eloquent opinion, declaring the Arkansas act unconstitutional because so-called "creation science" is only a version of Genesis read literally—a partisan (and narrowly sectarian) religious view, barred from public-school classrooms by the First Amendment. Legal language is often incomprehensible, but sometimes it is charming, and I enjoyed the wording of Overton's decision: ". . . judgment is hereby entered in favor of the plaintiffs and against the defendants. The relief prayed for is granted."

9   Support for Overton's equation of "creation science" with strident and sectarian fundamentalism comes from two sources. First, the leading creationists themselves released some frank private documents in response to plaintiffs' subpoenas. Overton's long list of citations seems to brand the claim for scientific creationism as simple hypocrisy. For example, Paul Ellwanger, the tireless advocate and drafter of the "model bill" that became Arkansas Act 590 of 1981, the law challenged by the ACLU, says in a letter to a state legislator that "I view this whole battle as one between God and anti-God forces, though I know there are a large number of evolutionists who believe in God. . . . it behooves Satan to do all he can to thwart our efforts . . ." In another letter, he refers to "the idea of killing evolution instead of playing these debating games that we've been playing for nigh over a decade already"—a reasonably clear statement of the creationists' ultimate aims, and an identification of their appeals for "equal time," "the American way of fairness," and "presenting them both and letting the kids decide" as just so much rhetoric.

10   The second source of evidence of the bill's unconstitutionality lies in the logic and character of creationist arguments themselves. The flood story is central to all creationist systems. It also has elicited the only specific and testable theory the creationists have offered; for the rest, they have only railed against evolutionary claims. The flood story was explicitly cited as one of the six defining characteristics of "creation science" in Arkansas Act 590: "explanation of the earth's geology by catastrophism, including the occurrence of a worldwide flood."

11   Creationism reveals its nonscientific character in two ways: its central tenets cannot be tested and its peripheral claims, which can be tested, have been proven false. At its core, the creationist account rests on "singularities"—that is to say, on miracles. The creationist God is not the noble clockwinder of Newton and Boyle, who set the laws of nature properly at the beginning of time and then released direct control in full confidence that his initial decisions would require no revision. He is, instead, a constant presence, who suspends his own laws when necessary to make the new or destroy the old. Since science can treat only natural phenomena occurring in

a context of invariant natural law, the constant invocation of miracles places creationism in another realm.

12   We have already seen how Whitcomb and Morris remove a divine finger from the dike of heaven to flood the earth from their vapor canopy. But the miracles surrounding Noah's flood do not stop there; two other supernatural assists are required. First, God acted "to gather the animals into the Ark." (The Bible tells us [Genesis 6:20] that they found their own way.) Second, God intervened to keep the animals "under control during the year of the Flood." Whitcomb and Morris provide a long disquisition on hibernation and suspect that some divinely ordained state of suspended animation relieved Noah's small and aged crew of most responsibility for feeding and cleaning (poor Noah himself was 600 years old at the time).

13   In candid moments, leading creationists will admit that the miraculous character of origin and destruction precludes a scientific understanding. Morris writes (and Judge Overton quotes): "God was there when it happened. We were not there.... Therefore, we are completely limited to what God has seen fit to tell us, and this information is in His written Word." Duane Gish, the leading creationist author, says: "We do not know how the Creator created, what processes He used, for He used processes which are not now operating anywhere in the natural universe.... We cannot discover by scientific investigation anything about the creative processes used by God." When pressed about these quotes, creationists tend to admit that they are purveying religion after all, but then claim that evolution is equally religious. Gish also says: "Creationists have repeatedly stated that neither creation nor evolution is a scientific theory (and each is equally religious)." But as Judge Overton reasoned, if creationists are merely complaining that evolution is religion, then they should be trying to eliminate it from the schools, not struggling to get their own brand of religion into science classrooms as well. And if, instead, they are asserting the validity of their own version of natural history, they must be able to prove, according to the demands of science, that creationism is scientific.

14   Scientific claims must be testable: we must, in principle, be able to envision a set of observations that would render them false. Miracles cannot be judged by this criterion, as Whitcomb and Morris have admitted. But is all creationist writing merely about untestable singularities? Are arguments never made in proper scientific form? Creationists do offer some testable statements, and these are amenable to scientific analysis. Why, then, do I continue to claim that creationism isn't science? Simply because these relatively few statements have been tested and conclusively refuted. Dogmatic assent to disproved claims is not scientific behavior. Scientists are as stubborn as the rest of us, but they must be able to change their minds.

15   In "flood geology," we find our richest source of testable creationist claims. Creationists have been forced into this uncharacteristically vulnera-

ble stance by a troubling fact too well known to be denied: namely, that the geological record of fossils follows a single, invariant order throughout the world. The oldest rocks contain only single-celled creatures; invertebrates dominate later strata, followed by the first fishes, then dinosaurs, and finally large mammals. One might be tempted to take a "liberal," or allegorical, view of Scripture and identify this sequence with the order of creation in Genesis 1, allowing millions or billions of years for the "days" of Moses. But creationists will admit no such reconciliation. Their fundamentalism is absolute and uncompromising. If Moses said "days," he meant periods of twenty-four hours, to the second. (Creationist literature is often less charitable to liberal theology than to evolution. As a subject for wrath, nothing matches the enemy within.)

16   Since God created with such alacrity, all creatures once must have lived simultaneously on the earth. How, then, did their fossil remains get sorted into an invariable order in the earth's strata? To resolve this particularly knotty dilemma, creationists invoke Noah's flood: all creatures were churned together in the great flood and their fossilized succession reflects the order of their settling as the waters receded. But what natural processes would produce such a predictable order from a singular chaos? The testable proposals of "flood geology" have been advanced to explain the causes of this sorting.

17   Whitcomb and Morris offer three suggestions. The first—hydrological— holds that denser and more streamlined objects would have descended more rapidly and should populate the bottom strata (in conventional geology, the oldest strata). The second—ecological—envisions a sorting responsive to environment. Denizens of the ocean bottom were overcome by the flood waters first, and should lie in the lower strata; inhabitants of mountaintops postponed their inevitable demise, and now adorn our upper strata. The third—anatomical or functional—argues that certain animals, by their high intelligence or superior mobility, might have struggled successfully for a time, and ended up at the top.

18   All three proposals have been proven false. The lower strata abound in delicate, floating creatures, as well as spherical globs. Many oceanic creatures—whales and teleost fishes in particular—appear only in upper strata, well above hordes of terrestrial forms. Clumsy sloths (not to mention hundreds of species of marine invertebrates) are restricted to strata lying well above others that serve as exclusive homes for scores of lithe and nimble small dinosaurs and pterosaurs.

19   The very invariance of the universal fossil sequence is the strongest argument against its production in a single gulp. Could exceptionless order possibly arise from a contemporaneous mixture by such dubious processes of sorting? Surely, somewhere, at least one courageous trilobite would have paddled on valiantly (as its colleagues succumbed) and won a place in the upper strata. Surely, on some primordial beach, a man would have suffered a

heart attack and been washed into the lower strata before intelligence had a chance to plot temporary escape. But if the strata represent vast stretches of sequential time, then invariant order is an expectation, not a problem. No trilobite lies in the upper strata because they all perished 225 million years ago. No man keeps lithified company with a dinosaur, because we were still 60 million years in the future when the last dinosaur perished.

20   True science and religion are not in conflict. The history of approaches to Noah's flood by scientists who were also professional theologians provides an excellent example of this important truth—and also illustrates just how long ago "flood geology" was conclusively laid to rest by religious scientists. I have argued that direct invocation of miracles and unwillingness to abandon a false doctrine deprive modern creationists of their self-proclaimed status as scientists. When we examine how the great scientist-theologians of past centuries treated the flood, we note that their work is distinguished by both a conscious refusal to admit miraculous events into their explanatory schemes and a willingness to abandon preferred hypotheses in the face of geological evidence. They were scientists *and* religious leaders—and they show us why modern creationists are not scientists.

21   On the subject of miracles, the Reverend Thomas Burnet published his century's most famous geological treatise in the 1680s, *Telluris theoria sacra (The Sacred Theory of the Earth)*. Burnet accepted the Bible's truth, and set out to construct a geological history that would be in accord with the events of Genesis. But he believed something else even more strongly: that, as a scientist, he must follow natural law and scrupulously avoid miracles. His story is fanciful by modern standards: the earth originally was devoid of topography, but was drying and cracking; the cracks served as escape vents for internal fluids, but rain sealed the cracks, and the earth, transformed into a gigantic pressure cooker, ruptured its surface skin; surging internal waters inundated the earth, producing Noah's flood. Bizarre, to be sure, but bizarre precisely because Burnet would not abandon natural law. It is not easy to force a preconceived story into the strictures of physical causality. Over and over again, Burnet acknowledges that his task would be much simpler if only he could invoke a miracle. Why weave such a complex tale to find water for the flood in a physically acceptable manner, when God might simply have made new water for his cataclysmic purification? Many of Burnet's colleagues urged such a course, but he rejected it as inconsistent with the methods of "natural philosophy" (the word "science" had not yet entered English usage):

> They say in short that God Almighty created waters on purpose to make the Deluge.... And this, in a few words, is the whole account of the business. This is to cut the knot when we cannot loose it.

22   Burnet's God, like the deity of Newton and Boyle, was a clock-winder, not a bungler who continually perturbed his own system with later corrections.

We think him a better Artist that makes a Clock that strikes regularly at every hour from the Springs and Wheels which he puts in the work, than he that hath so made his Clock that he must put his finger to it every hour to make it strike: And if one should contrive a piece of Clock-work so that it should beat all the hours, and make all its motions regularly for such a time, and that time being come, upon a signal given, or a Spring toucht, it should of its own accord fall all to pieces; would not this be look'd upon as a piece of greater Art, than if the Workman came at that time prefixt, and with a great Hammer beat it into pieces?

23   Flood geology was considered and tested by early-nineteenth-century geologists. They never believed that a single flood had produced all fossil-bearing strata, but they did accept and then disprove a claim that the uppermost strata contained evidence for a single, catastrophic, worldwide inundation. The science of geology arose in nations that were glaciated during the great ice ages, and glacial deposits are similar to the products of floods. During the 1820s, British geologists carried out an extensive empirical program to test whether these deposits represented the action of a single flood. The work was led by two ministers, the Reverend Adam Sedgwick (who taught Darwin his geology) and the Reverend William Buckland. Buckland initially decided that all the "superficial gravels" (as these deposits were called) represented a single event, and he published his *Reliquiae diluvianae (Relics of the Flood)* in 1824. However, Buckland's subsequent field work proved that the superficial gravels were not contemporaneous but represented several different events (multiple ice ages, as we now know). Geology proclaimed no worldwide flood but rather a long sequence of local events. In one of the great statements in the history of science, Sedgwick, who was Buckland's close colleague in both science and theology, publicly abandoned flood geology—and upheld empirical science—in his presidential address to the Geological Society of London in 1831.

Having been myself a believer, and, to the best of my power, a propagator of what I now regard as a philosophic heresy, and having more than once been quoted for opinions I do not now maintain, I think it right, as one of my last acts before I quit this Chair, thus publicly to read my recantation....

There is, I think, one great negative conclusion now incontestably established—that the vast masses of diluvial gravel, scattered almost over the surface of the earth, do not belong to one violent and transitory period....

We ought, indeed, to have paused before we first adopted the diluvian theory, and referred all our old superficial gravel to the action of the Mosaic flood.... In classing together distant unknown formations under one name; in giving them a simultaneous origin, and in determining their date, not by the organic remains we had discovered, but by those we expected hypothetically hereafter to discover, in them; we have given one more example of the passion with which the mind fastens upon general conclusions, and of the readiness with which it leaves the consideration of unconnected truths.

24   As I prepared to leave Little Rock last December, I went to my hotel room to gather my belongings and found a man sitting backward on my commode, pulling it apart with a plumber's wrench. He explained to me that a leak in the room below had caused part of the ceiling to collapse and he was seeking the source of the water. My commode, located just above, was the obvious candidate, but his hypothesis had failed, for my equipment was working perfectly. The plumber then proceeded to give me a fascinating disquisition on how a professional traces the pathways of water through hotel pipes and walls. The account was perfectly logical and mechanistic: it can come only from here, here, or there, flow this way or that way, and end up there, there, or here. I then asked him what he thought of the trial across the street, and he confessed his staunch creationism, including his firm belief in the miracle of Noah's flood.

25   As a professional, this man never doubted that water has a physical source and a mechanically constrained path of motion—and that he could use the principles of his trade to identify causes. It would be a poor (and unemployed) plumber indeed who suspected that the laws of engineering had been suspended whenever a puddle and cracked plaster bewildered him. Why should we approach the physical history of our earth any differently?

1982

Martin Luther King Jr.

LETTER FROM BIRMINGHAM JAIL

A "Public Statement by Eight Alabama Clergymen" appeared in a Birmingham, Alabama, newspaper in 1963. Martin Luther King Jr. wrote the response that follows it. He called his response a letter and addressed it directly to the clergymen, but he did not mail private copies to each of them. Instead, he published it in the newspaper and later revised it for inclusion in a collection of his writings. This suggests that he also had a wider audience in mind for his arguments.

King's "Letter" is a very complex document and can be analyzed profitably from a variety of points of view. But let us focus on audience—King does begin by addressing the clergymen, whose position certainly seems to present some moral problems. As a potential audience for this letter, they might be squirming. But soon they are not the only ones. King divides African-Americans into three groups: the violent separatists; the nonviolent activists like himself; and the others who are too complacent or too downtrodden to take a position. American whites, in King's analysis, break down similarly: the violent white racists; the few activist whites (mentioned in paragraph 32); and the many apathetic or nonactivist whites who view themselves as "moderate" on the issue of civil rights. Consider these last as a potential audience for this letter. They can read the early sections of this letter comfortably, feeling the justice of King's criticisms of the "Public Statement" and distancing themselves entirely from these clergymen who have hampered this eloquent and righteous man. But look what happens in paragraph 23. Now King is generalizing his concerns and expressing his grave disappointment with the white moderates, who favor civil rights but have done nothing to aid the struggle. Suddenly readers of King's letter are no longer so comfortably aloof. They must move to activism or the civil rights movement will be taken over by violent separatists—and it will be their fault.

As you go through the letter, you will see that ours is not the only way to read it. But do try to use King's own categories, his way of dividing up the world, to define his audience.

Public Statement by Eight Alabama Clergymen

April 12, 1963

1   We the undersigned clergymen are among those who, in January, issued "An Appeal for Law and Order and Common Sense," in dealing with racial problems in Alabama. We expressed understanding that honest convictions in racial matters could properly be pursued in the courts, but urged that decisions of those courts should in the meantime be peacefully obeyed.

2   Since that time there had been some evidence of increased forbearance and a willingness to face facts. Responsible citizens have undertaken to work on various problems which cause racial friction and unrest. In Birmingham, recent public events have given indication that we all have opportunity for a new constructive and realistic approach to racial problems.

3   However, we are now confronted by a series of demonstrations by some of our Negro citizens, directed and led in part by outsiders. We recognize the natural impatience of people who feel that their hopes are slow in being realized. But we are convinced that these demonstrations are unwise and untimely.

4   We agree rather with certain local Negro leadership which has called for honest and open negotiation of racial issues in our area. And we believe this kind of facing of issues can best be accomplished by citizens of our own metropolitan area, white and Negro, meeting with their knowledge and experience of the local situation. All of us need to face that responsibility and find proper channels for its accomplishment.

5   Just as we formerly pointed out that "hatred and violence have no sanction in our religious and political traditions," we also point out that such

actions as incite to hatred and violence, however technically peaceful those actions may be, have not contributed to the resolution of our local problems. We do not believe that these days of new hope are days when extreme measures are justified in Birmingham.

6   We commend the community as a whole, and the local news media and law enforcement officials in particular, on the calm manner in which these demonstrations have been handled. We urge the public to continue to show restraint should the demonstrations continue, and the law enforcement officials to remain calm and continue to protect our city from violence.

7   We further strongly urge our own Negro community to withdraw support from these demonstrations, and to unite locally in working peacefully for a better Birmingham. When rights are consistently denied, a cause should be pressed in the courts and in negotiations among local leaders, and not in the streets. We appeal to both our white and Negro citizenry to observe the principles of law and order and common sense.

Signed by:

C. C. J. Carpenter, D.D., LL.D., *Bishop of Alabama*

Joseph A. Durick, D.D., *Auxiliary Bishop, Diocese of Mobile, Birmingham*

Rabbi Milton L. Grafman, *Temple Emanu-El, Birmingham, Alabama*

Bishop Paul Hardin, *Bishop of the Alabama-West Florida Conference of the Methodist Church*

Bishop Nolan B. Harmon, *Bishop of the North Alabama Conference of the Methodist Church*

George M. Murray, D.D., LL.D., *Bishop Coadjutor, Episcopal Diocese of Alabama*

Edward V. Ramage, *Moderator, Synod of the Alabama Presbyterian Church in the United States*

Earl Stallings, *Pastor, First Baptist Church, Birmingham, Alabama*

Letter from Birmingham Jail[*]

April 16,1963

My Dear Fellow Clergymen:

1   While confined here in the Birmingham city jail, I came across your recent statement calling my present activities "unwise and untimely." Seldom do I pause to answer criticism of my work and ideas. If I sought to answer all the criticisms that cross my desk, my secretaries would have little

---

[*]*Author's Note:* This response to a published statement by eight fellow clergymen from Alabama . . . was composed under somewhat constricting circumstances. Begun on the margins of the newspaper in which the statement appeared while I was in jail, the letter was continued on scraps of writing paper supplied by a friendly Negro trusty, and concluded on a pad my attorneys were eventually permitted to leave me. Although the text remains in substance unaltered, I have indulged in the author's prerogative of polishing it for publication.

time for anything other than such correspondence in the course of the day, and I would have no time for constructive work. But since I feel that you are men of genuine good will and that your criticisms are sincerely set forth, I want to try to answer your statement in what I hope will be patient and reasonable terms.

2   I think I should indicate why I am here in Birmingham, since you have been influenced by the view which argues against "outsiders coming in." I have the honor of serving as president of the Southern Christian Leadership Conference, an organization operating in every southern state, with headquarters in Atlanta, Georgia. We have some eighty-five affiliated organizations across the South, and one of them is the Alabama Christian Movement for Human Rights. Frequently we share staff, educational and financial resources with our affiliates. Several months ago the affiliate here in Birmingham asked us to be on call to engage in a nonviolent direct-action program if such were deemed necessary. We readily consented, and when the hour came we lived up to our promise. So I, along with several members of my staff, am here because I was invited here. I am here because I have organizational ties here.

3   But more basically, I am in Birmingham because injustice is here. Just as the prophets of the eighth century B.C. left their villages and carried their "thus saith the Lord" far beyond the boundaries of their home towns, and just as the Apostle Paul left his village of Tarsus and carried the gospel of Jesus Christ to the far corners of the Greco-Roman world, so am I compelled to carry the gospel of freedom beyond my own home town. Like Paul, I must constantly respond to the Macedonian call for aid.

4   Moreover, I am cognizant of the interrelatedness of all communities and states. I cannot sit idly by in Atlanta and not be concerned about what happens in Birmingham. Injustice anywhere is a threat to justice everywhere. We are caught in an inescapable network of mutuality, tied in a single garment of destiny. Whatever affects one directly, affects all indirectly. Never again can we afford to live with the narrow, provincial "outside agitator" idea. Anyone who lives inside the United States can never be considered an outsider anywhere within its bounds.

5   You deplore the demonstrations taking place in Birmingham. But your statement, I am sorry to say, fails to express a similar concern for the conditions that brought about the demonstrations. I am sure that none of you would want to rest content with the superficial kind of social analysis that deals merely with effects and does not grapple with underlying causes. It is unfortunate that demonstrations are taking place in Birmingham, but it is even more unfortunate that the city's white power structure left the Negro community with no alternative.

6   In any nonviolent campaign there are four basic steps: collection of the facts to determine whether injustices exist; negotiation; self-purification; and direct action. We have gone through all these steps in Birmingham. There can

be no gainsaying the fact that racial injustice engulfs this community. Birmingham is probably the most thoroughly segregated city in the United States. Its ugly record of brutality is widely known. Negroes have experienced grossly unjust treatment in the courts. There have been more unsolved bombings of Negro homes and churches in Birmingham than in any other city in the nation. These are the hard, brutal facts of the case. On the basis of these conditions, Negro leaders sought to negotiate with the city fathers. But the latter consistently refused to engage in good-faith negotiation.

7   Then, last September, came the opportunity to talk with leaders of Birmingham's economic community. In the course of the negotiations, certain promises were made by the merchants—for example, to remove the stores' humiliating racial signs. On the basis of these promises, the Reverend Fred Shuttlesworth and the leaders of the Alabama Christian Movement for Human Rights agreed to a moratorium on all demonstrations. As the weeks and months went by, we realized that we were the victims of a broken promise. A few signs, briefly removed, returned; the others remained.

8   As in so many past experiences, our hopes had been blasted, and the shadow of deep disappointment settled upon us. We had no alternative except to prepare for direct action, whereby we would present our very bodies as a means of laying our case before the conscience of the local and the national community. Mindful of the difficulties involved, we decided to undertake a process of self-purification. We began a series of workshops on nonviolence, and we repeatedly asked ourselves: "Are you able to accept blows without retaliating?" "Are you able to endure the ordeal of jail?" We decided to schedule our direct-action program for the Easter season, realizing that except for Christmas, this is the main shopping period of the year. Knowing that a strong economic-withdrawal program would be the byproduct of direct action, we felt that this would be the best time to bring pressure to bear on the merchants for the needed change.

9   Then it occurred to us that Birmingham's mayoral election was coming up in March, and we speedily decided to postpone action until after election day. When we discovered that the Commissioner of Public Safety, Eugene "Bull" Connor, had piled up enough votes to be in the run-off, we decided again to postpone action until the day after the run-off so that the demonstrations could not be used to cloud the issues. Like many others, we wanted to see Mr. Connor defeated, and to this end we endured postponement after postponement. Having aided in this community need, we felt that our direct-action program could be delayed no longer.

10   You may well ask: "Why direct action? Why sit-ins, marches and so forth? Isn't negotiation a better path?" You are quite right in calling for negotiation. Indeed, this is the very purpose of direct action. Nonviolent direct action seeks to create such a crisis and foster such a tension that a community which has constantly refused to negotiate is forced to confront the issue. It seeks so to dramatize the issue that it can no longer be ignored. My citing the

creation of tension as part of the work of the nonviolent-resister may sound rather shocking. But I must confess that I am not afraid of the word "tension." I have earnestly opposed violent tension, but there is a type of constructive, nonviolent tension which is necessary for growth. Just as Socrates felt that it was necessary to create a tension in the mind so that individuals could rise from the bondage of myths and half-truths to the unfettered realm of creative analysis and objective appraisal, so must we see the need for nonviolent gadflies to create the kind of tension in society that will help men rise from the dark depths of prejudice and racism to the majestic heights of understanding and brotherhood.

11   The purpose of our direct-action program is to create a situation so crisis-packed that it will inevitably open the door to negotiation. I therefore concur with you in your call for negotiation. Too long has our beloved Southland been bogged down in a tragic effort to live in monologue rather than dialogue.

12   One of the basic points in your statement is that the action that I and my associates have taken in Birmingham is untimely. Some have asked: "Why didn't you give the new city administration time to act?" The only answer that I can give to this query is that the new Birmingham administration must be prodded about as much as the outgoing one, before it will act. We are sadly mistaken if we feel that the election of Albert Boutwell as mayor will bring the millennium to Birmingham. While Mr. Boutwell is a much more gentle person than Mr. Connor, they are both segregationists, dedicated to maintenance of the status quo. I have hope that Mr. Boutwell will be reasonable enough to see the futility of massive resistance to desegregation. But he will not see this without pressure from devotees of civil rights. My friends, I must say to you that we have not made a single gain in civil rights without determined legal and nonviolent pressure. Lamentably, it is an historical fact that privileged groups seldom give up their privileges voluntarily. Individuals may see the moral light and voluntarily give up their unjust posture; but, as Reinhold Niebuhr has reminded us, groups tend to be more immoral than individuals.

13   We know through painful experience that freedom is never voluntarily given by the oppressor; it must be demanded by the oppressed. Frankly, I have yet to engage in a direct-action campaign that was "well timed" in the view of those who have not suffered unduly from the disease of segregation. For years now I have heard the word "Wait!" It rings in the ear of every Negro with piercing familiarity. This "Wait" has almost always meant "Never." We must come to see, with one of our distinguished jurists, that "justice too long delayed is justice denied."

14   We have waited for more than 340 years for our constitutional and God-given rights. The nations of Asia and Africa are moving with jetlike speed toward gaining political independence, but we still creep at horse-and-buggy pace toward gaining a cup of coffee at a lunch counter. Perhaps it is easy for those who have never felt the stinging darts of segregation to say, "Wait." But

when you have seen vicious mobs lynch your mothers and fathers at will and drown your sisters and brothers at whim; when you have seen hate-filled policemen curse, kick and even kill your black brothers and sisters; when you see the vast majority of your twenty million Negro brothers smothering in airtight cage of poverty in the midst of an affluent society; when you suddenly find your tongue twisted and your speech stammering as you seek to explain to your six-year-old daughter why she can't go to the public amusement park that has just been advertised on television, and see tears welling up in her eyes when she is told that Funtown is closed to colored children, and see ominous clouds of inferiority beginning to form in her little mental sky, and see her beginning to distort her personality by developing an unconscious bitterness toward white people; when you have to concoct an answer for a five-year-old son who is asking: "Daddy, why do white people treat colored people so mean?"; when you take a cross-country drive and find it necessary to sleep night after night in the uncomfortable corners of your automobile because no motel will accept you; when you are humiliated day in and day out by nagging signs reading "white" and "colored"; when your first name becomes "nigger," your middle name becomes "boy" (however old you are) and your last name becomes "John," and your wife and mother are never given the respected title "Mrs."; when you are harried by day and haunted by night by the fact that you are a Negro, living constantly at tiptoe stance, never quite knowing what to expect next, and are plagued with inner fears and outer resentments; when you are forever fighting a degenerating sense of "nobodiness"—then you will understand why we find it difficult to wait. There comes a time when the cup of endurance runs over, and men are no longer willing to be plunged into the abyss of despair. I hope, sirs, you can understand our legitimate and unavoidable impatience.

15   You express a great deal of anxiety over our willingness to break laws. This is certainly a legitimate concern. Since we so diligently urge people to obey the Supreme Court's decision of 1954 outlawing segregation in the public schools, at first glance it may seem rather paradoxical for us consciously to break laws. One may well ask: "How can you advocate breaking some laws and obeying others?" The answer lies in the fact that there are two types of laws: just and unjust. I would be the first to advocate obeying just laws. One has not only a legal but a moral responsibility to obey just laws. Conversely, one has a moral responsibility to disobey unjust laws. I would agree with St. Augustine that "an unjust law is no law at all."

16   Now, what is the difference between the two? How does one determine whether a law is just or unjust? A just law is a man-made code that squares with the moral law or the law of God. An unjust law is a code that is out of harmony with the moral law. To put it in the terms of St. Thomas Aquinas: An unjust law is a human law that is not rooted in eternal law and natural law. Any law that uplifts human personality is just. Any law that degrades

human personality is unjust. All segregation statutes are unjust because segregation distorts the soul and damages the personality. It gives the segregator a false sense of superiority and the segregated a false sense of inferiority. Segregation, to use the terminology of the Jewish philosopher Martin Buber, substitutes an "I–it" relationship for an "I–thou" relationship and ends up relegating persons to the status of things. Hence segregation is not only politically, economically and sociologically unsound, it is morally wrong and sinful. Paul Tillich has said that sin is separation. Is not segregation an existential expression of man's tragic separation, his awful estrangement, his terrible sinfulness? Thus it is that I can urge men to obey the 1954 decision of the Supreme Court, for it is morally right; and I can urge them to disobey segregation ordinances, for they are morally wrong.

[17]   Let us consider a more concrete example of just and unjust laws. An unjust law is a code that a numerical or power majority group compels a minority group to obey but does not make binding on itself. This is *difference* made legal. By the same token, a just law is a code that a majority compels a minority to follow and that it is willing to follow itself. This is *sameness* made legal.

[18]   Let me give another explanation. A law is unjust if it is inflicted on a minority that, as a result of being denied the right to vote, had no part in enacting or devising the law. Who can say that the legislature of Alabama which set up that state's segregation laws was democratically elected? Throughout Alabama all sorts of devious methods are used to prevent Negroes from becoming registered voters, and there are some counties in which, even though Negroes constitute a majority of the population, not a single Negro is registered. Can any law enacted under such circumstances be considered democratically structured?

[19]   Sometimes a law is just on its face and unjust in its application. For instance, I have been arrested on a charge of parading without a permit. Now, there is nothing wrong in having an ordinance which requires a permit for a parade. But such an ordinance becomes unjust when it is used to maintain segregation and to deny citizens the First-Amendment privilege of peaceful assembly and protest.

[20]   I hope you are able to see the distinction I am trying to point out. In no sense do I advocate evading or defying the law, as would the rabid segregationist. That would lead to anarchy. One who breaks an unjust law must do so openly, lovingly, and with a willingness to accept the penalty. I submit that an individual who breaks a law that conscience tells him is unjust, and who willingly accepts the penalty of imprisonment in order to arouse the conscience of the community over its injustice, is in reality expressing the highest respect for law.

[21]   Of course, there is nothing new about this kind of civil disobedience. It was evidenced sublimely in the refusal of Shadrach, Meshach and Abednego to obey the laws of Nebuchadnezzar, on the ground that a higher moral law

was at stake. It was practiced superbly by the early Christians, who were willing to face hungry lions and the excruciating pain of chopping blocks rather than submit to certain unjust laws of the Roman Empire. To a degree, academic freedom is a reality today because Socrates practiced civil disobedience. In our own nation, the Boston Tea Party represented a massive act of civil disobedience.

22   We should never forget that everything Adolf Hitler did in Germany was "legal" and everything that Hungarian freedom fighters did in Hungary was "illegal." It was "illegal" to aid and comfort a Jew in Hitler's Germany. Even so, I am sure that, had I lived in Germany at the time, I would have aided and comforted my Jewish brothers. If today I lived in a Communist country where certain principles dear to the Christian faith are suppressed, I would openly advocate disobeying that country's antireligious laws.

23   I must make two honest confessions to you, my Christian and Jewish brothers. First, I must confess that over the past few years I have been gravely disappointed with the white moderate. I have almost reached the regrettable conclusion that the Negro's great stumbling block in his stride toward freedom is not the White Citizen's Counciler or the Ku Klux Klanner, but the white moderate, who is more devoted to "order" than to justice; who prefers a negative peace which is the absence of tension to a positive peace which is the presence of justice; who constantly says: "I agree with you in the goal you seek, but I cannot agree with your methods of direct action"; who paternalistically believes he can set the timetable for another man's freedom; who lives by a mythical concept of time and who constantly advises the Negro to wait for a "more convenient season." Shallow understanding from people of good will is more frustrating than absolute misunderstanding from people of ill will. Lukewarm acceptance is much more bewildering than outright rejection.

24   I had hoped that the white moderate would understand that law and order exist for the purpose of establishing justice and that when they fail in this purpose they become the dangerously structured dams that block the flow of social progress. I had hoped that the white moderate would understand that the present tension in the South is a necessary phase of the transition from an obnoxious negative peace, in which the Negro passively accepted his unjust plight, to a substantive and positive peace, in which all men will respect the dignity and worth of human personality. Actually, we who engage in nonviolent direct action are not the creators of tension. We merely bring to the surface the hidden tension that is already alive. We bring it out in the open, where it can be seen and dealt with. Like a boil that can never be cured so long as it is covered up but must be opened with all its ugliness to the natural medicines of air and light, injustice must be exposed, with all the tension its exposure creates, to the light of human conscience and the air of national opinion, before it can be cured.

25   In your statement you assert that our actions, even though peaceful, must be condemned because they precipitate violence. But is this a logical asser-

tion? Isn't this like condemning a robbed man because his possession of money precipitated the evil act of robbery? Isn't this like condemning Socrates because his unswerving commitment to truth and his philosophical inquiries precipitated the act by the misguided populace in which they made him drink hemlock? Isn't this like condemning Jesus because his unique God-consciousness and never-ceasing devotion to God's will precipitated the evil act of crucifixion? We must come to see that, as the federal courts have consistently affirmed, it is wrong to urge an individual to cease his efforts to gain his basic constitutional rights because the quest may precipitate violence. Society must protect the robbed and punish the robber.

26   I had also hoped that the white moderate would reject the myth concerning time in relation to the struggle for freedom. I have just received a letter from a white brother in Texas. He writes: "All Christians know that the colored people will receive equal rights eventually, but it is possible that you are in too great a religious hurry. It has taken Christianity almost two thousand years to accomplish what it has. The teachings of Christ take time to come to earth." Such an attitude stems from a tragic misconception of time, from the strangely irrational notion that there is something in the very flow of time that will inevitably cure all ills. Actually, time itself is neutral; it can be used either destructively or constructively. More and more I feel that the people of ill will have used time much more effectively than have the people of good will. We will have to repent in this generation not merely for the hateful words and actions of the bad people but for the appalling silence of the good people. Human progress never rolls in on wheels of inevitability; it comes through the tireless efforts of men willing to be coworkers with God, and without this hard work, time itself becomes an ally of the forces of social stagnation. We must use time creatively, in the knowledge that the time is always ripe to do right. Now is the time to make real the promise of democracy and transform our pending national elegy into a creative psalm of brotherhood. Now is the time to lift our national policy from the quicksand of racial injustice to the solid rock of human dignity.

27   You speak of our activity in Birmingham as extreme. At first I was rather disappointed that fellow clergymen would see my nonviolent efforts as those of an extremist. I began thinking about the fact that I stand in the middle of two opposing forces in the Negro community. One is a force of complacency, made up in part of Negroes who, as a result of long years of oppression, are so drained of self-respect and a sense of "somebodiness" that they have adjusted to segregation; and in part of a few middle-class Negroes who, because of a degree of academic and economic security and because in some ways they profit by segregation, have become insensitive to the problems of the masses. The other force is one of bitterness and hatred, and it comes perilously close to advocating violence. It is expressed in the various black nationalist groups that are springing up across the nation, the largest and best-known being Elijah Muhammad's Muslim movement. Nourished by the

Negro's frustration over the continued existence of racial discrimination, this movement is made up of people who have lost faith in America, who have absolutely repudiated Christianity, and who have concluded that the white man is an incorrigible "devil."

28   I have tried to stand between these two forces, saying that we need emulate neither the "do-nothingism" of the complacent nor the hatred and despair of the black nationalist. For there is the more excellent way of love and nonviolent protest. I am grateful to God that, through the influence of the Negro church, the way of nonviolence became an integral part of our struggle.

29   If this philosophy had not emerged, by now many streets of the South would, I am convinced, be flowing with blood. And I am further convinced that if our white brothers dismiss as "rabble-rousers" and "outside agitators" those of us who employ nonviolent direct action, and if they refuse to support our nonviolent efforts, millions of Negroes will, out of frustration and despair, seek solace and security in black-nationalist ideologies—a development that would inevitably lead to a frightening racial nightmare.

30   Oppressed people cannot remain oppressed forever. The yearning for freedom eventually manifests itself, and that is what has happened to the American Negro. Something within has reminded him of his birthright of freedom, and something without has reminded him that it can be gained. Consciously or unconsciously, he has been caught up by the *Zeitgeist*, and with his black brothers of Africa and his brown and yellow brothers of Asia, South America and the Caribbean, the United States Negro is moving with a sense of great urgency toward the promised land of racial justice. If one recognizes this vital urge that has engulfed the Negro community, one should readily understand why public demonstrations are taking place. The Negro has many pent-up resentments and latent frustrations, and he must release them. So let him march; let him make prayer pilgrimages to the city hall; let him go on freedom rides—and try to understand why he must do so. If his repressed emotions are not released in nonviolent ways, they will seek expression through violence; this is not a threat but a fact of history. So I have not said to my people: "Get rid of your discontent." Rather, I have tried to say that this normal and healthy discontent can be channeled into the creative outlet of nonviolent direct action. And now this approach is being termed extremist.

31   But though I was initially disappointed at being categorized as an extremist, as I continued to think about the matter I gradually gained a measure of satisfaction from the label. Was not Jesus an extremist for love: "Love your enemies, bless them that curse you, do good to them that hate you, and pray for them which despitefully use you, and persecute you." Was not Amos an extremist for justice: "Let justice roll down like waters and righteousness like an over-flowing stream." Was not Paul an extremist for the Christian gospel: "I bear in my body the marks of the Lord Jesus." Was not Martin Luther an extremist: "Here I stand; I cannot do otherwise, so help me God." And

John Bunyan: "I will stay in jail to the end of my days before I make a butchery of my conscience." And Abraham Lincoln: "This nation cannot survive half slave and half free." And Thomas Jefferson: "We hold these truths to be self-evident, that all men are created equal . . ." So the question is not whether we will be extremists, but what kind of extremists we will be. Will we be extremists for hate or for love? Will we be extremists for the preservation of injustice or for the extension of justice? In that dramatic scene on Calvary's hill three men were crucified. We must never forget that all three were crucified for the same crime—the crime of extremism. Two were extremists for immorality, and thus fell below their environment. The other, Jesus Christ, was an extremist for love, truth and goodness, and thereby rose above his environment. Perhaps the South, the nation and the world are in dire need of creative extremists.

32   I had hoped that the white moderate would see this need. Perhaps I was too optimistic; perhaps I expected too much. I suppose I should have realized that few members of the oppressor race can understand the deep groans and passionate yearnings of the oppressed race, and still fewer have the vision to see that injustice must be rooted out by strong, persistent and determined action. I am thankful, however, that some of our white brothers in the South have grasped the meaning of this social revolution and committed themselves to it. They are still all too few in quantity, but they are big in quality. Some—such as Ralph McGill, Lillian Smith, Harry Golden, James McBride Dabbs, Ann Braden and Sarah Patton Boyle—have written about our struggle in eloquent and prophetic terms. Others have marched with us down nameless streets of the South. They have languished in filthy, roach-infested jails, suffering the abuse and brutality of policemen who view them as "dirty nigger-lovers." Unlike so many of their moderate brothers and sisters, they have recognized the urgency of the moment and sensed the need for powerful "action" antidotes to combat the disease of segregation.

33   Let me take note of my other major disappointment. I have been so greatly disappointed with the white church and its leadership. Of course, there are some notable exceptions. I am not unmindful of the fact that each of you has taken some significant stands on this issue. I commend you, Reverend Stallings, for your Christian stand on this past Sunday, in welcoming Negroes to your worship service on a nonsegregated basis. I commend the Catholic leaders of this state for integrating Spring Hill College several years ago.

34   But despite these notable exceptions, I must honestly reiterate that I have been disappointed with the church. I do not say this as one of those negative critics who can always find something wrong with the church. I say this as a minister of the gospel, who loves the church; who was nurtured in its bosom; who has been sustained by its spiritual blessings and who will remain true to it as long as the cord of life shall lengthen.

35   When I was suddenly catapulted into the leadership of the bus protest in Montgomery, Alabama, a few years ago, I felt we would be supported by the white church. I felt that the white ministers, priests and rabbis of the South would be among our strongest allies. Instead, some have been outright opponents, refusing to understand the freedom movement and misrepresenting its leaders; all too many others have been more cautious than courageous and have remained silent behind the anesthetizing security of stained-glass windows.

36   In spite of my shattered dreams, I came to Birmingham with the hope that the white religious leadership of this community would see the justice of our cause and, with deep moral concern, would serve as the channel through which our just grievances could reach the power structure. I had hoped that each of you would understand. But again I have been disappointed.

37   I have heard numerous southern religious leaders admonish their worshipers to comply with a desegregation decision because it is the law, but I have longed to hear white ministers declare: "Follow this decree because integration is morally right and because the Negro is your brother." In the midst of blatant injustices inflicted upon the Negro, I have watched white churchmen stand on the sideline and mouth pious irrelevancies and sanctimonious trivialities. In the midst of a mighty struggle to rid our nation of racial and economic injustice, I have heard many ministers say: "Those are social issues, with which the gospel has no real concern." And I have watched many churches commit themselves to a completely otherworldly religion which makes a strange, un-Biblical distinction between body and soul, between the sacred and the secular.

38   I have traveled the length and breadth of Alabama, Mississippi and all the other southern states. On sweltering summer days and crisp autumn mornings I have looked at the South's beautiful churches with their lofty spires pointing heavenward. I have beheld the impressive outlines of her massive religious-education buildings. Over and over I have found myself asking: "What kind of people worship here? Who is their God? Where were their voices when the lips of Governor Barnett dripped with words of interposition and nullification? Where were they when Governor Wallace gave a clarion call for defiance and hatred? Where were their voices of support when bruised and weary Negro men and women decided to rise from the dark dungeons of complacency to the bright hills of creative protest?"

39   Yes, these questions are still in my mind. In deep disappointment I have wept over the laxity of the church. But be assured that my tears have been tears of love. There can be no deep disappointment where there is not deep love. Yes, I love the church. How could I do otherwise? I am in the rather unique position of being the son, the grandson and the great-grandson of preachers. Yes, I see the church as the body of Christ. But, oh! How we have blemished and scarred that body through social neglect and through fear of being nonconformists.

40   There was a time when the church was very powerful—in the time when the early Christians rejoiced at being deemed worthy to suffer for what they believed. In those days the church was not merely a thermometer that recorded the ideas and principles of popular opinion; it was a thermostat that transformed the mores of society. Whenever the early Christians entered a town, the people in power became disturbed and immediately sought to convict the Christians for being "disturbers of the peace" and "outside agitators." But the Christians pressed on, in the conviction that they were "a colony of heaven," called to obey God rather than man. Small in number, they were big in commitment. They were too God-intoxicated to be "astronomically intimidated." By their effort and example they brought an end to such ancient evils as infanticide and gladiatorial contests.

41   Things are different now. So often the contemporary church is a weak, ineffectual voice with an uncertain sound. So often it is an arch-defender of the status quo. Far from being disturbed by the presence of the church, the power structure of the average community is consoled by the church's silent—and often even vocal—sanction of things as they are.

42   But the judgment of God is upon the church as never before. If today's church does not recapture the sacrificial spirit of the early church, it will lose its authenticity, forfeit the loyalty of millions, and be dismissed as an irrelevant social club with no meaning for the twentieth century. Every day I meet young people whose disappointment with the church has turned into outright disgust.

43   Perhaps I have once again been too optimistic. Is organized religion too inextricably bound to the status quo to save our nation and the world? Perhaps I must turn my faith to the inner spiritual church, the church within the church, as the true *ekklesia* and the hope of the world. But again I am thankful to God that some noble souls from the ranks of organized religion have broken loose from the paralyzing chains of conformity and joined us as active partners in the struggle for freedom. They have left their secure congregations and walked the streets of Albany, Georgia, with us. They have gone down the highways of the South on tortuous rides for freedom. Yes, they have gone to jail with us. Some have been dismissed from their churches, have lost the support of their bishops and fellow ministers. But they have acted in the faith that right defeated is stronger than evil triumphant. Their witness has been the spiritual salt that has preserved the true meaning of the gospel in these troubled times. They have carved a tunnel of hope through the dark mountain of disappointment.

44   I hope the church as a whole will meet the challenge of this decisive hour. But even if the church does not come to the aid of justice, I have no despair about the future. I have no fear about the outcome of our struggle in Birmingham, even if our motives are at present misunderstood. We will reach the goal of freedom in Birmingham and all over the nation, because the goal of America is freedom. Abused and scorned though we may be, our destiny is tied up

with America's destiny. Before the pilgrims landed at Plymouth, we were here. Before the pen of Jefferson etched the majestic words of the Declaration of Independence across the pages of history, we were here. For more than two centuries our forebears labored in this country without wages; they made cotton king; they built the homes of their masters while suffering gross injustice and shameful humiliation—and yet out of a bottomless vitality they continued to thrive and develop. If the inexpressible cruelties of slavery could not stop us, the opposition we now face will surely fail. We will win our freedom because the sacred heritage of our nation and the eternal will of God are embodied in our echoing demands.

45   Before closing I feel impelled to mention one other point in your statement that has troubled me profoundly. You warmly commended the Birmingham police force for keeping "order" and "preventing violence." I doubt that you would have so warmly commended the police force if you had seen its dogs sinking their teeth into unarmed, nonviolent Negroes. I doubt that you would so quickly commend the policemen if you were to observe their ugly and inhumane treatment of Negroes here in the city jail; if you were to watch them push and curse old Negro women and young Negro girls; if you were to see them slap and kick old Negro men and young boys; if you were to observe them, as they did on two occasions, refuse to give us food because we wanted to sing our grace together. I cannot join you in your praise of the Birmingham police department.

46   It is true that the police have exercised a degree of discipline in handling the demonstrators. In this sense they have conducted themselves rather "nonviolently" in public. But for what purpose? To preserve the evil system of segregation. Over the past few years I have consistently preached that nonviolence demands that the means we use must be as pure as the ends we seek. I have tried to make clear that it is wrong to use immoral means to attain moral ends. But now I must affirm that it is just as wrong, or perhaps even more so, to use moral means to preserve immoral ends. Perhaps Mr. Connor and his policemen have been rather nonviolent in public, as was Chief Pritchett in Albany, Georgia, but they have used the moral means of nonviolence to maintain the immoral end of racial injustice. As T. S. Eliot has said: "The last temptation is the greatest treason: To do the right deed for the wrong reason."

47   I wish you had commended the Negro sit-inners and demonstrators of Birmingham for their sublime courage, their willingness to suffer and their amazing discipline in the midst of great provocation. One day the South will recognize its real heroes. They will be the James Merediths, with the noble sense of purpose that enables them to face jeering and hostile mobs, and with the agonizing loneliness that characterizes the life of the pioneer. They will be old, oppressed, battered Negro women, symbolized in a seventy-two-year-old woman in Montgomery, Alabama, who rose up with a sense of dignity and with her people decided not to ride segregated buses, and who responded with ungrammatical profundity to one who inquired about her

weariness: "My feets is tired, but my soul is at rest." They will be the young high school and college students, the young ministers of the gospel and a host of their elders, courageously and nonviolently sitting in at lunch counters and willingly going to jail for conscience' sake. One day the South will know that when these disinherited children of God sat down at lunch counters, they were in reality standing up for what is best in the American dream and for the most sacred values in our Judaeo-Christian heritage, thereby bringing our nation back to those great wells of democracy which were dug deep by the founding fathers in their formulation of the Constitution and the Declaration of Independence.

48   Never before have I written so long a letter. I'm afraid it is much too long to take your precious time. I can assure you that it would have been much shorter if I had been writing from a comfortable desk, but what else can one do when he is alone in a narrow jail cell, other than write long letters, think long thoughts and pray long prayers?

49   If I have said anything in this letter that overstates the truth and indicates an unreasonable impatience, I beg you to forgive me. If I have said anything that understates the truth and indicates my having a patience that allows me to settle for anything less than brotherhood, I beg God to forgive me.

50   I hope this letter finds you strong in the faith. I also hope that circumstances will soon make it possible for me to meet each of you, not as an integrationist or a civil-rights leader but as a fellow clergyman and a Christian brother. Let us all hope that the dark clouds of racial prejudice will soon pass away and the deep fog of misunderstanding will be lifted from our fear-drenched communities, and in some not too distant tomorrow the radiant stars of love and brotherhood will shine over our great nation with all their scintillating beauty.

Yours for the cause of Peace and Brotherhood,
Martin Luther King Jr.

Richard Selzer

LETTER TO A YOUNG SURGEON

Yes, here is another letter of advice. Selzer is a doctor and teaches medicine at Yale University. He is to surgery what Gould is to geology: one of the most widely read popularizers of the subject. This letter, one of a series published as a book, ostensibly addresses a particular young surgeon who has passed out in the operating room. However, his letter will work for a variety of young doctors experiencing a variety of degrees of squeamishness about their new profession, of which a fainting spell in the operating room (scalpel in hand, patient on the table) would only be an extreme example. Selzer here puts into written form what he must have said dozens of times orally while helping to train young physicians, much as Banning must have scolded poor Susan innumerable times before she moved away to college and began to receive those letters. As in the case of Banning, we should not define Selzer's audience too narrowly. Some of you may be considering a pre-med major, and for you Selzer's letters taken together could provide a realistic portrait of what it is like to be a doctor—and hence could help you decide if this is the profession for you. But even that is too narrow. Selzer knows perfectly well that his letters are going to be read primarily by non-doctors. He is trying to provide them with a humane portrait of his profession that may make them less inclined to jump like flushed birds when their surgeon speaks of a prospective operation. For reaching members of such an audience, what are the advantages of letting them imagine that they are eavesdropping on advice from an older doctor to a younger one?

1   All right. You fainted in the operating room, had to go sit on the floor in a corner and put your head down. You are making altogether too much of it. You have merely announced your humanity. Only the gods do not faint at the sight of the *mysterium tremendum;* they have too jaded a glance. At the same place in the novitiate I myself more than once slid ungracefully to the floor in the middle of things. It is less a sign of weakness than an expression of guilt. A flinching in the face of the forbidden.

2   The surgeon is an explorer in the tropical forest of the body. Now and then he reaches up to bring closer one of the wondrous fruits he sees there. Before he departs this place, he knows that he must pluck one of them. He knows, too, that it is forbidden to do so. But it is a trophy, no, a *spoil* that has been demanded of him by his patron, the patient, who has commissioned and outfitted him for this exploration. At last the surgeon holds the plucked organ in his hand, but he is never wholly at ease. For what man does not grow shy, fearful, before the occult uncovered?

3   Don't worry. The first red knife is the shakiest. This is as true for the assassin as it is for the surgeon. The assassin's task is easier, for he is more likely to be a fanatic. And nothing steadies the hand like zeal. The surgeon's work is madness icily reined in to a good purpose. Still I know that it is perverse to relieve pain by inflicting it. This requires that the patient give over to you his free will and his trust. It is too much to ask. Yet we do every day, and with the arrogance born of habit and custom, and grown casual, even charming.

4   "Come, lie down on this table," you say, and smile. Your voice is soft and reasonable.

5   "Where will you cut me open?" the patient asks. And he grips his belly as though he and it were orphan twins awaiting separate adoption. The patient's voice is *not* calm; it trembles and quavers.

6   "From here . . . to here," you reply, and you draw a fingernail across his shuddering flesh. His navel leaps like a flushed bird. Oh, God! He has heard the knell of disembowelment. You really *do* mean to do it! And you do, though not with the delectation that will be attributed to you by those who do not do this work.

7   The cadaver toward which I have again and again urged you is like an abundant nest from which the birds have long since flown. It is a dry, uninhabited place—already dusty. It is a "thing" that the medical student will pull apart and examine, seeking evidence, clues from which he can reconstruct the life that once flourished there. The living patient is a nest in which a setting bird huddles. She quivers, but does not move when you press aside leaves in order to see better. Your slightest touch frightens her. You hold your breath and let the leaves spring back to conceal her. You want so much for her to trust you.

8   In order to do good works throughout his lifetime, a man must strive ever higher to carry out his benefices; he must pray, defer pleasure and steel himself against temptation. And against fainting. The committing of surgery grows easier and easier, it seems, until the practice is second nature. Come, come! You fainted! Why don't you admit that you are imperfect, and that you strain to appeal to yourself and to others? Surgery is, in one sense, a judicious contrivance, like poetry. But . . . it is an elect life, here among the ranting machinery and brazen lamps of the operating room, where on certain days now the liquidity of the patient reminds me of the drought that is attacking my own flesh. Listen, I will tell you what you already know: There is nothing like an honest piece of surgery. Say what you will, there is nothing more satisfying to the spirit than . . . the lancing of a boil!

9   Behold the fierce, hot protuberance compressing the howling nerves about it. You sound it with your fingers. A light tap brings back a malevolent answering wave, and a groan from the patient. Now the questing knife rides in your hand. Go! And across the swelling gallops a thin red line. Again! Deeper, plowing. All at once there lifts a wave of green mud. Suddenly the patient's breathing comes more easily, his tense body relaxes, he smiles. For him it is like being touched by the hand of God. It is a simple act, requiring not a flicker of intellect nor a whisker of logic. To outwit disease it takes a peasant's cunning, not abstract brilliance. It is like the felling of a tree for firewood. Yet not poetry, nor music nor mathematics can bring such gladness, for riding out upon that wave of pus has come the black barque of pain. Just so will you come to love the boils and tumors of your patients.

10   I shall offer you two antidotes to fainting in the operating room.

11   1. Return as often as possible to the Anatomy Laboratory. As the sculptor must gain unlimited control over his marble, the surgeon must "own" the flesh. As drawing is to the painter, so is anatomy to the surgeon. You must continue to dissect for the rest of your life. To raise a flap of skin, to trace out

a nerve to its place of confluence, to carry a tendon to its bony insertion, these are things of grace and beauty. They are simple, nontheoretical, workaday acts which, if done again and again, will give rise to that profound sense of structure that is the birthplace of intuition.

12   It is only at the dissecting table that you can find the models of your art. Only there that you will internalize the structure and form of the body so that any variations or anomalies or unforeseen circumstances are not later met with dismay and surprise. Unlike the face, the internal organs bear a remarkable sameness to one another. True, there are differences in the size of normal kidneys, livers and spleens, and there are occasional odd lobulations and unusual arrangements of ducts and vessels, but by and large, one liver is very like another. A kidney is a kidney. Unlike a face, it bears no distinctive mark or expression that would stamp it as the kidney of Napoleon Bonaparte, say, or Herman Melville. It is this very sameness that makes of surgery a craft that can be perfected by repetition and industry. Therefore, return to the Anatomy Laboratory. Revere and follow your prosector. The worship and awe you show the cadavers will come back to you a thousandfold. Even now, such an old knife as I goes to that place to dissect, to probe, to delve. What is an operating room but a prosectorium that has been touched into life?

13   2. Do not be impatient to wield the scalpel. To become a surgeon is a gradual, imperceptible, subtle transformation. Do not hurry from the side of the one who instructs you, but stay with your "master" until he bids you to go. It is his office to warm you with his words, on rounds and in the operating room, to color the darkness and shade the brilliance of light until you have grown strong enough to survive. Then, yes, leave him, for no sapling can grow to fullness in the shade of a big tree.

14   Do these things that I have told you and you will not faint in the operating room. I do not any longer faint, nor have I for thirty years. But now and then, upon leaving the hospital after a long and dangerous operation has been brought to a successful close, I stroke the walls of the building as though it were a faithful animal that has behaved itself well.

                                                                    1982

Virginia Woolf

THE STORY OF SHAKESPEARE'S SISTER

Virginia Woolf, herself a writer of fiction, was asked in the 1920s to speak to two groups of educated British women on the subject of "Women and Fic-

tion." Her thesis was what she called a "minor point": "A woman must have money and a room of her own if she is to write fiction." Woolf revised the talks to form a book-length essay from which we reprint Chapter 3. The piece illustrates, among other things, that an argument can be meditative and associative, as well as factual and rigidly ordered, and that argumentative writing of this sort can have a strong effect on its audience. "I am going to do what I can to show you how I arrived at this opinion about the room and the money," she tells us. Much of her argument is indirect, and she uses a fiction, the story of Shakespeare's sister, to bring her point to life for her audience. How might you use narrative to strengthen an argument of your own? What are the possible dangers of such a strategy? What can you determine about the attitudes and beliefs of Woolf's audience? Does she seem to expect that her audience will be fairly sympathetic to her ideas or that they will resist quite strongly? What in the essay leads you to this conclusion? (The reference in the first sentence is to a trip to the library to research her subject.)

1   It was disappointing not to have brought back in the evening some important statement, some authentic fact. Women are poorer than men because—this or that. Perhaps now it would be better to give up seeking for the truth, and receiving on one's head an avalanche of opinion hot as lava, discoloured as dish-water. It would be better to draw the curtains; to shut out distractions; to light the lamp; to narrow the enquiry and to ask the historian, who records not opinions but facts, to describe under what conditions women lived, not throughout the ages, but in England, say in the time of Elizabeth.

2   For it is a perennial puzzle why no woman wrote a word of that extraordinary literature when every other man, it seemed, was capable of song or sonnet. What were the conditions in which women lived, I asked myself; for fiction, imaginative work that is, is not dropped like a pebble upon the ground, as science may be; fiction is like a spider's web, attached ever so lightly perhaps, but still attached to life at all four corners. Often the attachment is scarcely perceptible; Shakespeare's plays, for instance, seem to hang there complete by themselves. But when the web is pulled askew, hooked up at the edge, torn in the middle, one remembers that these webs are not spun in midair by incorporeal creatures, but are the work of suffering human beings, and are attached to grossly material things, like health and money and the houses we live in.

3   I went, therefore, to the shelf where the histories stand and took down one of the latest, Professor Trevelyan's *History of England*. Once more I looked up Women, found "position of," and turned to the pages indicated. "Wife-beating," I read, "was a recognized right of man, and was practised without shame by high as well as low.... Similarly," the historian goes on, "the daughter who refused to marry the gentleman of her parents' choice was liable to

be locked up, beaten and flung about the room, without any shock being inflicted on public opinion. Marriage was not an affair of personal affection, but of family avarice, particularly in the 'chivalrous' upper classes.... Betrothal often took place while one or both of the parties was in the cradle, and marriage when they were scarcely out of the nurses' charge." That was about 1470, soon after Chaucer's time. The next reference to the position of women is some two hundred years later, in the time of the Stuarts. "It was still the exception for women of the upper and middle class to choose their own husbands, and when the husband had been assigned, he was lord and master, so far at least as law and custom could make him. Yet even so," Professor Trevelyan concludes, "neither Shakespeare's women nor those of authentic seventeenth-century memoirs, like the Verneys and the Hutchinsons, seem wanting in personality and character." Certainly, if we consider it, Cleopatra must have had a way with her; Lady Macbeth, one would suppose, had a will of her own; Rosalind, one might conclude, was an attractive girl. Professor Trevelyan is speaking no more than the truth when he remarks that Shakespeare's women do not seem wanting in personality and character. Not being a historian, one might go even further and say that women have burnt like beacons in all the works of all the poets from the beginning of time—Clytemnestra, Antigone, Cleopatra, Lady Macbeth, Phèdre, Cressida, Rosalind, Desdemona, the Duchess of Malfi, among the dramatists; then among the prose writers: Millamant, Clarissa, Becky Sharp, Anna Karenine, Emma Bovary, Madame de Guermantes—the names flock to mind, nor do they recall women "lacking in personality and character." Indeed, if woman had no existence save in fiction written by men, one would imagine her a person of the utmost importance; very various; heroic and mean; splendid and sordid; infinitely beautiful and hideous in the extreme; as great as a man, some think even greater.[1] But this is woman in fiction. In fact, as Professor Trevelyan points out, she was locked up, beaten and flung about the room.

4   A very queer, composite being thus emerges. Imaginatively she is of the highest importance; practically she is completely insignificant. She pervades poetry from cover to cover; she is all but absent from history. She dominates

[1]"It remains a strange and almost inexplicable fact that in Athena's city, where women were kept in almost Oriental suppression as odalisques or drudges, the stage should yet have produced figures like Clytemnestra and Cassandra, Atossa and Antigone, Phèdre and Medea, and all the other heroines who dominate play after play of the 'misogynist' Euripides. But the paradox of this world where in real life a respectable woman could hardly show her face alone in the street, and yet on the stage woman equals or surpasses man, has never been satisfactorily explained. In modern tragedy the same predominance exists. At all events, a very cursory survey of Shakespeare's work (similarly with Webster, though not with Marlowe or Jonson) suffices to reveal how this dominance, this initiative of women, persists from Rosalind to Lady Macbeth. So too in Racine; six of his tragedies bear their heroines' names; and what male characters of his shall we set against Hermione and Andromaque, Bérénice and Roxane, Phèdre and Athalie? So again with Ibsen; what men shall we match with Solveig and Nora, Hedda and Hilda Wangel and Rebecca West?"—F. L. Lucas, *Tragedy*, pp. 114–15.

the lives of kings and conquerors in fiction; in fact she was the slave of any boy whose parents forced a ring upon her finger. Some of the most inspired words, some of the most profound thoughts in literature fall from her lips; in real life she could hardly read, could scarcely spell, and was the property of her husband.

5   It was certainly an odd monster that one made up by reading the historians first and the poets afterwards—a worm winged like an eagle; the spirit of life and beauty in a kitchen chopping up suet. But these monsters, however amusing to the imagination, have no existence in fact. What one must do to bring her to life was to think poetically and prosaically at one and the same moment, thus keeping in touch with fact—that she is Mrs. Martin, aged thirty-six, dressed in blue, wearing a black hat and brown shoes; but not losing sight of fiction either—that she is a vessel in which all sorts of spirits and forces are coursing and flashing perpetually. The moment, however, that one tries this method with the Elizabethan woman, one branch of illumination fails; one is held up by the scarcity of facts. One knows nothing detailed, nothing perfectly true and substantial about her. History scarcely mentions her. And I turned to Professor Trevelyan again to see what history meant to him. I found by looking at his chapter headings that it meant—

6   "The Manor Court and the Methods of Open-field Agriculture... The Cistercians and Sheep-farming... The Crusades... The University... The House of Commons... The Hundred Years' War... The Wars of the Roses... The Renaissance Scholars... The Dissolution of the Monasteries... Agrarian and Religious Strife... The Origin of English Sea-power... The Armada..." and so on. Occasionally an individual woman is mentioned, an Elizabeth, or a Mary; a queen or a great lady. But by no possible means could middle-class women with nothing but brains and character at their command have taken part in any one of the great movements which, brought together, constitute the historian's view of the past. Nor shall we find her in any collection of anecdotes. Aubrey hardly mentions her. She never writes her own life and scarcely keeps a diary; there are only a handful of her letters in existence. She left no plays or poems by which we can judge her. What one wants, I thought—and why does not some brilliant student at Newnham or Girton supply it?—is a mass of information; at what age did she marry; how many children had she as a rule; what was her house like; had she a room to herself; did she do the cooking; would she be likely to have a servant? All these facts lie somewhere, presumably, in parish registers and account books; the life of the average Elizabethan woman must be scattered about somewhere, could one collect it and make a book of it. It would be ambitious beyond my daring, I thought, looking about the shelves for books that were not there, to suggest to the students of those famous colleges that they should re-write history, though I own that it often seems a little queer as it is, unreal, lop-sided; but why should they not add a supplement to history? calling it, of course, by

some inconspicuous name so that women might figure there without impropriety? For one often catches a glimpse of them in the lives of the great, whisking away into the background, concealing, I sometimes think, a wink, a laugh, perhaps a tear. And, after all, we have lives enough of Jane Austen; it scarcely seems necessary to consider again the influence of the tragedies of Joanna Baillie upon the poetry of Edgar Allan Poe; as for myself, I should not mind if the homes and haunts of Mary Russell Mitford were closed to the public for a century at least. But what I find deplorable, I continued, looking about the bookshelves again, is that nothing is known about women before the eighteenth century. I have no model in my mind to turn about this way and that. Here am I asking why women did not write poetry in the Elizabethan age, and I am not sure how they were educated; whether they were taught to write; whether they had sitting-rooms to themselves; how many women had children before they were twenty-one; what, in short, they did from eight in the morning till eight at night. They had no money evidently; according to Professor Trevelyan they were married whether they liked it or not before they were out of the nursery, at fifteen or sixteen very likely. It would have been extremely odd, even upon this showing, had one of them suddenly written the plays of Shakespeare, I concluded, and I thought of that old gentleman, who is dead now, but was a bishop, I think, who declared that it was impossible for any woman, past, present, or to come, to have the genius of Shakespeare. He wrote to the papers about it. He also told a lady who applied to him for information that cats do not as a matter of fact go to heaven, though they have, he added, souls of a sort. How much thinking those old gentlemen used to save one! How the borders of ignorance shrank back at their approach! Cats do not go to heaven. Women cannot write the plays of Shakespeare.

7   Be that as it may, I could not help thinking, as I looked at the works of Shakespeare on the shelf, that the bishop was right at least in this; it would have been impossible, completely and entirely, for any woman to have written the plays of Shakespeare in the age of Shakespeare. Let me imagine, since facts are so hard to come by, what would have happened had Shakespeare had a wonderfully gifted sister, called Judith, let us say. Shakespeare himself went, very probably—his mother was an heiress—to the grammar school where he may have learnt Latin—Ovid, Virgil and Horace—and the elements of grammar and logic. He was, it is well known, a wild boy who poached rabbits, perhaps shot a deer, and had, rather sooner than he should have done, to marry a woman in the neighbourhood, who bore him a child rather quicker than was right. That escapade sent him to seek his fortune in London. He had, it seemed, a taste for the theatre; he began by holding horses at the stage door. Very soon he got work in the theatre, became a successful actor, and lived at the hub of the universe, meeting everybody, knowing everybody, practising his art on the boards, exercising his wits in the streets, and even

getting access to the palace of the queen. Meanwhile his extraordinarily gifted sister, let us suppose, remained at home. She was as adventurous, as imaginative, as agog to see the world as he was. But she was not sent to school. She had no chance of learning grammar and logic, let alone of reading Horace and Virgil. She picked up a book now and then, one of her brother's perhaps, and read a few pages. But then her parents came in and told her to mend the stockings or mind the stew and not moon about with books and papers. They would have spoken sharply but kindly, for they were substantial people who knew the conditions of life for a woman and loved their daughter—indeed, more likely than not she was the apple of her father's eye. Perhaps she scribbled some pages up in an apple loft on the sly, but was careful to hide them or set fire to them. Soon, however, before she was out of her teens, she was to be betrothed to the son of a neighbouring wool-stapler. She cried out that marriage was hateful to her, and for that she was severely beaten by her father. Then he ceased to scold her. He begged her instead not to hurt him, not to shame him in this matter of her marriage. He would give her a chain of beads or a fine petticoat, he said; and there were tears in his eyes. How could she disobey him? How could she break his heart? The force of her own gift alone drove her to it. She made up a small parcel of her belongings, let herself down by a rope one summer's night and took the road to London. She was not seventeen. The birds that sang in the hedge were not more musical than she was. She had the quickest fancy, a gift like her brother's, for the tune of words. Like him, she had a taste for the theatre. She stood at the stage door; she wanted to act, she said. Men laughed in her face. The manager—a fat, loose-lipped man—guffawed. He bellowed something about poodles dancing and women acting—no woman, he said, could possibly be an actress. He hinted—you can imagine what. She could get no training in her craft. Could she even seek her dinner in a tavern or roam the streets at midnight? Yet her genius was for fiction and lusted to feed abundantly upon the lives of men and women and the study of their ways. At last—for she was very young, oddly like Shakespeare the poet in her face, with the same grey eyes and rounded brows—at last Nick Greene the actor-manager took pity on her; she found herself with child by that gentleman and so—who shall measure the heat and violence of the poet's heart when caught and tangled in a woman's body?—killed herself one winter's night and lies buried at some cross-roads where the omnibuses now stop outside the Elephant and Castle.

8   That, more or less, is how the story would run, I think, if a woman in Shakespeare's day had had Shakespeare's genius. But for my part, I agree with the deceased bishop, if such he was—it is unthinkable that any woman in Shakespeare's day should have had Shakespeare's genius. For genius like Shakespeare's is not born among labouring, uneducated, servile people. It was not born in England among the Saxons and the Britons. It is not born

today among the working classes. How, then, could it have been born among women whose work began, according to Professor Trevelyan, almost before they were out of the nursery, who were forced to it by their parents and held to it by all the power of law and custom? Yet genius of a sort must have existed among women as it must have existed among the working classes. Now and again an Emily Brontë or a Robert Burns blazes out and proves its presence. But certainly it never got itself on to paper. When, however, one reads of a witch being ducked, of a woman possessed by devils, of a wise woman selling herbs, or even of a very remarkable man who had a mother, then I think we are on the track of a lost novelist, a suppressed poet, of some mute and inglorious Jane Austen, some Emily Brontë who dashed her brains out on the moor or mopped and mowed about the highways crazed with the torture that her gift had put her to. Indeed, I would venture to guess that Anon, who wrote so many poems without signing them, was often a woman. It was a woman Edward Fitzgerald, I think, suggested who made the ballads and the folk-songs, crooning them to her children, beguiling her spinning with them, or the length of the winter's night.

9   This may be true or it may be false—who can say?—but what is true in it, so it seemed to me, reviewing the story of Shakespeare's sister as I had made it, is that any woman born with a great gift in the sixteenth century would certainly have gone crazed, shot herself, or ended her days in some lonely cottage outside the village, half witch, half wizard, feared and mocked at. For it needs little skill in psychology to be sure that a highly gifted girl who had tried to use her gift for poetry would have been so thwarted and hindered by other people, so tortured and pulled asunder by her own contrary instincts, that she must have lost her health and sanity to a certainty. No girl could have walked to London and stood at a stage door and forced her way into the presence of actor-managers without doing herself a violence and suffering an anguish which may have been irrational—for chastity may be a fetish invented by a certain societies for unknown reasons—but were none the less inevitable. Chastity had then, it has even now, a religious importance in a woman's life, and has so wrapped itself round with nerves and instincts that to cut it free and bring it to the light of day demands courage of the rarest. To have lived a free life in London in the sixteenth century would have meant for a woman who was poet and playwright a nervous stress and dilemma which might well have killed her. Had she survived, whatever she had written would have been twisted and deformed, issuing from a strained and morbid imagination. And undoubtedly, I thought, looking at the shelf where there are no plays by women, her work would have gone unsigned. That refuge she would have sought certainly. It was the relic of the sense of chastity that dictated anonymity to women even so late as the nineteenth century. Currer Bell, George Eliot, George Sand, all the victims of inner strife as their writings prove, sought ineffectively to veil themselves by using the name of

a man. Thus they did homage to the convention, which if not implanted by the other sex was liberally encouraged by them (the chief glory of a woman is not to be talked of, said Pericles, himself a much-talked-of man), that publicity in women is detestable. Anonymity runs in their blood. The desire to be veiled still possesses them. They are not even now as concerned about the health of their fame as men are, and, speaking generally, will pass a tombstone or a signpost without feeling an irresistible desire to cut their names on it, as Alf, Bert or Chas. must do in obedience to their instinct, which murmurs if it sees a fine woman go by, or even a dog, *Ce chien est à moi.* And, of course, it may not be a dog, I thought, remembering Parliament Square, the Sieges Allee and other avenues; it may be a piece of land or a man with curly black hair. It is one of the great advantages of being a woman that one can pass even a very fine negress without wishing to make an Englishwoman of her.

10   That woman, then, who was born with a gift of poetry in the sixteenth century, was an unhappy woman, a woman at strife against herself. All the conditions of her life, all her own instincts, were hostile to the state of mind which is needed to set free whatever is in the brain. But what is the state of mind that is most propitious to the act of creation, I asked? Can one come by any notion of the state that furthers and makes possible that strange activity? Here I opened the volume containing the Tragedies of Shakespeare. What was Shakespeare's state of mind, for instance, when he wrote *Lear* and *Antony and Cleopatra?* It was certainly the state of mind most favourable to poetry that there has ever existed. But Shakespeare himself said nothing about it. We only know casually and by chance that he "never blotted a line." Nothing indeed was ever said by the artist himself about his state of mind until the eighteenth century perhaps. Rousseau perhaps began it. At any rate, by the nineteenth century self-consciousness had developed so far that it was the habit for men of letters to describe their minds in confessions and autobiographies. Their lives also were written, and their letters were printed after their deaths. Thus, though we do not know what Shakespeare went through when he wrote *Lear,* we do know what Carlyle went through when he wrote the *French Revolution;* what Flaubert went through when he wrote *Madame Bovary;* what Keats was going through when he tried to write poetry against the coming of death and the indifference of the world.

11   And one gathers from this enormous modern literature of confession and self-analysis that to write a work of genius is almost always a feat of prodigious difficulty. Everything is against the likelihood that it will come from the writer's mind whole and entire. Generally material circumstances are against it. Dogs will bark; people will interrupt; money must be made; health will break down. Further, accentuating all these difficulties and making them harder to bear is the world's notorious indifference. It does not ask people to write poems and novels and histories; it does not need them. It does not care whether Flaubert finds the right word or whether Carlyle scrupulously veri-

fies this or that fact. Naturally, it will not pay for what it does not want. And so the writer, Keats, Flaubert, Carlyle, suffers, especially in the creative years of youth, every form of distraction and discouragement. A curse, a cry of agony, rises from those books of analysis and confession. "Mighty poets in their misery dead"—that is the burden of their song. If anything comes through in spite of all this, it is a miracle, and probably no book is born entire and uncrippled as it was conceived.

[12]   But for women, I thought, looking at the empty shelves, these difficulties were infinitely more formidable. In the first place, to have a room of her own, let alone a quiet room or a sound-proof room, was out of the question, unless her parents were exceptionally rich or very noble, even up to the beginning of the nineteenth century. Since her pin money, which depended on the good will of her father, was only enough to keep her clothed, she was debarred from such alleviations as came even to Keats or Tennyson or Carlyle, all poor men, from a walking tour, a little journey to France, from the separate lodging which, even if it were miserable enough, sheltered them from the claims and tyrannies of their families. Such material difficulties were formidable; but much worse were the immaterial. The indifference of the world which Keats and Flaubert and other men of genius have found so hard to bear was in her case not indifference but hostility. The world did not say to her as it said to them, Write if you choose; it makes no difference to me. The world said with a guffaw, Write? What's the good of your writing? Here the psychologists of Newnham and Girton might come to our help, I thought, looking again at the blank spaces on the shelves. For surely it is time that the effect of discouragement upon the mind of the artist should be measured, as I have seen a dairy company measure the effect of ordinary milk and Grade A milk upon the body of the rat. They set two rats in cages side by side, and of the two one was furtive, timid and small, and the other was glossy, bold and big. Now what food do we feed women as artists upon? I asked, remembering, I suppose, that dinner of prunes and custard. To answer that question I had only to open the evening paper and to read that Lord Birkenhead is of the opinion—but really I am not going to trouble to copy out Lord Birkenhead's opinion upon the writing of women. What Dean Inge says I will leave in peace. The Harley Street specialist may be allowed to rouse the echoes of Harley Street with his vociferations without raising a hair on my head. I will quote, however, Mr. Oscar Browning, because Mr. Oscar Browning was a great figure in Cambridge at one time, and used to examine the students at Girton and Newnham. Mr. Oscar Browning was wont to declare "that the impression left on his mind, after looking over any set of examination papers, was that, irrespective of the marks he might give, the best woman was intellectually the inferior of the worst man." After saying that Mr. Browning went back to his rooms—and it is this sequel that endears him and makes him a human figure of some bulk and majesty—he went back to his rooms and found a stable-boy lying on the

sofa—"a mere skeleton, his cheeks were cavernous and sallow, his teeth were black, and he did not appear to have the full use of his limbs.... 'That's Arthur' [said Mr. Browning]. 'He's a dear boy really and most high-minded.'" The two pictures always seem to me to complete each other. And happily in this age of biography the two pictures often do complete each other, so that we are able to interpret the opinions of great men not only by what they say, but by what they do.

13   But though this is possible now, such opinions coming from the lips of important people must have been formidable enough even fifty years ago. Let us suppose that a father from the highest motives did not wish his daughter to leave home and become writer, painter or scholar. "See what Mr. Oscar Browning says," he would say; and there was not only Mr. Oscar Browning; there was the *Saturday Review;* there was Mr. Greg—the "essentials of a woman's being," said Mr. Greg emphatically, "are that *they are supported by, and they minister to, men*"—there was an enormous body of masculine opinion to the effect that nothing could be expected of women intellectually. Even if her father did not read out loud these opinions, any girl could read them for herself; and the reading, even in the nineteenth century, must have lowered her vitality, and told profoundly upon her work. There would always have been that assertion—you cannot do this, you are incapable of doing that—to protest against, to overcome. Probably for a novelist this germ is no longer of much effect; for there have been women novelists of merit. But for painters it must still have some sting in it; and for musicians, I imagine, is even now active and poisonous in the extreme. The woman composer stands where the actress stood in the time of Shakespeare. Nick Greene, I thought, remembering the story I had made about Shakespeare's sister, said that a woman acting put him in mind of a dog dancing. Johnson repeated the phrase two hundred years later of women preaching. And here, I said, opening a book about music, we have the very words used again in this year of grace, 1928, of women who try to write music. "Of Mlle. Germaine Tailleferre one can only repeat Dr. Johnson's dictum concerning a woman preacher, transposed into terms of music. 'Sir, a woman's composing is like a dog's walking on his hind legs. It is not done well, but you are surprised to find it done at all.'"[2] So accurately does history repeat itself.

14   Thus, I concluded, shutting Mr. Oscar Browning's life and pushing away the rest, it is fairly evident that even in the nineteenth century a woman was not encouraged to be an artist. On the contrary, she was snubbed, slapped, lectured and exhorted. Her mind must have been strained and her vitality lowered by the need of opposing this, of disproving that. For here again we come within range of that very interesting and obscure masculine complex which has had so much influence upon the woman's movement; that deep-

[2]*A Survey of Contemporary Music,* Cecil Gray, p. 246.

seated desire, not so much that *she* shall be inferior as that *he* shall be superior, which plants him wherever one looks, not only in front of the arts, but barring the way to politics too, even when the risk to himself seems infinitesimal and the suppliant humble and devoted. Even Lady Bessborough, I remembered, with all her passion for politics, must humbly bow herself and write to Lord Granville Leveson-Gower: "...notwithstanding all my violence in politics and talking so much on that subject, I perfectly agree with you that no woman has any business to meddle with that or any other serious business, farther than giving her opinion (if she is ask'd)." And so she goes on to spend her enthusiasm where it meets with no obstacle whatsoever upon that immensely important subject, Lord Granville's maiden speech in the House of Commons. The spectacle is certainly a strange one, I thought. The history of men's opposition to women's emancipation is more interesting perhaps than the story of that emancipation itself. An amusing book might be made of it if some young student at Girton or Newnham would collect examples and deduce a theory—but she would need thick gloves on her hands, and bars to protect her of solid gold.

15   But what is amusing now, I recollected, shutting Lady Bessborough, had to be taken in desperate earnest once. Opinions that one now pastes in a book labelled cock-a-doodle-dum and keeps for reading to select audiences on summer nights once drew tears, I can assure you. Among your grandmothers and great-grandmothers there were many that wept their eyes out. Florence Nightingale shrieked aloud in her agony.[3] Moreover, it is all very well for you, who have got yourselves to college and enjoy sitting-rooms—or is it only bed-sitting rooms?—of your own to say that genius should disregard such opinions; that genius should be above caring what is said of it. Unfortunately, it is precisely the men or women of genius who mind most what is said of them. Remember Keats. Remember the words he had cut on his tombstone. Think of Tennyson; think—but I need hardly multiply instances of the undeniable, if very unfortunate, fact that it is the nature of the artist to mind excessively what is said about him. Literature is strewn with the wreckage of men who have minded beyond reason the opinions of others.

16   And this susceptibility of theirs is doubly unfortunate, I thought, returning again to my original enquiry into what state of mind is most propitious for creative work, because the mind of an artist, in order to achieve the prodigious effort of freeing whole and entire the work that is in him, must be incandescent, like Shakespeare's mind, I conjectured, looking at the book which lay open at *Antony and Cleopatra*. There must be no obstacle in it, no foreign matter unconsumed.

17   For though we say that we know nothing about Shakespeare's state of mind, even as we say that, we are saying something about Shakespeare's

---

[3]See *Cassandra*, by Florence Nightingale, printed in *The Cause*, by R. Strachey.

state of mind. The reason perhaps why we know so little of Shakespeare—compared with Donne or Ben Jonson or Milton—is that his grudges and spites and antipathies are hidden from us. We are not held up by some "revelation" which reminds us of the writer. All desire to protest, to preach, to proclaim an injury, to pay off a score, to make the world the witness of some hardship or grievance was fired out of him and consumed. Therefore his poetry flows from him free and unimpeded. If ever a human being got his work expressed completely, it was Shakespeare. If ever a mind was incandescent, unimpeded, I thought, turning again to the bookcase, it was Shakespeare's mind.

1929

Reacting and Writing

Each of the readings in this section is prefaced by questions that direct you toward analyzing its implied audience. You could create a short, written response to any one of the questions, or you could use the questions to get you started on a longer written argument about the audience implied by the piece in question. Or you could contrast two pieces that seem to imply very different audiences. Remember that you need not identify the particular individuals addressed by an author. Instead, think about what attitudes and beliefs the implied audience seems to possess on the issue in question. You might also experiment with rewriting one of the pieces for a different audience. Does changing the audience change the argument itself? Or try telling a story that makes an argument, as Virginia Woolf does.

CHAPTER 2

The Idea of Intention

Having a clear idea of the audience for your argument is only a beginning. You must also have a clear idea of what you are trying to achieve with that audience in your essay. We call this general purpose, or goal, your intention. If your audience is a group of people whom you are guiding on a trip, your intention is the destination. Audience and intention are always inextricably linked, and one constantly informs the other. Only for ease of discussion do we treat them in separate chapters.

Even accomplished writers are often vague at first about what they hope to achieve. To clarify your intention, you must think hard about where you believe your audience stands when you begin your argument and where you hope they will be when you finish. Remember that you will start by considering a particular audience in the real world but that the process of writing your essay will transform it into an implied audience. When you are clear about your audience, you can begin to think concretely about your intention. What is realistic to expect of your audience? What is realistic to expect of yourself? You know where you stand on the issue in question—and, with some thought, you know where your audience stands. How far can you reasonably expect to move them in your direction?

Sometimes the answer to the last question is simple. Your intention is to change your audience's mind on some subject. Before reading your argument, your audience disagreed with you; after reading it, they will agree with you. Or so you hope. Sometimes, however, considering how to put your argument to your audience will lead you to modify your intention. Your audience may disagree with your position so strongly that the best you can hope for is to raise doubts so that they no longer automatically dismiss your position. Before, they thought astrology was for crackpots and charlatans; afterward, they at least understand how some intelligent person might believe in it. Or your audience may already largely agree with your position, and your intention is to get its members to act more consistently or enthusiastically on their own convictions. Before, they were going to vote for your candidate; afterward, they are going to contribute time and money to the campaign. Or perhaps members of your audience are so uninformed about certain aspects of the issue that you decide the best you can do is to provide them with important background information. Before, they did not know enough even to discuss an arms control treaty. Afterward, they know enough to start considering the various positions on it, including yours.

Imagine that you are a lawyer defending a client on criminal charges. The trial has not gone well for you, and now you have to give the final address to the jury members before they retire to make their decision. Of course, you still want to get your client off, but for his sake you should be more specific about your intention. Given the way the trial has gone and given your own sense of the jury, what is reasonable to expect?

You can still try for a complete acquittal. That means you have to clarify the central issues of the case to help the jury reach a consensus in favor of your client. Or you might decide that the best you can try for is a hung jury, one that can't come to a decision. Far from assisting the jury to reach a consensus, you will be using your last words to try to do whatever you can to prevent it. Rather than attempting to bring over to your side unsympathetic jurors, you will be trying to strengthen the resolve of the few who seem most sympathetic. Or you might decide to concede the loss and make the best of it. Although your client adamantly proclaims his innocence and refuses plea bargaining, you might still, with his best interests at heart, focus your remarks on the mitigating circumstances of the crime in the hope that the jury will find him guilty of a lesser charge or recommend clemency. In general, your client will be best served when you have carefully considered whether you intend to win, to draw, or to lose with minimal damage.

FOUR ARGUMENTS, FOUR INTENTIONS

The following are four of the most famous statements made by early Native American leaders. All are concerned with relations between the indigenous peoples and the colonists of European origin. Try to distinguish as precisely as possible the quite different intentions of these arguments. What does each speaker hope that his audience will believe when he finishes?

Powhatan led a great confederacy of Indian tribes in Virginia when the English were nearby, struggling to establish their first permanent colony in North America. Relations between him and the English leader John Smith were, at best, tense, but Powhatan successfully pursued a policy of peace between the two peoples, including permitting his daughter, Pocahontas, to marry a colonist.

Tachnechdorus, known to the colonists as Logan, had lost many of his family to the colonists' raids against his people, the Iroquois. Or so Thomas Jeffer-

son claimed when he included the following speech in his Notes on Virginia
(1785) as an example of eloquence equal to any produced in the Old World.

*The Shawnee leader Tecumseh, who grew up in the early days of the Amer-
ican republic, concluded that the colonists had an insatiable appetite for Indian
land and only a grand alliance of all Indian groups against them could prevent
further encroachments. This dream seemed still possible when Tecumseh
addressed the Osage who had recently been driven out of the Ohio Valley, their
ancestral home.*

*Few Indians were more widely revered in their lifetimes than Chief Seattle
(1786–1866), who pursued a policy of accommodation and compromise in the
Pacific Northwest. In the following selection he is reminding the governor of
the new Washington Territory of the obligations he still has to Seattle's people
in their decline.*

Powhatan

LETTER TO CAPTAIN JOHN SMITH

I am now grown old, and must soon die; and the succession must
descend, in order, to my brothers, *Opitchapan, Opekankanough,* and *Catataugh,*
and then to my two sisters, and their two daughters. I wish their experience
was equal to mine; and that your love to us might not be less than ours to you.
Why should you take by force that from us which you can have by love? Why
should you destroy us, who have provided you with food? What can you get
by war? We can hide our provisions, and fly into the woods; and then you
must consequently famish by wronging your friends. What is the cause of
your jealousy? You see us unarmed, and willing to supply your wants, if you
will come in a friendly manner, and not with swords and guns, as to invade
an enemy. I am not so simple, as not to know it is better to eat good meat, lie
well, and sleep quietly with my women and children; to laugh and be merry
with the English; and, being their friend, to have copper, hatchets, and whatever else I want, than to fly from all, to lie cold in the woods, feed upon
acorns, roots, and such trash, and to be so hunted, that I cannot rest, eat, or
sleep. In such circumstances, my men must watch, and if a twig should but
break, all would cry out, *"Here comes Capt. Smith";* and so, in this miserable
manner, to end my miserable life; and, Capt. Smith, this *might* be soon your
fate too, through your rashness and unadvisedness. I, therefore, exhort you
to peaceable councils; and, above all, I insist that the guns and swords, the
cause of all our jealousy and uneasiness, be removed and sent away.

1609

Logan

SPEECH AT THE END OF LORD DUNMORE'S WAR

1   I appeal to any white to say, if ever he entered Logan's cabin hungry, and he gave him not meat: if ever he came cold and naked and he clothed him not.

2   During the course of the last long bloody war, Logan remained idle in his cabin, an advocate for peace. Such was my love for the whites, that my countrymen pointed as they passed, and said, "Logan is the friend of white men."

3   I had even thought to have lived with you, but for the injuries of one man. Col. Cresap the last spring, in cold blood, and unprovoked, murdered all the relations of Logan; not even sparing my women and children.

4   There runs not a drop of my blood in the veins of any living creature. This called on me for revenge. I have sought it. I have killed many. I have fully glutted my vengeance. For my country, I rejoice at the beams of peace. But do not harbor a thought that mine is the joy of fear. Logan never felt fear. He will not turn on his heel to save his life. Who is there to mourn for Logan?—Not one!

1774

Tecumseh

WE ALL BELONG TO ONE FAMILY

1   Brothers—We all belong to one family; we are all children of the Great Spirit; we walk in the same path; slake our thirst at the same spring; and now affairs of the greatest concern lead us to smoke the pipe around the same council fire!

2   Brothers—We are friends; we must assist each other to bear our burdens. The blood of many of our fathers and brothers has run like water on the ground, to satisfy the avarice of the white men. We, ourselves, are threatened with a great evil; nothing will pacify them but the destruction of all the red men.

3   Brothers—When the white men first set foot on our grounds, they were hungry; they had no place on which to spread their blankets, or to kindle their fires. They were feeble; they could do nothing for themselves. Our fathers commiserated their distress, and shared freely with them whatever

the Great Spirit had given his red children. They gave them food when hungry, medicine when sick, spread skins for them to sleep on, and gave them grounds, that they might hunt and raise corn.

4   Brothers—The white people are like poisonous serpents: when chilled, they are feeble, and harmless, but invigorate them with warmth, and they sting their benefactors to death.

5   The white people came among us feeble; and now we have made them strong, they wish to kill us, or drive us back, as they would wolves and panthers.

6   Brothers—The white men are not friends to the Indians: at first, they only asked for land sufficient for a wigwam; now, nothing will satisfy them but the whole of our hunting grounds, from the rising to the setting sun.

7   Brothers—The white men want more than our hunting grounds; they wish to kill our warriors; they would even kill our old men, women, and little ones.

8   Brothers—Many winters ago, there was no land; the sun did not rise and set: all was darkness. The Great Spirit made all things. He gave the white people a home beyond the great waters. He supplied these grounds with game, and gave them to his red children; and he gave them strength and courage to defend them.

9   Brothers—My people wish for peace; the red men all wish for peace; but where the white people are, there is no peace for them, except it be on the bosom of our mother.

10   Brothers—The white men despise and cheat the Indians; they abuse and insult them; they do not think the red men sufficiently good to live.

11   The red men have borne many and great injuries; they ought to suffer them no longer. My people will not; they are determined on vengeance; they have taken up the tomahawk; they will make it fat with blood; they will drink the blood of the white people.

12   Brothers—My people are brave and numerous; but the white people are too strong for them alone. I wish you to take up the tomahawk with them. If we all unite, we will cause the rivers to stain the great waters with their blood.

13   Brothers—If you do not unite with us, they will first destroy us, and then you will fall an easy prey to them. They have destroyed many nations of red men because they were not united, because they were not friends to each other.

14   Brothers—The white people send runners amongst us; they wish to make us enemies, that they may sweep over and desolate our hunting grounds, like devastating winds, or rushing waters.

15   Brothers—Our Great Father over the great waters is angry with the white people, our enemies. He will send his brave warriors against them; he will send us rifles, and whatever else we want—he is our friend, and we are his children.

16   Brothers—Who are the white people that we should fear them? They cannot run fast, and are good marks to shoot at: they are only men; our fathers have killed many of them; we are not squaws, and we will stain the earth red with their blood.

17   Brothers—The Great Spirit is angry with our enemies; he speaks in thunder, and the earth swallows up villages, and drinks up the Mississippi. The great waters will cover their lowlands; their corn cannot grow; and the Great Spirit will sweep those who escape to the hills from the earth with his terrible breath.

18   Brothers—We must be united; we must smoke the same pipe; we must fight each other's battles; and more than all, we must love the Great Spirit; he is for us; he will destroy our enemies, and make his red children happy.

1810

Seattle

OUR PEOPLE ARE EBBING AWAY LIKE A RAPIDLY RECEDING TIDE

1   Yonder sky that has wept tears of compassion upon my people for centuries untold, and which to us appears changeless and eternal, may change. Today is fair. Tomorrow it may be overcast with clouds. My words are like the stars that never change. Whatever Seattle says the great chief at Washington can rely upon with as much certainty as he can upon the return of the sun or the seasons. The White Chief says that Big Chief at Washington sends us greetings of friendship and good will. This is kind of him for we know he has little need of our friendship in return. His people are many. They are like the grass that covers vast prairies. My people are few. They resemble the scattering trees of a storm-swept plain. The Great—and I presume—good White Chief sends us word that he wishes to buy our lands but is willing to allow us enough to live comfortably. This indeed appears just, even generous, for the Red Man no longer has rights that he need respect, and the offer may be wise also, as we are no longer in need of an extensive country.

2   There was a time when our people covered the land as the waves of a wind-ruffled sea cover its shell-paved floor, but that time long since passed away with the greatness of tribes that are now but a mournful memory. I will not dwell on, nor mourn over, our untimely decay, nor reproach my pale face brothers with hastening it as we too may have been somewhat to blame.

3   Youth is impulsive. When our young men grow angry at some real or imaginary wrong, and disfigure their faces with black paint, it denotes that their hearts are black—and then they are often cruel and relentless, and our old men and old women are unable to restrain them. Thus it has ever been. Thus it was when the white man first began to push our forefathers westward. But let us hope that the hostilities between us may never return. We

would have everything to lose and nothing to gain. Revenge by young braves is considered gain, even at the cost of their own lives, but old men who stay at home in times of war, and mothers who have sons to lose, know better.

4   Our good father at Washington—for I presume he is now our father as well as yours, since King George has moved his boundaries further north—our great and good father, I say, sends us word that if we do as he desires he will protect us. His brave warriors will be to us a bristling wall of strength, and his wonderful ships of war will fill our harbors so that our ancient enemies far to the northward—the Hidas and Timpsions—will cease to frighten our women, children and old men. Then in reality will he be our father and we his children. But can that ever be? Your God is not our God! Your God loves your people and hates mine. He folds his strong protecting arms lovingly about the pale face and leads him by the hand as a father leads his infant son—but He has forsaken His red children—if they are really His. Our God, the Great Spirit, seems also to have forsaken us. Your God makes your people wax strong every day. Soon they will fill all the land. Our people are ebbing away like a rapidly receding tide that will never return. The white man's God can not love our people or He would protect them. They seem to be orphans who can look nowhere for help. How then can we be brothers? How can your God become our God and renew our prosperity and awaken in us dreams of returning greatness? If we have a common Heavenly Father He must be partial—for He came to His pale-face children. We never saw Him. He gave you laws but had no word for His red children whose teeming multitudes once filled this vast continent as stars fill the firmament. No. We are two distinct races with separate origins and separate destinies. There is little in common between us.

5   To us the ashes of our ancestors are sacred and their resting place is hallowed ground. You wander far from the graves of your ancestors and seemingly without regret. Your religion was written on tables of stone by the iron finger of your God so that you could not forget. The Red Man could never comprehend nor remember it. Our religion is the traditions of our ancestors—the dreams of our old men, given them in the solemn hours of night by the Great Spirit; and the visions of our sachems, and is written in the hearts of our people.

6   Your dead cease to love you and the land of their nativity as soon as they pass the portals of the tomb and wander away beyond the stars. They are soon forgotten and never return. Our dead never forget the beautiful world that gave them being. They still love its verdant valleys, its murmuring rivers, its magnificent mountains, sequestered vales and verdant-lined lakes and bays, and ever yearn in tender, fond affection over the lonely hearted living, and often return from the Happy Hunting Ground to visit, guide, console and comfort them.

7   Day and night can not dwell together. The Red Man has ever fled the approach of the White Man as the morning mist flees before the rising sun.

8   However, your proposition seems fair, and I think that my folks will accept it and will retire to the reservation you offer them. Then we will dwell apart in peace for the words of the Great White Chief seem to be the voice of Nature speaking to my people out of dense darkness.

9   It matters little where we pass the remnant of our days. They will not be many. The Indian's night promises to be dark. Not a single star of hope hovers above his horizon. Sad-voiced winds moan in the distance. Grim Nemesis seems to be on the Red Man's trail, and wherever he goes he will hear the approaching footsteps of his fell destroyer and prepare to stolidly meet his doom, as does the wounded doe that hears the approaching footsteps of the hunter.

10   A few more moons. A few more winters—and not one of the descendants of the mighty hosts that once moved over this broad land or lived in happy homes, protected by the Great Spirit, will remain to mourn over the graves of a people—once more powerful and hopeful than yours. But why should I mourn at the untimely fate of my people? Tribe follows tribe, and nation follows nation, like the waves of the sea. It is the order of nature, and regret is useless. Your time of decay may be distant—but it will surely come, for even the White Man whose God walked and talked with him as friend with friend, can not be exempt from the common destiny. We may be brothers after all. We will see.

11   We will ponder your proposition and when we decide we will let you know. But should we accept it, I here and now make this condition—that we will not be denied the privilege without molestation, of visiting at any time the tombs of our ancestors, friends and children. Every part of this soil is sacred, in the estimation of my people. Every hillside, every valley, every plain and grove, has been hallowed by some sad or happy event in days long vanished. Even the rocks, which seem to be dumb and dead as they swelter in the sun along the silent shore thrill with memories of stirring events connected with the lives of my people, and the very dust upon which you now stand responds more lovingly to their footsteps than to yours, because it is rich with the dust of our ancestors and our bare feet are conscious of the sympathetic touch. Our departed braves, fond mothers, glad, happy-hearted maidens, and even the little children who lived here and rejoiced here for a brief season, still love these sombre solitudes and at eventide they grow shadowy of returning spirits. And when the last Red Man shall have perished, and the memory of my tribe shall have become a myth among the white man, these shores will swarm with the invisible dead of my tribe, and when your children's children think themselves alone in the field, the store, the shop, upon the highway, or in the silence of the pathless woods, they will not be alone. In all the earth there is no place dedicated to solitude. At night when the streets of your cities and villages are silent and you think them deserted, they will throng with the returning hosts that once filled them and still love this beautiful land. The White Man will never be alone.

12   Let him be just and deal kindly with my people, for the dead are not powerless. Dead—I say? There is no death. Only a change of worlds.

1855

You can see from these examples how your attempt to distinguish intentions was tied to your understanding of the audience for the piece. This understanding was subtler than simply asking whether the audience was primarily
red or white. For instance, Powhatan, unlike Seattle, was addressing an English
leader he knew personally. On the other hand, Tecumseh's argument extended
across tribal divisions. The intention of each leader was a combination of what
he most hoped for and what he perceived as possible in the context.

HOW INTENTION VARIES WITH AUDIENCE

Because your intention is intimately connected with your perception of
your audience, you will usually have to adapt your intention when you change
your audience. Suppose, for example, that the college librarian has decided that
he must cut back library hours as an economy measure, and you would very
much like to see those hours restored. If you are going to write a letter directly
to the librarian, you can see that it would not be wise to denounce his decision
as typical of the unfeeling attitude of moronic bureaucrats toward the needs of
the intellectual life—unless, that is, you have decided that the case is hopeless
and you simply want to let off steam. Assume, however, that your intention is
to get him to reconsider. How can you make that intention more concrete, more
manageable? You might decide to argue that other changes would save more
money and cause less hardship for students. You could then sympathize with
his budgetary plight and present your objection as a way of being helpful.

Suppose, however, that the librarian, moronic bureaucrat that he proves to
be, refuses to respond. And so you have to resort to the student newspaper to
make your case. Your desire to see the library stay open remains the same, but
your audience has now changed and your intention needs to be adapted. Instead
of asking someone to reverse a recent decision of his own, you are appealing to
a group of people with no direct authority to make this decision. You will need
to rouse them to demand action from someone else. Whereas the librarian has
definite budgetary reasons for not wanting to extend the library hours, your student audience will probably have no objections to having the library stay open
for 24 hours a day, 365 days a year, although they might not intend to be there
themselves. Unlike the librarian, however, they will have to be convinced that
this is a matter about which they should be concerned or on which they can
have any impact. Your intention will have to be adjusted accordingly.

In short, a skillful arguer has a purpose, but it is a purpose in regard to an
audience: to impress X on Y, to alert Y to the dangers of X, to show Y how

important X is, or to remind Y that X can no longer be neglected. If your intention is to alert Y to the dangers of over-the-counter drugs, it is important to consider whether Y is made up primarily of the consumers of these remedies, or of the manufacturers, or of government regulators. If it is the consumers, are you appealing directly to likely abusers of nonprescription drugs to try to educate them about the consequences? Or does it seem more effective to appeal to health-conscious people in general, who, once alerted to the problem, might be willing to campaign for better labelling and more consumer education by manufacturers? Even if your argument is likely to appear before a mixed group that represents the range of behaviors and attitudes toward nonprescription remedies, part of your strategy will be to decide which readers mean the most to you. Which are most likely to help you accomplish your particular purpose?

As you read the pieces in this chapter, it may help to think of their authors as facing the same kinds of problems that you have just imagined for yourself in these examples. When you try to state the author's intention, his or her purpose in regard to an audience, you need not think in terms of guessing the one right answer. In a sense, you are perfectly justified if your reaction to formulating an arguer's intention is to ask, "How on earth can I be expected to know what St. Paul or Chief Seattle had in mind?" What, short of a seance, could give you access to the thoughts of a long-dead writer from a different world? Think of yourself as making an argument based on a text, not communing with the spirits of the dead. Rather than ask whether your response is right or wrong, ask "How precise is its formulation?" and "How well is it supported by evidence from the text?"

St. Paul

ADDRESS TO THE JEWS OF ANTIOCH

The New Testament of the Christian Bible contains an extraordinary portrait of someone successfully adapting his intention to his audience while remaining true to his own convictions—this is the apostle Paul in the Acts of the Apostles. Let us just look at two examples from among many. Here is Paul addressing a Jewish audience in a synagogue.

1   Now Paul and his company set sail from Paphos, and came to Perga in Pamphylia. And John left them and returned to Jerusalem; but they passed on from Perga and came to Antioch of Pisidia. And on the sabbath day they went into the synagogue and sat down. After the reading of the law and the prophets, the rulers of the synagogue sent to them, saying, "Brethren, if you

have any word of exhortation for the people, say it." So Paul stood up, and monitoring with his hand said:

2 "Men of Israel, and you that fear God, listen. The God of this people Israel chose our fathers and made the people great during their stay in the land of Egypt, and with uplifted arm he led them out of it. And for about forty years he bore with them in the wilderness. And when he had destroyed seven nations in the land of Canaan, he gave them their land as an inheritance, for about four hundred and fifty years. And after that he gave them judges until Samuel the prophet. Then they asked for a king; and God gave them Saul the son of Kish, a man of the tribe of Benjamin, for forty years. And when he had removed him, he raised up David to be their king; of whom he testified and said, 'I have found in David the son of Jesse a man after my heart, who will do all my will.' Of this man's posterity God has brought to Israel a Savior, Jesus, as he promised. Before his coming John had preached a baptism of repentance to all the people of Israel. And as John was finishing his course, he said, 'What do you suppose that I am? I am not he. No, but after me one is coming, the sandals of whose feet I am not worthy to untie.'

3 "Brethren, sons of the family of Abraham, and those among you that fear God, to us has been sent the message of this salvation. For those who live in Jerusalem and their rulers, because they did not recognize him nor understand the utterances of the prophets which are read every sabbath, fulfilled these by condemning him. Though they could charge him with nothing deserving death, yet they asked Pilate to have him killed. And when they had fulfilled all that was written of him, they took him down from the tree, and laid him in a tomb.

4 But God raised him from the dead; and for many days he appeared to those who came up with him from Galilee to Jerusalem, who are now his witnesses to the people. And we bring you the good news that what God promised to the fathers, this he has fulfilled to us their children by raising Jesus; as also it is written in the second psalm,

'Thou art my Son,
today I have begotten thee.'

5 And as for the fact that he raised him from the dead, no more to return to corruption, he spoke in this way,

'I will give you the holy and sure
blessings of David.'

6 Therefore he says also in another psalm,

'Thou wilt not let thy Holy One see corruption.'

7 For David, after he had served the counsel of God in his own generation, fell asleep, and was laid with his fathers, and saw corruption; but he whom God raised up saw no corruption. Let it be known to you therefore, brethren, that through this man forgiveness of sins is proclaimed to you, and by him every one that believes is freed from everything from which you could not be

freed by the law of Moses. Beware, therefore, lest there come upon you what is said in the prophets:

'Behold, you scoffers, and wonder, and perish;
for I do a deed in your days,
a deed you will never believe, if one declares it to you.' "

(Acts 13:13–41)

ca. 85 A.D.

St. Paul

ADDRESS TO THE GREEK PHILOSOPHERS

Paul was seeking converts by using arguments that his Jewish audience could consider authoritative—namely, arguments from the Hebrew scriptures. Later, Paul addresses a quite different audience. He speaks to philosophers in Athens who initially regard him with amused contempt, as a superstitious babbler. In this hostile context, Paul first turns the tables by accusing his audience of the charge they hold against him and then uses authorities and principles that they themselves would likely accept. Notice that although his intention toward his audience changes, his beliefs do not.

1   Now while Paul was waiting for them at Athens, his spirit was provoked within him as he saw that the city was full of idols. So he argued in the synagogue with the Jews and the devout persons, and in the market place every day with those who chanced to be there. Some also of the Epicurean and Stoic philosophers met him. And some said, "What would this babbler say?" Others said, "He seems to be a preacher of foreign divinities"—because he preached Jesus and the resurrection. And they took hold of him and brought him to the Areopagus, saying, "May we know what this new teaching is which you present? For you bring some strange things to our ears; we wish to know therefore what these things mean." Now all the Athenians and the foreigners who lived there spent their time in nothing except telling or hearing something new.

2   So Paul, standing in the middle of the Areopagus, said: "Men of Athens, I perceive that in every way you are very superstitious. For as I passed along, and observed the objects of your worship, I found also an altar with this inscription, 'To the unknown god.' What therefore you worship as unknown, this I proclaim to you.

3   The God who made the world and everything in it, being Lord of heaven and earth, does not live in shrines made by man, nor is he served by human

hands, as though he needed anything, since he himself gives to all men life and breath and everything.

4   And he made from one every nation of men to live on all the face of the earth, having determined allotted periods and the boundaries of their habitation, that they should seek God, in the hope that they might feel after him and find him. Yet he is not far from each one of us, for

'In him we live and move and have our being';

as even some of your poets have said,

'For we are indeed his offspring.'

5   Being then God's offspring, we ought not to think that the Deity is like gold, or silver, or stone, a representation by the art and imagination of man. The times of ignorance God overlooked, but now he commands all men everywhere to repent, because he has fixed a day on which he will judge the world in righteousness by a man whom he has appointed, and of this he has given assurance to all men by raising him from the dead."

6   Now when they heard of the resurrection of the dead, some mocked; but others said, "We will hear you again about this."

(Acts 17: 16–32)

ca. 85 A.D.

We can say that Paul succeeds with this group when some say, "We will hear you again about this." This may seem to be a noncommittal reaction, but it was the most he could have hoped for.

Bartolomeo Vanzetti

THREE LETTERS FROM PRISON

Here is another example of how intention varies with audience. In 1920, Bartolomeo Vanzetti and Nicola Sacco were accused of robbing and murdering a paymaster and a guard at a shoe factory in South Braintree, Massachusetts. Both were Italian immigrants, Sacco a 29-year-old shoe-factory worker and Vanzetti a 31-year-old vendor in a fish market. Both were activists in an Italian anarchist group and had taken part in strikes and other kinds of agitation against the labor practices of their day. Neither knew English well at the time they were incarcerated, and Vanzetti in particular spent much of his seven years in prison

*reading and writing in both Italian and English. Up to the time of their execu-
tion, Sacco and Vanzetti firmly maintained that they had never committed a
crime in their lives. When asked by the court clerk at his last trial, "Have you
anything to say why sentence of death should not be passed upon you?," Vanzetti again stated that he had never committed this or any other crime, and
ended with this reflection on his situation:*

> *I am suffering because I am a radical and indeed I am a radical; I have suffered
> because I was an Italian, and indeed I am an Italian; I have suffered more for my
> family and for my beloved than for myself; but I am so convinced to be right that
> you can only kill me once but if you could execute me two times, and if I could be
> reborn two other times, I would live again to do what I have done already.*

*Assuming that Vanzetti's desire to proclaim his and Sacco's innocence and
to reaffirm their cause remains constant in these three letters, how would you
describe the way in which he adapts his intention to suit each audience? You
could begin by noticing that he goes into some specific details of the case and
of his circumstances in the letter to his father. To the college student Li Pei Kan,
he speaks in broad terms about the principles for which he stands. In writing to
the thirteen-year-old son of his friend and co-defendant Sacco, he emphasizes
neither factual details nor philosophical principles, but the motives and character of the boy's father.*

Dearest Father:

1   I have restrained until this moment the desire to write to you, since I had
hoped to be able to give you some good news.

2   Things have continued to go badly, so I decided to write to you. I know
how painful this occurrence in my life must be for all of you, it is this thought
that makes me suffer the most. I beg you to be as strong as I am, and to pardon
the pain that I am involuntarily causing you. I know that several people have
written to you, but I do not know if you are in possession of all the facts, since
several letters and collections of newspapers that friends sent to Italy have
never been received. This fact forces one to admit that either the Italian or the
American authorities are censoring all mail that concerns me. I do, however,
know that you have received some letters and are therefore acquainted with
the nature and outcome of my trial; it was a true crime against legality. A
friend sent me your greetings, your conviction that I am innocent, and the
happy news that you are feeling well. These are consolations of incalculable
worth. Yes: I am innocent, despite everything I am feeling well, and I do my
best to remain in good health. Now they are accusing me of murder. I have
never killed or wounded or robbed, but if things go as they did in the other
trial they would find even Christ, whom they have already crucified, guilty.
I have witnesses that I will call in my defense, and I will fight with all of my
energies. The weapons are unequal, and the fighting will be desperate. I will
have against me the law with all of its immense resources; the police with its

ages of experience in the art of condemning the innocent, a police whose actions are both uncontrolled and uncontrollable. Also arrayed against me are political and racial hate, and the great power that gold has in a country, and in a time, when the depth of human degeneration has been plumbed. The lust for gold has forced certain wretches to tell all sorts of vile lies about me. I have nothing to oppose this formidable coalition of enemies but my popularly acknowledged innocence, and the love and care of a handful of generous souls who love and aid me. The general public proclaims my innocence, demands my liberation. If you knew how much they have done, are doing and will do for me, you would be proud.

3   I hope that my Italian comrades will not deny me their support. In fact I'm sure they won't.

4   I have asked for the transcript of my trial. It will be translated into Italian and into other languages, and sent to Italy and to the other European nations.

5   Take heart therefore and be optimistic. Justice is always triumphant in the end, and so it will be in my case. Do not let this adversity oppress you, let it rather be an incentive to life, to living. Who knows what surprises destiny carries in its breast for us mortals? Who would have thought, a few days before my arrest, in what conditions I would now find myself? Who, therefore, can predict, from the terrible condition in which I now find myself, what tomorrow has in store for me? Let us, therefore, have faith and continue the struggle....

6   I wish to tell you and all my loved ones one other thing. Do not keep my arrest a secret. Do not be silent, I am innocent and you have nothing to be ashamed of. Do not be silent, broadcast the crime that has been committed against me from the rooftops. Tell the world that an honest man is being sent to jail to restore the reputation of the police, which has been lost in a hundred scandals and a hundred failures. The police have not been able to find one single criminal in all this rising sea of crime. I am being sent to jail because of an old sadist's attachment to his power and his position, and because of his desire to see me deprived of my liberty and my blood. Do not be silent, silence would be shameful.

7   For the moment I don't need any money. If I should need some I will let you know. The prisons here are much better than in Italy; I say this by intuition and from what I have heard, since I have never been in prison in Italy. We all have our own cells. Our furniture consists of an adequate bed, a closet, a table and a chair. The electric lights are on until nine at night. We are given three meals a day, and a hot drink once or even twice daily. We are allowed to write two letters a month, and an additional letter every third month. The warden allowed me to write several extra letters, this is one of them. There is a library which contains the world's scientific and artistic masterpieces. We work eight hours a day in a healthy atmosphere. We are allowed out into the courtyard every day. The inmates? Except for a few victims of circumstance, who are more to be pitied than censured, they are wretches. I treat everyone as well as I can, but I remain mostly in the company of those few who are able

to understand me, know my case and honor and love me. If you have kept the last letters that I sent you, send them back to the address of one of my friends, and insure them at the post office. They may be of great use to me.

8   I finish on a happy note: it is almost certain that there will be a retrial for the things that I was first accused of.

9   Be strong, therefore, and encourage my sisters and little brother, as well as all my relatives and friends.

July 23, 1927
Charlestown Prison

Dear Little Comrade [Li Pei Kan]:[1]

1   Your letter dated July 11th was given to me a few days ago, and it gives me joy each time I read it. I will not try to find words with which to thank you for your little picture you sent me. Youth is the hope of mankind, and my heart exults when I look at your photograph and say to myself "Lo! one of those who will pluck and uphold, highly, the flag of freedom, the flag of our supremely beautiful anarchy, which is now slowly falling down from our weakening hands,"—and a good one, as for that. You need to live for many other years, and hard ones, before to realize and understand what comfort and joy such a thought is to your old and dying Bartolo.

2   I have read of that—say, incident, and I thought it happened to you. It is less bad if it happened to an elderly one, because the elders are more worried and hardened by the vicissitude and adversities of life, so that they can bear better the hard blows of fate, while the young ones are more tender, and could be bent and split by black adversities. You will surely resist to all, and separate all, I am sure of it.

3   In regards to what you said of our Ideal in your letter, I fundamentally agree with all of it. My words on this subject, of my antecedent letter, were principally intended to fortify your spirit to better face the tremendous struggle for freedom and prevent future delusions by weakening fatalism and fortify voluntarism in you, as I do with all our young ones and neophites.

4   Perhaps you know Proudhon better than I, but if not, I advise you to study him. Read his *Peace and War*. I think he approached truth in many subjects nearer than other more recent great ones.

5   To my understanding, we are actually certainly dragged, with the rest of mankind, toward tyranny and darkness. Where will we land?

6   The relatively known history testifies, it is true, that mankind has continuously progressed, slowly, insteadily, with advances and retrocessions, yet, steadily progressed.

7   But the dead civilizations tell their tale as well and what came and passed before the dawn of our historical knowledge, we cannot know. History, like

---

[1]Li Pei Kan of Shanghai, China, a student at the Collège de Chateau Thierry, Aisne, France, during the last years of the Sacco-Vanzetti case. He wrote several pamphlets on the case in Chinese, the principal one being *On the Scaffold.*

evolution, as we know of it now, fails far from explaining the request of a deep thinker. Then, what will follow to this age of reversion and tyranny? A false democracy again, which in its turn would inevitably yield to another tide of tyranny? As it is happening from thousands of years?

8   Anarchy, the anarchists alone, we only can break these deadly circles and set life in such a way that by a natural synchronism, produced by the very nature of the things which create the new order, more exactly, which constitute the new order, history will be streamed toward the infinite sea of freedom, instead to turn in the above said dead, close circle, as, it seems, it did 'til now.

9   It is a titanic task—but humanly possible, and if we know, we will create the happy kingdom of Freedom when the traviated, misled tralignated working class, and people of all classes will, most instinctively, join us for the greatest emancipation of the history. But even then we will have to be at the brightness of our task, or else, only a new tyranny will be substitute to the present one as corollary of the immense holocaust.

10   These are the reasons why I tell you, young Comrade, heavy and hard words, just as your juvenile ardor, enthusiasm and faith bliss me, I hope my old experience will complete and fortify you.

11   My friends must have forgotten to send you *A Proletarian Life,*[2] or they are running short of the copies. But I hope to provide you with a copy in the near future. It is a poor thing, but you will take it for what it is. It was modified without my knowledge of it, to fit it to the Americans, to whom you can tell everything, and they like everything, except the pure, naked truth. In general, of course, but the exceptions to the rule are desperately few....

12   And now, dear Li, I embrace you with brotherly and glad heart.

August 21, 1927
From the Death House of Massachusetts State Prison

My Dear Dante:

1   I still hope, and we will fight until the last moment, to revindicate our right to live and to be free, but all the forces of the State and of the money and reaction are deadly against us because we are libertarians or anarchists.

2   I write little of this because you are now and yet too young to understand these things and other things of which I would like to reason with you.

3   But, if you do well, you will grow and understand your father's and my case and your father's and my principles, for which we will soon be put to death.

4   I tell you now that all that I know of your father, he is not a criminal, but one of the bravest men I ever knew. Some day you will understand what I am

---

[2]*The Story of a Proletarian Life,* an account of his own life written in Italian by Vanzetti during the first years of his imprisonment and published in a translation by Eugene Lyons in 1924 by the Defense Committee.

about to tell you. That your father has sacrificed everything dear and sacred to the human heart and soul for his fate in liberty and justice for all. That day you will be proud of your father, and if you come brave enough, you will take his place in the struggle between tyranny and liberty and you will vindicate his (our) names and our blood.

5   If we have to die now, you shall know, when you will be able to understand this tragedy in its fullest, how good and brave your father has been with you, your father and I, during these eight years of struggle, sorrow, passion, anguish and agony.

6   Even from now you shall be good, brave with your mother, with Ines, and with Susie—brave, good Susie[3]—and do all you can to console and help them.

7   I would like you to also remember me as a comrade and friend to your father, your mother and Ines, Susie and you, and I assure you that neither have I been a criminal, that I have committed no robbery and no murder, but only fought modestly to abolish crimes from among mankind and for the liberty of all.

8   Remember Dante, each one who will say otherwise of your father and I, is a liar, insulting innocent dead men who have been brave in their life. Remember and know also, Dante, that if your father and I would have been cowards and hypocrits and rinnegetors of our faith, we would not have been put to death. They would not even have convicted a lebbrous dog; not even executed a deadly poisoned scorpion on such evidence as that they framed against us. They would have given a new trial to a matricide and habitual felon on the evidence we presented for a new trial.

9   Remember, Dante, remember always these things; we are not criminals; they convicted us on a frame-up; they denied us a new trial; and if we will be executed after seven years, four months and seventeen days of unspeakable tortures and wrong, it is for what I have already told you; because we were for the poor and against the exploitation and oppression of the man by the man.

10   The documents of our case, which you and other ones will collect and preserve, will prove to you that your father, your mother, Ines, my family and I have sacrificed by and to a State Reason of the American Plutocratic reaction.

11   The day will come when you will understand the atrocious cause of the above written words, in all its fullness. Then you will honor us.

12   Now Dante, be brave and good always. I embrace you.

P.S. I left the copy of *An American Bible* to your mother now, for she will like to read it, and she will give it to you when you will be bigger and able to understand it. Keep it for remembrance. It will also testify to you how good and generous Mrs. Gertrude Winslow has been with us all. Good-bye Dante.

Bartolomeo

---

[3]Faithful friend of Mrs. Sacco, with whom she and her children lived during the last years of the case.

PREACHING TO THE CONVERTED: A COMMON INTENTION

When an arguer like St. Paul addresses his fellow Christians rather than trying to make new converts, he uses a different form of argument, even though
his religious message remains essentially the same. "Preaching to the converted" is in fact a surprisingly common intention. It is the intention of everything from simple pep talks to letters of condolence to political platforms. The
intention in such discourse is not to change opinions or beliefs; such discourse
intends to influence an audience by reaffirming and reassuring them about the
beliefs they already hold.

The Greeks called such discourse *epideictic* and considered it a type of
argument, even though it does not seek the same sort of change in its audience
that other types of argument strive for. It would be hard to overestimate the
importance of preaching to the converted as a means of increasing social solidarity or of establishing leadership. In the ancient world, as today, ritual occasions such as anniversaries, dedications, and funerals provided opportunities
for this sort of discourse. Here are some examples, the first taken from the Bible,
a funeral oration spoken by David for King Saul and Saul's son Jonathan.

The Book of Samuel

DAVID'S ELEGY FOR SAUL AND JONATHAN

*Notice that David is not just expressing his private grief, sincere as that is.
He is expressing the grief of his people, or rather the grief he thinks that they
should feel, at the death in battle of their annointed king. It seems that, in reality,
Saul had not been a particularly successful king. But that is beside the point
now. David's intention is to fuse private griefs, such as his own at the loss of
Jonathan, with public mourning at the loss of a king and a prince. In expressing
all this, David is demonstrating his own worthiness to be Saul's successor. Of
all the qualifications to be a leader, few are more important than the ability to
express effectively the feelings, the ideals, the goals of the governed.*

And David lamented with this lamentation over Saul and Jonathan his
son, and he said it should be taught to the people of Judah; behold, it is written in the Book of Jashar. He said:

> "Thy glory, O Israel, is slain upon thy high places!
>   How are the mighty fallen!
> Tell it not in Gath,
>   publish it not in the streets of Ashkelon;

lest the daughters of the Philistines rejoice,
　lest the daughters of the uncircumcised exult.

"Ye mountains of Gilboa,
　let there be no dew or rain upon you,
　nor upsurging of the deep!
10 For there the shield of the mighty was defiled,
　the shield of Saul, not anointed with oil.

"From the blood of the slain,
　from the fat of the mighty,
the bow of Jonathan turned not back,
　and the sword of Saul returned not empty.

"Saul and Jonathan, beloved and lovely!
　In life and in death they were not divided;
they were swifter than eagles,
　they were stronger than lions.

20 "Ye daughters of Israel, weep over Saul,
　who clothed you daintily in scarlet,
　who put ornaments of gold upon your apparel.

"How are the mighty fallen
　in the midst of the battle!

"Jonathan lies slain upon thy high places.
　I am distressed for you, my brother Jonathan;
very pleasant have you been to me;
　your love to me was wonderful,
　passing the love of women.

30 "How are the mighty fallen,
　and the weapons of war perished!"

(2 Sam. 1:17–27)

ca. 9th century, B.C.

Virgil
AENEAS TO HIS MEN*

In some contexts, the speaker may find it necessary to suppress a natural emotion, like grief. In the following passage from Virgil's Aeneid, *the hero,*

*Translated by Robert Fitzgerald.

Aeneas, has just lost a number of his ships and many of his most valued men in a disastrous storm. In telling his remaining men that, despite all the evidence, everything will work out, Aeneas tells them what they need to hear in order to continue struggling. He can draw on the earlier sufferings they have survived together to make this claim at least plausible. If he can keep his composure (no small task), he will be able to achieve his intention.

          Aeneas put in here,
With only seven ships from his full number,
And longing for the firm earth underfoot
The Trojans disembarked, to take possession
Of the desired sand-beach. Down they lay,
To rest their brinesoaked bodies on the shore.
Achatës promptly struck a spark from flint
And caught it in dry leaves; he added tinder
Round about and waved it for a flame-burst.
10   Then they brought out the grain of Ceres, tainted
By sea water, and Ceres' implements,
And, weary of their troubles, made all ready
To dry and grind with millstones what they had.

          Meanwhile, Aeneas climbed one of the peaks
For a long seaward view, hoping to sight
Gale-worn Antheus and the Phrygian biremes,
Capys, or high poops bearing Caïcus' arms.
He found no ship in sight, but on the shore
Three wandering stags. Behind them whole herds followed,
20   Grazing in a long line down the valleys.
Planting his feet, he took in hand the bow
And arrows carried by his aide, Achatës,
Then, aiming for the leaders with heads high
And branching antlers, brought them first to earth.
Next he routed the whole herd,
Driving them with his shafts through leafy places,
Shooting and shooting till he won the hunt
By laying seven carcasses on the ground,
A number equal to his ships. Then back
30   To port he went, and parcelled out the game
To his ships' companies. There he divided
The wine courtly Acestës had poured out
And given them on the Sicilian shore—
Full jugs of it—when they were about to sail.
By this and by a simple speech Aeneas
Comforted his people:

"Friends and companions,
Have we not known hard hours before this?
My men, who have endured still greater dangers,
God will grant us an end to these as well.
40   You sailed by Scylla's rage, her booming crags,
You saw the Cyclops' boulders. Now call back
Your courage, and have done with fear and sorrow.
Some day, perhaps, remembering even this
Will be a pleasure. Through diversities
Of luck, and through so many challenges,
We hold our course for Latium, where the Fates
Hold out a settlement and rest for us.
Troy's kingdom there shall rise again. Be patient:
Save yourselves for more auspicious days."

50   So ran the speech. Burdened and sick at heart,
He feigned hope in his look, and inwardly
Contained his anguish. Now the Trojan crews
Made ready for their windfall and their feast.
They skinned the deer, bared ribs and viscera,
Then one lot sliced the flesh and skewered it
On spits, all quivering, while others filled
Bronze cooking pots and tended the beach fires.
All got their strength back from the meal, reclining
On the wild grass, gorging on venison
60   And mellowed wine. When hunger had been banished,
And tables put away, they talked at length
In hope and fear about their missing friends:
Could one believe they might be still alive,
Or had they suffered their last hour,
Never again to hear a voice that called them?
Aeneas, more than any, secretly
Mourned for them all—for that fierce man, Orontës,
Then for Amycus, then for the bitter fate
Of Lycus, for brave Gyas, brave Cloanthus.

19 B.C.

◆   ◆   ◆

Sometimes less experienced writers write epideictic arguments unintentionally; they preach to the converted when they should be trying to change the
mind of an audience. Before you write an essay defending motherhood, deploring drug addiction, or praising honesty, ask yourself what your intention is and

whether there is an audience for such arguments. Are you beginning with a particular audience who despises motherhood, supports drug addiction, or distrusts honesty?

The problem of unintentionally preaching to the converted often arises from insufficient thought about audience and intention. A student might, for example, write an argument for legalizing prostitution strictly on the grounds that it could then be taxed and the government would have a new source of much-needed revenue. Legalizing prostitution might seem like a genuinely controversial proposal, and indeed for most people it is. But their objection to prostitution in most cases is not economic but social and moral. Thus, even though the proposal at first sounds controversial, arguing that legalizing prostitution will generate revenue is preaching to the converted. Who could deny that it would? Legalizing and taxing extortion, child pornography, or murder contracts would have a similar effect, but few are eager to legalize these practices. The arguer needs to rethink what exactly is at issue with his or her audience on this topic.

At other times, the problem of unintentionally preaching to the converted arises when the writer has conducted the argument at too high a level of generality. If you argue that the social and personal costs of drug addiction are terrible or that becoming addicted to a drug is undesirable, few will disagree, and you will in essence be preaching to the converted. But when you begin to be more specific—arguing, for example, that nicotine or caffeine or alcohol should be banned—you will have an unconverted audience whose views you will try to influence. The challenge is to find the point at which your issue becomes controversial for your audience.

Abraham Lincoln

THE GETTYSBURG ADDRESS

Sometimes a text will become so familiar that we will hardly impute to it an intention at all. For example, Lincoln's Gettysburg Address is usually read as if carved in stone.

1   Fourscore and seven years ago our fathers brought forth on this continent a new nation conceived in liberty and dedicated to the proposition that all men are created equal.

2   Now we are engaged in a great civil war testing whether that nation, or any nation so conceived and so dedicated, can long endure.

3 We are met on a great battlefield of that war. We have come to dedicate a portion of that field as a final resting-place for those who here gave their lives that that nation might live.

4 It is altogether fitting and proper that we should do this.

5 But, in a larger sense, we cannot dedicate, we cannot consecrate, we cannot hallow this ground. The brave men, living and dead, who struggled here have consecrated it far beyond our poor power to add or detract.

6 The world will little note nor long remember what we say here, but it can never forget what they did here.

7 It is for us the living rather to be dedicated here to the unfinished work which they who fought here have thus far so nobly advanced. It is rather for us to be here dedicated to the great task remaining before us—that from these honoured dead we take increased devotion to that cause for which they gave the last full measure of devotion—that this nation under God shall have a new birth of freedom, and that government of the people, by the people, for the people, shall not perish from the earth.

1863

Carl Sandburg

LINCOLN SPEAKS AT GETTYSBURG

Because of its fame, it is hard to think of the Gettysburg Address as anything but a self-sufficient masterpiece. We can praise its dignity of tone and brevity of expression. But who is to say that dignity or brevity was appropriate, except in terms of Lincoln's intention? Let us look at this speech again, this time in its context, at least as described in Carl Sandburg's biography of Lincoln.

1 Fifteen thousand, some said 30,000 or 50,000, people were on Cemetery Hill for the exercises the next day when the procession from Gettysburg arrived afoot and horseback representing the United States Government, the army and navy, governors of States, mayors of cities, a regiment of troops, hospital corps, telegraph-company representatives, Knights Templar, Masonic Fraternity, Odd Fellows, and other benevolent associations, the press, fire departments, citizens of Pennsylvania and other States. . . .

2 The United States House chaplain, the Reverend Thomas H. Stockton, offered a prayer while the thousands stood with uncovered heads.

3 "O God, our Father, for the sake of Thy Son, our Saviour, inspire us with Thy spirit, and sanctify us. . . . By this altar of sacrifice and on this field of

deliverance—on this mount of salvation—within the fiery and bloody line of these munitive rocks, looking back to the dark days of fear and trembling, and to the rapture of relief that came after, we multiply our thanksgiving, and confess our obligations to renew and perfect our personal and social consecration to Thy service and glory.... Bless the efforts to suppress this rebellion.... As the trees are not dead, though the foliage is gone, so our heroes are not dead though their forms have fallen—with their personality they are all with Thee, and the spirit of their example is here. It fills the air, it fills our hearts, and long as time shall last it will hover in these skies and rest on this landscape...."

4   The chaplain prayed as a master of liturgy and a familiar of sacred literature. The *Philadelphia Press* said that with the prayer "there was scarcely a dry eye in all that vast assemblage," while the *Cincinnati Daily Gazette* reporter wrote his observation: "The President evidently united in this adjuration in all the simplicity of his soul, and the falling tear declared the sincerity of his emotions."

5   Benjamin B. French, officer in charge of buildings in Washington, introduced the Honorable Edward Everett, orator of the day, who rose, bowed low to Lincoln, saying, "Mr. President." Lincoln responded, "Mr. Everett."

6   The orator of the day then stood in silence before a crowd that stretched to limits that would test his voice. Beyond and around were the wheat fields, the meadows, the peach orchards, long slopes of land, and five and seven miles farther the contemplative blue ridge of a low mountain range. His eyes could sweep them as he faced the audience. He had taken note of it in his prepared and rehearsed address. "Overlooking these broad fields now reposing from the labors of the waning year, the mighty Alleghanies dimly towering before us, the graves of our brethren beneath our feet, it is with hesitation that I raise my poor voice to break the eloquent silence of God and Nature. But the duty to which you have called me must be performed;—grant me, I pray you, your indulgence and your sympathy." Everett proceeded, "It was appointed by law in Athens," and gave an extended sketch of the manner in which the Greeks cared for their dead who fell in battle. He spoke of the citizens assembled to consecrate the day. "As my eye ranges over the fields whose sods were so lately moistened by the blood of gallant and loyal men, I feel, as never before, how truly it was said of old that it is sweet and becoming to die for one's country."

7   Northern cities would have been trampled in conquest but for "those who sleep beneath our feet," said the orator. He gave an outline of how the war began, traversed decisive features of the three days' battles at Gettysburg, discussed the doctrine of State sovereignty and denounced it, drew parallels from European history, and came to his peroration quoting Pericles on dead patriots: "The whole earth is the sepulchre of illustrious men." The men

of nineteen sister States had stood side by side on the perilous ridges. "Seminary Ridge, the Peach-Orchard, Cemetery, Culp, and Wolf Hill, Round Top, Little Round Top, humble names, henceforward dear and famous,—no lapse of time, no distance of space, shall cause you to be forgotten." He had spoken for an hour and fifty-seven minutes, some said a trifle over two hours, repeating almost word for word an address that occupied nearly two newspaper pages, as he had written it and as it had gone in advance sheets to many newspapers.

8   Everett came to his closing sentence without a faltering voice: "Down to the latest period of recorded time, in the glorious annals of our common country there will be no brighter page than that which relates THE BATTLES OF GETTYSBURG." It was the effort of his life and embodied the perfections of the school of oratory in which he had spent his career. His erect form and sturdy shoulders, his white hair and flung-back head at dramatic points, his voice, his poise, and chiefly some quality of inside goodheartedness, held most of his audience to him, though the people in the front rows had taken their seats three hours before his oration closed.

9   The Baltimore Glee Club sang an ode written for the occasion by Benjamin B. French, who had introduced Everett to the audience. The poets Longfellow, Bryant, Whittier, Lowell, George Boker, had been requested but none found time to respond with a piece to be set to music. The two closing verses of the ode by French immediately preceded the introduction of the President to the audience:

> Great God in Heaven!
> Shall all this sacred blood be shed?
> Shall we thus mourn our glorious dead?
> Oh, shall the end be wrath and woe,
> The knell of Freedom's overthrow,
>   A country riven?
>
> It will not be!
> We trust, O God! thy gracious power
> To aid us in our darkest hour.
> This be our prayer—"O Father! save
> A people's freedom from its grave.
>   All praise to Thee!"

10   Having read Everett's address, Lincoln knew when the moment drew near for him to speak. He took out his own manuscript from a coat pocket, put on his steel-bowed glasses, stirred in his chair, looked over the manuscript, and put it back in his pocket. The Baltimore Glee Club finished. The specially chosen Ward Hill Lamon rose and spoke the words "The President of the United States," who rose, and holding in one hand the two sheets of

paper at which he occasionally glanced, delivered the address in his high-pitched and clear-carrying voice. The *Cincinnati Commercial* reporter wrote, "The President rises slowly, draws from his pocket a paper, and, when commotion subsides, in a sharp, unmusical treble voice, reads the brief and pithy remarks." Hay wrote in his diary, "The President, in a firm, free way, with more grace than is his wont, said his half dozen words of consecration." Charles Hale of the *Boston Advertiser,* also officially representing Governor Andrew of Massachusetts, had notebook and pencil in hand, took down the slow-spoken words of the President, as follows:

> Fourscore and seven years ago, our fathers brought forth upon this continent a new nation, conceived in liberty and dedicated to the proposition that all men are created equal.
>
> Now we are engaged in a great civil war, testing whether that nation—or any nation, so conceived and so dedicated—can long endure.
>
> We are met on a great battle-field of that war. We are met to dedicate a portion of it as the final resting place of those who have given their lives that that nation might live.
>
> It is altogether fitting and proper that we should do this.
>
> But, in a larger sense, we cannot dedicate, we cannot consecrate, we cannot hallow, this ground. The brave men, living and dead, who struggled here, have consecrated it, far above our power to add or to detract.
>
> The world will very little note nor long remember what we say here; but it can never forget what they did here.
>
> It is for us, the living, rather, to be dedicated, here, to the unfinished work that they have thus far so nobly carried on. It is rather for us to be here dedicated to the great task remaining before us; that from these honored dead we take increased devotion to that cause for which they here gave the last full measure of devotion; that we here highly resolve that these dead shall not have died in vain; that the nation shall, under God, have a new birth of freedom, and that government of the people, by the people, for the people, shall not perish from the earth.

11   In a speech to serenaders just after the battle of Gettysburg four and a half months before, Lincoln had referred to the founding of the republic as taking place "eighty odd years since." Then he had hunted up the exact date, which was eighty-seven years since, and phrased it "Fourscore and seven years ago" instead of "Eighty-seven years since." Also in the final copy Lincoln wrote "We have come" instead of the second "We are met" that Hale reported.

12   In the written copy of his speech from which he read Lincoln used the phrase "our poor power." In other copies of the speech which he wrote out later he again used the phrase "our poor power." So it was evident that he meant to use the word "poor" when speaking to his audience, but he omitted it. Also in the copy held in his hands while facing the audience he had not

written the words "under God," though he did include those words in later copies which he wrote. Therefore the words "under God" were decided upon after he wrote the text the night before at the Wills residence.

13   The *New York Tribune* and many other newspapers indicated "[Applause.]" at five places in the address and "[Long continued applause.]" at the end. The applause, however, according to most of the responsible witnesses, was formal and perfunctory, a tribute to the occasion, to the high office, to the array of important men of the nation on the platform, by persons who had sat as an audience for three hours. Ten sentences had been spoken in five minutes, and some were surprised that it should end before the orator had really begun to get his outdoor voice.

14   The *New York Times* reporter gave his summary of the program by writing: "The opening prayer by Reverend Mr. Stockton was touching and beautiful, and produced quite as much effect upon the audience as the classic sentences of the orator of the day. President Lincoln's address was delivered in a clear loud tone of voice, which could be distinctly heard at the extreme limits of the large assemblage. It was delivered (or rather read from a sheet of paper which the speaker held in his hand) in a very deliberate manner, with strong emphasis, and with a most business-like air."

15   The *Philadelphia Press* man, John Russell Young, privately felt that Everett's speech was the performance of a great actor whose art was too evident, that it was "beautiful but cold as ice." The *New York Times* man noted: "Even while Mr. Everett was delivering his splendid oration, there were as many people wandering about the fields, made memorable by the fierce struggles of July, as stood around the stand listening to his eloquent periods. They seem to have considered, with President Lincoln, that it was not what was *said* here, but what was *done* here, that deserved their attention...."

16   The audience had expected, as the printed program stipulated, "Dedicatory Remarks, by the President of the United States." No eloquence was promised. Where eloquence is in flow the orator must have time to get tuned up, to expatiate and expand while building toward his climaxes, it was supposed. The *New York Tribune* man and other like observers merely reported the words of the address with the one preceding sentence: "The dedicatory remarks were then delivered by the President." These reporters felt no urge to inform their readers about how Lincoln stood, what he did with his hands, how he moved, vocalized, or whether he emphasized or subdued any parts of the address. Strictly, no address as such was on the program from him. He was down for just a few perfunctory "dedicatory remarks."

17   According to Lamon, Lincoln himself felt that about all he had given the audience was ordinary garden-variety dedicatory remarks, for Lamon wrote that Lincoln told him just after delivering the speech that he had regret over not having prepared it with greater care. "Lamon, that speech won't *scour*. It is a flat failure and the people are disappointed." On the farms where Lincoln

grew up as a boy when wet soil stuck to the mold board of a plow they said it didn't "scour."

[18] The near-by *Patriot and Union* of Harrisburg took its fling: "The President succeeded on this occasion because he acted without sense and without constraint in a panorama that was gotten up more for the benefit of his party than for the glory of the nation and the honor of the dead.... We pass over the silly remarks of the President; for the credit of the nation we are willing that the veil of oblivion shall be dropped over them and that they shall no more be repeated or thought of."

[19] The *Chicago Times* held that "Mr. Lincoln did most foully traduce the motives of the men who were slain at Gettysburg" in his reference to "a new birth of freedom," the *Times* saying, "They gave their lives to maintain the old government, and the only Constitution and Union." He had perverted history, misstated the cause for which they died, and with "ignorant rudeness" insulted the memory of the dead, the *Times* alleged: "Readers will not have failed to observe the exceeding bad taste which characterized the remarks of the President and Secretary of State at the dedication of the soldiers' cemetery at Gettysburg. The cheek of every American must tingle with shame as he reads the silly, flat, and dish-watery utterances of the man who has to be pointed out to intelligent foreigners as the President of the United States. And neither he nor Seward could refrain, even on that solemn occasion, from spouting their odious abolition doctrines. The readers of THE TIMES ought to know, too, that the valorous President did not dare to make this little journey to Gettysburg without being escorted by a bodyguard of soldiers. For the first time in the history of the country, the President of the United States, in traveling through a part of his dominions, on a peaceful, even a religious mission, had to be escorted by a bodyguard of soldiers ... It was fear of his own personal safety which led the President to go escorted as any other military despot might go." In the pronouncement of a funeral sermon Mr. Lincoln had intruded an "offensive exhibition of boorishness and vulgarity," had alluded to tribal differences that an Indian orator eulogizing dead warriors would have omitted, "which he knew would excite unnecessarily the bitter prejudices of his hearers." Therefore the *Chicago Times* would inquire, "Is Mr. Lincoln less refined than a savage?"

[20] A Confederate outburst of war propaganda related to Lincoln and the Gettysburg exercises was set forth in a *Richmond Examiner* editorial, and probably written by its editor, Edward A. Pollard, taking a day off from his merciless and occasionally wild-eyed criticism of President Jefferson Davis of the Confederacy. And the *Chicago Times*, which seldom let a day pass without curses on Lincoln for his alleged suppression of free speech and a free press, reprinted in full the long editorial from the *Examiner*. "The dramatic exhibition at Gettysburg is in thorough keeping with Yankee character, suited to the usual dignity of their chosen chief," ran part of the editorial

scorn. "Stage play, studied attitudes, and effective points were carefully elaborated and presented to the world as the honest outpourings of a nation's heart. In spite of shoddy contracts, of universal corruption, and cruel thirst for southern blood, these people have ideas...have read of them in books...and determined accordingly to have a grand imitation of them.... Mr. Everett was equal to the occasion. He "took down his Thucydides," and fancied himself a Pericles commemorating the illustrious dead. The music, the eloquence, the bottled tears and hermetically sealed grief, prepared for the occasion, were all properly brought out in honor of the heroes, whom they crimp in Ireland, inveigle in Germany, or hunt down in the streets of New York.

21   "So far the play was strictly classic. To suit the general public, however, a little admixture of the more irregular romantic drama was allowed. A vein of comedy was permitted to mingle with the deep pathos of the piece. This singular novelty, and deviation from classic propriety, was heighted by assigning this part to the chief personage. Kings are usually made to speak in the magniloquent language supposed to be suited to their elevated position. On the present occasion Lincoln acted the clown."

22   This was in the customary tone of the *Chicago Times* and relished by its supporting readers. Its rival, the *Chicago Tribune,* however, had a reporter who telegraphed (unless some editor who read the address added his own independent opinion) a sentence: "The dedicatory remarks of President Lincoln will live among the annals of man."

23   The *Cincinnati Gazette* reporter added after the text of the address, "That this was the right thing in the right place, and a perfect thing in every respect, was the universal encomium."

24   The American correspondent of the London *Times* wrote that "the ceremony was rendered ludicrous by some of the sallies of that poor President Lincoln.... Anything more dull and commonplace it would not be easy to produce."

25   Count Gurowski, the only man ever mentioned by Lincoln to Lamon as his possible assassin, wrote in a diary, "Lincoln spoke, with one eye to a future platform and to re-election."...

26   After the ceremonies at Gettysburg Lincoln lunched with Governor Curtin, Mr. Everett, and others at the Wills home, held a reception that had not been planned, handshaking nearly an hour, looking gloomy and listless but brightening sometimes as a small boy or girl came in line, and stopping one tall man for remarks as to just how high up he reached. At five o'clock he attended a patriotic meeting in the Presbyterian church, walking arm-in-arm with old John Burns, and listening to an address by Lieutenant Governor-elect Anderson of Ohio. At six-thirty he was on the departing Washington train. In the dining-car his secretary John Hay ate with Simon Cameron and Wayne MacVeagh. Hay had thought Cameron and MacVeagh hated each other, but he noted: "I

was more than usually struck by the intimate, jovial relations that exist between men that hate and detest each other as cordially as do those Pennsylvania politicians."

27   The ride to Washington took until midnight. Lincoln was weary, talked little, stretched out on one of the side seats in the drawing-room and had a wet towel laid across his eyes and forehead.

28   He had stood that day, the world's foremost spokesman of popular government, saying that democracy was yet worth fighting for. He had spoken as one in mist who might head on deeper yet into mist. He incarnated the assurances and pretenses of popular government, implied that it could and might perish from the earth. What he meant by "a new birth of freedom" for the nation could have a thousand interpretations. The taller riddles of democracy stood up out of the address. It had the dream touch of vast and furious events epitomized for any foreteller to read what was to come. He did not assume that the drafted soldiers, substitutes, and bounty-paid privates had died willingly under Lee's shot and shell, in deliberate consecration of themselves to the Union cause. His cadences sang the ancient song that where there is freedom men have fought and sacrificed for it, and that freedom is worth men's dying for. For the first time since he became President he had on a dramatic occasion declaimed, howsoever it might be read, Jefferson's proposition which had been a slogan of the Revolutionary War—"All men are created equal"—leaving no other inference than that he regarded the Negro slave as a man. His outwardly smooth sentences were inside of them gnarled and tough with the enigmas of the American experiment.

1939

From this account we can see something of the complexity of Lincoln's situation as a speaker. Which of these different listeners represented in Sandburg's account was Lincoln addressing? Surely he couldn't hope to reach those still loyal to the Confederacy, although they might of course be listening. Surely he also knew that the address would be widely printed in newspapers and hence would reach far beyond those physically present. You might try to imagine how you would have responded if you were the spokesperson for one constituency among Lincoln's contemporaries.

We needn't, by the way, identify Sandburg's evaluation of the speech with the judgment of history. A wide variety of responses to the speech is still possible today. One recent commentator dismissed the address as "disappointingly partisan"—and hence not worthy of the praise it usually receives. This critic regrets Lincoln's narrowness of intention, his failure to use the occasion to include sincere supporters of the Confederacy.

Reacting and Writing

The arguments in this chapter may seem distant at first from your own experience. Once you analyze their intentions, however, you should be able to think of numerous occasions when you might have a similar intention. You might, for example, remember a time when you had to address two distinct audiences on behalf of a single cause. You might actually try writing the letters to the librarian described in the first part of "How Intention Varies with Audience." Or you could write a pair of letters arguing some other issue of concern to you, addressing each to an audience with different interests. For example, how would a letter to the faculty differ from a letter to the students at a college or university if the issue were whether to incorporate the works of women and minorities into the school's survey of Western music, art, or literature? Can you then create a third letter that addresses the whole educational community without alienating one audience or the other?

◆ "Four Native Americans"

If you are interested in the four pieces by Native Americans, you might try creating a fifth argument, this time speaking from the point of view of the present. What would a present-day Native American leader say to a modern governor or President on behalf of his people? What argument might a modern Tecumseh address to the members of tribes other than his own? Such an essay makes a good group or class project, with everyone helping to amass information and then individuals writing arguments according to their own adopted audiences and intentions.

◆ "Three Letters from Prison"

The letters from Vanzetti lend themselves well to an analytical paper in which you look very carefully at the way in which Vanzetti's message is reshaped for each audience: his deeply worried father, a college student whom he does not know well but who shares his political views, and a thirteen-year-old boy, whose father is about to be executed. The boy, Dante Sacco, presumably cannot easily understand the consolation that Sacco and Vanzetti apparently derived from their belief in their cause. How does Vanzetti try to deal with this problem?

◆ "The Gettysburg Address"

You can also learn by putting yourself back imaginatively into the historical situations these readings recreate. Imagine yourself evaluating the Gettysburg Address for a specific group of your contemporaries (this would be your intention). What would you praise about the speech? What would you criticize? What would you make of the mixed response that the address received among its immediate contemporaries? How would you respond to Lincoln's own disappointment with the address? How might Lincoln's intention have to change if the North were losing at this point in the war instead of winning?

Additional Readings

THREE ESSAYS ON EDUCATION

William K. Kilpatrick

WHY JOHNNY CAN'T TELL RIGHT FROM WRONG

William Kilpatrick's essay, extracted from a recent book of the same title, makes an argument about moral values and post-1960s teaching practices. It appeared during a presidential campaign in which "family values" was a recurring but ill-defined slogan. Kilpatrick, a university professor, appears to make parents his primary audience, alerting them to his concerns about what is going on in their children's schools.

1   "It ought to be the oldest things that are taught to the youngest people," quipped G. K. Chesterton in 1910. If that guarded approach applies anywhere, moral education would seem to be the place. In learning right from wrong, young people ought to have the benefit of ideas that have been around for a while. After all, when researchers experiment with new treatments in medicine, the policy is to ask for adult volunteers, not to round up children. Common sense would seem to suggest a similarly cautious approach to experiments in teaching values.

2   For a long time that was the guiding policy in American schools. Teachers understood their main task to be the transmission of the culture: passing on to each new generation the lessons—some of them costly—that had been learned about right and wrong.

3   The 1960s, however, saw Chesterton's formula turned on its head. In that decade and the next, educators vied to outdo one another in rushing the newest developments and techniques into the classroom and into young heads. Nowhere was this done more avidly than in the field of moral education. The oldest ideas were, in effect, banished from the classroom. Almost overnight, concepts such as virtue, good example and character formation fell out of favor with educators.

4   In view of what was at stake, it was a surprisingly bloodless revolution. Teaching right from wrong has as much bearing on a culture's survival as

teaching reading, writing or science. Yet the radical innovations met with little resistance. For the most part they were embraced.

5   What accounts for this willing acceptance by the schools?

6   One possibility is that good behavior on the part of youngsters—aside from the normal quotient of rebellion and mischief—was something that educators were able to take for granted. Many educators at the time believed strongly in the idea of natural morality. And the relatively well-behaved youngsters in their classrooms seemed to prove the point. If their charges were, perhaps, somewhat more restive than students of the previous decade, that could be explained by the difficulty of adjusting to the new climate of freedom. What was generally ignored, of course, was the possibility that morality has more to do with culture than with nature: the possibility, that is, that character education had done its job well, and that the relative calm was not the fruit of nature but the lingering benefit of an earlier educational culture. Whatever the case, educators apparently felt they could afford to experiment.

7   Another explanation for this bloodless coup is simply that the time was ripe for it. Those were the days of the free speech movement, of flower children and campus sit-ins and Woodstock. It was also a time of violence—the murder of civil rights workers, the assassination of King and the Kennedys, the Vietnam War. Something was radically wrong with our culture—or so it seemed to many. And the revelations about Watergate in the early 1970s did not help matters. The main sentiment—and it was a sentiment widely shared by educators—was that the culture was something to be ashamed of, not transmitted. It would be better if students started from scratch and developed their own ideas about society.

8   This was the atmosphere into which the so-called decision-making model of moral education emerged. It was a model that relied on students to discover values for themselves, and it promised that this could be done without indoctrination of any sort. Students would be given tools for making decisions, but the decisions would be their own. The idea gained ready acceptance in schools. Decision making was exactly what educators were looking for, and they rushed to embrace it.

9   The decision-making model developed along two different lines. One approach, called "Values Clarification," emphasized feelings, personal growth and a totally non-judgmental attitude; the other, known as the "moral reasoning" approach, emphasized a "critical thinking" or cognitive approach to decision making. Although both shared many assumptions and methods, it is important to understand the differences.

10   Values Clarification got its start in 1966 with the publication of *Values and Teaching* by Louis Raths, Merrill Harmin and Sidney Simon—all professors of education. What the authors offered was not a way to teach values, but a way for students to "clarify" their own values. The authors took pains to distance

themselves from character education and traditional methods of teaching values. In fact, Simon once expressed a wish that parents would stop "fostering the immorality of morality." It was Simon, also, who took the lead in popularizing the new method. His *Values Clarification: A Handbook of Practical Strategies for Teachers and Students* was published in 1972, and quickly became a best-seller among teachers. According to the promotional blurb on the book's back cover, Values Clarification makes students "aware of *their own* feelings, *their own* ideas, *their own* beliefs . . . *their own* value systems."

[11]　But Values Clarification was not exactly a new idea. In reality, it was an outgrowth of human potential psychology. The developers of Values Clarification had simply taken Carl Rogers' nondirective, nonjudgmental therapy technique and applied it to moral education. Indeed, the authors of *Values and Teaching* were so committed to therapeutic non-judgmentalism that they felt obliged to note that "it is entirely possible that children will choose not to develop values. It is the teacher's responsibility to support this choice also."

[12]　True to its origins in the human potential movement, Values Clarification also puts a heavy emphasis on feelings—so much so that it virtually equates values with feelings. That this is the case is indicated in the very first strategy in the *Values Clarification* handbook. It is titled "Twenty Things You Love To Do." This exercise is not a prelude to deeper thought. Rather, it sets the tone for the whole book. A value is essentially what you like or love to do. It is not an ought-to but a want-to. In his book *Educating for Character,* Professor Thomas Lickona relates the story of an eighth-grade teacher who used this strategy with a low-achieving class only to find that the four most popular activities were "sex, drugs, drinking, and skipping school." The teacher was hamstrung. The Values Clarification framework gave her no way of persuading them otherwise. Her students had clarified their values, and they were able to justify their choices with answers they found satisfactory ("Everyone drinks and smokes dope"; "Sex is the best part of life").

[13]　Another problem with Values Clarification is that, despite its claim of being value-neutral, it actually conditions children to think of values as relative. This is apparent in strategy number three, "Values Voting." The exercise starts off innocuously enough with questions from the teacher such as, "How many of you like to go on long walks or hikes?" "How many enjoy going on a picnic?" "How many like yogurt?" and so on. But before long, questions of a weightier nature begin to appear in the list: "How many of you approve of premarital sex for boys? For girls?" "How many think we ought to legalize abortions?" "How many would approve of a marriage between homosexuals being sanctioned by a priest, minister or rabbi?"

[14]　No effort is made to set these loaded questions apart. They are simply interspersed with the innocuous questions in random fashion. In the context of picnics and long walks, however, some of these "items in life's cafeteria,"

as Simon once called them, seem wildly out of place—like a guest appearance by Madonna on *Mr. Rogers' Neighborhood.* At least it would seem that way to a thoughtful adult. But Values Clarification is about getting in touch with feelings, not thoughts. The exercises are designed so that a young student will come away with the impression that all values are simply a matter of personal taste—like eating yogurt. Reading through the *Values Clarification* book of strategies, one is forced to conclude that its authors are more interested in circumventing the rational mind than in stimulating it.

15   Values Clarification has suffered some setbacks in the last decade. The anti-intellectual bias is hard to ignore; so is the research, which shows Values Clarification to be ineffectual at best and potentially harmful. Moreover, Values Clarification has come under attack from parents' groups in dozens of states. Despite these difficulties, however, Values Clarification has shown amazing powers of survival. Those who favor the approach have adopted the simple tactic of changing the name while retaining the method. Values Clarification often shows up under the guise of drug education, sex education and life skills courses, which rely heavily on its techniques. For example, the initial curriculum for Quest, a popular drug education program, was written by Howard Kirschenbaum, co-author with Sidney Simon of the *Values Clarification* handbook. (The curriculum, which encourages students to follow their feelings and choose their own values, was recently dropped by Quest.)

16   The moral reasoning approach—the other strand within the decision making model—seemed to offer a good alternative to Values Clarification. It was the brainchild of Harvard psychologist Lawrence Kohlberg, a man who was, in many ways, the opposite of Sidney Simon. Whereas Simon was a laid-back popularizer with a mind singularly tuned to the changing moods of the 1960s, Kohlberg was a serious scholar whose ideas were buttressed by philosophical arguments, and whose research was highly regarded. Although Kohlberg, like Simon, rejected character education (he called it the "bag of virtues" approach), he had something other than feelings to offer in its place. Kohlberg wanted to turn children into moral thinkers, to teach them a valid process of moral reasoning. Children would still make their own decisions, but their decisions would be based on reason.

17   How could students be brought to higher levels of moral reasoning? Kohlberg felt that the Socratic dialogue—the method used by Socrates and Plato—was ideal. The Socratic dialogue provided a way of drawing out ideas without imposing values or moralizing. Moreover, the dialogue seemed to create an atmosphere of equality between student and teacher—a goal that, at the time, seemed highly desirable.

18   Accordingly, Kohlberg and his colleagues developed a curriculum based on the discussion of ethical dilemmas. Like Socrates or Plato, the teacher

poses one of these dilemmas and then encourages an exchange of ideas and opinions while keeping his own values in the background.

19   Here is an example of one such dilemma:

> Sharon and Jill were best friends. One day they went shopping together. Jill tried on a sweater and then, to Sharon's surprise, walked out of the store wearing the sweater under her coat. A moment later, the store's security officer stopped Sharon and demanded that she tell him the name of the girl who had walked out. He told the store owner that he had seen the two girls together, and that he was sure that the one who left had been shoplifting. The store owner told Sharon that she could really get in trouble if she didn't give her friend's name.

20   The dilemma, of course, is to decide what Sharon should do.

21   A skilled teacher could get quite a bit of mileage out of a quandary like this. Some of the issues that might come up would be lying versus loyalty, self-sacrifice versus self-protection, the cost to the public of shoplifting versus the cost to the girl if she's arrested.

22   In addition, the teacher may further complicate the situation by asking hypothetical questions: "Suppose Jill comes from a poor family and can't afford to buy new clothes?" or "Suppose you knew that other children had been making fun of Jill because of her unstylish clothing?" or "What if Sharon offers to pay for the sweater herself? Should the store agree to drop the matter?" The teacher may go a step farther and have students get the feel of the predicament by role-playing the various parts in the shoplifting scenario.

23   Here's another dilemma:

> Suppose a ten-year-old boy is hit by a car and brought by ambulance to the emergency room of a hospital. He needs surgery right away but the doctor needs the parents' permission. When the parents arrive they refuse consent for an operation. They are Christian Scientists and believe in the power of prayer rather than medicine to heal. The doctor could get a court order to override the parents but that might take too long. Should the doctor go ahead and operate despite the parents' objections?

24   You can see why the dilemma approach became popular. In the hands of any moderately capable teacher it's a surefire formula: the educational equivalent of a roller-coaster ride. Opinions go back and forth, up and down; the argument takes sudden, unexpected turns. Does the class favor an immediate operation? Then the teacher can play devil's advocate. He can say, "So you don't really care about freedom of religion. How would *you* like it if *your* freedom to practice *your* faith was taken away? Suppose your religion forbids you to salute the flag, and you are expelled from school for not saluting? Would that be right?" Or he may switch the focus to parental rights: "How would *you* feel if *you* were a parent and doctors operated on *your* child without your permission?" At any moment the discussion could go spinning off in a new direction.

25   Like a roller-coaster ride, the dilemma approach can leave its passengers a bit breathless. That is one of its attractions. But like a roller-coaster ride, it may also leave them a bit disoriented—or more than a bit. That, as a growing number of critics are suggesting, is one of its drawbacks.

26   The question to ask about this admittedly stimulating approach is this: do we want to concentrate on quandaries or on everyday morality? Not many children will grow up to face the doctor's dilemma described above. More to the point, it is not a dilemma any of them currently face. A great deal of a child's moral life—or an adult's, for that matter—is not made up of dilemmas at all. Most of our "moral decisions" have to do with temptations to do things we know we shouldn't do or temptations to avoid doing the things we know we should do. A temptation to steal money from her mother's purse is a more common problem for the average girl than deciding whether or not to turn in a friend who is shoplifting. It is certainly more common than deciding whether to perform surgery on an injured child.

27   The Jill and Sharon dilemma is actually a rather mild example of the form. Dilemmas about homosexuality, wife swapping, extramarital sex, abortion and even cannibalism are routine on the junior high and high school level and often make their way into elementary classrooms. The Donner Party dilemma, for example, tells the story of westward-bound settlers trapped by snow in the Sierra Nevada Mountains and faced with the alternative of death by starvation or cannibalism. Another Kohlberg dilemma concerns a mother who must choose between the lives of her two children. A Values Clarification dilemma places the student in the position of a government bureaucrat who must decide which of several people are to survive in a fallout shelter and which are to die of radiation poisoning.

28   The danger in focusing on problematic dilemmas such as these is that a student may begin to think that all of morality is similarly problematic. After being faced with quandary after quandary of the type that would stump Middle East negotiators, students will conclude that right and wrong are anybody's guess. They will gain the impression, as Cornell professor Richard Baer has pointed out, "that almost everything in ethics is either vague or controversial..."

29   Youngsters are often much more perceptive than adults in sensing where this line of reasoning leads. As one teacher admits, "I often discuss cheating this way, but I always get defeated because they will argue that cheating is all right. After you accept the idea that kids have the right to build a position with logical arguments, you have to accept what they come up with."

30   What Chesterton said about teaching "the oldest things" seems to apply here. Classroom time might be better spent in talking about the virtues of friendship, loyalty and honesty, and how to practice them, rather than in dredging up situations where honesty might not be the best policy or where

loyalty and honesty conflict or even where cannibalism might be a legitimate course of action.

[31]   Why isn't it done that way? The answer is that the developers of these curriculums are proceeding on the basis of a dubious assumption. They seem to assume that such things as honesty, property rights and human life are already highly valued by youngsters and, therefore, the only difficulty is to choose among these values when they conflict. That is, they assume a sort of natural goodness and integrity in the child, whereby he or she will always want to do the right thing. If there is a problem, it's only a problem of getting in touch with one's feelings or of learning to reason things out. The old idea that many of us suffer not from a defect in reasoning but a defect in character is not considered. Thus, in the Jill and Sharon dilemma, it is assumed that boys and girls have already mastered the ABC's of morality, that the kinds of dilemmas they are grappling with are of the higher-order kind that faces Sharon ("shall I be loyal to my friend or truthful to the authorities?") rather than the lower-order kind that faces Jill ("shall I take this sweater?"). But what if stealing a sweater is not a dilemma at all for me but my habitual mode of action?

[32]   Some of what is wrong with this assumption is revealed in a conversation Kohlberg had with Edwin Delattre shortly before Kohlberg's death. Delattre, who is professor of applied ethics at Boston University, tells it this way:

> He (Kohlberg) expressed perplexity about the ineffectiveness of his methods in prisons where he had been working. He told me that he posed for inmates one of his favorite dilemmas: "Your wife suffers from an incurable and potentially terminal disease for which she must take regular doses of a very expensive medicine. The medicine is manufactured by a single company, and you have exhausted all of your financial resources in past purchases of the medicine." The question he posed is whether you should let your wife die or steal the drug.
>
> The convicts were unperplexed. To a man, and without hesitation, they said, "Steal it." "But why," Larry Kohlberg asked them, "would you do that?" Laughing, they answered, "Because we steal things. *We wanna know why the stupid husband didn't steal it in the first place.*"

[33]   The point is that the decision whether or not to steal is only a dilemma for those who already think stealing is wrong. As Delattre observes, "no one can really *have* a dilemma or moral problem without already caring to be the kind of person who behaves well, the kind of person who wants to discover the right thing to do and to have what it takes to do it."

[34]   At issue here is the very nature of the moral life itself. Kohlberg's conception seems to be that morality has to do with solving difficult ethical problems. His tendency to view it this way may stem in part from his own experience. As a young man he was involved in the struggle to establish a Jewish homeland in Palestine. He and the men and women he worked with

were constantly faced with difficult, unprecedented and dangerous dilemmas involving the lives and freedom of others.

35   The superheated atmosphere in which Kohlberg worked may help to explain the system he later developed. The question remains, however, whether his emphasis on dilemmas is rightly placed. As one of Kohlberg's critics points out, "Not all of what constitutes one's morality consists of responding to problematic social situations . . . a person's morality is an ongoing quality of life and not disjointed responses to isolated situations."

36   In fact, as Delattre suggests, it is the kind of person one is in the first place that determines what will and will not be a "dilemma" in one's life. For a person of good character, a temptation to cheat on one's spouse or to cheat a business partner will be recognized as just that—a temptation and not a dilemma. On the other hand, for those lacking character, interesting "dilemmas" are always arising. For example, one Kohlberg exercise—the "swapping" dilemma—concerns a number of married couples who want to exchange partners for sexual purposes. Quite obviously, however, this is a dilemma only for people who allow themselves to entertain such possibilities.

37   "This approach," as Delattre observes of Kohlberg's model, "obscures the fact that relatively few of our moral failings are attributable to inept reasoning about dilemmas. Many more arise from moral indifference, disregard for other people, weakness of will, and bad or self-indulgent habits." The hard part of morality, in short, is not *knowing* what is right but *doing* it. And if this is so, the remedy lies not in forming opinions but in forming good habits.

38   This is not to say that the dilemma approach should never be used. If used judiciously and in an age-appropriate way, it can be a useful teaching tool—particularly in discussing policy issues or current events in the upper grades or in college. But as the first line of approach for developing values, it is woefully inadequate. It involves young people in repeatedly questioning values that may never have taken hold for them in the first place.

39   In short, it's a strange way to teach morality. An analogy would be an American history course in grade school that concentrated on the ambiguities rather than the achievements—for example on Jefferson's ownership of slaves rather than his authorship of the Declaration of Independence, or on Martin Luther King, Jr.'s adulteries rather than his leadership of the civil rights movement. There is a time and place for learning such facts, but to put them first in a child's experience and then expect him to develop much loyalty to the nation or its values would be foolish.

40   The same holds true for moral education. Debunking moral values before they are learned is not a good policy. Before students begin to think about the qualifications, exceptions and fine points that surround difficult cases they will seldom or never face, they need to build the kind of character that will allow them to act well in the very clear-cut situations they face daily.

The basics ought to come first. "We should not," as former Secretary of Education William Bennett points out, "use the fact that there are indeed many difficult and controversial moral questions as an argument against basic instruction in the subject. We do not argue . . . against teaching biology or chemistry because gene splicing and cloning are complex and controversial."

41   But what about Socrates? And what about Kohlberg's claim to be following in his path? There is certainly much to be admired in Socrates' calm, reasonable method of inquiry and in his patience and goodwill, but Kohlberg seems to have missed a key point about the Socratic method: it was not meant for youngsters. No one speaks more authoritatively about the Socratic method than Plato, and Plato maintained that it was to be reserved for mature men over the age of 30. "One great precaution," said Plato, "is not to let them [students] taste of arguments while they are young"—the danger being that they would develop a taste for arguments rather than a taste for truth. Young minds, like young puppies, said Plato, would only "pull and tear at arguments." Such a method might keep youngsters entertained but it would certainly not make them virtuous. For Plato it was much more important for young people to learn a love of virtue than to argue about it. The dialogue was for those for whom the love of virtue was already in place.

42   This is the problem with using the dialogue method prematurely. Another problem is that not everyone using it has the wisdom, integrity, or maturity of a Socrates.

43   I occasionally used a dialogue/dilemma approach when I was teaching eighth grade in the mid-sixties. Kohlberg hadn't come along with his curriculum at that time, but it was easy enough to find dilemmas or make them up. I thought I was allowing my students to think for themselves, but I can see now that I was more interested in having them think like me. That was not difficult to accomplish using the dilemma approach. It tended to knock my students off base. I could see that it sometimes also had the effect of alienating them from their parents' beliefs—particularly if their parents had traditional or conservative views. That didn't bother me at the time, but it bothers me now. (By the way, both Socrates and Plato were charged with leading youth away from their parents. I think most scholars of the classics would agree that the charge was not entirely without merit.)

44   In order to make reparations for my past misuse of the dilemma approach, I make a point each semester of telling my college students what is wrong with it. I find I can get the point across by making an analogy to television talk shows, the kind hosted by Phil Donahue and Oprah Winfrey. Such shows have a lot in common with current moral education classrooms: they thrive on the exchange of ideas and opinions, and they have the same ground rule—all views are to be respected. Moreover, the tendency of these programs to concentrate on the more unusual arrangements that crop up in life (swapping clubs, the Man/Boy Love Association, mothers and daughters who date

the same man) parallels the focus on thorny and rarely encountered dilemmas in the moral education class.

45   What is the cumulative effect of shows like this on the home viewer? Is he or she converted to swapping or to the cause of man-boy love? Probably not. But there is another effect. Watching the shows makes for increased tolerance for differing viewpoints and behaviors. The viewer may not adopt such viewpoints, but he now sees that there is something to them, or at least, that they can be defended in an articulate way. Living in a pluralistic society, we tend to think this is a desirable outcome. It is not stretching the point very much to say that in our culture, tolerance and open-mindedness have become the chief virtues.

46   It may be important to recall, however, that "tolerance" was not included in the four classical virtues or in the three Christian virtues that were later added to them. The notion that all ideas are to be respected is a fairly recent one—and not an easy notion to defend. Do the values of the Ku Klux Klan deserve respect? How about the values of the Mafia or the Colombian cocaine cartels? Do we owe respect to the values of the pornography industry? Christina Hoff Sommers, a professor of philosophy at Clark University, notes that this cultivation of tolerance also occurs in moral education classrooms. "But," she adds, "when tolerance is the sole virtue, students' capacity for moral indignation, so important for moral development, is severely inhibited." Whether in classrooms or on TV, a constant parade of alternative "values" tends to undermine the virtuous instinct that some things are and ought to be repugnant.

47   My question to my students about the talk show and the dilemma-centered classroom alike is whether such discussions can do more than develop a generalized—and sometimes excessive—tolerance. More precisely, can a person develop good moral character through participation in a talk show? Through classroom rap sessions? Is this the way to develop traits such as courage, self-restraint, perseverance or integrity? Students grasp the point immediately. Character is not about your skill in debate, it's about the kind of person you are.

48   Why then is the dilemma approach still in widespread use? One answer is that although it won't do much to develop a love of virtue or a hatred of vice, it will often do a lot for a teacher's popularity. Neil Postman, a professor of communications at New York University, suggests in a recent article that in order to compete with television, teaching has been reduced to a form of popular entertainment:

> Consequently, drawing an audience—rather than teaching—becomes the focus of education, and that is what television does. School is the one institution in the culture that should present a different worldview: a different way of knowing, of evaluating, of assessing. What worries me is that if school becomes so overwhelmed by entertainment's metaphors and metaphysics, then it becomes not

content-centered but attention-centered, like television, chasing "ratings" or class attendance. If school becomes that way, then the game may be lost, because school is using the same approach, epistemologically, as television. Instead of being something different from television, it is reduced to being just another kind of television.

[49] Kohlberg himself was quite serious about education; he never tried to be an entertainer. Nevertheless, his projects tended to produce educational fiascoes. In 1974, in an attempt to create not just a curriculum but a whole school based on his principles, Kohlberg founded the experimental Cluster School in Cambridge, Massachusetts. The "just community" school, as it was sometimes called, lasted only five years. According to Professor Sommers' account,

> these student-citizens were forever stealing from one another and using drugs during school hours. These transgressions provoked a long series of democratically conducted "town meetings" that to an outsider look very much like EST encounter groups. The students were frequently taken on retreats . . . where many of them broke the rules against sex and drugs. This provoked more democratic confrontations where, Kohlberg was proud to report, it was usually decided that for the sake of the group the students would police one another on subsequent retreats and turn in the names of the transgressors.

[50] None of this worked, however, and serious problems with drugs, theft, sex and racial division continued unabated. And this despite the fact that the school had only 30 students, who were tended to by six specially trained teachers, dozens of consultants and Kohlberg himself. In 1978, writing in *The Humanist*, Kohlberg said:

> Some years of active involvement with the practice of moral education at Cluster School has led me to realize that my notion . . . was mistaken . . . the educator must be a socializer teaching value content and behavior, and not only a Socratic or Rogerian process-facilitator of development . . . I no longer hold these negative views of indoctrinative moral education and I believe that the concepts guiding moral education must be partly "indoctrinative." This is true, by necessity, in a world in which children engage in stealing, cheating and aggression.

[51] But followers and enthusiasts of the Kohlberg approach seemed to tune out these second thoughts and reassessments. Since the failure of the Cluster School, 16 school systems have instituted "just community" schools—thus confirming Sommers' observation that "in American professional education nothing succeeds like failure." *Newsweek* recently described one such school in New York City:

> West Indians snub the Bronx blacks, Dominicans won't eat with Puerto Ricans. Today's meeting verges on chaos. Tessa, a sophomore from Belize, has the chair and the attention of perhaps a third of the kids there. The question: should RCS [Roosevelt Community School] make community service a requirement for graduation? Five sullen boys talk steadily in the rear. Kids wander to the sandwich table, chat, write in their diaries. Debaters shout: "Hey, Tiffany, why you opposed,

ya dumb bitch?" Allan Sternberg, the history teacher who runs the program, struggles to maintain order.

52   In the end, the students vote against mandatory community service. "Sternberg," reports *Newsweek*, "tries a plaintive note of regret, but they cut him off. 'You asked us, we said "no," now it's over with,' says one member." Somehow *Newsweek* manages to find a vague "fragmentary" progress in all this. But it's not, I think it safe to say, the sort of progress parents would like to see.

53   I have a question that I sometimes pose to groups of parents. It goes as follows: "Suppose your child's school was instituting a course or curriculum in moral education at the fifth- to seventh-grade level. As a parent which of the two models below would you prefer the school to use?

A. The first approach encourages students to develop their own values and value systems. This approach relies on presenting the students with provocative ethical dilemmas and encouraging open discussion and exchange of opinion. The ground rule for discussion is that there are no right or wrong answers. Each student must decide for himself/herself what is right or wrong. Students are encouraged to be nonjudgmental about values that differ from their own.

B. The second approach involves a conscious effort to teach specific virtues and character traits such as courage, justice, self-control, honesty, responsibility, charity, obedience to lawful authority, etc. These concepts are introduced and explained and then illustrated by memorable examples from history, literature, and current events. The teacher expresses a strong belief in the importance of these virtues and encourages his/her students to practice them in their own lives.

54   The vast majority of parents will choose B—the character education option. But when I ask groups of teachers and teachers-in-training which of the two models they would choose to teach, they invariably prefer model A. Many teachers say they would not use the second approach under any circumstances.

55   Parents and teachers in America have been on different wavelengths for quite some time, but I don't think it's necessarily the parents who need to make an adjustment. I believe they prefer character education over the experimental model not because of some knee-jerk conservatism, or because of their limited knowledge of theory, but because they have a better grasp of what is at stake, and because it is their own children who are in question.

56   A colleague who administered this "questionnaire" to parents in a working-class neighborhood overheard one of them say in reference to the decisionmaking model, "Make up his own mind? Are they serious?" Not very articulate, but I would wager that what she said was based on a lot of practical knowledge.

57   Sooner or later, each person does have to make up his or her own mind. However, a person who has learned something of courage, respect for truth and concern for others, who has begun to put these ideals into practice, and who cares about doing the right thing, is better equipped to reach sound moral judgments than one who has been schooled only to exchange opinions. To introduce a child to the complicated and controversial issues of the day without some prior attempt at forming character is a formula for confusing him, or worse. To do it in a format that suggests there are no right answers compounds the confusion, and amounts to a loading of the deck. One doesn't have to be exclusively liberal or conservative, religious or nonreligious to be troubled by this scheme.

58   Like the talk show, the dilemma approach leaves a boy or girl no objective criteria for deciding right and wrong. The only criteria is "what feels right to me," or—in the case of the better-managed classes—"what I can rationally defend." But, as we know from the talk show, rationality is an all-purpose tool that will serve any master. Morality seems to require acquaintance with something more basic which, for want of a better term, we can call "moral premises." Moral premises are not reasoned to but are seen or grasped by an intuitive act. And being able to grasp them, as Aristotle suggested, may well be a factor of being virtuous in the first place—or at least, beginning to practice the virtues. There are many things in life that can't be understood from the outside. We don't really understand tennis or chess, for instance, until we begin to play them. In the same way, we can't understand the rightness of charity until we begin to practice it. "Objective," noncommittal discussions of other people's moral behavior allows students to stay outside the "game" while misleading them to believe they are in it. In the absence of deeper foundations it seems likely that students will simply become adept at "pulling and tearing at arguments" like Plato's young puppies. At the same time, they will gain a facility for rationalizing whatever it is they have an inclination to do. Nothing more is being asked of them.

1992

Adrienne Rich

TAKING WOMEN STUDENTS SERIOUSLY[*]

Like William Kilpatrick's essay on values in education, Adrienne Rich's argument about the educational needs of female students remains timely, given

[*]The talk that follows was addressed to teachers of women.... It was given for the New Jersey College and University Coalition on Women's Education, May 9, 1978 [Rich's note].

some recent research suggesting that girls and boys do not receive equal atten-
tion and encouragement in school. Rich has taught at a variety of distinguished
institutions but is best known as a poet and essayist. In the essay that follows,
would you say that Rich is preaching to the converted (see the earlier section
of that title in this chapter), that is, is she strengthening the resolve of a group
already committed to feminist values? Or is she trying for new converts, show-
ing skeptics why they should think about educational needs particular to
female students? Or would you describe her audience in some other way?
Why?

1   I see my function here today as one of trying to create a context, delineate a background, against which we might talk about women as students and students as women. I would like to speak for awhile about this background, and then I hope that we can have, not so much a question period, as a raising of concerns, a sharing of questions for which we as yet may have no answers, an opening of conversations which will go on and on.

2   When I went to teach at Douglass, a women's college, it was with a particular background which I would like briefly to describe to you. I had graduated from an all-girls' school in the 1940s, where the head and the majority of the faculty were independent, unmarried women. One or two held doctorates, but had been forced by the Depression (and by the fact that they were women) to take secondary school teaching jobs. These women cared a great deal about the life of the mind, and they gave a great deal of time and energy—beyond any limit of teaching hours—to those of us who showed special intellectual interest or ability. We were taken to libraries, art museums, lectures at neighboring colleges, set to work on extra research projects, given extra French or Latin reading. Although we sometimes felt "pushed" by them, we held those women in a kind of respect which even then we dimly perceived was not generally accorded to women in the world at large. They were vital individuals, defined not by their relationships but by their personalities; and although under the pressure of the culture we were all certain we wanted to get married, their lives did not appear empty or dreary to us. In a kind of cognitive dissonance, we knew they were "old maids" and therefore supposed to be bitter and lonely; yet we saw them vigorously involved with life. But despite their existence as alternate models of women, the *content* of the education they gave us in no way prepared us to survive as women in a world organized by and for men.

3   From that school, I went on to Radcliffe, congratulating myself that now I would have great men as my teachers. From 1947 to 1951, when I graduated, I never saw a single woman on a lecture platform, or in front of a class, except when a woman graduate student gave a paper on a special topic. The "great men" talked of other "great men," of the nature of Man, the history of Mankind, the future of Man; and never again was I to experience, from a teacher,

the kind of prodding, the insistence that my best could be even better, that I had known in high school. Women students were simply not taken very seriously. Harvard's message to women was an elite mystification: we were, of course, part of Mankind; we were special, achieving women, or we would not have been there; but of course our real goal was to marry—if possible, a Harvard graduate.

4   In the late sixties, I began teaching at the City College of New York—a crowded, public, urban, multiracial institution as far removed from Harvard as possible. I went there to teach writing in the SEEK Program, which predated Open Admissions and which was then a kind of model for programs designed to open up higher education to poor, black, and Third World students. Although during the next few years we were to see the original concept of SEEK diluted, then violently attacked and betrayed, it was for a short time an extraordinary and intense teaching and learning environment. The characteristics of this environment were a deep commitment on the part of teachers to the minds of their students; a constant, active effort to create or discover the conditions for learning, and to educate ourselves to meet the needs of the new college population; a philosophical attitude based on open discussion of racism, oppression, and the politics of literature and language; and a belief that learning in the classroom could not be isolated from the student's experience as a member of an urban minority group in white America. Here are some of the kinds of questions we, as teachers of writing, found ourselves asking:

(1) What has been the student's experience of education in the inadequate, often abusively racist public school system, which rewards passivity and treats a questioning attitude or independent mind as a behavior problem? What has been her or his experience in a society that consistently undermines the selfhood of the poor and the nonwhite? How can such a student gain that sense of self which is necessary for active participation in education? What does all this mean for us as teachers?

(2) How do we go about teaching a canon of literature which has consistently excluded or depreciated nonwhite experience?

(3) How can we connect the process of learning to write well with the student's own reality, and not simply teach her/him how to write acceptable lies in standard English?

5   When I went to teach at Douglass College in 1976, and in teaching women's writing workshops elsewhere, I came to perceive stunning parallels to the questions I had first encountered in teaching the so-called disadvantaged students at City. But in this instance, and against the specific background of the women's movement, the questions framed themselves like this:

(1) What has been the student's experience of education in schools which reward female passivity, indoctrinate girls and boys in stereotypic sex roles, and do not take the female mind seriously? How does a woman gain a sense of her *self* in a system—in this case, patriarchal capitalism—which devalues work done by women, denies the importance and uniqueness of female experience, and is physically violent toward women? What does this mean for a woman teacher?

(2) How do we, as women, teach women students a canon of literature which has consistently excluded or depreciated female experience, and which often expresses hostility to women and validates violence against us?

(3) How can we teach women to move beyond the desire for male approval and getting "good grades" and seek and write their own truths that the culture has distorted or made taboo? (For women, of course, language itself is exclusive: I want to say more about this further on.)

6   In teaching women, we have two choices: to lend our weight to the forces that indoctrinate women to passivity, self-depreciation, and a sense of powerlessness, in which case the issue of "taking women students seriously" is a moot one; or to consider what we have to work against, as well as with, in ourselves, in our students, in the content of the curriculum, in the structure of the institution, in the society at large. And this means, first of all, taking ourselves seriously: Recognizing that central responsibility of a woman to herself, without which we remain always the Other, the defined, the object, the victim; believing that there is a unique quality of validation, affirmation, challenge, support, that one woman can offer another. Believing in the value and significance of women's experience, traditions, perceptions. Thinking of ourselves seriously, not as one of the boys, not as neuters, or androgynes, but *as women.*

7   Suppose we were to ask ourselves, simply: What does a woman need to know? Does she not, as a self-conscious, self-defining human being, need a knowledge of her own history, her much-politicized biology, an awareness of the creative work of women of the past, the skills and crafts and techniques and powers exercised by women in different times and cultures, a knowledge of women's rebellions and organized movements against our oppression and how they have been routed or diminished? Without such knowledge women live and have lived without context, vulnerable to the projections of male fantasy, male prescriptions for us, estranged from our own experience because our education has not reflected or echoed it. I would suggest that not biology, but ignorance of our selves, has been the key to our powerlessness.

8   But the university curriculum, the high-school curriculum, do not provide this kind of knowledge for women, the knowledge of Womankind, whose experience has been so profoundly different from that of Mankind. Only in the

precariously budgeted, much-condescended-to area of women's studies is such knowledge available to women students. Only there can they learn about the lives and work of women other than the few select women who are included in the "mainstream" texts, usually misrepresented even when they do appear. Some students, at some institutions, manage to take a majority of courses in women's studies, but the message from on high is that this is self-indulgence, soft-core education: the "real" learning is the study of Mankind.

9   If there is any misleading concept, it is that of "coeducation": that because women and men are sitting in the same classrooms, hearing the same lectures, reading the same books, performing the same laboratory experiments, they are receiving an equal education. They are not, first because the content of education itself validates men even as it invalidates women. Its very message is that men have been the shapers and thinkers of the world, and that this is only natural. The bias of higher education, including the so-called sciences, is white and male, racist and sexist; and this bias is expressed in both subtle and blatant ways. I have mentioned already the exclusiveness of grammar itself: "The student should test himself on the above questions"; "The poet is representative. He stands among partial men for the complete man." Despite a few half-hearted departures from custom, what the linguist Wendy Martyna has named "He-Man" grammar prevails throughout the culture. The efforts of feminists to reveal the profound ontological implications of sexist grammar are routinely ridiculed by academicians and journalists, including the professedly liberal *Times* columnist, Tom Wicker, and the professed humanist, Jacques Barzun. Sexist grammar burns into the brains of little girls and young women a message that the male is the norm, the standard, the central figure beside which we are the deviants, the marginal, the dependent variables. It lays the foundation for androcentric thinking, and leaves men safe in their solipsistic tunnel-vision.

10   Women and men do not receive an equal education because outside the classroom women are perceived not as sovereign beings but as prey. The growing incidence of rape on and off the campus may or may not be fed by the proliferations of pornographic magazines and X-rated films available to young males in fraternities and student unions; but it is certainly occurring in a context of widespread images of sexual violence against women, on billboards and in so-called high art. More subtle, more daily than rape is the verbal abuse experienced by the woman student on many campuses—Rutgers for example—where, traversing a street lined with fraternity houses, she must run a gauntlet of male commentary and verbal assault. The undermining of self, of a woman's sense of her right to occupy space and walk freely in the world, is deeply relevant to education. The capacity to think independently, to take intellectual risks, to assert ourselves mentally, is inseparable from our physical way of being in the world, our feelings of personal integrity. If it is dangerous for me to walk home late of an evening from the library, *because I am a woman and can be raped,* how self-possessed, how exuberant can I feel as

I sit working in that library? how much of my working energy is drained by the subliminal knowledge that, as a woman, I test my physical right to exist each time I go out alone? Of this knowledge, Susan Griffin has written:

> ...more than rape itself, the fear of rape permeates our lives. And what does one do from day to day, with *this* experience, which says, without words and directly to the heart, *your existence, your experience, may end at any moment.* Your experience may end, and the best defense against this is not to be, to deny being in the body, as a self, to...avert your gaze, make yourself, as a presence in the world, less felt.[1]

11   Finally, rape of the mind. Women students are more and more often now reporting sexual overtures by male professors—one part of our overall growing consciousness of sexual harassment in the workplace. At Yale a legal suit has been brought against the university by a group of women demanding an explicit policy against sexual advances toward female students by male professors. Most young women experience a profound mixture of humiliation and intellectual self-doubt over seductive gestures by men who have the power to award grades, open doors to grants and graduate school, or extend special knowledge and training. Even if turned aside, such gestures constitute mental rape, destructive to a woman's ego. They are acts of domination, as despicable as the molestation of the daughter by the father.

12   But long before entering college the woman student has experienced her alien identity in a world which misnames her, turns her to its own uses, denying her the resources she needs to become self-affirming, self-defined. The nuclear family teaches her that relationships are more important than selfhood or work; that "whether the phone rings for you, and how often," having the right clothes, doing the dishes, take precedence over study or solitude; that too much intelligence or intensity may make her unmarriageable; that marriage and children—service to others—are, finally, the points on which her life will be judged a success or a failure. In high school, the polarization between feminine attractiveness and independent intelligence comes to an absolute. Meanwhile, the culture resounds with messages. During Solar Energy Week in New York I saw young women wearing "ecology" T-shirts with the legend: CLEAN, CHEAP AND AVAILABLE; a reminder of the 1960s antiwar button which read: CHICKS SAY YES TO MEN WHO SAY NO. Department store windows feature female mannequins in chains, pinned to the wall with legs spread, smiling in positions of torture. Feminists are depicted in the media as "shrill," "strident," "puritanical," or "humorless," and the lesbian choice— the choice of the woman-identified woman—as pathological or sinister. The young woman sitting in the philosophy classroom, the political science lecture, is already gripped by tensions between her nascent sense of self-worth, and the battering force of messages like these.

---

[1]*Rape: The Power of Consciousness* (New York, 1979).

13   Look at a classroom: look at the many kinds of women's faces, postures, expressions. Listen to the women's voices. Listen to the silences, the unasked questions, the blanks. Listen to the small, soft voices, often courageously trying to speak up, voices of women taught early that tones of confidence, challenge, anger, or assertiveness, are strident and unfeminine. Listen to the voices of the women and the voices of the men; observe the space men allow themselves, physically and verbally, the male assumption that people will listen, even when the majority of the group is female. Look at the faces of the silent, and of those who speak. Listen to a woman groping for language in which to express what is on her mind, sensing that the terms of academic discourse are not her language, trying to cut down her thought to the dimensions of a discourse not intended for her (*for it is not fitting that a woman speak in public*); or reading her paper aloud at breakneck speed, throwing her words away, deprecating her own work by a reflex prejudgment: *I do not deserve to take up time and space.*

14   As women teachers, we can either deny the importance of this context in which women students think, write, read, study, project their own futures; or try to work with it. We can either teach passively, accepting these conditions, or actively, helping our students identify and resist them.

15   One important thing we can do is *discuss* the context. And this need not happen only in a women's studies course; it can happen anywhere. We can refuse to accept passive, obedient learning and insist upon critical thinking. We can become harder on our women students, giving them the kinds of "cultural prodding" that men receive, but on different terms and in a different style. Most young women need to have their intellectual lives, their work, legitimized against the claims of family, relationships, the old message that a woman is always available for service to others. We need to keep our standards very high, not to accept a woman's preconceived sense of her limitations; we need to be hard to please, while supportive of risk-taking, because self-respect often comes only when exacting standards have been met. At a time when adult literacy is generally low, we need to demand more, not less, of women, both for the sake of their futures as thinking beings, and because historically women have always had to be better than men to do half as well. A romantic sloppiness, an inspired lack of rigor, a self-indulgent incoherence, are symptoms of female self-depreciation. We should help our women students to look very critically at such symptoms, and to understand where they are rooted.

16   Nor does this mean we should be training women students to "think like men." Men in general think badly: in disjuncture from their personal lives, claiming objectivity where the most irrational passions seethe, losing, as Virginia Woolf observed, their senses in the pursuit of professionalism. It is not easy to think like a woman in a man's world, in the world of the professions; yet the capacity to do that is a strength which we can try to help our students develop. To think like a woman in a man's world means thinking critically,

refusing to accept the givens, making connections between facts and ideas which men have left unconnected. It means remembering that every mind resides in a body; remaining accountable to the female bodies in which we live; constantly retesting given hypotheses against lived experience. It means a constant critique of language, for as Wittgenstein (no feminist) observed, "The limits of my language are the limits of my world." And it means that most difficult thing of all: listening and watching in art and literature, in the social sciences, in all the descriptions we are given of the world, for the silences, the absences, the nameless, the unspoken, the encoded—for there we will find the true knowledge of women. And in breaking those silences, naming our selves, uncovering the hidden, making ourselves present, we begin to define a reality which resonates to *us,* which affirms *our* being, which allows the woman teacher and the woman student alike to take ourselves, and each other, seriously: meaning, to begin taking charge of our lives.

1978

Michael Gorra

LEARNING TO HEAR THE SMALL, SOFT VOICES

Michael Gorra is a writer and teacher. His essay originally appeared in the New York Times Magazine's *"About Men" column, and it raises some of the same issues that Adrienne Rich approaches from a different perspective in the preceding selection. If you have read the piece by Rich, you will recognize that Gorra's title is a quotation from it. Think about Gorra as a reader of Rich: how does his reading correspond to your own? How would you compare his intention to hers?*

1   "You at a women's college?" a friend said just after I'd been hired to teach English at Smith. "That's a scandal waiting to happen." He never made it clear if I was to be the debaucher or the debauchee. Another friend, a Smith alumna, told me its students saw the young male faculty, married or not, as "fair game." My mother told me to get a heavy doorstop for my office and to keep my wife's picture on my desk.

2   After three years at Smith, those comments seem far away, though by the time I got here I'd heard enough of them to make me decide I didn't really want to teach *Lolita* to my class of freshmen. And for the first few months I felt a sort of amused uneasiness walking around the place at night, wondering if the women I passed would start at my slouch-hatted shadow, or if campus security would stop me and demand to see an I.D.

3   But the experience of being a man at a women's college is both less lurid and more ambiguous than my friends had half-jokingly predicted. I remember being asked at my interview why I wanted to teach at a women's college. It's a disingenuous question, given the absence of a job market for English professors, particularly because it's hard for a man to have an ideological commitment to women's colleges the way some feminist women do. So I said I wanted good students at a good liberal arts college; and that once you get used to being at the teacher's end of the table, the other people in the room seem simply students, rather than members of one sex or the other. That's partly true.

4   Most days I don't feel any differently walking into a classroom full of women than I did walking into a coed classroom as a graduate teaching fellow. I don't notice that I'm the only man there. And I did notice my singularity, and felt uneasy with it, when I was an undergraduate myself, taking exchange courses at women's colleges.

5   That suggests I usually think of myself as a teacher rather than a male, that one role supersedes another. But sometimes at Smith College I do feel rather self-consciously male. Those times seem to fall into two categories. One is social—when a student invites me to dinner or a faculty-student tea at her dormitory. (Or when I meet a student at a door and hold it for her. That always seems to surprise and confuse the student, because it makes her see me suddenly as a man, rather than a teacher.)

6   The other is when discussion turns on questions of gender. Looking at posters advertising lectures or workshops—"Women Scholars of Judaism," "Bringing Girls to Math"—I often think that however interesting I might find such talks, I'm not really part of their intended audience. Some of that comes from the natural rift between faculty and student life and some doesn't, but it's not easy to say where the line falls. At a coed school, a workshop on eating disorders sponsored by the health service seems clearly for students; here it appears to be for women. Which makes me momentarily aware of myself as a member of a minority group, and produces some of the wariness that I imagine members of other minority groups feel in bumping against the white male hegemony of which I'm a part.

7   Now and then I feel that wariness in my own classroom. I'm preparing to teach Doris Lessing's *The Golden Notebook* for the first time, and am hesitant, nervous—and a bit excited—about how I'll handle it, in a room where some of my students will speak with more authority about it than I can. (I'm also terrified, in much the same way I would be in teaching *Lolita,* that somebody will ask me what Lessing means by equating a woman's orgasm with her integrity.) But I've also sought that wariness, or rather the self-consciousness that's a part of it, by trying to blur my two roles.

8   Each year in my freshmen writing class I have my students read Adrienne Rich's essay "Taking Women Students Seriously." There she asks us to

"Listen to the small, soft voices, often courageously trying to speak up, voices of women taught early that tones of confidence, challenge, anger, or assertiveness, are strident and unfeminine. Listen to the voices of the women and the voices of the men; observe the space men allow themselves, physically and verbally, the male assumption that people will listen, even when the majority of the group is female."

9   I ask my students to talk about their own behavior in the classroom, and mine. Most of them have chosen a women's college because they already know what Rich means about the difference between men and women—as students. But few of them have extended the argument to include their male teachers. So they always tell me, at first, that they defer to my opinion because I'm the teacher, not because I'm a man; because they're students, not because they're women. I'm not so sure—and neither, by the end of class, are they.

10   I'm satisfied when I can get my students to see the issue, but for me that's just the beginning. For I know now that I was naïve when I said at my interview that the students' sex doesn't matter. It matters profoundly, even or particularly when one isn't conscious of it. After a class on Orson Welles's *Citizen Kane* last year, my best student, an articulate and seemingly confident New Yorker, apologized to me for not having spoken that day. "I have a much different view of the movie than everyone else seems to," she said, "and I didn't want to disagree."

11   Our students still suffer, even at a women's college, from the lessons Rich says women are taught about unfemininity of assertiveness. They are uneasy with the prospect of having to defend their opinions, not only against my own devil's advocacy, but against each other. They would rather not speak if speaking means breaking with their classmates' consensus. Yet that consensus is usually more emotional, a matter of tone, than it is intellectual.

12   Last week I had two students, both of them bright and one speaking right after the other, offer diametrically opposed readings of a W. H. Auden poem. But the second student didn't define her interpretation against her predecessor's, as I think a man would have. She didn't begin by saying "I don't agree with that." She betrayed no awareness that she disagreed with her classmate, and seemed surprised when I pointed it out.

13   Such incidents have made me question my chief assumption about teaching—that people involved in a discussion will not only disagree with each other, but say so. I think they have made me a better teacher, a better listener, more able to gauge when silence means a real consensus and when it is a question of manners, to anticipate the ways in which a text might trouble my students, in case those "small, soft voices" can't summon the confidence to challenge it themselves.

14   But they have also made me use Rich's terms to question my own performance. The verbal space I allow myself, my assumption that people will lis-

ten—is that the teacher or the man? Does my maleness make me assume what I'm saying is worthwhile, even when it isn't? I don't have any answers to those questions. But I do know that having to ask them makes teaching here both more challenging, and more intriguing, than either my joking friends or I had imagined it could be.

1988

SIX ESSAYS ON THE ARTS

E. M. Forster

NOT LISTENING TO MUSIC

E. M. Forster is best known for his novels, including Howard's End *and* A Passage to India. *He also wrote critical essays on a variety of topics, particularly literature and the other arts. How does he justify his preference for music that is about nothing outside itself, when most people expect art to be about something? What audience would be receptive to such an argument? The philosopher Immanuel Kant said, "All art is a matter of taste, but you cannot discuss matters of taste with the tasteless." Forster's Bloomsbury circle of friends believed that good is undefinable: you cannot say what it is, you can only point to it as self-evident. Does Forster's argument imply an aesthetic elite that can recognize beauty as good in itself?*

1   Listening to music is such a muddle that one scarcely knows how to start describing it. The first point to get clear in my own case is that during the greater part of every performance I do not attend. The nice sounds make me think of something else. I wool-gather most of the time, and am surprised that others don't. Professional critics can listen to a piece as consistently and as steadily as if they were reading a chapter in a novel. This seems to me an amazing feat, and probably they only achieve it through intellectual training; that is to say, they find in the music the equivalent of a plot; they are following the ground bass or expecting the theme to re-enter in the dominant, and so on, and this keeps them on the rails. But I fly off every minute: after a bar or two I think how musical I am, or of something smart I might have said in conversation; or I wonder what the composer—dead a couple of centuries—can be feeling as the flames on the altar still flicker up; or how soon an H. E. bomb would extinguish them. Not to mention more obvious distractions: the tilt of the soprano's chin or chins; the antics of the conductor, that

impassioned beetle, especially when it is night time and he waves his shards; the affection of the pianist when he takes a top note with difficulty, as if he too were a soprano; the backs of the chairs; the bumps on the ceiling; the extreme physical ugliness of the audience. A classical audience is surely the plainest collection of people anywhere assembled for any common purpose; contributing my quota, I have the right to point this out. Compare us with a gang of navvies or with an office staff, and you will be appalled. This, too, distracts me.

2   What do I hear during the intervals when I do attend? Two sorts of music. They melt into each other all the time, and are not easy to christen, but I will call one of them "music that reminds me of something," and the other "music itself." I used to be very fond of music that reminded me of something, and especially fond of Wagner. With Wagner I always knew where I was; he never let the fancy roam; he ordained that one phrase should recall the ring, another the sword, another the blameless fool and so on; he was as precise in his indications as an oriental dancer. Since he is a great poet, that did not matter, but I accepted his leitmotiv system much too reverently and forced it onto other composers whom it did not suit, such as Beethoven and Franck. I thought that music must be the better for having a meaning. I think so still, but am less clear as to what "a meaning" is. In those days it was either a non-musical object, such as a sword or a blameless fool, or a non-musical emotion, such as fear, lust, or resignation. When music reminded me of something which was not music, I supposed it was getting me somewhere. "How like Monet!" I thought when listening to Debussy, and "How like Debussy!" when looking at Monet. I translated sounds into colours, saw the piccolo as apple-green, and the trumpets as scarlet. The arts were to be enriched by taking in one another's washing.

3   I still listen to some music this way. For instance, the slow start of Beethoven's Seventh Symphony invokes a gray-green tapestry of hunting scenes, and the slow movement of his Fourth Piano Concerto (the dialogue between piano and orchestra) reminds me of the dialogue between Orpheus and the Furies in Gluck. The climax of the first movement of the Appassionata (the "più allegro") seems to me sexual, although I can detect no sex in the Kreutzer, nor have I come across anyone who could, except Tolstoy. That disappointing work, Brahms' Violin Concerto, promises me clear skies at the opening, and only when the violin has squealed up in the air for page after page is the promise falsified. Wolf's "Ganymed" does give me sky—stratosphere beyond stratosphere. In these cases and in many others music reminds me of something non-musical, and I fancy that to do so is part of its job. Only a purist would condemn all visual parallels, all emotional labelings, all programs.

4   Yet there is a danger. Music that reminds does open the door to that imp of the concert hall, inattention. To think of a gray-green tapestry is not very

different from thinking of the backs of the chairs. We gather a superior wool from it, still we do wool-gather, and the sounds slip by blurred. The sounds! It is for them that we come, and the closer we can get up against them the better. So I do prefer "music itself" and listen to it and for it as far as possible. In this connection, I will try to analyze a mishap that has recently overtaken the Coriolanus Overture. I used to listen to the Coriolanus for "itself," conscious when it passed of something important and agitating, but not defining further. Now I learn that Wagner, endorsed by Sir Donald Tovey, has provided it with a Program: the opening bars indicate the hero's decision to destroy the Volscii, then a sweet tune for female influence, then the dotted-quaver-restlessness of indecision. This seems indisputable, and there is no doubt that this was, or was almost, Beethoven's intention. All the same, I have lost my Coriolanus. Its largeness and freedom have gone. The exquisite sounds have been hardened like a road that has been tarred for traffic. One has to go somewhere down them, and to pass through the same domestic crisis to the same military impasse, each time the overture is played.

5   Music is so very queer that an amateur is bound to get muddled when writing about it. It seems to be more "real" than anything, and to survive when the rest of civilization decays. In these days I am always thinking of it with relief. It can never be ruined or nationalized. So that the music which is untrammeled and untainted by reference is obviously the best sort of music to listen to; we get nearer the center of reality. Yet though it is untainted, it is never abstract; it is not like mathematics, even when it uses them. The Goldberg Variations, the last Beethoven Sonata, the Franck Quartet, the Schumann Piano Quintet and the Fourth Symphonies of Tchaikovsky and of Brahms certainly have a message. Though what on earth is it? I shall get tied up trying to say. There's an insistence in music—expressed largely through rhythm; there's a sense that it is trying to push across at us something which is neither an esthetic pattern nor a sermon. That's what I listen for specially.

6   So music that is itself seems on the whole better than music that reminds. And now to end with an important point: my own performances upon the piano. These grow worse yearly, but never will I give them up. For one thing, they compel me to attend—no wool-gathering or thinking myself clever here—and they drain off all non-musical matter. For another thing, they teach me a little about construction. I see what becomes of a phrase, how it is transformed or returned, sometimes bottom upward, and get some notion of the relation of keys. Playing Beethoven, as I generally do, I grow familiar with his tricks, his impatience, his sudden softnesses, his dropping of a tragic theme one semitone, his love, when tragic, for the key of C minor, and his aversion to the key of B major. This gives me a physical approach to Beethoven which cannot be gained through the slough of "appreciation." Even when people play as badly as I do, they should continue: it will help them to listen.

1939

Joan Didion

GEORGIA O'KEEFFE

Joan Didion's essay on Georgia O'Keeffe makes the claim that "style is char-acter." What does this seemingly plain statement mean, and how is it related to the point that Didion wants to make about O'Keeffe and her powerful paintings? For many women in the arts, a major concern is the lack of a woman's tradition comparable to the long and venerable traditions created by men. Mary Jo Salter addresses this issue in the essay that follows, as does Virginia Woolf in the selec-tion in Chapter 1. How do O'Keeffe's thoughts on painting the great American cow skull comment on this issue? How do Didion's thoughts on Georgia O'Keeffe and her work comment on it? How might the view of Georgia O'Keeffe held by Didion's audience change if Didion's essay realizes its intention?

1   "Where I was born and where and how I have lived is unimportant," Georgia O'Keeffe told us in the book of paintings and words published in her ninetieth year on earth. She seemed to be advising us to forget the beautiful face in the Stieglitz photographs. She appeared to be dismissing the rather condescending romance that had attached to her by then, the romance of extreme good looks and advanced age and deliberate isolation. "It is what I have done with where I have been that should be of interest." I recall an August afternoon in Chicago in 1973 when I took my daughter, then seven, to see what Georgia O'Keeffe had done with where she had been. One of the vast O'Keeffe "Sky Above Clouds" canvases floated over the back stairs in the Chicago Art Institute that day, dominating what seemed to be several sto-ries of empty light, and my daughter looked at it once, ran to the landing, and kept on looking. "Who drew it," she whispered after a while. I told her. "I need to talk to her," she said finally.

2   My daughter was making, that day in Chicago, an entirely unconscious but quite basic assumption about people and the work they do. She was assuming that the glory she saw in the work reflected a glory in its maker, that the painting was the painter as the poem is the poet, that every choice one made alone—every word chosen or rejected, every brush stroke laid or not laid down—betrayed one's character. *Style is character.* It seemed to me that afternoon that I had rarely seen so instinctive an application of this famil-iar principle, and I recall being pleased not only that my daughter responded to style as character but that it was Georgia O'Keeffe's particular style to which she responded: this was a hard woman who had imposed her 192 square feet of clouds on Chicago.

3   "Hardness" has not been in our century a quality much admired in women, nor in the past twenty years has it even been in official favor for men. When hardness surfaces in the very old we tend to transform it into "crustiness" or eccentricity, some tonic pepperiness to be indulged at a distance. On the evidence of her work and what she has said about it, Georgia O'Keeffe is neither "crusty" nor eccentric. She is simply hard, a straight shooter, a woman clean of received wisdom and open to what she sees. This is a woman who could early on dismiss most of her contemporaries as "dreamy," and would later single out one she liked as "a very poor painter." (And then add, apparently by way of softening the judgment: "I guess he wasn't a painter at all. He had no courage and I believe that to create one's own world in any of the arts takes courage.") This is a woman who in 1939 could advise her admirers that they were missing her point, that their appreciation of her famous flowers was merely sentimental. "When I paint a red hill," she observed coolly in the catalogue for an exhibition that year, "you say it is too bad that I don't always paint flowers. A flower touches almost everyone's heart. A red hill doesn't touch everyone's heart." This is a woman who could describe the genesis of one of her most well-known paintings—the "Cow's Skull: Red, White and Blue" owned by the Metropolitan—as an act of quite deliberate and derisive orneriness. "I thought of the city men I had been seeing in the East," she wrote. "They talked so often of writing the Great American Novel—the Great American Play—the Great American Poetry.... So as I was painting my cow's head on blue I thought to myself, "I'll make it an American painting. They will not think it great with the red stripes down the sides—Red, White and Blue—but they will notice it."

4   *The city men. The men. They.* The words crop up again and again as this astonishingly aggressive woman tells us what was on her mind when she was making her astonishingly aggressive paintings. It was those city men who stood accused of sentimentalizing her flowers: "I made you take time to look at what I saw and when you took time to really notice my flower you hung all your associations with flowers on my flower and you write about my flower as if I think and see what you think and see—and I don't." *And I don't.* Imagine those words spoken, and the sound you hear is *don't tread on me.* "The men" believed it impossible to paint New York, so Georgia O'Keeffe painted New York. "The men" didn't think much of her bright color, so she made it brighter. The men yearned toward Europe so she went to Texas, and then New Mexico. The men talked about Cézanne, "long involved remarks about the 'plastic quality' of his form and color," and took one another's long involved remarks, in the view of this angelic rattlesnake in their midst, altogether too seriously. "I can paint one of those dismal-colored paintings like the men," the woman who regarded herself always as an outsider remembers thinking one day in 1922, and she did: a painting of a shed "all low-toned and dreary with the tree beside the door." She called this act of rancor "The

Shanty" and hung it in her next show. "The men seemed to approve of it," she reported fifty-four years later, her contempt undimmed. "They seemed to think that maybe I was beginning to paint. That was my only low-toned dismal-colored painting."

5   Some women fight and others do not. Like so many successful guerrillas in the war between the sexes, Georgia O'Keeffe seems to have been equipped early with an immutable sense of who she was and a fairly clear understanding that she would be required to prove it. On the surface her upbringing was conventional. She was a child on the Wisconsin prairie who played with china dolls and painted watercolors with cloudy skies because sunlight was too hard to paint and, with her brother and sisters, listened every night to her mother read stories of the Wild West, of Texas, of Kit Carson and Billy the Kid. She told adults that she wanted to be an artist and was embarrassed when they asked what kind of artist she wanted to be: she had no idea "what kind." She had no idea what artists did. She had never seen a picture that interested her, other than a pen-and-ink Maid of Athens in one of her mother's books, some Mother Goose illustrations printed on cloth, a tablet cover that showed a little girl with pink roses, and the painting of Arabs on horseback that hung in her grandmother's parlor. At thirteen, in a Dominican convent, she was mortified when the sister corrected her drawing. At Chatham Episcopal Institute in Virginia she painted lilacs and sneaked time alone to walk out to where she could see the line of the Blue Ridge Mountains on the horizon. At the Art Institute in Chicago she was shocked by the presence of live models and wanted to abandon anatomy lessons. At the Art Students League in New York one of her fellow students advised her that, since he would be a great painter and she would end up teaching painting in a girls' school, any work of hers was less important than modeling for him. Another painted over her work to show her how the Impressionists did trees. She had not before heard how the Impressionists did trees and she did not much care.

6   At twenty-four she left all those opinions behind and went for the first time to live in Texas, where there were no trees to paint and no one to tell her how not to paint them. In Texas there was only the horizon she craved. In Texas she had her sister Claudia with her for a while, and in the late afternoons they would walk away from town and toward the horizon and watch the evening star come out. "That evening star fascinated me," she wrote. "It was in some way very exciting to me. My sister had a gun, and as we walked she would throw bottles into the air and shoot as many as she could before they hit the ground. I had nothing but to walk into nowhere and the wide sunset space with the star. Ten watercolors were made from that star." In a way one's interest is compelled as much by the sister Claudia with the gun as by the painter Georgia with the star, but only the painter left us this shining record. Ten watercolors were made from that star.

1976

Mary Jo Salter

A POEM OF ONE'S OWN

The American poet Mary Jo Salter reflects in this essay on a series of hard questions. How is a "woman poet" different from a poet? How do poets who are women deal with the maleness of our poetic tradition? Is a woman obliged on political grounds to set herself in opposition to such a tradition? Why have women distinguished themselves more frequently as fiction writers than as poets? Why is there no great poem of childbearing? As you read, you might ask yourself what similarities you see between the issues facing Salter and those that Didion treats in connection with Georgia O'Keeffe.

1   "I went to look for your new book at the store," a friend remarked some months ago, "and I couldn't find it in the poetry section. So I asked the guy behind the desk. 'Mary Jo Salter?' he said. 'Oh, she's in the women's section.'"

2   My first reaction on hearing this was, I admit, something not much less extreme than rage. The women's section? Why should my book of poems be placed next to *Our Bodies, Ourselves* or *New Guide to Breastfeeding* or *Women Workers in China*? All worthy books—but not poetry. Poetry is what I write, and the heroes I have kept in mind while writing it have included not only Dickinson and Moore and Bishop but Shakespeare and Auden and Frost. A stranger who for some reason had wanted to sample my poems, and who like me felt that poetry was essentially genderless, might not have checked the women's section, and would have walked out of the bookstore empty-handed.

3   But this image of empty-handedness made me reconsider. The women's section in bookstores has become big business, which is more than you can say for the poetry section. Most Americans, most Europeans—most book-buyers, I suppose, around the world—live in towns and cities where the poetry section at the local bookstore either doesn't exist or is too small to warrant a label. Who was I, then, to complain that my book of poems was taking up space in the women's section? Shouldn't I be glad to be misappropriated anywhere the well-meaning bookstore clerk should care to put me—the sports section, the gardening section, thrillers, knitting manuals, comics, calendars?

4   And besides, "ain't I a woman?" Had there been an American literature section in the bookstore, I would have been honored and delighted if a book of mine found a home there. I accept that I am an American and that every-

thing I write partakes in some way—although usually in an indirect and unconscious way—of my Americanness. Do I bristle at being placed in the women's section because I am displeased with—or, worse, ashamed of—being a woman?

5   Displeased? I think every woman of the late twentieth century is at least partly displeased with the practical experience of being female, to the extent that she realizes that the women's movement, and her own personal movement toward self-determination, are far from over. The continuing oppression of women around the globe is scandalous, and needs no confirming statistics from me. Ashamed? I hardly think so. But pride in being a woman, or in being an American, or in being a person with white skin—pride in any accident of birth with which our own talents have had and can have little to do—seems to me a foolhardy, blinkered excuse for a virtue. At its worst, such pride is nothing more exalted than bigotry. Better to say that one accepts, profits by, takes the knocks from, revels in being a woman than that one is proud of it; and better still to say that one enjoys being a poet who is a woman.

6   And yet, and yet. (Whenever we take up the slippery question of gender, there must be another "and yet.") Though pride may be a sin, or even just a snag, the exercising of a special sympathy with your own kind is one of many enlightenments to be wished for. The more I have thought about my indignation at being put in the women's section, the more I have realized that in certain ways I had put myself in the women's *poetry* section long ago.

7   Why, for instance, had I adopted Emily Dickinson as a sort of combination muse, mother, and teacher? For the past five or six years I have read her every week if not every day, written both poetry and prose about her, taught courses devoted to her. Of course, one must admire the originality and the precision that she brought to her craft, and her use of that craft to articulate the great abstractions of Life, Love, Death, Immortality. But having underscored that these sexless skills are the stuff of Dickinson's greatness, I must in all honesty confess that what first attracted me to her was the example she provided as a woman poet.

8   "I never had a mother," Dickinson remarked in a rare meeting with her literary mentor, Thomas Wentworth Higginson. In a letter she told him, "My Mother does not care for thought." Much has been written—indeed, too much with too little evidence has been written—about Dickinson's frustration with her mother's failure not only to think but to love and to communicate. But it does seem fair to remark that Dickinson sought a thinking female "role model," as we call it today, and took solace from the spiritual motherhood of certain women writers of her time.

9   Although her poems are more indebted to the Bible and Shakespeare than to any other sources, and although she turned to men for literary advice

and help early in her career, it's important to remember that the writers whose portraits she hung on her bedroom walls included Emily Brontë and George Eliot and Elizabeth Barrett Browning. Ellen Moers's thoroughly researched and fascinating book, *Literary Women* (1976), illustrates Dickinson's reading preferences even more forcefully: "The real hidden scandal of Emily Dickinson's life," Moers wrote,

> is not the romances upon which biographers try vainly to speculate, but her embarrassing ignorance of American literature. She knew Emerson's poetry well, and perhaps a little Thoreau and Hawthorne; but she pretended, at least, not to have read a line of Whitman, no Holmes, no Poe, no Irving; and none of the colonial New England poets. Instead she read and re-read every Anglo-American woman writer of her time: Helen Hunt Jackson and Lydia Maria Craik and Elizabeth Stuart Phelps and Rebecca Harding Davis and Francesca Alexander and Mathilde Mackarness and everything that George Eliot and Mrs. Browning and all the Brontës wrote. "Mrs. Hunt's poems," Dickinson wrote in an astonishing letter of 1871, "are stronger than any written by women since Mrs. Browning, with the exception of Mrs. Lewes."

10   Moers's reading list is a little misleading—Dickinson was versed in a great deal of male British literature—but her main point is a fertile one. Did it harm Dickinson in any way, one wonders, to read Mathilde Mackarness, whoever she was, instead of Walt Whitman? Apparently not—at least if you believe that "genius knows itself," as Adrienne Rich wrote in a fine essay on Dickinson. "[She] chose her seclusion, knowing she was exceptional and knowing what she needed. It was . . . a seclusion which included a wide range of people, of reading and correspondence."

11   Dickinson's judgment on that reading may differ quite broadly from our own. But if, like many people on both sides of the Atlantic, she overrated Elizabeth Barrett Browning's work, who can blame her? Elizabeth Barrett was already a successful poet before she met Robert Browning in her late 30s, and after marrying him she was so little inclined to "retire" from poetry that she went on to write *Aurora Leigh,* one of the best-selling, most ambitious, most feminist, and longest poems in the English language. One can imagine the vicarious thrill that Dickinson, who was only 30 when Barrett Browning died and just embarking on the most prolific period of her own career, must have felt on picking up *Aurora Leigh* and testing its published heft in her hands. Love of other authors is one of the essential pore-opening experiences that enables authorship. If Emily Dickinson had greater love for Elizabeth Barrett Browning, or even Mathilde Mackarness, than for Edgar Allan Poe or Herman Melville, and if that love helped her, in a world hostile both to women and to poets, to become a great poet, why on earth should we wish to fix what already worked?

12   And yet, and yet. To accept Dickinson's freedom to read and to love any writers who suit her is quite different, I think, from promoting those writers to Dickinson's league, simply by virtue of their sex. Two decades ago Tillie Olsen wrote that if we are to gauge contemporary writers' achievement by "appearance in twentieth-century literature courses, required reading lists, textbooks, quality anthologies, the year's best," and so on, only one woman is cited for every twelve men. This is an infuriating practice, and in recent years much has been done to retire it. But the process of allotting "equal time" to men and women has been a less sullied business in fiction than in poetry, for the novel is a genre at which women have excelled since its inception.

13   Men and women argue disinterestedly about whether Jane Austen was the greatest English novelist—or perhaps it was George Eliot. In the genre of poetry, women writing in English must pay our respects to Shakespeare, and to Milton, and to Chaucer, and a long list of others just a notch below them. Until recent times the writing of poetry was mostly the province of the learned, which in itself isn't a bad thing. The problem is that the learned, of course, were men. Thankful as we are to Virginia Woolf for making us see that if Shakespeare had had a sister, educational and social and psychological conditions would never have allowed her to become Shakespeare, so to speak, the fact remains that we have, as yet, no woman Shakespeare in English.

14   Male poets have had a double-barreled power behind them. The female muse inspired them; the male literary tradition, a tradition of accomplishment, gave them fathers both to revere and to try to usurp. Women have had a less accomplished literary tradition, though it grows more accomplished every century; and women writers may sometimes be seen deifying other women writers as a way, I suspect, of making them serve as both muse and tradition. Certainly, we don't have to accept the views of Eliot and Yeats and a host of others who align maleness with accomplishment and femaleness with inspiration. We may want to perform some violence upon the long-dead Pound when he writes, "Poetry speaks phallic direction." We may want to throttle Stevens for titling an essay "The Figure of the Youth as Virile Poet" and for composing this sentence in all complacent pride: "The centuries have a way of being male."

15   Irritating as it remains that male experience has for millennia been assumed to be normative, and female experience exceptional, we may, perhaps, forgive our male poets for finding inspiration in the female principle. The lunatic, the lover, and the poet are of imagination all compact, and as any poet, male or female, will tell you, a poem's first moment of inspiration is a sensation almost indistinguishable from that of falling in love. A heightened awareness of the reality of another person is the beginning of love; and that love is the beginning of a heightened awareness of the larger universe. Lovers may walk into doors or lose their wallets or forget their dentist appointments, but it is no accident that for their honeymoon they choose to go somewhere

beautiful, and that, more often than not, they see the natural world better than the loner. The world of the lover is suffused with the magic of connection, with links that go beyond words—links that the poet must therefore attempt to forge with words, for the poet is, as Shakespeare reminded us, a lunatic.

16   When that poet is a man, it is not surprising if, heterosexual or homosexual, he associates inspiration with femaleness, for what it really represents is otherness. Joseph Brodsky makes the leap that "the principle of rhyme," in particular, "enables one to sense that proximity between seemingly disparate entities." Rhyme is, in fact—as I've heard Brodsky remark in the classroom— a form of love. When the poet is a woman, is her muse usually male? In one way, yes, it would appear so: historically, most women's poetry has consisted of heterosexual love poetry. As deeply and as essentially as the woman poet learns from male writers, however, Dickinson's reading list suggests that the presence of any female "tradition"—however wobbly and uneven it is—will sometimes serve her as the most necessary muse of all. The male muse may not demand enough of us; for what men have usually wanted of us, their coy mistresses, is our bodies rather than our minds. The woman writer rarely has been able to find—or even imagine—a man who admired her enough to scold her, as Philip Sydney's muse scolded him, "Fool, look in thy heart and write." The tradition of accomplished women, then, may have to serve both as the exacting muse and the all-accepting mother. If we never had a mother, we adopt one.

17   The time is overdue to admit that there is something of a vacuum in women's poetry, and that we abhor it. For a woman to concede this is not disloyal to her sex; it's the first step in the creation of an environment in which women artists of the future will flourish. But what can be done about the fact that the list of beloved women poets is not anywhere near so long as the list of beloved poets who were born male?

18   The most liberating response to the problem was the one Elizabeth Bishop chose. As her admirer James Merrill writes, "Lowell called her one of the four best women poets ever—a wreath that can hardly have pleased Miss Bishop, who kept her work from appearing in the many recent 'women's anthologies.' Better, from her point of view, to be one of the forty, one of the forty thousand best *poets,* and have done with it." And he adds, "If I raise the issue at all, it's to dissociate her from these shopworn polarities." For the working poet, moved by the sexless sunset or the sex-indeterminate beetle, the polarities are indeed shopworn, but perhaps as readers we may pursue the issue an inch further. For one thing that we can do about these two unequal lists is to read women poets of the past who have never been much read, let alone famous, and to discover whether or not they deserve to be.

19   Emily Dickinson, after all, would never have become one of the most revered poets in the world had her sister Lavinia not rescued her poems from

the obscurity of a dresser drawer; and had her editor Mabel Loomis Todd not painstakingly, over years, transcribed nearly illegible scraps onto a bizarre typewriter that looked more like an astrolabe or an instrument of torture. Helen Hunt Jackson, that once celebrated, now nearly forgotten poet whose work Dickinson herself so admired, was another "sister" in this story, for she alone fully understood Dickinson's gifts while she was still alive. Jackson wrote to Dickinson urging her to publish: "You are a great poet—and it is a wrong to the day you live in, that you will not sing aloud," her letter went. "When you are what men call dead, you will be sorry you were so stingy." That has to be one of the most moving moments in American literary history.

20   And yet, and yet. Another reason so many of us are devoted to Dickinson is that we love the romance of her story. Not the lover's sort of romance, but the writer's. Dickinson suffered greatly in her love life, but she has to be one of the luckiest and unlikeliest great writers who ever lived. She chose to live in isolation, which meant she was saved from corruption at the hands of the literary crowd; no husband ever patted her head dismissively, no child ever interrupted her, and when her life was finished a team of disciples ensured her earthly immortality. If we do the necessary and difficult work of reappraising the literary "canon," and if we add some new names, new women's names, to the reading list, we will nonetheless have to settle for discoveries less dramatic than Lavinia Dickinson's, and we can't expect them to appear with a regular, democratic frequency.

21   For the fact is that we can't have it both ways. We can't simultaneously espouse Woolf's line that women haven't until recently been allowed the depth of education and the scope of experience to become Shakespeare, while also claiming that we really have an abundance of Shakespeares or even Woolfs, if anybody would just take the time to read us. Women's studies courses have mushroomed all over this country, with reading lists that combine established authors, forgotten authors, and women who never even thought of themselves as authors—farmers and factory workers and housewives whose letters and diaries carry a historical interest long after the deaths of the women themselves. This sort of social history can be fascinating, but I think it would be a great mistake to include it all under the heading of Literature in order to boast that women's output has been just as voluminous as men's.

22   But what is all this rating and counting and classifying of authors about anyway? If we set up one writer in competition against another, if we tally up writers of Type A against those of Type B, aren't we giving in to what some feminists tell us is the adversarial, aggressive mentality of patriarchal culture? We may think of Matthew Arnold's view of the function of criticism— "to learn and propagate the best that is known and thought"—and squirm in our chairs: Who's to say what is best, who's to say what is relevant?

23   Theoretically, these questions are of some interest. Practically speaking, most of us who are habitual, seasoned readers of poetry already have an answer. While acknowledging our profound differences of taste, we never doubt that there are good poems and terrible poems, and that the good ones are the only ones we have time for.

24   What else can be done about the fact that the list of the best women poets is not as long as the men's list? In addition to looking closely for unjustly neglected women, one might question whether some men poets have been overrated. I think, for some reason, of poets whose names contain double Ws—William Wordsworth, Walt Whitman, William Carlos Williams—and while I would be sorry to throw out the entire oeuvre of any of them, I confess that each of these estimable poets has at times bored me nearly to tears. It would do us no harm to be more judicious not only about poets but about poems, and to vow not to swallow a poet's whole menu unless all of it tastes good.

25   The problem with taking men poets down a peg, however, is that it's awfully hard to do so with discernment. The zeal to undo, and immediately, the centuries of neglect, condescension, and downright abuse endured by women poets—or lady poets, or poetesses, as they were once called—has resulted in the devaluation of some very great poets who were born male and (far worse) in the devaluation of poetry itself.

26   The big question, now, has to be asked: What *is* poetry? All sorts of definitions lodge in the mind. Dickinson said she knew it was poetry if she felt as if the top of her head were taken off, Moore said poetry was imaginary gardens with real toads in them, Pound insisted it had to be written at least as well as prose, Wordsworth claimed that it happened when emotion was recollected in tranquillity. Eliot took issue with Wordsworth: "Emotion recollected in tranquillity is an inexact formula," he wrote. "...Poetry is not a turning loose of emotion, but an escape from emotion; it is not the expression of personality, but an escape from personality. But, of course, only those who have personality and emotions know what it means to want to escape from these things."

27   When defining a vast object, often the best manner of proceeding is to catalog what it isn't. And yet we acknowledge the truth of each of these definitions—even, or perhaps especially, Stevens's assertion that no definition is possible. We accept that perhaps the closest thing to a definition of poetry is the aggregate of all definitions, suspended impossibly in the mind like the complex, conflicting, personal, impersonal, harmonious beauty of a poem itself. In any case, I hope we know that poetry is nothing less than any one of these writers would have it.

28   What do all these definitions have to do with the battle of the sexes? One wishes that the question were entirely irrelevant. But along with the recent

resurgence of interest in traditional and innovative verse forms among younger poets—a movement dubbed the New Formalism—a conflicting movement, or at least a bizarre set of assumptions, has taken shape. It contends that the formal tradition of English poetry—with its sonnets and rhymes royal and sestinas and villanelles, and even all the nameless nonce forms such as Herbert or Hardy devised for use in a single poem—is a male tradition, and thus must be rejected by women poets who want to find their own voices. Sandra Gilbert and Susan Gubar write that Eliot's concept of poetry as an "escape from emotion" has helped to construct "an implicitly masculine aesthetic of hard, abstract, learned verse that is opposed to the aesthetic of soft, effusive, personal verse supposedly written by women and the Romantics."

[29] One clings to that "supposedly"—to the notion that here is a division having less to do with innate character than social stereotype. And yet certain other feminists have unwittingly permitted themselves, and the rest of us women, to be pigeonholed. For them, the male poet who wrote in form stands, roughly speaking, for tranquillity, and the new woman poet who is honestly to address her subject matter stands for emotion. How can we fail to notice that when we divide poetry's function in half like this, we're left not with two groups of poems but with no real poems at all?

[30] In this connection, consider a passage from *Writing a Woman's Life,* a recent book by Carolyn Heilbrun, in which she reflects on the difficulty women have in resolving their relationships with their fathers. Heilbrun quotes Maxine Kumin as remarking that a poem about her father was the hardest she ever wrote, and then editorializes that Kumin "wrote it originally in syllabics and rhyme, using these as a defense between her and the material of the poem." She adds that Kumin herself emphasized, "That's how terrified I was of writing it." Now, I don't know what proportion of blame Heilbrun and Kumin should each be assigned for this passage, but this is shameful stuff. What a suffocating prescription it is—that we must not only come to terms with our fathers, but must do so without benefit of meter or rhyme!

[31] I suppose that Marianne Moore's penchant for syllabics is one reason that she is not widely taken up by women who believe in the legitimacy of "women's poetry." Another reason might be that she tends to write about animals, when she is supposed to write about her father. Well, we can always hope that her father *was* something of an animal, in which case Moore is all right. Yet we will not be able to argue away the claims for meter and rhyme so easily. Not all poets are interested in formal meters or rhyme, of course; and some of this century's best poems are free-form creations. But most of these have been written with *some* idea of form, *some* attention to a measurable music, and with an unreckonable indebtedness to the formal masters of the past.

[32] Are we really ready to throw out Shakespeare and Milton for using their meters as a "defense," in Heilbrun's terms, between themselves and their

material? The imaginary garden of poetry may be wilder looking than it used to be, but it is still a garden. And even if you or I choose not to plant a garden in neat rows, we will not be able to quash the garden-planting impulse in everybody else.

33   Ironically enough, what I—who would champion formal poetry—am arguing for is freedom. Freedom to write about our fathers or not, to write in meter or not. Freedom to think of ourselves as Women Poets, in capitals, or in lower case, or as Poets, in capitals, who hardly ever think about being women. When subject matter reigns supreme in poetry, the next step is to prescribe the subject matter. And a short step from there is prescribing the proper feelings about the subject matter. Heilbrun offers, again unwittingly, a cautionary passage: "What does it mean unambiguously to be a woman?" she asks, and answers that historically it has meant "to put a man at the center of one's life and to allow to occur only what honors his prime position." So far, so good; it's in the next sentence that I get scared. "Occasionally, women have put God or Christ in the place of a man," she adds, and remarks either scornfully or sorrowfully, "the results are the same: one's own desires and quests are always secondary."

34   Now undoubtedly, to many of us the Judeo-Christian tradition has seemed to offer women a bad deal. Suffice it to say that the adoration of Mary and the greatness of the women saints may never entirely erase for women a consciousness of the ways we have been wronged in both Old Testament and New. Tillie Olsen has set forth some of these wrongs in telegraphic style: "Religion when all believed. In sorrow shalt thou bring forth children. May the wife's womb never cease from bearing. Neither was the man created for the woman but the woman for the man. Let the woman learn in silence and in all subjection. Contrary to biological birth fact: Adam's rib. The Jewish male morning prayer: thank God I was not born a woman."

35   When we women are reminded of our place in the Judeo-Christian hierarchy—and I'd guess that many of us daily spend a good deal of subconscious energy trying to forget it—Heilbrun's implicit suggestion that women writers, or women in general, must dethrone God or Christ looks pretty inviting. The real point, however, is that our personal desires and quests are always secondary, whether we are Christians or atheists. Is there a mature adult who honestly believes that he or she comes first? Even more to the point, has there ever been a mature, great poet of any stripe who did not seek access to something greater than him- or herself?

36   And what if our desire *is* God? If that form of desire is to be disallowed, then the achievement of all sorts of women writers who put themselves second after God—writers from the twelfth-century Heloise to the twentieth-century Flannery O'Connor—dissolves into nothingness. And a good chunk of English poetry, particularly of the seventeenth century—the devotional poetry of the dean of St. Paul's, John Donne, and the country parson George Herbert—dissolves away, too.

37   Such misgivings must be at the bottom of my discomfort at having my book of poems assigned to the women's section of the bookstore. My books, however modest, represent an effort to speak not only of being a woman, and not only to women. Joyce Carol Oates, in a brief essay titled "The (Woman) Writer," puts the word "woman" in parentheses, and this, it seems to me, strikes precisely the right note. We cannot excise the word, or excise it all the time, since all women writers begin as women. But if we hope to play the resounding chords of human experience, and even extrahuman experience, the word "writer" will have to be the tonic key in which we do it.

38   And yet, and yet. We have arrived at a resounding chord, and now must acknowledge that it is dissonant. For the means by which most men writers throughout history have discovered how to speak selflessly of the broadly human, the universal, the spiritual is through selfishly shutting themselves off from domestic distractions. True, male writers have had to pay the bills with hack work that threatened to kill high art altogether. But women writers have had not only plenty of breadwinning to do, but the childbearing and the child-raising and the laundry and the potato-peeling too. Woolf put this memorably over half a century ago: she said she had to kill the Angel of the House before it killed her.

39   Woolf belonged to a subspecies of woman writer—the fiction writer— that has generally had much better luck than the poet in juggling the thousand tasks of women. Some fiction writers actually make money at their work, which frees at least a little time for the next story. Poets generally make no money, and thus they make no time. And that is a serious problem, for although the poet is apt to write at shorter length than the fiction writer, she evidently needs more uninterrupted time. She can accommodate herself less to daily social distractions, partly because she is usually not writing about society to the degree the novelist is, partly because a poet, if worth her salt, is writing with a more concentrated attentiveness to language.

40   In any case, though fiction-writing is never easy, it is apparently easier if you don't have children. Most women writers of fiction in history have been childless and it is only now that we can amass a long list of distinguished women fiction writers and remark with nothing less than joy at how many are mothers: Doris Lessing, Nadine Gordimer, Hortense Calisher, Edna O'Brien, Cynthia Ozick, Joan Didion, Alison Lurie, Muriel Spark, Alice Munro, etc., etc. The list of the best women poets in our language, by contrast, is a nearly unbroken catalog of childlessness: Elizabeth Barrett Browning (who had one child, late), Emily Dickinson, Christina Rossetti, Charlotte Mew, Marianne Moore, Louise Bogan, Elizabeth Bishop, May Swenson, etc., etc. If we take comfort in remembering that Sylvia Plath was a mother, it is not for long: we know what happened to her.

41   Since childbearing is the experience that may most radically distinguish the lives of women from the lives of men, and since women writers who want

to be mothers ought to be able to make this choice with no more than the usual amount of terror, I take the dearth of excellent mother-poets to be very disturbing indeed. I want to disbelieve what the statistics seem to tell us. They seem to be telling me, in any case, that the physical and emotional energy I put into my children is teaching me selflessness every day, and that if I don't learn to be selfish soon I will lack both the time and the assertiveness of spirit to have even a chance at writing the best poems I am capable of. Meanwhile, of course, I want to transcend the sense of self altogether, as Donne and Herbert hoped to do. The paradox simply will not go away.

42   Yet I hope there's a more cheerful way of looking at these conflicts and paradoxes. Women in our time understand them better than any generation of women in history. If no great English poem has yet been written about childbirth, maybe one of us will be the one to juggle the paradoxes just long enough to achieve it. And we will not address ourselves only to "women's subjects," either. We will see the word "woman" in italics in some poems, and in parentheses in others, and we won't read it at all in others. If artistic freedom means anything, it means that every poet, and every poem by every poet, is unique. And it means that we will sometimes (or often) speak in the bold voice too little heard yet from women, the voice that dares to serve as arbiter of taste and ethics, analyst of politics and religion, champion of the purity of art—the voice that won't die of mortification if somebody else disagrees. This is the voice that the 31-year-old Emily Dickinson, writing in 1862, had already mastered:

> I reckon—when I count at all—
> First—Poets—then the sun
> Then Summer—Then the Heaven of God—
> And then—the List is done—
>
> But—looking back—the First so seems
> To Comprehend the Whole—
> The Others look a needless Show—
> So I write—Poets—All—

1991

Below are three reviews of the same film, *Dances With Wolves* (1990). One might at first be inclined to say that all three reviewers have the same intention: to acquaint an audience of potential moviegoers with the reviewer's opinion of the film in question. Is *Dances With Wolves* worth the time and the price of admission? But if you look closely at the three reviews and try to articulate each writer's intention in detail, we think that you will find striking differences. What does each reviewer expect from a film? What does each reviewer assume about his or her audience?

David Denby

HOW THE WEST WAS LOST

David Denby wrote this review for New York Magazine. *Dances With* Wolves *was promoted by its makers for its sensitivity to cultural issues. For example, many characters speak in Lakota, the language of the Sioux, a rare event in the portrayal of American Indians in the movies. The film won twelve Academy Awards, and Denby's largely positive review stresses both its respectful portrait of the Sioux and its appeal as a work of art.*

1   The single most exciting moment in Kevin Costner's three-hour epic Western *Dances With Wolves* is neither a battle nor a stampede but a bravura bit of posturing by an angry Indian. The Indian (Rodney A. Grant), a Sioux, gallops directly toward the hero, Lieutenant Dunbar (Costner), who is standing, too frightened to run, with his cocked revolver held straight out in front of him. The Sioux screams (in Lakota), "I am Wind in His Hair. Can you see I am not afraid of you?" He screams it again: The moment has a crazy grandeur. Dunbar never shoots, but then, after the brave rides off, he faints dead away. It's the 1860s, and the Sioux are approaching their violent end as a powerful civilization. There isn't much left to them besides desperate gestures.

2   Costner, who directed and produced *Dances With Wolves,* has licked the problem moviemakers have been struggling with at least since Delmer Daves made *Broken Arrow* in 1950. How does one honor a destroyed or diminished culture without sentimentalizing it? The movie is not deeply imagined; it's overdeliberate and more illustrative than dramatic. Costner works the horizon like a man who has just discovered silhouettes and sunsets. There are too many tight close-ups—as if truth resided in a quavering eyelid. But even if the camera technique is occasionally laughable, this is also an enjoyable, stirring, and extremely conscientious old-fashioned movie, with some essential things done right. It's the best movie Robert Redford never made.

3   The doomed Sioux in *Dances With Wolves* are heroic—dignified and fierce and strange—but not stiff-jointed or incomprehensible. Costner may simply have applied his loose-limbed instincts as an actor to what he knows about Indians. His kind of humor, which undercuts appearances and gets to the heart of the matter, humanizes the Sioux. So does having them speak at length in their own language. They have real conversations (subtitled), with shades of meaning that go way beyond the "many moons have passed since soldiers come" school of Hollywood Indian palaver. Yet these same Indians go on murderous rampages, shrieking as they scalp their victims.

4   The story of *Dances With Wolves* has been told, in one form or another, many times before, but it's a good story—as close as white Americans are likely to come to a central ethical myth—and perhaps it needs to be told in every generation. Dunbar, a Civil War hero on the Union side, requests a post in the West. Sent to the Dakota territory, he lives in a "fort" (more like a shack) all by himself, deep in Sioux country. He approaches a tribe living nearby, gains their trust, learns their ways, and becomes one of them. Eventually, he fights with them against their enemies and in return is treated as a traitor by the Army, whose soldiers, a low, scruffy bunch, are hell-bent on annihilating the savages. Dunbar's dreary task is to prepare the Sioux to accept that there will be many, many more whites coming their way.

5   It's also a story that once would have been told in 100 minutes, and when I first heard about the length of *Dances With Wolves,* I thought, This is what happens when a movie star becomes a director and producer. But now I think the movie needs some—though perhaps not all—of the spaciousness Costner gives it. A good part of the "story" is how a man experiences the hush that falls over the Western landscape. A new terrain for movies, South Dakota is less overtly dramatic than Wyoming or Montana. There are no big mountains, no rock formations suitable for gunfights. Dunbar goes out there from the East, eager to experience the frontier, and for a while, he doesn't understand the land. The flat plains, golden or dull brown, with slight rises that afford views for miles, take on an alien cast.

6   *Dances With Wolves,* shot in extreme wide-screen format, reclaims the open spaces that have been lost to American movies since the Western genre collapsed. Characters ride to the tops of mesas and peer down. There's a stirring moment when Dunbar first sees the tents and fires of the Sioux villages arrayed near a river, and the sight of a complete community astonishes him. In the West, to spot someone else first is to control him. This is a movie about land—*turf,* finally, what the Indians have and the whites want. Costner, I would bet, took a good look at *Lawrence of Arabia* before going to work. Mixed in with the banal horizon shots are beautiful views, in the expansive David Lean style, of animals and men, seen from great distances as they move across plains between buttes.

7   Costner began developing the project with Michael Blake years ago, urging him to write and publish the story as a novel (he did) before turning it into a screenplay. In other words, the role of Dunbar was tailored, from the beginning, to Costner. Dunbar keeps a journal, and as he writes, Costner reads the words to us in a flat, rather affectless voice. This hero is an attentive, straightforward man, a little dull, perhaps, but a natural observer; he's always waiting, watching, sizing up the situation—or *being* sized up by someone else. Costner doesn't stand on his dignity like Gary Cooper or John Wayne. But he doesn't trust language much more than they did.

8   Yet Dunbar, uninteresting in himself, does something remarkable: He breaks through to the Sioux. By accident, he faces his first Indian stark naked. He hides nothing, presenting himself only as a man. Later he comes across a Sioux woman (Mary McDonnell) who has lost her husband and is slashing herself in grief. (It turns out she is a white, captured as a little girl.) He brings her to the village and later marries her. The tribe makes a space for him.

9   As a director, Costner is good at first meetings—the fumbling initial encounters between Dunbar and the fierce, distrusting Sioux, who sit in baffled counsel, trying to take him in. But once he carries the relationships past their first hazards, he doesn't bring them to a boil. The movie needs more in the way of conflict. And there are narrative holes. A Sioux war party leaves the village to fight the rival Pawnee, and, to our amazement, a Pawnee war party attacks the village while the men are away. In revenge? Did the two war parties crisscross? We never hear.

10   The Indians are ruthless but moral, emotional, loyal. They kill to survive. The whites, on the other hand, are often horrifying—pathetic scum who kill for sport and pleasure. There's a touch of white self-loathing here, though perhaps no more than the case deserves. *Dances With Wolves*, unlike the Vietnam-haunted movies of the early seventies, doesn't end in a massacre—just Wind in His Hair making another spectacular gesture. More effectively than any movie in years, *Dances With Wolves* mourns the magnificence that ended when the settlers came.

1990

Michael Dorris

INDIANS IN ASPIC

You will quickly see that Michael Dorris disagrees with David Denby about the portrayal of Native Americans in Dances With Wolves. *Where else do they agree and disagree? Among Dorris's own ancestors were Modoc Indians, and he lived for a time on a Montana reservation when he was young. He and his wife, the writer Louise Erdrich, have both written extensively on the experiences of contemporary Native Americans. What does Dorris expect from a film that takes on a deeply problematic issue in the history of the United States? His review appeared in the* New York Times, *a few months later than Denby's, after the film's popular success was evident. How might he respond to Denby's positive remarks about the film's entertainment and artistic value?*

1   The Sioux and Lieut. John Dunbar, the character enthusiastically played by Kevin Costner in *Dances With Wolves,* meet auspiciously: He's naked, and that so disconcerts a group of mounted warriors that the naïve young soldier lives to tell the tale, a sort of Boy Scout Order of the Arrow ritual carried to the nth power.

2   Dunbar, renamed Dances With Wolves, quickly earns merit badges in Pawnee-bashing and animal telepathy, and marries Stands With a Fist (Mary McDonnell), a passionate young widow who just happens to be a white captive cum Campfire Girl of impressive cross-cultural accomplishments. Eventually the "With" family strikes out on their own—the nucleus of a handsome new Anglo tribe—sadder, wiser and certainly more sensitive as a result of their native American immersion.

3   Mr. Costner follows in a long tradition of literary and cinematic heroes who have discovered Indians. Robinson Crusoe did it off the coast of Brazil, Natty Bumppo did it in New York State and everyone from Debra Paget (*Broken Arrow,* 1950) and Natalie Wood (*The Searchers,* 1956) to Dustin Hoffman (*Little Big Man,* 1970) and Richard Harris (*A Man Called Horse,* 1970) has done it in Hollywood.

4   Usually these visits do not bode well for the aboriginal hosts—just ask the Mohicans. Appreciative white folks always seem to show up shortly before the cavalry (who are often looking for them) or Manifest Destiny, and record the final days of peace before the tribe is annihilated. Readers and viewers of such sagas are left with a predominant emotion of regret for a golden age now but a faint memory. In the imaginary mass media world of neat beginnings, middles and ends, American Indian society, whatever its virtues and fascinations as an arena for Euro-American consciousness-raising, is definitely past tense.

5   Thematically virtually all of these works share a subtle or not so subtle message: Indians may be poor, they may at first seem strange or forbidding or primitive, but by golly once you get to know them they have a thing or two to teach us about The Meaning of Life.

6   The tradition goes back a long way. Europeans like Jean-Jacques Rousseau and Karl May (the turn-of-this-century novelist whose books, a mixture of Louis L'Amour and the Hardy Boys, have been a rite of passage for generations of German youth) laid out a single range for Indians to inhabit: savage-savage to noble-savage. Indians embody the concept of "the other"—a foreign, exotic, even cartoonish panorama against which "modern" (that is, white) men can measure and test themselves, and eventually, having proved their mettle in battle, be dubbed as natural leaders by their hosts.

7   Placed within the genre, *Dances With Wolves* shows some signs of evolution. Kevin Costner obviously spared no expense to achieve a sense of authenticity in his production. He filmed on the Pine Ridge reservation in South Dakota and defied conventional Hollywood wisdom to assemble a large and talented native American supporting cast. Great attention was paid

to ethnographically correct costumes, and if the streets in the native camp seem a tad too spotless to be believed, at least the tepees are museum quality.

8   Impressively, large segments of the film are spoken in Lakota, the language of the western Sioux, and though the subtitles are stilted—Indians in the movies seem incapable of using contractions—they at least convey the impression that native Americans had an intellectual life.

9   When I saw *Dances With Wolves* at an advance screening, I predicted that it would be less than a box-office smash. Though spectacular to look at, it struck me as too long, too predictable, too didactic to attract a large audience. Twelve Academy Award nominations and $100 million in revenue later, was I ever wrong. In fact, the movie probably sells tickets precisely *because* it delivers the old-fashioned Indians that the ticket-buying audience expects to find. Dunbar is our national myth's everyman—handsome, sensitive, flexible, right-thinking. He passes the test of the frontier, out-Indians the Indians, achieves a pure soul by encountering and surmounting the wilderness.

10   Yet, if *Dances With Wolves* had been about *people* who happen to be Indians, rather than about *Indians* (uniformly stoic, brave, nasty to their enemies, nice to their friends), it might have stood a better chance of acting as a bridge between societies that have for too long woodenly characterized each other.

11   With such tremendous popularity, the film is sure to generate a bubble of sympathy for the Sioux, but hard questions remain: Will this sentiment be practical, translating into public support for native American religious freedom cases before the Supreme Court, for restoration of Lakota sacred lands (the Black Hills) or water rights, for tribal sovereignty, for providing the money desperately needed by reservation health clinics? Pine Ridge is the most economically impoverished corner of America today, the Census Bureau says, but will its modern Indian advocates in business suits, men and women with lap-top computers and perfect English, be the recipients of a tidal wave of good will?

12   Or will it turn out, once again, that the only good Indians—the only Indians whose causes and needs we can embrace—are lodged safely in the past, wrapped neatly in the blankets of history, magnets for our sympathy because they require nothing of us but tears in a dark theater?

1991

Pauline Kael

A NEW AGE DAYDREAM

Like Michael Dorris, Pauline Kael dissents from the positive view of Dances With Wolves *taken by David Denby in his review as well as by the Motion Pic-*

ture Academy, who awarded it twelve Oscars, and the viewers who made it a huge success at the box office. Again, ask yourself what this reviewer expects from a film. Kael's objections to the film are quite different from Dorris's, but do her observations contradict his? Kael's reviews appear in The New Yorker. *How would you describe her relationship to and her purpose regarding her audience?*

1   A friend of mine broke up with his woman friend after they went to see *Field of Dreams:* she liked it. As soon as I got home from *Dances with Wolves,* I ran to the phone and warned him not to go to it with his new woman friend. Set during the Civil War, this new big Indians-versus-Cavalry epic is about how the white men drove the Native Americans from their land. But Kevin Costner, who directed *Dances with Wolves* and stars in it, is not a man who lets himself be ripped apart by the violent cruelty of what happened. He's no extremist: it's a middle-of-the-road epic. Lieutenant Dunbar (Costner), a Union officer, sees that the Sioux have a superior culture—they're held up as models for the rest of us—and he changes sides. Costner must have heard Joseph Campbell on PBS advising people to "follow your bliss." This is a nature-boy movie, a kid's daydream of being an Indian. When Dunbar has become a Sioux named Dances with Wolves, he writes in his journal that he knows for the first time who he really is. Costner has feathers in his hair and feathers in his head.

2   Once our hero has become an Indian, we don't have to feel torn or divided. We can see that the white men are foulmouthed, dirty louts. The movie—Costner's debut as a director—is childishly naïve. When Lieutenant Dunbar is alone with his pet wolf, he's like Robinson Crusoe on Mars. When he tries to get to know the Sioux, and he and they are feeling each other out, it's a sci-fi film that has the hero trying to communicate with an alien race. But in this movie it's the white men who are the aliens: the smelly brutes are even killing each other, in the war between the North and the South. Luckily, we Indians are part of a harmonious community. Dances with Wolves has never seen people "so dedicated to their families." And he loves their humor.

3   At the beginning, there's a bizarre Civil War battle sequence with the wounded Lieutenant Dunbar riding on horseback between rows of Union and Confederate soldiers, his arms outstretched, welcoming bullets in a Christlike embrace, and throughout the movie he is brutalized, seems dead, but rises again. (Does getting beaten give Costner a self-righteous feeling? Even when it's as unconvincingly staged as it is here?) There's nothing really campy or shamelessly flamboyant after the opening. There isn't even anything with narrative power or bite to it. This Western is like a New Age social-studies lesson. It isn't really revisionist; it's the old stuff toned down and sensitized.

4   Costner and his friend Michael Blake, who worked up the material with him in mind and then wrote the novel and the screenplay, are full of good will. They're trying to show the last years of the Sioux as an independent nation

from the Sioux point of view. And it's that sympathy for the Indians that (I think) the audience is responding to. But Costner and Blake are moviemaking novices. Instead of helping us understand the Sioux, they simply make the Sioux like genial versions of us. The film provides the groovy wisdom of the Sioux on the subjects of peace and togetherness: you never fight among yourselves—you negotiate. Each of the Indian characters is given a trait or two; they all come across as simpleminded, but so does the hero. Even the villains are endearingly dumb, the way they are in stories children write.

5   There's nothing affected about Costner's acting or directing. You hear his laid-back, surfer accent; you see his deliberate goofy faints and falls, and all the closeups of his handsomeness. This epic was made by a bland megalomaniac. (The Indians should have named him Plays with Camera.) You look at that untroubled face and know he can make everything lightweight. How is he as a director? Well, he has moments of competence. And the movie has an authentic vastness. The wide-screen cinematography, by Dean Semler, features the ridges, horizons, and golden sunsets of South Dakota; it's pictorial rather than emotionally expressive, but it's spacious and open at times, and there are fine images of buffalo pounding by.

6   Mostly, the action is sluggish and the scenes are poorly shaped. Crowds of moviegoers love the movie, though—maybe partly because the issues have been made so simple. As soon as you see the Indians, amused, watch the hero frolicking with his wolf, you know that the white men will kill it. Maybe, also, crowds love this epic because it's so innocent: Costner shows us his bare ass like a kid at camp feeling one with the great outdoors. He's the boyish man of the hour: the Sioux onscreen revere him, because he's heroic and modest, too. TV interviewers acclaim him for the same qualities. He's the Orson Welles that everybody wants—Orson Welles with no belly.

1990

FIVE ARGUMENTS USING PERSONAL EXPERIENCE

Maxine Hong Kingston

NO NAME WOMAN

Maxine Hong Kingston writes that her mother told stories "to grow up on." We might ask of all these personal experiences, including Kingston's, "What growing up did they occasion for the author?" This will help us understand what growing up the recounting of these experiences is intended to achieve in the audience. For instance, how is the growing up that Kingston does in this essay different from what her mother intends? Kingston teaches us by drawing us into her own specifically Chinese background.

1   "You must not tell anyone," my mother said, "what I am about to tell you. In China your father had a sister who killed herself. She jumped into the family well. We say that your father has all brothers because it is as if she had never been born.

2   "In 1924 just a few days after our village celebrated seventeen hurry-up weddings—to make sure that every young man who went 'out on the road' would responsibly come home—your father and his brothers and your grandfather and his brothers and your aunt's new husband sailed for America, the Gold Mountain. It was your grandfather's last trip. Those lucky enough to get contracts waved goodbye from the decks. They fed and guarded the stowaways and helped them off in Cuba, New York, Bali, Hawaii. 'We'll meet in California next year,' they said. All of them sent money home.

3   "I remember looking at your aunt one day when she and I were dressing; I had not noticed before that she had such a protruding melon of a stomach. But I did not think, 'She's pregnant,' until she began to look like other pregnant women, her skirt pulling and the white tops of her black pants showing. She could not have been pregnant, you see, because her husband had been gone for years. No one said anything. We did not discuss it. In early summer she was ready to have the child, long after the time when it could have been possible.

4   "The village had also been counting. On the night the baby was to be born the villagers raided our house. Some were crying. Like a great saw, teeth strung with lights, files of people walked zigzag across our land, tearing the rice. Their lanterns doubled in the disturbed black water, which drained away through the broken bunds. As the villagers closed in, we could see that some of them, probably men and women we knew well, wore white masks. The people with long hair hung it over their faces. Women with short hair made it stand up on end. Some had tied white bands around their foreheads, arms, and legs.

5   "At first they threw mud and rocks at the house. Then they threw eggs and began slaughtering our stock. We could hear the animals scream their deaths—the roosters, the pigs, a last great roar from the ox. Familiar wild heads flared in our night windows; the villagers encircled us. Some of the faces stopped to peer at us, their eyes rushing like searchlights. The hands flattened against the panes, framed heads, and left red prints.

6   "The villagers broke in the front and the back doors at the same time, even though we had not locked the doors against them. Their knives dripped with the blood of our animals. They smeared blood on the doors and walls. One woman swung a chicken, whose throat she had slit, splattering blood in red arcs about her. We stood together in the middle of our house, in the family

hall with the pictures and tables of the ancestors around us, and looked straight ahead.

7   "At that time the house had only two wings. When the men came back, we would build two more to enclose our courtyard and a third one to begin a second courtyard. The villagers pushed through both wings, even your grandparents' rooms, to find your aunt's, which was also mine until the men returned. From this room a new wing for one of the younger families would grow. They ripped up her clothes and shoes and broke her combs, grinding them underfoot. They tore her work from the loom. They scattered the cooking fire and rolled the new weaving in it. We could hear them in the kitchen breaking our bowls and banging the pots. They overturned the great waist-high earthenware jugs; duck eggs, pickled fruits, vegetables burst out and mixed in acrid torrents. The old woman from the next field swept a broom through the air and loosed the spirits-of-the-broom over our heads. 'Pig.' 'Ghost.' 'Pig,' they sobbed and scolded while they ruined our house.

8   "When they left, they took sugar and oranges to bless themselves. They cut pieces from the dead animals. Some of them took bowls that were not broken and clothes that were not torn. Afterward we swept up the rice and sewed it back up into sacks. But the smells from the spilled preserves lasted. Your aunt gave birth in the pigsty that night. The next morning when I went for the water, I found her and the baby plugging up the family well.

9   "Don't let your father know that I told you. He denies her. Now that you have started to menstruate, what happened to her could happen to you. Don't humiliate us. You wouldn't like to be forgotten as if you had never been born. The villagers are watchful."

10   Whenever she had to warn us about life, my mother told stories that ran like this one, a story to grow up on. She tested our strength to establish realities. Those in the emigrant generations who could not reassert brute survival died young and far from home. Those of us in the first American generations have had to figure out how the invisible world the emigrants built around our childhoods fit in solid America.

11   The emigrants confused the gods by diverting their curses, misleading them with crooked streets and false names. They must try to confuse their offspring as well, who, I suppose, threaten them in similar ways—always trying to get things straight, always trying to name the unspeakable. The Chinese I know hide their names; sojourners take new names when their lives change and guard their real names with silence.

12   Chinese-Americans, when you try to understand what things in you are Chinese, how do you separate what is peculiar to childhood, to poverty, insanities, one family, your mother who marked your growing with stories, from what is Chinese? What is Chinese tradition and what is the movies?

13   If I want to learn what clothes my aunt wore, whether flashy or ordinary, I would have to begin, "Remember Father's drowned-in-the-well sister?" I cannot ask that. My mother has told me once and for all the useful parts. She

will add nothing unless powered by Necessity, a riverbank that guides her life. She plants vegetable gardens rather than lawns; she carries the odd-shaped tomatoes home from the fields and eats food left for the gods.

14 Whenever we did frivolous things, we used up energy; we flew high kites. We children came up off the ground over the melting cones our parents brought home from work and the American movie on New Year's Day—*Oh, You Beautiful Doll* with Betty Grable one year, and *She Wore a Yellow Ribbon* with John Wayne another year. After the one carnival ride each, we paid in guilt; our tired father counted his change on the dark walk home.

15 Adultery is extravagance. Could people who hatch their own chicks and eat the embryos and the heads for delicacies and boil the feet in vinegar for party food, leaving only the gravel, eating even the gizzard lining—could such people engender a prodigal aunt? To be a woman, to have a daughter in starvation time was a waste enough. My aunt could not have been the lone romantic who gave up everything for sex. Women in the old China did not choose. Some man had commanded her to lie with him and be his secret evil. I wonder whether he masked himself when he joined the raid on her family.

16 Perhaps she encountered him in the fields or on the mountain where the daughters-in-law collected fuel. Or perhaps he first noticed her in the market-place. He was not a stranger because the village housed no strangers. She had to have dealings with him other than sex. Perhaps he worked an adjoining field, or he sold her the cloth for the dress she sewed and wore. His demand must have surprised, then terrified her. She obeyed him; she always did as she was told.

17 When the family found a young man in the next village to be her husband, she stood tractably beside the best rooster, his proxy, and promised before they met that she would be his forever. She was lucky that he was her age and she would be the first wife, an advantage secure now. The night she first saw him, he had sex with her. Then he left for America. She had almost forgotten what he looked like. When she tried to envision him, she only saw the black and white face in the group photograph the men had taken before leaving.

18 The other man was not, after all, much different from her husband. They both gave orders: she followed. "If you tell your family, I'll beat you. I'll kill you. Be here again next week." No one talked sex, ever. And she might have separated the rapes from the rest of living if only she did not have to buy her oil from him or gather wood in the same forest. I want her fear to have lasted just as long as rape lasted so that the fear could have been contained. No drawn-out fear. But women at sex hazarded birth and hence lifetimes. The fear did not stop but permeated everywhere. She told the man, "I think I'm pregnant." He organized the raid against her.

19 On nights when my mother and father talked about their life back home, sometimes they mentioned an "outcast table" whose business they still seemed to be settling, their voices tight. In a commensal tradition, where food

is precious, the powerful older people made wrongdoers eat alone. Instead of letting them start separate new lives like the Japanese, who could become samurais and geishas, the Chinese family, faces averted but eyes glowering sideways, hung on to the offenders and fed them leftovers. My aunt must have lived in the same house as my parents and eaten at an outcast table. My mother spoke about the raid as if she had seen it, when she and my aunt, a daughter-in-law to a different household, should not have been living together at all. Daughters-in-law lived with their husbands' parents, not their own; a synonym for marriage in Chinese is "taking a daughter-in-law." Her husband's parents could have sold her, mortgaged her, stoned her. But they had sent her back to her own mother and father, a mysterious act hinting at disgraces not told me. Perhaps they had thrown her out to deflect the avengers.

20   She was the only daughter; her four brothers went with her father, husband, and uncles "out on the road" and for some years became western men. When the goods were divided among the family, three of the brothers took land, and the youngest, my father, chose an education. After my grandparents gave their daughter away to her husband's family, they had dispensed all the adventure and all the property. They expected her alone to keep the traditional ways, which her brothers, now among the barbarians, could fumble without detection. The heavy, deep-rooted women were to maintain the past against the flood, safe for returning. But the rare urge west had fixed upon our family, and so my aunt crossed boundaries not delineated in space.

21   The work of preservation demands that the feelings playing about in one's guts not be turned into action. Just watch their passing like cherry blossoms. But perhaps my aunt, my forerunner, caught in a slow life, let dreams grow and fade and after some months or years went toward what persisted. Fear at the enormities of the forbidden kept her desires delicate, wire and bone. She looked at a man because she liked the way the hair was tucked behind his ears, or she liked the question-mark line of a long torso curving at the shoulder and straight at the hip. For warm eyes or a soft voice or a slow walk—that's all—a few hairs, a line, a brightness, a sound, a pace, she gave up family. She offered us up for a charm that vanished with tiredness, a pigtail that didn't toss when the wind died. Why, the wrong lighting could erase the dearest thing about him.

22   It could very well have been, however, that my aunt did not take subtle enjoyment of her friend, but, a wild woman, kept rollicking company. Imagining her free with sex doesn't fit, though. I don't know any women like that, or men either. Unless I see her life branching into mine, she gives me no ancestral help.

23   To sustain her being in love, she often worked at herself in the mirror, guessing at the colors and shapes that would interest him, changing them frequently in order to hit on the right combination. She wanted him to look back.

24   On a farm near the sea, a woman who tended her appearance reaped a reputation for eccentricity. All the married women blunt-cut their hair in

flaps about their ears or pulled it back in tight buns. No nonsense. Neither style blew easily into heart-catching tangles. And at their weddings they displayed themselves in their long hair for the last time. "It brushed the backs of my knees," my mother tells me. "It was braided, and even so, it brushed the backs of my knees."

25   At the mirror my aunt combed individuality into her bob. A bun could have been contrived to escape into black streamers blowing in the wind or in quiet wisps about her face, but only the older women in our picture album wear buns. She brushed her hair back from her forehead, tucking the flaps behind her ears. She looped a piece of thread, knotted into a circle between her index fingers and thumbs, and ran the double strand across her forehead. When she closed her fingers as if she were making a pair of shadow geese bite, the string twisted together catching the little hairs. Then she pulled the thread away from her skin, ripping the hairs out neatly, her eyes watering from the needles of pain. Opening her fingers, she cleaned the thread, then rolled it along her hairline and the tops of her eyebrows. My mother did the same to me and my sisters and herself. I used to believe that the expression "caught by the short hairs" meant a captive held with a depilatory string. It especially hurt at the temples, but my mother said we were lucky we didn't have to have our feet bound when we were seven. Sisters used to sit on their beds and cry together, she said, as their mothers or their slave removed the bandages for a few minutes each night and let the blood gush back into their veins. I hope that the man my aunt loved appreciated a smooth brow, and that he wasn't just a tits-and-ass man.

26   Once my aunt found a freckle on her chin, at a spot that the almanac said predestined her for unhappiness. She dug it out with a hot needle and washed the wound with peroxide.

27   More attention to her looks than these pullings of hairs and pickings at spots would have caused gossip among the villagers. They owned work clothes and good clothes, and they wore good clothes for feasting the new seasons. But since a woman combing her hair hexes beginnings, my aunt rarely found an occasion to look her best. Women looked like great sea snails—the corded wood, babies, and laundry they carried were the whorls on their backs. The Chinese did not admire a bent back; goddesses and warriors stood straight. Still there must have been a marvelous freeing of beauty when a worker laid down her burden and stretched and arched.

28   Such commonplace loveliness, however, was not enough for my aunt. She dreamed of a lover for the fifteen days of New Year's, the time for families to exchange visits, money, and food. She plied her secret comb. And sure enough she cursed the year, the family, the village, and herself.

29   Even as her hair lured her imminent lover, many other men looked at her. Uncles, cousins, nephews, brothers would have looked, too, had they been home between journeys. Perhaps they had already been restraining their

curiosity, and they left, fearful that their glances, like a field of nesting birds, might be startled and caught. Poverty hurt, and that was their first reason for leaving. But another, final reason for leaving the crowded house was the never-said.

30   She may have been unusually beloved, the precious only daughter, spoiled and mirror gazing because of the affection the family lavished on her. When her husband left, they welcomed the chance to take her back from the in-laws; she could live like the little daughter for just a while longer. There are stories that my grandfather was different from other people, "crazy ever since the little Jap bayoneted him in the head." He used to put his naked penis on the dinner table, laughing. And one day he brought home a baby girl, wrapped up inside his brown western-style greatcoat. He had traded one of his sons, probably my father, the youngest, for her. My grandmother made him trade back. When he finally got a daughter of his own, he doted on her. They must have all loved her, except perhaps my father, the only brother who never went back to China, having once been traded for a girl.

31   Brothers and sisters, newly men and women, had to efface their sexual color and present plain miens. Disturbing hair and eyes, a smile like no other, threatened the ideal of five generations living under one roof. To focus blurs, people shouted face to face and yelled from room to room. The immigrants I know have loud voices, unmodulated to American tones even after years away from the village where they called their friendships out across the fields. I have not been able to stop my mother's screams in public libraries or over telephones. Walking erect (knees straight, toes pointed forward, not pigeon-toed, which is Chinese-feminine) and speaking in an inaudible voice, I have tried to turn myself American-feminine. Chinese communication was loud, public. Only sick people had to whisper. But at the dinner table, where the family members came nearest one another, no one could talk, not the outcasts nor any eaters. Every word that falls from the mouth is a coin lost. Silently they gave and accepted food with both hands. A preoccupied child who took his bowl with one hand got a sideways glare. A complete moment of total attention is due everyone alike. Children and lovers have no singularity here, but my aunt used a secret voice, a separate attentiveness.

32   She kept the man's name to herself throughout her labor and dying; she did not accuse him that he be punished with her. To save her inseminator's name she gave silent birth.

33   He may have been somebody in her own household, but intercourse with a man outside the family would have been no less abhorrent. All the village were kinsmen, and the titles shouted in loud country voices never let kinship be forgotten. Any man within visiting distance would have been neutralized as a lover—"brother," "younger brother," "older brother"—one hundred and fifteen relationship titles. Parents researched birth charts probably not so much to assure good fortune as to circumvent incest in a population that has

but one hundred surnames. Everybody has eight million relatives. How useless then sexual mannerisms, how dangerous.

34   As if it came from an atavism deeper than fear, I used to add "brother"
silently to boys' names. It hexed the boys, who would or would not ask me
to dance, and made them less scary and as familiar and deserving of benevolence as girls.

35   But, of course, I hexed myself also—no dates. I should have stood up,
both arms waving, and shouted out across libraries, "Hey you! Love me
back." I had no idea, though, how to make attraction selective, how to control
its direction and magnitude. If I made myself American-pretty so that the five
or six Chinese boys in the class fell in love with me, everyone else—the Cau-
casian, Negro, and Japanese boys—would too. Sisterliness, dignified and
honorable, made much more sense.

36   Attraction eludes control so stubbornly that whole societies designed to
organize relationships among people cannot keep order, not even when they
bind people to one another from childhood and raise them together. Among
the very poor and the wealthy, brothers married their adopted sisters, like
doves. Our family allowed some romance, paying adult bride's prices and
providing dowries so that their sons and daughters could marry strangers.
Marriage promises to turn strangers into friendly relatives—a nation of sib-
lings.

37   In the village structure, spirits shimmered among the live creatures, balanced and held in equilibrium by time and land. But one human being flaring
up into violence could open up a black hole, a maelstrom that pulled in the sky.
The frightened villagers, who depended on one another to maintain the real,
went to my aunt to show her a personal, physical representation of the break
she had made in the "roundness." Misallying couples snapped off the future,
which was to be embodied in true offspring. The villagers punished her for
acting as if she could have a private life, secret and apart from them.

38   If my aunt had betrayed the family at a time of large grain yields and
peace, when many boys were born, and wings were being built on many
houses, perhaps she might have escaped such severe punishment. But the
men—hungry, greedy, tired of planting in dry soil, cuckolded—had had to
leave the village in order to send food-money home. There were ghost
plagues, bandit plagues, wars with the Japanese, floods. My Chinese brother
and sister had died of an unknown sickness. Adultery, perhaps only a mistake during good times, became a crime when the village needed food.

39   The round moon cakes and round doorways, the round tables of graduated size that fit one roundness into another, round windows and rice
bowls—these talismans had lost their power to warn this family of the law: a
family must be whole, faithfully keeping the descent line by having sons to
feed the old and the dead, who in turn look after the family. The villagers
came to show my aunt and her lover-in-hiding a broken house. The villagers
were speeding up the circling of events because she was too shortsighted to

see that her infidelity had already harmed the village, that waves of consequences would return unpredictably, sometimes in disguise, as now, to hurt her. This roundness had to be made coinsized so that she would see its circumference: punish her at the birth of her baby. Awaken her to the inexorable. People who refused fatalism because they could invest small resources insisted on culpability. Deny accidents and wrest fault from the stars.

40   After the villagers left, their lanterns now scattering in various directions toward home, the family broke their silence and cursed her. "Aiaa, we're going to die. Death is coming. Death is coming. Look what you've done. You've killed us. Ghost! Dead ghost! Ghost! You've never been born." She ran out into the fields, far enough from the house so that she could no longer hear their voices, and pressed herself against the earth, her own land no more. When she felt the birth coming, she thought that she had been hurt. Her body seized together. "They've hurt me too much," she thought. "This is gall, and it will kill me." With forehead and knees against the earth, her body convulsed and then relaxed. She turned on her back, lay on the ground. The black well of sky and stars went out and out and out forever; her body and her complexity seemed to disappear. She was one of the stars, a bright dot in blackness, without home, without a companion, in eternal cold and silence. An agoraphobia rose in her, speeding higher and higher, bigger and bigger; she would not be able to contain it; there would be no end to fear.

41   Flayed, unprotected against space, she felt pain return, focusing her body. This pain chilled her—a cold, steady kind of surface pain. Inside, spasmodically, the other pain, the pain of the child, heated her. For hours she lay on the ground, alternately body and space. Sometimes a vision of normal comfort obliterated reality: she saw the family in the evening gambling at the dinner table, the young people massaging their elders' backs. She saw them congratulating one another, high joy on the mornings the rice shoots came up. When these pictures burst, the stars drew yet further apart. Black space opened.

42   She got to her feet to fight better and remembered that old-fashioned women gave birth in their pigsties to fool the jealous, pain-dealing gods, who do not snatch piglets. Before the next spasms could stop her, she ran to the pigsty, each step a rushing out into emptiness. She climbed over the fence and knelt in the dirt. It was good to have a fence enclosing her, a tribal person alone.

43   Laboring, this woman who had carried her child as a foreign growth that sickened her every day, expelled it at last. She reached down to touch the hot, wet, moving mass, surely smaller than anything human, and could feel that it was human after all—fingers, toes, nails, nose. She pulled it up on to her belly, and it lay curled there, butt in the air, feet precisely tucked one under the other. She opened her loose shirt and buttoned the child inside. After resting, it squirmed and thrashed and she pushed it up to her breast. It turned its head this way and that until it found her nipple. There, it made little snuffling noises. She clenched her teeth at its preciousness, lovely as a young calf, a piglet, a little dog.

44   She may have gone to the pigsty as a last act of responsibility: she would protect this child as she had protected its father. It would look after her soul, leaving supplies on her grave. But how would this tiny child without family find her grave when there would be no marker for her anywhere, neither in the earth nor the family hall? No one would give her a family hall name. She had taken the child with her into the wastes. At its birth the two of them had felt the same raw pain of separation, a wound that only the family pressing tight could close. A child with no descent line would not soften her life but only trail after her, ghostlike, begging her to give it purpose. At dawn the villagers on their way to the fields would stand around the fence and look.

45   Full of milk, the little ghost slept. When it awoke, she hardened her breasts against the milk that crying loosens. Toward morning she picked up the baby and walked to the well.

46   Carrying the baby to the well shows loving. Otherwise abandon it. Turn its face into the mud. Mothers who love their children take them along. It was probably a girl; there is some hope of forgiveness for boys.

47   "Don't tell anyone you had an aunt. Your father does not want to hear her name. She has never been born." I have believed that sex was unspeakable and words so strong and fathers so frail that "aunt" would do my father mysterious harm. I have thought that my family, having settled among immigrants who had also been their neighbors in the ancestral land, needed to clean their name, and a wrong word would incite the kinspeople even here. But there is more to this silence: they want me to participate in her punishment. And I have.

48   In the twenty years since I heard this story I have not asked for details nor said my aunt's name; I do not know it. People who can comfort the dead can also chase after them to hurt them further—a reverse ancestor worship. The real punishment was not the raid swiftly inflicted by the villagers, but the family's deliberately forgetting her. Her betrayal so maddened them, they saw to it that she should suffer forever, even after death. Always hungry, always needing, she would have to beg food from other ghosts, snatch and steal it from those whose living descendants give them gifts. She would have to fight the ghosts massed at crossroads for the buns a few thoughtful citizens leave to decoy her away from village and home so that the ancestral spirits could feast unharassed. At peace, they could act like gods, not ghosts, their descent lines providing them with paper suits and dresses, spirit money, paper houses, paper automobiles, chicken, meat, and rice into eternity—essences delivered up in smoke and flames, steam and incense rising from each rice bowl. In an attempt to make the Chinese care for people outside the family, Chairman Mao encourages us now to give our paper replicas to the spirits of outstanding soldiers and workers, no matter whose ancestors they may be. My aunt remains forever hungry. Goods are not distributed evenly among the dead.

⁴⁹   My aunt haunts me—her ghost drawn to me because now, after fifty years of neglect, I alone devote pages of paper to her, though not origamied into houses and clothes. I do not think she always means me well. I am telling on her, and she was a spite suicide, drowning herself in the drinking water. The Chinese are always very frightened of the drowned one, whose weeping ghost, wet hair hanging and skin bloated, waits silently by the water to pull down a substitute.

1975

Enrique López

BACK TO BACHIMBA

You will see a kinship between Enrique López's essay and the previous piece by Maxine Hong Kingston, different as their transplanted cultures are. Like Kingston, López selects details that will give the reader the feel of his parents' culture. Like many "hyphenated Americans," as he calls himself in paragraph 22, López is particularly interested in the politics of naming: in what others call him and in what he chooses to call himself. How is the issue of naming related to what you see as the intention of this piece in regard to its audience?

¹   I am a *pocho* from Bachimba, a rather small Mexican village in the state of Chihuahua, where my father fought with the army of Pancho Villa.[1] He was, in fact, the only private in Villa's army.

²   *Pocho* is ordinarily a derogatory term in Mexico (to define it succinctly, a *pocho* is a Mexican slob who has pretensions of being a gringo sonofabitch), but I use it in a very special sense. To me that word has come to mean "uprooted Mexican," and that's what I have been all my life. Though my entire upbringing and education took place in the United States, I have never felt completely American, and when I am in Mexico, I sometimes feel like a displaced gringo with a curiously Mexican name—Enrique Preciliano López y Martinez de Sepulveda de Sapien de Quien-sabe-quien. One might conclude that I'm either a schizo-cultural Mexican or a cultured schizoid American.

³   In any event, the schizo-ing began a long time ago, when my father and many of Pancho Villa's troops fled across the border to escape the oncoming *federales* who eventually defeated Villa. My mother and I, traveling across the hot desert plains in a buckboard wagon, joined my father in El Paso, Texas, a

---

[1]*Pancho Villa*: Mexican revolutionary (1878–1923).

few days after his hurried departure. With more and more Villistas swarming into El Paso every day, it was quickly apparent that jobs would be exceedingly scarce and insecure; so my parents packed our few belongings and we took the first available bus to Denver. My father had hoped to move to Chicago because the name sounded so Mexican, but my mother's meager savings were hardly enough to buy tickets for Colorado.

4   There we moved into a ghetto of Spanish-speaking residents who chose to call themselves Spanish Americans and resented the sudden migration of their brethren from Mexico, whom they sneeringly called *surumatos* (slang for "southerners"). These so-called Spanish Americans claimed direct descent from the original *conquistadores* of Spain. They also insisted that they had *never* been Mexicans, since their region of New Spain (later annexed to the United States) was never a part of Mexico. But what they claimed most vociferously—and erroneously—was an absence of Indian ancestry. It made no difference that any objective observer could see by merely looking at them the results of considerable fraternization between the conquering Spaniards and the Comanche and Navaho women who crossed their paths. Still, these *manitos,* as they were snidely labeled by the *surumatos,* stubbornly refused to be identified with Mexico, and would actually fight anyone who called them Mexican. So intense was this intergroup rivalry that the bitterest "race riots" I have ever witnessed—and engaged in—were between the look-alike, talk-alike *surumatos* and *manitos* who lived near Denver's Curtis Park. In retrospect the harsh conflicts between us were all the more silly and self-defeating when one recalls that we were all lumped together as "spiks" and "greasers" by the Anglo-Saxon community.

5   Predictably enough, we *surumatos* began huddling together in a sub-neighborhood within the larger ghetto, and it was there that I became painfully aware that my father had been the only private in Pancho Villa's army. Most of my friends were the sons of captains, colonels, majors, and even generals, though a few fathers were admittedly mere sergeants and corporals. My father alone had been a lowly private in that famous Division del Norte. Naturally, I developed a most painful complex, which led me to all sorts of compensatory fibs. During one brief spell I fancied my father as a member of the dreaded *los dorados,* the "golden ones," who were Villa's favorite henchmen. (Later I was to learn that my father's cousin, Martin López, was a genuine and quite notorious *dorado.*) But all my inventions were quickly un-invented by my very own father, who seemed to take a perverse delight in being Pancho's only private.

6   No doubt my chagrin was accentuated by the fact that Pancho Villa's exploits were a constant topic of conversation in our household. My entire childhood seems to be shadowed by his presence. At our dinner table, almost every night, we would listen to endlessly repeated accounts of this battle, that stratagem, or some great act of Robin Hood kindness by *el centauro del norte.*

I remember how angry my parents were when they saw Wallace Beery in *Viva Villa!* "Garbage by stupid gringos," they called it. They were particularly offended by the sweaty, unshaven sloppiness of Beery's portrayal. "Pancho Villa was clean and orderly, no matter how much he chased after women. This man's a dirty swine."

7   As if to deepen our sense of *Villismo,* my parents also taught us "Adelita" and *"Se llevaron el cañon para Bachimba"* ("They took the cannons to Bachimba"), the two most famous songs of the Mexican revolution. Some twenty years later (during my stint at Harvard Law School), while strolling along the Charles River, I would find myself softly singing *"Se llevaron el cañon para Bachimba, para Bachimba, para Bachimba"* over and over again. That's all I could remember of that poignant rebel song. Though I had been born there, I had always regarded *"Bachimba"* as a fictitious, made-up, Lewis Carroll kind of word. So that eight years ago, when I first returned to Mexico, I was literally stunned when I came to a crossroad south of Chihuahua and saw an old road marker: "Bachimba 18 km." Then it really exists—I shouted inwardly—Bachimba is a real town! Swinging onto the narrow, poorly paved road, I gunned the motor and sped toward the town I'd been singing about since infancy. It turned out to be a quiet, dusty village with a bleak worn-down plaza that was surrounded by nondescript buildings of uncertain vintage.

8   Aside from the songs about Bachimba and Adelita and all the folk tales about Villa's guerrilla fighters, my early years were strongly influenced by our neighborhood celebrations of Mexico's two most important patriotic events: Mexican Independence Day on September 16 and the anniversary of the battle of Puebla on May 5. On those two dates Mexicans all over the world are likely to become extremely chauvinistic. In Denver we would stage annual parades that included three or four floats skimpily decorated with crepe paper streamers, a small band, several adults in threadbare battle dress, and hundreds of kids marching in wild disorder. It was during one of these parades—I was ten years old then—that I was seized with acute appendicitis and had to be rushed to a hospital. The doctor subsequently told my mother that I had made a long, impassioned speech about the early revolutionist Miguel Hidalgo while the anesthetic was taking hold, and she explained with pardonable pride that it was the speech I was to make at Turner Hall that evening. Mine was one of the twenty-three *discursos* scheduled on the post-parade program, a copy of which my mother still retains. My only regret was missing the annual *discurso* of Don Miguel Gómez, my godfather, a deep-throated orator who would always climax his speech by falling to his knees and dramatically kissing the floor, almost weeping as he loudly proclaimed: *"Ay, Mexico! Beso tu tierra, tu mero corazon"* ("Ah, Mexico! I kiss your sacred soil, the very heart of you"). He gave the same oration for seventeen years, word for word and gesture for gesture, and it never failed to bring tears to his eyes. But not once did he return to Chihuahua, even for a brief visit.

9   My personal Mexican-ness eventually produced serious problems for me. Upon entering grade school I learned English rapidly, and rather well, always ranking either first or second in my class; yet the hard core of me remained stubbornly Mexican. This chauvinism may have been a reaction to the constant racial prejudice we encountered on all sides. The neighborhood cops were always running us off the streets and calling us "dirty greasers," and most of our teachers frankly regarded us as totally inferior. I still remember the galling disdain of my sixth-grade teacher, whose constant mimicking of our heavily accented speech drove me to a desperate study of *Webster's Dictionary* in the hope of acquiring a vocabulary larger than hers. Sadly enough, I succeeded only too well, and for the next few years I spoke the most ridiculous high-flown rhetoric in the Denver public schools. One of my favorite words was "indubitably," and it must have driven everyone mad. I finally got rid of my accent by constantly reciting "Peter Piper picked a peck of pickled peppers" with little round pebbles in my mouth. Somewhere I had read about Demosthenes.

10   During this phase of my childhood the cultural tug of war known as "Americanization" almost pulled me apart. There were moments when I would identify completely with the gringo world (what could have been more American than my earnest high-voiced portrayal of George Washington, however ridiculous the cotton wig my mother had fashioned for me?); then quite suddenly I would feel so acutely Mexican that I would stammer over the simplest English phrase. I was so ready to take offense at the slightest slur against Mexicans that I would imagine prejudice where none existed. But on other occasions, in full confidence of my belonging, I would venture forth into social areas that I should have realized were clearly forbidden to little chicanos from Curtis Park. The inevitable rebuffs would leave me floundering in self-pity; it was small comfort to know that other minority groups suffered even worse rebuffs than we did.

11   The only non-Mexican boy on our street was a Negro named Leroy Logan, who was probably my closest childhood friend. Leroy was the best athlete, the best whistler, the best liar, the best horseshoe player, the best marble shooter, the best mumblety-pegger, and the best shoplifter in our neighborhood. He was also my "partner," and I thus entitled myself to a fifty-fifty share of all his large triumphs and petty thefts. Because he considered "Mexican" a derogatory word bordering on obscenity, Leroy would pronounce it "Mesican" so as to soften its harshness. But once in a while, when he'd get angry with me, he would call me a "lousy Mesican greasy spik" with the most extraordinarily effective hissing one can imagine. And I'm embarrassed to admit that I would retaliate by calling him "alligator bait." As a matter of fact, just after I had returned from the hospital, he came to visit me, and I thoughtlessly greeted him with a flippant, "Hi, alligator ba—" I never fin-

ished the phrase because Leroy whacked me on the stomach with a Ping-Pong paddle and rushed out of my house with great, sobbing anger.

12   Weeks later, when we had re-established a rather cool rapport, I tried to make up for my stupid insult by helping him steal cabbages from the vegetable trucks that rumbled through our neighborhood on their way to the produce markets. They would come down Larimer Street in the early dawn, and Leroy and I would sneak up behind them at the 27th Street stop sign, where they were forced to pause for cross traffic. Then Leroy, with a hooked pole he had invented, would stab the top cabbages and roll them off the truck. I would be waiting below to catch them with an open gunny sack. Our system was fabulously successful for a while, and we found a ready market for the stolen goods; but one morning, as I started to unfurl my sack, a fairly large cabbage conked me on the head. Screaming with pain, I lunged at Leroy and tried to bite him. He, laughing all the while—it was obviously a funny scene—glided out of my reach, and finally ran into a nearby alley. We never engaged in commercial affairs thereafter.

13   Still and all, I remember him with great affection and a touch of sadness. I say sadness because eventually Leroy was to suffer the misery of being an outsider in an already outside ghetto. As he grew older, it was apparent that he longed to be a Mexican, that he felt terribly dark and alone. "Sometimes," he would tell me, "I feel like my damn skin's too tight, like I'm gonna bust out of it." One cold February night I found him in the coal shed behind Pacheco's store, desperately scraping his forearm with sandpaper, the hurt tears streaming down his face. "I got to get this off, man. I can't stand all this blackness." We stood there quietly staring at the floor for a long, anguished moment, both of us miserable beyond word or gesture. Finally he drew a deep breath, blew his nose loudly, and mumbled half audibly, "Man, you sure lucky to be a Mesican."

14   Not long after this incident Leroy moved out of Denver to live with relatives in Georgia. When I saw him off at the bus station, he grabbed my shoulder and whispered huskily, "You gonna miss me, man. You watch what I tellya." "Indubitably," I said. "Aw, man, cut that stuff. You the most fancy-pants Mesican I know." Those were his last words to me, and they caused a considerable dent in my ego. Not enough, however, to diminish my penchant for fancy language. The dictionary continued to be my comic book well into high school.

15   Speaking of language, I am reminded of a most peculiar circumstance: almost every Mexican American lawyer that I've ever met speaks English with a noticeable Spanish accent, this despite the fact that they have all been born, reared, and educated exclusively in America. Of the forty-eight lawyers I have in mind, only three of us are free of any accent. Needless to say, our "cultural drag" has been weighty and persistent. And one must presume that our ethnic hyphens shall be with us for many years to come.

16   My own Mexican-ness, after years of decline at Harvard University, suddenly burst forth again when I returned to Chihuahua and stumbled on the town of Bachimba. I had long conversations with an uncle I'd never met before, my father's younger brother, Ramón. It was Tio Ramón who chilled my spine with eyewitness stories about Pancho Villa's legendary *dorados,* one of whom was Martin López. "He was your second cousin. The bravest young buck in Villa's army. And he became a *dorado* when he was scarcely seventeen years old because he dared to defy Pancho Villa himself. As your papa may have told you, Villa had a bad habit of burying treasure up in the mountains and also burying the man he took with him to dig the hole for it. Well, one day he chose Martin López to go with him. Deep in the mountains they went, near Parral. And when they got to a suitably lonely place, Pancho Villa told him to dig a hole with pick and shovel. Then, when Martin had dug down to his waist, Villa leveled a gun at the boy. "Say your prayers, *muchacho.* You shall stay here with the gold—forever." But Martin had come prepared. In his large right boot he had a gun, and when he rose from his bent position, he was pointing that gun at Villa. They stood there, both ready to fire, for several seconds, and finally Don Pancho started to laugh in that wonderful way of his. "*Bravo, bravo, muchacho!* You've got more guts than a man. Get out of that hole, boy. I need you for my *dorados.*"

17   Tio Ramón's eyes were wet with pride. "But what is more important, he died with great valor. Two years later, after he had terrorized the *federales* and Pershing's gringo soldiers, he was finally wounded and captured here in Bachimba. It was a bad wound in his leg, finally turning to gangrene. Then one Sunday morning they hauled Martin López and three other prisoners to the plaza. One by one they executed the three lesser prisoners against the wall. I was up on the church tower watching it all. Finally it was your uncle's turn. They dragged him off the buckboard wagon and handed him his crutches. Slowly, painfully, he hobbled to the wall and stood there. Very straight he stood. "Do you have any last words?" asked the captain of the firing squad. With great pride Martin tossed his crutches aside and stood very tall on his one good leg. 'Give me, you yellow bastards, give me a gun—and I'll show you who is the man among . . .' Eight bullets crashed into his chest and face, and I never heard that final word. That was your second cousin. You would have been proud to know him."

18   As I listened to Tio Ramón's soft nostalgic voice that evening, there in the sputtering light of the kerosene lamp on his back patio, I felt as intensely Mexican as I shall ever feel.

19   But not for long. Within six weeks I was destined to feel *less* Mexican than I had ever felt. The scene of my trauma was the Centro Mexicano de Escritores, where the finest young writers of Mexico met regularly to discuss works in progress and to engage in erudite literary and philosophical discussions. Week after week I sat among them, dumbstruck by my inadequacy in Spanish

and my total ignorance of their whole frame of reference. How could I have possibly imagined that I was Mexican? Those conversations were a dense tangle of local and private allusions, and the few threads I could grasp only magnified my ignorance. The novelist Juan Rulfo was then reading the initial drafts of his *Pedro Páramo,* later to be acclaimed the best avant-garde fiction in Mexican literature. Now that I have soaked myself in the *ambiance* of Mexico, Rulfo's novel intrigues me beyond measure; but when he first read it at the Centro, he might just as well have been reading "Jabberwocky" in Swahili for all I understood of it. And because all of the other Mexican writers knew and greatly appreciated *Páramo,* I could only assume that I was really "too gringo" to comprehend it. For this reason, I, a person with no great talent for reticence, never opened my mouth at the Centro. In fact, I was so shell-shocked by those sessions that I even found it difficult to converse with my housekeeper about such simple matters as dirty laundry or the loose doorknob in the bathroom.

20   Can any of us really go home again? I, for one, am convinced that I have no true home, that I must reconcile myself to a schizo-cultural limbo, with a mere hyphen to provide some slight cohesion between my split selves. This inevitable splitting is a plague and a pleasure. Some mornings as I glide down the Paseo de la Reforma, perhaps the most beautiful boulevard in the world, I am suddenly angered by the *machismo,* or aggressive maleness, of Mexican drivers who crowd and bully their screeching machines through dense traffic. What terrible insecurity, what awful dread of emasculation, produces such assertive bully-boy conduct behind a steering wheel? Whatever the reasons, there is a part of me that can never accept this much-celebrated *machismo.* Nor can I accept the exaggerated nationalism one so frequently encounters in the press, on movie screens, over the radio, in daily conversations—that shrill barrage of slogans proclaiming that "there is only one Mexico."

21   Recently, when I expressed these views to an old friend, he smiled quite knowingly: "Let's face it, Hank, you're not really a Mexican—despite that long, comical name of yours. You're an American through and through." But that, of course, is a minority view and almost totally devoid of realism. One could just as well say that Martin Luther King was not a Negro, that he was merely an American. But the plain truth is that neither I nor the Martin Luther Kings of our land can escape the fact that we are Mexican and Negro with roots planted so deeply in the United States that we have grown those strong little hyphens that make us Mexican-American and Negro-American. This assertion may not please some idealists who would prefer to blind themselves to our obvious ethnic and racial differences, who are unwittingly patronizing when they insist that we are all alike and indistinguishable. But the politicians, undoubtedly the most pragmatic creatures in America, are completely aware that ethnic groups *do* exist and that they seem to huddle together, bitch together, and sometimes vote together.

22   When all is said and done, we hyphenated Americans are here to stay, bubbling happily or unhappily in the great non-melting pot. Much has been gained and will be gained from the multiethnic aspects of the United States, and there is no useful purpose in attempting to wish it away or to homogenize it out of existence. In spite of the race riots in Watts and ethnic unrest elsewhere, there would appear to be a kind of *modus vivendi* developing on almost every level of American life.

23   And if there are those of us who may never feel completely at home, we can always make that brief visit to Bachimba.

1967

E. B. White

ONCE MORE TO THE LAKE

Although he wrote many fine essays, E. B. White may be remembered most warmly for Charlotte's Web, *the story of a spider who was "a true friend and a good writer." In this essay, he uses an experience particular to his own life to make a universally applicable point. The ending comes as a surprise at first, but can you find preparation for it when you reread the piece? Why would White want to remind us that we are mortal, something we already know? Why might we need a reminder?*

1   One summer, along about 1904, my father rented a camp on a lake in Maine and took us all there for the month of August. We all got ringworm from some kittens and had to rub Pond's Extract on our arms and legs night and morning, and my father rolled over in a canoe with all his clothes on; but outside of that the vacation was a success and from then on none of us ever thought there was any place in the world like that lake in Maine. We returned summer after summer—always on August 1st for one month. I have since become a salt-water man, but sometimes in summer there are days when the restlessness of the tides and the fearful cold of the sea water and the incessant wind which blows across the afternoon and into the evening make me wish for the placidity of a lake in the woods. A few weeks ago this feeling got so strong I bought myself a couple of bass hooks and a spinner and returned to the lake where we used to go, for a week's fishing and to revisit old haunts.

2   I took along my son, who had never had any fresh water up his nose and who had seen lily pads only from train windows. On the journey over to the lake I began to wonder what it would be like. I wondered how time would

have marred this unique, this holy spot—the coves and streams, the hills that the sun set behind, the camps and the paths behind the camps. I was sure the tarred road would have found it out and I wondered in what other ways it would be desolated. It is strange how much you can remember about places like that once you allow your mind to return into the grooves which lead back. You remember one thing, and that suddenly reminds you of another thing. I guess I remembered clearest of all the early mornings, when the lake was cool and motionless, remembered how the bedroom smelled of the lumber it was made of and of the wet woods whose scent entered through the screen. The partitions in the camp were thin and did not extend clear to the top of the rooms, and as I was always the first up I would dress softly so as not to wake the others, and sneak out into the sweet outdoors and start out in the canoe, keeping close along the shore in the long shadows of the pines. I remembered being very careful never to rub my paddle against the gunwale for fear of disturbing the stillness of the cathedral.

3   The lake had never been what you would call a wild lake. There were cottages sprinkled around the shores, and it was in farming country although the shores of the lake were quite heavily wooded. Some of the cottages were owned by nearby farmers, and you would live at the shore and eat your meals at the farmhouse. That's what our family did. But although it wasn't wild, it was a fairly large and undisturbed lake and there were places in it which, to a child at least, seemed infinitely remote and primeval.

4   I was right about the tar: it led to within half a mile of the shore. But when I got back there, with my boy, and we settled into a camp near a farmhouse and into the kind of summertime I had known, I could tell that it was going to be pretty much the same as it had been before—I knew it, lying in bed the first morning, smelling the bedroom, and hearing the boy sneak quietly out and go off along the shore in a boat. I began to sustain the illusion that he was I, and therefore, by simple transposition, that I was my father. This sensation persisted, kept cropping up all the time we were there. It was not an entirely new feeling, but in this setting it grew much stronger. I seemed to be living a dual existence. I would be in the middle of some simple act, I would be picking up a bait box or laying down a table fork, or I would be saying something, and suddenly it would be not I but my father who was saying the words or making the gesture. It gave me a creepy sensation.

5   We went fishing the first morning. I felt the same damp moss covering the worms in the bait can, and saw the dragonfly alight on the tip of my rod as it hovered a few inches from the surface of the water. It was the arrival of this fly that convinced me beyond any doubt that everything was as it always had been, that the years were a mirage and there had been no years. The small waves were the same, chucking the rowboat under the chin as we fished at anchor, and the boat was the same boat, the same color green and the ribs broken in the same places, and under the floor-boards the same fresh-water leav-

ings and débris—the dead helgramite, the wisps of moss, the rusty discarded fishook, the dried blood from yesterday's catch. We stared silently at the tips of our rods, at the dragonflies that came and went. I lowered the tip of mine into the water tentatively, pensively dislodging the fly, which darted two feet away, poised, darted two feet back, and came to rest again a little farther up the rod. There had been no years between the ducking of this dragonfly and the other one—the one that was part of memory. I looked at the boy, who was silently watching his fly, and it was my hands that held his rod, my eyes watching. I felt dizzy and didn't know which rod I was at the end of.

6　　We caught two bass, hauling them in briskly as though they were mackerel, pulling them over the side of the boat in a businesslike manner without any landing net, and stunning them with a blow on the back of the head. When we got back for a swim before lunch, the lake was exactly where we had left it, the same number of inches from the dock, and there was only the merest suggestion of a breeze. This seemed an utterly enchanted sea, this lake you could leave to its own devices for a few hours and come back to, and find that it had not stirred, this constant and trustworthy body of water. In the shallows, the dark, water-soaked sticks and twigs, smooth and old, were undulating in clusters on the bottom against the clean ribbed sand, and the track of the mussel was plain. A school of minnows swam by, each minnow with its small individual shadow, doubling the attendance, so clear and sharp in the sunlight. Some of the other campers were in swimming, along the shore, one of them with a cake of soap, and the water felt thin and clear and unsubstantial. Over the years there had been this person with the cake of soap, this cultist, and here he was. There had been no years.

7　　Up to the farmhouse to dinner through the teeming, dusty field, the road under our sneakers was only a two-track road. The middle track was missing, the one with the marks of the hooves and the splotches of dried, flaky manure. There had always been three tracks to choose from in choosing which track to walk in; now the choice was narrowed down to two. For a moment I missed terribly the middle alternative. But the way led past the tennis court, and something about the way it lay there in the sun reassured me; the tape had loosened along the backline, the alleys were green with plantains and other weeds, and the net (installed in June and removed in September) sagged in the dry noon, and the whole place steamed with midday heat and hunger and emptiness. There was a choice of pie for dessert, and one was blueberry and one was apple, and the waitresses were the same country girls, there having been no passage of time, only the illusion of it as in a dropped curtain—the waitresses were still fifteen; their hair had been washed, that was the only difference—they had been to the movies and seen the pretty girls with the clean hair.

8　　Summertime, oh summertime, pattern of life indelible, the fade-proof lake, the woods unshatterable, the pasture with the sweetfern and the juniper forever and ever, summer without end; this was the background, and the life along the shore was the design, the cottagers with their innocent and tranquil design, their tiny docks with the flagpole and the American flag floating against the white clouds in the blue sky, the little paths over the roots of the trees leading from camp to camp and the paths leading back to the outhouses and the can of lime for sprinkling, and at the souvenir counters at the store the miniature birch-bark canoes and the post cards that showed things looking a little better than they looked. This was the American family at play, escaping the city heat, wondering whether the newcomers in the camp at the head of the cove were "common" or "nice," wondering whether it was true that the people who drove up for Sunday dinner at the farmhouse were turned away because there wasn't enough chicken.

9   It seemed to me, as I kept remembering all this, that those times and those summers had been infinitely precious and worth saving. There had been jollity and peace and goodness. The arriving (at the beginning of August) had been so big a business in itself, at the railway station the farm wagon drawn up, the first smell of the pine-laden air, the first glimpse of the smiling farmer, and the great importance of the trunks and your father's enormous authority in such matters, and the feel of the wagon under you for the long ten-mile haul, and at the top of the last long hill catching the first view of the lake after eleven months of not seeing this cherished body of water. The shouts and cries of the other campers when they saw you, and the trunks to be unpacked, to give up their rich burden. (Arriving was less exciting nowadays, when you sneaked up in your car and parked it under a tree near the camp and took out the bags and in five minutes it was all over, no fuss, no loud wonderful fuss about trunks.)

10   Peace and goodness and jollity. The only thing that was wrong now, really, was the sound of the place, an unfamiliar nervous sound of the outboard motors. This was the note that jarred, the one thing that would sometimes break the illusion and set the years moving. In those other summertimes all motors were inboard; and when they were at a little distance, the noise they made was a sedative, an ingredient of summer sleep. They were one-cylinder and two-cylinder engines, and some were make-and-break and some were jump-spark, but they all made a sleepy sound across the lake. The onelungers throbbed and fluttered, and the twin-cylinder ones purred and purred, and that was a quiet sound too. But now the campers all had outboards. In the daytime, in the hot mornings, these motors made a petulant, irritable sound; at night, in the still evening when the afterglow lit the water, they whined about one's ears like mosquitoes. My boy loved our rented outboard, and his great desire was to achieve singlehanded mastery over it, and authority, and he soon learned the trick of choking it a little (but not too much), and the adjustment of the needle valve. Watching him I would remember the things you could do with the old one-cylinder engine with the heavy flywheel, how

you could have it eating out of your hand if you got really close to it spiritually. Motor boats in those days didn't have clutches, and you would make a landing by shutting off the motor at the proper time and coasting in with a dead rudder. But there was a way of reversing them, if you learned the trick, by cutting the switch and putting it on again exactly on the final dying revolution of the flywheel, so that it would kick back against compression and begin reversing. Approaching a dock in a strong following breeze, it was difficult to slow up sufficiently by the ordinary coasting method, and if a boy felt he had complete mastery over his motor, he was tempted to keep it running beyond its time and then reverse it a few feet from the dock. It took a cool nerve, because if you threw the switch a twentieth of a second too soon you would catch the flywheel when it still had speed enough to go up past center, and the boat would leap ahead, charging bull-fashion at the dock.

11   We had a good week at the camp. The bass were biting well and the sun shone endlessly, day after day. We would be tired at night and lie down in the accumulated heat of the little bedrooms after the long hot day and the breeze would stir almost imperceptibly outside and the smell of the swamp drift in through the rusty screens. Sleep would come easily and in the morning the red squirrel would be on the roof, tapping out his gay routine. I kept remembering everything, lying in bed in the mornings—the small steamboat that had a long rounded stern like the lip of a Ubangi, and how quietly she ran on the moonlight sails, when the older boys played their mandolins and the girls sang and we ate doughnuts dipped in sugar, and how sweet the music was on the water in the shining night, and what it had felt like to think about girls then. After breakfast we would go up to the store and the things were in the same place—the minnows in a bottle, the plugs and spinners disarranged and pawed over by the youngsters from the boys' camp, the fig newtons and the Beeman's gum. Outside, the road was tarred and cars stood in front of the store. Inside, all was just as it had always been, except there was more Coca-Cola and not so much Moxie and root beer and birch beer and sarsaparilla. We would walk out with a bottle of pop apiece and sometimes the pop would backfire up our noses and hurt. We explored the streams, quietly, where the turtles slid off the sunny logs and dug their way into the soft bottom; and we lay on the town wharf and fed worms to the tame bass. Everywhere we went I had trouble making out which was I, the one walking at my side, the one walking in my pants.

12   One afternoon while we were there at that lake a thunderstorm came up. It was like the revival of an old melodrama that I had seen long ago with childish awe. The second-act climax of the drama of the electrical disturbance over a lake in America had not changed in any important respect. This was the big scene, still the big scene. The whole thing was so familiar, the first feeling of oppression and heat and a general air around camp of not wanting to go very far away. In midafternoon (it was all the same) a curious darkening

of the sky, and a lull in everything that had made life tick; and then the way the boats suddenly swung the other way at their moorings with the coming of a breeze out of the new quarter, and the premonitory rumble. Then the kettle drum, then the snare, then the bass drum and cymbals, then crackling light against the dark, and the gods grinning and licking their chops in the hills. Afterward the calm, the rain steadily rustling in the calm lake, the return of light and hope and spirits, and the campers running out in joy and relief to go swimming in the rain, their bright cries perpetuating the deathless joke about how they were getting simply drenched, and the children screaming with delight at the new sensation of bathing in the rain, and the joke about getting drenched linking the generations in a strong indestructible chain. And the comedian who waded in carrying an umbrella.

13 When the others went swimming my son said he was going in too. He pulled his dripping trunks from the line where they had hung all through the shower, and wrung them out. Languidly, and with no thought of going in, I watched him, his hard little body, skinny and bare, saw him wince slightly as he pulled up around his vitals the small, soggy, icy garment. As he buckled the swollen belt suddenly my groin felt the chill of death.

1941

Paule Marshall

FROM THE POETS IN THE KITCHEN

Many authors write at some point an account of the influences most important in shaping their writing careers. Paule Marshall's "From the Poets in the Kitchen" is such an essay. Her novels and short stories often take place in the Caribbean settings from which her family originated or else in transplanted Caribbean communities in New York, where she grew up. Her intention goes beyond reporting major influences on her writing. If you agree that she tries to change or at least adjust her audience's views, try to decide what attitudes and beliefs are at issue and how she seeks to change them.

1 Some years ago, when I was teaching a graduate seminar in fiction at Columbia University, a well known male novelist visited my class to speak on his development as a writer. In discussing his formative years, he didn't realize it but he seriously endangered his life by remarking that women writers are luckier than those of his sex because they usually spend so much time as children around their mothers and their mothers' friends in the kitchen.

2   What did he say that for? The women students immediately forgot about being in awe of him and began readying their attack for the question and answer period later on. Even I bristled. There again was the awful image of women locked away from the world in the kitchen with only each other to talk to, and their daughters locked in with them.

3   But my guest wasn't really being sexist or trying to be provocative or even spoiling for a fight. What he meant—when he got around to explaining himself more fully—was that, given the way children are (or were) raised in our society, with little girls kept closer to home and their mothers, the woman writer stands a better chance of being exposed, while growing up, to the kind of talk that goes on among women, more often than not in the kitchen; and that this experience gives her an edge over her male counterpart by instilling in her an appreciation for ordinary speech.

4   It was clear that my guest lecturer attached great importance to this, which is understandable. Common speech and the plain, workaday words that make it up are, after all, the stock in trade of some of the best fiction writers. They are the principal means by which characters in a novel or story reveal themselves and give voice sometimes to profound feelings and complex ideas about themselves and the world. Perhaps the proper measure of a writer's talent is skill in rendering everyday speech—when it is appropriate to the story—as well as the ability to tap, to exploit, the beauty, poetry and wisdom it often contains.

5   "If you say what's on your mind in the language that comes to you from your parents and your street and friends you'll probably say something beautiful." Grace Paley tells this, she says, to her students at the beginning of every writing course.

6   It's all a matter of exposure and training of the ear for the would-be writer in those early years of apprenticeship. And, according to my guest lecturer, this training, the best of it, often takes place in as unglamorous a setting as the kitchen.

7   He didn't know it, but he was essentially describing my experience as a little girl. I grew up among poets. Now they didn't look like poets—whatever that breed is supposed to look like. Nothing about them suggested that poetry was their calling. They were just a group of ordinary housewives and mothers, my mother included, who dressed in a way (shapeless housedresses, dowdy felt hats and long, dark, solemn coats) that made it impossible for me to imagine they had ever been young.

8   Nor did they do what poets were supposed to do—spend their days in an attic room writing verses. They never put pen to paper except to write occasionally to their relatives in Barbados. "I take my pen in hand hoping these few lines will find you in health as they leave me fair for the time being," was the way their letters invariably began. Rather, their day was spent "scrubbing floor," as they described the work they did.

9   Several mornings a week these unknown bards would put an apron and a pair of old house shoes in a shopping bag and take the train or streetcar from our section of Brooklyn out to Flatbush. There, those who didn't have steady jobs would wait on certain designated corners for the white housewives in the neighborhood to come along and bargain with them over pay for a day's work cleaning their houses. This was the ritual even in the winter.

10   Later, armed with the few dollars they had earned, which in their vocabulary became "a few raw-mouth pennies," they made their way back to our neighborhood, where they would sometimes stop off to have a cup of tea or cocoa together before going home to cook dinner for their husbands and children.

11   The basement kitchen of the brownstone house where my family lived was the usual gathering place. Once inside the warm safety of its walls the women threw off the drab coats and hats, seated themselves at the large center table, drank their cups of tea or cocoa, and talked. While my sister and I sat at a smaller table over in a corner doing our homework, they talked—endlessly, passionately, poetically, and with impressive range. No subject was beyond them. True, they would indulge in the usual gossip: whose husband was running with whom, whose daughter looked slightly "in a way" (pregnant) under her bridal gown as she walked down the aisle. That sort of thing. But they also tackled the great issues of the time. They were always, for example, discussing the state of the economy. It was the mid and late 30's then, and the aftershock of the Depression, with its soup lines and suicides on Wall Street, was still being felt.

12   Some people, they declared, didn't know how to deal with adversity. They didn't know that you had to "tie up your belly" (hold in the pain, that is) when things got rough and go on with life. They took their image from the bellyband that is tied around the stomach of a newborn baby to keep the navel pressed in.

13   They talked politics. Roosevelt was their hero. He had come along and rescued the country with relief and jobs, and in gratitude they christened their sons Franklin and Delano and hoped they would live up to the names.

14   If F. D. R. was their hero, Marcus Garvey was their God. The name of the fiery, Jamaican-born black nationalist of the 20's was constantly invoked around the table. For he had been their leader when they first came to the United States from the West Indies shortly after World War I. They had contributed to his organization, the United Negro Improvement Association (UNIA), out of their meager salaries, bought shares in his ill-fated Black Star Shipping Line, and at the height of the movement they had marched as members of his "nurses' brigade" in their white uniforms up Seventh Avenue in Harlem during the great Garvey Day parades. Garvey: He lived on through the power of their memories.

15   And their talk was of war and rumors of wars. They raged against World War II when it broke out in Europe, blaming it on the politicians. "It's these

politicians. They're the ones always starting up all this lot of war. But what they care? It's the poor people go to suffer and mothers with their sons." If it was *their* sons, they swore they would keep them out of the Army by giving them soap to eat each day to make their hearts sound defective. Hitler? He was for them "the devil incarnate."

16   Then there was home. They reminisced often and at length about home. The old country. Barbados—or Bimshire, as they affectionately called it. The little Caribbean island in the sun they loved but had to leave. "Poor—poor but sweet" was the way they remembered it.

17   And naturally they discussed their adopted home. America came in for both good and bad marks. They lashed out at it for the racism they encountered. They took to task some of the people they worked for, especially those who gave them only a hardboiled egg and a few spoonfuls of cottage cheese for lunch. "As if anybody can scrub floor on an egg and some cheese that don't have no taste to it!"

18   Yet although they caught H in "this man country," as they called America, it was nonetheless a place where "you could at least see your way to make a dollar." That much they acknowledged. They might even one day accumulate enough dollars, with both them and their husbands working, to buy the brownstone houses which, like my family, they were only leasing at that period. This was their consuming ambition: to "buy house" and to see the children through.

19   There was no way for me to understand it at the time, but the talk that filled the kitchen those afternoons was highly functional. It served as therapy, the cheapest kind available to my mother and her friends. Not only did it help them recover from the long wait on the corner that morning and the bargaining over their labor, it restored them to a sense of themselves and reaffirmed their self-worth. Through language they were able to overcome the humiliations of the work-day.

20   But more than therapy, that freewheeling, wide-ranging, exuberant talk functioned as an outlet for the tremendous creative energy they possessed. They were women in whom the need for self-expression was strong, and since language was the only vehicle readily available to them they made of it an art form that—in keeping with the African tradition in which art and life are one—was an integral part of their lives.

21   And their talk was a refuge. They never really ceased being baffled and overwhelmed by America—its vastness, complexity and power. Its strange customs and laws. At a level beyond words they remained fearful and in awe. Their uneasiness and fear were even reflected in their attitude toward the children they had given birth to in this country. They referred to those like myself, the little Brooklyn-born Bajans (Barbadians), as "these New York children" and complained that they couldn't discipline us properly because of

the laws here. "You can't beat these children as you would like, you know, because the authorities in this place will dash you in jail for them. After all, these is New York children." Not only were we different, American, we had, as they saw it, escaped their ultimate authority.

22   Confronted therefore by a world they could not encompass, which even limited their rights as parents, and at the same time finding themselves permanently separated from the world they had known, they took refuge in language. "Language is the only homeland," Czeslaw Milosz, the emigré Polish writer and Nobel Laureate, has said. This is what it became for the women at the kitchen table.

23   It served another purpose also, I suspect. My mother and her friends were after all the female counterpart of Ralph Ellison's invisible man. Indeed, you might say they suffered a triple invisibility, being black, female and foreigners. They really didn't count in American society except as a source of cheap labor. But given the kind of women they were, they couldn't tolerate the fact of their invisibility, their powerlessness. And they fought back, using the only weapon at their command: the spoken word.

24   Those late afternoon conversations on a wide range of topics were a way for them to feel they exercised some measure of control over their lives and the events that shaped them. "Soully-gal, talk yuh talk!" they were always exhorting each other. "In this man world you got to take yuh mouth and make a gun!" They were in control, if only verbally and if only for the two hours or so that they remained in our house.

25   For me, sitting over in the corner, being seen but not heard, which was the rule for children in those days, it wasn't only what the women talked about—the content—but the way they put things—their style. The insight, irony, wit and humor they brought to their stories and discussions and their poet's inventiveness and daring with language—which of course I could only sense but not define back then.

26   They had taken the standard English taught them in the primary schools of Barbados and transformed it into an idiom, an instrument that more adequately described them—changing around the syntax and imposing their own rhythm and accent so that the sentences were more pleasing to their ears. They added the few African sounds and words that had survived, such as the derisive suck-teeth sound and the word "yam," meaning to eat. And to make it more vivid, more in keeping with their expressive quality, they brought to bear a raft of metaphors, parables, Biblical quotations, sayings and the like:

27   "The sea ain' got no back door," they would say, meaning that it wasn't like a house where if there was a fire you could run out the back. Meaning that it was not to be trifled with. And meaning perhaps in a larger sense that man should treat all of nature with caution and respect.

28   "I has read hell by heart and called every generation blessed!" They sometimes went in for hyperbole.

29   A woman expecting a baby was never said to be pregnant. They never used that word. Rather, she was "in the way" or, better yet, "tumbling big." "Guess who I butt up on in the market the other day tumbling big again!"

30   And a woman with a reputation of being too free with her sexual favors was known in their book as a "thoroughfare"—the sense of men like a steady stream of cars moving up and down the road of her life. Or she might be dubbed "a free-bee," which was my favorite of the two. I liked the image it conjured up of a woman scandalous perhaps but independent, who flitted from one flower to another in a garden of male beauties, sampling their nectar, taking her pleasure at will, the roles reversed.

31   And nothing, no matter how beautiful, was ever described as simply beautiful. It was always "beautiful-ugly": the beautiful-ugly dress, the beautiful-ugly house, the beautiful-ugly car. Why the word "ugly," I used to wonder, when the thing they were referring to was beautiful, and they knew it. Why the antonym, the contradiction, the linking of opposites? It used to puzzle me greatly as a child.

32   There is the theory in linguistics which states that the idiom of a people, the way they use language, reflects not only the most fundamental views they hold of themselves and the world but their very conception of reality. Perhaps in using the term "beautiful-ugly" to describe nearly everything, my mother and her friends were expressing what they believed to be a fundamental dualism in life: the idea that a thing is at the same time its opposite, and that these opposites, these contradictions make up the whole. But theirs was not a Manichaean brand of dualism that sees matter, flesh, the body, as inherently evil, because they constantly addressed each others as "soully-gal"—soul: spirit; gal: the body, flesh, the visible self. And it was clear from their tone that they gave one as much weight and importance as the other. They had never heard of the mind/body split.

33   As for God, they summed up His essential attitude in a phrase. "God," they would say, "don't love ugly and He ain't stuck on pretty."

34   Using everyday speech, the simple commonplace words—but always with imagination and skill—they gave voice to the most complex ideas. Flannery O'Connor would have approved of how they made ordinary language work, as she put it, "doubletime," stretching, shading, deepening its meaning. Like Joseph Conrad they were always trying to infuse new life in the "old old words worn thin ... by ... careless usage." And the goals of their oral art were the same as his: "to make you hear, to make you feel ... to make you *see*." This was their guiding esthetic.

35   By the time I was 8 or 9, I graduated from the corner of the kitchen to the neighborhood library, and thus from the spoken to the written word. The Macon Street Branch of the Brooklyn Public Library was an imposing half block long edifice of heavy gray masonry, with glass-paneled doors at the front and two tall metal torches symbolizing the light that comes of learning flanking the wide steps outside.

36   The inside was just as impressive. More steps—of pale marble with gleaming brass railings at the center and sides—led up to the circulation desk, and a great pendulum clock gazed down from the balcony stacks that faced the entrance. Usually stationed at the top of the steps like the guards outside Buckingham Palace was the custodian, a stern-faced West Indian type who for years, until I was old enough to obtain an adult card, would immediately shoo me with one hand into the Children's Room and with the other threaten me into silence, a finger to his lips. You would have thought he was the chief librarian and not just someone whose job it was to keep the brass polished and the clock wound. I put him in a story called "Barbados" years later and had terrible things happen to him at the end.

37   I sheltered from the storm of adolescence in the Macon Street library, reading voraciously, indiscriminately, everything from Jane Austen to Zane Grey, but with a special passion for the long, full-blown, richly detailed 18th- and 19th-century picaresque tales: "Tom Jones," "Great Expectations," "Vanity Fair."

38   But although I loved nearly everything I read and would enter fully into the lives of the characters—indeed, would cease being myself and become them—I sensed a lack after a time. Something I couldn't quite define was missing. And then one day, browsing in the poetry section, I came across a book by someone called Paul Laurence Dunbar, and opening it I found the photograph of a wistful, sad-eyed poet who to my surprise was black. I turned to a poem at random. "Little brown-baby wif spa'klin/eyes/Come to yo' pappy an' set on his knee." Although I had a little difficulty at first with the words in dialect, the poem spoke to me as nothing I had read before of the closeness, the special relationship I had had with my father, who by then had become an ardent believer in Father Divine and gone to live in Father's "kingdom" in Harlem. Reading it helped to ease somewhat the tight knot of sorrow and longing I carried around in my chest that refused to go away. I read another poem. "'Lias! 'Lias! Bless de Lawd!/Don' you know de day's/erbroad?/Ef you don' get up, you scamp/Dey'll be trouble in dis camp." I laughed. It reminded me of the way my mother sometimes yelled at my sister and me to get out of bed in the mornings.

39   And another: "Seen my lady home las' night/jump back, honey, jump back./Hel' huh han' an' sque'z it tight..." About love between a black man and a black woman. I had never seen that written about before and it roused in me all kinds of delicious feelings and hopes.

40   And I began to search then for books and stories and poems about "The Race" (as it was put back then), about my people. While not abandoning Thackeray, Fielding, Dickens and the others, I started asking the reference librarian, who was white, for books by Negro writers, although I must admit I did so at first with a feeling of shame—the shame I and many others used to experience in those days whenever the word "Negro" or "colored" came up.

41 No grade school literature teacher of mine had ever mentioned Dunbar or James Weldon Johnson or Langston Hughes. I didn't know that Zora Neale Hurston existed and was busy writing and being published during those years. Nor was I made aware of people like Frederick Douglass and Harriet Tubman—their spirit and example—or the great 19th-century abolitionist and feminist Sojourner Truth. There wasn't even Negro History Week when I attended P.S. 35 on Decatur Street!

42 What I needed, what all the kids—West Indian and native black American alike—with whom I grew up needed, was an equivalent of the Jewish shul, someplace where we could go after school—the schools that were short-changing us—and read works by those like ourselves and learn about our history.

43 It was around that time also that I began harboring the dangerous thought of someday trying to write myself. Perhaps a poem about an apple tree, although I had never seen one. Or the story of a girl who could magically transplant herself to wherever she wanted to be in the world—such as Father Divine's kingdom in Harlem. Dunbar—his dark, eloquent face, his large volume of poems—permitted me to dream that I might someday write, and with something of the power with words my mother and her friends possessed.

44 When people at readings and writers' conferences ask me who my major influences were, they are sometimes a little disappointed when I don't immediately name the usual literary giants. True, I am indebted to those writers, white and black, whom I read during my formative years and still read for instruction and pleasure. But they were preceded in my life by another set of giants whom I always acknowledge before all others: the group of women around the table long ago. They taught me my first lessons in the narrative art. They trained my ear. They set a standard of excellence. This is why the best of my work must be attributed to them; it stands as testimony to the rich legacy of language and culture they so freely passed on to me in the word-shop of the kitchen.

1983

Richard Wilbur

THE WRITER

A distinguished poet and translator, Richard Wilbur was named Poet Laureate of the United States in 1987 and his New and Collected Poems *won a Pulitzer prize in 1989. This poem, "The Writer," makes a slender but serious argument both about artistic creativity and about parenthood. How does the image of the "dazed starling" battering against the bright window help to bring home Wilbur's point?*

In her room at the prow of the house
Where light breaks, and the windows are tossed with linden,
My daughter is writing a story.

I pause in the stairwell, hearing
From her shut door a commotion of typewriter-keys
Like a chain hauled over a gunwale.

Young as she is, the stuff
Of her life is a great cargo, and some of it heavy:
I wish her a lucky passage.

10   But now it is she who pauses,
As if to reject my thought and its easy figure.
A stillness greatens, in which

The whole house seems to be thinking,
And then she is at it again with a bunched clamor
Of strokes, and again is silent.

I remember the dazed starling
Which was trapped in that very room, two years ago;
How we stole in, lifted a sash

And retreated, not to affright it;
20   And how for a helpless hour, through the crack of the door,
We watched the sleek, wild, dark

And iridescent creature
Batter against the brilliance, drop like a glove
To the hard floor, or the desk-top,

And wait then, humped and bloody,
For the wits to try it again; and how our spirits
Rose when, suddenly sure,

It lifted off from a chair-back,
Beating a smooth course for the right window
30   And clearing the sill of the world.

It is always a matter, my darling,
Of life or death, as I had forgotten. I wish
What I wished you before, but harder.

1976

Reacting and Writing

All the essays and the poem in these groupings are admirable arguments, but no one will agree with all of them. Their intentions are incompatible with one another. When read critically, they force you to choose among them. You might try defining the issue at stake in two or more of the works, and then writing an essay of your own, taking sides. Note that the differences of opinion extend across the groupings; the essays on the arts, for example, have important implications for education. Moreover, just because you agree with an author does not mean you have to employ his or her techniques; you could, for instance, use a personal experience to argue for the position taken by one of the educators. As you read these arguments, analyzing their intentions and weighing their relative merits, you might imagine yourself overhearing a great conversation to which you have your own contribution to make.

◆ Three Essays on Education

Have you ever engaged in any of the values clarification activities described by Kilpatrick? How do you respond to his criticism of them? If you agree with him, try writing a letter from the parent of a school child to the local superintendent, explaining your concern about such exercises. If you disagree, write a letter from the superintendent to a parent who has objected to this form of education, explaining its value and answering the concerns raised by Kilpatrick.

Both Rich and Gorra are concerned with the issue of gender in education. What differences do you detect in their attitudes toward gender differences? Toward the aims of the teacher in the classroom?

All three essays assume that the classroom is a place where serious moral issues are at stake. Yet many people have argued that public education in particular should not concern itself with values, that the schools should leave such teaching to parents. What do you think?

◆ Six Essays on the Arts

Some readers might object to Forster's argument on the grounds that it is elitist. It implies that real appreciation of art requires a connoisseur like himself; ordinary people cannot understand art properly. Do you agree that this is his position? If not, can you formulate it in your own words? What do you think about the qualifications for art appreciation? How applicable are Forster's arguments to the type of music you most enjoy?

If you are interested in Didion's analysis of Georgia O'Keeffe and her work, you might find a reproduction of "Cow Skull: Red, White and Blue" and try writing a description of it. Even though you might consider yours an objective description, simply an account of what you see, when you compare it to those of your classmates, you will find that a description generally implies an aesthetic, a set of opinions about what is ugly and what is beautiful. Thus, your description makes an argument. In a revision, you could try to make your view of the painting more persuasive to a classmate who saw it quite differently.

As we mention in the headnote to "A Poem of One's Own," Mary Jo Salter addresses herself in this essay to a series of difficult questions. Choose one of these questions and then briefly summarize her answer. Then go on to add a thought of your own, agreeing or disagreeing with some aspect of Salter's response.

The three reviews of *Dances With Wolves* offer a good opportunity to sharpen your skills in analyzing intention. All could be said to have the same purpose—evaluating the film for potential viewers. Yet each seems to have a somewhat different notion of what an audience will look for in a film. What makes a worthwhile film, according to each reviewer? You might view *Dances With Wolves* and write your own analysis, for *your* audience, of its strengths and shortcomings. Or you could take a more recent film of your choosing and try to relate it to a larger issue, as Dorris does in "Indians in Aspic." (What is "aspic" and what does he mean when he claims that the film offers its Indians in it?)

◆ **Five Arguments Using Personal Experience**

These accounts of personal experiences offer a rich variety of ways to connect the private events of one's own life to wider human issues. Taking the essay that speaks most directly to you, analyze how the author makes the link from personal to public issues. Or you could take a pair of related essays and use their differences to help you see each one more clearly. For example, Kingston, López, and Marshall all reflect on the experiences of "hyphenated Americans," as López calls himself. What do they have in common and what distinguishes their experiences as Chinese-, Mexican-, and Caribbean-Americans? White uses a particular experience to make a point about the transience of human life. The pieces by Marshall and Wilbur both reflect on the sources of a writer's creativity—Kingston, Marshall, and White all look at the past from the perspective of the present. Nearly all the pieces in this section use vividly detailed but often ordinary events to convey the warmth and the tensions of life in a family, but what differences do you detect in the intention of each author toward his or her audience?

CHAPTER 3

Three Basic Tools for Making an Argument Persuasive

Once you have an audience and an intention, you are ready to begin constructing your argument. You will probably find that both your audience and your intention change as you think, write, and revise. We have already discussed how an implied audience results when you transform a particular audience in the real world into one implied by your written text. You have also seen how an intention evolves as you think about your audience and what you want it to realize or reconsider. Ancient students of argument distinguished three ways to ask for the attention and assent of an audience. They called them the three rhetorical appeals and gave them the Greek names *ethos, pathos,* and *logos.* Think of an appeal in this context as a tool with which one tries to make an argument worthy of an audience's assent.

ETHOS APPEALS

If we regard a communication as made up of three elements—the speaker or writer, the audience, and the subject—we can consider *ethos* as most closely allied to the first element. *Ethos* appeals are attempts to persuade an audience by using *the character of the speaker* as a reason for the audience to assent to the argument. (Because *ethical* has another meaning in English, we speak of *ethos* appeals rather than "ethical appeals." Unfortunately, not all *ethos* appeals are ethical.) Some writers or speakers bring a powerful *ethos* with them before they utter a word. A Nobel prize in physics makes one's opinions authoritative on the subject, especially to nonphysicists. Aristotle called this external information the speaker's "accidental *ethos*": It is made up of factors that the speaker can't change for the sake of the speech, factors such as his or her age and reputation. Frequently your accidental *ethos* is unknown to your readers, and so you have to create an appropriate image for yourself in the text, much as you created an appropriate role for your audience. Humility, wit, sincerity, candor, openmindedness—whatever the audience admires in the character of a person can be used in an *ethos* appeal. A successful *ethos* will depend in large part on the audience in question. Arguers who choose the wrong *ethos* may come on too strong or too cool or appear too arrogant (when they only mean to seem confident). Other arguers will bring to their arguments bad reputations that they will have a hard time overcoming. When members of the audience start asking themselves, "Would I buy a used car from this person?," the argument—any argument—is in deep trouble.

Some qualities will rarely appeal to any audience: pomposity, narrowmindedness, dishonesty. But whether an argument comes across as appealingly self-confident or irritatingly arrogant will depend in part on the audience. Imagine an outsider with a new idea trying to show an established, experienced group that its traditions or customary practices are wrongheaded. Tact and diplomacy will usually get that person further with his audience than bragging. He may need to admit his inexperience openly before his audience will even listen to his ideas. But in another situation, an acknowledgment of inexperience might sound too timid or defensive. These adjustments to audience are easier in person, when one can, for example, accompany an assertive remark with a modest voice and facial expression. In writing, you have only your choice of words and their arrangement to convey whatever subtleties your *ethos* may require.

A useful way to study *ethos* is to look at the introductions to essays. Authors and speakers have to introduce themselves, by their tone if nothing else. Some will introduce themselves as authorities. Thus, an essayist on student protests will begin his essay: "In several years of fighting for, fighting against, and simply observing student revolts in the U.S. and Europe, I have been struck by certain recurring patterns of action and internationally common styles in the rhetoric of confrontation. Leaving out the student revolts in Turkey, Czechoslovakia, and Spain—all of which have special features—and confining ourselves to the U.S. and the advanced western democracies of Western Europe, it seems to me. . . ." The author has made sure that the "me" to whom "it seems" is someone whose opinion is more authoritative than the opinions of almost all of his readers. Who among his readers knows about the special features of the recent student unrest in Turkey?

In an essay arguing for the legalization of marijuana, the author is concerned that we know immediately that he is an authority who has no personal stake in the legalization. So he begins: "There are an estimated 10,000,000 Americans who smoke marijuana either regularly or occasionally, and they have very obvious reasons for wishing that pot were treated more sensibly by the law. As one of the 190,000,000 who have never smoked marijuana, I also favor decriminalizing its use, but for less personal reasons. It is my considered opinion, after studying drug use and drug laws in 30 nations and dealing with drug abuse problems professionally for 15 years. . . ."

Frequently an author will try to have his cake and eat it too—that is, he or she will try to be both an expert and also someone with whom the audience can identify. In the following introduction, for instance, C. P. Snow is at pains to make sure his readers do not feel inferior to him just because he has become famous for having written a brilliant book deploring what he called the two cultures of science and humanities.

1   It is about three years since I made a sketch in print of a problem which had been on my mind for some time. It was a problem I could not avoid just because of the circumstances of my life. The only credentials I had to ruminate on the subject at all came through those circumstances, through nothing more than a set of chances. Anyone with similar experience would have seen much the same things and I think made very much the same comments about them. It just happened to be an unusual experience. By training I was a scientist; by vocation I was a writer. That was all. It was a piece of luck, if you like, that arose through coming from a poor home.

2   But my personal history isn't the point now. All that I need say is that I came to Cambridge and did a bit of research here at a time of major scientific activity. I was privileged to have a ringside view of one of the most wonderful creative periods in all physics. And it happened through the flukes of war—including meeting W. L. Bragg in the buffet on Kettering station on a very cold morning in 1939, which had a determining influence on my practical life—that I was able, and indeed morally forced, to keep that ringside view ever since. So for thirty years I have had to be in touch with scientists not only out of curiosity, but as a part of a working existence. During the same thirty years I was trying to shape the books I wanted to write, which in due course took me among writers.

Morris Zuckerman, on the other hand, gains the attention of members of his audience by telling them that he used to agree with them on the subject at hand, U. S. policy in Central America. It is only now, after having had special experience, that he knows better. He is going to share that experience with them so that they can find agreement once again.

1   Because of enormous public confusion over the United States' involvement in Central America, I recently visited the region with a delegation of Congressmen to see it first-hand. I went holding political views of El Salvador and Nicaragua shared by many liberals and centrists in our nation. I returned impressed with the effectiveness of United States policy and convinced that we need to be involved.

2   I had thought that in El Salvador we were engaged in wrong-headed and dangerous military action on behalf of a repressive Government, and that Washington had failed to address economic and political grievances built up after decades of injustice. I went with the impression that the guerrillas seemed to have won popular support for their efforts to revolutionize the political system. My instinct was that this was only an internal struggle, not an East-West competition, and that once again we were backing the wrong side for the wrong reason.

3   But I returned home with the sense that United States military support was critical for physical security in the countryside, which, in turn, is necessary to guarantee ordinary Salvadorans [the] ability to make free choices. I also concluded that our military support is essential. . . .

In these cases *ethos* is being used to prepare for the main body of the argument. Sometimes, however, the *ethos* can carry a whole argument. A twelve-year-old boy writes to Supreme Court Justice Felix Frankfurter to ask how he can start preparing himself for the bar. Frankfurter responds by telling him to "forget all about any technical preparation for the law.... Stock your mind with the deposit of much good reading, and widen and deepen your feelings by experiencing vicariously as much as possible the wonderful mysteries of the universe and forget all about your future career." Why should the boy be persuaded? To put it crudely, because of the letterhead; Justice Frankfurter would know what it takes to be a good lawyer, if anyone would. And why would he lie?

Of course, *ethos* can cut both ways. A story is told of an old justice on the Supreme Court who stayed on long after he could follow the technicalities of the cases. He was asked by a sympathetic friend how he could continue in good conscience under the circumstances. He replied that he always knew exactly how to vote on controversial cases. He would just find out how the Chief Justice was voting and then vote the contrary.

Sometimes the very intensity of conviction that a writer or speaker expresses will carry an audience along, especially if the audience is already sympathetic to the point of view. So Martin Luther King Jr.'s most famous speech was carried along by the refrain, "I have a dream." The audience is invited to identify with and be uplifted by that visionary *ethos* so like the *ethos* of the prophets in the Bible.

Sometimes a work will be carried by the self-deprecation of the author. The essays of Montaigne have been cherished for four hundred years by a succession of readers who have found his humble and humbling *ethos* irresistible, an *ethos* that is first evoked in his gently ironic preface.

1 This book was written in good faith, reader. It warns you from the outset that in it I have set myself no goal but a domestic and private one. I have had no thought of serving either you or my own glory. My powers are inadequate for such a purpose. I have dedicated it to the private convenience of my relatives and friends, so that when they have lost me (as soon they must), they may recover here some features of my habits and temperament, and by this means keep the knowledge they have had of me more complete and alive.

2 If I had written to seek the world's favor, I should have bedecked myself better, and should present myself in a studied posture. I want to be seen here in my simple, natural, ordinary fashion, without straining or artifice; for it is myself that I portray. My defects will here be read to the life, and also my natural form, as far as respect for the public has allowed. Had I been placed among those nations which are said to live still in the sweet freedom of nature's first laws, I assure you I should very gladly have portrayed myself here entire and wholly naked.

3 Thus, reader, I am myself the matter of my book; you would be unreasonable to spend your leisure on so frivolous and vain a subject.

4 So farewell. Montaigne, this first day of March, fifteen hundred and eighty.

Sometimes authors will entirely efface themselves in order to have their readers forget about their existence. They are purely objective and dispassionate reporters concerning their subject. Hence, the philosopher George Santayana begins an essay on liberty: "When ancient peoples defended what they called their liberty the word stood for a plain and urgent interest of theirs: that their cities should not be destroyed, their territories pillaged, and they themselves sold into slavery. For the Greeks in particular liberty means even more than this." Forgetting about Santayana as an individual, we might be lulled into thinking that we are just getting the facts, rather than Santayana's interpretation of them (which, by the way, is quite idiosyncratic).

Most of us, if we are candid, will admit that at least as many of our decisions are based on the character of others as on our own independent investigation of the issues. All you have to do is look at the endorsements on both sides of an issue to be pretty sure how you will decide. And the issue in question can be anything from AIDS funding to the merits of a recent action movie. (President Clinton wants more funding, but Congress doesn't; Siskel and Ebert vote thumbs down, but *USA Today* loves it.) And to be persuasive we have to learn how to control our own *ethos*. In the following excerpt, Benjamin Franklin has just realized that he is in the decided minority on an issue being considered by the convention that is establishing the constitution for the United States.

> It is with reluctance that I rise to express a disapprobation of any one article of the plan, for which we are so much obliged to the honorable gentleman who laid it before us. From its first reading, I have borne a good will to it, and, in general, wished it success. In this particular of salaries to the executive branch, I happen to differ; and, as my opinion may appear new and chimerical, it is only from a persuasion that it is right, and from a sense of duty, that I hazard it. The Committee will judge of my reasons when they have heard them, and their judgment may possibly change mine.

Reading that paragraph, you realize that Franklin was not often in the minority for long.

M. F. K. Fisher

THE GASTRONOMICAL ME

The opening paragraph of this brief selection states succinctly the ethos *problem that Fisher faces: can an audience take a "food writer" seriously as a writer? This piece was originally the foreword to a volume of her collected writings, and it answers in a very small space what she imagines to be her audience's questions on picking up such a book: Am I going to read a whole book about food? About the preparation and serving of food? And yet not a cook-*

book, but a book? Do you find Fisher's answer to this question persuasive? How does her writing style help to enhance her ethos? This piece is followed by one of her longer essays, "The Measure of My Powers." As you read that selection, consider how well it bears out her claim here that "when I write of hunger, I am really writing about love and the hunger for it."

1   People ask me: Why do you write about food, and eating and drinking? Why don't you write about the struggle for power and security, and about love, the way others do?

2   They ask it accusingly, as if I were somehow gross, unfaithful to the honor of my craft.

3   The easiest answer is to say that, like most other humans, I am hungry. But there is more than that. It seems to me that our three basic needs, for food and security and love, are so mixed and mingled and entwined that we cannot straightly think of one without the others. So it happens that when I write of hunger, I am really writing about love and the hunger for it, and warmth and the love of it and the hunger for it . . . and then the warmth and richness and fine reality of hunger satisfied . . . and it is all one.

4   I tell about myself, and how I ate bread on a lasting hillside, or drank red wine in a room now blown to bits, and it happens without my willing it that I am telling too about the people with me then, and their other deeper needs for love and happiness.

5   There is food in the bowl, and more often than not, because of what honesty I have, there is nourishment in the heart, to feed the wilder, more insistent hungers. We must eat. If, in the face of that dread fact, we can find other nourishment, and tolerance and compassion for it, we'll be no less full of human dignity.

6   There is a communion of more than our bodies when bread is broken and wine drunk. And that is my answer, when people ask me: Why do you write about hunger, and not wars or love?

1937

M. F. K. Fisher

THE MEASURE OF MY POWERS

In the previous piece, we saw Fisher carefully establishing her ethos, considering in what way a "food writer" can be a real writer. Here, she spends the first half of her essay describing dismal failures in the kitchen, an early effort at pudding that made her mother sick and an ill-fated invention called "Hindu Eggs" that blistered her little sister's lips. Clearly she can afford to make herself vulnerable as a cook; these events were long ago and she has had so many triumphs since that she does not spare herself—if anything, one wonders if she has exaggerated a bit. If one of her aims is to involve her reader in the joys of nourishing one's "beloved few," why might she begin with an account of these calamities? How do you feel about her as a person and as a cook when you finish the essay?

1   The first thing I cooked was pure poison. I made it for Mother, after my little brother David was born, and within twenty minutes of the first swallow she was covered with great itching red welts. The doctor came, soda compresses were laid on, sedatives and mild physic were scattered about, and all subsided safely…except my feeling of deep shock and hurt professional pride. As the nurse, Miss Faulck, pointed out, I should have been content to let well enough alone.

2   The pudding was safe enough: a little round white shuddering milky thing I had made that morning under the stern eye of Miss Faulck and whoever it was that succeeded mad Ora in the kitchen. It had "set" correctly. It was made according to the directions for Invalid Cookery in Mother's best recipe book, and I had cleaned my fingernails until tears filled my eyes before I touched so much as the box of cornstarch.

3   Then, in the middle of the afternoon, when the pudding slid with a chill plop into the saucer, I knew that I could not stand to present it, my first culinary triumph, in its naked state. It was obscenely pure, obscenely colorless.

4   A kind of loyalty to Ora rose in me, and without telling Miss Faulck I ran into the back yard and picked ten soft ripe blackberries. I blew off the alley-dust, and placed them gently in a perfect circle around the little pudding. Its cool perfection leaped into sudden prettiness, like Miss America when the winning ribbon is hung across her high-breasted symmetry.

5   And even a little while later, when Mother lay covered with compresses and Miss Faulck pursed her lips and David howled for a meal he couldn't have because he might drink hive-juice, Mother smiled at my shocked anxious confusion, and said, "Don't worry, sweet…it was the loveliest pudding I have ever seen."

6   I agreed with her in spite of the despair.

7   I can't remember ever learning anything, that is, I don't hear Mother's voice saying to me, "Now this is a teaspoon, and this is the way you sift flour, and warm eggs won't make mayonnaise…." But evidently I loved to cook, and she taught me several things without making them into lessons, because in the next few years I knew how to make white sauce, and cup cakes with grated orange rind in them. (Father was always very complimentary about them, and Anne and I loved to save ours until the rest of the family had left

the table, and then cover them with cream and sugar and eat them with a spoon.)

8   I could make jelly rolls, too, which seems odd now; I don't think I've even tasted one since I was about ten, much less had any interest in putting one together.

9   I loved to read cookbooks (unlike my feeling for jelly roll that passion has grown stronger with the years), and inevitably I soon started to improve on what I had read. Once I made poor Anne share my proud misery with something I called Hindu Eggs. I was sure I had read about it in Fanny Farmer; all you did was add curry powder to a white sauce and pour it over sliced hard-boiled eggs.

10   When Mother said she and Father would be away one night, and I might get supper alone, I hid the gleam in my eye when she told me to put the sauce and the eggs in a casserole, and be sure to drink milk, and open a jar of plums or something for dessert.

11   "Yes, Mother, I know I can do it," I said smoothly, and the word *Hindu* danced sensuously in my mind, safely unsaid until Mother was out of the house.

12   The casserole was handsome, too, when Anne and I sat down to it in exciting solitude at the big table. Anne admired me, there was no doubt of it . . . and I admired myself. The rich brown sauce bubbled and sent out puffs of purely Oriental splendor. I sat in Father's place, and served each of us generously.

13   The first bite, and perhaps the next two or three, were all right; we were hungry, and in a hurry to feel the first warmth in our little bellies. Then Anne put down her fork. She beat me to it, so I continued to hold mine, determined like any honest cook to support my product.

14   "It's too hot, it burns," my little sister said, and gulped at her milk.

15   "Blow on it," I instructed. "Mother's not here."

16   We blew, and I ate three more bites to Anne's dutiful one. The heat seemed to increase. My influence over Anne must have been persuasive as well as autocratic in those far days, because she ate most of what was on her plate before the tears started rolling down her round brown cheeks.

17   I ate all mine, proudly, but inside I was cold with the new knowledge that I had been stupid. I had thought I remembered a recipe when I didn't, and I had used curry without knowing anything about it, and when the sauce looked boringly white I had proceeded to make it richly darker with probably five tablespoonfuls of the exotic powder.

18   I ate all I could, for fear Father would see how much we threw into the garbage pail, and then after my sweet forgiving little sister helped me straighten the kitchen we went upstairs and, with the desperate intuition of burned animals, sat on the edge of the bathtub for a long time with our mouths full of mineral oil. She never said anything more about it, either; and the next morning there were only a few blisters, just inside our lips.

19   When I was eleven we all moved to the country. We had a cow and chickens, and partly because of that and partly because Grandmother had died we began to eat more richly.

20   We had chocolate puddings with chopped nuts and heavy cream. The thought of them makes me dizzy now, but we loved them. And lots of butter: I was good at churning, and learned very well how to sterilize the wooden churn and make the butter and then roll it into fine balls and press it into molds. I liked that. And we could have mayonnaise, rich yellow with eggs and oil, instead of the boiled dressing Grandmother's despotic bowels and stern palate called for.

21   Mother, in an orgy of baking brought on probably by all the beautiful eggs and butter lying around, spent every Saturday morning making cakes. They were piled high with icings. They were filled with crushed almonds, chopped currants, and an outrageous number of calories. They were beautiful. Saturday afternoons they sat cooling, along with Mother and the kitchen after the hectic morning, and by Sunday night they were already a pleasant if somewhat bilious memory.

22   After about a year of this luscious routine, Mother retired more or less permanently to the front part of the house, perhaps with half an eye on the bathroom scales, but before she gave up cooking, I learned a lot about cakes from her. The fact that I have never made one since then—at least, the kind with many layers and fillings and icings and all that—has little to do with the gratitude I have often felt for knowing how to measure and sift and be patient and not be daunted by disappointment.

23   Mother, like all artists, was one-sided. She only cooked what she herself liked. She knew very little about meats, so I gradually learned all that myself. She hated gravies, and any sauces but "white sauce" (probably a hangover from Grandmother's training), so I made some hideous mistakes with them. And there was always an element of surprise, if not actual danger, in my meals; the Hindu eggs had larned me but not curbed my helpless love of anything rare or racy.

24   But in spite of all that, I was the one who got dinner on the cook's off-night. I improved, there is no doubt about it, and it was taken for granted that I would step into the kitchen at the drop of a hat.

25   Perhaps Anne would have liked a chance at having all the family's attention for those few hours. If so she never got it. The stove, the bins, the cupboards, I had learned forever, make an inviolable throne room. From them I ruled; temporarily I controlled. I felt powerful, and I loved that feeling.

26   I am more modest now, but I still think that one of the pleasantest of all emotions is to know that I, I with my brain and my hands, have nourished my beloved few, that I have concocted a stew or a story, a rarity or a plain dish, to sustain them truly against the hungers of the world.

1954

A. J. Liebling

AHAB AND NEMESIS

If M. F. K. Fisher anticipates a certain skepticism in her audience about whether food can be a serious subject for a writer, Liebling has a challenge as great or greater in winning an audience for a demanding and thoughtful essay about boxing. Notice that his very first sentence is about a "durable account" of a boxing match by an earlier writer. Liebling thus raises for his audience the possibility that at least some writing about boxing is of enduring interest, even after most people have forgotten the match in question. Notice how easily Liebling's first paragraph moves from boxers to the writer Gertrude Stein and to nonrepresentational painting. In paragraph 3, we find another boxing writer, one who was, according to Liebling, "the Edward Gibbon and Sir Thomas Malory of the old London prize ring." By comparing a boxing writer to Gibbon, author of the monumental Decline and Fall of the Roman Empire, *and Malory, author of an epic account of King Arthur and his knights, Liebling establishes both that he has a sense of humor and that his reading is not limited to sports coverage. By beginning with his predecessors, Liebling skillfully creates a tradition for himself of serious and lasting writing about boxing. If he had chosen to write about Gertrude Stein, or nonrepresentational painting, or the Roman Empire, or King Arthur, establishing this tradition might not be necessary. But, given the nature of his subject, attention to* ethos *might be important in determining whether his writing proves "durable" and whether it finds an audience outside the world of sports writing.*

1 Back in 1922, the late Heywood Broun, who is not remembered primarily as a boxing writer, wrote a durable account of a combat between the late Benny Leonard and the late Rocky Kansas for the lightweight championship of the world. Leonard was the greatest practitioner of the era, Kansas just a rough, optimistic fellow. In the early rounds Kansas messed Leonard about, and Broun was profoundly disturbed. A radical in politics, he was a conservative in the arts, and Kansas made him think of Gertrude Stein, *Les Six*, and nonrepresentational painting, all novelties that irritated him.

2 "With the opening gong, Rocky Kansas tore into Leonard," he wrote, "He was gauche and inaccurate, but terribly persistent." The classic verities prevailed, however. After a few rounds, during which Broun continued to yearn for a return to a culture with fixed values, he was enabled to record, "The young child of nature who was challenging for the championship dropped his guard, and Leonard hooked a powerful and entirely orthodox blow to the conventional point of the jaw. Down went Rocky Kansas. His past life flashed

before him during the nine seconds in which he remained on the floor, and he wished that he had been more faithful as a child in heeding the advice of his boxing teacher. After all, the old masters did know something. There is still a kick in style, and tradition carries a nasty wallop."

3   I have often thought of Broun's words in the years since Rocky Marciano, the reigning heavyweight champion, scaled the fistic summits, as they say in *Journal-Americanese,* by beating Jersey Joe Walcott. The current Rocky is gauche and inaccurate, but besides being persistent he is a dreadfully severe hitter with either hand. The predominative nature of this asset has been well stated by Pierce Egan, the Edward Gibbon and Sir Thomas Malory of the old London prize ring, who was less preoccupied than Broun with ultimate implications. Writing in 1821 of a milling cove named Bill Neat, the Bristol Butcher, Egan said, "He possesses a requisite above all the art that *teaching* can achieve for any boxer; namely, *one hit* from his right hand, given in proper distance, can gain a victory; but three of them are positively enough to dispose of a giant." This is true not only of Marciano's right hand but of his left hand, too—provided he doesn't miss the giant entirely. Egan doubted the advisability of changing Neat's style, and he would have approved of Marciano's. The champion has an apparently unlimited absorptive capacity for percussion (Egan would have called him an "insatiable glutton") and inexhaustible energy ("a prime bottom fighter"). "Shifting," or moving to the side, and "milling in retreat," or moving back, are innovations of the late eighteenth century that Rocky's advisers have carefully kept from his knowledge, lest they spoil his natural prehistoric style. Egan excused these tactics only in boxers of feeble constitution.

4   Archie Moore, the light-heavyweight champion of the world, who hibernates in San Diego, California, and estivates in Toledo, Ohio, is a Brounian rather than an Eganite in his thinking about style, but he naturally has to do more than think about it. Since the rise of Marciano, Moore, a cerebral and hyper-experienced light-colored pugilist who has been active since 1936, has suffered the pangs of a supreme exponent of *bel canto* who sees himself crowded out of the opera house by a guy who can only shout. As a sequel to a favorable review I wrote of one of his infrequent New York appearances, when his fee was restricted to a measly five figures, I received a sad little note signed "The most unappreciated fighter in the world, Archie Moore." A fellow who has as much style as Moore tends to overestimate the intellect—he develops the kind of Faustian mind that will throw itself against the problem of perpetual motion, or of how to pick horses first, second, third, *and* fourth in every race. Archie's note made it plain to me that he was honing his harpoon for the White Whale.

5   When I read newspaper items about Moore's decisioning a large, playful porpoise of a Cuban heavyweight named Nino Valdes and scoop-netting a minnow like Bobo Olson, the middleweight champion, for practice, I thought

of him as a lonely Ahab, rehearsing to buck Herman Melville, Pierce Egan, and the betting odds. I did not think that he could bring it off, but I wanted to be there when he tried. What would *Moby Dick* be if Ahab had succeeded? Just another fish story. The thing that is eternally diverting is the struggle of man against history—or what Albert Camus, who used to be an amateur middleweight, has called the Myth of Sisyphus. (Camus would have been a great man to cover the fight, but none of the syndicates thought of it.) When I heard that the boys had been made for September 20, 1955, at the Yankee Stadium, I shortened my stay abroad in order not to miss the Encounter of the Two Heroes, as Egan would have styled the rendezvous.

6   In London on the night of September 13, a week before the date set for the Encounter, I tried to get my eye in for fight-watching by attending a bout at the White City greyhound track between Valdes, who had been imported for the occasion, and the British Empire heavyweight champion, Don Cockell, a fat man whose gift for public suffering has enlisted the sympathy of a sentimental people. Since Valdes had gone fifteen rounds with Moore in Las Vegas the previous May, and Cockell had excruciated for nine rounds before being knocked out by Marciano in San Francisco in the same month, the bout offered a dim opportunity for establishing what racing people call a "line" between Moore and Marciano. I didn't get much of an optical workout, because Valdes disposed of Cockell in three rounds. It was evident that Moore and Marciano had not been fighting the same class of people this season.

7   This was the only fight I ever attended in a steady rainstorm. It had begun in the middle of the afternoon, and, while there was a canopy over the ring, the spectators were as wet as speckled trout. "The weather, it is well known, has no terrors to the admirers of Pugilism of Life," Egan once wrote, and on his old stamping ground this still holds true. As I took my seat in a rock pool that had collected in the hollow of my chair, a South African giant named Ewart Potgieter, whose weight had been announced as 22 stone 10, was ignoring the doctrine of apartheid by leaning on a Jamaican colored man who weighed a mere 16 stone, and by the time I had transposed these statistics to 318 pounds and 224 pounds, respectively, the exhausted Jamaican had acquiesced in resegregation and retired. The giant had not struck a blow, properly speaking, but had shoved downward a number of times, like a man trying to close an overfilled trunk.

8   The main bout proved an even less grueling contest. Valdes, eager to get out of the chill, struck Cockell more vindictively than is his wont, and after a few gestures invocative of commiseration, the fat man settled in one corner of the ring as heavily as suet pudding upon the unaccustomed gastric system. He had received what Egan would have called a "ribber" and a "nobber," and when he arose it was seen that the latter had raised a cut on his forehead. At the end of the third round, his manager withdrew him from competition. It was not an inspiring occasion, but after the armistice eight or nine shivering

Cubans appeared in the runway behind the press section and jumped up and down to register emotion and restore circulation. *"Ahora Marciano!"* they yelled. "Now for Marciano!" Instead of being grateful for the distraction, the other spectators took a poor view of it. "Sit down, you chaps!" one of them cried. "We want to see the next do!" They were still parked out there in the rain when I tottered into the Shepherd's Bush underground station and collapsed, sneezing, on a train that eventually disgorged me at Oxford Circus, with just enough time left to buy a revivifying draught before eleven o'clock, when the pubs closed. How the mugs I left behind cured themselves I never knew. They had to do it on Bovril.

9   Because I had engagements that kept me in England until a few days before the Encounter, I had no opportunity to visit the training camps of the rival American Heroes. I knew all the members of both factions, however, and I could imagine what they were thinking. In the plane on the way home, I tried to envision the rival patterns of ratiocination. I could be sure that Marciano, a kind, quiet, imperturbable fellow, would plan to go after Moore and make him fight continuously until he tired enough to become an accessible target. After that he would expect concussion to accentuate exhaustion and exhaustion to facilitate concussion, until Moore came away from his consciousness, like everybody else Rocky had ever fought. He would try to remember to minimize damage to himself in the beginning, while there was still snap in Moore's arms, because Moore is a sharp puncher. (Like Bill Neat of old, Marciano hits at his opponent's arms when he cannot hit past them. "In one instance, the arm of Oliver [a Neat adversary] received so paralyzing a shock in stopping the blow that it appeared almost useless," Egan once wrote.) Charlie Goldman would have instructed Marciano in some rudimentary maneuver to throw Moore's first shots off, I felt sure, but after a few minutes Rocky would forget it, or Archie would figure it out. But there would always be Freddie Brown, the "cut man," in the champion's corner to repair superficial damage. One reason Goldman is a great teacher is that he doesn't try to teach a boxer more than he can learn. What he had taught Rocky in the four years since I had first seen him fight was to shorten the arc of most of his blows without losing power thereby, and always to follow one hard blow with another—"for insurance"—delivered with the other hand, instead of recoiling to watch the victim fall. The champion had also gained confidence and presence of mind; he has a good fighting head, which is not the same thing as being a good mechanical practitioner.

10   "A *boxer* requires a *nob* as well as a *statesman* does a HEAD, coolness and calculation being essential to *second* his efforts," Egan wrote, and the old historiographer was never more correct. Rocky was thirty-one, not in the first flush of youth for a boxer, but Moore was only a few days short of thirty-nine, so age promised to be in the champion's favor if he kept pressing.

11   Moore's strategic problem, I reflected on the plane, offered more choices and, as a corollary, infinitely more chances for error. It was possible, but not probable, that jabbing and defensive skill would carry him through fifteen

rounds, even on those old legs, but I knew that the mere notion of such a *gambade* would revolt Moore. He is not what Egan would have called a shy fighter. Besides, would Ahab have been content merely to go the distance with the White Whale? I felt sure that Archie planned to knock the champion out, so that he could sign his next batch of letters "The most appreciated and deeply opulent fighter in the world." I surmised that this project would prove a mistake, like Mr. Churchill's attempt to take Gallipoli in 1915, but it would be the kind of mistake that would look good in his memoirs.

12 The basis of what I rightly anticipated would prove a miscalculation went back to Archie's academic background. As a young fighter of conventional tutelage, he must have heard his preceptors say hundreds of times, "They will all go if you hit them right." If a fighter did not believe that, he would be in the position of a Euclidian without faith in the 180-degree triangle. Moore's strategy, therefore, would be based on working Marciano into a position where he could hit him right. He would not go in and slug with him, because that would be wasteful, distasteful, and injudicious, but he might try to cut him up, in an effort to slow him down so he could hit him right, or else try to hit him right and then cut him up. The puzzle he reserved for me—and Marciano—was the tactic by which he would attempt to attain his strategic objective. In the formation of his views, I believed, Moore would be handicapped, rather than aided, by his active, skeptical mind. One of the odd things about Marciano is that he isn't terribly big. It is hard for a man like Moore, just under six feet tall and weighing about 180 pounds, to imagine that a man approximately the same size can be immeasurably stronger than he is. This is particularly true when, like the light-heavyweight champion, he has spent his whole professional life contending with boxers—some of them considerably bigger—whose strength has proved so near his own that he could move their arms and bodies by cunning pressures. The old classicist would consequently refuse to believe what he was up against.

13 The light-heavyweight limit is 175 pounds, and Moore can get down to that when he must, in order to defend his title, but in a heavyweight match each Hero is allowed to weigh whatever he pleases. I was back in time to attend the weighing-in ceremonies, held in the lobby of Madison Square Garden at noon on the day set for the Encounter, and learned that Moore weighed 188 and Marciano 188¼—a lack of disparity that figured to encourage the rationalist's illusions. I also learned that, in contrast to Jack Solomons—the London promoter who held the Valdes-Cockell match in the rain—the I.B.C., which was promoting the Encounter, had decided to postpone it for twenty-four hours, although the weather was clear. The decision was based on apprehension of Hurricane Ione, which, although apparently veering away from New York, might come around again like a lazy left hook and drop in on the point of the Stadium's jaw late in the evening. Nothing like that happened, but the postponement brought the town's theaters and bars another evening of good business from the out-of-town fight trade, such as they always get on the eve of a memorable Encounter. ("Not a bed could be

had at any of the villages at an early hour on the preceding evening; and Uxbridge was crowded beyond all former precedent," Egan wrote of the night before Neat beat Oliver.) There was no doubt that the fight had caught the public imagination, ever sensitive to a meeting between Hubris and Nemesis, as the boys on the quarterlies would say, and the bookies were laying eighteen to five on Nemesis, according to the boys on the dailies who always seem to hear. (A friend of mine up from Maryland with a whim and a five-dollar bill couldn't get ten against it in ordinary barroom money anywhere, although he wanted Ahab.)

14   The enormous—by recent precedent—advance sale of tickets had so elated the I.B.C. that it had decided to replace the usual card of bad preliminary fights with some not worth watching at all, so there was less distraction than usual as we awaited the appearance of the Heroes on the fateful evening. The press seats had been so closely juxtaposed that I could fit in only sidewise between two colleagues—the extra compression having been caused by the injection of a prewar number of movie stars and politicos.

15   The tight quarters were an advantage, in a way, since they facilitated my conversation with Peter Wilson, an English prize-ring correspondent, who happened to be in the row behind me. I had last seen Mr. Wilson at White City the week before, at a time when the water level had already reached his shredded-Latakia mustache. I had feared that he had drowned at ringside, but when I saw him at the Stadium, he assured me that by buttoning the collar of his mackintosh tightly over his nostrils, he had been able to make the garment serve as a diving lung, and so survive. Like all British fight writers when they are relieved of the duty of watching British fighters, he was in a holiday mood, and we chatted happily.

16   There is something about the approach of a good fight that renders the spirit insensitive to annoyance; it is only when the amateur of the Sweet Science has some doubts as to how good the main bout will turn out to be that he is avid for the satisfaction to be had from the preliminaries. This is because after the evening is over, he may have only a good supporting fight to remember. There were no such doubts—even in the minds of the mugs who had paid for their seats—on the evening of September 21.

17   At about ten-thirty the champion and his faction entered the ring. It is not customary for the champion to come in first, but Marciano has never been a stickler for protocol. He is a humble, kindly fellow, who even now will approach an acquaintance on the street and say bashfully, "Remember me? I'm Rocky Marciano." The champion doesn't mind waiting five or ten minutes to give anybody a punch in the nose. In any case, once launched from his dressing room under the grandstand, he could not have arrested his progress to the ring, because he had about forty policemen pushing behind him, and three more clearing a path in front of him. Marciano, tucked in behind the third cop like a football ball-carrier behind his interference, had to run or be

trampled to death. Wrapped in a heavy blue bathrobe and with a blue monk's cowl pulled over his head, he climbed the steps to the ring with the cumbrous agility of a medieval executioner ascending the scaffold. Under the hood he seemed to be trying to look serious. He has an intellectual appreciation of the anxieties of a champion, but he has a hard time forgetting how strong he is; while he remembers that, he can't worry as much as he knows a champion should. His attendants—quick, battered little Goldman; Al Weill, the stout, excitable manager, always stricken just before the bell with the suspicion that he may have made a bad match; Al Columbo—are all as familiar to the crowd as he is.

18   Ahab's party arrived in the ring a minute or so later, and Charlie Johnston, his manager—a calm sparrow hawk of a man, as old and wise in the game as Weill—went over to watch Goldman put on the champion's gloves. Freddie Brown went to Moore's corner to watch *his* gloves being put on. Moore wore a splendid black silk robe with a gold lamé collar and belt. He sports a full mustache above an imperial, and his hair, sleeked down under pomade when he opens operations, invariably rises during the contest, as it gets water sloshed on it between rounds and the lacquer washes off, until it is standing up like the top of a shaving brush. Seated in his corner in the shadow of his personal trainer, a brown man called Cheerful Norman, who weighs 235 pounds, Moore looked like an old Japanese print I have of a "Shogun Engaged in Strategic Contemplation in the Midst of War." The third member of his group was Bertie Briscoe, a rough, chipper little trainer, whose more usual charge is Sandy Saddler, the featherweight champion—also a Johnston fighter. Mr. Moore's features in repose rather resemble those of Orson Welles, and he was reposing with intensity.

19   The procession of other fighters and former fighters to be introduced was longer than usual. The full galaxy was on hand, including Jack Dempsey, Gene Tunney, and Joe Louis, the *têtes de cuvée* of former-champion society; ordinary former heavyweight champions, like Max Baer and Jim Braddock, slipped through the ropes practically unnoticed. After all the celebrities had been in and out of the ring, an odd dwarf, advertising something or other— possibly himself—was lifted into the ring by an accomplice and ran across it before he could be shooed out. The referee, a large, craggy, oldish man named Harry Kessler, who, unlike some of his better-known colleagues, is not an ex-fighter, called the men to the center of the ring.

20   This was his moment; he had the microphone. "Now, Archie and Rocky, I want a nice, clean fight," he said, and I heard a peal of silvery laughter behind me from Mr. Wilson, who had seen both of them fight before. "Protect yourself at all times," Mr. Kessler cautioned them unnecessarily. When the principals shook hands, I could see Mr. Moore's eyebrows rising like storm clouds over the Sea of Azov. His whiskers bristled and his eyes glowed like dark coals as he scrunched his eyebrows down again and enveloped the

Whale with the Look, which was intended to dominate his willpower. Mr. Wilson and I were sitting behind Marciano's corner, and as he came back to it, I observed his expression, to determine what effect the Look had had upon him. More than ever, he resembled a Great Dane who has heard the word "bone."

21   A moment later the bell rang, and the Heroes came out for the first round. Marciano, training in the sun for weeks, had tanned to a slightly deeper tint than Moore's old ivory, and Moore, at 188, looked, if anything, bigger and more muscular than Marciano; much of the champion's weight is in his legs, and his shoulders slope. Marciano advanced, but Moore didn't go far away. As usual, he stood up nicely, his arms close to his body and his feet not too far apart, ready to go anywhere but not without a reason—the picture of a powerful, decisive intellect unfettered by preconceptions. Marciano, pulling his left arm back from the shoulder, flung a left hook. He missed, but not by enough to discourage him, and then walked in and hooked again. All through the round he threw those hooks, and some of them grazed Moore's whiskers; one even hit him on the side of the head. Moore didn't try much offensively; he held a couple of times when Marciano worked in close.

22   Marciano came back to his corner as he always does, unimpassioned. He hadn't expected to catch Moore with those left hooks anyway, I imagine; all he had wanted was to move him around. Moore went to his corner inscrutable. They came out for the second, and Marciano went after him in brisker fashion. In the first round he had been throwing the left hook, missing with it, and then throwing a right and missing with that, too. In the second he tried a variation—throwing a right and then pulling a shoulder back to throw the left. It appeared for a moment to have Moore confused, as a matador might be confused by a bull who walked in on his hind legs. Marciano landed a couple of those awkward hooks, but not squarely. He backed Moore over toward the side of the ring farthest from me, and then Moore knocked him down.

23   Some of the reporters, describing the blow in the morning papers, called it a "sneak punch," which is journalese for one the reporter didn't see but technically means a lead thrown before the other man has warmed up or while he is musing about the gate receipts. This had been no lead, and although I certainly hadn't seen Moore throw the punch, I knew that it had landed inside the arc of Marciano's left hook. ("Marciano missed with the right, trun the left, and Moore stepped inside it," my private eye, Whitey Bimstein, said next day, confirming my diagnosis, and the film of the fight bore both of us out.) So Ahab had his harpoon in the Whale. He had hit him right if ever I saw a boxer hit right, with a classic brevity and conciseness. Marciano stayed down for two seconds. I do not know what took place in Mr. Moore's breast when he saw him get up. He may have felt, for the moment, like Don Giovanni when the Commendatore's statue grabbed at him—startled because he thought he had killed the guy already—or like Ahab when he

saw the Whale take down Fedallah, harpoons and all. Anyway, he hesitated a couple of seconds, and that was reasonable. A man who took nine to come up after a punch like that would be doing well, and the correct tactic would be to go straight in and finish him. But a fellow who came up on two was so strong he would bear investigation.

24   After that, Moore did go in, but not in a crazy way. He hit Marciano some good, hard, classic shots, and inevitably Marciano, a trader, hit him a few devastating swipes, which slowed him. When the round ended, the edge of Moore's speed was gone, and he knew that he would have to set a new and completely different trap, with diminished resources. After being knocked down, Marciano had stopped throwing that patterned right-and-left combination; he has a good nob. "He never trun it again in the fight," Whitey said next day, but I differ. He threw it in the fifth, and again Moore hit him a peach of a right inside it, but the steam was gone; this time Ahab couldn't even stagger him. Anyway, there was Moore at the end of the second, dragging his shattered faith in the unities and humanities back to his corner. He had hit a guy right, and the guy hadn't gone. But there is no geezer in Moore, any more than there was in the master of the Pequod.

25   Both came out for the third very gay, as Egan would have said. Marciano had been hit and cut, so he felt acclimated, and Moore was so mad at himself for not having knocked Marciano out that he almost displayed animosity toward him. He may have thought that perhaps he had not hit Marciano *just* right; the true artist is always prone to self-reproach. He would try again. A minute's attention from his squires had raised his spirits and slaked down his hair. At this point, Marciano set about him. He waddled in, hurling his fists with a sublime disregard of probabilities, content to hit an elbow, a biceps, a shoulder, the top of a head—the last supposed to be the least profitable target in the business, since, as every beginner learns, "the head is the hardest part of the human body," and a boxer will only break his hands on it. Many boxers make the systematic presentation of the cranium part of their defensive scheme. The crowd, basically anti-intellectual, screamed encouragement. There was Moore, riding punches, picking them off, slipping them, rolling with them, ducking them, coming gracefully out of his defensive efforts with sharp, patterned blows—and just about holding this parody even on points. His face, emerging at instants from under the storm of arms—his own and Rocky's—looked like that of a swimming walrus. When the round ended, I could see that he was thinking deeply. Marciano came back to his corner at a kind of suppressed dogtrot. He didn't have a worry in the world.

26   It was in the fourth, though, that I think Sisyphus began to get the idea he couldn't roll back the Rock. Marciano pushed him against the ropes and swung at him for what seemed a full minute without ever landing a punch that a boxer with Moore's background would consider a credit to his workmanship. He kept them coming so fast, though, that Moore tired just getting

out of their way. One newspaper account I saw said that at this point Moore "swayed uncertainly," but his motions were about as uncertain as Margot Fonteyn's, or Artur Rubinstein's. He is the most premeditated and best-synchronized swayer in his profession. After the bell rang for the end of the round, the champion hit him a right for good measure—he usually manages to have something on the way all the time—and then pulled back to disclaim any uncouth intention. Moore, no man to be conned, hit him a corker of a punch in return, when he wasn't expecting it. It was a gesture of moral reprobation and also a punch that would give any normal man something to think about between rounds. It was a good thing Moore couldn't see Marciano's face as he came back to his corner, though, because the champion was laughing.

27   The fifth was a successful round for Moore, and I had him ahead on points that far in the fight. But it took no expert to know where the strength lay. There was even a moment in the round when Moore set himself against the ropes and encouraged Marciano to swing at him, in the hope the champion would swing himself tired. It was a confession that he himself was too tired to do much hitting.

28   In the sixth Marciano knocked Moore down twice—once, early in the round, for four seconds, and once, late in the round, for eight seconds, with Moore getting up just before the bell rang. In the seventh, after that near approach to obliteration, the embattled intellect put up its finest stand. Marciano piled out of his corner to finish Moore, and the stylist made him miss so often that it looked, for a fleeting moment, as if the champion were indeed punching himself arm-weary. In fact, Moore began to beat him to the punch. It was Moore's round, certainly, but an old-timer I talked to later averred that one of the body blows Marciano landed in that round was the hardest of the fight.

29   It was the eighth that ended the competitive phase of the fight. They fought all the way, and in the last third of the round the champion simply overflowed Archie. He knocked him down with a right six seconds before the bell, and I don't think Moore could have got up by ten if the round had lasted that long. The fight by then reminded me of something that Sam Langford, one of the most profound thinkers—and, according to all accounts, one of the greatest doers—of the prize ring, once said to me: "Whatever that other man wants to do, don't let him do it." Merely by moving in all the time and punching continually, Marciano achieves the same strategic effect that Langford gained by finesse. It is impossible to think, or to impose your thought, if you have to keep on avoiding punches.

30   Moore's "game," as old Egan would have called his courage, was beyond reproach. He came out proudly for the ninth, and stood and fought back with all he had, but Marciano slugged him down, and he was counted out with his left arm hooked over the middle rope as he tried to rise. It was a crushing

defeat for the higher faculties and a lesson in intellectual humility, but he had made a hell of a fight.

31 The fight was no sooner over than hundreds of unsavory young yokels with New England accents began a kind of mountain-goat immigration from the bleachers to ringside. They leaped from chair to chair and, after they reached the press section, from typewriter shelf to typewriter shelf and, I hope, from movie star to movie star. "Rocky!" they yelled. "Brockton!" Two of them, as dismal a pair of civic ambassadors as I have seen since I worked on the Providence *Journal & Evening Bulletin,* stood on Wilson's typewriter and yelled "Providence!" After the fighters and the hick delinquents had gone away, I made my way out to Jerome Avenue, where the crowd milled, impenetrable, under the el structure.

32 If you are not in a great hurry to get home (and why should you be at eleven-thirty or twelve on a fight night?), the best plan is to walk up to the station north of the Stadium and have a beer in a saloon, or a cup of tea in the 167th Street Cafeteria, and wait until the whole mess clears away. By that time you may even get a taxi. After this particular fight I chose the cafeteria, being in a contemplative rather than a convivial mood. The place is of a genre you would expect to find nearer Carnegie Hall, with blond woodwork and modern functional furniture imported from Italy—an appropriate background for the evaluation of an aesthetic experience. I got my tea and a smoked-salmon sandwich on a soft onion roll at the counter and made my way to a table, where I found myself between two young policemen who were talking about why Walt Disney has never attempted a screen version of Kafka's *Metamorphosis.* As I did not feel qualified to join in that one, I got out my copy of the official program of the fights and began to read the high-class feature articles as I munched my sandwich.

33 One reminded me that I had seen the first boxing show ever held in Yankee Stadium—on May 12, 1923. I had forgotten that it *was* the first show, and even that 1923 was the year the Stadium opened. In my true youth the Yankees used to share the Polo Grounds with the Giants, and I had forgotten that, too, because I never cared much about baseball, although, come to think of it, I used to see the Yankees play occasionally in the nineteen-'teens, and should have remembered. I remembered the boxing show itself very well, though. It happened during the spring of my second suspension from college, and I paid five dollars for a high-grandstand seat. The program merely said that it had been "an all-star heavyweight bill promoted by Tex Rickard for the Hearst Milk Fund," but I found that I could still remember every man and every bout on the card.

34 One of the main events was between old Jess Willard, the former heavyweight champion of the world, who had lost the title to Jack Dempsey in 1919, and a young heavyweight named Floyd Johnson. Willard had been coaxed from retirement to make a comeback because there was such a dearth

of heavyweight material that Rickard thought he could still get by, but as I remember the old fellow, he couldn't fight a lick. He had a fair left jab and a right uppercut that a fellow had to walk into to get hurt by, and he was big and soft. Johnson was a mauler worse than Rex Layne, and the old man knocked him out. The other main event, *ex aequo*, had Luis Angel Firpo opposing a fellow named Jack McAuliffe II, from Detroit, who had had only fifteen fights and had never beaten anybody, and had a glass jaw. The two winners, of whose identity there was infinitesimal preliminary doubt, were to fight each other for the right to meet the great Jack Dempsey. Firpo was so crude that Marciano would be a Fancy Dan in comparison. He could hit with only one hand—his right—he hadn't the faintest idea of what to do in close, and he never cared much for the business anyway. He knocked McAuliffe out, of course, and then, in a later "elimination" bout, stopped poor old Willard. He subsequently became a legend by going one and a half sensational rounds with Dempsey, in a time that is now represented to us as the golden age of American pugilism.

35   I reflected with satisfaction that old Ahab Moore could have whipped all four principals on that card within fifteen rounds, and that while Dempsey may have been a great champion, he had less to beat than Marciano. I felt the satisfaction because it proved that the world isn't going backward, if you can just stay young enough to remember what it was really like when you were really young.

1958

Lars Eighner

ON DUMPSTER DIVING

Eighner is the author of Travels with Lizbeth, *an account of a period of homelessness, as is this piece, which originally appeared in* The Threepenny Review. *The ethos problem facing a homeless author proposing to write about how to scavenge in a dumpster for food goes without saying. He begins with the origins of the word "dumpster," which he capitalizes out of consideration for its status as a trademark of the Dempsey Dumpster company. Why might he choose such an opening? In paragraph 7, he proposes to move from the practical art of dumpster diving to the abstract contemplation of it. As you read the essay, think about what abstractions he wants us to consider, and about how these values and concerns reflect on him as author. How does the ethos Eighner*

*creates for himself affect the reader's attitude toward the potentially repulsive
subject of scavenging in a dumpster?*

1   Long before I began Dumpster diving I was impressed with Dumpsters, enough so that I wrote the Merriam-Webster research service to discover what I could about the word "Dumpster." I learned from them that "Dumpster" is a proprietary word belonging to the Dempsey Dumpster company.

2   Since then I have dutifully capitalized the word although it was lowercased in almost all of the citations Merriam-Webster photocopied for me. Dempsey's word is too apt. I have never heard these things called anything but Dumpsters, I do not know anyone who knows the generic name for these objects. From time to time, however, I hear a wino or hobo give some corrupted credit to the original and call them Dipsy Dumpsters.

3   I began Dumpster diving about a year before I became homeless.

4   I prefer the term "scavenging" and use the word "scrounging" when I mean to be obscure. I have heard people, evidently meaning to be polite, using the word "foraging," but I prefer to reserve that word for gathering nuts and berries and such which I do also according to the season and the opportunity. "Dumpster diving" seems to me to be a little too cute and, in my case, inaccurate because I lack the athletic ability to lower myself into the Dumpsters as the true divers do, much to their increased profit.

5   I like the frankness of the word "scavenging," which I can hardly think of without picturing a big black snail on an aquarium wall. I live from the refuse of others. I am a scavenger. I think it a sound and honorable niche, although if I could I would naturally prefer to live the comfortable consumer life, perhaps—and only perhaps—as a slightly less wasteful consumer owing to what I have learned as a scavenger.

6   While my dog Lizbeth and I were still living in the house on Avenue B in Austin, as my savings ran out, I put almost all my sporadic income into rent. The necessities of daily life I began to extract from Dumpsters. Yes, we ate from Dumpsters. Except for jeans, all my clothes came from Dumpsters. Boom boxes, candles, bedding, toilet paper, medicine, books, a typewriter, a virgin male love doll, change sometimes amounting to many dollars: I acquired many things from the Dumpsters.

7   I have learned much as a scavenger. I mean to put some of what I have learned down here, beginning with the practical art of Dumpster diving and proceeding to the abstract.

8   What is safe to eat?

9   After all, the finding of objects is becoming something of an urban art. Even respectable employed people will sometimes find something tempting sticking out of a Dumpster or standing beside one. Quite a number of people, not all of them of the bohemian type, are willing to brag that they found this

or that piece in the trash. But eating from Dumpsters is the thing that separates the dilettanti from the professionals.

10   Eating safely from the Dumpsters involves three principles: using the senses and common sense to evaluate the condition of the found materials, knowing the Dumpsters of a given area and checking them regularly, and seeking always to answer the question "Why was this discarded?"

11   Perhaps everyone who has a kitchen and a regular supply of groceries has, at one time or another, made a sandwich and eaten half of it before discovering mold on the bread or got a mouthful of milk before realizing the milk had turned. Nothing of the sort is likely to happen to a Dumpster diver because he is constantly reminded that most food is discarded for a reason. Yet a lot of perfectly good food can be found in Dumpsters.

12   Canned goods, for example, turn up fairly often in the Dumpsters I frequent. All except the most phobic people would be willing to eat from a can even if it came from a Dumpster. Canned goods are among the safest of foods to be found in Dumpsters, but are not utterly foolproof.

13   Although very rare with modern canning methods, botulism is a possibility. Most other forms of food poisoning seldom do lasting harm to a healthy person. But botulism is almost certainly fatal and often the first symptom is death. Except for carbonated beverages, all canned goods should contain a slight vacuum and suck air when first punctured. Bulging, rusty, dented cans and cans that spew when punctured should be avoided, especially when the contents are not very acidic or syrupy.

14   Heat can break down the botulin, but this requires much more cooking than most people do to canned goods. To the extent that botulism occurs at all, of course, it can occur in cans on pantry shelves as well as in cans from Dumpsters. Need I say that home-canned goods found in Dumpsters are simply too risky to be recommended.

15   From time to time one of my companions, aware of the source of my provisions, will ask, "Do you think these crackers are really safe to eat?" For some reason it is most often the crackers they ask about.

16   This question always makes me angry. Of course I would not offer my companion anything I had doubts about. But more than that I wonder why he cannot evaluate the condition of the crackers for himself. I have no special knowledge and I have been wrong before. Since he knows where the food comes from, it seems to me he ought to assume some of the responsibility for deciding what he will put in his mouth.

17   For myself I have few qualms about dry foods such as crackers, cookies, cereal, chips, and pasta if they are free of visible contaminates and still dry and crisp. Most often such things are found in the original packaging, which is not so much a positive sign as it is the absence of a negative one.

18   Raw fruits and vegetables with intact skins seem perfectly safe to me, excluding of course the obviously rotten. Many are discarded for minor

imperfections which can be pared away. Leafy vegetables, grapes, cauliflower, broccoli, and similar things may be contaminated by liquids and may be impractical to wash.

19   Candy, especially hard candy, is usually safe if it has not drawn ants. Chocolate is often discarded only because it has become discolored as the cocoa butter de-emulsified. Candying after all is one method of food preservation because pathogens do not like very sugary substances.

20   All of these foods might be found in any Dumpster and can be evaluated with some confidence largely on the basis of appearance. Beyond these are foods which cannot be correctly evaluated without additional information.

21   I began scavenging by pulling pizzas out of the Dumpster behind a pizza delivery shop. In general prepared food requires caution, but in this case I knew when the shop closed and went to the Dumpster as soon as the last of the help left.

22   Such shops often get prank orders, called "bogus." Because help seldom stays long at these places pizzas are often made with the wrong topping, refused on delivery for being cold, or baked incorrectly. The products to be discarded are boxed up because inventory is kept by counting boxes: a boxed pizza can be written off; an unboxed pizza does not exist.

23   I never placed a bogus order to increase the supply of pizzas and I believe no one else was scavenging in this Dumpster. But the people in the shop became suspicious and began to retain their garbage in the shop overnight.

24   While it lasted I had a steady supply of fresh, sometimes warm pizza. Because I knew the Dumpster I knew the source of the pizza, and because I visited the Dumpster regularly I knew what was fresh and what was yesterday's.

25   The area I frequent is inhabited by many affluent college students. I am not here by chance; the Dumpsters in this area are very rich. Students throw out many good things, including food. In particular they tend to throw everything out when they move at the end of a semester, before and after breaks, and around midterm when many of them despair of college. So I find it advantageous to keep an eye on the academic calendar.

26   The students throw food away around the breaks because they do not know whether it has spoiled or will spoil before they return. A typical discard is a half jar of peanut butter. In fact nonorganic peanut butter does not require refrigeration and is unlikely to spoil in any reasonable time. The student does not know that, and since it is Daddy's money, the student decides not to take a chance.

27   Opened containers require caution and some attention to the question "Why was this discarded?" But in the case of discards from student apartments, the answer may be that the item was discarded through carelessness, ignorance, or wastefulness. This can sometimes be deduced when the item is found with many others, including some that are obviously perfectly good.

28   Some students, and others, approach defrosting a freezer by chucking out the whole lot. Not only do the circumstances of such a find tell the story, but also the mass of frozen goods stays cold for a long time and items may be found still frozen or freshly thawed.

29   Yogurt, cheese, and sour cream are items that are often thrown out while they are still good. Occasionally I find a cheese with a spot of mold, which of course I just pare off, and because it is obvious why such a cheese was discarded, I treat it with less suspicion than an apparently perfect cheese found in similar circumstances. Yogurt is often discarded, still sealed, only because the expiration date on the carton had passed. This is one of my favorite finds because yogurt will keep for several days, even in warm weather.

30   Students throw out canned goods and staples at the end of semesters and when they give up college at midterm. Drugs, pornography, spirits, and the like are often discarded when parents are expected—Dad's day, for example. And spirits also turn up after big party weekends, presumably discarded by the newly reformed. Wine and spirits, of course, keep perfectly well even once opened.

31   My test for carbonated soft drinks is whether they still fizz vigorously. Many juices or other beverages are too acid or too syrupy to cause much concern provided they are not visibly contaminated. Liquids, however, require some care.

32   One hot day I found a large jug of Pat O'Brien's Hurricane mix. The jug had been opened, but it was still ice cold. I drank three large glasses before it became apparent to me that someone had added the rum to the mix, and not a little rum. I never tasted the rum and by the time I began to feel the effects I had already ingested a very large quantity of the beverage. Some divers would have considered this a boon, but being suddenly and thoroughly intoxicated in a public place in the early afternoon is not my idea of a good time.

33   I have heard of people maliciously contaminating discarded food and even handouts, but mostly I have heard of this from people with vivid imaginations who have had no experience with the Dumpsters themselves. Just before the pizza shop stopped discarding its garbage at night, jalapeños began showing up on most of the discarded pizzas. If indeed this was meant to discourage me it was a wasted effort because I am native Texan.

34   For myself, I avoid game, poultry, pork, and egg-based foods whether I find them raw or cooked. I seldom have the means to cook what I find, but when I do I avail myself of plentiful supplies of beef which is often in very good condition. I suppose fish becomes disagreeable before it becomes dangerous. The dog is happy to have any such thing that is past its prime and, in fact, does not recognize fish as food until it is quite strong.

35   Home leftovers, as opposed to surpluses from restaurants, are very often bad. Evidently, especially among students, there is a common type of personality that carefully wraps up even the smallest leftover and shoves it into the

back of the refrigerator for six months or so before discarding it. Characteristic of this type are the reused jars and margarine tubs which house the remains.

36   I avoid ethnic foods I am unfamiliar with. If I do not know what it is supposed to look like when it is good, I cannot be certain I will be able to tell if it is bad.

37   No matter how careful I am I still get dysentery at least once a month, oftener in warm weather. I do not want to paint too romantic a picture. Dumpster diving has serious drawbacks as a way of life.

38   I learned to scavenge gradually, on my own. Since then I have initiated several companions into the trade. I have learned that there is a predictable series of stages a person goes through in learning to scavenge.

39   At first the new scavenger is filled with disgust and self-loathing. He is ashamed of being seen and may lurk around, trying to duck behind things, or he may try to dive at night.

40   (In fact, most people instinctively look away from a scavenger. By skulking around, the novice calls attention to himself and arouses suspicion. Diving at night is ineffective and needlessly messy.)

41   Every grain of rice seems to be a maggot. Everything seems to stink. He can wipe the egg yolk off the found can, but he cannot erase the stigma of eating garbage out of his mind.

42   That stage passes with experience. The scavenger finds a pair of running shoes that fit and look and smell brand-new. He finds a pocket calculator in perfect working order. He finds pristine ice cream, still frozen, more than he can eat or keep. He begins to understand: people do throw away perfectly good stuff, a lot of perfectly good stuff.

43   At this stage, Dumpster shyness begins to dissipate. The diver, after all, has the last laugh. He is finding all manner of good things which are his for the taking. Those who disparage his profession are the fools, not he.

44   He may begin to hang onto some perfectly good things for which he has neither a use nor a market. Then he begins to take note of the things which are not perfectly good but are nearly so. He mates a Walkman with broken earphones and one that is missing a battery cover. He picks up things which he can repair.

45   At this stage he may become lost and never recover. Dumpsters are full of things of some potential value to someone and also of things which never have much intrinsic value but are interesting. All the Dumpster divers I have known come to the point of trying to acquire everything they touch. Why not take it, they reason, since it is all free.

46   This is, of course, hopeless. Most divers come to realize that they must restrict themselves to items of relatively immediate utility. But in some cases the diver simply cannot control himself. I have met several of these pack-rat

types. Their ideas of the values of various pieces of junk verge on the psychotic. Every bit of glass may be a diamond, they think, and all that glistens, gold.

[47]   I tend to gain weight when I am scavenging. Partly this is because I always find far more pizza and doughnuts than water-packed tuna, nonfat yogurt, and fresh vegetables. Also, I have not developed much faith in the reliability of Dumpsters as a food source, although it has been proven to me many times. I tend to eat as if I have no idea where my next meal is coming from. But mostly I just hate to see food go to waste and so I eat much more than I should. Something like this drives the obsession to collect junk.

[48]   As for collecting objects, I usually restrict myself to collecting one kind of small object at a time, such as pocket calculators, sunglasses, or campaign buttons. To live on the street I must anticipate my needs to a certain extent: I must pick up and save warm bedding I find in August because it will not be found in Dumpsters in November. But even if I had a home with extensive storage space I could not save everything that might be valuable in some contingency.

[49]   I have proprietary feelings about my Dumpsters. As I have suggested, it is no accident that I scavenge from Dumpsters where good finds are common. But my limited experience with Dumpsters in other areas suggests to me that it is the population of competitors rather than the affluence of the Dumpers that most affects the feasibility of survival by scavenging. The large number of competitors is what puts me off the idea of trying to scavenge in places like Los Angeles.

[50]   Curiously, I do not mind my direct competition, other scavengers, so much as I hate the can scroungers.

[51]   People scrounge cans because they have to have a little cash. I have tried scrounging cans with an able-bodied companion. Afoot a can scrounger simply cannot make more than a few dollars a day. One can extract the necessities of life from the Dumpsters directly with far less effort than would be required to accumulate the equivalent value in cans.

[52]   Can scroungers, then, are people who *must* have small amounts of cash. These are drug addicts and winos, mostly the latter because the amounts of cash are so small.

[53]   Spirits and drugs do, like all other commodities, turn up in Dumpsters and the scavenger will from time to time have a half bottle of a rather good wine with his dinner. But the wino cannot survive on these occasional finds; he must have his daily dose to stave off the DTs. All the cans he can carry will buy about three bottles of Wild Irish Rose.

[54]   I do not begrudge them the cans, but can scroungers tend to tear up the Dumpsters, mixing the contents and littering the area. They become so specialized that they can see only cans. They earn my contempt by passing up change, canned goods, and readily hockable items.

55   There are precious few courtesies among scavengers. But it is a common practice to set aside surplus items: pairs of shoes, clothing, canned goods, and such. A true scavenger hates to see good stuff go to waste and what he cannot use he leaves in good condition in plain sight.

56   Can scroungers lay waste to everything in their path and will stir one of a pair of good shoes to the bottom of a Dumpster, to be lost or ruined in the muck. Can scroungers will even go through individual garbage cans, something I have never seen a scavenger do.

57   Individual garbage cans are set out on the public easement only on garbage days. On other days going through them requires trespassing close to a dwelling. Going through individual garbage cans without scattering litter is almost impossible. Litter is likely to reduce the public's tolerance of scavenging. Individual garbage cans are simply not as productive as Dumpsters; people in houses and duplexes do not move as often and for some reason do not tend to discard as much useful material. Moreover, the time required to go through one garbage can that serves one household is not much less than the time required to go through a Dumpster that contains the refuse of twenty apartments.

58   But my strongest reservation about going through individual garbage cans is that this seems to me a very personal kind of invasion to which I would object if I were a householder. Although many things in Dumpsters are obviously meant never to come to light, a Dumpster is somehow less personal.

59   I avoid trying to draw conclusions about the people who dump in the Dumpsters I frequent. I think it would be unethical to do so, although I know many people will find the idea of scavenger ethics too funny for words.

60   Dumpsters contain bank statements, bills, correspondence, and other documents, just as anyone might expect. But there are also less obvious sources of information. Pill bottles, for example. The labels on pill bottles contain the name of the patient, the name of the doctor, and the name of the drug. AIDS drugs and antipsychotic medicines, to name but two groups, are specific and are seldom prescribed for any other disorders. The plastic compacts for birth control pills usually have complete label information.

61   Despite all of this sensitive information, I have had only one apartment resident object to my going through the Dumpster. In that case it turned out the resident was a university athlete who was taking bets and who was afraid I would turn up his wager slips.

62   Occasionally a find tells a story. I once found a small paper bag containing some unused condoms, several partial tubes of flavored sexual lubricant, a partially used compact of birth control pills, and the torn pieces of a picture of a young man. Clearly, she was through with him and planning to give up sex altogether.

63   Dumpster things are often sad—abandoned teddy bears, shredded wedding books, despaired-of sales kits. I find many pets lying in state in Dumpsters. Although I hope to get off the streets so that Lizbeth can have a long and comfortable old age, I know this hope is not very realistic. So I suppose when her time comes she too will go into a Dumpster. I will have no better place for her. And after all, for most of her life her livelihood has come from the Dumpster. When she finds something I think is safe that has been spilled from the Dumpster I let her have it. She already knows the route around the best Dumpsters. I like to think that if she survives me she will have a chance of evading the dog catcher and of finding her sustenance on the route.

64   Silly vanities also come to rest in the Dumpsters. I am a rather accomplished needleworker. I get a lot of materials from the Dumpsters. Evidently sorority girls, hoping to impress someone, perhaps themselves, with their mastery of a womanly art, buy a lot of embroider-by-number kits, work a few stitches horribly, and eventually discard the whole mess. I pull out their stitches, turn the canvas over, and work an original design. Do not think I refrain from chuckling as I make original gifts from these kits.

65   I find diaries and journals. I have often thought of compiling a book of literary found objects. And perhaps I will one day. But what I find is hopelessly commonplace and bad without being, even unconsciously, camp. College students also discard their papers. I am horrified to discover the kind of paper which now merits an A in an undergraduate course. I am grateful, however, for the number of good books and magazines the students throw out.

66   In the area I know best I have never discovered vermin in the Dumpsters, but there are two kinds of kitty surprise. One is alley cats which I meet as they leap, claws first, out of Dumpsters. This is especially thrilling when I have Lizbeth in tow. The other kind of kitty surprise is a plastic garbage bag filled with some ponderous, amorphous mass. This always proves to be used cat litter.

67   City bees harvest doughnut glaze and this makes the Dumpster at the doughnut shop more interesting. My faith in the instinctive wisdom of animals is always shaken whenever I see Lizbeth attempt to catch a bee in her mouth, which she does whenever bees are present. Evidently some birds find Dumpsters profitable, for birdie surprise is almost as common as kitty surprise of the first kind. In hunting season all kinds of small game turn up in Dumpsters, some of it, sadly, not entirely dead. Curiously, summer and winter, maggots are uncommon.

68   The worst of the living and near-living hazards of the Dumpsters are the fire ants. The food that they claim is not much of a loss, but they are vicious and aggressive. It is very easy to brush against some surface of the Dumpster and pick up half a dozen or more fire ants, usually in some sensitive area such as the underarm. One advantage of bringing Lizbeth along as I make Dumpster rounds is that, for obvious reasons, she is very alert to ground-based fire ants. When Lizbeth recognizes the signs of fire ant infestation around our feet she does the Dance of the Zillion Fire Ants. I have learned not to ignore this warning from Lizbeth, whether I perceive the tiny ants or not, but to remove

ourselves at Lizbeth's first pas de bourée. All the more so because the ants are the worst in the months I wear flip-flops, if I have them.

69   (Perhaps someone will misunderstand the above. Lizbeth does the Dance of the Zillion Fire Ants when she recognizes more fire ants than she cares to eat, not when she is being bitten. Since I have learned to react promptly, she does not get bitten at all. It is the isolated patrol of fire ants that falls in Lizbeth's range that deserves pity. Lizbeth finds them quite tasty.)

70   By far the best way to go through a Dumpster is to lower yourself into it. Most of the good stuff tends to settle at the bottom because it is usually weightier than the rubbish. My more athletic companions have often demonstrated to me that they can extract much good material from a Dumpster I have already been over.

71   To those psychologically or physically unprepared to enter a Dumpster, I recommend a stout stick, preferably with some barb or hook at one end. The hook can be used to grab plastic garbage bags. When I find canned goods or other objects loose at the bottom of a Dumpster I usually can roll them into a small bag that I can then hoist up. Much Dumpster diving is a matter of experience for which nothing will do except practice.

72   Dumpster diving is outdoor work, often surprisingly pleasant. It is not entirely predictable; things of interest turn up every day and some days there are finds of great value. I am always very pleased when I can turn up exactly the thing I most wanted to find. Yet in spite of the element of chance, scavenging more than most other pursuits tends to yield returns in some proportion to the effort and intelligence brought to bear. It is very sweet to turn up a few dollars in change from a Dumpster that has just been gone over by a wino.

73   The land is now covered with cities. The cities are full of Dumpsters. I think of scavenging as a modern form of self-reliance. In any event, after ten years of government service, where everything is geared to the lowest common denominator, I find work that rewards initiative and effort refreshing. Certainly, I would be happy to have a sinecure again, but I am not heartbroken not to have one anymore.

74   I find from the experience of scavenging two rather deep lessons. The first is to take what I can use and let the rest go by. I have come to think that there is no value in the abstract. A thing I cannot use or make useful, perhaps by trading, has no value however fine or rare it may be. I mean useful in a broad sense—so, for example, some art I would think useful and valuable, but other art might be otherwise for me.

75   I was shocked to realize that some things are not worth acquiring, but now I think it is so. Some material things are white elephants that eat up the possessor's substance.

76   The second lesson is of the transience of material being. This has not quite converted me to a dualist, but it has made some headway in that direction. I do not suppose that ideas are immortal, but certainly mental things are longer-lived than other material things.

77   Once I was the sort of person who invests material objects with sentimental value. Now I no longer have those things, but I have the sentiments yet.

[78] Many times in my travels I have lost everything but the clothes I was wearing and Lizbeth. The things I find in Dumpsters, the love letters and rag dolls of so many lives, remind me of this lesson. Now I hardly pick up a thing without envisioning the time I will cast it away. This I think is a healthy state of mind. Almost everything I have now has already been cast out at least once, proving that what I own is valueless to someone.

[79] Anyway, I find my desire to grab for the gaudy bauble has been largely sated. I think this is an attitude I share with the very wealthy—we both know there is plenty more where what we have came from. Between us are the rat-race millions who have confounded their selves with the objects they grasp and who nightly scavenge the cable channels looking for they know not what.

[80] I am sorry for them.

1991

PATHOS APPEALS

Pathos appeals are those based on specific inclinations of the audience, especially their feelings. These are emotional appeals in the broadest sense. You may remember the *pathos* appeal contained in the magazine advertisement that showed a wide-eyed and bedraggled child with a caption reading, "You can help her or you can turn the page." We speak of these appeals as *pathos* appeals rather than "pathetic appeals" because the most common meaning of *pathetic* is "pitifully unsuccessful." Only some *pathos* appeals are pathetic. All are volatile, however, and must be handled with care. Think of a blaring, shrieking, drum-beating television advertisement meant to fire you with enthusiasm for the product—when in reality each repetition of the ad strengthens your determination never to buy that product under any circumstances. Think about a story that was meant to draw your tears and instead made you laugh at its sentimentality. When *pathos* appeals succeed, they are extremely effective; when they fail, they are often an embarrassment to their author.

William Shakespeare
ANTONY'S SPEECH OVER THE BODY OF CAESAR

A famous illustration of how an argument can hinge on pathos *appeals is Mark Antony's funeral oration at the center of Shakespeare's* Julius Caesar *(III.ii).*

Some conspirators headed by Brutus and Cassius have assassinated Caesar. They are concerned about what reactions Caesar's death will provoke, both among important political figures and among the masses. A powerful supporter of Caesar, Mark Antony, has just heard of the assassination. He asks the conspirators for permission to speak to the masses at Caesar's funeral. The conspirator Cassius is uneasy at the prospect of Antony's speech and cautions Brutus:

> You know not what you do. Do not consent
> That Antony speak in his funeral.
> Know you how much the people may be mov'd
> By that which he will utter?

But Brutus wants Caesar to have the proper rituals of burial. He assures Cassius that he will speak before Antony. He will make certain that the crowd understands that the conspirators had to kill Caesar to prevent him from becoming a dictator. He tells Antony that he is free to praise Caesar, but forbids him to attack the conspirators. Both Brutus and Antony address the crowd; the differences in their rhetoric are striking.

SCENE: *Rome. The Forum*

[*Enter* BRUTUS *and* CASSIUS, *and* CITIZENS.]

CITIZENS.   We will be satisfied.[1] Let us be satisfied.
BRUTUS.   Then follow me, and give me audience, friends.
     Cassius, go you into the other street,
     And part the numbers.
     Those that will hear me speak, let 'em stay here;
     Those that will follow Cassius, go with him;
     And public reasons shall be rendered
     Of Caesar's death.
FIRST CITIZEN.   I will hear Brutus speak.
10 SECOND CITIZEN.   I will hear Cassius, and compare their reasons,
     When severally[2] we hear them rendered.

              [*Exit* CASSIUS, *with some* CITIZENS. BRUTUS *goes into the pulpit.*]

THIRD CITIZEN.   The noble Brutus is ascended. Silence!
BRUTUS.   Be patient till the last.
     Romans, countrymen, and lovers, hear me for my cause, and be silent,
     that you may hear. Believe me for mine honour, and have respect to mine
     honour, that you may believe. Censure me in your wisdom, and awake
     your senses, that you may the better judge. If there be any in this assembly, any dear friend of Caesar's, to him I say, that Brutus' love to Caesar

---

[1]*satisfied*: given an adequate explanation (for Caesar's death)
[2]*severally*: individually

20 was no less than his. If then, that friend demand, why Brutus rose against Caesar, this is my answer—not that I loved Caesar less; but that I loved Rome more. Had you rather Caesar were living, and die all slaves, than that Caesar were dead, to live all free men? As Caesar loved me, I weep for him; as he was fortunate, I rejoice at it; as he was valiant, I honour him: but as he was ambitious, I slew him. There is tears, for his love; joy, for his fortune; honour, for his valour; and death, for his ambition. Who is here so base, that would be a bondman? If any, speak, for him have I offended. Who is here so rude, that would not be a Roman? If any, speak, for him have I offended. Who is here so vile, that will not love his country? If any, speak, for him have I offended. I pause for a reply.

30 CITIZENS.   None Brutus, none.

BRUTUS.   Then none have I offended. I have done no more to Caesar than you shall do to Brutus. The question of his death is enrolled[3] in the Capitol; his glory not extenuated,[4] wherein he was worthy; nor his offences enforced,[5] for which he suffered death.

[*Enter* ANTONY *with* CAESAR'S *body.*]

Here comes his body, mourned by Mark Antony, who though he had no hand in his death, shall receive the benefit of his dying, a place in the commonwealth, as which of you shall not? With this I depart, that as I slew my best lover for the good of Rome, I have the same dagger for myself, when it shall please my country to need my death.

40 CITIZENS.   Live Brutus, live, live!

FIRST CITIZEN.   Bring him with triumph home unto his house.

SECOND CITIZEN.   Give him a statue with his ancestors.

THIRD CITIZEN.   Let him be Caesar.

FOURTH CITIZEN.   Caesar's better parts
    Shall be crowned in Brutus.

FIRST CITIZEN.   We'll bring him to his house, with shouts and clamours.

BRUTUS.   My countrymen—

SECOND CITIZEN.   Peace, silence, Brutus speaks.

FIRST CITIZEN.   Peace ho!

50 BRUTUS.   Good countrymen, let me depart alone,
    And for my sake, stay here with Antony:
    Do grace to Caesar's corpse, and grace his speech
    Tending to Caesar's glories, which Mark Antony
    By our permission is allowed to make.
    I do entreat you, not a man depart,
    Save I alone, till Antony have spoke. [*Exit.*]

[3]*enrolled*: recorded
[4]*extenuated*: lessened
[5]*enforced*: exaggerated

FIRST CITIZEN.   Stay ho, and let us hear Mark Antony.
THIRD CITIZEN.   Let him go up into the public chair,
   We'll hear him. Noble Antony go up.
60 ANTONY.   For Brutus' sake, I am beholding to you. [*Goes up.*]
FOURTH CITIZEN.   What does he say of Brutus?
THIRD CITIZEN.   He says, for Brutus' sake
   He finds himself beholding to us all.
FOURTH CITIZEN.   'Twere best he speak no harm of Brutus here.
FIRST CITIZEN.   This Caesar was a tyrant.
THIRD CITIZEN.   Nay that's certain.
   We are blest that Rome is rid of him.
SECOND CITIZEN.   Peace, let us hear what Antony can say.
ANTONY.   You gentle Romans—
70 CITIZENS. Peace ho, let us hear him.
ANTONY.   Friends, Romans, countrymen, lend me your ears.
   I come to bury Caesar not to praise him.
   The evil that men do, lives after them,
   The good is oft interred with their bones;
   So let it be with Caesar. The noble Brutus
   Hath told you Caesar was ambitious;
   If it were so, it was a grievous fault,
   And grievously hath Caesar answered it.
   Here, under leave of Brutus, and the rest—
80   For Brutus is an honourable man,
   So are they all, all honourable men—
   Come I to speak in Caesar's funeral.
   He was my friend, faithful, and just to me;
   But Brutus says, he was ambitious,
   And Brutus is an honourable man.
   He hath brought many captives home to Rome,
   Whose ransoms did the general coffers fill.
   Did this in Caesar seem ambitious?
   When that the poor have cried, Caesar hath wept.
90   Ambition should be made of sterner stuff,
   Yet Brutus says, he was ambitious;
   And Brutus is an honourable man.
   You all did see, that on the Lupercal[6]
   I thrice presented him a kingly crown,
   Which he did thrice refuse. Was this ambition?
   Yet Brutus says, he was ambitious;
   And sure he is an honourable man.

[6]*Lupercal*: a Roman fertility celebration

I speak not to disprove what Brutus spoke,
But here I am, to speak what I do know;
100   You all did love him once, not without cause,
What cause withholds you then to mourn for him?
O judgement, thou art fled to brutish beasts,
And men have lost their reason. Bear with me;
My heart is in the coffin there with Caesar,
And I must pause, till it come back to me.
FIRST CITIZEN.   Methinks there is much reason in his sayings.
SECOND CITIZEN.   If you consider rightly of the matter,
Caesar has had great wrong.
THIRD CITIZEN.   Has he masters?
110   I fear there will a worse come in his place.
FOURTH CITIZEN.   Marked ye his words? He would not take the crown.
Therefore 'tis certain, he was not ambitious.
FIRST CITIZEN.   If it be found so, some will dear abide it.
SECOND CITIZEN.   Poor soul, his eyes are red as fire with weeping.
THIRD CITIZEN.   There's not a nobler man in Rome than Antony.
FOURTH CITIZEN.   Now mark him, he begins again to speak.
ANTONY.   But yesterday, the word of Caesar might
Have stood against the world. Now lies he there,
And none so poor to[7] do him reverence.
120   O masters, if I were disposed to stir
Your hearts and minds to mutiny and rage,
I should do Brutus wrong, and Cassius wrong,
Who you all know are honourable men.
I will not do them wrong. I rather choose
To wrong the dead, to wrong myself and you,
Than I will wrong such honourable men.
But here's a parchment, with the seal of Caesar,
I found it in his closet, 'tis his will.
Let but the commons hear this testament—
130   Which, pardon me, I do not mean to read—
And they would go and kiss dead Caesar's wounds,
And dip their napkins in his sacred blood;
Yea, beg a hair of him for memory,
And dying, mention it within their wills,
Bequeathing it as a rich legacy
Unto their issue.
FOURTH CITIZEN.   We'll hear the will, read it Mark Antony.
CITIZENS.   The will, the will! We will hear Caesar's will.

[7]*none so poor to*: no one so insignificant as to

ANTONY. Have patience gentle friends, I must not read it.
140   It is not meet you know[8] how Caesar loved you.
       You are not wood, you are not stones, but men;
       And being men, hearing the will of Caesar,
       It will inflame you, it will make you mad.
       'Tis good you know not that you are his heirs,
       For if you should, O what would come of it?
FOURTH CITIZEN. Read the will, we'll hear it Antony.
       You shall read us the will, Caesar's will.
ANTONY. Will you be patient? Will you stay awhile?
       I have o'ershot myself to tell you of it.
150   I fear I wrong the honourable men
       Whose daggers have stabbed Caesar; I do fear it.
FOURTH CITIZEN. They were traitors. Honourable men?
CITIZENS. The will! The testament!
SECOND CITIZEN. They were villains, murderers. The will, read the will.
ANTONY. You will compel me then to read the will?
       Then make a ring about the corpse of Caesar,
       And let me show you him that made the will.
       Shall I descend? And will you give me leave?
CITIZENS. Come down.
160 SECOND CITIZEN. Descend.
THIRD CITIZEN. You shall have leave. [ANTONY *comes down.*]
FOURTH CITIZEN. A ring, stand around.
FIRST CITIZEN. Stand from the hearse, stand from the body.
SECOND CITIZEN. Room for Antony, most noble Antony.
ANTONY. Nay, press not so upon me; stand far off.
CITIZENS. Stand back; room; bear back.
ANTONY. If you have tears, prepare to shed them now.
       You all do know this mantle, I remember
       The first time ever Caesar put it on;
170   Twas on a summer's evening in his tent,
       That day he overcame the Nervii.[9]
       Look, in this place ran Cassius' dagger through.
       See what a rent the envious Casca made.
       Through this, the well-beloved Brutus stabbed,
       And as he plucked his cursed steel away,
       Mark how the blood of Caesar followed it,
       As rushing out of doors, to be resolved[10]
       If Brutus so unkindly knocked, or no;

[8]*It is not meet you know*: it is best that you not know
[9]*Overcame the Nervii*: the defeat of the Nervii was one of Caesar's great military triumphs
[10]*As . . . resolved*: As if rushing out to determine

For Brutus, as you know, was Caesar's angel.
180   Judge, O you gods, how dearly Caesar loved him.
This was the most unkindest cut of all;
For when the noble Caesar saw him stab,
Ingratitude, more strong than traitors' arms,
Quite vanquished him. Then burst his mighty heart,
And in his mantle muffling up his face,
Even at the base of Pompey's statue,
Which all the while ran blood, great Caesar fell.
O what a fall was there, my countrymen!
Then I, and you, and all of us fell down,
190   Whilst bloody treason flourished over us.
O now you weep, and I perceive you feel
The dint of pity. These are gracious drops.
Kind souls, what weep you, when you but behold
Our Caesar's vesture[11] wounded? Look you here,
Here is himself, marred as you see with traitors.

FIRST CITIZEN.   O piteous spectacle!

SECOND CITIZEN.   O noble Caesar!

THIRD CITIZEN.   O woeful day!

FOURTH CITIZEN.   O traitors, villains!

200 FIRST CITIZEN.   O most bloody sight!

SECOND CITIZEN.   We will be revenged.

CITIZENS.   Revenge! About! Seek! Burn! Fire! Kill! Slay!
    Let not a traitor live.

ANTONY.   Stay countrymen.

FIRST CITIZEN.   Peace there, hear the noble Antony.

SECOND CITIZEN.   We'll hear him, we'll follow him, we'll die with him.

ANTONY.   Good friends, sweet friends, let me not stir you up
    To such a sudden flood of mutiny.
    They that have done this deed are honourable.
210   What private griefs they have, alas I know not,
    That made them do it. They are wise, and honourable,
    And will no doubt with reasons answer you.
    I come not, friends, to steal away your hearts,
    I am no orator as Brutus is;
    But, as you know me all, a plain blunt man
    That love my friend, and that they know full well,
    That gave me public leave to speak of him.
    For I have neither wit, nor words, nor worth,
    Action, nor utterance,[12] nor the power of speech

[11]*vesture*: clothing

[12]*Action, nor utterance*: appropriate gestures, nor skillful delivery

220 To stir men's blood; I only speak right on.
I tell you that which you yourselves do know,
Show you sweet Caesar's wounds, poor, poor dumb mouths,
And bid them speak for me. But were I Brutus,
And Brutus Antony, there were an Antony
Would ruffle up your spirits, and put a tongue
In every wound of Caesar, that should move
The stones of Rome to rise and mutiny.
CITIZENS.   We'll mutiny.
FIRST CITIZEN.   We'll burn the house of Brutus.
230 THIRD CITIZEN.   Away then, come, seek the conspirators.
ANTONY.   Yet hear me countrymen, yet hear me speak.
CITIZENS.   Peace ho, hear Antony, most noble Antony.
ANTONY.   Why friends, you go to do you know not what.
Wherein hath Caesar thus deserved your loves?
Alas you know not, I must tell you then.
You have forgot the will I told you of.
CITIZEN.   Most true, the will, let's stay and hear the will.
ANTONY.   Here is the will, and under Caesar's seal.
To every Roman citizen he gives,
240 To every several man, seventy-five drachmas.
SECOND CITIZEN.   Most noble Caesar, we'll revenge his death.
THIRD CITIZEN.   O royal Caesar!
ANTONY.   Hear me with patience.
CITIZENS.   Peace ho!
ANTONY.   Moreover, he hath left you all his walks.
His private arbours, and new-planted orchards,
On this side Tiber; he hath left them you,
And to your heirs for ever—common pleasures,[13]
To walk abroad, and recreate yourselves.
250 Here was a Caesar! When comes such another?
FIRST CITIZEN.   Never, never. Come, away, away!
We'll burn his body in the holy place,
And with the brands fire the traitors' houses.
Take up the body.
SECOND CITIZEN.   Go fetch fire.
THIRD CITIZEN.   Pluck down benches.
FOURTH CITIZEN.   Pluck down forms,[14] windows, any thing.

[*Exeunt* CITIZENS *with the body.*]

[13]*common pleasures*: public parks
[14]*forms*: benches

ANTONY.   Now let it work. Mischief thou art afoot,
  Take thou what course thou wilt.

1599

Notice that, although it has its own subtleties, Brutus's speech is relatively plain, admirably compact, and ends with a piece of logical reasoning:

Only those of you who wish to be slaves can object to the death of a tyrant.
None of you wishes to be a slave.
Therefore, none of you can object to the death of a tyrant.

In contrast, Antony's speech reads like a manual of *pathos* appeals. By stressing his own grief, Antony works to evoke a similar response in his audience. At one point, he apologizes for being unable to speak:

  Bear with me;
My heart is in the coffin there with Caesar,
And I must pause, till it come back to me.

You probably noticed that Antony makes generous use of what we now call the power of suggestion. The best example is his uncovering Caesar's body with the line "if you have tears, prepare to shed them now." He cannot read Caesar's will to the crowd because "hearing the will of Caesar,/It will inflame you, it will make you mad." Of course, Antony intends all along to read the will for this very purpose. In the act of claiming that he will not wrong the conspirators, Antony also manages to unite himself with the audience—"to wrong *myself and you*"—in opposition to Brutus and Cassius.

Antony frequently assures his audience that he will not do precisely what he intends to do or is in the very process of doing; he *is* praising Caesar and he *does* intend to stir his audience up to mutiny. To remove any doubt we might have about Antony's intentions, Shakespeare has him say after everyone else has left the stage: "Now let it work. Mischief, thou art afoot,/Take thou what course thou wilt." What reasons can you suggest for Antony's continued assurances that he isn't doing what he's doing?

Another place to watch for *pathos* appeals is in figurative language, especially in the author's use of comparisons to make an impression or a mental picture more vivid and therefore more moving. In lines 220 to 227 Antony compares Caesar's wounds to mouths and declares that a skilled orator ought to be able to put a tongue in each "mouth," a tongue that will incite the very stones of Rome to rise up against those who inflicted the wounds. These stylistic devices, taken together with the large-scale devices we have already noted, contribute a great deal to creating the desired effect. An effective style can be *in itself* persuasive, just as a poorly written piece will fail with some audiences on that ground alone.

Although we've chosen this speech to illustrate *pathos* appeals, Antony's speech also demonstrates a speaker's efforts to establish a credible *ethos*. From the perspective of *ethos,* the most important part of the speech is the one in which Antony defines himself as a speaker in relation to his audience:

> I come not, friends, to steal away your hearts,
> I am no orator as Brutus is;
> But, as you know me all, a plain blunt man
> That love my friend, and that they know full well
> That gave me public leave to speak of him.
> For I have neither wit, nor words, nor worth,
> Action, nor utterance, nor the power of speech
> To stir men's blood; I only speak right on.
> I tell you that which you yourselves do know,
> Show you sweet Caesar's wounds, poor, poor, dumb mouths,
> And bid them speak for me. But were I Brutus,
> And Brutus Antony, there were an Antony
> Would ruffle up your spirits, and put a tongue
> In every wound of Caesar, that should move
> The stones of Rome to rise and mutiny.

Antony's claim that he has no rhetorical powers is an age-old rhetorical device. No skilled rhetorician wants to call his audience's attention to his success in rousing their passions. We can imagine the less critical members of Antony's audience shaking their heads in bafflement: which of the two speakers they have just heard is the "plain blunt man" lacking "the power of speech to stir men's blood," and which the highly skilled orator? Although the style of his speech is elaborate, Antony also creates a feeling of spontaneity and intimacy by interrupting his sentences with little asides like the "friends" and the "as you know me all" in the lines just quoted. These interruptions add a casual, conversational note to Antony's otherwise rather formal oratory. Thus he appeals to his audience by projecting an image of himself as a frank, plainspoken man, one who is grieving over a dead friend and confiding in other close friends.

How can attention to Antony's stylistically elaborate *pathos* appeals in poetry help you to write a relatively straightforward essay in prose? And because Shakespeare had Brutus lose, do we assume that clever, scheming emotional appeals are to be preferred to rational thought? Once again, the answer lies with audience. Shakespeare chose to present the Roman mob as fickle, irrational, and easily led. Those who address their writing to audiences they respect will want to think twice about employing Antony's strategies.

In fact, some of you might wonder whether *pathos* appeals are ever a legitimate argumentative procedure. Modern history has given us some horrifying examples of what can happen when a powerful speaker grips his audience's emotions and uses the power he gains over them to accomplish his own ends. We'll devote the whole of Chapter 4 to the question of ethics in argumentation, and you may want to return to Brutus's and Antony's speeches after you have read that chapter. For now, imagine a parent pleading with a would-be murderer for a child's life. Would we condemn a parent as manipulative for trying to appeal to the emotions of someone threatening to harm his or her child? You will want to weigh these issues for yourself; our belief is that much of the best we do as human beings is based on compassion, "feeling with" others. *Pathos* is language applied toward encouraging others to "feel with" us. If we disapprove, it will be of the motive behind the appeal, not of the appeal itself.

Jonathan Edwards

SINNERS IN THE HANDS OF AN ANGRY GOD

In the following reading, Jonathan Edwards, the great eighteenth-century American preacher, is literally trying to scare the hell out of his audience. He is not trying to convince the members of his audience of the fact of hell and damnation; by virtue of their being in his congregation he can be sure they already believe. But he is trying to use fear to help them act more consistently on their conviction, to strive more mightily to be numbered among the elect.

1   That world of misery, that lake of burning brimstone, is extended abroad under you. There is the dreadful pit of the glowing flames of the wrath of God; there is hell's wide gaping mouth open; and you have nothing to stand upon, nor anything to take hold of. There is nothing between you and hell but the air; it is only the power and mere pleasure of God that holds you up.

2   You probably are not sensible of this; you find you are kept out of hell, but do not see the hand of God in it; but look at other things, as the good state of your bodily constitution, your care of your own life, and the means you use for your own preservation. But indeed these things are nothing; if God should withdraw His hand, they would avail no more to keep you from falling, than the thin air to hold up a person that is suspended in it.

3   Your wickedness makes you as it were heavy as lead, and to tend downwards with great weight and pressure towards hell; and, if God should let you go, you would immediately sink and swiftly descend and plunge into the bottomless gulf, and your healthy constitution, and your own care and prudence, and best contrivance, and all your righteousness, would have no more influence to uphold you and keep you out of hell, than a spider's web would have to stop a falling rock. Were it not that so is the sovereign pleasure of God, the earth would not bear you one moment; for you are a burden to it; the creation groans with you; the creature is made subject to the bondage of your corruption, not willingly; the sun does not willingly shine upon you to give you light to serve sin and Satan; the earth does not willingly yield her increase to satisfy your lusts; nor is it willingly a stage for your wickedness to be acted upon; the air does not willingly serve you for breath to maintain the flame of life in your vitals, while you spend your life in the service of God's enemies. God's creatures are good, and were made for men to serve God with, and do not will-

ingly subserve to any other purpose, and groan when they are abused to purposes so directly contrary to their nature and end. And the world would spew you out, were it not for the sovereign hand of Him who hath subjected it in hope. There are the black clouds of God's wrath now hanging directly over your heads, full of the dreadful storm, and big with thunder; and were it not for the restraining hand of God, it would immediately burst forth upon you. The sovereign pleasure of God, for the present, stays His rough wind; otherwise it would come with fury, and your destruction would come like a whirlwind, and you would be like the chaff of the summer threshing floor.

4   The wrath of God is like great waters that are dammed for the present; they increase more and more, and rise higher and higher, till an outlet is given; and, the longer the stream is stopped, the more rapid and mighty is its course, when once it is let loose. It is true, that judgment against your evil work has not been executed hitherto; the floods of God's vengeance have been withheld; but your guilt in the meantime is constantly increasing, and you are every day treasuring up more wrath; the waters are continually rising and waxing more and more mighty; and there is nothing but the mere pleasure of God, that holds the waters back, that are unwilling to be stopped, and press hard to go forward. If God should only withdraw His hand from the floodgate, it would immediately fly open, and the fiery floods of the fierceness and wrath of God, would rush forth with inconceivable fury, and would come upon you with omnipotent power; and if your strength were ten thousand times greater than it is, yea, ten thousand times greater than the strength of the stoutest, sturdiest devil in hell, it would be nothing to withstand or endure it.

5   The bow of God's wrath is bent, and the arrow made ready on the string, and justice bends the arrow at your heart, and strains the bow, and it is nothing but the mere pleasure of God, and that of an angry God, without any promise or obligation at all, that keeps the arrow one moment from being made drunk with your blood.

6   Thus are all you that never passed under a great change of heart, by the mighty power of the Spirit of God upon your souls; all that were never born again, and made new creatures, and raised from being dead in sin, to a state of new, and before altogether unexperienced light and life (however you may have reformed your life in many things, and may have had religious affections, and may keep up a form of religion in your families and closets, and in the houses of God, and may be strict in it), you are thus in the hands of an angry God; it is nothing but His mere pleasure that keeps you from being this moment swallowed up in everlasting destruction.

7   However unconvinced you may now be of the truth of what you hear, by and by you will be fully convinced of it. Those that are gone from being in the like circumstances with you, see that it was so with them; for destruction came suddenly upon most of them; when they expected nothing of it, and while they were saying, Peace and safety: now they see that those things that they depended on for peace and safety were nothing but thin air and empty shadows.

8   The God that holds you over the pit of hell, much as one holds a spider, or some loathsome insect, over the fire, abhors you, and is dreadfully provoked; His wrath towards you burns like fire; He looks upon you as worthy of nothing else, but to be cast into the fire; He is of purer eyes than to bear to have you in His sight; you are ten thousand times so abominable in His eyes, as the most hateful and venomous serpent is in ours. You have offended him infinitely more than ever a stubborn rebel did his prince. And yet, it is nothing but His hand that holds you from falling into the fire every moment. It is ascribed to nothing else, that you did not go to hell the last night; that you were suffered to awake again in this world, after you closed your eyes to sleep. And there is no other reason to be given why you have not dropped into hell since you arose in the morning, but that God's hand has held you up. There is no other reason to be given why you have not gone to hell, since you have sat here in the house of God, provoking His pure eyes by your sinful wicked manner of attending His solemn worship: yea, there is nothing else that is to be given as a reason why you do not this very moment drop down into hell.

9   O sinner! consider the fearful danger you are in: it is a great furnace of wrath, a wide and bottomless pit, full of the fire of wrath, that you are held over in the hand of that God, whose wrath is provoked and incensed as much against you, as against many of the damned in hell. You hang by a slender thread, with the flames of divine wrath flashing about it, and ready every moment to singe it, and burn it asunder; and you have no interest in any Mediator, and nothing to lay hold of to save yourself, nothing to keep off the flames of wrath, nothing of your own, nothing that you ever have done, nothing that you can do, to induce God to spare you one moment.

1741

Carl Sandburg

A FENCE

The early twentieth century American poet, Carl Sandburg, liked to celebrate ordinary people, preferring them to the privileged elites whom he thought dominated literature. In the following poem, he tries to outrage his readers by contrasting the "masterpiece" of a fence that is designed to keep out the "rabble" with those "hungry men" and "wandering children" who are the ones really being excluded. Note the threat suggested by his ending the poem with "To-morrow," a time when—Sandburg seems to be saying—such fences will be breached by force. Note how few words are required to charge the poem with pathos. In what circumstances do you think this minimalist approach to pathos will work better than a flat-out, heart-wrenching appeal on behalf of the home-less and their children?

> Now the stone house on the lake front is finished and the
>   workmen are beginning the fence.
> The palings are made of iron bars with steel points that can
>   stab the life out of any man who falls on them.
> As a fence, it is a masterpiece, and will shut off the
>   rabble and all vagabonds and hungry men and all
>   wandering children looking for a place to play.
> Passing through the bars and over the steel points will go
>   nothing except Death and the Rain and To-morrow.

1916

LOGOS APPEALS

Finally, there are *logos* appeals. While *ethos* appeals derive from charac-teristics of the arguer and *pathos* appeals derive from characteristics of the audi-ence, *logos* appeals derive from the intellectual understanding shared by the arguer and the audience. Of the three appeals, *logos* appeals connect most directly with the subject of the communication. Much of the essay writing you do for college courses rests primarily on *logos* appeals. Once again, we refer to them as *logos* appeals rather than "logical appeals" because the modern word *logical* covers only a small part of the territory inhabited by *logos* appeals. In addition to logic or reasoning, *logos* appeals can include facts, statistics, defi-nitions, analogies, quotations from authorities, and other kinds of evidence offered in support of a speaker's or writer's arguable claims.

As we have said, *logos* appeals generally rely on the common ground between arguer and audience—their common respect for logic, justice, effi-ciency, accuracy, or whatever. As an example, let's say that a state commission decides that adding an hour to the public school day would contribute substan-tially to the education of the state's schoolchildren. The teachers, they hasten to add, would of course be compensated for the extra work. The teachers might dis-agree with the commission's proposal for a number of reasons, prominent among them the addition to their already heavy workload. They might also regard the promised salary increase as far too small in return for the work involved. Although both sides might have reasonable claims, as long as the commissioners are talking exclusively about benefits to schoolchildren and the teachers are talk-ing exclusively about harm to teachers, the argument can go nowhere: it lacks a common ground on which teachers and commissioners can meet.

In preparing to make their views public, the teachers might recognize that this absence of a common ground means that their argument, although highly compelling to teachers, is unlikely to persuade others. The teachers could spend their time telling each other that increased work for inadequate pay is a raw deal, but this argument is unlikely to change the mind of anyone strongly committed to the idea of improving education by lengthening the school day.

As an alternative, the teachers could think about the issue from the perspective of their audience and see whether a genuine dialogue could be initiated. They too want their pupils to receive a rich, full education. Should they support the longer day while insisting that they be guaranteed fair pay? Would the commissioners' plan work, they might ask, even if the teachers were fully compensated? No! As experienced educators, they are convinced that, especially in the earlier grades, children do not have the power of concentration and the self-discipline to make such a long day worthwhile. The teachers' preparation would be wasted, and the children would quickly grow frustrated with school. In skeletal form, their revised argument might run: "Adding an hour to the school day would injure our children's education because it would exhaust and frustrate young pupils." Now at least the two groups can talk about how best to reach a goal they hold in common: educating schoolchildren.

Your common sense will generally tell you if those involved in an argument have established a common ground. If the citizens of a community argue that a local chemical plant should be closed down because its air pollution is making them sick, and the chemical company argues that it should be allowed to remain open because it contributes mightily to the local economy, you can see that the two are arguing at cross purposes, that they haven't established a common ground. One side is operating on the assumption that public health is the most crucial factor in ensuring the public good; the other side assumes that economic prosperity is the central concern. To turn the disagreement into a dialogue, they need to sit down together and weigh the relative importance of health and prosperity and perhaps see if both can be preserved.

Let us take another example. Suppose our community is considering a rent-control law by which landlords would be regulated as to how much they could increase rents. We are a nonpartisan group, like the League of Women Voters, and are trying to assess the potential arguments on both sides. We might classify the potential *logos* appeals into three subgroups: appeals to more particular facts, appeals to more general principles, and appeals to analogous cases. The opposing sides agree that the community must have ample, affordable rental housing; that is our common ground. So we might look first at relevant facts. Is the cost of housing going up in our community faster than inflation or the renters' ability to pay? Is the amount of available housing going down because landlords are not getting a high enough return on their investments? (We might actually conduct interviews with individual renters and landlords.) And then we might look at analogous cases. What were the effects when other communities enacted similar legislation? What were the effects when our community regulated similar enterprises? And then we might seek more general principles. Is the kind of rent-control law being considered itself constitutional in the limits it puts on property rights? Is it inherently just or fair to renters and landlords?

We cannot expect that these inquiries are themselves going to decide the issue for us; they are only meant to help us clarify the basis for our decision. If the facts seem to show that landlords are leaving our community because of regulations already in place, we might consider outlawing conversions to condominiums to make it more difficult for them to leave without losing their investment—or argue that they are leaving already, so rent control will make no difference in an already inevitable flight. If an analogous case shows that rent-control laws have had an unexpected adverse effect on another community, we might question whether that community is really like ours. (The community was much smaller, the law was different, there was no university nearby, or the national economy was stronger then.) If an appeal to "justice" seems to demand rent control, we might ask whether the notion of justice being invoked squares with ours or whether there are alternative definitions. Or if law cases seem to support the constitutionality of the law, we might see if there are other rules of law that at least make the issue doubtful and then raise the question of whether our community can afford expensive litigation at this time. In short, we should be able to anticipate most of the *logos* appeals made by both sides and also possible responses to these appeals. We will survey possibly relevant facts, explore possibly revealing analogies, and seek out possibly applicable authorities.

What we are trying to avoid is a debate in which each side lines up and slings mud at the other. This is possible only because we began by finding common ground. Both sides agreed that they were committed to ample, affordable rentals. In the course of the discussion, it may become clear that some on each side are not sincerely committed to this common ground. Some on one side may be only interested in whatever will maximize profits for the landlords; some on the other side may privately believe that the only fair rent is no rent at all. In such cases, we must either find new common ground or—more likely—ignore these factions in future discussions, for their minds are already closed on the subject. We have learned what we can from them, and they refuse to learn from us or from each other.

Marcus Tullius Cicero

MILO'S INNOCENCE*

Because arguers and audiences generally share a faith in logical reasoning, facts, statistics, definitions, examples, and pronouncements by authorities, these are among the most commonly used logos appeals. The following extract is an argument based on the respect for logical reasoning shared by the speaker and his audience. Two Roman noblemen have had a brawl and one has killed the other, allegedly in self-defense. Here the Roman orator Cicero argues from

---

*Translated by Michael Grant.

probability that the dead man, Clodius, must have been the aggressor, making a premeditated attack on Cicero's unsuspecting client, Milo. Rather than piling up facts, Cicero is reasoning out the situation, arguing for those conclusions most favorable to his client's case.

Gentlemen, it all fits in. To Milo it was positively advantageous that Clodius should stay alive. But for Clodius, if he was ever going to attain his principal ambition, the death of Milo was very greatly to be desired. Clodius detested Milo, but Milo did not hate Clodius at all. Clodius had habitually and continually initiated violence, whereas all Milo had done was to resist aggression. Clodius had openly declared and proclaimed that Milo was going to die; but nothing of the kind was ever heard from Milo. Clodius had known the day of Milo's departure, while Milo for his part had no knowledge whatever of the date when Clodius was likely to come back. Milo's journey was unavoidable, but Clodius' trip had no purpose, and was indeed positively inconvenient to him. Milo had openly announced that he would be leaving Rome on the date in question; Clodius had concealed the fact that he was going to return on the very same day. Milo made not the smallest change in his plans, while Clodius invented reasons to explain why his own movements were changed. And, finally, Milo, if he was engaged in a plot, would have taken up his position near the city and waited until nightfall, whereas Clodius, quite regardless of any apprehensions he might have felt about Milo, still had every reason to be afraid of coming to the city after dark.

52 B.C.

Robin Lakoff

TAG QUESTIONS

Student writers often feel unqualified to argue about the subjects suggested to them because they have an insufficient number of facts on that subject. Knowing the facts is absolutely critical, of course. No one will be persuaded by an argument that contains fundamental errors of fact. But we find that sometimes our students overlook the sources of evidence that they do possess, such as the common experiences and perceptions that unite them to their audiences. In this selection from her essay "You Are What You Say," Robin Lakoff uses evidence from daily life to support her argument that our society conditions women to use unassertive, "ladylike" speech. One of her examples of such speech is the tag question, which, she argues, turns an ordinary statement into "a statement that doesn't demand to be believed by anyone but the speaker." Using a tag question is "a way of giving leeway, of not forcing the addressee to go along with the views of the speaker." Note that Lakoff doesn't offer her reader a scientific study of tag questions, only some examples that she hopes will correspond to her audience's experiences. Her use of the phrase, "as far as I know," ensures that the strength of her claim is in proportion to the casual evidence she gives to support it. Rather than making absolute claims, she speaks of "likely consequences" and what factors "may explain" why women's language sounds as it does. Lakoff is a professor of linguistics, and both her arguments and her evidence would be different if she were addressing other scholars in her field. But this essay appeared in Ms. magazine; its arguments are meant to be accessible to the nonspecialist reader.

1   The tag question allows a speaker to avoid commitment, and thereby avoid conflict with the addressee. The problem is that, by so doing, speakers may also give the impression of not really being sure of themselves, or looking to the addressee for confirmation of their views. This uncertainty is reinforced in more subliminal ways, too. There is a peculiar sentence intonation-pattern, used almost exclusively by women, as far as I know, which changes a declarative answer into a question. The effect of using the rising inflection typical of a yes-no question is to imply that the speaker is seeking confirmation, even though the speaker is clearly the only one who has the requisite information, which is why the question was put to her in the first place:

(Q) When will dinner be ready?
(A) Oh . . . around six o'clock . . . ?

It is as though the second speaker were saying, "Six o'clock—if that's okay with you, if you agree." The person being addressed is put in the position of having to provide confirmation. One likely consequence of this sort of speech-pattern in a woman is that, often unbeknownst to herself, the speaker builds a reputation of tentativeness, and others will refrain from taking her seriously. . . .

2   Such idiosyncrasies may explain why women's language sounds much more "polite" than men's. It is polite to leave a decision open, not impose your mind, or views, or claims, on anyone else. So a tag question is a kind of polite statement, in that it does not force agreement or belief on the addressee. In the same way a request is a polite command, in that it does not force obedience on the addressee, but rather suggests something to be done as a favor to the speaker. A clearly stated order implies a threat of certain consequences if it is not followed, and—even more impolite—implies that the speaker is in a superior position and able to enforce the order. By couching wishes in the form of a request, on the other hand, a speaker implies that if the request is not carried out, only the speaker will suffer; noncompliance cannot harm the addressee. So the decision is really up to the addressee. The distinction becomes clear in these examples:

Close the door.
Please close the door.

Will you close the door?
Will you please close the door?
Won't you close the door?

1974

Charles Darwin

EVIDENCE FOR THE HIGH RATE OF INCREASE AMONG LIVING BEINGS

Some arguments require a substantial amount of specialized evidence. Charles Darwin's views on evolution were somewhat unwelcome to his original readers, who had no desire to believe that they were descended from the same ancestors as the apes. In the following passage from Origin of Species, *Charles Darwin moves from theoretical projections to demonstrable fact in his effort to prove that the high rate at which organisms reproduce must lead to a struggle for survival.*

1   There is no exception to the rule that every organic being naturally increases at so high a rate, that if not destroyed, the earth would soon be covered by the progeny of a single pair. Even slow-breeding man has doubled in twenty-five years and at this rate, in a few thousand years, there would literally not be standing room for his progeny. Linnaeus has calculated that if an annual plant produced only two seeds—and there is no plant so unproductive as this—and their seedlings next year produced two, and so on, then in twenty years there would be a million plants. The elephant is reckoned to be the slowest breeder of all known animals, and I have taken some pains to estimate its probable minimum rate of natural increase: it will be under the mark to assume that it breeds when thirty years old, and goes on breeding till ninety years old, bringing forth three pairs of young in this interval; if this be so, at the end of the fifth century there would be alive fifteen million elephants, descended from the first pair.

2   But we have better evidence on this subject than mere theoretical calculations, namely, the numerous recorded cases of the astonishingly rapid increase of various animals in a state of nature, when circumstances have been favourable to them during two or three following seasons. Still more striking is the evidence from our domestic animals of many kinds which have run wild in several parts of the world: if the statements of the rate of increase of slow-breeding cattle and horses in South America, and latterly in Austra-

lia, had not been well authenticated, they would have been quite incredible. So it is with plants: cases could be given of introduced plants which have become common throughout whole islands in a period of less than ten years. Several of the plants now most numerous over the wide plains of La Plata, clothing square leagues of surface almost to the exclusion of all other plants, have been introduced from Europe; and there are plants which now range in India, as I hear from Dr Falconer, from Cape Comorin to the Himalaya, which have been imported from America since its discovery. In such cases, and endless instances could be given, no one supposes that the fertility of these animals or plants has been suddenly and temporarily increased in any sensible degree. The obvious explanation is that the conditions of life have been very favourable, and that there has consequently been less destruction of the old and young, and that nearly all the young have been enabled to breed. In such cases the geometrical ratio of increase, the result of which never fails to be surprising, simply explains the extraordinarily rapid increase and wide diffusion of naturalised productions in their new homes. . . .

1859

USING THE THREE APPEALS IN CONSTRUCTING AN ARGUMENT

Let's say that you have been thinking about the nature of racial prejudice and want to communicate your ideas to an audience. One possibility is to define carefully for yourself and your audience exactly what prejudice is. A definition would be a type of *logos* appeal.

Gordon Allport

THE NATURE OF PREJUDICE

In the following passage, Gordon Allport, a Harvard psychologist, chooses to develop a definition of prejudice. Notice that he uses examples as well as more formal definitions to make his point.

> *For myself, earth-bound and fettered to the scene of my activities, I confess that I do feel the differences of mankind, national and individual. . . . I am, in plainer words, a bundle of prejudices—made up of likings and dislikings— the veriest thrall to sympathies, apathies, antipathies.*
>
> Charles Lamb

1   In Rhodesia a white truck driver passed a group of idle natives and muttered, "They're lazy brutes." A few hours later he saw natives heaving two-hundred pound sacks of grain onto a truck, singing in rhythm to their work. "Savages," he grumbled. "What do you expect?"

2   In one of the West Indies it was customary at one time for natives to hold their noses conspicuously whenever they passed an American on the street. And in England, during the war, it was said, "The only trouble with the Yanks is that they are over-paid, over-sexed, and over here."

3   Polish people often called the Ukrainians "reptiles" to express their contempt for a group they regarded as ungrateful, revengeful, wily, and treacherous. At the same time Germans called their neighbors to the east "Polish cattle." The Poles retaliated with "Prussian swine"—a jibe at the presumed uncouthness and lack of honor of the Germans.

4   In South Africa, the English, it is said, are against the Afrikaner; both are against the Jews; all three are opposed to the Indians; while all four conspire against the native black.

5   In Boston, a dignitary of the Roman Catholic Church was driving along a lonesome road on the outskirts of the city. Seeing a small Negro boy trudging along, the dignitary told his chauffeur to stop and give the boy a lift. Seated together in the back of the limousine, the cleric, to make conversation, asked, "Little Boy, are you a Catholic?" Wide-eyed with alarm, the boy replied, "No sir, it's bad enough being colored without being one of those things."

6   Pressed to tell what Chinese people really think of Americans, a Chinese student reluctantly replied, "Well, we think they are the best of the foreign devils." This incident occurred before the Communist revolution in China. Today's youth in China are trained to think of Americans as the *worst* of the foreign devils.

7   In Hungary, the saying is, "An anti-Semite is a person who hates the Jews more than is absolutely necessary."

8   No corner of the world is free from group scorn. Being fettered to our respective cultures, we, like Charles Lamb, are bundles of prejudice.

Two Cases

9   An anthropologist in his middle thirties had two young children, Susan and Tom. His work required him to live for a year with a tribe of American Indians in the home of a hospitable Indian family. He insisted, however, that his own family live in a community of white people several miles distant from the Indian reservation. Seldom would he allow Tom and Susan to come to the tribal village, though they pleaded for the privilege. And on rare occasions when they made the visit, he sternly refused to allow them to play with the friendly Indian children.

10   Some people, including a few of the Indians, complained that the anthropologist was untrue to the code of his profession—that he was displaying race prejudice.

11   The truth is otherwise. This scientist knew that tuberculosis was rife in the tribal village, and that four of the children in the household where he lived had already died of the disease. The probability of infection for his own children, if they came much in contact with the natives, was high. His better judgment told him that he should not take the risk. In this case, his ethnic avoidance was based on rational and realistic grounds. There was no feeling of antagonism involved. The anthropologist had no generally negative attitude toward the Indians. In fact he liked them very much.

12   Since this case fails to illustrate what we mean by racial or ethnic prejudice, let us turn to another.

13   In the early summer season two Toronto newspapers carried between them holiday advertisements from approximately 100 different resorts. A Canadian social scientist, S. L. Wax, undertook an interesting experiment.[1] To each of these hotels and resorts he wrote two letters, mailing them at the same time, and asking for room reservations for exactly the same dates. One letter he signed with the name "Mr. Greenberg," the other with the name "Mr. Lockwood." Here are the results:

> To "Mr. Greenberg":
>   52 percent of the resorts replied;
>   36 percent offered him accommodations.
> To "Mr. Lockwood":
>   95 percent of the resorts replied;
>   93 percent offered him accommodations.

Thus, nearly all of the resorts in question welcomed Mr. Lockwood as a correspondent and as a guest; but nearly half of them failed to give Mr. Greenberg the courtesy of a reply, and only slightly more than a third were willing to receive him as a guest.

14   None of the hotels knew "Mr. Lockwood" or "Mr. Greenberg." For all they knew "Mr. Greenberg" might be a quiet, orderly gentleman, and "Mr. Lockwood" rowdy and drunk. The decision was obviously made not on the merits of the individual, but on "Mr. Greenberg's" supposed membership in a group. He suffered discourtesy and exclusion *solely* because of his name, which aroused a prejudgment of his desirability in the eyes of the hotel managers.

15   Unlike our first case, this incident contains the two essential ingredients of ethnic prejudice. (1) There is definite hostility and rejection. The majority of the hotels wanted nothing to do with "Mr. Greenberg." (2) The basis of the rejection was categorical. "Mr. Greenberg" was not evaluated as an individual. Rather, he was condemned on the basis of his presumed group membership.

> A close reasoner might at this point ask the question: What basic difference exists between the cases of the anthropologist and the hotels in the matter of "categorical rejection"? Did not the anthropologist reason from the high probability

[1]S. L. Wax. A survey of restrictive advertising and discrimination by summer resorts in the Province of Ontario. Canadian Jewish Congress: *Information and comment,* 1948, 7, 10–13.

of infection that it would be safer not to risk contact between his children and the Indians? And did not the hotelkeepers reason from a high probability that Mr. Greenberg's ethnic membership would in fact bring them an undesirable guest? The anthropologist knew that tubercular contagion was rampant; did not the innkeepers know that "Jewish vices" were rampant and not to be risked?

This question is legitimate. If the innkeepers were basing their rejection on facts (more accurately, on a high probability that a given Jew will have undesirable traits), their action would be as rational and defensible as the anthropologist's. But we can be sure that such is not the case.

Some managers may never have had any unpleasant experiences with Jewish guests—a situation that seems likely in view of the fact that in many cases Jewish guests had never been admitted to the hotels. Or, if they have had such experiences, they have not kept a record of their frequency in comparison with objectionable non-Jewish guests. Certainly they have not consulted scientific studies concerning the relative frequency of desirable and undesirable traits in Jews and non-Jews. If they sought such evidence, they would, as we shall learn . . . find no support for their policy of rejection.

It is, of course, possible that the manager himself was free from personal prejudice, but, if so, he was reflecting the anti-Semitism of his gentile guests. In either event our point is made.

Definition

[16]   The word *prejudice,* derived from the Latin noun *praejudicium,* has, like most words, undergone a change of meaning since classical times. There are three stages in the transformation.[2]

(1) To the ancients, *praejudicium* meant a *precedent*—a judgment based on previous decisions and experiences.

(2) Later, the term, in English, acquired the meaning of a judgment formed before due examination and consideration of the facts—a premature or hasty judgment.

(3) Finally the term acquired also its present emotional flavor of favorableness or unfavorableness that accompanies such a prior and unsupported judgment.

[17]   Perhaps the briefest of all definitions of prejudice is: *thinking ill of others without sufficient warrant.*[3] This crisp phrasing contains the two essential ingredients of all definitions—reference to unfounded judgment and to a feeling-tone. It is, however, too brief for complete clarity.

---

[2]Cf. *A New English Dictionary.* (Sir James A. H. Murray, ed.) Oxford: Clarendon Press, 1909, Vol. VII, Pt. II, 1275.

[3]This definition is derived from the Thomistic moralists who regard prejudice as "rash judgment." The author is indebted to the Reverend J. H. Fichter, S. J., for calling this treatment to his attention. The definition is more fully discussed by the Reverend John LaFarge, S. J., in *The Race Question and the Negro,* New York: Longmans, Green, 1945, 174 ff.

18   In the first place, it refers only to *negative* prejudice. People may be prejudiced in favor of others; they may think *well* of them without sufficient warrant. The wording offered by the *New English Dictionary* recognizes positive as well as negative prejudice:

> *A feeling, favorable or unfavorable, toward a person or thing, prior to, or not based on, actual experience.*

While it is important to bear in mind that biases may be *pro* as well as *con*, it is none the less true that *ethnic* prejudice is mostly negative. A group of students was asked to describe their attitudes toward ethnic groups. No suggestion was made that might lead them toward negative reports. Even so, they reported eight times as many antagonistic attitudes as favorable attitudes. In this volume, accordingly, we shall be concerned chiefly with prejudice *against*, not with prejudice *in favor of*, ethnic groups.

19   The phrase "thinking ill of others" is obviously an elliptical expression that must be understood to include feelings of scorn or dislike, of fear and aversion, as well as various forms of antipathetic conduct: such as talking against people, discriminating against them, or attacking them with violence.

20   Similarly, we need to expand the phrase "without sufficient warrant." A judgment is unwarranted whenever it lacks basis in fact. A wit defined prejudice as "being down on something you're not up on."

21   It is not easy to say how much fact is required in order to justify a judgment. A prejudiced person will almost certainly claim that he has sufficient warrant for his views. He will tell of bitter experiences he has had with refugees, Catholics, or Orientals. But, in most cases, it is evident that his facts are scanty and strained. He resorts to a selective sorting of his own few memories, mixes them up with hearsay, and overgeneralizes. No one can possibly know *all* refugees, Catholics, or Orientals. Hence any negative judgment of these groups *as a whole* is, strictly speaking, an instance of thinking ill without sufficient warrant.

22   Sometimes, the ill-thinker has no first-hand experience on which to base his judgment. A few years ago most Americans thought exceedingly ill of Turks—but very few had ever seen a Turk nor did they know any person who had seen one. Their warrant lay exclusively in what they had heard of the Armenian massacres and of the legendary crusades. On such evidence they presumed to condemn all members of a nation.

23   Ordinarily, prejudice manifests itself in dealing with individual members of rejected groups. But in avoiding a Negro neighbor, or in answering "Mr. Greenberg's" application for a room, we frame our action to accord with our categorical generalization of the group as a whole. We pay little or no attention to individual differences, and overlook the important fact that Negro X, our neighbor, is not Negro Y, whom we dislike for good and sufficient reason;

that Mr. Greenberg, who may be a fine gentleman, is not Mr. Bloom, whom we have good reason to dislike.

24   So common is this process that we might define prejudice as:

> an avertive or hostile attitude toward a person who belongs to a group, simply because he belongs to that group, and is therefore presumed to have the objectionable qualities ascribed to the group.

This definition stresses the fact that while ethnic prejudice in daily life is ordinarily a matter of dealing with individual people it also entails an unwarranted idea concerning a group as a whole.

25   Returning to the question of "sufficient warrant," we must grant that few if any human judgments are based on absolute certainty. We can be reasonably, but not absolutely, sure that the sun will rise tomorrow, and that death and taxes will finally overtake us. The sufficient warrant for any judgment is always a matter of probabilities. Ordinarily our judgments of natural happenings are based on firmer and higher probabilities than our judgments of people. Only rarely do our categorical judgments of nations or ethnic groups have a foundation in high probability.

26   Take the hostile view of Nazi leaders held by most Americans during World War II. Was it prejudiced? The answer is No, because there was abundant available evidence regarding the evil policies and practices accepted as the official code of the party. True, there may have been good individuals in the party who at heart rejected the abominable program; but the probability was so high that the Nazi group constituted an actual menace to world peace and to humane values that a realistic and justified conflict resulted. The high probability of danger removes an antagonism from the domain of prejudice into that of realistic social conflict.

27   In the case of gangsters, our antagonism is not a matter of prejudice, for the evidence of their antisocial conduct is conclusive. But soon the line becomes hard to draw. How about an ex-convict? It is notoriously difficult for an ex-convict to obtain a steady job where he can be self-supporting and self-respecting. Employers naturally are suspicious if they know the man's past record. But often they are more suspicious than the facts warrant. If they looked further they might find evidence that the man who stands before them is genuinely reformed, or even that he was unjustly accused in the first place. To shut the door merely because a man has a criminal record has *some* probability in its favor, for many prisoners are never reformed; but there is also an element of unwarranted prejudgment involved. We have here a true borderline instance.

28   We can never hope to draw a hard and fast line between "sufficient" and "insufficient" warrant. For this reason we cannot always be sure whether we are dealing with a case of prejudice or nonprejudice. Yet no one will deny that often we form judgments on the basis of scant, even nonexistent, probabilities.

29   *Overcategorization* is perhaps the commonest trick of the human mind. Given a thimbleful of facts we rush to make generalizations as large as a tub. One young boy developed the idea that all Norwegians were giants because he was impressed by the gigantic stature of Ymir in the saga, and for years was fearful lest he meet a living Norwegian. A certain man happened to know three Englishmen personally and proceeded to declare that the whole English race had the common attributes that he observed in these three.

30   There is a natural basis for this tendency. Life is so short, and the demands upon us for practical adjustments so great, that we cannot let our ignorance detain us in our daily transactions. We have to decide whether objects are good or bad by classes. We cannot weigh each object in the world by itself. Rough and ready rubrics, however coarse and broad, have to suffice.

31   Not every overblown generalization is a prejudice. Some are simply *misconceptions*, wherein we organize wrong information. One child had the idea that all people living in Minneapolis were "monopolists." And from his father he had learned that monopolists were evil folk. When in later years he discovered the confusion, his dislike of dwellers in Minneapolis vanished.

32   Here we have the test to help us distinguish between ordinary errors of prejudgment and prejudice. If a person is capable of rectifying his erroneous judgments in the light of new evidence, he is not prejudiced. *Prejudgments become prejudices only if they are not reversible when exposed to new knowledge.* A prejudice, unlike a simple misconception, is actively resistant to all evidence that would unseat it. We tend to grow emotional when a prejudice is threatened with contradiction. Thus the difference between ordinary prejudgments and prejudice is that one can discuss and rectify a prejudgment without emotional resistance.

33   Taking these various considerations into account, we may now attempt a final definition of negative ethnic prejudice—one that will serve us throughout this book. Each phrase in the definition represents a considerable condensation of the points we have been discussing:

> Ethnic prejudice is an antipathy based upon a faulty and inflexible generalization. It may be felt or expressed. It may be directed toward a group as a whole, or toward an individual because he is a member of that group.

The net effect of prejudice, thus defined, is to place the object of prejudice at some disadvantage not merited by his own misconduct. . . .

1954

◆ ◆ ◆

Perhaps your idea about prejudice is quite personal, and your intention is to affect your audience's attitude by showing how living in a prejudiced society has influenced your own character. You might wonder why an audience should be interested in you in particular. They will be if your insights are new to them, if you show that you have given the subject the careful thought that they have not had the time or inclination to give it, or if the image you create of yourself and your ideas is appealing in some other way. This emphasis on you yourself as arguer suggests that you will be using an *ethos* appeal.

Zora Neale Hurston

HOW IT FEELS TO BE COLORED ME

One might expect that an ethos *appeal concerning prejudice would be based on anger or outrage. Zora Neale Hurston, however, in her productive career as an essayist and novelist, thrived on doing the unexpected. Her writing frequently charms the reader into submission. You might want to compare her* ethos *to those of the other authors in this section. What do her many allusions, some of them quite obscure, contribute to her persuasiveness?*

1   I am colored but I offer nothing in the way of extenuating circumstances except the fact that I am the only Negro in the United States whose grandfather on the mother's side was *not* an Indian chief.

2   I remember the very day that I became colored. Up to my thirteenth year I lived in the little Negro town of Eatonville, Florida. It is exclusively a colored town. The only white people I knew passed through the town going to or coming from Orlando. The native whites rode dusty horses, the Northern tourists chugged down the sandy village road in automobiles. The town knew the Southerners and never stopped cane chewing when they passed. But the Northerners were something else again. They were peered at cautiously from behind curtains by the timid. The more venturesome would come out on the porch to watch them go past and got just as much pleasure out of the tourists as the tourists got out of the village.

3   The front porch might seem a daring place for the rest of the town, but it was a gallery seat for me. My favorite place was atop the gate-post. Proscenium box for a born first-nighter. Not only did I enjoy the show, but I didn't mind the actors knowing that I liked it. I usually spoke to them in passing. I'd wave at them and when they returned my salute, I would say something like this: "Howdy-do-well-I-thank-you-where-you-goin'?" Usually automobile or the horse paused at this, and after a queer exchange of compliments, I would probably "go a piece of the way" with them, as we say in farthest Florida. If one of my family happened to come to the front in time to see me, of course negotiations would be rudely broken off. But even so, it is clear that I

was the first "welcome-to-our-state" Floridian, and I hope the Miami Chamber of Commerce will please take notice.

4   During this period, white people differed from colored to me only in that they rode through town and never lived there. They liked to hear me "speak pieces" and sing and wanted to see me dance the parse-me-la, and gave me generously of their small silver for doing these things, which seemed strange to me for I wanted to do them so much that I needed bribing to stop. Only they didn't know it. The colored people gave no dimes. They deplored any joyful tendencies in me, but I was their Zora nevertheless. I belonged to them, to the nearby hotels, to the county—everybody's Zora.

5   But changes came in the family when I was thirteen, and I was sent to school in Jacksonville. I left Eatonville, the town of the oleanders, as Zora. When I disembarked from the river-boat at Jacksonville, she was no more. It seemed that I had suffered a sea change. I was not Zora of Orange County any more, I was now a little colored girl. I found it out in certain ways. In my heart as well as in the mirror, I became a fast brown—warranted not to rub nor run.

6   But I am not tragically colored. There is no great sorrow dammed up in my soul, nor lurking behind my eyes. I do not mind at all. I do not belong to the sobbing school of Negrohood who hold that nature somehow has given them a lowdown dirty deal and whose feelings are all hurt about it. Even in the helter-skelter skirmish that is my life, I have seen that the world is to the strong regardless of a little pigmentation more or less. No, I do not weep at the world—I am too busy sharpening my oyster knife.

7   Someone is always at my elbow reminding me that I am the granddaughter of slaves. It fails to register depression with me. Slavery is sixty years in the past. The operation was successful and the patient is doing well, thank you. The terrible struggle that made me an American out of a potential slave said "On the line!" The Reconstruction said "Get set!"; and the generation before said "Go!" I am off to a flying start and I must not halt in the stretch to look behind and weep. Slavery is the price I paid for civilization, and the choice was not with me. It is a bully adventure and worth all that I have paid through my ancestors for it. No one on earth ever had a greater chance for glory. The world to be won and nothing to be lost. It is thrilling to think—to know that for any act of mine, I shall get twice as much praise or twice as much blame. It is quite exciting to hold the center of the national stage, with the spectators not knowing whether to laugh or to weep.

8   The position of my white neighbor is much more difficult. No brown specter pulls up a chair beside me when I sit down to eat. No dark ghost thrusts its leg against mine in bed. The game of keeping what one has is never so exciting as the game of getting.

9   I do not always feel colored. Even now I often achieve the unconscious Zora of Eatonville before the Hegira. I feel most colored when I am thrown against a sharp white background.

10   For instance at Barnard. "Beside the waters of the Hudson" I feel my race. Among the thousand white persons, I am a dark rock surged upon, and overswept, but through it all, I remain myself. When covered by the waters, I am; and the ebb but reveals me again.

11   Sometimes it is the other way around. A white person is set down in our midst, but the contrast is just as sharp for me. For instance, when I sit in the drafty basement that is The New World Cabaret with a white person, my color comes. We enter chatting about any little nothing that we have in common and are seated by the jazz waiters. In the abrupt way that jazz orchestras have, this one plunges into a number. It loses no time in circumlocutions, but gets right down to business. It constricts the thorax and splits the heart with its tempo and narcotic harmonies. This orchestra grows rambunctious, rears on its hind legs and attacks the tonal veil with primitive fury, rending it, clawing it until it breaks through to the jungle beyond. I follow those heathen— follow them exultingly. I dance wildly inside myself; I yell within, I whoop; I shake my assegai above my head, I hurl it true to the mark *yeeeeooww*! I am in the jungle and living in the jungle way. My face is painted red and yellow and my body is painted blue. My pulse is throbbing like a war drum. I want to slaughter something—give paid, give death to what, I do not know. But the piece ends. The men of the orchestra wipe their lips and rest their fingers. I creep back slowly to the veneer we call civilization with the last tone and find the white friend sitting motionless in his seat, smoking calmly.

12   "Good music they have here," he remarks, drumming the table with his fingertips.

13   Music. The great blobs of purple and red emotion have not touched him. He has only heard what I felt. He is far away and I see him but dimly across the ocean and the continent that have fallen between us. He is so pale with his whiteness then and I am *so* colored.

14   At certain times I have no race, I am *me*. When I set my hat at a certain angle and saunter down Seventh Avenue, Harlem City, feeling as snooty as the lions in front of the Forty-Second Street Library, for instance. So far as my feelings are concerned, Peggy Hopkins Joyce on the Boule Mich with her gorgeous raiment, stately carriage, knees knocking together in a most aristocratic manner, has nothing on me. The cosmic Zora emerges. I belong to no race nor time. I am the eternal feminine with its string of beads.

15   I have no separate feeling about being an American citizen and colored. I am merely a fragment of the Great Soul that surges within the boundaries. My country, right or wrong.

16   Sometimes, I feel discriminated against, but it does not make me angry. It merely astonishes me, How *can* any deny themselves the pleasure of my company? It's beyond me.

17   But in the main, I feel like a brown bag of miscellany propped against a wall. Against a wall in company with other bags, white, red and yellow. Pour out the contents, and there is discovered a jumble of small things priceless and worthless. A first-water diamond, an empty spool, bits of broken glass, lengths of string, a key to a door long since crumbled away, a rusty knife-blade, old shoes saved for a road that never was and never will be, a nail bent under the weight of things too heavy for any nail, a dried flower or two still a little fragrant. In your hand is the brown bag. On the ground before you is the jumble it held—so much like the jumble in the bags, could they be emptied, that all might be dumped in a single heap and the bags refilled without altering the content of any greatly. A bit of colored glass more or less would not matter. Perhaps that is how the Great Stuffer of Bags filled them in the first place—who knows?

1928

Perhaps you think that your audience has become too complacent or apathetic on the subject of prejudice, that their emotions need to be engaged before you can change their minds. You might then choose to employ a *pathos* appeal.

Roy Wilkins

AN ESCAPE FROM JUDGE LYNCH

Wilkins asks his audience to imagine the experience of racial discrimination by identifying with his grandfather. You might compare Wilkins's pathos appeal here with the one that Martin Luther King Jr. employs in paragraph 14 of his "Letter from Birmingham Jail," reprinted in Chapter 1.

1   When Grandfather Wilkins got up off his knees on Emancipation Day, his old master and the overseers were still standing there looking at him, and he obviously had a problem. He had been a slave one minute, a freedman the next; but he was still black all day long, and not a white planter in Holly Springs was eager to help him. To say that the vanquished whites of Marshall County merely opposed his liberation would be to do them an injustice; they considered it a war crime against them—and they did everything they could to undo it. He owned no house or land, no mule, no seed, no tools, no food,

not even the clothes on his back. By force of brutal necessity, his first free choice was a hard one: to stay on the plantation.

2   It didn't take long for the white planters and politicians of Mississippi to get together in Jackson to patch up their losses in the Civil War. "Ours is and ever shall be government for white men," Governor Benjamin Humphreys promised the state in his 1865 inaugural address, and the legislature lost no time in translating the rhetoric into action: it passed the notorious and ferocious Black Code, which all but reestablished slavery in Mississippi.

3   Given the provisions of this code, Grandfather Wilkins's decision to stay put was probably the better part of valor. He had just turned fourteen. One of the new statutes bound all Negro orphans under eighteen—and all Negroes under eighteen who had no job—as "apprentices" to masters who could work them, beat them, and run them to the ground if they ran away. Another "antivagrancy" statute stipulated that by the second Monday in January 1866, all freedmen, free Negroes, and mulattoes in Mississippi had to produce written evidence proving that they had a job and a place to live. Local mayors, aldermen, and justices of the peace were given the power to arrest anyone charged with violating the law and to conduct trials without juries for the hapless suspects. Those convicted could be fined $50 and clapped in jail for ten days. To pay the fines, local sheriffs had the power to hire out penniless violators to their old masters.

4   The penalty for speaking up against the Black Code or insulting a white man or preaching without a license was a fine of up to $100 and thirty days in jail. As things stood, Grandfather Wilkins could be arrested almost as quickly for kicking a mule as for mixing with white folks. He could not carry a knife or gun, and the penalty for intermarriage, an idea I'm sure never occurred to him, was life in prison. The code was so transparently evil that radical reconstructionists in the U.S. Congress seized upon it to justify imposing martial law upon Mississippi and granting suffrage to the freedmen, the two devices of Reconstruction that the white folks of Holly Springs hated above all others.

5   It never fails to astonish me when members of white ethnic groups ask in indignation why Negroes should represent a special historical case, why they haven't made the same progress as the Irish or the Italians, the East European or Jewish immigrants. The question bespeaks a hostile indifference to the great gap between the starting points of black Americans and other ethnics. In the beginning Grandfather Wilkins had only two assets to count: the patrollers no longer dogged his every step, and he didn't have to sneak off into the woods simply to worship as a Christian. To keep black people out of the white pews in Holly Springs, planters encouraged the freedmen to build their own churches. Before long, chapels were sprouting on hilltop and bottom all over the county. Freed slaves from the Wilkins plantations built a church at the foot of a high hill near the farm of Moses Wilkins, politely call-

ing it Wilkins Chapel. On Sundays the little church resounded with hymns, prayers, and sermons. Grandfather Wilkins and the others gathered there to talk out their troubles and to plan for the future, violating three or four Mississippi race laws every time they said amen.

6   The little country chapels were the only organizations Grandfather Wilkins and the other blacks of Marshall County could call their own. Bishop Elias Cottrell, who learned preaching by studying the sermons of a white minister over a pine-knot fire at night, rode circuit among them and later rose to great prominence in the colored Methodist Episcopal Church (now the Christian Methodist Episcopal Church). Hiram Revels, who represented Mississippi in the U.S. Senate during Reconstruction, was also a Baptist preacher in Holly Springs for a time. His flock called him "Parson Revels." He got on so well with the white folks that he was buried under an imposing monument in the main cemetery in Holly Springs, a long way from the weedy patch of ground where Grandfather Wilkins now lies.

7   My grandfather was a Methodist until the day he died. I believe his first name represents a corruption of Asbury, taken after Bishop Francis Asbury, an early saddle-back revivalist of the Methodist Episcopal Church who imported a rugged article of Methodist faith from England: "Slavery is contrary to the laws of God and man and hurtful to society." That tenet gave the Methodists an early and strong call on the loyalties of black Christians like Grandfather Wilkins. John Wesley himself laid claim to converting the first black believer to the faith that has sometimes sustained and sometimes subdued Negroes for more than two hundred years. In his diary for November 29, 1758, Wesley recorded that he had ridden

> ... to Wandsworth and baptized two Negroes belonging to Mr. Gilbert, a gentleman lately from Antigua. One of these is deeply convinced of sin; the other is rejoicing in God her saviour, and is the first African Christian I have ever known. But shall not God, in his own time, have these heathen as his inheritance?

8   I find it harder to say who will be redeemed and who will be had when Judgment Day arrives. But no matter how it comes out, the Methodist Church supplied Grandfather Wilkins with a faith that served him well all his life.

9   At a prayer meeting one night he met my grandmother, a thin young girl named Emma. She had a quick smile, bright eyes, and the neck of a swan. Her skin was very black; she had small delicate hands—and that scar. Grandfather Wilkins was twenty-two years old, and she swept him away. Late in December 1873, he enlisted his brother Nelson to go with him to the courthouse in Holly Springs to take out a marriage license. The two brothers walked five miles over hill and ridge to reach the courthouse, a brick building two stories high, topped by a cupola and the town clock. They made their way through the town square, past mules and horses, goats and squawking chickens. Penetrating the high cool corridors of the courthouse, the two

young men found the Marshall County clerk's office, a bailiwick run by a one-armed Confederate war hero named George B. Myers. Myers listened while they swore to a bond of $200 guaranteeing that Grandfather Wilkins's marriage plans were proper and in good order. In a bold hand, Myers signed the license for them, and they scratched their X's, the signatures of men forcibly deprived of education as slaves, where Myers told them to. Those timid little crosses comprise the earliest literary relics of my family.

10   Two days before Christmas, the Reverend B. H. Ford married my grandparents. The neighbors came from farms all around for the wedding. In later years Grandfather Wilkins would smile to himself when he thought back on that day. The celebration was just like when white folks got married, he would say, "'cept the bride didn't have no white dress and there wasn't no fancy cookin' for a weddin' supper."

11   At the peak of Reconstruction, Grandfather Wilkins was a married man and a sharecropper. His old master staked him to a mule, seed, manure, food, clothes, and a cabin, in return for his labor and a 50–50 split of his cotton crop at harvest time, an arrangement that left him half slave and half free. The white planters kept the power to sell the cotton crop in Holly Springs, setting prices, collecting what they could, and returning what they chose to their croppers, a system built for boodling. Year after year, Grandfather Wilkins finished the harvest feeling that he had been outwitted or just plain cheated. But he was able to put aside a little bit of cash. Finally, he managed to rent a small farm several miles up the road from the Wilkins plantation, within shouting distance of Beverly Chapel, where he had become an elder. That move upward from cropper to tenant farmer imparted its kinetic energy to the Wilkins family, and we have been driven onward ever since.

12   Reconstruction opened the ballot to black people around Holly Springs, and Grandfather Wilkins became as fervent a Republican as he was a Methodist. In Marshall County, the G.O.P. was made up of Negroes, a few highly principled old-line Whigs who hated Democrats more than they hated black people, some Southern scalawags snuffling after postwar spoils, and a few carpetbaggers from up North. All through Reconstruction, the Republicans spent most of their energy figuring out how to outfox or outhate the Democrats.

13   The leading carpetbagger in Holly Springs was a tall, thin, ugly fellow named Nelson Gill. Gill organized the freedmen into political clubs called Loyal Leagues. The leagues encouraged the blacks of Holly Springs to vote a solid Republican line, partly for their own benefit, even more for the greater glory of Gill himself, who held more offices than any other man around: postmaster, head of the Freedmen's Bureau, president of the Board of Supervisors, and sergeant-at-arms in the state legislature. In Jackson he outraged Southern Bourbons by replacing white page boys with black children.

14   Gill was a greater talker and organizer, and the Loyal League gave my grandfather and the other freedmen their first instruction in the political harangue. The annals of Holly Springs record that there were great parades, processions a mile long of freedmen dressed in flaming-red sashes and great badges of red and blue marching through the streets. At night blazing torches lit the way, and in the day a horn and drum beat out a cadence for the marchers. During one particularly hot campaign, there was a float carrying a tree with branches full of possums, next to which stood a giant black man sharpening a knife. As the float passed through the streets he shouted, "Carve that possum, nigger, carve him to the heart." Then he yelled at the shuddering whites, "Carve that white man, nigger, carve *him* to the heart."

15   On Election Day the black voters of Marshall County rode to the polls four abreast on horses and mules. Gill met them at the courthouse gate, handing out great wads of Republican ballots, from a carpetbag at his feet. The performance outraged white Democrats, who quickly took to stuffing ballot boxes and stealing elections themselves. They got so good at it that in the election of 1875 they wangled back all the power Reconstruction had cost them.

16   Politics thereafter became a dangerous game for Grandfather Wilkins. Henry C. Myers, the brother of the county clerk who signed my grandfather's wedding license, was elected sheriff in 1875. According to local historians, Sheriff Myers also happened to be Cyclops in the Ku Klux Klan, which had about fifteen dens in Marshall County. The Klansmen of Marshall County wore red and black regalia and practiced a catechism so simple that the dimmest cracker could master it. ("Question: What are the objectives of the Ku Klux Klan? Answer: To suppress the Negro and keep him in the position where he belongs and to see that the Democratic Party controls this country.") After Reconstruction, torchlight parades and black political power flickered out, not to reappear for nearly one hundred years.

17   As Reconstruction waned, our family began to grow. Grandfather Wilkins's first son, Robert, was born in May 1876; my father two years later; a daughter and two more sons—Eula, John, and Oran—followed in the 1880s. By the time the census takers came around in 1900, there were three sons, a daughter, a grandson named Sam, and a granddaughter named Beatrice living with Grandfather Wilkins, and his little farmhouse could barely hold all the clan.

18   My father hated farming. He was a stocky man with brown skin and a chronic scowl. Around Holly Springs everyone called him Willie. He went to a one-room school for black children near Beverly Chapel, spending all the time he could steal from the chores with his nose buried in Grandfather Wilkins's Bible. Grandfather Wilkins strapped him for lazing, but encouraged him to get an education. Eventually he managed to talk his way into Rust College in Holly Springs, which was run by the African Methodist Episcopal Church. Back then Rust was more like a high school than a modern col-

lege but it was an improvement over the unpainted, one-room shacks that Mississippi considered good enough schools for its black children.

19   At Rust, my father began to court my mother, a willowy young country schoolmarm named Mayfield Edmundson, who taught in a little school near Beverly Chapel. She was very pretty and rather frail. She wore dresses that buttoned up to her chin and down to he wrists, and she had a look of perpetually surprised innocence. Her friends called her Sweetie Mayfield.

20   My mother had a café-au-lait complexion. Her sister Elizabeth was fairer. Their father was Peyton Edmundson, one of the first black Baptist preachers in Marshall County. The Edmundsons provide the second of the two anomalies in my family tree: a paternal grandfather named Jeffries and, on my mother's side of the family, a great-grandfather who was probably white. The fair skin of the Edmundson sisters had to come from somewhere. There is no way to know for sure, but I suspect that Parson Edmundson or his wife—perhaps both of them—were light-skinned children from one of those unions white masters so commonly forced on black women in the slave quarters or the woods after dark.

21   In early June 1900, my father proposed to Sweetie Mayfield and made the same trip to the Marshall County courthouse that Grandfather Wilkins had made before him. There was, however, an improvement in the marriage license Willie Wilkins obtained: he signed the document himself in a clear, confident hand. No more X's—we were making progress.

22   William Wilkins and Mayfield Edmundson were married on June 7, 1900. For a while my father worked as a porter, the best job he could get after graduating from Rust College. The work was bone-wearying and poorly paid. He had to call the son of his boss "sir," even though the white boy was younger than he was. He had to step out of the way every time a white man approached him on the street. In return, the white folks of Holly Springs saluted him as "boy"—or "nigger."

23   My father had enough education to realize that the equality of all men as set forth in the Declaration of Independence wasn't exactly common policy around Marshall County; he became the family's first hell-raiser. Since he talked back to white people whenever he felt like it, people around Holly Springs began to worry about him. They said he was on his way to becoming a troublemaker, bum, and all-round bad nigger. I have the same traits buried somewhere in my chromosomes. I don't like to be mistreated. I don't like to see other people mistreated. I believe in fighting back.

24   The rebelliousness of my father finally broke into open insurrection in midsummer 1900. One day not long after his marriage, he was walking down a dirt road near Grandfather Wilkins's farm. It was a hot day, and dust kicked up in red whirls as he scuffed along, deep in thought. Suddenly he heard a voice bellow behind him: "Nigger, get out of my way."

25   For a second he stood there transfixed. When he turned around, he saw a white farmer sitting on a wagon in the middle of the road. The farmer was leering at him, waiting confidently for him to jump out of the way. A lifetime of insult finally boiled up and over within my father. He took a quick step forward, swung up onto the wagon, and smashed the smirk off his tormentor's face. Then he kept right on swinging until the white man lay in the wagon bed, bloody and groaning. Finally, trembling with rage, he stepped back down into the road and walked home to the farm.

26   In those days, by the book of Judge Lynch, for a Negro to hit a white man meant death in the Deep South. Word of what had happened quickly raced through the county. Late that afternoon, a worried white friend for whom Grandfather Wilkins did chores came calling at the farm.

27   "Uncle Asberry," he said, "you better get that boy Willie out of town. He's making trouble for both of us. There's nothing I can do for him. He's heading for a lynching sure."

28   The same night, in the darkness, Grandfather Wilkins anxiously bundled Willie and Sweetie Mayfield into a wagon and drove them to a railroad station up the line from Holly Springs. Early the next morning, they caught the first train north. Willie Wilkins had lifted us from mute suffering to open war against the injustices of race. The Lord may have delivered Daniel from the lion's den and Grandfather Wilkins from slavery, but it was the Illinois Central that delivered my father from Mississippi—one step ahead of a lynch rope.

1982

These three examples of ways to make an argument about prejudice use all three appeals, and you will probably mix your own appeals as well. Your choice of *ethos, pathos,* and *logos* appeals will proceed from your choices about audience and intention in a way that is unique to your essay.

Reacting and Writing

◆ *Ethos* Appeals

To begin to develop a sense of your own *ethos,* you might think of an area in which you have some expertise—training to make an athletic team, running for a campus office, preparing yourself for college, adjusting to its demands once there. Try writing a letter of advice to someone in your high school, giving him or her the fruits of your experience and knowledge. How might you establish yourself as someone worth listening to?

◆   *Pathos* **Appeals**

To experiment with *pathos,* make a list of four issues, large or small, that matter to you. Then think of a forum in which you might express your views on these subjects (school newspaper, letter to a local or national newspaper, petition to a congressman, etc.). For each issue, write a paragraph that seeks to engage your audience's feelings: to stir their compassion, to rouse them from inactivity, to focus their attention strongly on your subject, or to accomplish some other goal that seems reasonable given the audience and the subject.

◆   *Logos* **Appeals**

Using evidence that you gather from your own experience and that of your fellow students, argue in favor of or against the structure of the curriculum at your college or university. Remember that some undergraduate programs have no requirements beyond the courses needed for the major, some have a carefully designed curriculum in which all the students take the same courses, and some have distribution requirements to ensure that students take a sufficiently wide variety of courses. Decide whether you think your school's program is flexible enough and coherent enough to give students the best possible education.

Or you can practice gathering evidence from your own experience by writing a new essay entitled "You Are What You Say," the title of Robin Lakoff's article from which we drew the selection, "Tag Questions." Think of another way in which the language we use affects our way of seeing the world or the way that the world sees us. Do your research by listening carefully to yourself and your friends.

You can also practice using *logos* appeals by writing definitions. Look at Allport's definition of *prejudice* and then write a definition of your own of some important word that means different things to different people.

ORGANIZING YOUR APPEALS

Suppose that you have decided on an audience and an intention, and you have also settled on the various appeals you are going to make. The ancient rhetoricians would say that you have finished with the invention stage of your composition, and you now have to consider disposition—how you are going to order your appeals. If the paper is like a trip, the audience is someone being taken for the ride, and the intention is the destination, then the disposition or organization maps the stages of the journey. The classical rhetoricians thought that each stage or part of a composition should have its own specific intention or objective. The work of composition then is divided up into tasks of manageable size and scope. How far can one reasonably expect to go on each leg of the journey?

Cicero, probably the greatest of the ancient Roman rhetoricians, suggested a conventional way to organize a piece of argumentative discourse. He certainly did not think that his was the only way. But he did think it was important to have such a conventional structure in mind to make sure both that nothing crucial is left out and that too much isn't attempted in any one section. He was also worried about having to speak extemporaneously, as you might be worried occasionally about writing answers for essay examinations or about having to write papers the night before they are due. We are going to review Cicero's method here by using a familiar piece of discourse that was much influenced by it, Thomas Jefferson's Declaration of Independence.

> When in the Course of human events, it becomes necessary for one people to dissolve the political bands which have connected them with another, and to assume among the Powers of the earth, the separate and equal station to which the Laws of Nature and of Nature's God entitle them, a decent respect to the opinions of mankind requires that they should declare the causes which impel them to the separation.

The first section, of course, is the introduction, or *exordium* as Cicero would have called it. Here the author usually gives a preliminary sense of the kinds of *logos, pathos,* and *ethos* appeals he will use. The case at hand—*logos*—is the dissolution of political bands. The appeal is going to be made to a most generalized audience, virtually all "mankind." This significantly limits the utility of *pathos* appeals. The *ethos* is dignified in the extreme; these revolutionaries, far from being wild radicals, have a decent respect for the opinions of mankind, the laws of nature, and the God of nature—or so they insist.

After the introduction, the author then has to evaluate what the audience needs to know even to consider the case at hand. This Cicero called the *narration;* here should be reviewed matters that are not in dispute. In a court case, it might be the facts on which both sides agree. If—to use our earlier example—the argument is over rent control, we might feel the need to recount for those who have just moved here the recent history of the issue in our city or review the discussions at the last city council meeting. Of course, there are opportunities to color the narration so that it anticipates the position eventually to be argued, but Cicero would have regarded this as sophistry.

Jefferson wants to convince his very general audience that the revolutionaries are behaving responsibly, that their decision to declare their independence is a rational one. He knows that the view of reason commonly held in the eighteenth century is one based on mathematics, especially geometry. To argue rationally in this context, one must argue from self-evident truths. So Jefferson's narration is a listing of the self-evident truths on the basis of which he and his fellows have reached their decision.

> We hold these truths to be self-evident, that all men are created equal, that they are endowed by their Creator with certain unalienable Rights, that among these are Life, Liberty and the pursuit of Happiness. That to secure these rights, Governments are instituted among Men, deriving their just powers from the consent of the governed. That whenever any Form of Government becomes destructive of these ends, it is the Right of the People to alter or to abolish it, and to institute a new Govern-

ment, laying its foundation on such principles and organizing its powers in such form, as to them shall seem most likely to effect their Safety and Happiness.

After the audience has been informed by the narration, it still might not be ready to hear the argument. It might hold certain opinions that have to be removed before the author can expect to get a fair hearing. This section is usually called the *refutation,* but that is a misnomer. The usual technique in such a section is to concede the general correctness of the audience's opinion—but to claim that it does not apply in the case at hand. So Jefferson will agree that, no matter how self-evident his principles, we cannot always act on them.

> Prudence, indeed, will dictate that Governments long established should not be changed for light and transient causes; and accordingly all experience hath shown, that mankind are more disposed to suffer, while evils are sufferable, than to right themselves by abolishing the forms to which they are accustomed. But when a long train of abuses and usurpations, pursuing invariably the same Object evinces a design to reduce them under absolute Despotism, it is their right, it is their duty, to throw off such Government, and to provide new Guards for their future security.

The audience now knows about the principles on which the revolutionaries have based their decision and knows too that the revolutionaries claim to have considered the dictates of prudence. Note that Jefferson is not yet asking his audience to agree that this decision is prudent; he is asking it only to suspend its judgment of the revolutionaries, because he has shown that he shares its concerns. In short, he gets what he temporarily needs through his *ethos.*

So the narration and refutation-concession are finished. Jefferson has presented them in the order suggested by Cicero, but that does not mean they always have to appear in this order. An audience bitterly prejudiced against you might need a concession or refutation as soon as possible. You might even have to tuck it into your introduction. Remember the essay for the legalization of marijuana, in which the author said in his second sentence that he did not smoke pot; before even getting to his qualifications he had to refute implicitly the proposition, "Everyone who supports legalization is a pothead."

What Cicero and the other ancient rhetoricians were offering were rules of thumb that could be adapted to circumstances. And we should feel free to adapt them to ours. In academic writing, for instance, it is commonplace to combine the narration and refutation into a single section. In their classic paper on the structure of DNA, Watson and Crick survey the various earlier attempts to propose a model and then show why each has been inadequate. So, too, an historian will survey earlier attempts to understand why many seventeenth-century European governments faced a crisis at about the same time, the literary critic will survey other interpretations of the ghost in *Hamlet,* or the anthropologist will praise his predecessors who collected data on kinship relations among the Apache, but, in each case, these surveys are simply preparing the ground for the argument. The author shows the importance of his subject and how knowl-

edgeable he is, but, most significantly, he removes what he perceives as imped-
iments in his audience—the ignorance in some members, the sense in others
that the problem has already been resolved.

Now Jefferson's audience is finally ready to hear his argument. He will provide it, as Cicero advises, in clearly marked stages. First, Cicero suggests, we
must have the *definition.* Jefferson must make certain that the audience understands exactly what the issue is, or perhaps what specifically his thesis is. He is
not yet asking for assent only understanding. To return to the rent control example we used earlier, say that our thesis is that rent control is probably unconstitutional. Before we present our specific evidence, we had better be sure our
audience knows exactly what we mean by "rent control" and by "probably
unconstitutional." (For instance: "By 'probably unconstitutional,' I mean that,
barring a new decision by the U.S. Supreme Court on property rights, we will
lose any appeal of this law.") This can be a crucial portion of an argument, but
it is an easy section for Jefferson because he has already been careful about
defining his terms. His definition then flows naturally right out of his concession.

> Such has been the patient sufferance of these Colonies; and such is now the neces-
> sity which constrains them to alter their former Systems of Government. The history
> of the present King of Great Britain is a history of repeated injuries and usurpations,
> all having in direct object the establishment of an absolute Tyranny over these
> States. To prove this, let Facts be submitted to a candid world.

Now that he has his audience clear about his thesis, Jefferson can present
his evidence—and he does, at length.

> He has refused his Assent to Laws, the most wholesome and necessary for the
> public good.
> He has forbidden his Governors to pass Laws of immediate and pressing impor-
> tance, unless suspended in their operation till his Assent should be obtained; and
> when so suspended, he has utterly neglected to attend to them.
> He has refused to pass other laws for the accommodation of large districts of
> people, unless those people would relinquish the right of Representation in the Leg-
> islature, a right unestimable to them and formidable to tyrants only.
> He has called together legislative bodies at places unusual, uncomfortable, and
> distant from the depository of their Public Records, for the sole purpose of fatiguing
> them into compliance with his measures.
> He has dissolved Representative Houses repeatedly, for opposing with manly
> firmness his invasions on the rights of the people.
> He has refused for a long time, after such dissolutions, to cause others to be
> elected; whereby the Legislative Powers, incapable of Annihilation, have returned
> to the People at large for their exercise; the State remaining in the mean time
> exposed to all the dangers of invasion from without, and convulsions within.
> He has endeavoured to prevent the population of these States; for that purpose
> obstructing the Laws for Naturalization of Foreigners; refusing to pass others to
> encourage their migration hither, and raising the conditions of new Appropriations
> of Lands.

He has obstructed the Administration of Justice, by refusing his Assent to Laws for establishing Judiciary Powers.

He has made Judges dependent on his Will alone, for the tenure of their offices, and the amount and payment of their salaries.

He has erected a multitude of New Offices, and sent hither swarms of Officers to harass our People, and eat out their substance.

He has kept among us, in times of peace, Standing Armies without the Consent of our legislature.

He has affected to render the Military independent of and superior to the Civil Power.

He has combined with others to subject us to a jurisdiction foreign to our constitution, and unacknowledged by our law; giving his Assent to their acts of pretended Legislation:

For quartering large bodies of armed troops among us:

For protecting them, by a mock Trial, from Punishment for any Murders which they should commit on the Inhabitants of these States:

For cutting off our trade with all parts of the world:

For imposing taxes on us without our Consent:

For depriving us in many cases, of the benefits of Trial by Jury:

For transporting us beyond Seas to be tried for pretended offences:

For abolishing the free System of English Laws in a neighbouring Province, establishing therein an Arbitrary government, and enlarging its Boundaries so as to render it at once an example and fit instrument for introducing the same absolute rule into these Colonies:

For taking away our Charters, abolishing our most valuable Laws, and altering fundamentally the Forms of our Governments:

For suspending our own Legislatures, and declaring themselves invested with Power to legislate for us in all cases whatsoever.

He has abdicated Government here, by declaring us out of his Protection and waging War against us.

He has plundered our seas, ravaged our Coasts, burnt our towns, and destroyed the lives of our people.

He is at this time transporting large armies of foreign mercenaries to compleat the works of death, desolation and tyranny, already begun with circumstances of Cruelty & perfidy scarcely paralleled in the most barbarous ages, and totally unworthy the Head of a civilized nation.

He has constrained our fellow Citizens taken Captive on the High Seas to bear Arms against their Country, to become the executioners of their friends and Brethren, or to fall themselves by their Hands.

He has excited domestic insurrections amongst us, and has endeavoured to bring on the inhabitants of our frontiers, the merciless Indian Savages, whose Known rule of warfare, is an undistinguished destruction of all ages, sexes and conditions.

Jefferson's work, however, is still not done, as Cicero would have reminded him. While you are presenting your evidence, you should think about possible objections. In other words, you should be able to anticipate what your opponent will say, by way of rebuttal, to your particular contentions. Note here that you are not worrying about the prejudices or ignorance from which your audience suffered going into your discussion, but about the objections that are occasioned by the specific argument you have used. This the ancient rhetoricians called the *prolepsis,* from the Greek word for anticipation. Because Jefferson has focused his attack on King George, he anticipates the objection that this focus is too narrow, that the Americans should appeal to other British authorities. He also anticipates this objection that King George himself would fix things if he only were made aware of the grievances of the colonists.

> In every stage of these Oppressions We have Petitioned for Redress in the most humble terms: Our repeated Petitions have been answered only by repeated injury. A Prince, whose character is thus marked by every act which may define a Tyrant, is unfit to be the ruler of a free People.
>
> Nor have We been wanting in attention to our British brethren. We have warned them from time to time of attempts by their legislature to extend an unwarrantable jurisdiction over us. We have reminded them of the circumstances of our emigration and settlement here. We have appealed to their native justice and magnanimity, and we have conjured them by the ties of our common kindred to disavow these usurpations, which, would inevitably interrupt our connections and correspondence. They too have been deaf to the voice of justice and of consanguinity. We must, therefore, acquiesce in the necessity, which denounces our Separation, and hold them, as we hold the rest of mankind, Enemies in War, in Peace Friends.

Now, finally, Jefferson is almost finished. He must hope that he has persuaded his audience. For whatever is left of his discourse, he will be preaching to the recently converted. He now can build to a climax in what Cicero called the *peroration.* If an author is ever going to go for *pathos,* it is in the peroration, when the audience is most likely to be on his side, and he can try, with whatever resources he has at hand, to increase the degree of their adherence.

> We, therefore, the Representatives of the united States of America, in General Congress, Assembled, appealing to the Supreme Judge of the world for the rectitude of our intentions, do, in the Name, and by Authority of the good People of these Colonies, solemnly publish and declare, That these United Colonies are, and of Right ought to be Free and Independent States, that they are Absolved from all Allegiance to the British Crown, and that all political connection between them and the State of Great Britain, is and ought to be totally dissolved; and that as Free and Independent States, they have full Power to levy War, conclude Peace, contract Alliances, establish Commerce, and to do all other Acts and Things which Independent States may of right do. And for the support of this Declaration, with a firm reliance on the Protection of Divine Providence, we mutually pledge to each other our Lives, our Fortunes and our Sacred Honor.

1776

◆ ◆ ◆

Of course, some of you will never—and none of you will always—follow this Ciceronian structure when organizing your arguments. However, you still might wish to remember it as a way of checking whether you are doing all that you need to do: Is there background information that I should have provided and haven't? Are there terms in my thesis I still need to define? Are there objections that I should have anticipated? After a while, these questions will become second nature to you. But until then, using Cicero or the Declaration of Independence to jog your memory may help.

Additional Readings

We chose the readings that follow for their use of the three rhetorical appeals. As you read them, regard identifying an appeal as arising from *ethos, pathos,* or *logos* as only a first step. Think about the writer's intention and what views you think the implied audience holds. Why does the arguer choose this type of appeal for this particular audience and intention? How do the various appeals work together? Do you find the speaker or writer skillful in the choice of appeals? If you were the arguer, how might you alter the choice of appeals?

Carlos Fuentes

HIGH NOON IN LATIN AMERICA

Carlos Fuentes, a noted Mexican novelist, published in the New York Times *this essay critical of U.S. policy. Notice how he uses his own* ethos *as well as analogies from outside Central American affairs to forward his argument. Can you separate out his peroration where he assumes that he and his audience are finally in agreement? Can you find many* pathos *appeals earlier?*

1   Some time ago, I was traveling in the state of Morelos in central Mexico, looking for the birthplace of Emiliano Zapata, the village of Anenecuilco. I stopped on the way and asked a *campesino,* a laborer of the fields, how far it was to that village. He answered me: "If you had left at daybreak, you would be there now." This man had an internal clock which marked his own time and that of his culture. For the clocks of all men and women, of all civilizations, are not set at the same hour. One of the wonders of our menaced globe is the variety of its experiences, its memories and its desires. Any attempt to impose a uniform politics on this diversity is like a prelude to death.

2   The daybreak of a movement of social and political renewal cannot be set by calendars other than those of the people involved. Revolutions cannot be exported. With Lech Walesa and Solidarity, it was the internal clock of the people of Poland that struck the morning hour. So it has always been: with the people of Massachusetts in 1776; with the people of my country during our revolutionary experience; with the people of Central America in the hour we are all living. The dawn of revolution reveals the total history of a community. This is a self-knowledge that a society cannot be deprived of without grave consequences.

3   The Mexican Revolution was the object of constant harassment pressures, menaces, boycotts, and even a couple of armed interventions between 1910 and 1932. It was extremely difficult for the United States administrations of the time to deal with violent and rapid change on the southern border of your country. Calvin Coolidge convened both houses of Congress in 1927 and—talkative for once—denounced Mexico as the source of "Bolshevik" subversion in Central America. This set the scene for the third invasion of Nicaragua by U. S. Marines in this century. We were the first domino. But precisely because of our revolutionary policies (favoring agrarian reform, secular education, collective bargaining, and recovery of natural resources)—all of them opposed by the successive governments in Washington, from Taft to Hoover—Mexico became a modern, contradictory, self-knowing and self-questioning nation.

4   The revolution did not make an instant democracy out of my country. Mexico first had to become a nation. What the revolution gave us all was the totality of our history and the possibility of a culture. "The revolution," wrote my compatriot, the great poet Octavio Paz, "is a sudden immersion of Mexico in its own being. In the revolutionary explosion . . . each Mexican . . . finally recognizes, in a mortal embrace, the other Mexican." How can we stand by as this experience is denied, through ignorance and arrogance, to other people, our brothers, in Central America and the Caribbean?

5   The United States is the only major power of the West that was born beyond the Middle Ages, modern at birth. As part of the fortress of the Counter-Reformation, Latin America has had to do constant battle with the past. We did not acquire freedom of speech, freedom of belief, freedom of enterprise as our birthrights, as you did. We have had to fight desperately for them. The complexity of the cultural struggles underlying our political and economic struggles has to do with unresolved tensions, sometimes as old as the conflict between pantheism and monotheism, or as recent as the conflict between tradition and modernity. This is our cultural baggage, both heavy and rich.

6   The problems of Nicaragua are Nicaraguan, but they will cease to be so if that country is deprived of all possibility for normal survival. Why is the United States so impatient with four years of Sandinismo, when it was so tolerant of forty-five years of Somocismo? Why is it so worried about free elec-

tions in Nicaragua, but so indifferent to free elections in Chile? And why, if it respects democracy so much, did the United States not rush to the defense of the democratically elected president of Chile, Salvador Allende, when he was overthrown by the Latin American Jaruzelski, General Augusto Pinochet? How can we live and grow together on the basis of such hypocrisy?

7   Nicaragua is being attacked and invaded by forces sponsored by the United States. It is being invaded by counter-revolutionary bands led by former commanders of Somoza's national guard who are out to overthrow the revolutionary government and reinstate the old tyranny. Who will stop them from doing so if they win? These are not freedom fighters. They are Benedict Arnolds.

8   The problems of El Salvador, are Salvadoran. The Salvadoran rebellion did not originate and is not manipulated from outside El Salvador. To believe this is akin to crediting Soviet accusations that the Solidarity movement in Poland is somehow the creature of the United States.

9   The real struggle for Latin America is then, as always, a struggle with ourselves, within ourselves. We must solve it by ourselves. Nobody else can truly know it; we are living through our family quarrels. We must assimilate this conflicted past. Sometimes we must do it—as has occurred in Mexico, Cuba, El Salvador and Nicaragua—through violent means. We need time and culture. We also need patience. Both ours and yours.

10   What happens between the daybreak of revolution in a marginal country and its imagined destiny as a Soviet base? If nothing happens but harassment, blockades, propaganda, pressures, and invasions against the revolutionary country, then that prophecy will become self-fulfilling.

11   But if power with historical memory and diplomacy with historical imagination come into play, we, the United States and Latin America, might end up with something very different: a Latin America of independent states building institutions of stability, renewing the culture of national identity, diversifying our economic interdependence, and wearing down the dogmas of two musty nineteenth-century philosophies. And a United States giving the example of a tone in relations that is present, active, co-operative, respectful, aware of cultural differences, and truly proper for a great power unafraid of ideological labels, capable of coexisting with diversity in Latin America as it has learned to coexist with diversity in black Africa.

12   Precisely twenty years ago, John F. Kennedy said at another commencement ceremony: "If we cannot end now our differences, at least we can help make the world safe for diversity." This, I think, is the greatest legacy of the sacrificed statesman whose death we all mourned. Let us understand that legacy, by which death ceased to be an enigma and became, not a lament for what might have been, but a hope for what can be. This can be.

13   Let us remember, let us imagine, let us reflect. The United States can no longer go it alone in Central America and the Caribbean. It cannot, in today's

world, practice the anachronistic policies of the "big stick." It will only achieve, if it does so, what it cannot truly want. Many of our countries are struggling to cease being banana republics. They do not want to become balalaika republics. Do not force them to choose between appealing to the Soviet Union or capitulating to the United States.

14   My plea is this one: Do not practice negative overlordship in this hemisphere. Practice positive leadership. Join the forces of change and patience and identity in Latin America.

15   "If we had started out at daybreak, we would be there now." Our times have not coincided. Your daybreak came quickly. Our night has been long. But we can overcome the distance between our times if we can both recognize that the true duration of the human heart is in the present, this present in which we remember and we desire; this present where our past and our future are gone.

16   We need your memory and your imagination or ours shall never be complete. You need our memory to redeem your past, and our imagination to complete your future. We may be here on this hemisphere for a long time. Let us remember one another. Let us respect one another. Let us walk together outside the night of repression and hunger and intervention, even if for you the sun is high noon and for us at a quarter to twelve.

1983

Homer

THE EMBASSY TO ACHILLES[*]

In Homer's epic poem, the Iliad, *the greatest Greek warrior has withdrawn from fighting the war against the Trojans because he feels that he has been slighted by the commander-in-chief, Agamemnon. Personal honor was of paramount importance to the Greeks, and Agamemnon has affronted Achilles by unjustly keeping his war prize, the girl Briseis. With the war going so badly for the Greeks in the absence of Achilles, Agamemnon declares himself willing to make restitution and sends three envoys to persuade Achilles to come back to the fight. He chooses his envoys carefully: Odysseus, whose distinguishing characteristic is his resourcefulness, both in battle and in human affairs; Phoinix, who taught and nurtured Achilles as a child; and Ajax, the great warrior. Odysseus'*

---

[*]Translated by Richmond Lattimore. Lattimore uses the Greek spelling "Achilleus" for the hero's name.

speech shows shrewd knowledge of his audience. Achilles is not one to underestimate his own capacities, and Odysseus stresses that the Greeks are lost without their greatest warrior. Not accidentally, Odysseus ends with a veiled challenge: the greatest Trojan warrior, Hector, is looking for a worthy opponent among the Greeks. Because Achilles' answer makes clear that the core of his resistance is emotional—his anger at the slight—Phoinix makes one of the most famous pathos *appeals of antiquity when he reminds Achilles of how he held him on his knee as a little child, how he cut up his food, and how Achilles spat up his wine on Phoinix's shirt. Phoinix makes the self-destructive nature of anger a central issue in his argument and tells the cautionary tale of Meleager. Ajax's speech is a last-ditch attempt, often the place for a high-risk strategy. Thus, Ajax is the most frank and critical, calling Achilles proud and pitiless. Ajax brings the three speeches full circle when he returns to the offer of restitution with which Odysseus had begun. Notice how each of the suppliants tries to find something he in particular can use to persuade Achilles. Ancient rhetoricians pointed to this scene from Book IX of the* Iliad *as vividly illustrating all three rhetorical appeals.*

Now they came beside the shelters and ships of the Myrmidons
and they found Achilleus delighting his heart in a lyre, clear-sounding,
splendid and carefully wrought, with a bridge of silver upon it,
which he won out of the spoils when he ruined Eëtion's city.
With this he was pleasuring his heart, and singing of men's fame,
as Patroklos was sitting over against him, alone, in silence,
watching Aiakides[1] and the time he would leave off singing.
Now these two came forward, as brilliant Odysseus led them,
and stood in his presence. Achilleus rose to his feet in amazement
10   holding the lyre as it was, leaving the place where he was sitting.
In the same way Patroklos, when he saw the men come, stood up.
And in greeting Achilleus the swift of foot spoke to them:
'Welcome. You are my friends who have come, and greatly I need you,
who even to this my anger are dearest of all the Achaians.'
So brilliant Achilleus spoke, and guided them forward,
and caused them to sit down on couches with purple coverlets
and at once called over to Patroklos who was not far from him:
'Son of Menoitios, set up a mixing-bowl that is bigger,
and mix us stronger drink, and make ready a cup for each man,
20   since these who have come beneath my roof are the men that I love best.'
So he spoke, and Patroklos obeyed his beloved companion,
and tossed down a great chopping-block into the firelight,
and laid upon it the back of a sheep, and one of a fat goat,
with the chine of a fatted pig edged thick with lard, and for him

---

[1]*Aiakides:* another name for Achilleus

Automedon held the meats, and brilliant Achilleus carved them,
and cut it well into pieces and spitted them, as meanwhile
Menoitios' son, a man like a god, made the fire blaze greatly.
But when the fire had burned itself out, and the flames had died down,
he scattered the embers apart, and extended the spits across them
30 lifting them to the andirons, and sprinkled the meats with divine salt.
Then when he had roasted all, and spread the food on the platters,
Patroklos took the bread and set it out on a table
in fair baskets, while Achilleus served the meats. Thereafter
he himself sat over against the godlike Odysseus
against the further wall, and told his companion, Patroklos,
to sacrifice to the gods; and he threw the firstlings in the fire.
They put their hands to the good things that lay ready before them.
But when they had put aside their desire for eating and drinking,
Aias nodded to Phoinix, and brilliant Odysseus saw it,
40 and filled a cup with wine, and lifted it to Achilleus:
'Your health, Achilleus. You have no lack of your equal portion
either within the shelter of Atreus' son, Agamemnon,
nor here now in your own. We have good things in abundance
to feast on; here it is not the desirable feast we think of,
but a trouble all too great, beloved of Zeus, that we look on
and are afraid. There is doubt if we save our strong-benched vessels
or if they will be destroyed, unless you put on your war strength.
The Trojans in their pride, with their far-renowned companions,
have set up an encampment close by the ships and the rampart,
50 and lit many fires along their army, and think no longer
of being held, but rather to drive in upon the black ships.
And Zeus, son of Kronos, lightens upon their right hand, showing them
portents of good, while Hektor in the huge pride of his strength rages
irresistibly, reliant on Zeus, and gives way to no one
neither god nor man, but the strong fury has descended upon him.
He prays now that the divine Dawn will show most quickly,
since he threatens to shear the uttermost horns from the ship-sterns,
to light the ships themselves with ravening fire, and to cut down
the Achaians themselves as they stir from the smoke beside them.
60 All this I fear terribly in my heart, lest immortals
accomplish all these threats, and lest for us it be destiny
to die here in Troy, far away from horse-pasturing Argos.
Up, then! if you are minded, late though it be, to rescue
the afflicted sons of the Achaians from the Trojan onslaught.
It will be an affliction to you hereafter, there will be no remedy
found to heal the evil thing when it has been done. No, beforehand
take thought to beat the evil day aside from the Danaans.

Dear friend, surely thus your father Peleus advised you
that day when he sent you away to Agamemnon from Phthia:

70 "My child, for the matter of strength, Athene and Hera will give it
if it be their will, but be it yours to hold fast in your bosom
the anger of the proud heart, for consideration is better.
Keep from the bad complication of quarrel, and all the more for this
the Argives will honour you, both their younger men and their elders."
So the old man advised, but you have forgotten. Yet even now
stop, and give way from the anger that hurts the heart. Agamemnon
offers you worthy recompense if you change from your anger.
Come then, if you will, listen to me, while I count off for you
all the gifts in his shelter that Agamemnon has promised:

80 Seven unfired tripods; ten talents' weight of gold; twenty
shining cauldrons; and twelve horses, strong, race-competitors
who have won prizes in the speed of their feet. That man would not be
poor in possessions, to whom were given all these have won him,
nor be unpossessed of dearly honoured gold, were he given
all the prizes Agamemnon's horses won in their speed for him.
He will give you seven women of Lesbos, the work of whose hands
is blameless, whom when you yourself captured strong-founded Lesbos
he chose, and who in their beauty surpassed the races of women.
He will give you these, and with them shall go the one he took from you,

90 the daughter of Briseus. And to all this he will swear a great oath
that he never entered into her bed and never lay with her
as is natural for human people, between men and women.
All these gifts shall be yours at once; but again, if hereafter
the gods grant that we storm and sack the great city of Priam,
you may go to your ship and load it deep as you please with
gold and bronze, when we Achaians divide the war spoils,
and you may choose for yourself twenty of the Trojan women,
who are the loveliest of all after Helen of Argos.
And if we come back to Achaian Argos, pride of the tilled land,

100 you could be his son-in-law; he would honour you with Orestes,
his growing son, who is brought up there in abundant luxury.
Since, as he has three daughters there in his strong-built castle,
Chrysothemis and Laodike and Iphianassa,
you may lead away the one of these that you like, with no bride-price,
to the house of Peleus; and with the girl he will grant you as dowry
many gifts, such as no man ever gave with his daughter.
He will grant you seven citadels, strongly settled:
Kardamyle and Enope and Hire of the grasses,
Pherai the sacrosanct, and Antheia deep in the meadows,

110 with Aipeia the lovely, and Pedasos of the vineyards.

All these lie near the sea, at the bottom of sandy Pylos,
and men live among them rich in cattle and rich in sheepflocks,
who will honour you as if you were a god with gifts given
and fulfil your prospering decrees underneath your sceptre.
All this he will bring to pass for you, if you change from your anger.
But if the son of Atreus is too much hated in your heart,
himself and his gifts, at least take pity on all the other
Achaians, who are afflicted along the host, and will honour you
as a god. You may win very great glory among them.
¹²⁰ For now you might kill Hektor, since he would come very close to you
with the wicked fury upon him, since he thinks there is not his equal
among the rest of the Danaans the ships carried hither.'
     Then in answer to him spoke Achilleus of the swift feet:
'Son of Laertes and seed of Zeus, resourceful Odysseus:
without consideration for you I must make my answer,
the way I think, and the way it will be accomplished, that you may not
come one after another, and sit by me, and speak softly.
For as I detest the doorways of Death, I detest that man, who
hides one thing in the depths of his heart, and speaks forth another.
¹³⁰ But I will speak to you the way it seems best to me: neither
do I think the son of Atreus, Agamemnon, will persuade me,
nor the rest of the Danaans, since there was no gratitude given
for fighting incessantly forever against your enemies.
Fate is the same for the man who holds back, the same if he fights hard.
We are all held in a single honour, the brave with the weaklings.
A man dies still if he has done nothing, as one who has done much.
Nothing is won for me, now that my heart has gone through its afflictions
in forever setting my life on the hazard of battle.
For as to her unwinged young ones the mother bird brings back
¹⁴⁰ morsels, wherever she can find them, but as for herself it is suffering,
such was I, as I lay through all the many nights unsleeping,
such as I wore through the bloody days of the fighting,
striving with warriors for the sake of these men's women.
But I say that I have stormed from my ships twelve cities
of men, and by land eleven more through the generous Troad.
From all these we took forth treasures, goodly and numerous,
and we would bring them back, and give them to Agamemnon,
Atreus' son; while he, waiting back beside the swift ships,
would take them, and distribute them little by little, and keep many.
¹⁵⁰ All the other prizes of honour he gave the great men and the princes
are held fast by them, but from me alone of all the Achaians
he has taken and keeps the bride of my heart. Let him lie beside her
and be happy. Yet why must the Argives fight with the Trojans?

And why was it the son of Atreus assembled and led here
these people? Was it not for the sake of lovely-haired Helen?
Are the sons of Atreus alone among mortal men the ones
who love their wives? Since any who is a good man, and careful,
loves her who is his own and cares for her, even as I now
loved this one from my heart, though it was my spear that won her.
160 Now that he has deceived me and taken from my hands my prize of honour,
let him try me no more. I know him well. He will not persuade me.
Let him take counsel with you, Odysseus, and the rest of the princes
how to fight the ravening fire away from his vessels.
Indeed, there has been much hard work done even without me;
he has built himself a wall and driven a ditch about it,
making it great and wide, and fixed the sharp stakes inside it.
Yet even so he cannot hold the strength of manslaughtering
Hektor; and yet when I was fighting among the Achaians
Hektor would not drive his attack beyond the wall's shelter
170 but would come forth only so far as the Skaian gates and the oak tree.
There once he endured me alone, and barely escaped my onslaught.
But, now I am unwilling to fight against brilliant Hektor,
tomorrow, when I have sacrificed to Zeus and to all gods,
and loaded well my ships, and rowed out on to the salt water,
you will see, if you have a mind to it and if it concerns you,
my ships in the dawn at sea on the Hellespont where the fish swarm
and my men manning them with good will to row. If the glorious
shaker of the earth should grant us a favouring passage
on the third day thereafter we might raise generous Phthia.
180 I have many possessions there that I left behind when I came here
on this desperate venture, and from here there is more gold, and red bronze,
and fair-girdled women, and grey iron I will take back;
all that was allotted to me. But my prize: he who gave it,
powerful Agamemnon, son of Atreus, has taken it back again
outrageously. Go back and proclaim to him all that I tell you,
openly, so other Achaians may turn against him in anger
if he hopes yet one more time to swindle some other Danaan,
wrapped as he is forever in shamelessness; yet he would not,
bold as a dog though he be, dare look in my face any longer.
190 I will join with him in no counsel, and in no action.
He cheated me and he did me hurt. Let him not beguile me
with words again. This is enough for him. Let him of his own will
be damned, since Zeus of the counsels has taken his wits away from him.
I hate his gifts. I hold him light as the strip of a splinter.
Not if he gave me ten times as much, and twenty times over
as he possesses now, not if more should come to him from elsewhere,

or gave all that is brought in to Orchomenos, all that is brought in
to Thebes of Egypt, where the greatest possessions lie up in the houses,
Thebes of the hundred gates, where through each of the gates two hundred
²⁰⁰ fighting men come forth to war with horses and chariots;
not if he gave me gifts as many as the sand or the dust is,
not even so would Agamemnon have his way with my spirit
until he had made good to me all this heartrending insolence.
Nor will I marry a daughter of Atreus' son, Agamemnon,
not if she challenged Aphrodite the golden for loveliness,
not if she matched the work of her hands with grey-eyed Athene;
not even so will I marry her; let him pick some other Achaian,
one who is to his liking and is kinglier than I am.
For if the gods will keep me alive, and I win homeward,
²¹⁰ Peleus himself will presently arrange a wife for me.
There are many Achaian girls in the land of Hellas and Phthia,
daughters of great men who hold strong places in guard. And of these
any one that I please I might make my beloved lady.
And the great desire in my heart drives me rather in that place
to take a wedded wife in marriage, the bride of my fancy,
to enjoy with her the possessions won by aged Peleus. For not
worth the value of my life are all the possessions they fable
were won for Ilion, that strong-founded citadel, in the old days
when there was peace, before the coming of the sons of the Achaians;
²²⁰ not all that the stone doorsill of the Archer holds fast within it,
of Phoibos Apollo in Pytho of the rocks. Of possessions
cattle and fat sheep are things to be had for the lifting,
and tripods can be won, and the tawny high heads of horses,
but a man's life cannot come back again, it cannot be lifted
nor captured again by force, once it has crossed the teeth's barrier.
For my mother Thetis the goddess of the silver feet tells me
I carry two sorts of destiny toward the day of my death. Either,
if I stay here and fight beside the city of the Trojans,
my return home is gone, but my glory shall be everlasting;
²³⁰ but if I return home to the beloved land of my fathers,
the excellence of my glory is gone, but there will be a long life
left for me, and my end in death will not come to me quickly.
And this would be my counsel to others also, to sail back
home again, since no longer shall you find any term set
on the sheer city of Ilion, since Zeus of the wide brows has strongly
held his own hand over it, and its people are made bold.
Do you go back therefore to the great men of the Achaians,
and take them this message, since such is the privilege of the prices:
that they think out in their minds some other scheme that is better,

240 which might rescue their ships, and the people of the Achaians,
who man the hollow ships, since this plan will not work for them
which they thought of by reason of my anger. Let Phoinix
remain here with us and sleep here, so that tomorrow
he may come with us in our ships to the beloved land of our fathers,
if he will; but I will never use force to hold him.'
    So he spoke, and all of them stayed stricken to silence
in amazement at his words. He had spoken to them very strongly.
But at long last Phoinix the aged horseman spoke out
in a stormburst of tears, and fearing for the ships of the Achaians:
250 'If it is going home, glorious Achilleus, you ponder
in your heart, and are utterly unwilling to drive the obliterating
fire from the fast ships, since anger has descended on your spirit,
how then shall I, dear child, be left in this place behind you
all alone? Peleus the aged horseman sent me forth with you
on that day when he sent you from Phthia to Agamemnon
a mere child, who knew nothing yet of the joining of battle
nor of debate where men are made pre-eminent. Therefore
he sent me along with you to teach you of all these matters,
to make you a speaker of words and one who accomplished in action.
260 Therefore apart from you, dear child, I would not be willing
to be left behind, not were the god in person to promise
he would scale away my old age and make me a young man blossoming
as I was that time when I first left Hellas, the land of fair women,
running from the hatred of Ormenos' son Amyntor,
my father, who hated me for the sake of a fair-haired mistress.
For he made love to her himself, and dishonoured his own wife,
my mother; who was forever taking my knees and entreating me
to lie with this mistress instead so that she would hate the old man.
I was persuaded and did it; and my father when he heard of it straightway
270 called down his curses, and invoked against me the dreaded furies
that I might never have any son born of my seed to dandle
on my knees; and the divinities, Zeus of the underworld
and Persephone the honoured goddess, accomplished his curses.
Then I took it into my mind to cut him down with the sharp bronze,
but some one of the immortals checked my anger, reminding me
of rumour among the people and men's maledictions repeated,
that I might not be called a parricide among the Achaians.
But now no more could the heart in my breast be ruled entirely
to range still among these halls when my father was angered.
280 Rather it was the many kinsmen and cousins about me
who held me closed in the house, with supplications repeated,
and slaughtered fat sheep in their numbers, and shambling horn-curved

cattle, and numerous swine with the fat abundant upon them
were singed and stretched out across the flame of Hephaistos,
and much wine was drunk that was stored in the jars of the old man.
Nine nights they slept nightlong in their places beside me,
and they kept up an interchange of watches, and the fire was never
put out; one below the gate of the strong-closed courtyard,
and one in the ante-chamber before the doors of the bedroom.
290 But when the tenth night had come to me in its darkness,
then I broke the close-compacted doors of the chamber
and got away, and overleapt the fence of the courtyard
lightly, unnoticed by the guarding men and the women servants.
Then I fled far away through the wide spaces of Hellas
and came as far as generous Phthia, mother of sheepflocks,
and to lord Peleus, who accepted me with a good will
and gave me his love, even as a father loves his own son
who is a single child bought up among many possessions.
He made me a rich man, and granted me many people,
300 and I lived, lord over the Dolopes, in remotest Phthia,
and, godlike Achilleus, I made you all that you are now,
and loved you out of my heart, for you would not go with another
out to any feast, nor taste any food in your own halls
until I had set you on my knees, and cut little pieces
from the meat, and given you all you wished, and held the wine for you.
And many times you soaked the shirt that was on my body
with wine you would spit up in the troublesomeness of your childhood.
So I have suffered much through you, and have had much trouble,
thinking always how the gods would not bring to birth any children
310 of my own; so that it was you, godlike Achilleus, I made
my own child, so that some day you might keep hard affliction from me.
Then, Achilles, beat down your great anger. It is not
yours to have a pitiless heart. The very immortals
can be moved; their virtue and honour and strength are greater than ours are,
and yet with sacrifices and offerings for endearment,
with libations and with savour men turn back even the immortals
in supplication, when any man does wrong and transgresses.
For there are also the spirits of Prayer, the daughters of great Zeus,
and they are lame of their feet, and wrinkled, and cast their eyes sidelong,
320 who toil on their way left far behind by the spirit of Ruin:
but she, Ruin, is strong and sound on her feet, and therefore
far outruns all Prayers, and wins into every country
to force men astray; and the Prayers follow as healers after her.
If a man venerates these daughters of Zeus as they draw near,
such a man they bring great advantage, and hear his entreaty;

but if a man shall deny them, and stubbornly with a harsh word
refuse, they go to Zeus, son of Kronos, in supplication
that Ruin may overtake this man, that he be hurt, and punished.
So, Achilleus: grant, you also, that Zeus' daughters be given
330 their honour, which, lordly though they be, curbs the will of others.
Since, were he not bringing gifts and naming still more hereafter,
Atreus' son; were he to remain still swollen with rancour,
even I would not bid you throw your anger aside, nor
defend the Argives, though they needed you sorely. But see now,
he offers you much straightway, and has promised you more hereafter;
he has sent the best men to you to supplicate you, choosing them
out of the Achain host, those who to yourself are the dearest
of all the Argives. Do not you make vain their argument
nor their footsteps, though before this one could not blame your anger.
340 Thus it was in the old days also, the deeds that we hear of
from the great men, when the swelling anger descended upon them.
The heroes would take gifts; they would listen and be persuaded.
For I remember this action of old, it is not a new thing,
and how it went; you are all my friends, I will tell it among you.
    The Kouretes and the steadfast Aitolians were fighting
and slaughtering one another about the city of Kalydon,
the Aitolians in lovely Kalydon's defence, the Kouretes
furious to storm and sack it in war. For Artemis,
she of the golden chair, had driven this evil upon them,
350 angered that Oineus had not given the pride of the orchards
to her, first fruits; the rest of the gods were given due sacrifice,
but alone to this daughter of great Zeus he had given nothing.
He had forgotten, or had not thought, in his hard delusion,
and in wrath at his whole mighty line the Lady of Arrows
sent upon them the fierce wild boar with the shining teeth, who
after the way of his kind did much evil to the orchards of Oineus.
For he ripped up whole tall trees from the ground and scattered them
headlong roots and all, even to the very flowers of the orchard.
The son of Oineus killed this boar, Meleagros, assembling
360 together many hunting men out of numerous cities
with their hounds; since the boar might not have been killed by a few men,
so huge was he, and had put many men on the sad fire for burning.
But the goddess again made a great stir of anger and crying
battle, over the head of the boar and the bristling boar's hide,
between Kouretes and the high-hearted Aitolians. So long
as Meleagros lover of battle stayed in the fighting
it went the worse for the Kouretes, and they could not even
hold their ground outside the wall, though they were so many.

But when the anger came upon Meleagros, such anger
370 as wells in the hearts of other also, though their minds are careful,
he, in the wrath of his heart against his own mother, Althaia,
lay apart with his wedded bride, Kleopatra the lovely,
daughter of sweet-stepping Marpessa, child of Euenos,
and Idas, who was the strongest of all men upon earth
in his time; for he even took up the bow to face the King's onset,
Phoibos Apollo, for the sake of the sweet-stepping maiden;
a girl her father and honoured mother had named in their palace
Alkyone, sea-bird, as a by-name, since for her sake
her mother with the sorrow-laden cry of a sea-bird
380 wept because far-reaching Phoibos Apollo had taken her;
with this Kleopatra he lay mulling his heart-sore anger,
raging by reason of his mother's curses, which she called down
from the gods upon him, in deep grief for the death of her brother,
and many times beating with her hands on the earth abundant
she called on Hades and on honoured Persephone, lying
at length along the ground, and the tears were wet on her bosom,
to give death to her son; and Erinys, the mist-walking,
she of the heart without pity, heard her out of the dark places.
Presently there was thunder about the gates, and the sound rose
390 of towers under assault, and the Aitolian elders
supplicated him, sending their noblest priests of the immortals,
to come forth and defend them; they offered him a great gift:
wherever might lie the richest ground in lovely Kalydon,
there they told him to choose out a piece of land, an entirely
good one, of fifty acres, the half of it to be vineyard
and the half of it unworked ploughland of the plain to be furrowed.
And the aged horseman Oineus again and again entreated him,
and took his place at the threshold of the high-vaulted chamber
and shook against the bolted doors, pleading with his own son.
400 And again and again his honoured mother and his sisters
entreated him, but he only refused the more; then his own friends
who were the most honoured and dearest of all entreated him;
but even so they could not persuade the heart within him
until, as the chamber was under close assault, the Kouretes
were mounting along the towers and set fire to the great city.
And then at last his wife, the fair-girdled bride, supplicated
Meleagros, in tears, and rehearsed in their numbers before him
all the sorrows that come to men when their city is taken:
they kill the men, and the fire leaves the city in ashes,
410 and strangers lead the children away and the deep-girdled women.
And the heart, as he listened to all this evil, was stirred within him,

and he rose, and went, and closed his body in shining armour.
So he gave way in his own heart, and drove back the day of evil
from the Aitolians; yet these no longer would make good
their many and gracious gifts; yet he drove back the evil from them.
 Listen, then; do not have such a thought in your mind; let not
the spirit within you turn you that way, dear friend. It would be worse
to defend the ships after they are burning. No, with gifts promised
go forth. The Achaians will honour you as they would an immortal.
420 But if without gifts you go into the fighting where men perish,
your honour will no longer be as great, though you drive back the battle.'
 Then in answer to him spoke Achilleus of the swift feet:
'Phoinix my father, aged, illustrious, such honour is a thing
I need not. I think I am honoured already in Zeus' ordinance
which will hold me here beside my curved ships as long as life's wind
stays in my breast, as long as my knees have their spring beneath me.
And put away in your thoughts this other thing I tell you.
Stop confusing my heart with lamentation and sorrow
for the favour of great Atreides. It does not become you
430 to love this man, for fear you turn hateful to me, who love you.
It should be your pride with me to hurt whoever shall hurt me.
Be king equally with me; take half of my honour.
These men will carry back the message; you stay here and sleep here
in a soft bed, and we shall decide tomorrow, as dawn shows,
whether to go back home again or else to remain here.'
 He spoke, and, saying nothing, nodded with his brows to Patroklos
to make up a neat bed for Phoinix, so the others might presently
think of going home from his shelter. The son of Telamon,
Aias the godlike, saw it, and now spoke his word among them:
440 'Son of Laertes and seed of Zeus, resourceful Odysseus:
let us go. I think that nothing will be accomplished
by argument on this errand; it is best to go back quickly
and tell this story, though it is not good, to the Danaans
who sit there waiting for us to come back, seeing that Achilleus
has made savage the proud-hearted spirit within his body.
He is hard, and does not remember that friends' affection
wherein we honoured him by the ships, far beyond all others.
Pitiless. And yet a man takes from his brother's slayer
the blood price, or the price for a child who was killed, and the guilty
450 one, when he has largely repaid, stays still in the country,
and the injured man's heart is curbed, and his pride, and his anger
when he has taken the price; but the gods put in your breast a spirit
not to be placated, bad, for the sake of one single
girl. Yet now we offer you seven, surpassingly lovely,

and much beside these. Now make gracious the spirit within you.
Respect your own house; see, we are under the same roof with you,
from the multitude of the Danaans, we who desire beyond all
others to have your honour and love, out of all the Achaians.'
    Then in answer to him spoke Achilleus of the swift feet:
460 'Son of Telamon, seed of Zeus, Aias, lord of the people:
all that you have said seems spoken after my own mind.
Yet still the heart in me swells up in anger, when I remember
the disgrace that he wrought upon me before the Argives,
the son of Atreus, as if I were some dishonoured vagabond.
Do you then go back to him, and take him this message:
that I shall not think again of the bloody fighting
until such time as the son of wise Priam, Hektor the brilliant,
comes all the way to the ships of the Myrmidons, and their shelters,
slaughtering the Argives, and shall darken with fire our vessles.
470 But around my own shelter, I think, and beside my black ship
Hektor will be held, though he be very hungry for battle.'
    He spoke, and they taking each a two-handled cup poured out
a libation, then went back to their ships, and Odysseus led them.
Now Patroklos gave the maids and his followers orders
to make up without delay a neat bed for Phoinix.
And these obeyed him and made up the bed as he had commanded,
laying fleeces on it, and a blanket, and a sheet of fine linen.
There the old man lay down and waited for the divine Dawn.
But Achilleus slept in the inward corner of the strong-built shelter,
480 and a woman lay beside him, one he had taken from Lesbos,
Phorbas' daughter, Diomede of the fair colouring.
In the other corner Patroklos went to bed; with him also
was a girl, Iphis the fair-girdled, whom brilliant Achilleus
gave him, when he took sheer Skyros, Enyeus' citadel.
    Now when these had come back to the shelters of Agamemnon,
the sons of the Achaians greeted them with their gold cups
uplifted, one after another, standing, and asked them questions.
And the first to question them was the lord of men, Agamemnon:
'Tell me, honoured Odysseus, great glory of the Achaians:
490 is he willing to fight the ravening fire away from our vessels,
or did he refuse, and does the anger still hold his proud heart?'
    Then long-suffering great Odysseus spoke to him in answer:
'Son of Atreus, most lordly, king of men, Agamemnon.
That man will not quench his anger, but still more than ever
is filled with rage. He refuses you and refuses your presents.
He tells you yourself to take counsel among the Argives
how to save your ships, and the people of the Achaians.

And he himself has threatened that tomorrow as dawn shows
he will drag down his strong-benched, oarswept ships to the water.
500 He said it would be his counsel to others also, to sail back
home again, since no longer will you find any term set
on the sheer city of Ilion, since Zeus of the wide brows has strongly
held his own hand over it, and its people are made bold.
So he spoke. There are these to attest it who went there with me
also, Aias, and the two heralds, both men of good counsel.
But aged Phoinix stayed there for the night, as Achilleus urged him,
so he might go home in the ships to the beloved land of his fathers
if Phoinix will; but he will never use force to persuade him.'
　　So he spoke, and all of them stayed stricken to silence
510 in amazement at his words. He had spoken to them very strongly.
For a long time the sons of the Achains said nothing, in sorrow,
but at long last Diomedes of the great war cry spoke to them:
'Son of Atreus, most lordly and king of men, Agamemnon,
I wish you had not supplicted the blameless son of Peleus
with innumerable gifts offered. He is a proud man without this,
and now you have driven him far deeper into his pride. Rather
we shall pay him no more attention, whether he comes in with us
or stays away. He will fight again, whenever the time comes
that the heart in his body urges him to, and the god drives him.
520 Come then, do as I say, and let us all be won over.
Go to sleep, now that the inward heart is made happy
with food and drink, for these are the strength and courage within us.
But when the lovely dawn shows forth with rose fingers, Atreides,
rapidly form before our ships both people and horses
stirring them on, and yourself be ready to fight in the foremost.'
　　So he spoke, and all the kings gave him their approval,
acclaiming the word of Diomedes, breaker of horses.
Then they poured a libation, and each man went to his shelter,
where they went to their beds and took the blessing of slumber.

ca. **8th century,** B.C.

Virginia Woolf

THE DEATH OF THE MOTH

Much of this essay by the British novelist Virginia Woolf is devoted to a minute description of the actions of the dying moth. On first glance it could hardly be called an argument at all. But in paragraph 3, she makes a remark about "the true nature of life," which suggests that she does take a position, even if that position is rather abstract and rather indirectly stated. What do you take her to mean in the last paragraph when she speaks of "this minute wayside triumph of so great a force over so mean an antagonist"? If you agree that the essay makes an argument, try to decide what Woolf argues for and how she combines her appeals in constructing that argument.

1   Moths that fly by day are not properly to be called moths; they do not excite that pleasant sense of dark autumn nights and ivy-blossom which the commonest yellow-underwing asleep in the shadow of the curtain never fails to rouse in us. They are hybrid creatures, neither gay like butterflies nor sombre like their own species. Nevertheless the present specimen, with his narrow hay-coloured wings, fringed with a tassel of the same colour, seemed to be content with life. It was a pleasant morning, mid-September, mild, benignant, yet with a keener breath than that of the summer months. The plough was already scoring the field opposite the window, and where the share had been, the earth was pressed flat and gleamed with moisture. Such vigour came rolling in from the fields and the down beyond that it was difficult to keep the eyes strictly turned upon the book. The rooks too were keeping one of their annual festivities; soaring round the tree tops until it looked as if a vast net with thousands of black knots in it had been cast up into the air; which, after a few moments sank slowly down upon the trees until every twig seemed to have a knot at the end of it. Then, suddenly, the net would be thrown into the air again in a wider circle this time, with the utmost clamour and vociferation, as though to be thrown into the air and settle slowly down upon the tree tops were a tremendously exciting experience.

2   The same energy which inspired the rooks, the ploughmen, the horses, and even, it seemed, the lean bare-backed downs, sent the moth fluttering from side to side of his square of the window-pane. One could not help watching him. One was, indeed, conscious of a queer feeling of pity for him. The possibilities of pleasure seemed that morning so enormous and so various that to have only a moth's part in life, and a day moth's at that, appeared a hard fate, and his zest in enjoying his meagre opportunities to the full, pathetic. He flew vigorously to one corner of his compartment, and, after waiting there a second, flew across to the other. What remained for him but to fly to a third corner and then to a fourth? That was all he could do, in spite of the size of the downs, the width of the sky, the far-off smoke of houses, and the romantic voice, now and then, of a steamer out at sea. What he could do he did. Watching him, it seemed as if a fibre, very thin but pure, of the enormous energy of the world had been thrust into his frail and diminutive body. As often as he crossed the pane, I could fancy that a thread of vital light became visible. He was little or nothing but life.

3   Yet, because he was so small, and so simple a form of the energy that was rolling in at the open window and driving its way through so many narrow

and intricate corridors in my own brain and in those of other human beings, there was something marvellous as well as pathetic about him. It was as if someone had taken a tiny bead of pure life and decking it as lightly as possible with down and feathers, had set it dancing and zigzagging to show us the true nature of life. Thus displayed one could not get over the strangeness of it. One is apt to forget all about life, seeing it humped and bossed and garnished and cumbered so that it has to move with the greatest circumspection and dignity. Again, the thought of all that life might have been had he been born in any other shape caused one to view his simple activities with a kind of pity.

4   After a time, tired by his dancing apparently, he settled on the window ledge in the sun, and, the queer spectacle being at an end, I forgot about him. Then, looking up, my eye was caught by him. He was trying to resume his dancing, but seemed either so stiff or so awkward that he could only flutter to the bottom of the window-pane; and when he tried to fly across it he failed. Being intent on other matters I watched these futile attempts for a time without thinking, unconsciously waiting for him to resume his flight, as one waits for a machine, that has stopped momentarily, to start again without considering the reason of its failure. After perhaps a seventh attempt he slipped from the wooden ledge and fell, fluttering his wings, on to his back on the window sill. The helplessness of his attitude roused me. It flashed upon me that he was in difficulties; he could no longer raise himself; his legs struggled vainly. But, as I stretched out a pencil, meaning to help him to right himself, it came over me that the failure and awkwardness were the approach of death. I laid the pencil down again.

5   The legs agitated themselves once more. I looked as if for the enemy against which he struggled. I looked out of doors. What had happened there? Presumably it was midday, and work in the fields had stopped. Stillness and quiet had replaced the previous animation. The birds had taken themselves off to feed in the brooks. The horses stood still. Yet the power was there all the same, massed outside indifferent, impersonal, not attending to anything in particular. Somehow it was opposed to the little hay-coloured moth. It was useless to try to do anything. One could only watch the extraordinary efforts made by those tiny legs against an oncoming doom which could, had it chosen, have submerged an entire city, not merely a city, but masses of human beings; nothing, I knew, had any chance against death. Nevertheless after a pause of exhaustion the legs fluttered again. It was superb this last protest, and so frantic that he succeeded at last in righting himself. One's sympathies, of course, were all on the side of life. Also, when there was nobody to care or to know, this gigantic effort on the part of an insignificant little moth, against a power of such magnitude, to retain what no one else valued or desired to keep, moved one strangely. Again, somehow, one saw life, a pure bead. I lifted the pencil again, useless though I knew it to be. But even as I did so, the

unmistakable tokens of death showed themselves. The body relaxed, and instantly grew stiff. The struggle was over. The insignificant little creature now knew death. As I looked at the dead moth, this minute wayside triumph of so great a force over so mean an antagonist filled me with wonder. Just as life had been strange a few minutes before, so death was now as strange. The moth having righted himself now lay most decently and uncomplainingly composed. O yes, he seemed to say, death is stronger than I am.

1942

Reacting and Writing

Using any one of the essays in this section, write an analysis of the use of the three appeals. Begin by making decisions about implied audience and about intention. Then you can decide which appeal seems to you to dominate (if any), and what effects the arguer achieves by using the appeals that he or she does.

You might also turn back to the readings in Chapters 1 and 2, especially those that you found most persuasive. Re-read them, and try to distinguish their appeals. Try to decide which appeal contributed most to the essay's ability to persuade you. This exercise, too, could serve as an essay topic.

C H A P T E R   4

Argument's Ethical Dimension

Knowledge in the wrong hands is dangerous. We all recognize this principle when it is applied to a modern concern, such as technology. Our knowledge of how matter works gives us power over it. We can use this knowledge for good or for ill, to cure or to kill, to free or to enslave, for hospitals or for concentration camps. The power that machines give us is itself morally neutral. And so we in the twentieth century worry if our control over nature has too far outstripped our ability to make the right choices about how to use it.

Rhetoric is verbal engineering. It shows us how to do things with words. Like technology, language is an instrument that can be put to moral or to immoral uses. What is to prevent the unscrupulous among us from using their persuasive abilities to exploit the very society that they should seek to improve?

The ancients had a word for a moral person who could speak persuasively and well; they called such a person a *rhetor*. It is interesting that we rarely hear this word today. But we have adapted an ancient term to refer to an immoral person who speaks and writes persuasively and well; we call him or her a *sophist*. The modern, derogatory meaning of the term is probably not fair to the original sophists who were simply the first individuals in the West to teach persuasion systematically. Yet they were attacked even in their own time. To sharpen their skills, some of them practiced coming up with ingenious arguments first on one side of an issue and then on the other, an activity that led some critics to think of them as unprincipled and irresponsible. From the start, it was clear that the study of argument, however well intentioned, could enable an unscrupulous speaker to make the worse side of a case appear more convincing than the better side.

ETHICS AND THE THREE APPEALS

Part of the difficulty posed by rhetoric arises from its tools—the three appeals that we discussed in Chapter 3. We mentioned there that audiences are often particularly suspicious of *pathos* appeals, appeals to an audience's emotions. One of the reasons that rhetoric frequently has a bad name in ordinary speech is that people associate it with attempts to use people's loves, hates, and fears to mislead them. In the modern world, audiences have reason to be wary of being manipulated, but it is not *pathos* appeals themselves that are sophistical. If appeals to the emotions were banned from speaking and writing, we would probably find the resulting discourse flat, inhuman, and unengaging. Like all rhetorical tools, *pathos* appeals are in themselves morally neutral, and their use determines their legitimacy. Is a horrifyingly graphic description of death by a fiery car crash a justifiable *pathos* appeal? To answer, we must ask how it will be used. To warn against reckless driving? To sell an expensive and useless so-called safety device? To reduce the crowds on the freeways by terrifying commuters into taking mass transit? Or to advertise the latest Charles Bronson movie?

Each time you evaluate a *pathos* appeal, you need to weigh a number of factors. How vulnerable is the intended audience to such appeals? How clear, complete, and accurate is the general presentation of the argument? Does the argument appeal to the whole person—judgment as well as emotions—or only to the latter? These are decisions you will have to make for yourself. What one person considers an honest sales pitch can strike the next person as questionable tactics and seem to a third to be a swindle in the making.

Ethos appeals are, of course, open to the same problems. A person with a reputation for sharp dealing may alienate an audience by trying to appear fresh-faced and innocent. Posing as more expert than one is, trying to disguise obvious self-interest in one's argument, shifting the blame, trying to laugh off serious concerns—all of these can damage one's *ethos* to the extent that an audience rejects the argument largely out of distaste for the arguer.

Because of the faith most people have in reasoning, facts, and authorities, *logos* appeals have the best reputation of the three. But a logical argument can easily be technically correct and thus sound convincing, without being true. Take, for example, this line of reasoning. All New Englanders live in neat, white houses. Mary Jones is a New Englander. Therefore, Mary Jones lives in a neat, white house. The conclusion drawn, that Mary Jones must live in a neat, white house, is technically valid. If *all* members of a class possess this attribute and Mary Jones belongs to the class, then she too must possess the attribute. But it is not true that all New Englanders live in neat, white houses, and thus the conclusion about the condition and the color of Mary Jones's dwelling is worthless.

This example is harmless enough, but think about the kind of logic that runs, "Because he's Irish, he probably drinks too much," or "Because there is a welfare recipient in the room, you'd better guard your purse." All of us are constantly assaulted by arguments, good and bad. If they sound logically consistent, we don't always stop to scrutinize their truth. Our lack of scrutiny can be the sophist's gain.

Even factual evidence can be used unethically. You will sometimes hear someone say, "Let's clear away all the rhetoric and look at the hard facts." As you know, one problem with this idea is that *logos* appeals are a type of rhetoric, and hard facts—and soft ones, too—always have a rhetorical dimension. As an example, although many people think of statistics as factual, they are extremely slippery. A couple with an ordinary income might try to impress their more status-conscious friends by pointing out that they live on a street where the average household income is more than $500,000 a year. This could indeed be a "fact," and the neighborhood would sound very posh unless their friends realized that the street in question has just five houses, four of them inhabited by families of modest means and one of them occupied by a miserly billionaire. Thus, nearly every family on the street would make much less than the average income for the street. This kind of irresponsible use of evidence is sometimes found in the graphs used in newspaper and magazine articles. As you know, you can draw a perfectly accurate graph that makes a tiny increase look like one side of Mount Everest, or you can make the same increase look negligible by drawing the graph on a much larger scale.

EVALUATING ETHICAL AND UNETHICAL ARGUMENTS

The temptation to sophistry for the skillful speaker or writer is far stronger than one might at first suspect. To illustrate this, the analogy with technology is again helpful. The modern admirer of technology may mistake the means for the end. We seem to assume at times that we should build a bridge, keep a patient alive, or send human beings to Mars, simply because we have the technology to do so. We may be lured into favoring technologies that show our ingenuity to best advantage, rather than pursuing less spectacular innovations that fill concrete human needs.

Understandably, skilled rhetoricians, proud of their skills, seek occasions to display those skills to the fullest extent. However, if displaying skills is the sole motivation, then the arguer may be attracted to the worse side of a debate. How better for a lawyer to display his skills than to get an obviously guilty murderer off scot-free? How better for an advertising executive than to get a corrupt politician accepted by the electorate as a candidate of reform, or to make cigarettes appear to be good for your lungs? A sophistical argument is generally quite showy and sounds great at first, but upon thought and examination, it turns out to be flawed in some basic way. In the words of one wit, a sophistical argument is like a dead mackerel by moonlight. It's brilliant, but it stinks.

Judging ethical and unethical uses of rhetoric is not simply a matter of determining which side of an issue someone favors. Abortion, mercy killing, nuclear research, capital punishment—all are complex issues, and thoughtful, responsible people are found on both sides. In addition, not all issues are two-sided: some have as many facets as an elaborately cut gem. A skilled rhetor, like anyone else, can simply end up taking what seems to us an immoral position on an issue. He is simply mistaken, and we can hope that an exchange of opinions will help him to correct his ideas on the subject in dispute, or help us to correct ours. So too, sophists can be on the right side of issues. Even good causes have their opportunists. The ethical dimension of any subject is almost always complex, and a generally responsible argument for an excellent cause can contain some breathtakingly sophistical moves.

One familiar way to judge the ethics of an argument is to ask whether you would care to have that argument used on you. Sophists use arguments they would not accept themselves if they were in the audience. No one wishes to be manipulated, but a sophist doesn't hesitate to manipulate others. Sophists feel no responsibility to represent their true opinions, or to make their actions consistent with their words. They are willing to argue anything to anybody if there are sufficient prospects for success.

Suppose we presented the facts of a legal case to an experienced attorney—say this one is a man—and told him that he was going to participate in the trial. He does not know what his role will be, defense or prosecution, defendant or plaintiff, jury member or judge. Now we present him with an argument and ask him if it should be used in the case. If he is a responsible arguer, he will weigh the validity and the truth of the argument and its relevance to the case. If he is a sophist, he will not be able to decide whether to approve the argument until he knows his own role in the trial and thus where his interests lie. Justice, the common good, will have no final place in his decision.

ETHICS AND YOUR OWN ARGUMENTS

As a writer of arguments, you may at times find yourself in a position that feels somewhat sophistical to you. You may, for example, feel compelled to write an argument in support of your teacher's views, whatever your own may be. Or you may be unable to reach a position of your own on an assigned issue, and hence you find yourself tossing around arguments first for one side and then the other. To make matters worse, you have been advised to adapt your argument to suit your audience. Such advice, if taken to mean "tell people what they want to hear," may seem to jeopardize your integrity. How do you create an argument that is sound both technically and ethically?

First, of course, you can apply the sophist-rhetor test and avoid argumentative strategies that you would not like used on yourself. Deliberately confusing the issue, using inflammatory language, falsifying evidence—these transgressions are fairly simple to identify and to avoid. But what about the queasy feeling that your argument is more clever than right? Recognize that writing is itself a good way to discover your own views. There is nothing sophistical about veering from side to side because you don't yet know what you believe. You can avoid sophistry by making your argument an honest statement of your best thoughts on this issue *so far.* Don't feel that you have to make a definitive decision for all time or a prescription for immediate action. Your essay will be more—not less—persuasive if you acknowledge obvious problems with your case and explain why you still think that it is worthwhile. Are the problems not as serious as they seem? Can they be avoided? Are the alternatives worse? If your audience even suspects you of ignoring or camouflaging the flaws in your case, you have damaged your *ethos,* and your audience will be suspicious of your claims.

Finally, you can make some decisions about the ethics of persuasion by thinking, reading, talking, and writing about the issue. You will construct a great many arguments in your lifetime, but you will also be the audience for a great many. The best defense against a sophist is a sophisticated audience. The dangers posed by sophistry can range from a consumer being fast-talked into buying a useless product to an entire society being plunged into war by the sophistical machinations of its leaders. Equipping yourself to deal with an argument's ethical dimension will make you a more critical listener as well as a more enlightened arguer.

The arguments in this chapter all embody ethical problems of some sort. (Can you think of an important argument that doesn't have an ethical dimension?) In the readings, you'll find an assortment of arguments, some contemptible, some meritorious, and most debatable in between. We know, by the way, that these selections are debatable because some early readers of this chapter objected that there are almost no real sophists represented, and others objected that it is weighted far too heavily in the direction of sophistry. In each case, ask yourself to what extent the arguments presented are ethically sound.

Thucydides

THE CORCYRAEANS*

In the fifth century, B.C., a conflict between the residents of Corcyra (the Greek island now called Corfu) and of Corinth led to a war that destroyed much of Greek political life, one of the great tragedies of the ancient world. Some readers of the following passage believe that the ancient Greek historian Thucydides meant to portray the Corcyraeans as blunt and honest realists who admit that they are motivated by self-interest, whereas the Corinthians make posturing

*Adapted from the translation by Benjamin Jowett.

speeches about their honor. Others brand the arguments of the Corcyraeans as sophistical, in the modern negative sense. What do you think? Why? Given the view of human nature Thucydides expresses here, how would he have voted on this debate—with Corcyra or Corinth?

1   The Corinthians, exasperated by the war with Corcyra, spent the next two years busily building ships. They made great sacrifices to create a great navy: rowers were collected from the Peloponnesus and from the rest of Greece by the attraction of generous pay. The Corcyraeans were alarmed at the report of their preparations, for they were without allies. They had not entered in the league either of the Athenians or of the Lacedaemonians. They decided to go to Athens to join the Athenian alliance, and get what help they could from them. The Corinthians, hearing of their intentions, also sent ambassadors to Athens, fearing lest the combination of the Athenian and Corcyraean navies might prevent them from bringing the war to a satisfactory conclusion. Accordingly an assembly was held at which both parties came forward to plead their respective causes. The Corcyraeans spoke first as follows.

2   "Men of Athens, those who, like ourselves, come to others who are not their allies and to whom they have never rendered any significant service and ask help of them, are bound to show, in the first place, that the granting of their request is expedient, or at any rate not inexpedient, and secondly, that their gratitude will be lasting. If they fulfill neither requirement, they have no right to complain at a refusal. Now the Corcyraeans, when they sent us here to ask for an alliance, were confident that they could establish to your satisfaction both these points. But, unfortunately, we have had a practice inconsistent with this request which we are about to make and contrary to our own interest at the present moment. Up till now we have never, if we could avoid it, been the allies of others, and now we come and ask you to enter into an alliance with us. Through this practice we find ourselves isolated in our war with the Corinthians. The policy of not making alliances lest they should endanger us at another's bidding, instead of being wisdom, as we once imagined, has now unmistakably proved to be weakness and folly. True, in the last naval engagement we repelled the Corinthians single-handedly. But now they are on the point of attacking us with a much greater force which they have drawn together from the Peloponnesus and from all Greece. We know that we are too weak to resist them unaided, and may expect the worst if we fall into their hands. We are therefore compelled to ask assistance of you and of all the world; and you must not be hard on us if now, renouncing our lazy neutrality (which was an error but not a crime), we dare to be inconsistent.

3   "To you at this moment the request which we are making offers a glorious opportunity. In the first place, you will assist the oppressed and not the oppressors; secondly, you will admit us to your alliance at a time when our interests are at stake, and will lay up a treasure of gratitude in our hearts.

Lastly, we have a navy greater than any but your own. Think about it. What good fortune can be more extraordinary, what more annoying to your enemies than the voluntary agreement of a power to an alliance for which you would have given any amount of money and could never have been too thankful? This power now places herself at your disposal; you are to incur no danger and no expense, and she brings you a good name in the world, gratitude from those who seek your aid, and an increase of your own strength. Few have ever had all these advantages offered them at once; equally few when they come asking an alliance are able to give in the way of security and honour as much as they hope to receive.

4   "And if any one thinks that the war in which our services may be needed will never arrive, he is mistaken. He does not see that the Lacedaemonians, fearing the growth of your empire, are eager to take up arms, and that the Corinthians, who are your enemies, are all-powerful with them. The Corinthians are beginning with us, and only then will they go on to you, so that we may not stand united against them in the bond of a common enmity; they will not miss the chance of weakening us or strengthening themselves. And it is in our mutual interest to strike first, we offering and you accepting our alliance, and to forestall their designs instead of waiting to counteract them.

5   "If they say that we are their colony and that therefore you have no right to receive us, they should be made to understand that all colonies honor their mother-city when she treats them well, but are estranged from her by injustice. For colonists are not meant to be the servants but the equals of those who remain at home. And the injustice of their conduct to us is manifest: for we proposed an arbitration in the matter of Epidamnus, but they insisted on prosecuting their quarrel by arms and would not hear of a legal trial. When you see how they treat us who are their own kinsmen, take warning: if they try deception, do not be misled by them; and if they make a direct request to you, refuse. Concessions to enemies only end in regret. Avoiding them is the safest way.

6   "Moreover, you will not be breaking the treaty with the Lacedaemonians by receiving us; for we are not allies either of you or of them. What does the treaty say? 'Any Hellenic city which is the ally of no one may join whichever league it pleases.' And how monstrous that they should man their ships, not only from their own confederacy, but from Greece in general, even from your subjects, while they would debar us from the alliance which naturally offers us safety, and will denounce it as a crime if you accede to our request. With far better reason shall we complain of you if you refuse. For you will be thrusting away us who are not your enemies and are in peril; and, far from restraining the enemy and the aggressor, you will be allowing him to gather fresh forces out of your own dominions. How unjust is this! Surely if you would be impartial, you should either prevent the Corinthians from hiring soldiers in your dominions, or send to us such help as you can; but it would be best of all if you would openly receive and assist us. Many, as we have

already explained, are the advantages which we offer. Above all, our enemies are your enemies, which is the best guarantee of fidelity in an ally; and they are not weak but well able to injure those who secede from them. Again, when the offered alliance is that of a maritime and not of a land power, it is a far more serious matter to refuse. You should, if possible, allow no one to have a fleet but yourselves; or, if this is impossible, whoever is strongest at sea, make him your friend.

7   "Someone may think that the course which we recommend is expedient, but he may be afraid that if he is convinced by our arguments he will break the treaty. To him we reply that as long as he is strong he may make a present of his fears to the enemy, but that if he reject the alliance he will be weak, and then his confidence, however reassuring to himself, will be anything but terrifying to enemies who are strong. It is Athens about which he is advising, and not Corcyra: will he be providing for her best interests if, when war is imminent and almost at the door, he is so anxious about the chances of the hour that he hesitates to attach to him a state which cannot be made a friend or enemy without momentous consequences? Corcyra, besides offering many other advantages, is conveniently situated for the coastal voyage to Italy and Sicily; it stands in the way of any fleet coming from there to the Peloponnesus, and can also protect a fleet on its way to Sicily. One word more, which is the sum of all and everything we have to say, and should convince you that you must not abandon us. Greece has only three considerable navies: there is ours, and there is yours, and there is the Corinthian. Now, if the Corinthians get hold of ours, and you allow the two to become one, you will have to fight against the united navies of Corcyra and the Peloponnesus. But, if you make us your allies, you will have our navy in addition to your own ranged at your side in the impending conflict."

8   Thus spoke the Corcyraeans. The Corinthians replied as follows.

9   "These Corcyraeans have chosen to speak not only of their proposed alliance with you, but also of our alleged misdoings and of the unjust war which they say has been forced upon them by us. So we too must touch on these two points before we proceed to our main argument. You will then be better prepared to appreciate our claim upon you, and will have good reason for rejecting their petition. They pretend that they have up to now refused to make alliances from wisdom and moderation, but they really adopted this policy from an evil, not a good motive. They did not want to have an ally who might go and tell of their crimes, and who would put them to shame whenever they called him in. Their geographical position makes them judges of their own offences against others, and they can therefore afford to dispense with judges appointed under treaties; for they hardly ever visit their neighbors, but foreign ships are constantly driven to their shores by bad weather. And all the time they screen themselves under the specious name of neutrality, making believe that they are unwilling to be the accomplices of other men's crimes.

But the truth is that they wish to keep their own criminal acts to themselves. Where they are strong they oppress; where they cannot be found out, they defraud; and whatever they may steal they are never ashamed. If they were really the upright men they profess to be, they would submit differences with others to arbitration to show that honesty for all to see.

10   "But they have not shown themselves honest either towards us or towards any others. Although they are our colony, they have always stood aloof from us; and now they are fighting against us on the plea that they were not sent out to be exploited. To this we respond that we did not send them out to be insulted by them, but only expected to be recognized as their leaders and receive proper respect. Our other colonies at any rate honour us; no city is more loved by her colonies than Corinth. That we are popular with the majority shows that the Corcyraeans have no reason to dislike us; and, if it seems extraordinary that we should go to war with them, our defence is that they are doing us extraordinary injury. Even if we had been misled by passion, it would have been honorable in them to make allowances for us, and dishonorable in us to use violence when they showed moderation. But they have wronged us over and over again in their insolence and pride of wealth; and now there is our colony of Epidamnus. The Corinthians would not help Epidamnus in her distress; and then when we came to her rescue, they seized the colony and are now holding it by force.

11   "They pretend that they first offered to have the matter decided by arbitration. This appeal to justice might have some meaning in the mouth of someone whose actions have been consistent with his words. But it is not in someone who has already taken dishonest advantage. These men began by laying siege to Epidamnus, and only when they feared our vengeance did they put forward their specious offer of arbitration. And as if the wrong which they have themselves done at Epidamnus were not enough, they now come here and ask you to be, not their allies, but their accomplices in crime and would have you receive them when they are at odds with us. But they should have come when they were out of danger, not at a time when we are smarting under an injury and they have good reason to be afraid. You have never derived any benefit from their power, but they will now benefit by yours. Although innocent of their crimes, you will be held equally responsible by us. If they expect you now to share the disadvantages of their crimes, they should have long ago shared with you the benefits of their power.

12   "We have argued that our complaints are justified and that our adversaries are tyrannical and dishonest. We will now show you that you have no right to receive them. Although the treaty allows any neutral cities to join either league, this provision does not apply to any who have in view the injury of others, but only to any who is in need of protection. It certainly does not apply to one who forsakes his allegiance and who will bring war instead of peace to those who receive him. In such a situation any who are wise will not receive him. And Corcyraeans will bring war to you if you listen to them

and not to us. For if you become the allies of the Corcyraeans you will be no longer at peace with us, but will be transformed into enemies; and we must, if you take their part, defend ourselves against them by defending ourselves against you. But you ought in common justice to stand aloof from both; or, if you must join either side, you should join us and go to war against them; to Corinth you are in any event bound by treaty, but with Corcyra you never even entered into a temporary negotiation. And do not set the precedent of receiving the rebellious subjects of others. At the revolt of Samos, when the other Peloponnesians were divided upon the question of giving aid to the rebels, we voted in your favour and expressly maintained that 'every one should be allowed to chastise his own allies.' If you mean to receive and assist evil-doers, we shall assuredly gain as many allies of yours as you will of ours; and you will establish a principle which will tell against yourselves more than against us.

13   "Such are the grounds of right which we urge; and they are sufficient according to Hellenic law. And may we venture to recall to your minds an obligation of which we claim the repayment in our present need? There was a time before the Persian invasion when you were in want of ships for the Aeginetan war, and we Corinthians lent you twenty. This service which we then rendered to you gave you the victory over the Aeginetans, just as the other, which prevented the Peloponnesians from aiding the Samians, enabled you to punish Samos. Both benefits were conferred on one of those critical occasions when men in the act of attacking their enemies are utterly oblivious to everything but victory, and deem him who assists them a friend though he may have previously been a foe, him who opposes them a foe, even though he may happen to be a friend; they will even often neglect their own interests in the excitement of the struggle.

14   "Think of these things; let the younger be informed of them by their elders, and resolve all of you to render like for like. Do not say to yourselves that although this is just, in the event of war something else is expedient; for the true path of expediency is the path of right. The war with which the Corcyraeans would frighten you into doing wrong is distant, and may never come. Is it worthwhile to be so carried away by the prospect of it that you bring upon yourselves the hatred of the Corinthians which is both near and certain? Would you not be wiser in seeking to mitigate the ill-feeling which your treatment of the Megarians has already inspired? The later kindness done in season, though small in comparison, may cancel a greater previous offence. And do not be attracted by their offer of a great naval alliance; for to do no wrong to a neighbor is a surer source of strength than to gain a perilous advantage under the influence of a momentary illusion.

15   "We are now ourselves in the same situation in which you were, when we declared at Sparta that every one so placed should be allowed to chastise his own allies; and we demand to receive the same measure at your hands. You gained by our vote, and we ought not to be injured by yours. Pay what you

owe, knowing that this is our time of need, in which a man's best friend is he who does him a service, while he who opposes him is his worst enemy. Do not receive these Corcyraeans into alliance despite us, and do not support them in injustice. In acting thus you will act rightly, and will also act in your true interests."

[16]   Such were the words of the Corinthians.

[17]   The Athenians heard both sides, and they held two assemblies; in the first of them they were more influenced by the words of the Corinthians, but in the second they changed their minds and inclined towards the Corcyraeans. They would not go so far as to make an alliance both offensive and defensive with them; for then, if the Corcyraeans had required them to join in an expedition against Corinth, the treaty with the Peloponnesians would have been broken. But they concluded a defensive league, by which the two states promised to aid each other if an attack were made on the territory or on the allies of either. For they believed that in any case the war with Peloponnesus was inevitable, and they had no mind to let Corcyra and her navy fall into the hands of the Corinthians. Their plan was to embroil them more and more with one another; and then, when the war came, the Corinthians and the other naval powers would be weaker. They also considered that Corcyra was conveniently situated for the coast voyage to Italy and Sicily.

[18]   Under the influence of these feelings, they received the Corcyraeans into alliance; the Corinthians departed; and the Athenians now despatched to Corcyra ten ships commanded by Lacedaemonius the son of Cimon, Diotimus the son of Strombichus, and Proteas the son of Epicles. The commanders received orders not to engage with the Corinthians unless they sailed against Corcyra or to any place belonging to the Corcyraeans, and attempted to land there, in which case they were to resist them to the utmost. These orders were intended to prevent a breach of the treaty. But the Corinthians, when their preparations were completed, sailed against Corcyra with a hundred and fifty ships—ten Elean, twelve Megarian, ten Leucadian, twenty-seven Ambraciot, one from Anactorium, and ninety of their own.

[19]   The subsequent naval battle became the first of the Peloponnesian War, for the Corinthians insisted that the Athenian fleet in taking part with the Corcyraeans had fought against them in time of truce.

◆ ◆ ◆

Thucydides later describes the eventual outcome of events in Corcyra: the outbreak of a bloody civil war. What does his description reveal about his attitude toward the Corcyraeans?

[1]   The Corcyraeans continued slaughtering those of their fellow-citizens whom they thought their enemies; they professed to punish them for their designs against the democracy, but in fact some were killed from personal

motives, of hatred or because of debts. Every form of death was to be seen; and everything, and more than everything, that commonly happens in revolutions, happened then. The father slew the son, and the suppliants were torn from the temples and slain near them; some of them were even walled up in the temple of Dionysus, and there perished. To such extremes of cruelty did the revolution go; and this seemed to be the worst of revolutions, because it was the first.

2   For not long afterwards nearly the whole Hellenic world was in commotion; in every city the chiefs of the democracy and of the oligarchy were struggling, the one to bring in the Athenians, the other the Lacedaemonians. In time of peace, men would have had no excuse for introducing either, and no desire to do so; but when they were at war, the introduction of a foreign alliance on one side or the other to the hurt of their enemies and the advantage of themselves was easily effected by the dissatisfied party. And revolution brought upon the cities of Greece many terrible calamities, which will continue to recur as long as human nature remains the same, but which are more or less aggravated and differ in character with every new combination of circumstances. In peace and prosperity both states and individuals are actuated by higher motives, because they do not fall under the dominion of dire necessity; but war, which takes away the comfortable provision of daily life, is a hard master and tends to assimilate men's characters to their conditions.

3   Once troubles had begun in the cities, the revolutionary spirit was carried further, until these revolutionaries seemed determined to outdo all others by the ingenuity of their enterprises and the atrocity of their revenges. The meaning of words had no longer a stable relation to things, but was changed by them as they thought proper. Reckless daring was held to be loyal courage; prudent delay was the excuse of a coward; moderation was the disguise of unmanly weakness; to be intelligently informed was to be ineffective. Fanaticism was the true quality of a man. To betray was to be prudent. The lover of violence was always trusted, and the proponent of peace suspected. He who succeeded in a plot was deemed knowing, but a still greater master in craft was he who detected one. On the other hand, he who decided from the first to have nothing to do with plots was a breaker up of parties and a coward who was afraid of the enemy. In a word, he who could outstrip another in a bad action was applauded, and so was he who encouraged to evil one who had no idea of it. The tie of party was stronger than the tie of blood, because a partisan was more ready to dare without asking why. (For party associations are not based upon any established law, nor do they seek the public good; they are formed to circumvent the laws and from self-interest.) The seal of good faith was not divine law, but fellowship in crime. If an enemy when he was successful offered generous words, the opposite party received them in a partisan spirit. Revenge was dearer than self-preservation. Any agreements sworn to by either party, when they could do nothing else, were binding only as long as both were powerless. But he who on a favourable opportunity first

took courage, and struck at his enemy when he saw him off his guard, had greater pleasure in a perfidious act than he would have had in an open act of revenge; he congratulated himself that he had taken the safer course, and also that he had outwitted his enemy and gained the advantage by superior ability. In general, the dishonest more easily gain credit for cleverness than the honest for goodness; men take a pride in the one, but are ashamed of the other.

4   The cause of all these evils was the love of power, originating in avarice and ambition, and the party-spirit which is engendered by them when men are deeply committed to a contest. For the leaders on either side used specious names, the one party professing to uphold the constitutional equality of the many, the other the wisdom of the few. All the while they made the public good, to which in name they were devoted, but a cover for their pursuit of private gain. Striving in every way to defeat each other, they committed the most monstrous crimes; yet even these were surpassed by the magnitude of their revenges which they pursued to the very utmost, neither party observing any definite limits either of justice or public expediency, but both alike making the caprice of the moment their law. Either by the help of an unrighteous sentence, or grasping power with the strong hand, they were eager to satisfy the fanaticism of party-spirit. Neither faction cared for religion; but any fair pretence which succeeded in effecting some odious purpose was greatly lauded. And the citizens who were of neither party fell a prey to both; either they were disliked because they held aloof, or men were jealous of their surviving.

5   Thus revolution gave birth to every form of wickedness in Greece. The simplicity which is so large an element in a noble nature was laughed to scorn and disappeared. Ideological antagonism everywhere prevailed; for there was no word binding enough, nor oath terrible enough to reconcile enemies. Each man was strong only in the conviction that nothing was secure; he must look to his own safety, and could not afford to trust others. The less intelligent generally succeeded best. For, aware of their own deficiencies, and fearing the capacity of their opponents, for whom they were no match in powers of speech, and whose subtle wits were likely to anticipate them in contriving evil, they struck boldly and at once. But the cleverer sort, presuming in their arrogance that they would be aware in time, and disdaining to act when they could think, were taken off their guard and easily destroyed.

6   Now in Corcyra most of these deeds were perpetrated, and for the first time. There was every crime which men could commit in revenge who had been governed not wisely, but tyrannically, and now had the oppressor at their mercy. There were the dishonest designs of others who were longing to be relieved from their habitual poverty, and were naturally animated by a passionate desire for their neighbor's goods; and there were crimes of another class which men commit, not from the covetousness, but from the enmity which equals foster towards one another until they are carried away by their blind rage into the extremes of pitiless cruelty. At such a time the life

of the city was all in disorder, and human nature, which is always ready to transgress the laws, having now trampled them under foot, delighted to show that its passions were ungovernable, that it was stronger than justice, and the enemy of everything above it. If malignity had not exercised a fatal power, how could any one have preferred revenge to piety, and gain to innocence? But, when men are retaliating upon others, they are reckless of the future, and do not hesitate to annul those common laws of humanity to which every individual trusts for his own hope of deliverance should he ever be overtaken by calamity; they forget that in their own hour of need they will look for them in vain.

ca. **431–403** B.C.

George Orwell

THE CASE FOR THE PIGS

In George Orwell's political satire, Animal Farm, *the barnyard animals have taken over the farm for themselves, overthrowing Jones, the farmer. Here Snowball, Napoleon, and the other pigs argue that they have a plan for furthering everyone's interests.*

1   'Now, comrades,' said Snowball, throwing down the paint-brush, 'to the hayfield! Let us make it a point of honour to get in the harvest more quickly than Jones and his men could do.'

2   But at this moment the three cows, who had seemed uneasy for some time past, set up a loud lowing. They had not been milked for twenty-four hours, and their udders were almost bursting. After a little thought, the pigs sent for buckets and milked the cows fairly successfully, their trotters being well adapted to this task. Soon there were five buckets of frothing creamy milk at which many of the animals looked with considerable interest.

3   'What is going to happen to all that milk?' said someone.

4   'Jones used sometimes to mix some of it in our mash,' said one of the hens.

5   'Never mind the milk, comrades!' cried Napoleon, placing himself in front of the buckets. 'That will be attended to. The harvest is more important. Comrade Snowball will lead the way. I shall follow in a few minutes. Forward, comrades! The hay is waiting.'

6   So the animals trooped down to the hayfield to begin the harvest, and when they came back in the evening it was noticed that the milk had disappeared.

7   How they toiled and sweated to get the hay in! But their efforts were rewarded, for the harvest was an even bigger success than they had hoped.

8   Sometimes the work was hard; the implements had been designed for human beings and not for animals, and it was a great drawback that no animal was able to use any tool that involved standing on his hind legs. But the pigs were so clever that they could think of a way round every difficulty. As for the horses, they knew every inch of the field, and in fact understood the business of mowing and raking far better than Jones and his men had ever done. The pigs did not actually work, but directed and supervised the others. With their superior knowledge it was natural that they should assume the leadership. Boxer and Clover would harness themselves to the cutter or the horserake (no bits or reins were needed in these days, of course) and tramp steadily round and round the field with a pig walking behind and calling out 'Gee up, comrade!' or 'Whoa back, comrade!' as the case might be. And every animal down to the humblest worked at turning the hay and gathering it. Even the ducks and hens toiled to and fro all day in the sun, carrying tiny wisps of hay in their beaks. In the end they finished the harvest in two days' less time than it had usually taken Jones and his men. Moreover, it was the biggest harvest that the farm had ever seen. There was no wastage whatever; the hens and ducks with their sharp eyes had gathered up the very last stalk. And not an animal on the farm had stolen so much as a mouthful.

9   All through that summer the work of the farm went like clockwork. The animals were happy as they had never conceived it possible to be. Every mouthful of food was an acute positive pleasure, now that it was truly their own food, produced by themselves and for themselves, not doled out to them by a grudging master. With the worthless parasitical human beings gone, there was more for everyone to eat. There was more leisure too, inexperienced though the animals were. They met with many difficulties—for instance, later in the year, when they harvested the corn, they had to tread it out in the ancient style and blow away the chaff with their breath, since the farm possessed no threshing machine—but the pigs with their cleverness and Boxer with his tremendous muscles always pulled them through. Boxer was the admiration of everybody. He had been a hard worker even in Jones's time, but now he seemed more like three horses than one; there were days when the entire work of the farm seemed to rest upon his mighty shoulders. From morning to night he was pushing and pulling, always at the spot where the work was hardest. He had made an arrangement with one of the cockerels to call him in the mornings half an hour earlier than anyone else, and would put in some volunteer labour at whatever seemed to be most needed, before the regular day's work began. His answer to every problem, every setback, was 'I will work harder!'—which he had adopted as his personal motto.

10   But everyone worked according to his capacity. The hens and ducks, for instance, saved five bushels of corn at the harvest by gathering up the stray

grains. Nobody stole, nobody grumbled over his rations, the quarrelling and biting and jealousy which had been normal features of life in the old days had almost disappeared. Nobody shirked—or almost nobody. Mollie, it was true, was not good at getting up in the morning, and had a way of leaving work early on the ground that there was a stone in her hoof. And the behaviour of the cat was somewhat peculiar. It was soon noticed that when there was work to be done the cat could never be found. She would vanish for hours on end, and then reappear at mealtimes, or in the evening after work was over, as though nothing had happened. But she always made such excellent excuses, and purred so affectionately, that it was impossible not to believe in her good intentions. Old Benjamin, the donkey, seemed quite unchanged since the Rebellion. He did his work in the same slow obstinate way as he had done it in Jones's time, never shirking, and never volunteering for extra work either. About the Rebellion and its results he would express no opinion. When asked whether he was not happier now that Jones was gone, he would say only 'Donkeys live a long time. None of you has ever seen a dead donkey,' and the others had to be content with this cryptic answer.

11   On Sundays there was no work. Breakfast was an hour later than usual, and after breakfast there was a ceremony which was observed every week without fail. First came the hoisting of the flag. Snowball had found in the harness-room an old green tablecloth of Mrs Jones's and had painted on it a hoof and a horn in white. This was run up the flagstaff in the farmhouse garden every Sunday morning. The flag was green, Snowball explained, to represent the green fields of England, while the hoof and horn signified the future Republic of the Animals which would arise when the human race had been finally overthrown. After the hoisting of the flag all the animals trooped into the big barn for a general assembly which was known as the Meeting. Here the work of the coming week was planned out and resolutions were put forward and debated. It was always the pigs who put forward the resolutions. The other animals understood how to vote, but could never think of any resolutions of their own. Snowball and Napoleon were by far the most active in the debates. But it was noticed that these two were never in agreement: whatever suggestion either of them made, the other could be counted on to oppose it. Even when it was resolved—a thing no one could object to in itself—to set aside a small paddock behind the orchard as a home of rest for animals who were past work, there was a stormy debate over the correct retiring age for each class of animal. The Meeting always ended with the singing of 'Beasts of England,' and the afternoon was given up to recreation.

12   The pigs had set aside the harness-room as a headquarters for themselves. Here, in the evening, they studied blacksmithing, carpentering, and other necessary arts from books which they had brought out of the farmhouse. Snowball also busied himself with organizing the other animals into what he called Animal Committees. He was indefatigable at this. He formed

the Egg Production Committee for the hens, the Clean Tails League for the cows, the Wild Comrades' Reeducation Committee (the object of this was to tame the rats and rabbits), the Whiter Wool Movement for the sheep, and various others, besides instituting classes in reading and writing. On the whole, these projects were a failure. The attempt to tame the wild creatures, for instance, broke down almost immediately. They continued to behave very much as before, and when treated with generosity, simply took advantage of it. The cat joined the Re-education Committee and was very active in it for some days. She was seen one day sitting on a roof and talking to some sparrows who were just out of her reach. She was telling them that all animals were now comrades and that any sparrow who chose could come and perch on her paw; but the sparrows kept their distance.

13   The reading and writing classes, however, were a great success. By the autumn almost every animal on the farm was literate in some degree.

14   As for the pigs, they could already read and write perfectly. The dogs learned to read fairly well, but were not interested in reading anything except the Seven Commandments. Muriel, the goat, could read somewhat better than the dogs, and sometimes used to read to the others in the evenings from scraps of newspaper which she found on the rubbish heap. Benjamin could read as well as any pig, but never exercised his faculty. So far as he knew, he said, there was nothing worth reading. Clover learnt the whole alphabet, but could not put words together. Boxer could not get beyond the letter D. He would trace out A, B, C, D, in the dust with his great hoof, and then would stand staring at the letters with his ears back, sometimes shaking his forelock, trying with all his might to remember what came next and never succeeding. On several occasions, indeed, he did learn E, F, G, H, but by the time he knew them, it was always discovered that he had forgotten A, B, C, and D. Finally he decided to be content with the first four letters, and used to write them out once or twice every day to refresh his memory. Mollie refused to learn any but the six letters which spelt her own name. She would form these very neatly out of pieces of twig, and would then decorate them with a flower or two and walk round them admiring them.

15   None of the other animals on the farm could get further than the letter A. It was also found that the stupider animals, such as the sheep, hens, and ducks, were unable to learn the Seven Commandments by heart. After much thought Snowball declared that the Seven Commandments could in effect be reduced to a single maxim, namely: 'Four legs good, two legs bad.' This, he said, contained the essential principle of Animalism. Whoever had thoroughly grasped it would be safe from human influences. The birds at first objected, since it seemed to them that they also had two legs, but Snowball proved to them that this was not so.

16 'A bird's wing, comrades,' he said, 'is an organ of propulsion and not of manipulation. It should therefore be regarded as a leg. The distinguishing mark of Man is the *hand*, the instrument with which he does all his mischief.'

17 The birds did not understand Snowball's long words, but they accepted his explanation, and all the humbler animals set to work to learn the new maxim by heart. FOUR LEGS GOOD, TWO LEGS BAD, was inscribed on the end wall of the barn, above the Seven Commandments and in bigger letters. When they had once got it by heart, the sheep developed a great liking for this maxim, and often as they lay in the field they would all start bleating 'Four legs good, two legs bad! Four legs good, two legs bad!' and keep it up for hours on end, never growing tired of it.

18 Napoleon took no interest in Snowball's committees. He said that the education of the young was more important than anything that could be done for those who were already grown up. It happened that Jessie and Bluebell had both whelped soon after the hay harvest, giving birth between them to nine sturdy puppies. As soon as they were weaned, Napoleon took them away from their mothers, saying that he would make himself responsible for their education. He took them up into a loft which could only be reached by a ladder from the harnessroom, and there kept them in such seclusion that the rest of the farm soon forgot their existence.

19 The mystery of where the milk went to was soon cleared up. It was mixed every day into the pigs' mash. The early apples were now ripening, and the grass of the orchard was littered with windfalls. The animals had assumed as a matter of course that these would be shared out equally; one day, however, the order went forth that all the windfalls were to be collected and brought to the harnessroom for the use of the pigs. At this some of the other animals murmured, but it was no use. All the pigs were in full agreement on this point, even Snowball and Napoleon. Squealer was sent to make the necessary explanation to the others.

20 'Comrades!' he cried. 'You do not imagine, I hope, that we pigs are doing this in a spirit of selfishness and privilege? Many of us actually dislike milk and apples. I dislike them myself. Our sole object in taking these things is to preserve our health. Milk and apples (this has been proved by Science, comrades) contain substances absolutely necessary to the well-being of a pig. We pigs are brainworkers. The whole management and organization of this farm depend on us. Day and night we are watching over your welfare. It is for *your* sake that we drink that milk and eat those apples. Do you know what would happen if we pigs failed in our duty? Jones would come back! Yes, Jones would come back! Surely, comrades,' cried Squealer almost pleadingly, skipping from side to side and whisking his tail, 'surely there is no one among you who wants to see Jones come back?'

21   Now if there was one thing that the animals were completely certain of, it was that they did not want Jones back. When it was put to them in this light, they had no more to say. The importance of keeping the pigs in good health was all too obvious. So it was agreed without further argument that the milk and the windfall apples (and also the main crop of apples when they ripened) should be reserved for the pigs alone.

1945

Jonathan Swift

A MODEST PROPOSAL

Jonathan Swift, the author of Gulliver's Travels, *wrote this essay in 1729. Swift himself was born in Ireland, and thus the treatment of the impoverished Irish by the English concerned him deeply. Why do you suppose that the essay has become a classic? What judgment would you make on the ethics of this argument? How would you support your view?*

A modest proposal for preventing the children of poor people in Ireland from being a burden to their parents or country, and for making them beneficial to the public

1   It is a melancholy object to those who walk through this great town or travel in the country, when they see the streets, the roads, and cabin doors, crowded with beggars of the female-sex, followed by three, four, or six children, all in rags and importuning every passenger for an alms. These mothers, instead of being able to work for their honest livelihood, are forced to employ all their time in strolling to beg sustenance for their helpless infants, who, as they grow up, either turn thieves for want of work, or leave their dear native country to fight for the Pretender in Spain, or sell themselves to the Barbadoes.

2   I think it is agreed by all parties that this prodigious number of children in the arms, or on the backs, or at at the heels of their mothers, and frequently of their fathers, is in the present deplorable state of the kingdom a very great additional grievance; and therefore whoever could find out a fair, cheap, and easy method of making these children sound, useful members of the commonwealth would deserve so well of the public as to have his statue set up for a preserver of the nation.

3   But my intention is very far from being confined to provide only for the children of professed beggars; it is of a much greater extent, and shall take in

the whole number of infants at a certain age who are born of parents in effect as little able to support them as those who demand our charity in the streets.

4   As to my own part, having turned my thoughts for many years upon this important subject, and maturely weighed the several schemes of other projectors, I have always found them grossly mistaken in their computation. It is true, a child just dropped from its dam may be supported by her milk for a solar year, with little other nourishment; at most not above the value of two shillings, which the mother may certainly get, or the value in scraps, by her lawful occupation of begging; and it is exactly at one year old that I propose to provide for them in such a manner as instead of being a charge upon their parents or the parish, or wanting food and raiment for the rest of their lives, they shall on the contrary contribute to the feeding, and partly to the clothing, of many thousands.

5   There is likewise another great advantage in my scheme, that it will prevent those voluntary abortions, and that horrid practice of women murdering their bastard children, alas, too frequent among us, sacrificing the poor innocent babes, I doubt, more to avoid the expense than the shame, which would move tears and pity in the most savage and inhuman breast.

6   The number of souls in this kingdom being usually reckoned one million and a half, of these I calculate there may be about two hundred thousand couples whose wives are breeders; from which number I subtract thirty thousand couples who are able to maintain their own children, although I apprehend there cannot be so many under the present distresses of the kingdom; but this being granted, there will remain an hundred and seventy thousand breeders. I again subtract fifty thousand for those women who miscarry, or whose children die by accident or disease within the year. There only remain an hundred and twenty thousand children of poor parents annually born. The question therefore is, how this number shall be reared and provided for, which, as I have already said, under the present situation of affairs, is utterly impossible by all the methods hitherto proposed. For we can neither employ them in handicraft or agriculture; we neither build houses (I mean in the country) nor cultivate land. They can very seldom pick up a livelihood by stealing till they arrive at six years old, except where they are of towardly parts, although I confess they learn the rudiments much earlier, during which time they can however be looked upon only as probationers, as I have been informed by a principal gentleman in the county of Cavan, who protested to me that he never knew above one or two instances under the age of six, even in a part of the kingdom so renowned for the quickest proficiency in that art.

7   I am assured by our merchants that a boy or a girl before twelve years old is no salable commodity; and even when they come to this age they will not yield above three pounds, or three pounds and half a crown at most of the Exchange; which cannot turn to account either to the parents or the kingdom, the charge of nutriment and rags having been at least four times that value.

8   I shall now therefore humbly propose my own thoughts, which I hope will not be liable to the least objection.

9   I have been assured by a very knowing American of my acquaintance in London, that a young healthy child well nursed is at a year old a most delicious, nourishing, and wholesome food, whether stewed, roasted, baked, or boiled; and I make no doubt that it will equally serve in a fricassee or a ragout.

10   I do therefore humbly offer it to public consideration that of the hundred and twenty thousand children, already computed, twenty thousand may be reserved for breed, whereof only one fourth part to be males, which is more than we allow to sheep, black cattle, or swine; and my reason is that these children are seldom the fruits of marriage, a circumstance not much regarded by our savages, therefore one male will be sufficient to serve four females. That the remaining hundred thousand may at a year old be offered in sale to the persons of quality and fortune through the kingdom, always advising the mother to let them suck plentifully in the last month, so as to render them plump and fat for a good table. A child will make two dishes at an entertainment for friends; and when the family dines alone, the fore or hind quarter will make a reasonable dish, and seasoned with a little pepper or salt will be very good boiled on the fourth day, especially in winter.

11   I have reckoned upon a medium that a child just born will weigh twelve pounds, and in a solar year if tolerably nursed increaseth to twenty-eight pounds.

12   I grant this food will be somewhat dear, and therefore very proper for landlords, who, as they have already devoured most of the parents, seem to have the best title to the children.

13   Infant's flesh will be in season throughout the year, but more plentiful in March, and a little before and after. For we are told by a grave author, an eminent French physician, that fish being a prolific diet, there are more children born in Roman Catholic countries about nine months after Lent than at any other season; therefore, reckoning a year after Lent, the markets will be more glutted than usual, because the number of popish infants is at least three to one in this kingdom; and therefore it will have one other collateral advantage, by lessening the number of Papists among us.

14   I have already computed the charge of nursing a beggar's child (in which list I reckon all cottagers, laborers, and four fifths of the farmers) to be about two shillings per annum, rags included; and I believe no gentleman would repine to give ten shillings for the carcass of a good fat child, which, as I have said, will make four dishes of excellent nutritive meat, when he hath only some particular friend of his own family to dine with him. Thus the squire will learn to be a good landlord, and grow popular among the tenants; the mother will have eight shillings net profit, and be fit for work till she produces another child.

15   Those who are more thrifty (as I must confess the times require) may flay the carcass; the skin of which artifically dressed will make admirable gloves for ladies, and summer boots for fine gentlemen.

16   As to our city of Dublin, shambles may be appointed for this purpose in the most convenient parts of it, and butchers we may be assured will not be wanting; although I rather recommend buying the children alive, and dressing them hot from the knife as we do roasting pigs.

17   A very worthy person, a true lover of this country, and whose virtues I highly esteem, was lately pleased in discoursing on this matter to offer a refinement upon my scheme. He said that many gentlemen of this kingdom, having of late destroyed their deer, he conceived that the want of venison might be well supplied by the bodies of young lads and maidens, not exceeding fourteen years of age nor under twelve, so great a number of both sexes in every county being now ready to starve for want of work and service; and these to be disposed of by their parents, if alive, or otherwise by their nearest relations. But with due deference to so excellent a friend and so deserving a patriot, I cannot be altogether in his sentiments; for as to the males, my American acquaintance assured me from frequent experience that their flesh was generally tough and lean, like that of our schoolboys, by continual exercise, and their taste disagreeable; and to fatten them would not answer the charge. Then as to the females, it would, I think with humble submission, be a loss to the public, because they soon would become breeders themselves: and besides, it is not improbable that some scrupulous people might be apt to censure such a practice (although indeed very unjustly) as a little bordering upon cruelty; which, I confess, hath always been with me the strongest objection against any project, how well soever intended.

18   But in order to justify my friend, he confessed that this expedient was put into his head by the famous Psalmanazar, a native of the island Formosa, who came from thence to London above twenty years ago, and in conversation told my friend that in his country when any young person happened to be put to death, the executioner sold the carcass to persons of quality as a prime dainty; and that in his time the body of a plump girl of fifteen, who was crucified for an attempt to poison the emperor, was sold to his Imperial Majesty's prime minister of state, and other great mandarins of the court, in joints from the gibbet, at four hundred crowns. Neither indeed can I deny that if the same use were made of several plump young girls in this town, who without one single groat to their fortunes cannot stir abroad without a chair; and appear at the playhouse and assemblies in foreign fineries which they never will pay for, the kingdom would not be the worse.

19   Some persons of a desponding spirit are in great concern about that vast number of poor people who are aged, diseased, or maimed, and I have been desired to employ my thoughts what course may be taken to ease the nation of so grievous an encumbrance. But I am not in the least pain upon that matter, because it is very well known that they are every day dying and rotting by cold and famine, and filth and vermin, as fast as can be reasonably expected. And as to the younger laborers, they are now in almost as hopeful a condition. They cannot get work, and consequently pine away for want of nourishment to a degree that if at any time they are accidentally hired to com-

mon labor, they have not strength to perform it; and thus the country and themselves are happily delivered from the evils to come.

20   I have too long digressed, and therefore shall return to my subject. I think the advantages by the proposal which I have made are obvious and many, as well as of the highest importance.

21   For first, as I have already observed, it would greatly lessen the number of Papists, with whom we are yearly overrun, being the principal breeders of the nation as well as our most dangerous enemies; and who stay at home on purpose to deliver the kingdom to the Pretender, hoping to take their advantage by the absence of so many good Protestants, who have chosen rather to leave their country than to stay at home and pay tithes against their conscience to an Episcopal curate.

22   Secondly, the poorer tenants will have something valuable of their own, which by law may be made liable to distress, and help to pay their landlord's rent, their corn and cattle being already seized and money a thing unknown.

23   Thirdly, whereas the maintenance of an hundred thousand children, from two years old and upwards, cannot be computed at less than ten shillings a piece per annum, the nation's stock will be thereby increased fifty thousand pounds per annum, besides the profit of a new dish introduced to the tables of all gentlemen of fortune in the kingdom who have any refinement in taste. And the money will circulate among ourselves, the goods being entirely of our own growth and manufacture.

24   Fourthly, the constant breeders, besides the gain of eight shillings sterling per annum by the sale of their children, will be rid of the charge of maintaining them after the first year.

25   Fifthly, this food would likewise bring great custom to taverns, where the vintners will certainly be so prudent as to procure the best receipts for dressing it to perfection, and consequently have their houses frequented by all the fine gentlemen, who justly value themselves upon their knowledge in good eating; and a skillful cook, who understands how to oblige his guests, will contrive to make it as expensive as they please.

26   Sixthly, this would be a great inducement to marriage, which all wise nations have either encouraged by rewards or enforced by laws and penalties. It would increase the care and tenderness of mothers toward their children, when they were sure of a settlement for life to the poor babes, provided in some sort by the public, to their annual profit instead of expense. We should see an honest emulation among the married women, which of them could bring the fattest child to the market. Men would become as fond of their wives during the time of their pregnancy as they are now of their mares in foal, their cows in calf, or sows when they are ready to farrow; not offer to beat or kick them (as is too frequent a practice) for fear of a miscarriage.

27   Many other advantages might be enumerated. For instance, the addition of some thousand carcasses in our exportation of barreled beef, the propaga-

tion of swine's flesh, and improvement in the art of making good bacon, so much wanted among us by the great destruction of pigs, too frequent at our tables, which are no way comparable in taste or magnificence to a well-grown, fat, yearling child, which roasted whole will make a considerable figure at a lord mayor's feast or any other public entertainment. But this and many others I omit, being studious of brevity.

28   Supposing that one thousand families in this city would be constant customers for infants' flesh, besides others who might have it at merry meetings, particularly weddings and christenings, I compute that Dublin would take off annually about twenty thousand carcasses, and the rest of the kingdom (where probably they will be sold somewhat cheaper) the remaining eighty thousand.

29   I can think of no one objection that will possibly be raised against this proposal, unless it should be urged that the number of people will be thereby much lessened in the kingdom. This I freely own, and it was indeed one principal design in offering it to the world. I desire the reader will observe, that I calculate my remedy for this one individual kingdom of Ireland and for no other that ever was, is, or I think ever can be upon earth. Therefore let no man talk to me of other expedients: of taxing our absentees at five shillings a pound: of using neither clothes nor household furniture except what is of our own growth and manufacture; of utterly rejecting the materials and instruments that promote foreign luxury; of curing the expensiveness of pride, vanity, idleness, and gaming in our women; of introducing a vein of parsimony prudence, and temperance; of learning to love our country, in the want of which we differ even from Laplanders and the inhabitants of Topinamboo: of quitting our animosities and factions, nor acting any longer like the Jews, who were murdering one another at the very moment their city was taken: of being a little cautious not to sell our country and conscience for nothing: of teaching landlords to have at least one degree of mercy toward their tenants; lastly, of putting a spirit of honesty, industry, and skill into our shopkeepers; who, if a resolution could now be taken to buy only our native goods, would immediately unite to cheat and exact upon us in the price, the measure, and the goodness, nor could ever yet be brought to make one fair proposal of just dealing, though often and earnestly invited to it.

30   Therefore I repeat, let no man talk to me of these and the like expedients, till he hath at least some glimpse of hope that there will ever be some hearty and sincere attempt to put them in practice.

31   But as to myself, having been wearied out for many years with offering vain, idle, visionary thoughts, and at length utterly despairing of success, I fortunately fell upon this proposal, which, as it is wholly new, so it hath something solid and real, of no expense and little trouble, full in our own power, and whereby we can incur no danger in disobliging England. For this kind of commodity will not bear exportation, the flesh being of too tender a

304　◆　Argument's Ethical Dimension

consistence to admit a long continuance in salt, although perhaps I could name a country which would be glad to eat up our whole nation without it.

32　　After all, I am not so violently bent upon my own opinion as to reject any offer proposed by wise men, which shall be found equally innocent, cheap, easy, and effectual. But before something of that kind shall be advanced in contradiction to my scheme, and offering a better, I desire the author or authors will be pleased maturely to consider two points. First, as things now stand, how they will be able to find food and raiment for an hundred thousand useless mouths and backs. And secondly, there being a round million of creatures in human figure throughout this kingdom, whose sole subsistence put into a common stock would leave them in debt two millions of pounds sterling, adding those who are beggars by profession to the bulk of farmers, cottagers, and laborers, with their wives and children who are beggars in effect; I desire those politicians who dislike my overture, and may perhaps be so bold to attempt an answer, that they will first ask the parents of these mortals whether they would not at this day think it a great happiness to have been sold for food at a year old in the manner I prescribe, and thereby have avoided such a perpetual scene of misfortunes as they have since gone through by the oppression of landlords, the impossibility of paying rent without money or trade, the want of common sustenance, with neither house nor clothes to cover them from the inclemencies of the weather, and the most inevitable prospect of entailing the like or greater miseries upon their breed forever.

33　　I profess, in the sincerity of my heart, that I have not the least personal interest in endeavoring to promote this necessary work, having no other motive than the public good of my country, by advancing our trade, providing for infants, relieving the poor, and giving some pleasure to the rich. I have no children by which I can propose to get a single penny; the youngest being nine years old, and my wife past childbearing.

1729

Plato

CRITO*

The ancient philosopher Socrates left no writings to record his teachings. One of his pupils, Plato, recreated in writing dialogues between Socrates and other speakers in an attempt to preserve both Socrates's teachings and the distinctive way that he conveyed his ideas to his listeners. In Crito, *Socrates, "con-*

*Translated by Hugh Tredennick.

demned to death for allegedly corrupting the youth of Athens," is being urged to escape from Athens. Think about both Crito and Socrates as arguers. Do you agree with Socrates that there are experts in morality to whom we should defer, just as we might to athletic trainers? Should we act against our principles when our country orders us to do something that we think is wrong?

SOCRATES.   Here already, Crito? Surely it is still early?

CRITO.   Indeed it is.

SOCRATES.   About what time?

CRITO.   Just before dawn.

SOCRATES.   I wonder that the warder paid any attention to you.

CRITO.   He is used to me now, Socrates, because I come here so often. Besides, he is under some small obligation to me.

SOCRATES.   Have you only just come, or have you been here for long?

CRITO.   Fairly long.

10 SOCRATES.   Then why didn't you wake me at once, instead of sitting by my bed so quietly?

CRITO.   I wouldn't dream of such a thing, Socrates. I only wish I were not so sleepless and depressed myself. I have been wondering at you, because I saw how comfortably you were sleeping, and I deliberately didn't wake you because I wanted you to go on being as comfortable as you could. I have often felt before in the course of my life how fortunate you are in your disposition, but I feel it more than ever now in your present misfortune when I see how easily and placidly you put up with it.

SOCRATES.   Well, really, Crito, it would be hardly suitable for a man of my age

20   to resent having to die.

CRITO.   Other people just as old as you are get involved in these misfortunes, Socrates, but their age doesn't keep them from resenting it when they find themselves in your position.

SOCRATES.   Quite true. But tell me, why have you come so early?

CRITO.   Because I bring bad news, Socrates—not so bad from your point of view, I suppose, but it will be very hard to bear for me and your other friends, and I think that I shall find it hardest of all.

SOCRATES.   Why, what is this news? Has the boat come in from Delos—the boat which ends my reprieve when it arrives?

30 CRITO.   It hasn't actually come in yet, but I expect that it will be here today, judging from the report of some people who have just arrived from Sunium and left it there. It's quite clear from their account that it will be here today, and so by tomorrow, Socrates, you will have to . . . to end your life.

SOCRATES.   Well, Crito, I hope that it may be for the best. If the gods will it so, so be it. All the same, I don't think it will arrive today.

CRITO.   What makes you think that?

SOCRATES.   I will try to explain. I think I am right in saying that I have to die on the day after the boat arrives?

40 CRITO.   That's what the authorities say, at any rate.

SOCRATES.   Then I don't think it will arrive on this day that is just beginning, but on the day after. I am going by a dream that I had in the night, only a little while ago. It looks as though you were right not to wake me up.

CRITO.   Why, what was the dream about?

SOCRATES.   I thought I saw a gloriously beautiful woman dressed in white robes, who came up to me and addressed me in these words: 'Socrates, to the pleasant land of Phthia on the third day thou shalt come.'

CRITO.   Your dream makes no sense, Socrates.

SOCRATES.   To my mind, Crito, it is perfectly clear.

50 CRITO.   Too clear, apparently. But look here, Socrates, it is still not too late to take my advice and escape. Your death means a double calamity for me. I shall not only lose a friend whom I can never possibly replace, but besides a great many people who don't know you and me very well will be sure to think that I let you down, because I could have saved you if I had been willing to spend the money. And what could be more contemptible than to get a name for thinking more of money than of your friends? Most people will never believe that it was you who refused to leave this place although we tried our hardest to persuade you.

SOCRATES.   But my dear Crito, why should we pay so much attention to what
60 'most people' think? The really reasonable people, who have more claim to be considered, will believe that the facts are exactly as they are.

CRITO.   You can see for yourself, Socrates, that one has to think of popular opinion as well. Your present position is quite enough to show that the capacity of ordinary people for causing trouble is not confined to petty annoyances, but has hardly any limits if you once get a bad name with them.

SOCRATES.   I only wish that ordinary people *had* an unlimited capacity for doing harm; then they might have an unlimited power for doing good, which would be a splendid thing, if it were so. Actually they have nei-
70 ther. They cannot make a man wise or stupid; they simply act at random.

CRITO.   Have it that way if you like, but tell me this, Socrates. I hope that you aren't worrying about the possible effects on me and the rest of your friends, and thinking that if you escape we shall have trouble with informers for having helped you to get away, and have to forfeit all our property or pay an enormous fine, or even incur some further punishment? If any idea like that is troubling you, you can dismiss it altogether. We are quite entitled to run that risk in saving you, and even worse, if necessary. Take my advice, and be reasonable.

SOCRATES.   All that you say is very much in my mind, Crito, and a great deal
80 more besides.

CRITO.   Very well, then, don't let it distress you. I know some people who are willing to rescue you from here and get you out of the country for quite a moderate sum. And then surely you realize how cheap these informers are to buy off; we shan't need much money to settle them, and I think you've got enough of my money for yourself already. And then even supposing that in your anxiety for my safety you feel that you oughtn't to spend my money, there are these foreign gentlemen staying in Athens who are quite willing to spend theirs. One of them, Simmias of Thebes, has actually brought the money with him for this very purpose, and Cebes and a number of others are quite ready to do the same. So, as I say, you mustn't let any fears on these grounds make you slacken your efforts to escape, and you mustn't feel any misgivings about what you said at your trial—that you wouldn't know what to do with yourself if you left this country. Wherever you go, there are plenty of places where you will find a welcome, and if you choose to go to Thessaly, I have friends there who will make much of you and give you complete protection, so that no one in Thessaly can interfere with you.

Besides, Socrates, I don't even feel that it is right for you to try to do what you are doing, throwing away your life when you might save it. You are doing your best to treat yourself in exactly the same way as your enemies would, or rather did, when they wanted to ruin you. What is more, it seems to me that you are letting your sons down too. You have it in your power to finish their bringing-up and education, and instead of that you are proposing to go off and desert them, and so far as you are concerned they will have to take their chance. And what sort of chance are they likely to get? The sort of thing that usually happens to orphans when they lose their parents. Either one ought not to have children at all, or one ought to see their upbringing and education through to the end. It strikes me that you are taking the line of least resistance, whereas you ought to make the choice of a good man and a brave one, considering that you profess to have made goodness your object all through life. Really, I am ashamed, both on your account and on ours, your friends'. It will look as though we had played something like a coward's part all through this affair of yours. First there was the way you came into court when it was quite unnecessary—that was the first act. Then there was the conduct of the defense—that was the second. And finally, to complete the farce, we get this situation, which makes it appear that we have let you slip out of our hands through some lack of courage and enterprise on our part, because we didn't save you, and you didn't save yourself, when it would have been quite possible and practicable, if we had been any use at all.

There, Socrates, if you aren't careful, besides the suffering there will be all this disgrace for you and us to bear. Come, make up your mind.

Really it's too late for that now; you ought to have it made up already. There is no alternative; the whole thing must be carried through during this common night. If we lose any more time, it can't be done; it will be too late. I appeal to you, Socrates, on every ground; take my advice and please don't be unreasonable!

SOCRATES. My dear Crito, I appreciate your warm feelings very much—that is, assuming that they have some justification. If not, the stronger they are, the harder they will be to deal with. Very well, then, we must consider whether we ought to follow your advice or not. You know that this is not a new idea of mine; it has always been my nature never to accept advice from any of my friends unless reflection shows that it is the best course that reason offers. I cannot abandon the principles which I used to hold in the past simply because this accident has happened to me; they seem to me to be much as they were, and I respect and regard the same principles now as before. So unless we can find better principles on this occasion, you can be quite sure that I shall not agree with you—not even if the power of the people conjures up fresh hordes of bogies to terrify our childish minds, by subjecting us to chains and executions and confiscations of our property.

Well, then, how can we consider the question most reasonably? Suppose that we begin by reverting to this view which you hold about people's opinions. Was it always right to argue that some opinions should be taken seriously but not others? Or was it always wrong? Perhaps it was right before the question of my death arose, but now we can see clearly that it was a mistaken persistence in a point of view which was really irresponsible nonsense. I should like very much to inquire into this problem, Crito, with your help, and to see whether the argument will appear in any different light to me now that I am in this position, or whether it will remain the same, and whether we shall dismiss it or accept it.

Serious thinkers, I believe, have always held some such view as the one which I mentioned just now, that some of the opinions which people entertain should be respected, and others should not. Now I ask you, Crito, don't you think that this is a sound principle? You are safe from the prospect of dying tomorrow, in all human probability, and you are not likely to have your judgment upset by this impending calamity. Consider, then, don't you think that this is a sound enough principle, that one should not regard all the opinions that people hold, but only some and not others? What do you say? Isn't that a fair statement?

CRITO. Yes, it is.

SOCRATES. In other words, one should regard the good ones and not the bad?

CRITO. Yes.

SOCRATES. The opinions of the wise being good, and the opinions of the foolish bad?

CRITO. Naturally.

SOCRATES. To pass on, then, what do you think of the sort of illustration that I used to employ? When a man is in training, and taking it seriously, does he pay attention to all praise and criticism and opinion indiscriminately,
170 or only when it comes from the one qualified person, the actual doctor or trainer?

CRITO. Only when it comes from the one qualified person.

SOCRATES. Then he should be afraid of the criticism and welcome the praise of the one qualified person, but not those of the general public.

CRITO. Obviously.

SOCRATES. So he ought to regulate his actions and exercises and eating and drinking by the judgment of his instructor, who has expert knowledge, rather than by the opinions of the rest of the public.

CRITO. Yes, that is so.

180 SOCRATES. Very well. Now if he disobeys the one man and disregards his opinion and commendations, and pays attention to the advice of the many who have no expert knowledge, surely he will suffer some bad effect?

CRITO. Certainly.

SOCRATES. And what is this bad effect? Where is it produced? I mean, in what part of the disobedient person?

CRITO. His body, obviously; that is what suffers.

SOCRATES. Very good. Well now, tell me, Crito—we don't want to go through all the examples one by one—does this apply as a general rule, and above all to the sort of actions which we are trying to decide about, just and
190 unjust, honorable and dishonorable, good and bad? Ought we to be guided and intimidated by the opinion of the many or by that of the one—assuming that there is someone with expert knowledge? Is it true that we ought to respect and fear this person more than all the rest put together, and that if we do not follow his guidance we shall spoil and mutilate that part of us which, as we used to say, is improved by right conduct and destroyed by wrong? Or is this all nonsense?

CRITO. No, I think it is true, Socrates.

SOCRATES. Then consider the next step. There is a part of us which is improved by healthy actions and ruined by unhealthy ones. If we spoil it
200 by taking the advice of nonexperts, will life be worth living when this part is once ruined? The part I mean is the body. Do you accept this?

CRITO. Yes.

SOCRATES. Well, is life worth living with a body which is worn out and ruined in health?

CRITO. Certainly not.

SOCRATES. What about the part of us which is mutilated by wrong actions and benefited by right ones? Is life worth living with this part ruined? Or do we believe that this part of us, whatever it may be, in which right and wrong operate, is of less importance than the body?

210 CRITO.   Certainly not.

SOCRATES.   It is really more precious?

CRITO.   Much more.

SOCRATES.   In that case, my dear fellow, what we ought to consider is not so much what people in general will say about us but how we stand with the expert in right and wrong, the one authority, who represents the actual truth. So in the first place your proposition is not correct when you say that we should consider popular opinion in questions of what is right and honorable and good, or the opposite. Of course one might object; all the same, the people have the power to put us to death.

220 CRITO.   No doubt about that! Quite true, Socrates. It is a possible objection.

SOCRATES.   But so far as I can see, my dear fellow, the argument which we have just been through is quite unaffected by it. At the same time I should like you to consider whether we are still satisfied on this point, that the really important thing is not to live, but to live well.

CRITO.   Why, yes.

SOCRATES.   And that to live well means the same thing as to live honorably or rightly?

CRITO.   Yes.

SOCRATES.   Then in the light of this agreement we must consider whether or

230 not it is right for me to try to get away without an official discharge. If it turns out to be right, we must make the attempt; if not, we must let it drop. As for the considerations you raise about expense and reputation and bringing up children, I am afraid, Crito, that they represent the reflections of the ordinary public, who put people to death, and would bring them back to life if they could, with equal indifference to reason. Our real duty, I fancy, since the argument leads that way, is to consider one question only, the one which we raised just now. Shall we be acting rightly in paying money and showing gratitude to these people who are going to rescue me, and in escaping or arranging the escape ourselves, or

240 shall we really be acting wrongly in doing all this? If it becomes clear that such conduct is wrong, I cannot help thinking that the question whether we are sure to die, or to suffer any other ill effect for that matter, if we stand our ground and take no action, ought not to weigh with us at all in comparison with the risk of doing what is wrong.

CRITO.   I agree with what you say, Socrates, but I wish you would consider what we ought to *do*.

SOCRATES.   Let us look at it together, my dear fellow; and if you can challenge any of my arguments, do so and I will listen to you; but if you can't, be a good fellow and stop telling me over and over again that I ought to leave

250 this place without official permission. I am very anxious to obtain your approval before I adopt the course which I have in mind. I don't want to act against your convictions. Now give your attention to the starting

point of this inquiry—I hope that you will be satisfied with my way of stating it—and try to answer my questions to the best of your judgment.

CRITO.   Well, I will try.

SOCRATES.   Do we say that one must never willingly do wrong, or does it depend upon circumstances? Is it true, as we have often agreed before, that there is no sense in which wrongdoing is good or honorable? Or have we jettisoned all our former convictions in these last few days? Can you and I at our age, Crito, have spent all these years in serious discussions without realizing that we were no better than a pair of children? Surely the truth is just what we have always said. Whatever the popular view is, and whether the alternative is pleasanter than the present one or even harder to bear, the fact remains that to do wrong is in every sense bad and dishonorable for the person who does it. Is that our view, or not?

CRITO.   Yes, it is.

SOCRATES.   Then in no circumstances must one do wrong.

CRITO.   No.

SOCRATES.   In that case one must not even do wrong when one is wronged, which most people regard as the natural course.

CRITO.   Apparently not.

SOCRATES.   Tell me another thing, Crito. Ought one to do injuries or not?

CRITO.   Surely not, Socrates.

SOCRATES.   And tell me, is it right to do an injury in retaliation, as most people believe, or not?

CRITO.   No, never.

SOCRATES.   Because, I suppose, there is no difference between injuring people and wronging them.

CRITO.   Exactly.

SOCRATES.   So one ought not to return a wrong or an injury to any person, whatever the provocation is. Now be careful, Crito, that in making these single admissions you do not end by admitting something contrary to your real beliefs. I know that there are and always will be few people who think like this, and consequently between those who do think so and those who do not there can be no agreement on principle; they must always feel contempt when they observe one another's decisions. I want even you to consider very carefully whether you share my views and agree with me, and whether we can proceed with our discussion from the established hypothesis that it is never right to do a wrong or return a wrong or defend oneself against injury by retaliation, or whether you dissociate yourself from any share in this view as a basis for discussion. I have held it for a long time, and still hold it, but if you have formed any other opinion, say so and tell me what it is. If, on the other hand, you stand by what we have said, listen to my next point.

CRITO.   Yes, I stand by it and agree with you. Go on.

SOCRATES.   Well, here is my next point, or rather question. Ought one to fulfill all one's agreements, provided that they are right, or break them?

CRITO.   One ought to fulfill them.

SOCRATES.   Then consider the logical consequence. If we leave this place without first persuading the state to let us go, are we or are we not doing an injury, and doing it in a quarter where it is least justifiable? Are we or are we not abiding by our just agreements?

CRITO.   I can't answer your questions, Socrates. I am not clear in my mind.

SOCRATES.   Look at it in this way. Suppose that while we were preparing to run away from here—or however one should describe it—the laws and constitution of Athens were to come and confront us and ask this question, Now, Socrates, what are you proposing to do? Can you deny that by this act which you are contemplating you intend, so far as you have the power, to destroy us, the laws, and the whole state as well? Do you imagine that a city can continue to exist and not be turned upside down, if the legal judgments which are pronounced in it have no force but are nullified and destroyed by private persons?

How shall we answer this question, Crito, and others of the same kind? There is much that could be said, especially by a professional advocate, to protest against the invalidation of this law which enacts that judgments once pronounced shall be binding. Shall we say, Yes, I do intend to destroy the laws, because the state wronged me by passing a faulty judgment at my trial? Is this to be our answer, or what?

CRITO.   What you have just said, by all means, Socrates.

SOCRATES.   Then what supposing the laws say, Was there provision for this in the agreement between you and us, Socrates? Or did you undertake to abide by whatever judgments the state pronounced?

If we expressed surprise at such language, they would probably say, Never mind our language, Socrates, but answer our questions; after all, you are accustomed to the method of question and answer. Come now, what charge do you bring against us and the state, that you are trying to destroy us? Did we not give you life in the first place? Was it not through us that your father married your mother and begot you? Tell us, have you any complaint against those of us laws that deal with marriage?

No, none, I should say.

Well, have you any against the laws which deal with children's upbringing and education, such as you had yourself? Are you not grateful to those of us laws which were instituted for this end, for requiring your father to give you a cultural and physical education?

Yes, I should say.

Very good. Then since you have been born and brought up and educated, can you deny, in the first place, that you were our child and servant, both you and your ancestors? And if this is so, do you imagine that what is right for us is equally right for you, and that whatever we try to do to you, you are justified in retaliating? You did not have equality of rights with your father, or your employer—supposing that you had had one—to enable you to retaliate. You were not allowed to answer back when you were scolded or to hit back when you were beaten, or to do a great many other things of the same kind. Do you expect to have such license against your country and its laws that if we try to put you to death in the belief that it is right to do so, you on your part will try your hardest to destroy your country and us its laws in return? And will you, the true devotee of goodness, claim that you are justified in doing so? Are you so wise as to have forgotten that compared with your mother and father and all the rest of your ancestors your country is something far more precious, more venerable, more sacred, and held in greater honor both among gods and among all reasonable men? Do you not realize that you are even more bound to respect and placate the anger of your country than your father's anger? That if you cannot persuade your country you must do whatever it orders, and patiently submit to any punishment that it imposes, whether it be flogging or imprisonment? And if it leads you out to war, to be wounded or killed, you must comply, and it is right that you should do so. You must not give way or retreat or abandon your position. Both in war and in the law courts and everywhere else you must do whatever your city and your country command, or else persuade them in accordance with universal justice, but violence is a sin even against your parents, and it is a far greater sin against your country.

What shall we say to this, Crito—that what the laws say is true, or not?

CRITO.   Yes, I think so.

SOCRATES.   Consider, then, Socrates, the laws would probably continue, whether it is also true for us to say that what you are now trying to do to us is not right. Although we have brought you into the world and reared you and educated you, and given you and all your fellow citizens a share in all the good things at our disposal, nevertheless by the very fact of granting our permission we openly proclaim this principle, that any Athenian, on attaining to manhood and seeing for himself the political organization of the state and us its laws, is permitted, if he is not satisfied with us, to take his property and go away wherever he likes. If any of you chooses to go to one of our colonies, supposing that he should not be satisfied with us and the state, or to emigrate to any other country, not one of us laws hinders or prevents him from going away wherever he likes, without any loss of property. On the other hand, if any one of you stands his ground when he can see how we administer justice and the rest of our public organization, we hold that by so doing he has in fact undertaken to do anything that we tell him. And we maintain that anyone who disobeys is guilty of doing wrong on three separate counts: first because we are his parents, and secondly because we are his guardians, and thirdly because, after promising obedience, he is neither obeying us nor persuading us to change our decision if we are at fault in any way. And although all our orders are in the form of proposals, not of savage commands, and we give him the choice of either persuading us or doing what we say, he is actually doing neither. These are the charges, Socrates, to which we say that you will be liable if you do what you are contemplating, and you will not be the least culpable of your fellow countrymen, but one of the most guilty.

If I asked why, they would no doubt pounce upon me with perfect justice and point out that there are very few people in Athens who have entered into this agreement with them as explicitly as I have. They would say, Socrates, we have substantial evidence that you are satisfied with us and with the state. You would not have been so exceptionally reluctant to cross the borders of your country if you had not been exceptionally attached to it. You have never left the city to attend a festival or for any other purpose, except on some military expedition. You have never traveled abroad as other people do, and you have never felt the impulse to acquaint yourself with another country or constitution. You have been content with us and with our city. You have definitely chosen us, and undertaken to observe us in all your activities as a citizen, and as the crowning proof that you are satisfied with our city, you have begotten children in it. Furthermore, even at the time of your trial you could have proposed the penalty of banishment, if you had chosen to do so—that is, you could have done then with the sanction of the state what you are now trying to do without it. But whereas at that time you made a noble show of indifference if you had to die, and in fact preferred death, as you said, to banishment, now you show no respect for your earlier professions, and no regard for us, the laws, whom you are trying to destroy. You are behaving like the lowest type of menial, trying to run away in spite of the contracts and undertakings by which you agreed to live as a member of our state. Now first answer this question. Are we or are we not speaking the truth when we say that you have undertaken, in deed if not in word, to live your life as a citizen in obedience to us?

What are we to say to that, Crito? Are we not bound to admit it?

CRITO.   We cannot help it, Socrates.

SOCRATES.   It is a fact, then, they would say, that you are breaking covenants and undertakings made with us, although you made them under no compulsion or misunderstanding, and were not compelled to decide in a limited time. You had seventy years in which you could have left the country, if you were not satisfied with us or felt that the agreements were unfair. You did not choose Sparta or Crete—your favorite models of good government—or any other Greek or foreign state. You could not have

absented yourself from the city less if you had been lame or blind or decrepit in some other way. It is quite obvious that you stand by yourself above all other Athenians in your affection for this city and for us its laws. Who would care for a city without laws? And now, after all this, are
430   you not going to stand by your agreement? Yes, you are, Socrates, if you will take our advice, and then you will at least escape being laughed at for leaving the city.

We invite you to consider what good you will do to yourself or your friends if you commit this breach of faith and stain your conscience. It is fairly obvious that the risk of being banished and either losing their citizenship or having their property confiscated will extend to your friends as well. As for yourself, if you go to one of the neighboring states, such as Thebes or Megara, which are both well governed, you will enter them as an enemy to their constitution, and all good patriots will eye you with
440   suspicion as a destroyer of law and order. Incidentally you will confirm the opinion of the jurors who tried you that they gave a correct verdict; a destroyer of laws might very well be supposed to have a destructive influence upon young and foolish human beings. Do you intend, then, to avoid well-governed states and the higher forms of human society? And if you do, will life be worth living? Or will you approach these people and have the impudence to converse with them? What arguments will you use, Socrates? The same which you used here, that goodness and integrity, institutions and laws, are the most precious possessions of mankind? Do you not think that Socrates and everything about him will
450   appear in a disreputable light? You certainly ought to think so.

But perhaps you will retire from this part of the world and go to Crito's friends in Thessaly? That is the home of indiscipline and laxity, and no doubt they would enjoy hearing the amusing story of how you managed to run away from prison by arraying yourself in some costume or putting on a shepherd's smock or some other conventional runaway's disguise, and altering your personal appearance. And will no one comment on the fact that an old man of your age, probably with only a short time left to live, should dare to cling so greedily to life, at the price of violating the most stringent laws? Perhaps not, if you avoid irritating anyone. Oth-
460   erwise, Socrates, you will hear a good many humiliating comments. So you will live as the toady and slave of all the populace, literally 'roistering in Thessaly,' as though you had left this country for Thessaly to attend a banquet there. And where will your discussions about goodness and uprightness be then, we should like to know? But of course you want to live for your children's sake, so that you may be able to bring them up and educate them. Indeed! By first taking them off to Thessaly and making foreigners of them, so that they may have that additional enjoyment? Or if that is not your intention, supposing that they are brought up here with you still alive, will they be better cared for and educated without you,

470   because of course your friends will look after them? Will they look after your children if you go away to Thessaly, and not if you go away to the next world? Surely if those who profess to be your friends are worth anything, you must believe that they would care for them.

     No, Socrates, be advised by us your guardians, and do not think more of your children or of your life or of anything else than you think of what is right, so that when you enter the next world you may have all this to plead in your defense before the authorities there. It seems clear that if you do this thing, neither you nor any of your friends will be the better for it or be more upright or have a cleaner conscience here in this world, 480   nor will it be better for you when you reach the next. As it is, you will leave this place, when you do, as the victim of a wrong done not by us, the laws, but by your fellow men. But if you leave in that dishonorable way, returning wrong for wrong and evil for evil, breaking your agreements and covenants with us, and injuring those whom you least ought to injure—yourself, your friends, your country, and us—then you will have to face our anger in your lifetime, and in that place beyond when the laws of the other world know that you have tried, so far as you could, to destroy even us their brothers, they will not receive you with a kindly welcome. Do not take Crito's advice, but follow ours.

490   That, my dear friend Crito, I do assure you, is what I seem to hear them saying, just as a mystic seems to hear the strains of music, and the sound of their arguments rings so loudly in my head that I cannot hear the other side. I warn you that, as my opinion stands at present, it will be useless to urge a different view. However, if you think that you will do any good by it, say what you like.

CRITO.   No, Socrates, I have nothing to say.

SOCRATES.   Then give it up, Crito, and let us follow this course, since God points out the way.

ca. 370 B.C.

Simone Weil

ON HUMAN OBLIGATIONS*

The French philosopher Simone Weil argues a position here that is interesting in itself and in relation to Plato's Crito. *As you think about her argument and*

*Translated by Richard Rees.

its ethical basis, you might compare it to the speeches of Socrates in Crito. *Unlike many recent thinkers, Socrates and Weil believe in moral absolutes: some actions are universally immoral, some universally moral. Weil assumes that at the heart of all human beings is a longing for what is good. Thus many of her appeals rely on that longing in the hearts of her own audience. You will notice that Weil's main mode of discourse is the assertion. Under what circumstances is assertion likely to be persuasive? Rather than an argument, some might call her essay a* credo: *a statement of what she believes. As you think about her argument's ethical dimension, you might also think about how persuasive it is. Are you part of her audience?*

Profession of Faith

1   There is a reality outside the world, that is to say, outside space and time, outside man's mental universe, outside any sphere whatsoever that is accessible to human faculties.

2   Corresponding to this reality, at the centre of the human heart, is the longing for an absolute good, a longing which is always there and is never appeased by any object in this world.

3   Another terrestrial manifestation of this reality lies in the absurd and insoluble contradictions which are always the terminus of human thought when it moves exclusively in this world.

4   Just as the reality of this world is the sole foundation of facts, so that other reality is the sole foundation of good.

5   That reality is the unique source of all the good that can exist in this world: that is to say, all beauty, all truth, all justice, all legitimacy, all order, and all human behaviour that is mindful of obligations.

6   Those minds whose attention and love are turned towards that reality are the sole intermediary through which good can descend from there and come among men.

7   Although it is beyond the reach of any human faculties, man has the power of turning his attention and love towards it.

8   Nothing can ever justify the assumption that any man, whoever he may be, has been deprived of this power.

9   It is a power which is only real in this world in so far as it is exercised. The sole condition for exercising it is consent.

10   This act of consent may be expressed, or it may not be, even tacitly; it may not be clearly conscious, although it has really taken place in the soul. Very often it is verbally expressed although it has not in fact taken place. But whether expressed or not, the one condition suffices: that it shall in fact have taken place.

11   To anyone who does actually consent to directing his attention and love beyond the world, towards the reality that exists outside the reach of all

human faculties, it is given to succeed in doing so. In that case, sooner or later, there descends upon him a part of the good, which shines through him upon all that surrounds him.

12   The combination of these two facts—the longing in the depth of the heart for absolute good, and the power, though only latent, of directing attention and love to a reality beyond the world and of receiving good from it—constitutes a link which attaches every man without exception to that other reality.

13   Whoever recognizes that reality recognizes also that link. Because of it, he holds every human being without any exception as something sacred to which he is bound to show respect.

14   This is the only possible motive for universal respect towards all human beings. Whatever formulation of belief or disbelief a man may choose to make, if his heart inclines him to feel this respect, then he in fact also recognizes a reality other than this world's reality. Whoever in fact does not feel this respect is alien to that other reality also.

15   The reality of the world we live in is composed of variety. Unequal objects unequally solicit our attention. Certain people personally attract our attention, either through the hazard of circumstances or some chance affinity. For the lack of such circumstance or affinity other people remain unidentified. They escape our attention or, at the most, it only sees them as items of a collectivity.

16   If our attention is entirely confined to this world it is entirely subject to the effect of these inequalities, which it is all the less able to resist because it is unaware of it.

17   It is impossible to feel equal respect for things that are in fact unequal unless the respect is given to something that is identical in all of them. Men are unequal in all their relations with the things of this world, without exception. The only thing that is identical in all men is the presence of a link with the reality outside the world.

18   All human beings are absolutely identical in so far as they can be thought of as consisting of a centre, which is an unquenchable desire for good, surrounded by an accretion of psychical and bodily matter.

19   Only by really directing the attention beyond the world can there be real contact with this central and essential fact of human nature. Only an attention thus directed possesses the faculty, always identical in all cases, of irradiating with light any human being whatsoever.

20   If anyone possesses this faculty, then his attention is in reality directed beyond the world, whether he is aware of it or not.

21   The link which attaches the human being to the reality outside the world is, like the reality itself, beyond the reach of human faculties. The respect that it inspires as soon as it is recognized cannot be expressed to that part of man which exists in the reality of this world.

22   This respect cannot, in this world, find any form of direct expression. But unless it is expressed it has no existence. There is a possibility of indirect expression for it.

23   The respect inspired by the link between man and the reality outside the world can be expressed to that part of man which exists in the reality of this world.

24   The reality of this world is necessity. The part of man which is in this world is the part which is in bondage to necessity and subject to the misery of need.

25   The one possibility of indirect expression of respect for the human being is offered by men's needs, the needs of the soul and of the body, in this world.

26   It is based upon the connection in human nature between the desire for good, which is the essence of man, and his sensibility. There is never any justification for doubting the existence in any man of this connection.

27   Because of it, when a man's life is destroyed or damaged by some wound or privation of soul or body, which is due to other men's actions or negligence, it is not only his sensibility that suffers but also his aspiration towards the good. Therefore there has been sacrilege towards that which is sacred in him.

28   On the other hand, there are cases where it is only a man's sensibility that is affected; for example, where his wound or privation is solely the result of the blind working of natural forces, or where he recognizes that the people who seem to be making him suffer are far from bearing him any ill will, but are acting solely in obedience to a necessity which he also acknowledges.

29   The possibility of indirect expression of respect for the human being is the basis of obligation. Obligation is concerned with the needs in this world of the souls and bodies of human beings, whoever they may be. For each need there is a corresponding obligation; for each obligation a corresponding need. There is no other kind of obligation, so far as human affairs are concerned.

30   If there seem to be others, they are either false or else it is only by error that they have not been classed among the obligations mentioned.

31   Anyone whose attention and love are really directed towards the reality outside the world recognizes at the same time that he is bound, both in public and private life, by the single and permanent obligation to remedy, according to his responsibilities and to the extent of his power, all the privations of soul and body which are liable to destroy or damage the earthly life of any human being whatsoever.

32   This obligation cannot legitimately be held to be limited by the insufficiency of power or the nature of the responsibilities until everything possible has been done to explain the necessity of the limitation to those who will suffer by it; the explanation must be completely truthful and must be such as to make it possible for them to acknowledge the necessity.

33   No combination of circumstances ever cancels this obligation. If there are circumstances which seem to cancel it as regards a certain man or category of men, they impose it in fact all the more imperatively.

34   The thought of this obligation is present to all men, but in very different forms and in very varying degrees of clarity. Some men are more and some are less inclined to accept—or to refuse—it as their rule of conduct.

35   Its acceptance is usually mixed with self-deception, and even when it is quite sincere it is not consistently acted upon. To refuse it is to become criminal.

36   The proportions of good and evil in any society depend partly upon the proportion of consent to that of refusal and partly upon the distribution of power between those who consent and those who refuse.

37   If any power of any kind is in the hands of a man who has not given total, sincere, and enlightened consent to this obligation, such power is misplaced.

38   If a man has willfully refused to consent, then it is in itself a criminal activity for him to exercise any function, major or minor, public or private, which gives him control over people's lives. All those who, with knowledge of his mind, have acquiesced in his exercise of the function are accessories to the crime.

39   Any State whose whole official doctrine constitutes an incitement to this crime is itself wholly criminal. It can retain no trace of legitimacy.

40   Any State whose official doctrine is not primarily directed against this crime in all its forms is lacking in full legitimacy.

41   Any legal system which contains no provisions against this crime is without the essence of legality. Any legal system which provides against some forms of this crime but not others is without the full character of legality.

42   Any government whose members commit this crime, or authorize it in their subordinates, has betrayed its function.

43   Any collectivity, institution, or form of collective life whatsoever whose normal functioning implies or induces the practice of this crime is convicted *ipso facto* of illegitimacy and should be reformed or abolished.

44   Any man who has any degree of influence, however small, upon public opinion becomes an accessory to this crime if he refrains from denouncing it whenever it comes to his knowledge, or if he purposely avoids knowledge of it in order not to have to denounce it.

45   A country is not innocent of this crime if public opinion, being free to express itself, does not denounce any current examples of it, or if, freedom of expression being forbidden, the crime is not denounced clandestinely.

46   It is the aim of public life to arrange that all forms of power are entrusted, so far as possible, to men who effectively consent to be bound by the obligation towards all human beings which lies upon everyone, and who understand the obligation.

47   Law is the quality of the permanent provisions for making this aim effective.

48   To understand the obligation involves two things: understanding the principle and understanding its application.

49   Since it is with human needs in this world that the application is concerned, it is for the intelligence to conceive the idea of need and to discern, discriminate, and enumerate, with all the accuracy of which it is capable, the earthly needs of the soul and of the body.

50   This is a study which is permanently open to revision.

Statement of Obligations

51   A concrete conception of obligation towards human beings and a subdivision of it into a number of obligations is obtained by conceiving the earthly needs of the body and of the human soul. Each need entails a corresponding obligation.

52   The needs of a human being are sacred. Their satisfaction cannot be subordinated either to reasons of state, or to any consideration of money, nationality, race, or colour, or to the moral or other value attributed to the human being in question, or to any consideration whatsoever.

53   There is no legitimate limit to the satisfaction of the needs of a human being except as imposed by necessity and by the needs of other human beings. The limit is only legitimate if the needs of all human beings receive an equal degree of attention.

54   The fundamental obligation towards human beings is subdivided into a number of concrete obligations by the enumeration of the essential needs of the human being. Each need is related to an obligation, and each obligation to a need.

55   The needs in question are earthly needs, for those are the only ones that man can satisfy. They are needs of the soul as well as of the body; for the soul has needs whose non-satisfaction leaves it in a state analogous to that of a starved or mutilated body.

56   The principal needs of the human body are food, warmth, sleep, health, rest, exercise, fresh air.

57   The needs of the soul can for the most part be listed in pairs of opposites which balance and complete one another.

58   The human soul has need of equality and of hierarchy.

59   Equality is the public recognition, effectively expressed in institutions and manners, of the principle that an equal degree of attention is due to the needs of all human beings. Hierarchy is the scale of responsibilities. Since attention is inclined to direct itself upwards and remain fixed, special provisions are necessary to ensure the effective compatibility of equality and hierarchy.

60   The human soul has need of consented obedience and of liberty.

61   Consented obedience is what one concedes to an authority because one judges it to be legitimate. It is not possible in relation to a political power established by conquest or *coup d' état* nor to an economic power based upon money.

62   Liberty is the power of choice within the latitude left between the direct constraint of natural forces and the authority accepted as legitimate. The latitude should be sufficiently wide for liberty to be more than a fiction, but it should include only what is innocent and should never be wide enough to permit certain kinds of crime.

63   The human soul has need of truth and of freedom of expression.

64   The need for truth requires that intellectual culture should be universally accessible, and that it should be able to be acquired in an environment neither physically remote nor psychologically alien. It requires that in the domain of thought there should never be any physical or moral pressure exerted for any purpose other than an exclusive concern for truth; which implies an absolute ban on all propaganda without exception. It calls for protection against error and lies; which means that every avoidable material falsehood publicly asserted becomes a punishable offence. It calls for public health measures against poisons in the domain of thought.

65   But, in order to be exercised, the intelligence requires to be free to express itself without control by any authority. There must therefore be a domain of pure intellectual research, separate but accessible to all, where no authority intervenes.

66   The human soul has need of some solitude and privacy and also of some social life.

67   The human soul has need of both personal property and collective property.

68   Personal property never consists in the possession of a sum of money, but in the ownership of concrete objects like a house, a field, furniture, tools, which seem to the soul to be an extension of itself and of the body. Justice requires that personal property, in this sense, should be, like liberty, inalienable.

69   Collective property is not defined by a legal title but by the feeling among members of a human milieu that certain objects are like an extension or development of the milieu. This feeling is only possible in certain objective conditions.

70   The existence of a social class defined by the lack of personal and collective property is as shameful as slavery.

71   The human soul has need of punishment and of honour.

72   Whenever a human being, through the commission of a crime, has become exiled from good, he needs to be reintegrated with it through suffering. The suffering should be inflicted with the aim of bringing the soul to recognize freely some day that its infliction was just. This reintegration with the good is what punishment is. Every man who is innocent, or who has finally expiated guilt, needs to be recognized as honourable to the same extent as anyone else.

73   The human soul has need of disciplined participation in a common task of public value, and it has need of personal initiative within this participation.

74   The human soul has need of security and also of risk. The fear of violence or of hunger or of any other extreme evil is a sickness of the soul. The boredom produced by a complete absence of risk is also a sickness of the soul.

75   The human soul needs above all to be rooted in several natural environments and to make contact with the universe through them.

76   Examples of natural human environments are: a man's country, and places where his language is spoken, and places with a culture or a historical past which he shares, and his professional milieu, and his neighbourhood.

77   Everything which has the effect of uprooting a man or of preventing him from becoming rooted is criminal.

78   Any place where the needs of human beings are satisfied can be recognized by the fact that there is a flowering of fraternity, joy, beauty, and happiness. Wherever people are lonely and turned in on themselves, wherever there is sadness or ugliness, there are privations that need remedying.

1943

Adolf Hitler

ON PROPAGANDA[*]

At first, there might seem to be little to say about the ethics of a piece by Adolf Hitler, arguing that the correct use of propaganda is "a true art." But it is worthwhile to look carefully at his argument, thinking about it in isolation as well as in connection with the almost incomprehensible fact of his responsibility for the deaths of millions of innocents. Propaganda was an important part of the rise to power of Hitler's Nazi Party in the 1920s, and this selection is taken from his programatic statement, Mein Kampf, *published in 1925. Two questions to ask as you read are, What is the relation of propaganda to rhetoric? Is Hitler's understanding of propaganda the same as our notion of sophistry, or would you distinguish the two? In paragraph 9, Hitler bases an assumption on the famous dictim that the end justifies the means. What do you think about this principle, both in itself and in connection with this argument?*

1   Ever since I have been scrutinizing political events, I have taken a tremendous interest in propagandist activity. I saw that the Socialist-Marxist

[*]Translated by Ralph Manheim.

organizations mastered and applied this instrument with astounding skill. And I soon realized that the correct use of propaganda is a true art which has remained practically unknown to the bourgeois parties. Only the Christian-Social movement, especially in Lueger's time, achieved a certain virtuosity on this instrument, to which it owed many of its successes.

2   But it was not until the War that it became evident what immense results could be obtained by a correct application of propaganda. Here again, unfortunately, all our studying had to be done on the enemy side, for the activity on our side was modest, to say the least. The total miscarriage of the German 'enlightenment' service stared every soldier in the face, and this spurred me to take up the question of propaganda even more deeply than before.

3   There was often more than enough time for thinking, and the enemy offered practical instruction which, to our sorrow, was only too good.

4   For what we failed to do, the enemy did, with amazing skill and really brilliant calculation. I, myself, learned enormously from this enemy war propaganda. But time passed and left no trace in the minds of all those who should have benefited; partly because they considered themselves too clever to learn from the enemy, partly owing to lack of good will.

5   Did we have anything you could call propaganda?

6   I regret that I must answer in the negative. Everything that actually was done in this field was so inadequate and wrong from the very start that it certainly did no good and sometimes did actual harm.

7   The form was inadequate, the substance was psychologically wrong: a careful examination of German war propaganda can lead to no other diagnosis.

8   There seems to have been no clarity on the very first question: Is propaganda a means or an end?

9   It is a means and must therefore be judged with regard to its end. It must consequently take a form calculated to support the aim which it serves. It is also obvious that its aim can vary in importance from the standpoint of general need, and that the inner value of the propaganda will vary accordingly. The aim for which we were fighting the War was the loftiest, the most overpowering, that man can conceive: it was the freedom and independence of our nation, the security of our future food supply, and—our national honor; a thing which, despite all contrary opinions prevailing today, nevertheless exists, or rather should exist, since peoples without honor have sooner or later lost their freedom and independence, which in turn is only the result of a higher justice, since generations of rabble without honor deserve no freedom. Any man who wants to be a cowardly slave can have no honor, or honor itself would soon fall into general contempt.

10   The German nation was engaged in a struggle for a human existence, and the purpose of war propaganda should have been to support this struggle; its aim to help bring about victory.

11   When the nations on this planet fight for existence—when the question of destiny, 'to be or not to be,' cries out for a solution—then all considerations of humanitarianism or aesthetics crumble into nothingness; for all these concepts do not float about in the ether, they arise from man's imagination and are bound up with man. When he departs from this world, these concepts are again dissolved into nothingness, for Nature does not know them. And even among mankind, they belong only to a few nations or rather races, and this in proportion as they emanate from the feeling of the nation or race in question. Humanitarianism and aesthetics would vanish even from a world inhabited by man if this world were to lose the races that have created and upheld these concepts.

12   But all such concepts become secondary when a nation is fighting for its existence; in fact, they become totally irrelevant to the forms of the struggle as soon as a situation arises where they might paralyze a struggling nation's power of self-preservation. And that has always been their only visible result.

13   As for humanitarianism, Moltke said years ago that in war it lies in the brevity of the operation, and that means that the most aggressive fighting technique is the most humane.

14   But when people try to approach these questions with drivel about aesthetics, etc., really only one answer is possible: where the destiny and existence of a people are at stake, all obligation toward beauty ceases. The most unbeautiful thing there can be in human life is and remains the yoke of slavery. Or do these Schwabing decadents view the present lot of the German people as 'aesthetic'? Certainly we don't have to discuss these matters with the Jews, the most modern inventors of this cultural perfume. Their whole existence is an embodied protest against the aesthetics of the Lord's image.

15   And since these criteria of humanitarianism and beauty must be eliminated from the struggle, they are also inapplicable to propaganda.

16   Propaganda in the War was a means to an end, and the end was the struggle for the existence of the German people; consequently, propaganda could only be considered in accordance with the principles that were valid for this struggle. In this case the most cruel weapons were humane if they brought about a quicker victory; and only those methods were beautiful which helped the nation to safeguard the dignity of its freedom.

17   This was the only possible attitude toward war propaganda in a life-and-death struggle like ours.

18   If the so-called responsible authorities had been clear on this point, they would never have fallen into such uncertainty over the form and application of this weapon: for even propaganda is no more than a weapon, though a frightful one in the hand of an expert.

19   The second really decisive question was this: To whom should propaganda be addressed? To the scientifically trained intelligentsia or to the less educated masses?

20   It must be addressed always and exclusively to the masses.

21   What the intelligentsia—or those who today unfortunately often go by that name—what they need is not propaganda but scientific instruction. The content of propaganda is not science any more than the object represented in a poster is art. The art of the poster lies in the designer's ability to attract the attention of the crowd by form and color. A poster advertising an art exhibit must direct the attention of the public to the art being exhibited; the better it succeeds in this, the greater is the art of the poster itself. The poster should give the masses an idea of the significance of the exhibition, it should not be a substitute for the art on display. Anyone who wants to concern himself with the art itself must do more than study the poster; and it will not be enough for him just to saunter through the exhibition. We may expect him to examine and immerse himself in the individual works, and thus little by little form a fair opinion.

22   A similar situation prevails with what we today call propaganda.

23   The function of propaganda does not lie in the scientific training of the individual, but in calling the masses' attention to certain facts, processes, necessities, etc., whose significance is thus for the first time placed within their field of vision.

24   The whole art consists in doing this so skillfully that everyone will be convinced that the fact is real, the process necessary, the necessity correct, etc. But since propaganda is not and cannot be the necessity in itself, since its function, like the poster, consists in attracting the attention of the crowd, and not in educating those who are already educated or who are striving after education and knowledge, its effect for the most part must be aimed at the emotions and only to a very limited degree at the so-called intellect.

25   All propaganda must be popular and its intellectual level must be adjusted to the most limited intelligence among those it is addressed to. Consequently, the greater the mass it is intended to reach, the lower its purely intellectual level will have to be. But if, as in propaganda for sticking out a war, the aim is to influence a whole people, we must avoid excessive intellectual demands on our public, and too much caution cannot be exerted in this direction.

26   The more modest its intellectual ballast, the more exclusively it takes into consideration the emotions of the masses, the more effective it will be. And this is the best proof of the soundness or unsoundness of a propaganda campaign, and not success in pleasing a few scholars or young aesthetes.

27   The art of propaganda lies in understanding the emotional ideas of the great masses and finding, through a psychologically correct form, the way to the attention and thence to the heart of the broad masses. The fact that our bright boys do not understand this merely shows how mentally lazy and conceited they are.

28   Once we understand how necessary it is for propaganda to be adjusted to the broad mass, the following rule results:

29   It is a mistake to make propaganda many-sided, like scientific instruction, for instance.

30   The receptivity of the great masses is very limited, their intelligence is small, but their power of forgetting is enormous. In consequence of these facts, all effective propaganda must be limited to a very few points and must harp on these in slogans until the last member of the public understands what you want him to understand by your slogan. As soon as you sacrifice this slogan and try to be many-sided, the effect will piddle away, for the crowd can neither digest nor retain the material offered. In this way the result is weakened and in the end entirely cancelled out.

31   Thus we see that propaganda must follow a simple line and correspondingly the basic tactics must be psychologically sound.

32   For instance, it was absolutely wrong to make the enemy ridiculous, as the Austrian and German comic papers did. It was absolutely wrong because actual contact with an enemy soldier was bound to arouse an entirely different conviction, and the results were devastating; for now the German soldier, under the direct impression of the enemy's resistance, felt himself swindled by his propaganda service. His desire to fight, or even to stand firm, was not strengthened, but the opposite occurred. His courage flagged.

33   By contrast, the war propaganda of the English and Americans was psychologically sound. By representing the Germans to their own people as barbarians and Huns, they prepared the individual soldier for the terrors of war, and thus helped to preserve him from disappointments. After this, the most terrible weapon that was used against him seemed only to confirm what his propagandists had told him; it likewise reinforced his faith in the truth of his government's assertions, while on the other hand it increased his rage and hatred against the vile enemy. For the cruel effects of the weapon, whose use by the enemy he now came to know, gradually came to confirm for him the 'Hunnish' brutality of the barbarous enemy, which he had heard all about; and it never dawned on him for a moment that his own weapons possibly, if not probably, might be even more terrible in their effects.

34   And so the English soldier could never feel that he had been misinformed by his own countrymen, as unhappily was so much the case with the German soldier that in the end he rejected everything coming from this source as 'swindles' and 'bunk.' All this resulted from the idea that any old simpleton (or even somebody who was intelligent 'in other things') could be assigned to propaganda work, and the failure to realize that the most brilliant psychologists would have been none too good.

35   And so the German war propaganda offered an unparalleled example of an 'enlightenment' service working in reverse, since any correct psychology was totally lacking.

36   There was no end to what could be learned from the enemy by a man who kept his eyes open, refused to let his perceptions be classified, and for

four and a half years privately turned the storm-flood of enemy propaganda over in his brain.

37   What our authorities least of all understood was the very first axiom of all propagandist activity: to wit, the basically subjective and one-sided attitude it must take toward every question it deals with. In this connection, from the very beginning of the War and from top to bottom, such sins were committed that we were entitled to doubt whether so much absurdity could really be attributed to pure stupidity alone.

38   What, for example, would we say about a poster that was supposed to advertise a new soap and that described other soaps as 'good'?

39   We would only shake our heads.

40   Exactly the same applies to political advertising.

41   The function of propaganda is, for example, not to weigh and ponder the rights of different people, but exclusively to emphasize the one right which it has set out to argue for. Its task is not to make an objective study of the truth, in so far as it favors the enemy, and then set it before the masses with academic fairness; its task is to serve our own right, always and unflinchingly.

42   It was absolutely wrong to discuss war-guilt from the standpoint that Germany alone could not be held responsible for the outbreak of the catastrophe; it would have been correct to load every bit of the blame on the shoulders of the enemy, even if this had not really corresponded to the true facts, as it actually did.

43   And what was the consequence of this half-heartedness?

44   The broad mass of a nation does not consist of diplomats, or even professors of political law, or even individuals capable of forming a rational opinion; it consists of plain mortals, wavering and inclined to doubt and uncertainty. As soon as our own propaganda admits so much as a glimmer of right on the other side, the foundation for doubt in our own right has been laid. The masses are then in no position to distinguish where foreign injustice ends and our own begins. In such a case they become uncertain and suspicious, especially if the enemy refrains from going in for the same nonsense, but unloads every bit of blame on his adversary. Isn't it perfectly understandable that the whole country ends up by lending more credence to enemy propaganda, which is more unified and coherent, than to its own? And particularly a people that suffers from the mania of objectivity as much as the Germans. For, after all this, everyone will take the greatest pains to avoid doing the enemy any injustice, even at the peril of seriously besmirching and even destroying his own people and country.

45   Of course, this was not the intent of the responsible authorities, but the people never realize that.

46   The people in their overwhelming majority are so feminine by nature and attitude that sober reasoning determines their thoughts and actions far less than emotion and feeling.

47   And this sentiment is not complicated, but very simple and all of a piece. It does not have multiple shadings; it has a positive and a negative; love or

hate, right or wrong, truth or lie, never half this way and half that way, never partially, or that kind of thing.

48   English propagandists understood all this most brilliantly—and acted accordingly. They made no half statements that might have given rise to doubts.

49   Their brilliant knowledge of the primitive sentiments of the broad masses is shown by their atrocity propaganda, which was adapted to this condition. As ruthless as it was brilliant, it created the preconditions for moral steadfastness at the front, even in the face of the greatest actual defeats, and just as strikingly it pilloried the German enemy as the sole guilty party for the outbreak of the War: the rabid, impudent bias and persistence with which this lie was expressed took into account the emotional, always extreme, attitude of the great masses and for this reason was believed.

50   How effective this type of propaganda was is most strikingly shown by the fact that after four years of war it not only enabled the enemy to stick to its guns, but even began to nibble at our own people.

51   It need not surprise us that our propaganda did not enjoy this success. In its inner ambiguity alone, it bore the germ of ineffectualness. And finally its content was such that it was very unlikely to make the necessary impression on the masses. Only our featherbrained 'statesmen' could have dared to hope that this insipid pacifistic bilge could fire men's spirits till they were willing to die.

52   As a result, their miserable stuff was useless, even harmful in fact.

53   But the most brilliant propagandist technique will yield no success unless one fundamental principle is borne in mind constantly and with unflagging attention. It must confine itself to a few points and repeat them over and over. Here, as so often in this world, persistence is the first and most important requirement for success.

54   Particularly in the field of propaganda, we must never let ourselves be led by aesthetes or people who have grown blasé: not by the former, because the form and expression of our propaganda would soon, instead of being suitable for the masses, have drawing power only for literary teas; and of the second we must beware, because, lacking in any fresh emotion of their own, they are always on the lookout for new stimulation. These people are quick to weary of everything; they want variety, and they are never able to feel or understand the needs of their fellow men who are not yet so callous. They are always the first to criticize a propaganda campaign, or rather its content, which seems to them too old-fashioned, too hackneyed, too out-of-date, etc. They are always after novelty, in search of a change, and this makes them mortal enemies of any effective political propaganda. For as soon as the organization and the content of propaganda begin to suit their tastes, it loses all cohesion and evaporates completely.

55   The purpose of propaganda is not to provide interesting distraction for blasé young gentlemen, but to convince, and what I mean is to convince the masses. But the masses are slow-moving, and they always require a certain

time before they are ready even to notice a thing, and only after the simplest ideas are repeated thousands of times will the masses finally remember them.

56   When there is a change, it must not alter the content of what the propaganda is driving at, but in the end must always say the same thing. For instance, a slogan must be presented from different angles, but the end of all remarks must always and immutably be the slogan itself. Only in this way can the propaganda have a unified and complete effect.

57   This broadness of outline from which we must never depart, in combination with steady, consistent emphasis, allows our final success to mature. And then, to our amazement, we shall see what tremendous results such perseverance leads to—to results that are almost beyond our understanding.

58   All advertising, whether in the field of business or politics, achieves success through the continuity and sustained uniformity of its application.

59   Here, too, the example of enemy war propaganda was typical; limited to a few points, devised exclusively for the masses, carried on with indefatigable persistence. Once the basic ideas and methods of execution were recognized as correct, they were applied throughout the whole War without the slightest change. At first the claims of the propaganda were so impudent that people thought it insane; later, it got on people's nerves; and in the end, it was believed. After four and a half years, a revolution broke out in Germany; and its slogans originated in the enemy's war propaganda.

60   And in England they understood one more thing: that this spiritual weapon can succeed only if it is applied on a tremendous scale, but that success amply covers all costs.

61   There, propaganda was regarded as a weapon of the first order, while in our country it was the last resort of unemployed politicians and a comfortable haven for slackers.

62   And, as was to be expected, its results all in all were zero.

1925

Winston Churchill

THE BATTLE OF BRITAIN

Here is a speech by one of the major leaders and orators of the twentieth century, Winston Churchill. Although Churchill was widely admired for his leadership during World War II, more recently some writers have argued that his leadership had a demagogic side—that is, he gained power over people by stirring their emotions and prejudices. On the basis of the following speech, what do you think? It was given before the British House of Commons and then broadcast to the public.

1   I spoke the other day of the colossal military disaster which occurred when the French High Command failed to withdraw the northern armies from Belgium at the moment when they knew that the French front was decisively broken at Sedan and on the Meuse. This delay entailed the loss of fifteen or sixteen French divisions and threw out of action for the critical period the whole of the British Expeditionary Force. Our Army and 120,000 French troops were indeed rescued by the British Navy from Dunkirk but only with the loss of their cannon, vehicles and modern equipment. This loss inevitably took some weeks to repair, and in the first two of those weeks the battle in France has been lost. When we consider the heroic resistance made by the French Army against heavy odds in this battle, the enormous losses inflicted upon the enemy and the evident exhaustion of the enemy, it may well be thought that these twenty-five divisions of the best-trained and best-equipped troops might have turned the scale. However, General Weygand had to fight without them. Only three British divisions or their equivalent were able to stand in the line with their French comrades. They have suffered severely, but they have fought well. We sent every man we could to France as fast as we could re-equip and transport their formations.

2   I am not reciting these facts for the purpose of recrimination. That I judge to be utterly futile and even harmful. We cannot afford it. I recite them in order to explain why it was we did not have, as we could have had, between twelve and fourteen British divisions fighting in the line in this great battle instead of only three. Now I put all this aside. I put it on the shelf, from which the historians, when they have time, will select their documents to tell their stories. We have to think of the future and not of the past. This also applies in a small way to our own affairs at home. There are many who would hold an inquest in the House of Commons on the conduct of the Governments—and of Parliaments, for they are in it, too—during the years which led up to this catastrophe. They seek to indict those who were responsible for the guidance of our affairs. This also would be a foolish and pernicious process. There are too many in it. Let each man search his conscience and search his speeches. I frequently search mine.

3   Of this I am quite sure, that if we open a quarrel between the past and the present, we shall find that we have lost the future. Therefore, I cannot accept the drawing of any distinctions between Members of the present Government. It was formed at a moment of crisis in order to unite all the parties and all sections of opinion. It has received the almost unanimous support of both Houses of Parliament. Its Members are going to stand together, and, subject to the authority of the House of Commons, we are going to govern the country and fight the war. It is absolutely necessary at a time like this that every

Minister who tries each day to do his duty shall be respected; and their sub-ordinates must know that their chiefs are not threatened men, men who are here today and gone tomorrow, but that their directions must be punctually and faithfully obeyed. Without this concentrated power we cannot face what lies before us. I should not think it would be very advantageous for the House to prolong this Debate this afternoon under conditions of public stress. Many facts are not clear that will be clear in a short time. We are to have a Secret Session on Thursday, and I should think that would be a better opportunity for the many earnest expressions of opinion which Members will desire to make and for the House to discuss vital matters without having everything read the next morning by our dangerous foes.

4   The disastrous military events which have happened during the past fortnight have not come to me with any sense of surprise. Indeed, I indicated a fortnight ago as clearly as I could to the House that the worst possibilities were open; and I made it perfectly clear then that whatever happened in France would make no difference to the resolve of Britain and the British Empire to fight on, 'if necessary for years, if necessary alone'. During the last few days we have successfully brought off the great majority of the troops we had on the lines of communication in France; and seven-eighths of the troops we have sent to France since the beginning of the war—that is to say, about 350,000 out of 400,000 men—are safely back in this country. Others are still fighting with the French, and fighting with considerable success in their local encounters against the enemy. We have also brought back a great mass of stores, rifles and munitions of all kinds which had been accumulated in France during the last nine months.

5   We have, therefore, in this island today a very large and powerful military force. This force comprises all our best trained and our finest troops, including scores of thousands of those who have already measured their quality against the Germans and found themselves at no disadvantage. We have under arms at the present time in this island over a million and a quarter men. Behind these we have the Local Defence Volunteers, numbering half a million, only a portion of whom, however, are yet armed with rifles or other firearms. We have incorporated into our defence forces every man for whom we have a weapon. We expect very large additions to our weapons in the near future, and in preparation for this we intend forthwith to call up, drill and train further large numbers. Those who are not called up, or else are employed upon the vast business of munitions production in all its branches—and their ram-ifications are innumerable—will serve their country best by remaining at their ordinary work until they receive their summons. We have also over here Dominions armies. The Canadians had actually landed in France, but have now been safely withdrawn, much disappointed, but in perfect order, with all their artillery and equipment. And these very high-class forces from the Dominions will now take part in the defence of the Mother Country.

6   Lest the account which I have given of these large forces should raise the question: Why did they not take part in the great battle in France? I must

make it clear that, apart from the divisions training and organizing at home, only twelve divisions were equipped to fight upon a scale which justified their being sent abroad. And this was fully up to the number which the French had been led to expect would be available in France at the ninth month of the war. The rest of our forces at home have a fighting value for home defence which will, of course, steadily increase every week that passes. Thus, the invasion of Great Britain would at this time require the transportation across the sea of hostile armies on a very large scale, and after they had been so transported they would have to be continually maintained with all the masses of munitions and supplies which are required for continuous battle—as continuous battle it will surely be.

7   Here is where we come to the Navy—and after all, we have a Navy. Some people seem to forget that we have a Navy. We must remind them. For the last thirty years I have been concerned in discussions about the possibilities of oversea invasion, and I took the responsibility on behalf of the Admiralty, at the beginning of the last war, of allowing all regular troops to be sent out of the country. That was a very serious step to take, because our Territorials had only just been called up and were quite untrained. Therefore, this island was for several months practically denuded of fighting troops. The Admiralty had confidence at that time in their ability to prevent a mass invasion even though at that time the Germans had a magnificent battle fleet in the proportion of ten to sixteen, even though they were capable of fighting a general engagement every day and any day, whereas now they have only a couple of heavy ships worth speaking of—the *Scharnhorst* and the *Gneisenau*. We are also told that the Italian Navy is to come out and gain sea superiority in these waters. If they seriously intend it, I shall only say that we shall be delighted to offer Signor Mussolini a free and safeguarded passage through the Straits of Gibraltar in order that he may play the part to which he aspires. There is a general curiosity in the British Fleet to find out whether the Italians are up to the level they were at in the last war or whether they have fallen off at all.

8   Therefore, it seems to me that as far as seaborne invasion on a great scale is concerned, we are far more capable of meeting it today than we were at many periods in the last war and during the early months of this war, before our other troops were trained, and while the BEF had proceeded abroad. Now, the Navy have never pretended to be able to prevent raids by bodies of 5,000 or 10,000 men flung suddenly across and thrown ashore at several points on the coast some dark night or foggy morning. The efficiency of seapower, especially under modern conditions, depends upon the invading force being of large size. It has to be of large size, in view of our military strength, to be of any use. If it is of large size, then the Navy have something they can find and meet and, as it were, bite on. Now we must remember that even five divisions, however lightly equipped, would require 200 to 250 ships, and with modern air reconnaissance and photography it would not be easy to collect such an armada, marshal it, and conduct it across the sea without any powerful naval forces to escort it; and there would be very great pos-

sibilities, to put it mildly, that this armada would be intercepted long before it reached the coast, and all the men drowned in the sea or, at the worst, blown to pieces with their equipment while they were trying to land. We also have a great system of minefields, recently strongly reinforced, through which we alone know the channels. If the enemy tries to sweep passages through these minefields, it will be the task of the Navy to destroy the mine-sweepers and any other forces employed to protect them. There should be no difficulty in this, owing to our great superiority at sea.

9   Those are the regular, well-tested, well-proved arguments on which we have relied during many years in peace and war. But the question is whether there are any new methods by which those solid assurances can be circumvented. Odd as it may seem, some attention has been given to this by the Admiralty, whose prime duty and responsibility it is to destroy any large seaborne expedition before it reaches, or at the moment when it reaches these shores. It would not be a good thing for me to go into details of this. It might suggest ideas to other people which they have not thought of, and they would not be likely to give us any of their ideas in exchange. All I will say is that untiring vigilance and mind-searching must be devoted to the subject, because the enemy is crafty and cunning and full of novel treacheries and stratagems. The House may be assured that the utmost ingenuity is being displayed and imagination is being evoked from large numbers of competent officers, well-trained in tactics and thoroughly up to date, to measure and counterwork novel possibilities. Untiring vigilance and untiring searching of the mind is being, and must be, devoted to the subject, because, remember, the enemy is crafty and there is no dirty trick he will not do.

10   Some people will ask why, then, was it that the British Navy was not able to prevent the movement of a large army from Germany into Norway across the Skagerrak? But the conditions in the Channel and in the North Sea are in no way like those which prevail in the Skagerrak. In the Skagerrak, because of the distance, we could give no air support to our surface ships, and consequently, lying as we did close to the enemy's main air power, we were compelled to use only our submarines. We could not enforce the decisive blockade or interruption which is possible from surface vessels. Our submarine took a heavy toll but could not, by themselves, prevent the invasion of Norway. In the Channel and in the North Sea, on the other hand, our superior naval surface forces, aided by our submarines, will operate with close and effective air assistance.

11   This brings me, naturally, to the great question of invasion from the air, and of the impending struggle between the British and German Air Forces. It seems quite clear that no invasion on a scale beyond the capacity of our land forces to crush speedily is likely to take place from the air until our Air Force has been definitely overpowered. In the meantime, there may be raids by parachute troops and attempted descents of airborne soldiers. We should be

able to give those gentry a warm reception, both in the air and on the ground, if they reach it in any condition to continue the dispute. But the great question is: Can we break Hitler's air weapon? Now, of course, it is a very great pity that we have not got an Air Force at least equal to that of the most powerful enemy within striking distance of these shores. But we have a very powerful Air Force which has proved itself far superior in quality, both in men and in many types of machine, to what we have met so far in the numerous and fierce air battles which have been fought with the Germans. In France, where we were at a considerable disadvantage and lost many machines on the ground when they were standing around the aerodromes, we were accustomed to inflict in the air losses of as much as two to two-and-a-half to one. In the fighting over Dunkirk, which was a sort of no-man's-land, we undoubtedly beat the German Air Force, and gained the mastery of the local air, inflicting here a loss of three or four to one day after day. Anyone who looks at the photographs which were published a week or so ago of the re-embarkation, showing the masses of troops assembled on the beach and forming an ideal target for hours at a time, must realize that this re-embarkation would not have been possible unless the enemy had resigned all hope of recovering air superiority at that time and at that place.

12   In the defence of this island the advantages to the defenders will be much greater than they were in the fighting around Dunkirk. We hope to improve on the rate of three or four to one which was realized at Dunkirk; and in addition all our injured machines and their crews which get down safely—and, surprisingly, a very great many injured machines and men do get down safely in modern air fighting—all of these will fall, in an attack upon these islands, on friendly soil and live to fight another day; whereas all the injured enemy machines and their complements will be total losses as far as the war is concerned.

13   During the great battle in France, we gave very powerful and continuous aid to the French Army, both by fighters and bombers; but in spite of every kind of pressure we never would allow the entire metropolitan fighter strength of the Air Force to be consumed. This decision was painful, but it was also right, because the fortunes of the battle in France could not have been decisively affected even if we had thrown in our entire fighter force. That battle was lost by the unfortunate strategical opening, by the extraordinary and unforeseen power of the armored columns and by the great preponderance of the German Army in numbers. Our fighter Air Force might easily have been exhausted as a mere accident in that great struggle, and then we should have found ourselves at the present time in a very serious plight. But as it is, I am happy to inform the House that our fighter strength is stronger at the present time relatively to the Germans, who have suffered terrible losses, than it has ever been; and consequently we believe ourselves possessed of the capacity to continue the war in the air under better conditions

than we have ever experienced before. I look forward confidently to the exploits of our fighter pilots—these splendid men, this brilliant youth—who will have the glory of saving their native land, their island home, and all they love, from the most deadly of all attacks.

14   There remains, of course, the danger of bombing attacks, which will certainly be made very soon upon us by the bomber forces of the enemy. It is true that the German bomber force is superior in numbers to ours; but we have a very large bomber force also, which we shall use to strike at military targets in Germany without intermission. I do not at all underrate the severity of the ordeal which lies before us; but I believe our countrymen will show themselves capable of standing up to it, like the brave men of Barcelona, and will be able to stand up to it, and carry on in spite of it, at least as well as any other people in the world. Much will depend upon this; every man and every woman will have the chance to show the finest qualities of their race, and render the highest service to their cause. For all of us, at this time, whatever our sphere, our station, our occupation or our duties, it will be a help to remember the famous lines:

> He nothing common did or mean,
> Upon that memorable scene.

15   I have thought it right upon this occasion to give the House and the country some indication of the solid, practical grounds upon which we base our inflexible resolve to continue the war. There are a good many people who say, 'Never mind. Win or lose, sink or swim, better die than submit to tyranny— and such a tyranny.' And I do not dissociate myself from them. But I can assure them that our professional advisers of the three Services unitedly advise that we should carry on the war, and that there are good and reasonable hopes of final victory. We have fully informed and consulted all the self-governing Dominions, these great communities far beyond the oceans who have been built up on our laws and on our civilization, and who are absolutely free to choose their course, but are absolutely devoted to the ancient Motherland, and who feel themselves inspired by the same emotions which lead me to stake our all upon duty and honour. We have fully consulted them, and I have received from their Prime Ministers, Mr Mackenzie King of Canada, Mr Menzies of Australia, Mr Fraser of New Zealand and General Smuts of South Africa—that wonderful man, with his immense profound mind, and his eye watching from a distance the whole panorama of European affairs—I have received from all these eminent men, who all have Governments behind them elected on wide franchises, who are all there because they represent the will of their people, messages couched in the most moving terms in which they endorse our decision to fight on, and declare themselves ready to share our fortunes and to persevere to the end. That is what we are going to do.

16   We may now ask ourselves: In what way has our position worsened since the beginning of the war? It has worsened by the fact that the Germans have

conquered a large part of the coastline of Western Europe, and many small countries have been overrun by them. This aggravates the possibilities of air attack and adds to our naval preoccupations. It in no way diminishes, but on the contrary definitely increases, the power of our long-distance blockade. Similarly, the entrance of Italy into the war increases the power of our long-distance blockade. We have stopped the worst leak by that. We do not know whether military resistance will come to an end in France or not, but should it do so, then of course the Germans will be able to concentrate their forces, both military and industrial, upon us. But for the reasons I have given to the House these will not be found so easy to apply. If invasion has become more imminent, as no doubt it has, we, being relieved from the task of maintaining a large army in France, have far larger and more efficient forces to meet it.

17   If Hitler can bring under his despotic control the industries of the countries he has conquered, this will add greatly to his already vast armament output. On the other hand, this will not happen immediately, and we are now assured of immense, continuous and increasing support in supplies and munitions of all kinds from the United States; and especially of aeroplanes and pilots from the Dominions and across the oceans, coming from regions which are beyond the reach of enemy bombers.

18   I do not see how any of these factors can operate to our detriment on balance before the winter comes; and the winter will impose a strain upon the Nazi regime, with almost all Europe writhing and starving under its cruel heel, which, for all their ruthlessness, will run them very hard. We must not forget that from the moment when we declared war on September 3 it was always possible for Germany to turn all her Air Force upon this country, together with any other devices of invasion she might conceive, and that France could have done little or nothing to prevent her doing so. We have, therefore, lived under this danger, in principle and in a slightly modified form, during all these months. In the meanwhile, however, we have enormously improved our methods of defence, and we have learned, what we had no right to assume at the beginning, namely, that the individual aircraft and the individual British pilot have a sure and definite superiority. Therefore, in casting up this dread balance-sheet and contemplating our dangers with a disillusioned eye, I see great reason for intense vigilance and exertion, but none whatever for panic or despair.

19   During the first four years of the last war the Allies experienced nothing but disaster and disappointment. That was our constant fear: one blow after another, terrible losses, frightful dangers. Everything miscarried. And yet at the end of those four years the morale of the Allies was higher than that of the Germans who had moved from one aggressive triumph to another, and who stood everywhere triumphant invaders of the lands into which they had broken. During that war we repeatedly asked ourselves the question: How are we going to win? and no one was able to ever to answer it with much precision, until at the end, quite suddenly, quite unexpectedly, our terrible foe

collapsed before us, and we were so glutted with victory that in our folly we threw it away.

[20]   We do not yet know what will happen in France or whether the French resistance will be prolonged, both in France and in the French Empire overseas. The French Government will be throwing away great opportunities and casting adrift their future if they do not continue the war in accordance with their treaty obligations, from which we have not felt able to release them. The House will have read the historic declaration in which, at the desire of many Frenchmen—and our own hearts—we have proclaimed our willingness at the darkest hour in French history to conclude a union of common citizenship in this struggle. However matters may go in France or with the French Government, or other French Governments, we in this island and in the British Empire will never lose our sense of comradeship with the French people. If we are now called upon to endure what they have been suffering, we shall emulate their courage, and if final victory rewards our toils they shall share the gains, aye, and freedom shall be restored to all. We abate nothing of our just demands; not one jot or tittle do we recede. Czechs, Poles, Norwegians, Dutch, Belgians have joined their causes to our own. All these shall be restored.

[21]   What General Weygand called the Battle of France is over. I expect that the battle of Britain is about to begin. Upon this battle depends the survival of Christian civilization. Upon it depends our own British life, and the long continuity of our institutions and our Empire. The whole fury and might of the enemy must very soon be turned on us. Hitler knows that he will have to break us in this island or lose the war. If we can stand up to him, all Europe may be free and the life of the world may move forward into broad, sunlit uplands. But if we fail, then the whole world, including the United States, including all that we have known and cared for, will sink into the abyss of a new dark age made more sinister, and perhaps more protracted, by the lights of perverted science. Let us therefore brace ourselves to our duties, and so bear ourselves that, if the British Empire and its Commonwealth last for a thousand years, men will still say, 'This was their finest hour.'

June 18, 1940

Hannah Arendt

WHY EICHMANN MUST HANG

In her book Eichmann in Jerusalem: A Report on the Banality of Evil, *Hannah Arendt argues that the Nazi official Adolf Eichmann was not the horrific butcher that most people imagined him to be when he first came to trial in 1961 for his war crimes. Her conclusion is that Eichmann did not participate in the murder of millions of men, women, and children out of sadism or racial hatred. Instead, she depicts him as horrific in a different way: a bureaucratic paper-pusher who prided himself on following orders with great exactness and effi-ciency, even when those orders involved the slaughter of huge numbers of innocent people. Arendt uses evidence from Eichmann's trial to argue that he had never been able to see his actions as morally wrong. Because he literally regarded his superiors' words as law, he saw himself as a reliable worker and a good, law-abiding citizen. Arendt poses herself the difficult problem of whether society can justly condemn Eichmann to death if he had no intention to do wrong and little sense that what he did was wrong. In the following selection, she first summarizes the problem of intent and then imagines a powerful epi-deictic speech that seeks to communicate to Eichmann, but more importantly to the world watching the trial, why society is justified in taking Eichmann's life.*

1   Foremost among the larger issues at stake in the Eichmann trial was the assumption current in all modern legal systems that intent to do wrong is necessary for the commission of a crime. On nothing, perhaps, has civilized jurisprudence prided itself more than on this taking into account of the sub-jective factor. Where this intent is absent, where, for whatever reasons, even reasons of moral insanity, the ability to distinguish between right and wrong is impaired, we feel no crime has been committed. We refuse, and consider as barbaric, the propositions "that a great crime offends nature, so that the very earth cries out for vengeance; that evil violates a natural harmony which only retribution can restore; that a wronged collectivity owes a duty to the moral order to punish the criminal."[1] And yet I think it is undeniable that it was pre-cisely on the ground of these long-forgotten propositions that Eichmann was brought to justice to begin with, and that they were, in fact, the supreme jus-tification for the death penalty. Because he had been implicated and had played a central role in an enterprise whose open purpose was to eliminate forever certain "races" from the surface of the earth, he had to be eliminated. And if it is true that "justice must not only be done but must be seen to be done," then the justice of what was done in Jerusalem would have emerged to be seen by all if the judges had dared to address their defendant in some-thing like the following terms:

2   "You admitted that the crime committed against the Jewish people dur-ing the war was the greatest crime in recorded history, and you admitted your role in it. But you said you had never acted from base motives, that you had never had any inclination to kill anybody, that you had never hated Jews,

---

[1]Yosel Rogat, *The Eichmann Trial and the Rule of Law* (Santa Barbara, CA: Center for the Study of Democratic Institutions, 1961).

and still that you could not have acted otherwise and that you did not feel guilty. We find this difficult, though not altogether impossible, to believe; there is some, though not very much, evidence against you in this matter of motivation and conscience that could be proved beyond reasonable doubt. You also said that your role in the Final Solution was an accident and that almost anybody could have taken your place, so that potentially almost all Germans are equally guilty. What you meant to say was that where all, or almost all, are guilty, nobody is. This is an indeed quite common conclusion, but one we are not willing to grant you. And if you don't understand our objection, we would recommend to your attention the story of Sodom and Gomorrah, two neighboring cities in the Bible, which were destroyed by fire from Heaven because all the people in them had become equally guilty. This, incidentally, has nothing to do with the newfangled notion of 'collective guilt,' according to which people supposedly are guilty of, or feel guilty about, things done in their name but not by them—things in which they did not participate and from which they did not profit. In other words, guilt and innocence before the law are of an objective nature, and even if eighty million Germans had done as you did, this would not have been an excuse for you.

3 "Luckily, we don't have to go that far. You yourself claimed not the actuality but only the potentiality of equal guilt on the part of all who lived in a state whose main political purpose had become the commission of unheard-of crimes. And no matter through what accidents of exterior or interior circumstances you were pushed onto the road of becoming a criminal, there is an abyss between the actuality of what you did and the potentiality of what others might have done. We are concerned here only with what you did, and not with the possible noncriminal nature of your inner life and of your motives or with the criminal potentialities of those around you. You told your story in terms of a hard-luck story, and, knowing the circumstances, we are, up to a point, willing to grant you that under more favorable circumstances it is highly unlikely that you would ever have come before us or before any other criminal court. Let us assume, for the sake of argument, that it was nothing more than misfortune that made you a willing instrument in the organization of mass murder; there still remains the fact that you have carried out, and therefore actively supported, a policy of mass murder. For politics is not like the nursery; in politics obedience and support are the same. And just as you supported and carried out a policy of not wanting to share the earth with the Jewish people and the people of a number of other nations—as though you and your superiors had any right to determine who should and who should not inhabit the world—we find that no one, that is, no member of the human race, can be expected to want to share the earth with you. This is the reason, and the only reason, you must hang."

1963

Henrik Ibsen

STOCKMANN'S SPEECH*

In the climactic scene of Henrik Ibsen's An Enemy of the People, *Dr. Stockmann addresses an assembly of his fellow townspeople. Stockmann has discovered that the center of the town's prosperity, its popular therapeutic bathing establishment, is a menace to the health of its users. Naively, as it turns out, Stockmann assumed that the bathing establishment would be immediately closed and measures taken to eliminate the source of the contamination. Stockmann's brother, the town's burgomaster (mayor), persuades several influential citizens that this will cost the taxpayers dearly and that the damage to the reputation of the baths might be irreparable. Instead of closing the baths, the leading citizens and the ordinary townspeople unite to discredit Stockmann and thus preserve their prosperity, possibly at the expense of the health, or even of the lives, of the invalids who come to bathe. Although we expect at this point that Stockmann will prove his claims by producing the results of water-sample tests he has received from a university laboratory, he speaks instead on a more general issue. Is Stockmann persuasive? What would you judge him to be—a sophist or a rhetor—or can you come up with a term that better describes his attempt at persuasion?*

DR. STOCKMANN.   Can I speak?

ASLAKSEN [*Ringing the bell*].   Dr. Stockmann will address the meeting.

DR. STOCKMANN.   A few days ago, I should have liked to see any one venture upon such an attempt to gag me as has been made here to-night! I would have fought like a lion for my sacred rights! But now I care little enough; for now I have more important things to speak of.

[*The people crowd closer round him.* MORTEN KIIL *comes in sight among the bystanders.*]

DR. STOCKMANN [*Continuing*].   I have been pondering a great many things during these last days—thinking such a multitude of thoughts, that at last my head was positively in a whirl——

10 BURGOMASTER [*Coughing*].   H'm——!

DR. STOCKMANN.   But presently things seemed to straighten themselves out, and I saw them clearly in all their bearings. That is why I stand here this

*Translated by Eleanor Marx-Aveling.

evening. I am about to make great revelations, my fellow citizens! I am going to announce to you a far-reaching discovery, beside which the trifling fact that our water-works are poisoned, and that our health-resort is built on pestilential ground, sinks into insignificance.

MANY VOICES [*Shouting*]. Don't speak about the Baths! We won't listen to that! No more of that!

DR. STOCKMANN. I have said I would speak of the great discovery I have
20   made within the last few days—the discovery that all our sources of spiritual life are poisoned, and that our whole society rests upon a pestilential basis of falsehood.

SEVERAL VOICES [*In astonishment and half aloud*]. What's he saying?

BURGOMASTER. Such an insinuation——!

ASLAKSEN [*With his hand on the bell*]. I must call upon the speaker to moderate his expressions.

DR. STOCKMANN. I have loved my native town as dearly as any man can love the home of his childhood. I was young when I left our town, and distance, homesickness and memory threw, as it were, a glamour over the
30   place and its people.

[*Some applause and cries of approval.*]

DR. STOCKMANN. Then for years I was imprisoned in a horrible hole, far away in the north. As I went about among the people scattered here and there over the stony wilderness, it seemed to me, many a time, that it would have been better for these poor famishing creatures to have had a cattle-doctor to attend them, instead of a man like me.

[*Murmurs in the room.*]

BILLING [*Laying down his pen*]. Strike me dead if I've ever heard——!

HOVSTAD. What an insult to an estimable peasantry!

DR. STOCKMANN. Wait a moment!—I don't think any one can reproach me with forgetting my native town up there. I sat brooding like an eider duck
40   and what I hatched was—the plan of the Baths.

[*Applause and expressions of dissent.*]

DR. STOCKMANN. And when, at last, fate ordered things so happily that I could come home again—then, fellow citizens, it seemed to me that I hadn't another desire in the world. Yes, one desire I had: an eager, constant, burning desire to be of service to my birthplace, and to its people.

BURGOMASTER [*Gazing into vacancy*]. A strange method to select—

DR. STOCKMANN. So I went about revelling in my happy illusions. But yesterday morning—no, it was really two nights ago—my mind's eyes were opened wide, and the first thing I saw was the colossal stupidity of the authorities—

[*Noise, cries, and laughter.* MRS. STOCKMANN *coughs repeatedly.*]

50 BURGOMASTER.   Mr. Chairman!

ASLAKSEN [*Ringing his bell*].   In virtue of my position——!

DR. STOCKMANN.   It's petty to catch me up on a word, Mr. Aslaksen! I only mean that I became alive to the extraordinary muddle our leading men had been guilty of, down at the Baths. I cannot for the life of me abide leading men—I've seen enough of them in my time. They are like goats in a young plantation: they do harm at every point; they block the path of a free man wherever he turns—and I should be glad if we could exterminate them like other noxious animals——

[*Uproar in the room.*]

BURGOMASTER.   Mr. Chairman, are such expressions permissible?

60 ASLAKSEN [*With his hand on the bell*].   Dr. Stockmann——

DR. STOCKMANN. I can't conceive how it is that I have only now seen through these gentry; for haven't I had a magnificent example before my eyes here every day—my brother Peter—slow of understanding, tenacious in prejudice——

[*Laughter, noise, and whistling.* MRS. STOCKMANN *coughs.* ASLAKSEN *rings violently.*]

THE DRUNKEN MAN [*Who has come in again*].   Is it me you're alluding to? Sure enough, my name's Petersen; but devil take me if——

ANGRY VOICES.   Out with that drunken man! Turn him out!

[*The man is again turned out.*]

BURGOMASTER.   Who is that person?

A BYSTANDER.   I don't know him, Burgomaster.

70 ANOTHER.   He doesn't belong to the town.

A THIRD.   I believe he's a timber-dealer from——   [*The rest is inaudible.*]

ASLAKSEN.   The man was evidently intoxicated.—Continue, Dr. Stockmann; but pray endeavour to be moderate.

DR. STOCKMANN.   Well, fellow citizens, I shall say no more about our leading men. If any one imagines, from what I have just said, that it's these gentlemen I want to make short work of to-night, he is mistaken—altogether mistaken. For I cherish the comfortable conviction that these laggards, these relics of a decaying order of thought, are diligently cutting their own throats. They need no doctor to hasten their end. And it is not people

80   of that sort that constitute the real danger to society; it is not they who are most active in poisoning the sources of our spiritual life and making a plague-spot of the ground beneath our feet; it is not they who are the most dangerous enemies of truth and freedom in our society.

CRIES FROM ALL SIDES.   Who, then? Who is it? Name, name!

DR. STOCKMANN. Yes, you may be sure I shall name them! For this is the great discovery I made yesterday: [*In a louder tone.*] The most dangerous foe to truth and freedom in our midst is the compact majority. Yes, it's the confounded, compact, liberal majority—that, and nothing else! There, I've told you.

[*Immense disturbance in the room. Most of the audience are shouting, stamping, and whistling. Several elderly gentlemen exchange furtive glances and seem to be enjoying the scene.* MRS. STOCKMANN *rises in alarm.* EILIF *and* MORTEN *advance threateningly towards the schoolboys, who are making noises.* ASLAKSEN *rings the bell and calls for order.* HOVSTAD *and* BILLING *both speak, but nothing can be heard. At last quiet is restored.*]

90 ASLAKSEN.   I must request the speaker to withdraw his ill-considered expressions.

DR. STOCKMANN.   Never, Mr. Aslaksen! For it's this very majority that robs me of my freedom, and wants to forbid me to speak the truth.

HOVSTAD.   The majority always has right on its side.

BILLING.   Yes, and truth too, strike me dead!

DR. STOCKMANN.   The majority never has right on its side. Never I say! That is one of the social lies that a free, thinking man is bound to rebel against. Who make up the majority in any given country? Is it the wise men or the fools? I think we must agree that the fools are in a terrible, overwhelming
100   majority, all the wide world over. But how in the devil's name can it ever be right for the fools to rule over the wise men?   [*Uproar and yells.*]

DR. STOCKMANN.   Yes, yes, you can shout me down, but you cannot gainsay me. The majority has might—unhappily—but right it has not. It is I, and the few, the individuals, that are in the right. The minority is always right.
                                                            [*Renewed uproar.*]

HOVSTAD.   Ha ha! Dr. Stockmann has turned aristocrat since the day before yesterday!

DR. STOCKMANN.   I have said that I have no words to waste on the little, narrow-chested, short-winded crew that lie in our wake. Pulsating life has nothing more to do with them. I am speaking of the few, the individuals
110   among us, who have made all the new, germinating truths their own. These men stand, as it were, at the outposts, so far in the van that the compact majority has not yet reached them—and there they fight for truths that are too lately born into the world's consciousness to have won over the majority.

HOVSTAD.   So the Doctor's a revolutionist now!

DR. STOCKMANN.   Yes, by Heaven, I am, Mr. Hovstad! I am going to revolt against the lie that truth belongs exclusively to the majority. What sort of truths do the majority rally round? Truths so stricken in years that they

are sinking into decrepitude. When a truth is so old as that, gentlemen,
it's in a fair way to become a lie.   [*Laughter and jeers.*]

DR. STOCKMANN.   Yes, yes, you may believe me or not, as you please; but
truths are by no means the wiry Methusalehs some people think them. A
normally-constituted truth lives—let us say—as a rule, seventeen or
eighteen years; at the outside twenty; very seldom more. And truths so
patriarchal as that are always shockingly emaciated; yet it's not till then
that the majority takes them up and recommends them to society as
wholesome food. I can assure you there's not much nutriment in that sort
of fare; you may take my word as a doctor for that. All these majority-
truths are like last year's salt pork; they're like rancid, mouldy ham, producing all the moral scurvy that devastates society.

ASLAKSEN.   It seems to me that the honourable speaker is wandering rather
far from the subject.

BURGOMASTER.   I beg to endorse the Chairman's remark.

DR. STOCKMANN.   Why you're surely mad, Peter! I'm keeping as closely to my
text as I possibly can; for my text is precisely this—that the masses, the
majority, this devil's own compact majority—it's that, I say, that's poisoning the sources of our spiritual life, and making a plague-spot of the
ground beneath our feet.

HOVSTAD.   And you make this charge against the great, independent majority, just because they have the sense to accept only certain and acknowledged truths?

DR. STOCKMANN.   Ah, my dear Mr. Hovstad, don't talk about certain truths!
The truths acknowledged by the masses, the multitude, were certain
truths to the vanguard in our grandfathers' days. We, the vanguard of
today, don't acknowledge them any longer; and I don't believe there
exists any other certain truth but this—that no society can live a healthy
life upon truths so old and marrowless.

HOVSTAD.   But instead of all this vague talk, suppose you were to give us
some specimens of these old marrowless truths that we are living upon.

[*Approval from several quarters.*]

DR. STOCKMANN.   Oh, I could give you no end of samples from the rubbish-
heap; but, for the present, I shall keep to one acknowledged truth, which
is a hideous lie at bottom, but which Mr. Hovstad, and the *Messenger,* and
all adherents of the *Messenger,* live on all the same.

HOVSTAD.   And that is——?

DR. STOCKMANN.   That is the doctrine you have inherited from your forefathers, and go on thoughtlessly proclaiming far and wide—the doctrine
that the multitude, the vulgar herd, the masses, are the pith of the people—
that they are the people—that the common man, the ignorant, undevel-

oped member of society, has the same right to sanction and to condemn, to counsel and to govern, as the intellectually distinguished few.

BILLING.   Well, now, strike me dead——!

HOVSTAD [*Shouting at the same time*].   Citizens, please note this!

ANGRY VOICES.   Ho-ho! Aren't we the people? Is it only the grand folks that are to govern?

A WORKING MAN.   Out with the fellow that talks like that!

OTHERS.   Turn him out!

A CITIZEN [*Shouting*].   Blow your horn, Evensen.

[*The deep notes of a horn are heard; whistling, and terrific noise in the room.*]

DR. STOCKMANN [*When the noise has somewhat subsided*].   Now do be reasonable! Can't you bear even for once in a way to hear the voice of truth? I don't ask you all to agree with me on the instant. But I certainly should have expected Mr. Hovstad to back me up, as soon as he had collected himself a bit. Mr. Hovstad sets up to be a freethinker——

SEVERAL VOICES [*Subdued and wondering*].   Freethinker, did he say? What? Mr. Hovstad a freethinker?

HOVSTAD [*Shouting*].   Prove it, Dr. Stockmann. When have I said so in print?

DR. STOCKMANN [*Reflecting*].   No, upon my soul, you're right there; you've never had the frankness to do that. Well, well, I won't put you on the rack, Mr. Hovstad. Let me be the freethinker then. And now I'll make it clear to you all, and on scientific grounds too, that the *Messenger* is leading you shamefully by the nose, when it tells you that you, the masses, the crowd, are the true pith of the people. I tell you that's only a newspaper lie. The masses are nothing but the raw material that must be fashioned into a People.

[*Murmurs, laughter, and disturbance in the room.*]

DR. STOCKMANN.   Is it not so with all other living creatures? What a difference between a cultivated and an uncultivated breed of animals! Just look at a common barn-door hen. What meat do you get from such a skinny carcase? Not much, I can tell you! And what sort of eggs does she lay? A decent crow or raven can lay nearly as good. Then take a cultivated Spanish or Japanese hen, or take a fine pheasant or turkey—ah! then you'll see the difference! And now look at the dog, our near relation. Think first of an ordinary vulgar cur—I mean one of those wretched, ragged, plebeian-mongrels that haunt the gutters, and soil the sidewalks. Then place such a mongrel by the side of a poodle-dog, descended through many generations from an aristocratic stock, who have lived on delicate food, and heard harmonious voices and music. Do you think the brain of the poodle isn't very differently developed from that of the mongrel? Yes, you may be sure it is! It's well-bred poodle-pups like this that jugglers train to perform the most marvellous tricks. A common peasant-cur could never learn anything of the sort—not if he tried till doomsday.

[*Noise and laughter are heard all round.*]

200 A CITIZEN [*Shouting*].   Do you want to make dogs of us now?

ANOTHER MAN.   We're not animals, Doctor!

DR. STOCKMANN.   Yes, on my soul, but we are animals, my good sir! We're one and all of us animals, whether we like it or not. But truly there are few enough aristocratic animals among us. Oh, there's a terrible difference between poodle-men and mongrel-men! And the ridiculous part of it is, that Mr. Hovstad quite agrees with me so long as it's four-legged animals we're talking of—

HOVSTAD.   Oh, beasts are only beasts.

DR. STOCKMANN.   Well and good—but no sooner do I apply the law to two-
210   legged animals, than Mr. Hovstad stops short; then he daren't hold his own opinions, or think out his own thoughts; then he turns the whole principle upside down, and proclaims in the *People's Messenger* that the barndoor hen and the gutter-mongrel are precisely the finest specimens in the menagerie. But that's always the way, so long as the commonness still lingers in your system, and you haven't worked your way up to spiritual distinction.

HOVSTAD.   I make no pretense to any sort of distinction. I come of simple peasant folk, and I am proud that my root should lie deep down among the common people, who are here being insulted.

220 WORKMEN.   Hurrah for Hovstad. Hurrah! hurrah!

DR. STOCKMANN.   The sort of common people I am speaking of are not found among the lower classes alone; they crawl and swarm all around us—up to the very summits of society. Just look at your own smug, respectable Burgomaster! Why, my brother Peter belongs as clearly to the common people as any man that walks on two legs——   [*Laughter and hisses.*]

BURGOMASTER.   I protest against such personalities.

DR. STOCKMANN [*Imperturbably*].   —and that not because, like myself, he's descended from a good-for-nothing old pirate from Pomerania, or there abouts—for that's our ancestry——

230 BURGOMASTER.   An absurd tradition! Utterly groundless.

DR. STOCKMANN.   —but he is so because he thinks the thoughts and holds the opinions of his official superiors. Men who do that, belong, intellectually-speaking, to the common people; and that is why my distinguished brother Peter is at bottom so undistinguished,—and consequently so illiberal.

BURGOMASTER.   Mr. Chairman——!

HOVSTAD.   So that the distinguished people in this country are the Liberals? That's quite a new light on the subject.   [*Laughter.*]

DR. STOCKMANN.   Yes, that is part of my new discovery. And this, too, follows:
240   that liberality of thought is almost precisely the same thing as morality.
Therefore I say it's absolutely unpardonable of the *Messenger* to proclaim,
day out, day in, the false doctrine that it's the masses, the multitude, the
compact majority, that monopolize liberality and morality,—and that
vice and corruption and all sorts of spiritual uncleanness ooze out of culture, as all that filth oozes down to the Baths from the Mill Dale tan-
works!   [*Noise and interruptions.*]
DR. STOCKMANN [*Goes on imperturbably, smiling in his eagerness*].   And yet this
same *Messenger* can preach about elevating the masses and the multitude
to a higher level of well-being! Why, deuce take it, if the *Messenger's* own
250   doctrine holds good, the elevation of the masses would simply mean
hurling them straight to perdition! But, happily, the notion that culture
demoralises is nothing but an old traditional lie. No it's stupidity, poverty, the ugliness of life, that do the devil's work! In a house that isn't
aired and swept every day—my wife maintains that the floors ought to
be scrubbed too, but perhaps that is going too far;—well,—in such a
house, I say, within two or three years, people lose the power of thinking
or acting morally. Lack of oxygen enervates the conscience. And there
seems to be precious little oxygen in many and many a house in this
town, since the whole compact majority is unscrupulous enough to want
260   to found its future upon a quagmire of lies and fraud.
ASLAKSEN.   I cannot allow so gross an insult to be levelled against a whole
community.
A GENTLEMAN.   I move that the Chairman order the speaker to sit down.
EAGER VOICES.   Yes, yes! That's right! Sit down! Sit down!
DR. STOCKMANN [*Flaring up*].   Then I shall proclaim the truth at every street
corner! I shall write to newspapers in other towns! The whole country
shall know how matters stand here!
HOVSTAD.   It almost seems as if the Doctor's object were to ruin the town.
DR. STOCKMANN.   Yes, so well do I love my native town that I would rather
270   ruin it than see it flourishing upon a lie.
ASLAKSEN.   That's plain speaking.

[*Noise and whistling.* MRS. STOCKMANN *coughs in vain; the* DOCTOR *no longer heeds
her.*]

HOVSTAD [*Shouting amid the tumult*].   The man who would ruin a whole community must be an enemy to his fellow citizens!
DR. STOCKMANN [*With growing excitement*].   What does it matter if a lying
community is ruined! Let it be levelled to the ground, say I! All men who
live upon a lie ought to be exterminated like vermin! You'll end by poisoning the whole country; you'll bring it to such a pass that the whole

country will deserve to perish. And if ever it comes to that, I shall say, from the bottom of my heart: Perish the country! Perish all its people!

280 A MAN [*In the crowd*]. Why, he talks like a regular enemy of the people!

BILLING. Strike me dead but there spoke the people's voice!

THE WHOLE ASSEMBLY [*Shouting*]. Yes! yes! yes! He's an enemy of the people! He hates his country! He hates the whole people!

ASLAKSEN. Both as a citizen of this town and as a human being, I am deeply shocked at what it has been my lot to hear to-night. Dr. Stockmann has unmasked himself in a manner I should never have dreamt of. I must reluctantly subscribe to the opinion just expressed by some estimable citizens; and I think we ought to formulute this opinion in a resolution. I therefore beg to move, "That this meeting declares the medical officer of

290 the Baths, Dr. Thomas Stockmann, to be an enemy of the people."

[*Thunders of applause and cheers.*]

1882

Choderlos de Laclos

VALMONT EXPLAINS THE APPEARANCES*

Les Liaisons Dangereuses, *an eighteenth-century French novel by Choderlos de Laclos, is made up of the fictional letters of a group of aristocratic correspondents, particularly the Vicomte de Valmont, a single man, and the Marquise de Merteuil, a young widow. Most of Valmont's letters to his confidante, the Marquise, describe his efforts to seduce a virtuous married woman, Madame de Tourvel. He finally succeeds, and the letters that follow show him writing his way out of a difficulty with his newly won love. (Madame de Rosemonde is an older friend and confidante of Madame de Tourvel.) How does Valmont persuade Madame de Tourvel that he is innocent of infidelity toward her? What comment would you make on the ethics of Valmont's argument? In some ways his letter to the Marquise is the most intriguing. How does he convince her that he is sincere? What makes this question particularly interesting is that, in this novel made up only of fictional letters, we have no "true" account of the events, only the reports of the various correspondents. Thus, everything we know is embedded in a rhetorical context; all of the correspondents have their*

---

*Translated by Richard Aldington.

own interests to further. Are we justified in assuming that Valmont lies to Madame de Tourvel and tells the truth to the Marquise?

Letter 135

Madame de Tourvel to Madame de Rosemonde

1   I am trying to write to you without knowing if I shall be able to do so. Ah! Heaven, when I think that in my last letter it was the excess of my happiness which prevented my continuing it! And now it is the excess of my despair which overwhelms me, which leaves me no strength except to feel my pain, and takes away from me the strength to express it.

2   Valmont . . . Valmont loves me no more, he never loved me. Love does not disappear in this way. He deceives me, he betrays me, he outrages me. I endure all the misfortunes and humiliations which can be gathered together, and they come upon me from him.

3   And do not think this is a mere suspicion; I was so far from having any! I have not the happiness to be able to doubt. I saw him; what can he say to justify himself? . . . But what does it matter to him! He will not even attempt it. . . . Wretch that I am! What will my tears and reproaches matter to him? What does he care for me! . . .

4   It is true that he has sacrificed me, surrendered me . . . and to whom? . . . a vile creature. . . . But what am I saying? Ah? I have lost even the right to scorn her. She has betrayed fewer duties, she is less guilty than I. Oh! How painful is grief when it is founded on remorse! I feel my tortures increase. Farewell, my dear friend; however unworthy of your pity I have rendered myself, you will yet have some pity for me if you can form any idea of what I am suffering.

5   I have just re-read my letter, and I see that it tells you nothing; I will try to have the courage to relate this cruel event. It was yesterday; for the first time since my return I was to dine out. Valmont came to see me at five; never had he seemed so tender. He let me know that my plan of going out vexed him, and, as you may suppose, I soon decided to stay at home. However, suddenly, two hours later his manner and tone changed perceptibly. I do not know if anything escaped me which could offend him; but in any case, a little later he pretended to recollect an engagement which forced him to leave me and he went away; yet it was not without expressing very keen regrets which seemed to me tender and which I then thought sincere.

6   Left to myself, I thought it more polite not to avoid my first engagement since I was free to carry it out. I completed my toilet and entered my carriage. Unhappily my coachman took me by the Opera and I found myself in the confusion of the exit; a few steps in front of me in the next line I saw Valmont's carriage. My heart beat at once, but it was not from fear; and the one idea which filled me was the desire that my carriage would go forward.

Instead of that, his was forced to retire, and stopped opposite mine. I leaned forward at once; what was my astonishment to see at his side a woman of ill repute, well known as such! I leaned back, as you may suppose; this alone was enough to rend my heart; but, what you will scarcely believe, this same creature, apparently informed by an odious confidence, did not leave her carriage window, kept looking at me, and laughed so loudly it might have made a scene.

7   In the state of prostration I was in I allowed myself to be driven to the house where I was to sup, but it was impossible to remain there; every moment I felt ready to faint and I could not restrain my tears.

8   When I returned I wrote to M. de Valmont and sent him my letter immediately; he was not at home. Desirous, at any price, to emerge from this state of death or to have it confirmed forever, I sent the man back with orders to wait, but my servant returned before midnight and told me that the coachman, who had come back, had said that his master would not be in that night. This morning I thought there was nothing to do but to ask for my letters once more and to request him never to come to my house again. I gave orders to that effect; but doubtless they were useless. It is nearly midday; he has not yet arrived and I have not even received a word from him.

9   And now, my dear friend, I have nothing more to add; you know all about it and you know my heart. My one hope is that I shall not be here long to distress your tender friendship.

Paris, 15th of November, 17—

Letter 136

Madame de Tourvel to the Vicomte de Valmont

10   Doubtless, Monsieur, after what happened yesterday you will not expect to be received in my house again and, doubtless, you have no great wish to do so! The object of this note, then, is not so much to ask you not to come again as to request from you once more those letters which ought never to have existed; letters which, if they may have amused you for a moment as proofs of the delusion you created, cannot but be indifferent to you now that it is dissipated and now that they express nothing but a sentiment you have destroyed.

11   I recognize and confess I was wrong to give you a confidence by which so many other women before me have been victimized; in this I blame myself alone; but I thought at least I did not deserve from you that I should be abandoned to contempt and insult. I thought that in sacrificing myself to you, in losing for you alone my rights to the esteem of others and of myself, that I might expect not to be judged by you with more severity than by the public, whose opinion still recognizes an immense difference between a weak woman and a depraved woman. These wrongs, which would be wrongs to

anyone, are the only ones of which I speak. I am silent upon those of love; your heart would not understand mine. Farewell, Monsieur.

Paris, 15th of November, 17—

Letter 137

The Vicomte de Valmont to Madame de Tourvel

[12]   Your letter, Madame, has only just been handed to me; I shuddered on reading it, and it has left me scarcely strength to reply. What a dreadful idea of me you hold! Ah! No doubt I have done wrong, and such wrong that I shall never forgive myself for it in my life, even if you should hide it with your indulgence. But how far from my soul those wrongs you reproach me with have ever been! What I! I humiliate you! I degrade you! When I respect you as much as I cherish you, when my pride dates from the moment when you thought me worthy of you! Appearances have deceived you; and I confess they may have been against me; but why have you not in your heart that which should combat them? Why was it not revolted at the mere idea that it could have any reason to complain of mine? Yet you believed this! So you not only thought me capable of this atrocious madness, but you even feared you had made yourself liable to it by your favours to me. Ah! Since you feel yourself so degraded by your love I am then very vile in your eyes?

[13]   Oppressed by the painful feeling this idea causes me, I am wasting in resenting it the time I should employ in destroying it. I will confess all; but another consideration still restrains me. Must I then relate facts I wish to annihilate and fix your attention and mine upon a moment of error which I should like to atone for by the remainder of my life, whose cause I have yet to comprehend, whose memory must forever bring me humiliation and despair? Ah! If by accusing myself I must excite your anger, you will at least not have to seek far for your vengeance; it will suffice you to leave me to my remorse.

[14]   Yet—who would believe it?—the first cause of this event is the all-powerful charm I feel in your presence. It was that which made me forget too long an important engagement which could not be postponed. When I left you it was too late and I did not find the person I was looking for. I hoped to find him at the Opera and this step was equally fruitless. Emilie, whom I found there, whom I knew at a time when I was far from knowing either you or love; Emilie had no carriage and asked me to take her to her home close at hand. I saw no objection and consented. But it was then that I met you and I felt at once that you would be tempted to think me guilty.

[15]   The fear of displeasing or distressing you is so powerful in me that it must have been, and was indeed, speedily noticed. I confess even that it made me request the woman not to show herself; this precaution of delicacy turned against my love. Accustomed, like all those of her condition, never to be certain of a power which is always usurped, except through the abuse they

allow themselves to make of it, Emilie took care not to allow so striking an opportunity to escape. The more she saw my embarrassment increase the more pains she took to show herself, and her silly mirth—I blush to think that you could have believed for a moment that you were its object—was only caused by the cruel anxiety I felt, which was itself the result of my respect and my love.

16   So far I am certainly more unfortunate than guilty; and these wrongs which would be wrongs to anyone and are the only ones of which you speak cannot be blamed upon me since they do not exist. But it is in vain that you are silent upon the wrongs of love; I shall not keep the same silence about them; too great an interest compels me to break it.

17   In my shame at this inconceivable aberration I cannot recall its memory without extreme pain. I am deeply convinced of my errors and would consent to bear their punishment or to await their forgiveness from time, from my unending affection, and from my repentance. But how can I be silent when what I have to say is important to your sensibility?

18   Do not think I am looking for a roundabout way to excuse or palliate my error; I confess myself guilty. But I do not confess, I will never confess that this humiliating fault can be regarded as a wrong to love. Ah! What can there be in common between a surprisal of the senses, between a moment of self-forgetfulness soon followed by shame and regret, and a pure sentiment which can only be born in a delicate soul, can only be sustained there by esteem, and whose fruit is happiness! Ah! Do not profane love thus! Above all, fear to profane yourself by collecting under the same point of view what can never be confounded. Let vile and degraded women dread a rivalry they feel can be established in spite of them, let them endure the torments of a jealousy which is both cruel and humiliating; but you, turn your eyes away from objects which sully your gaze and, pure as the Divinity itself, punish, like it, the offence without resenting it.

19   But what punishment can you inflict upon me which could be more painful than that I feel, which can be compared with the regret of having displeased you, to the despair of having distressed you, to the crushing idea of having rendered myself less worthy of you? You are thinking how to punish me! And I ask you for consolation; not that I deserve it, but because it is necessary to me and can only come to me from you.

20   If, suddenly forgetting my love and yours and setting no value upon my happiness, you wish, on the contrary, to give me over to an eternal pain, you have the right to do so; strike; but if, being more indulgent or more tender, you remember still the sweet feelings which united our hearts—that pleasure of the soul, always reborn and always more deeply felt; those days, so sweet, so happy, which each of us owes to the other; all those treasures of love which love alone procures—perhaps you may prefer the power of re-creating them to that of destroying them. What more shall I say? I have lost everything, and

lost it through my own fault; but I can regain all by your benefaction. It is for you to decide now. I add only one word. Yesterday you swore to me that my happiness was certain as long as it depended on you! Ah! Madame, will you abandon me today to an eternal despair?

Paris, 15th of November, 17—

Letter 138

The Vicomte de Valmont to the Marquise de Merteuil

21   I persist, my fair friend; no, I am not in love; and it is not my fault if circumstances force me to play the part. Only consent and come back; you will soon see for yourself that I am sincere. I gave proofs of it yesterday and they cannot be destroyed by what is happening today.

22   I went to see the tender prude and went without having any other engagement; for the Volanges girl, in spite of her age, was to spend the whole night at Madame V...'s precocious ball. At first, lack of occupation made me desire to prolong this evening with her and I had even, with this purpose, exacted a small sacrifice; but scarcely was it granted when the pleasure I promised myself was disturbed by the idea of this love which you persist in believing of me, or at least in accusing me of; to such an extent that I felt no other desire than that of being able at the same time to assure myself and to convince you that it was a pure calumny on your part.

23   I therefore adopted a violent course; and on some slight pretext I left my Beauty in great surprise and doubtless even more distress. For myself, I went off calmly to meet Emilie at the Opera; and she can inform you that no regret troubled our pleasures until we separated this morning.

24   Yet I had a fair enough cause for anxiety if my perfect indifference had not preserved me from it; for you must know that I was barely four houses from the Opera, with Emilie in my carriage, when the austere devotee's carriage came up exactly opposite mine and a block kept us for nearly ten minutes beside one another. We could see each other as plainly as at midday and there was no way to escape.

25   But that is not all; it occurred to me to confide to Emilie that this was the woman of the letter. (Perhaps you will remember that jest and that Emilie was the writing-table.) She had not forgotten it; she is a merry creature; and she had no rest until she had observed at her ease 'that virtue', as she called it, and that with peals of laughter outrageous enough to provoke a temper.

26   That is still not all; did not the jealous creature send to my house that very evening? I was not there; but, in her obstinacy, she sent there a second time with orders to wait for me. As soon as I had decided to remain with Emilie I sent back my carriage with no orders to the coachman except to come for me there next morning; when he got back he found the messenger of love, and thought it quite simple to say that I was not returning that night. You can

guess the effect of this news and that when I returned I found my dismissal expressed with all the dignity demanded by the situation.

27   So this adventure which you think interminable might have been ended this morning, as you see; if it is not ended the reason is not, as you will think, that I set any value on its continuance; the reason is that, on the one hand, I did not think it decent to allow myself to be deserted; and, on the other hand, that I wished to reserve the honour of this sacrifice for you.

28   I have therefore replied to the severe note by a long sentimental letter; I gave lengthy reasons and I relied on love to get them accepted as good. I have just received a second note, still very rigorous and still confirming the eternal breach, as was to be expected; but its tone was not the same. She will above all things not see me; this determination is announced four times in the most irrevocable manner. I concluded I ought not to lose a moment before presenting myself, I have already sent my servant to get hold of the door-porter, and in a moment I shall go myself to have my pardon signed; for in wrongs of this kind there is only one formula which gives a general absolution and that can only be obtained in person.

29   Good-bye, my charming friend; I am now going to attempt this great event.

Paris, 15th of November, 17—

Letter 139

Madame de Tourvel to Madame de Rosemonde

30   How I blame myself, my tender friend, for having spoken to you of my passing troubles too much and too soon! It is because of me that you are now in distress; the grief which came to you from me still lasts while I am happy. Yes, all is forgotten, forgiven; let me express it better, all is retrieved. Calm and bliss have succeeded grief and anguish. O joy of my heart, how shall I express you! Valmont is innocent—a man who loves so much cannot be guilty. He had not done me the heavy, offensive injuries for which I blamed him with such bitterness; and if I needed to be indulgent in one point, had I not my own injustices to repair?

31   I will not tell you in detail the facts or reasons which justify him; perhaps the mind would not thoroughly appreciate them: the heart alone is capable of feeling them. Yet if you suspect me of weakness, I shall appeal to your own judgment in support of mine. For men, you said yourself, infidelity is not inconstancy.

32   It is not that I do not feel that this distinction, which opinion authorizes in vain, wounds my susceptibility; but how can mine complain when Valmont's susceptibility suffers even more? Do not think that he pardons or can console himself for this very fault which I forgive; and yet, how he has retrieved this little error by the excess of his love and of my happiness!

³³ Either my felicity is greater or I am more conscious of its value since I feared I had lost it; in any case I can say that if I felt I had the strength to endure again distress as cruel as that I have just passed through, I should not think I was buying too dearly this increase of happiness I have since enjoyed. O! my tender mother, scold your inconsiderate daughter for having troubled you over-much by her hastiness; scold her for having judged rashly and calumniated him whom she ought never to have ceased to adore; but as you recognise that she is imprudent, see that she is happy, and increase her joy by sharing it.

Paris, 16th of November, 17—, in the evening.
1781

Euripides
JASON EXPLAINS[*]

This argument is taken from the story of Jason and Medea as dramatized by the ancient Greek playwright Euripides (fifth century, B.C.). It shows a man leaving his wife and children for a beautiful young princess. Euripides's original Greek audience would already know the final outcome of this story: Medea will take her revenge by killing not only the new wife but also her own children, to leave Jason with nothing. At the time of this argument, Creon, the new bride's father, has already banished Medea for making violent threats against Jason and the young princess. Medea has heard only indirectly about Jason's plans, and this is their first confrontation. The Chorus—in this play a group of local women—is a convention of Greek drama used to provide a commentary on the action. Here one can also imagine the Chorus as another audience for the arguments put forward by Jason and Medea.

What kind of role do Jason's speeches create for Medea? Because Euripides makes clear that Medea cares deeply for her children, we might assume that Jason's arguments about providing for their future are well chosen. Does the manner in which he presents those arguments seem persuasive, or would you present them differently? Do you find one of the speakers to be more responsible than the other?

CHORUS.   Flow backward to your sources, sacred rivers,
    And let the world's great order be reversed.
    It is the thoughts of *men* that are deceitful,

[*]Translated by Rex Warner.

Their pledges that are loose.
Story shall now turn my condition to a fair one,
Women are paid their due.
No more shall evil-sounding fame be theirs.

Cease now, you muses of the ancient singers,
To tell the tale of my unfaithfulness;
For not on us did Phoebus, lord of music,
Bestow the lyre's divine
Power, for otherwise I should have sung an answer
To the other sex. Long time
Has much to tell of us, and much of them.

You sailed away from your father's home,
With a heart on fire you passed
The double rocks of the sea.
And now in a foreign country
You have lost your rest in a widowed bed,
And are driven forth, a refugee
In dishonor from the land.

Good faith has gone, and no more remains
In great Greece a sense of shame.
It has flown away to the sky.
No father's house for a haven
Is at hand for you now, and another queen
Of your bed has dispossessed you and
Is mistress of your home.

[*Enter* JASON, *with attendants.*]

JASON.   This is not the first occasion that I have noticed
How hopeless it is to deal with a stubborn temper.
For, with reasonable submission to our ruler's will,
You might have lived in this land and kept your home.
As it is you are going to be exiled for your loose speaking.
Not that I mind myself. You are free to continue
Telling everyone that Jason is a worthless man.
But as to your talk about the king, consider
Yourself most lucky that exile is your punishment.
I, for my part, have always tried to calm down
The anger of the king, and wished you to remain.

But you will not give up your folly, continually
Speaking ill of him, and so you are going to be banished.
All the same, and in spite of your conduct, I'll not desert

My friends, but have come to make some provision for you,
So that you and the children may not be penniless
Or in need of anything in exile. Certainly
Exile brings many troubles with it. And even
If you hate me, I cannot think badly of you.

MEDEA.   O coward in every way—that is what I call you,
With bitterest reproach for your lack of manliness,
50   You have come, you, my worst enemy, have come to me!
It is not an example of overconfidence
Or of boldness thus to look your friends in the face,
Friends you have injured—no, it is the worst of all
Human diseases, shamelessness. But you did well
To come, for I can speak ill of you and lighten
My heart, and you will suffer while you are listening.
And first I will begin from what happened first.
I saved your life, and every Greek knows I saved it,
Who was a shipmate of yours aboard the Argo,
60   When you were sent to control the bulls that breathed fire
And yoke them, and when you would sow that deadly field.
Also that snake, who encircled with his many folds
The Golden Fleece and guarded it and never slept,
I killed, and so gave you the safety of the light.
And I myself betrayed my father and my home,
And came with you to Pelias' land of Iolcus.
And then, showing more willingness to help than wisdom,
I killed him, Pelias, with a most dreadful death
At his own daughters' hands, and took away your fear.
70   This is how I behaved to you, you wretched man,
And you forsook me, took another bride to bed,
Though you had children; for, if that had not been,
You would have had an excuse for another wedding.
Faith in your word has gone. Indeed, I cannot tell
Whether you think the gods whose names you swore by then
Have ceased to rule and that new standards are set up,
Since you must know you have broken your word to me.
O my right hand, and the knees which you often clasped
In supplication, how senselessly I am treated
80   By this bad man, and how my hopes have missed their mark!
Come, I will share my thoughts as though you were a friend—
You! Can I think that you would ever treat me well?
But I will do it, and these questions will make you
Appear the baser. Where am I to go? To my father's?

Him I betrayed and his land when I came with you.
To Pelias' wretched daughters? What a fine welcome
They would prepare for me who murdered their father!
For this is my position—hated by my friends
At home, I have, in kindness to you, made enemies
90   Of others whom there was no need to have injured.
And how happy among Greek women you have made me
On your side for all this! A distinguished husband
I have—for breaking promises. When in misery
I am cast out of the land and go into exile,
Quite without friends and all alone with my children,
That will be a fine shame for the new-wedded groom,
For his children to wander as beggars and she who saved him.
O God, you have given to mortals a sure method
Of telling the gold that is pure from the counterfeit;
100   Why is there no mark engraved upon men's bodies,
By which we could know the true ones from the false ones?
  CHORUS.   It is a strange form of anger, difficult to cure,
When two friends turn upon each other in hatred.
  JASON.   As for me, it seems I must be no bad speaker.
But, like a man who has a good grip of the tiller,
Reef up his sail, and so run away from under
This mouthing tempest, woman, of your bitter tongue.
Since you insist on building up your kindness to me,
My view is that Cypris was alone responsible
110   Of men and gods for the preserving of my life.
You are clever enough—but really I need not enter
Into the story of how it was love's inescapable
Power that compelled you to keep my person safe.
On this I will not go into too much detail.
In so far as you helped me, you did well enough.
But on this question of saving me, I can prove
You have certainly got from me more than you gave.
Firstly, instead of living among barbarians,
You inhabit a Greek land and understand our ways,
120   How to live by law instead of the sweet will of force.
And all the Greeks considered you a clever woman.
You were honored for it; while, if you were living at
The ends of the earth, nobody would have heard of you.
For my part, rather than stores of gold in my house
Or power to sing even sweeter songs than Orpheus,
I'd choose the fate that made me a distinguished man.

There is my reply to your story of my labors.
Remember it was you who started the argument.
Next for your attack on my wedding with the princess:
130 Here I will prove that, first, it was a clever move,
Secondly, a wise one, and, finally, that I made it
In your best interests and the children's. Please keep calm.
When I arrived here from the land of Iolcus,
Involved, as I was, in every kind of difficulty,
What luckier chance could I have come across than this,
An exile to marry the daughter of the king?
It was not—the point that seems to upset you—that I
Grew tired of your bed and felt the need of a new bride;
Nor with any wish to outdo your number of children.
140 We have enough already. I am quite content.
But—this was the main reason—that we might live well,
And not be short of anything. I know that all
A man's friends leave him stone-cold if he becomes poor.
Also that I might bring my children up worthily
Of my position, and, by producing more of them
To be brothers of yours, we would draw the families
Together and all be happy. You need no more children.
And it pays me to do good to those I have now
By having others. Do you think this a bad plan?
150 You wouldn't if the love question hadn't upset you.
But you women have got into such a state of mind
That, if your life at night is good, you think you have
Everything; but, if in that quarter things go wrong,
You will consider your best and truest interests
Most hateful. It would have been better far for men
To have got their children in some other way, and women
Not to have existed. Then life would have been good.
CHORUS.   Jason, though you have made this speech of yours look well,
Still I think, even though others do not agree,
160 You have betrayed your wife and are acting badly.
MEDEA.   Surely in many ways I hold different views
From others, for I think that the plausible speaker
Who is a villain deserves the greatest punishment.
Confident in his tongue's power to adorn evil,
He stops at nothing. Yet he is not really wise.
As in your case. There is no need to put on the airs
Of a clever speaker, for one word will lay you flat.
If you were not a coward, you would not have married
Behind my back, but discussed it with me first.

170 JASON.   And you, no doubt, would have furthered the proposal,
    If I had told you of it, you who even now
    Are incapable of controlling your bitter temper.
    MEDEA.   It was not that. No, you thought it was not respectable
    As you got on in years to have a foreign wife.
    JASON.   Make sure of this: it was not because of a woman
    I made the royal alliance in which I now live,
    But, as I said before, I wished to preserve you
    And breed a royal progeny to be brothers
    To the children I have now, a sure defense to us.
180 MEDEA.   Let me have no happy fortune that brings pain with it,
    Or prosperity which is upsetting to the mind!
    JASON.   Change your ideas of what you want, and show more sense.
    Do not consider painful what is good for you,
    Nor, when you are lucky, think yourself unfortunate.
    MEDEA.   You can insult me. You have somewhere to turn to.
    But I shall go from this land into exile, friendless.
    JASON.   It was what you chose yourself. Don't blame others for it.
    MEDEA.   And how did I choose it? Did I betray my husband?
    JASON.   You called down wicked curses on the king's family.
190 MEDEA.   A curse, that is what I am become to your house too.
    JASON.   I do not propose to go into all the rest of it;
    But, if you wish for the children or for yourself
    In exile to have some of my money to help you,
    Say so, for I am prepared to give with open hand,
    Or to provide you with introductions to my friends
    Who will treat you well. You are a fool if you do not
    Accept this. Cease your anger and you will profit.
    MEDEA.   I shall never accept the favors of friends of yours,
    Nor take a thing from you, so you need not offer it.
200   There is no benefit in the gifts of a bad man.
    JASON.   Then, in any case, I call the gods to witness that
    I wish to help you and the children in every way,
    But you refuse what is good for you. Obstinately
    You push away your friends. You are sure to suffer for it.
    MEDEA.   Go! No doubt you hanker for your virginal bride,
    And are guilty of lingering too long out of her house.
    Enjoy your wedding. But perhaps—with the help of God—
    You will make the kind of marriage that you will regret.

[JASON *goes out with his attendants.*]

CHORUS.   When love is in excess
210   It brings a man no honor

Nor any worthiness.
But if in moderation Cypris comes,
There is no other power at all so gracious.
O goddess, never on me let loose the unerring
Shaft of your bow in the poison of desire.

Let my heart be wise.
It is the gods' best gift.
On me let mighty Cypris
Inflict no wordy wars or restless anger
220 To urge my passion to a different love.
But with discernment may she guide women's weddings,
Honoring most what is peaceful in the bed.

O country and home,
Never, never may I be without you,
Living the hopeless life,
Hard to pass through and painful,
Most pitiable of all.
Let death first lay me low and death
Free me from this daylight.
230 There is no sorrow above
The loss of a native land.
I have seen it myself,
Do not tell of a secondhand story.
Neither city nor friend
Pitied you when you suffered
The worst of sufferings.
O let him die ungraced whose heart
Will not reward his friends,
Who cannot open an honest mind
240 No friend will he be of mine.

◆ ◆ ◆

In this later speech, Medea pretends to be finally reconciled with Jason, but she is in fact plotting her revenge on him. Is there any way to tell from the speech itself that Medea is insincere?

JASON.   I have come at your request. Indeed, although
You are bitter against me, this you shall have: I will listen
To what new thing you want, woman, to get from me.
MEDEA.   Jason, I beg you to be forgiving toward me
For what I said. It is natural for you to bear with

My temper, since we have had much love together.
I have talked with myself about this and I have
Reproached myself. "Fool" I said, "why am I so mad?
Why am I set against those who have planned wisely?
Why make myself an enemy of the authorities
And of my husband, who does the best thing for me
By marrying royalty and having children who
Will be as brothers to my own? What is wrong with me?
Let me give up anger, for the gods are kind to me.
Have I not children, and do I not know that we
In exile from our country must be short of friends?"
When I considered this I saw that I had shown
Great lack of sense, and that my anger was foolish.
Now I agree with you. I think that you are wise
In having this other wife as well as me, and I
Was mad. I should have helped you in these plans of yours,
Have joined in the wedding, stood by the marriage bed,
Have taken pleasure in attendance on your bride.
But we women are what we are—perhaps a little
Worthless; and you men must not be like us in this,
Nor be foolish in return when we are foolish.
Now, I give in, and admit that then I was wrong.
I have come to a better understanding now.

431 B.C.

Gary Soto

THE PIE

Gary Soto's books frequently describe his recollections of poverty, hot sun, and hard work as part of his boyhood in a Chicano family in California's Central Valley. For his powerful writing, he has won a number of distinguished awards, including a Guggenheim Fellowship and the American Book Award. Here is a piece from his 1990 collection, A Summer Life. *In a gracefully written essay that is lighter than many in this chapter, Soto reflects on guilt, sin, and pie stealing.*

1   I knew enough about hell to stop me from stealing. I was holy in almost every bone. Some days I recognized the shadows of angels flopping on the backyard grass, and other days I heard faraway messages in the plumbing

that howled underneath the house when I crawled there looking for something to do.

2   But boredom made me sin. Once, at the German Market, I stood before a rack of pies, my sweet tooth gleaming and the juice of guilt wetting my underarms. I gazed at the nine kinds of pie, pecan and apple being my favorites, although cherry looked good, and my dear, fat-faced chocolate was always a good bet. I nearly wept trying to decide which to steal and, forgetting the flowery dust priests give off, the shadow of angels and the proximity of God howling in the plumbing underneath the house, sneaked a pie behind my coffee-lid frisbee and walked to the door, grinning to the bald grocer whose forehead shone with a window of light.

3   "No one saw," I muttered to myself, the pie like a discus in my hand, and hurried across the street, where I sat on someone's lawn. The sun wavered between the branches of a yellowish sycamore. A squirrel nailed itself high on the trunk, where it forked into two large bark-scabbed limbs. Just as I was going to work my cleanest finger into the pie, a neighbor came out to the porch for his mail. He looked at me, and I got up and headed for home. I raced on skinny legs to my block, but slowed to a quick walk when I couldn't wait any longer. I held the pie to my nose and breathed in its sweetness. I licked some of the crust and closed my eyes as I took a small bite.

4   In my front yard, I leaned against a car fender and panicked about stealing the apple pie. I knew an apple got Eve in deep trouble with snakes because Sister Marie had shown us a film about Adam and Eve being cast into the desert, and what scared me more than falling from grace was being thirsty for the rest of my life. But even that didn't stop me from clawing a chunk from the pie tin and pushing it into the cavern of my mouth. The slop was sweet and gold-colored in the afternoon sun. I laid more pieces on my tongue, wet finger-dripping pieces, until I was finished and felt like crying because it was about the best thing I had ever tasted. I realized right there and then, in my sixth year, in my tiny body of two hundred bones and three or four sins, that the best things in life came stolen. I wiped my sticky fingers on the grass and rolled my tongue over the corners of my mouth. A burp perfumed the air.

5   I felt bad not sharing with Cross-Eyed Johnny, a neighbor kid. He stood over my shoulder and asked, "Can I have some?" Crust fell from my mouth, and my teeth were bathed with the jam-like filling. Tears blurred my eyes as I remembered the grocer's forehead. I remembered the other pies on the rack, the warm air of the fan above the door and the car that honked as I crossed the street without looking.

6   "Get away," I had answered Cross-Eyed Johnny. He watched my fingers greedily push big chunks of pie down my throat. He swallowed and said in a whisper, "Your hands are dirty," then returned home to climb his roof and sit watching me eat the pie by myself. After a while, he jumped off and hobbled away because the fall had hurt him.

7   I sat on the curb. The pie tin glared at me and rolled away when the wind picked up. My face was sticky with guilt. A car honked, and the driver knew.

Mrs. Hancock stood on her lawn, hands on hip, and she knew. My mom, peeling a mountain of potatoes at the Redi-Spud factory, knew. I got to my feet, stomach taut, mouth tired of chewing, and flung my frisbee across the street, its shadow like the shadow of an angel fleeing bad deeds. I retrieved it, jogging slowly. I flung it again until I was bored and thirsty.

8   I returned home to drink water and help my sister glue bottle caps onto cardboard, a project for summer school. But the bottle caps bored me, and the water soon filled me up more than the pie. With the kitchen stifling with heat and lunatic flies, I decided to crawl underneath our house and lie in the cool shadows listening to the howling sound of plumbing. Was it God? Was it Father, speaking from death, or Uncle with his last shiny dime? I listened, ear pressed to a cold pipe, and heard a howl like the sea. I lay until I was cold and then crawled back to the light, rising from one knee, then another, to dust off my pants and squint in the harsh light. I looked and saw the glare of a pie tin on a hot day. I knew sin was what you take and didn't give back.

1990

Reacting and Writing

The questions that introduce most of the readings in this section ask you to make decisions about whether you think that the arguer's methods are ethical. Our introduction to this chapter suggests a number of ways in which you could make and support such a decision. Another possibility is to ask whether the arguer's audience had a fair chance. Can you think of other ways to decide whether you are dealing with an ethical arguer?

You might go back to some of the readings in previous chapters to evaluate them in ethical terms. Look, for example, at the attempts to advise young people in Chapter I or at Antony's speech in Chapter 3. Your class might want to bring in outside examples of ethical and unethical arguments that have been directed at them lately.

If you think that an arguer in a given case is clearly a sophist, how would you go about unmasking him or her? Are the arguments themselves flawed? Are they valid without being true, for example? Or are the arguments fine and the speaker's motives sophistical?

You could make any of the readings in this book the subject of scrutiny on ethical grounds. Try to do more than label the arguments as good or bad. Instead, imagine yourself persuading an admirer of the arguer that this arguer's techniques are unfair, or imagine persuading a critic of the arguer's techniques that the arguer is justified in using them. Be sure to support your claims with evidence from the argument itself, as well as with whatever reasoning and outside examples you need.

◆ "The Corcyraeans"

A way into this difficult piece is to distinguish those points on which all sides agree from those that are at issue. For instance, everyone seems to agree that an Athenian decision in favor of the Corcyraeans will lead to war; the Corcyraeans just contend that war is inevitable, anyway. What can we learn about the real situation from the dispute between Corinth and Corcyra over Epidamnus? (Notice that the Corcyraeans scarcely mention the dispute.) What is the likely outcome of the war between Corcyra and Corinth if Athens does not intervene? (Note that the Corcyraeans scarcely mention *that*.) Should the Athenian leaders govern their decisions by the "glorious opportunity" offered by the Corcyraeans or by the past service rendered by the Corinthians? One way to respond in writing would be to write two editorial columns, one on each side of this debate (see a reputable newspaper for models). Does this reading suggest any modern parallels?

◆ **"The Case for the Pigs"**

Look carefully at Squealer's question at the end of paragraph 20. It is a fine example of the manipulative use of the either/or fallacy, a deliberate misrepresentation of two alternatives as though they were the only ones. Squealer's rhetoric may seem obviously sophistical, but to what extent is that diagnosis dependent upon the earlier narrative? If we didn't know what was really happening, could we unmask Squealer just from his words?

◆ **"A Modest Proposal"**

Why is satire so important a tool in attacking sophistry? In part, perhaps, because the satirist says to his or her opponent, in effect, "You can't be serious." Anyone who contends that the problem of poverty in Ireland is being honestly addressed is a charlatan and a knave—or so Swift seems to be arguing. You may have written a satirical argument before, but you might try writing one in direct response to the piece in this chapter that you find most sophistical.

◆ **"Crito"**

Plato surely intended to depict Socrates as the good man speaking well, as the Romans later were to phrase it. Socrates's assertion that we should not change our principles to suit our circumstances suggests one way to guard against sophistry. Nonetheless, there is another side to this argument. Refusing to adjust one's principles in light of one's experiences can lead to a moral rigidity that can itself be dangerous. Could the Athenians have been right that Socrates was corrupting the Athenian youth? The form that Socrates's argument takes—the dialogue—is worth experimenting with as a way of making an argument. Try giving some good points and tough questions to the opposing voice you create. The exercise of thinking in dialogic terms helps an arguer to understand the give-and-take that is essential to persuasion.

◆ **"On Human Obligations"**

Weil's pronouncements will seem very abstract on a first reading, and it is often hard to tell whether one agrees with a statement until it is made more concrete. You might take one of her statements and relate it to an issue that interests you. Look, for example, at her statements about government and law in paragraphs 36-47. Would our state and our laws pass Weil's criteria for legitimacy? To what particular issues might you tie her pronouncements?

◆ **"On Propaganda"**

Reading Hitler's piece today will make many people think about commercial advertising and about those "public service announcements" that try to encourage some behaviors and discourage others. What ethical principles govern such practices? What seems to you to be Hitler's justification for his use of propaganda?

◆ **"The Battle of Britain"**

Can you think of a situation in which you might have to strengthen the resolve of your audience rather than changing its mind? Emotional appeals seem the obvious choice for such a rhetorical situation, and yet that choice brings us again to the line between persuasion and manipulation. Analyze the appeals that Churchill makes, asking whether any could be labeled demagogic. Can you think of appeals that he might have made that would have been unquestionably sophistical? Construct an argument of your own that strengthens your audience's resolve to support a cause you believe in, keeping in mind the issues raised by Churchill's speech.

◆ **"Why Eichmann Must Hang"**

Arendt's *Eichmann in Jerusalem* remains a controversial work. Many readers believe that, by characterizing Eichmann as a "banal" paper pusher, Arendt minimizes or trivializes the atrocious crimes committed against the Jews under the Nazi regime. Others find her thesis about Eichmann convincing and extremely important as an insight into the dangers of a modern bureaucratic society in which no individual has enough personal authority to exercise genuine moral choice. If, like Eichmann, a middle manager or civil servant claims just to be doing his job, just following orders, to what extent can we hold him responsible for moral transgressions that he did not initiate? In the imaginary speech that Arendt wrote for the judges, she gives her views about the way in which Eichmann might be held accountable. The ethical issues here are many and complex: what do you think about Eichmann's moral culpability? About the ethics of the speech Arendt gives to the judges?

◆ **"Stockmann's Speech"**

Most readers begin by sympathizing with Stockmann. He has the truth on his side, but he is brought down by his own idealism, just as Plato believed that Socrates was. The sophists in this case, it seems obvious, are Stockmann's brother and the newspaper editor who play to the prejudices of the crowd. But why does Ibsen have Stockmann attack the majority so openly and ineptly? Why didn't Stockmann stick to his hard evidence about the danger of the water? Ibsen seems to suggest that Stockmann has willed his own failure. Could Winston Churchill have expected to rally his countrymen in his "Battle of Britain" speech if he had told them that he would rather ruin Britain than see it flourish upon a lie, as Stockmann says about his town? One explanation for Stockmann's behavior may be contained in his idea of the truth as what is rejected by the majority. This point of view makes him sound like the artist who must get bad reviews to assure himself that he is really an artist—to be accepted is to be a commercial hack. But if, as he says, truth is constantly changing, why does he feel justified in preferring the truth to the survival of his native town? Try rewriting the speech, endeavoring to show the majority its mistake, rather than condemning it as an entity.

◆   **"Valmont Explains the Appearances"**

The obvious way to respond to this selection is with a letter of your own. For example, you could write your own answer to letter 139, having Madame de Rosemonde try to dissuade her friend from any further contact with Valmont. How would a Margaret Banning (see her letters in Chapter 1) ride to the epistolary rescue? Or, to bring the exercise closer to your own experience, you could write a letter to a friend whom you see being duped by someone else. How could you bring that person to his or her senses? Notice how skillfully Laclos informs the real audience (us) about events between the characters, as his correspondents address their various fictional audiences. See if you can inform your audience about your friend's circumstances, even as you address the letter to that friend.

◆   **"Jason Explains"**

An interesting aspect of this piece is Euripides's ironic use of the Chorus. To us, its sententious responses always seem woefully inadequate to what is happening. How could an analysis of the exchange between the two main characters help you to construct another possible Chorus—one that argues with Jason and Medea effectively and responsibly?

◆   **"The Pie"**

If Soto's essay reminds you of a chapter in the history of your own moral development, write an essay recounting the experience. You might even take Soto's last sentence: "I knew sin was _____." (Or fill in some other word in place of *sin*.) Try to select the details you include on the basis of their relevance to your overall intention for the piece.

CHAPTER 5

Four Symposia

A symposium was in ancient times an occasion for feasting, joking, and drinking, together with serious conversation. The word is now used to describe a conference, a roundtable discussion, or, as we use it here, a variety of points of view on a central concern. A symposium is not the same as a debate, although it can involve debates. One side wins a debate, but no one wins a symposium. Ideally, a symposium is a cooperative inquiry, and the participants reach a higher level of understanding than any one participant could achieve alone. The readings in this chapter are meant to start discussions, not to end them. The four broad topics are "Censorship and Freedom of Expression," "Our Relationship to Our Natural Environment," "Sex, Gender, Family," and "Politics, Principles, and Practicalities."

Notice that these four symposia also draw in the readings from previous chapters. The essays on art and on education in Chapter 2 relate to the first symposium, for example. The pieces in Chapter 2 by Kilpatrick, Salter, Kingston, López, White, Marshall, and Wilbur complement the selections in the third symposium. The selection in Chapter 3 from Shakespeare raises issues relevant to the symposium on politics, as does Martin Luther King Jr.'s "Letter from Birmingham Jail" in Chapter 1. You will undoubtedly make other connections as you read.

I. CENSORSHIP AND FREEDOM OF EXPRESSION

The *Republic,* one of Plato's best known works, describes his conception of an ideal state. No aspect of this work has attracted more hostility than his infamous banning of the poets from his ideal community and his straightforward declaration that "Most of the stories now in use [for educating young people] must be discarded." Written about 2,500 years ago, Plato's argument raises a fundamental question with which our society continues to struggle. Do works of art or entertainment affect the formation of our characters in serious and lasting ways?

The career of the German filmmaker, Leni Riefenstahl, provides us with a good test case for these questions of art and morality. Few people contest the judgment that Riefenstahl's films are admirable works of art. Visually, they can be intoxicatingly beautiful. But she worked in close cooperation with Adolf Hitler, and her films glorify the Nazi party. The debate over whether she should be honored for her filmmaking accomplishments illustrates some of the complexities of the questions we are considering. There is no proof, for example, that Riefenstahl personally inflicted suffering on the Jews and the others persecuted by the Nazis. But there is little question that her films—especially a compelling documentary called *Triumph of the Will*—aided Hitler in consolidating his power. *Triumph of the Will* (Hitler himself named it) celebrates the then-emerging Nazi party and its ambitious leader, Adolf Hitler. Riefenstahl has always maintained that she is an artist, not a propagandist, and that her films reflect the realities of her day. Her supporters argue that unpopular political views should not affect her right to be heard or the assessment of her artistic merit. Her critics charge that because the films promoted the Third Reich, Riefenstahl must share in the moral responsibility for the deeds of the Nazis. When, in 1974, an American film festival decided to honor her work, a strong outcry arose. While her defenders argued that they were honoring the art and not the personal life or the political views of the artist, one of her detractors carried a placard with the declaration, "The greater the artist, the greater the responsibility."

The readings in this symposium have something to say about Plato's argument, although many do not intentionally respond to his views. As you read, ask yourself where you stand in this long and important dialogue. You may not have large and sweeping opinions like Plato's, but you can begin with how you stand on specific contemporary applications of the problems the readings raise. Can books corrupt people? Can song lyrics? *Should* Leni Riefenstahl be honored for the artistic excellence of her films? Is criticizing its moral implications a legitimate approach to a work of art or literature?

Plato

ON THE NEED FOR CENSORSHIP[*]

In ancient Greece, schoolchildren learned what we now call the language arts by studying their culture's great poets. It is important to remember that the

---

[*]Translated and condensed by Francis Cornford.

poetry in question addresses adult concerns and that the elementary readers often used in our schools would probably strike Plato as sanitized well beyond his own requirements. Our ideas may in fact be more restrictive, not less, than Plato's, where reading matter for schoolchildren is concerned. You may find yourself put off by the moralistic tone of Socrates's speeches in this dialogue— for many, his objection to immoderate laughter seems like the last straw. But Plato's fundamental claim, that artistic representations have a strong impact on the formation of character, has never been refuted.

Notice that in the last paragraphs, Plato's interests seem to shift from censorship in primary education to a general ban on poetry—from our point of view, a very different issue. The first speaker is Socrates; the second, a man named Adeimantus.

1   What is this education to be, then? Perhaps we shall hardly invent a system better than the one which long experience has worked out, with its two branches for the cultivation of the mind and of the body. And I suppose we shall begin with the mind, before we start physical training.

2   Naturally.

3   Under that head will come stories; and of these there are two kinds: some are true, others fictitious. Both must come in, but we shall begin our education with the fictitious kind.

4   I don't understand, he said.

5   Don't you understand, I replied, that we begin by telling children stories, which, taken as a whole, are fiction, though they contain some truth? Such story-telling begins at an earlier age than physical training; that is why I said we should start with the mind.

6   You are right.

7   And the beginning, as you know, is always the most important part, especially in dealing with anything young and tender. That is the time when the character is being moulded and easily takes any impress one may wish to stamp on it.

8   Quite true.

9   Then shall we simply allow our children to listen to any stories that anyone happens to make up, and so receive into their minds ideas often the very opposite of those we shall think they ought to have when they are grown up?

10   No, certainly not.

11   It seems, then, our first business will be to supervise the making of fables and legends, rejecting all which are unsatisfactory; and we shall induce nurses and others to tell their children only those which we have approved, and to think more of moulding their souls with these stories than they now do of rubbing their limbs to make them strong and shapely. Most of the stories now in use must be discarded.

12   What kind do you mean?

13   If we take the great ones, we shall see in them the pattern of all the rest, which are bound to be of the same stamp and to have the same effect.

14   No doubt; but which do you mean by the great ones?

15   The stories in Hesiod and Homer and the poets in general, who have at all times composed fictitious tales and told them to mankind.

16   Which kind are you thinking of, and what fault do you find in them?

17   The worst of all faults, especially if the story is ugly and immoral as well as false—misrepresenting the nature of gods and heroes, like an artist whose picture is utterly unlike the object he sets out to draw.

18   That is certainly a serious fault; but give me an example.

19   A signal instance of false invention about the highest matters is that foul story, which Hesiod repeats, of the deeds of Uranus and the vengeance of Cronos; and then there is the tale of Cronos's doings and his son's treatment of him. Even if such tales were true, I should not have supposed they should be lightly told to thoughtless young people. If they cannot be altogether suppressed, they should only be revealed in a mystery, to which access should be as far as possible restricted by requiring the sacrifice, not of a pig, but of some victim such as very few could afford.

20   It is true: those stories are objectionable.

21   Yes, and not to be repeated in our commonwealth, Adeimantus. We shall not tell a child that, if he commits the foulest crimes or goes to any length in punishing his father's misdeeds, he will be doing nothing out of the way, but only what the first and greatest of the gods have done before him.

22   I agree; such stories are not fit to be repeated.

23   Nor yet any tales of warfare and intrigues and battles of gods against gods, which are equally untrue. If our future Guardians are to think it a disgrace to quarrel lightly with one another, we shall not let them embroider robes with the Battle of the Giants or tell them of all the other feuds of gods and heroes with their kith and kin. If by any means we can make them believe that no one has ever had a quarrel with a fellow citizen and it is a sin to have one, that is the sort of thing our old men and women should tell children from the first; and as they grow older, we must make the poets write for them in the same strain. Stories like those of Hera being bound by her son, or of Hephaestus flung from heaven by his father for taking his mother's part when she was beaten, and all those battles of the gods in Homer, must not be admitted into our state, whether they be allegorical or not. A child cannot distinguish the allegorical sense from the literal, and the ideas he takes in at that age are likely to become indelibly fixed; hence the great importance of seeing that the first stories he hears shall be designed to produce the best possible effect on his character.

24   Yes, that is reasonable. But if we were asked which of these stories in particular are of the right quality, what should we answer?

25   I replied: You and I, Adeimantus, are not, for the moment, poets, but founders of a commonwealth. As such, it is not our business to invent stories ourselves, but only to be clear as to the main outlines to be followed by the poets in making their stories and the limits beyond which they must not be allowed to go.

26   True; but what are these outlines for any account they may give of the gods?

27   Of this sort, said I. A poet, whether he is writing epic, lyric, or drama, surely ought always to represent the divine nature as it really is. And the truth is that that nature is good and must be described as such.

28   Unquestionably.

29   Well, nothing that is good can be harmful; and if it cannot do harm, it can do no evil; and so it cannot be responsible for any evil.

30   I agree.

31   Again, goodness is beneficent, and hence the cause of well-being.

32   Yes.

33   Goodness, then, is not responsible for everything, but only for what is as it should be. It is not responsible for evil.

34   Quite true.

35   It follows, then, that the divine, being good, is not, as most people say, responsible for everything that happens to mankind, but only for a small part; for the good things in human life are far fewer than the evil, and, whereas the good must be ascribed to heaven only, we must look elsewhere for the cause of evils.

36   I think that is perfectly true.

37   So we shall condemn as a foolish error Homer's description of Zeus as the 'dispenser of both good and ill.' We shall disapprove when Pandarus' violation of oaths and treaties is said to be the work of Zeus and Athena, or when Themis and Zeus are said to have caused strife among the gods. Nor must we allow our young people to be told by Aeschylus that 'Heaven implants guilt in man, when his will is to destroy a house utterly.' If a poet writes of the sorrows of Niobe or the calamities of the house of Pelops or of the Trojan war, either he must not speak of them as the work of a god, or, if he does so, he must devise some such explanation as we are now requiring: he must say that what the god did was just and good, and the sufferers were the better for being chastised. One who pays a just penalty must not be called miserable, and his misery then laid at heaven's door. The poet will only be allowed to say that the wicked were miserable because they needed chastisement, and the punishment of heaven did them good. If our commonwealth is to be well-ordered, we must fight to the last against any member of it being suffered to speak of the divine, which is good, being responsible for evil. Neither young nor old must listen to such tales, in prose or verse. Such doctrine would be impious, self-contradictory, and disastrous to our commonwealth.

38   I agree, he said, and I would vote for a law to that effect.

39   Well then, that shall be one of our laws about religion. The first principle to which all must conform in speech or writing is that heaven is not responsible for everything, but only for what is good.

40   I am quite satisfied.

41   Now what of this for a second principle? Do you think of a god as a sort of magician who might, for his own purposes, appear in various shapes, now actually passing into a number of different forms, now deluding us into believing he has done so; or is his nature simple and of all things the least likely to depart from its proper form?

42   I cannot say offhand.

43   Well, if a thing passes out of its proper form, must not the change come either from within or from some outside cause?

44   Yes.

45   Is it not true, then, that things, in the most perfect condition are the least affected by changes from outside? Take the effect on the body of food and drink or of exertion, or the effect of sunshine and wind on a plant: the healthiest and strongest suffer the least change. Again, the bravest and wisest spirit is least disturbed by external influence. Even manufactured things—furniture, houses, clothes—suffer least from wear and tear when they are well made and in good condition. So this immunity to change from outside is characteristic of anything which, thanks to art or nature or both, is in a satisfactory state.

46   That seems true.

47   But surely the state of the divine nature must be perfect in every way, and would therefore be the last thing to suffer transformations from any outside cause.

48   Yes.

49   Well then, would a god change or alter himself?

50   If he changes at all, it can only be in that way.

51   Would it be a change for the better or for the worse?

52   It could only be for the worse; for we cannot admit any imperfection in divine goodness or beauty.

53   True; and that being so, do you think, Adeimantus, that anyone, god or man, would deliberately make himself worse in any respect?

54   That is impossible.

55   Then a god cannot desire to change himself. Being as perfect as he can be, every god, it seems, remains simply and for ever in his own form.

56   That is the necessary conclusion.

57   If so, my friend, the poets must not tell us that 'the gods go to and fro among the cities of men, disguised as strangers of all sorts from far countries'; nor must they tell any of those false tales of Proteus and Thetis transforming

themselves, or bring Hera on the stage in the guise of a priestess collecting alms for 'the life-giving children of Inachus, the river of Argos.' Mothers, again, are not to follow these suggestions and scare young children with mischievous stories of spirits that go about by night in all sorts of outlandish shapes. They would only be blaspheming the gods and at the same time making cowards of their children.

58   No, that must not be allowed.

59   But are we to think that the gods, though they do not really change, trick us by some magic into believing that they appear in many different forms?

60   Perhaps.

61   What? said I; would a god tell a falsehood or act one by deluding us with an apparition?

62   I cannot say.

63   Do you not know that the true falsehood—if that is a possible expression—is a thing that all gods and men abominate?

64   What do you mean?

65   This, I replied: no one, if he could help it, would tolerate the presence of untruth in the most vital part of his nature concerning the most vital matters. There is nothing he would fear so much as to harbour falsehood in that quarter.

66   Still I do not understand.

67   Because you think I mean something out of the ordinary. All I mean is the presence of falsehood in the soul concerning reality. To be deceived about the truth of things and so to be in ignorance and error and to harbour untruth in the soul is a thing no one would consent to. Falsehood in that quarter is abhorred above everything.

68   It is indeed.

69   Well then, as I was saying, this ignorance in the soul which entertains untruth is what really deserves to be called the true falsehood; for the spoken falsehood is only the embodiment or image of a previous condition of the soul, not pure unadulterated falsity. Is it not so?

70   It is.

71   This real falsehood, then, is hateful to gods and men equally. But is the spoken falsehood always a hateful thing? Is it not sometimes helpful—in war, for instance, or as a sort of medicine to avert some fit of folly or madness that might make a friend attempt some mischief? And in those legends we were discussing just now, we can turn fiction to account; not knowing the facts about the distant past, we can make our fiction as good an embodiment of truth as possible.

72   Yes, that is so.

73   Well, in which of these ways would falsehood be useful to a god? We cannot think of him as embodying truth in fiction for lack of information about the past.

74   No, that would be absurd.

75   So there is no room in his case for poetical inventions. Would he need to tell untruths because he has enemies to fear?

76   Of course not.

77   Or friends who are mad or foolish?

78   No; a fool or a madman could hardly enjoy the friendship of the gods.

79   Gods, then, have no motive for lying. There can be no falsehood of any sort in the divine nature.

80   None.

81   We conclude, then, that a god is a being of entire simplicity and truthfulness in word and in deed. In himself he does not change, nor does he delude others, either in dreams or in waking moments, by apparitions or oracles or signs.

82   I agree, after all you have said.

83   You will assent, then, to this as a second principle to guide all that is to be said or written about the gods: that they do not transform themselves by any magic or mislead us by illusions or lies. For all our admiration of Homer, we shall not approve his story of the dream Zeus sent to Agamemnon; nor yet those lines of Aeschylus where Thetis tells how Apollo sang at her wedding:

> Boding good fortune for my child, long life
> From sickness free, in all things blest by heaven,
> His song, so crowned with triumph, cheered my heart.
> I thought those lips divine, with prophecy
> Instinct, could never lie. But he, this guest,
> Whose voice so rang with promise at the feast,
> Even he, has slain my son.

If a poet writes of the gods in this way, we shall be angry and refuse him the means to produce his play. Nor shall we allow such poetry to be used in educating the young, if we mean our Guardians to be godfearing and to reproduce the divine nature in themselves so far as man may.

84   I entirely agree with your principles, he said, and I would have them observed as laws.

85   So far, then, as religion is concerned, we have settled what sorts of stories about the gods may, or may not, be told to children who are to hold heaven and their parents in reverence and to value good relations with one another.

86   Yes, he said; and I believe we have settled right.

87   We also want them to be brave. So the stories they hear should be such as to make them unafraid of death. A man with that fear in his heart cannot be brave, can he?

88   Surely not.

89   And can a man be free from that fear and prefer death in battle to defeat and slavery, if he believes in a world below which is full of terrors?

90   No.

91   Here again, then, our supervision will be needed. The poets must be told to speak well of that other world. The gloomy descriptions they now give must be forbidden, not only as untrue, but as injurious to our future warriors. We shall strike out all lines like these:

> I would rather be on earth as the hired servant of another, in the house of a landless man with little to live on, than be king over all the dead;

or these:

> Alack, there is, then, even in the house of Death a spirit or a shade; but the wits dwell in it no more.

We shall ask Homer and the poets in general not to mind if we cross out all passages of this sort. If most people enjoy them as good poetry, that is all the more reason for keeping them from children or grown men who are to be free, fearing slavery more than death.

92   I entirely agree.

93   We must also get rid of all that terrifying language, the very sound of which is enough to make one shiver: 'loathsome Styx,' 'the River of Wailing,' 'infernal spirits,' 'anatomies,' and so on. For other purposes such language may be well enough; but we are afraid that fever consequent upon such shivering fits may melt down the fine-tempered spirit of our Guardians. So we will have none of it; and we shall encourage writing in the opposite strain.

94   Clearly.

95   Another thing we must banish is the wailing and lamentations of the famous heroes. For this reason: if two friends are both men of high character, neither of them will think that death has any terrors for his comrade; and so he will not mourn for his friend's sake, as if something terrible had befallen him.

96   No.

97   We also believe that such a man, above all, possesses within himself all that is necessary for a good life and is least dependent on others, so that he has less to fear from the loss of a son or brother or of his wealth or any other possession. When such misfortune comes, he will bear it patiently without lamenting.

98   True.

99   We shall do well, then, to strike out descriptions of the heroes bewailing the dead, and make over such lamentations to women (and not to women of good standing either) and to men of low character, so that the Guardians we are training for our country may disdain to imitate them.

100   Quite right.

101   Once more, then, we shall ask Homer and the other poets not to represent Achilles, the son of a goddess, as 'tossing from side to side, now on his face, now on his back,' and then as rising up and wandering distractedly on the seashore, or pouring ashes on his head with both hands, with all those tears

and wailings the poet describes; nor to tell how Priam, who was near akin to the gods, 'rolled in the dung as he made entreaty, calling on each man by name.' Still more earnestly shall we ask them not to represent gods as lamenting, or at any rate not to dare to misrepresent the highest god by making him say: 'Woe is me that Sarpedon, whom I love above all men, is fated to die at the hands of Patroclus.' For if our young men take such unworthy descriptions seriously instead of laughing at them, they will hardly feel themselves, who are but men, above behaving in that way or repress any temptation to do so. They would not be ashamed of giving way with complaints and outcries on every trifling occasion; and that would be contrary to the principle we have deduced and shall adhere to, until someone can show us a better.

102   It would.

103   Again, our Guardians ought not to be overmuch given to laughter. Violent laughter tends to provoke an equally violent reaction. We must not allow poets to describe men of worth being overcome by it; still less should Homer speak of the gods giving way to 'unquenchable laughter' at the sight of Hephaestus 'bustling from room to room.' That will be against your principles.

104   Yes, if you choose to call them mine.

105   Again, a high value must be set upon truthfulness. If we were right in saying that gods have no use for falsehood and it is useful to mankind only in the way of a medicine, obviously a medicine should be handled by no one but a physician.

106   Obviously.

107   If anyone, then, is to practice deception, either on the country's enemies or on its citizens, it must be the Rulers of the commonwealth, acting for its benefit; no one else may meddle with this privilege. For a private person to mislead such Rulers we shall declare to be a worse offence than for a patient to mislead his doctor or an athlete his trainer about his bodily condition, or for a seaman to misinform his captain about the state of the ship or of the crew. So, if anyone else in our commonwealth 'of all that practice crafts, physician, seer, or carpenter,' is caught not telling the truth, the Rulers will punish him for introducing a practice as fatal and subversive in a state as it would be in a ship.

108   It would certainly be as fatal, if action were suited to the word.

109   Next, our young men will need self-control; and for the mass of mankind that chiefly means obeying their governors, and themselves governing their appetite for the pleasures of eating and drinking and sex. Here again we shall disapprove of much that we find in Homer.

110   I agree.

111   Whereas we shall allow the poets to represent any examples of self-control and fortitude on the part of famous men, and admit such lines as these: 'Odysseus smote his breast, chiding his heart: Endure, my heart; thou has borne worse things than these.'

¹¹² Yes, certainly.

¹¹³ Nor again must these men of ours be lovers of money, or ready to take bribes. They must not hear that 'gods and great princes may be won by gifts.'

¹¹⁴ No, that sort of thing cannot be approved.

¹¹⁵ If it were not for my regard for Homer, I should not hesitate to call it downright impiety to make Achilles say to Apollo: 'Thou has wronged me, thou deadliest of gods; I would surely requite thee, if I had but the power.' And all those stories of Achilles dragging Hector round the tomb of Patroclus and slaughtering captives on the funeral pyre we shall condemn as false, and not let our Guardians believe that Achilles, who was the son of a goddess and of the wise Peleus, third in descent from Zeus, and the pupil of the sage Chiron, was so disordered that his heart was a prey to two contrary maladies, mean covetousness and arrogant contempt of gods and men.

¹¹⁶ You are right.

¹¹⁷ We have now distinguished the kinds of stories that may and may not be told about gods and demigods, heroes, and the world below. There remains the literature concerned with human life.

¹¹⁸ Clearly.

¹¹⁹ We cannot lay down rules for that at our present stage.

¹²⁰ Why not?

¹²¹ Because, I suspect, we shall find both poets and prose-writers guilty of the most serious misstatements about human life, making out that wrongdoers are often happy and just men miserable; that injustice pays, if not detected; and that my being just is to another man's advantage, but a loss to myself. We shall have to prohibit such poems and tales and tell them to compose others in the contrary sense. Don't you think so?

¹²² I am sure of it.

¹²³ Well, as soon as you admit that I am right there, may I not claim that we shall have reached agreement on the subject of all this inquiry?

¹²⁴ That is a fair assumption.

¹²⁵ Then we must postpone any decision as to how the truth is to be told about human life, until we have discovered the real nature of justice and proved that it is intrinsically profitable to its possessor, no matter what reputation he may have in the eyes of the world.

¹²⁶ That is certainly true.

¹²⁷ So much for the content of literature. If we consider next the question of form, we shall then have covered the whole field.

¹²⁸ I don't understand what you mean by form, said Adeimantus.

¹²⁹ I must explain then, said I. Let me put it in this way. Any story in prose or verse is always a setting forth of events, past, present, or future, isn't it?

¹³⁰ Yes.

131   And that can be done either in pure narrative or by means of representation or in both ways.

132   I am still rather in the dark.

133   I seem to be a poor hand at explaining; I had better give a particular illustration. You remember the beginning of the *Iliad*, which describes how Chryses begged Agamemnon to release his daughter, and Agamemnon was angry, and Chryses called on his god to avenge the refusal on the Greeks. So far the poet speaks in his own person, but later on he speaks in the character of Chryses and tries to make us feel that the words come, not from Homer, but from an aged priest. Throughout the *Iliad* and *Odyssey*, the events are set forth in these two different forms. All the time, both in the speeches and in the narrative parts in between, he is telling his story; but where he is delivering a speech in character, he tries to make his manner resemble that of the person he has introduced as speaker. Any poet who does that by means of voice and gesture, is telling his story by way of dramatic representation; whereas, if he makes no such attempt to suppress his own personality, the events are set forth in simple narrative.

134   Now I understand.

135   Observe, then, that, if you omit the intervening narrative and leave only the dialogue, you get the opposite form.

136   Yes, I see; that occurs in tragedy, for instance.

137   Exactly, said I. Now I think you see the distinction I failed to make clear. All story-telling, in prose or poetry, is in one of three forms. It may be wholly dramatic: tragedy, as you say, or comedy. Or the poet may narrate the events in his own person; perhaps the best example of that is the dithyramb. Or again both methods may be used, as in epic and several other kinds of poetry.

138   Yes, he said, I see now what you meant.

139   Remember, too, I began by saying that, having done with the content, we had still to consider the form. I meant that we should have to decide whether to allow our poets to tell their story in dramatic form, wholly, or in part (and, if so, in what parts), or not at all.

140   You mean, I suspect, the question whether we shall admit tragedy and comedy into our commonwealth.

141   Perhaps, I replied, or the question may be wider still. I do not know yet; but we must go wherever the wind of the argument carries us.

142   That is good advice.

143   Here then, Adeimantus, is a question for you to consider: Do we want our Guardians to be capable of playing many parts? Perhaps the answer follows from our earlier principle that a man can only do one thing well; if he tries his hand at several, he will fail to make his mark in any of them. Does not that principle apply to acting? The same man cannot act many parts so well as he can act one.

144   No, he cannot.

145   Then he will hardly be able to pursue some worthy occupation and at the same time represent a variety of different characters. Even in the case of two forms of representation so closely allied as tragedy and comedy, the same poet cannot write both with equal success. Again, the recitation of epic poetry and acting on the stage are distinct professions; and even on the stage different actors perform in tragedy and comedy.

146   That is so.

147   And human talent, Adeimantus, seems to be split up into subdivisions even minuter than these; so that no man can successfully represent many different characters in the field of art or pursue a corresponding variety of occupations in real life.

148   Quite true.

149   If, then, we are to hold fast to our original principle that our Guardians shall be set free from all manual crafts to be the artificers of their country's freedom, with the perfect mastery which comes of working only at what conduces to that end, they ought not to play any other part in dramatic representation any more than in real life; but if they act, they should, from childhood upward, impersonate only the appropriate types of character, men who are brave, religious, self-controlled, generous. They are not to do anything mean or dishonourable; no more should they be practiced in representing such behavior, for fear of becoming infected with the reality. You must have noticed how the reproduction of another person's gestures or tones of voice or states of mind, if persisted in from youth up, grows into a habit which becomes second nature.

150   Yes, I have.

151   So these charges of ours, who are to grow up into men of worth, will not be allowed to enact the part of a woman, old or young, railing against her husband, or boasting of a happiness which she imagines can rival the gods', or overwhelmed with grief and misfortune; much less a woman in love, or sick, or in labour; nor yet slaves of either sex, going about their menial work; nor men of a low type, behaving with cowardice and all the qualities contrary to those we mentioned, deriding one another and exchanging coarse abuse whether drunk or sober, and otherwise using language and behaviour that are an offence against themselves as well as their neighbours; nor must they copy the words and actions of madmen. Knowledge they must have of baseness and insanity both in men and women, but not reproduce such behaviour in life or in art.

152   Quite true.

153   Again, are they to impersonate men working at some trade, such as a smith's, or rowing a galley or giving the time to the oarsmen?

154   How should they, when they are not even to take any notice of such occupations?

155   And may they take part in performances which imitate horses neighing and bulls bellowing or the noise of rivers and sea and thunder?

156   We have already forbidden them to represent the ravings of insanity.

157   If I understand you, then, there are two contrasted forms of expression in which any series of events may be set forth: one which will always be used by a man of fine character and breeding, the other by one whose nature and upbringing are of a very different sort.

158   Yes, there are those two forms.

159   One of them involves little change and variety; when the words have been fitted to a suitable musical mode and rhythm, the recitation can keep almost to the same mode and rhythm throughout, the modulations required being slight. The other, on the contrary, involves every sort of variation and demands the use of all the modes and rhythms there are.

160   Quite true.

161   Now all writers and composers fall into one or other of these styles, or a mixture of both. What shall we do? Are we to admit into our commonwealth one or other of the extreme styles, or the mixed one, or all three?

162   If my judgement is to prevail, the simple one which serves to represent a fine character.

163   On the other hand, Adeimantus, the mixed style has its attractions; and children and their attendants, not to mention the great mass of the public, find the opposite of the one you chose the most attractive of all.

164   No doubt they do.

165   But perhaps you think it will not suit our commonwealth, where no man is to be two or more persons or a jack of all trades; this being the reason why ours is the only state in which we shall find a shoemaker who cannot also take command of a ship, a farmer who does not leave his farm to serve on juries, a soldier who is not a tradesman into the bargain.

166   Quite true.

167   Suppose, then, that an individual clever enough to assume any character and give imitations of anything and everything should visit our country and offer to perform his compositions, we shall bow down before a being with such miraculous powers of giving pleasure; but we shall tell him that we are not allowed to have any such person in our commonwealth; we shall crown him with fillets of wool, anoint his head with myrrh, and conduct him to the borders of some other country. For our own benefit, we shall employ the poets and story-tellers of the more austere and less attractive type, who will reproduce only the manner of a person of high character and, in the substance of their discourse, conform to those rules we laid down when we began the education of our warriors.

168   Yes, we shall do that, if it lies in our power.

169   So now, my dear Adeimantus, we have discussed both the content and the form of literature, and we have finished with that part of education.

170   Yes, I think so.

ca. 375 B.C.

John Stuart Mill

THE HARM PRINCIPLE

One fundamental question that bears directly on the issue of censorship is the extent to which government should intervene in the everyday lives and conduct of citizens. John Stuart Mill, a nineteenth-century philosopher, proposed that we decide whether to permit or prohibit actions and speech on the basis of whether that action or speech harms someone else. An individual's behavior, he argues, should be entirely his own affair if it harms no one else. The saying "your right to swing your arms around ends where the other fellow's nose begins" is a version of the harm principle. As excerpted here, the selection works from general claims about limiting government intervention in the lives of citizens to specific statements about freedom of expression (beginning in paragraph 6). If you have read the preceding argument from Plato's Republic, *you will notice a complete reorientation of priorities. Socrates thinks about how to shape the citizens to suit the commonwealth, and Mill thinks about how to shape the commonwealth to suit the needs of the individual citizens.*

1   The object of this essay is to assert one very simple principle, as entitled to govern absolutely the dealings of society with the individual in the way of compulsion and control, whether the means used be physical force in the form of legal penalties or the moral coercion of public opinion. That principle is that the sole end for which mankind are warranted, individually or collectively, in interfering with the liberty of action of any of their number is self-protection. That the only purpose for which power can be rightfully exercised over any member of a civilized community, against his will, is to prevent harm to others. His own good, either physical or moral, is not a sufficient warrant. He cannot rightfully be compelled to do or forbear because it will be better for him to do so, because it will make him happier, because, in the opinions of others, to do so would be wise or even right. These are good reasons for remonstrating with him, or reasoning with him, or persuading him, or entreating him, but not for compelling him or visiting him with any evil in case he do otherwise. To justify that, the conduct from which it is desired to deter him must be calculated to produce evil to someone else. The only part of the conduct of anyone for which he is amenable to society is that which concerns others. In the part which merely concerns himself, his independence is, of right, absolute. Over himself, over his own body and mind, the individual is sovereign.

2   It is, perhaps, hardly necessary to say that this doctrine is meant to apply only to human beings in the maturity of their faculties. We are not speaking of children or of young persons below the age which the law may fix as that of manhood or womanhood. Those who are still in a state to require being taken care of by others must be protected against their own actions as well as against external injury. For the same reason we may leave out of consideration those backward states of society in which the race itself may be considered as in its nonage. The early difficulties in the way of spontaneous progress are so great that there is seldom any choice of means for overcoming them; and a ruler full of the spirit of improvement is warranted in the use of any expedients that will attain an end perhaps otherwise unattainable. Despotism is a legitimate mode of government in dealing with barbarians, provided the end be their improvement and the means justified by actually effecting that end. Liberty, as a principle, has no application to any state of things anterior to the time when mankind have become capable of being improved by free and equal discussion. Until then, there is nothing for them but implicit obedience to an Akbar or a Charlemagne, if they are so fortunate as to find one. But as soon as mankind have attained the capacity of being guided to their own improvement by conviction or persuasion (a period long since reached in all nations with whom we need here concern ourselves), compulsion, either in the direct form or in that of pains and penalties for noncompliance, is no longer admissible as a means to their own good, and justifiable only for the security of others. . . .

3   There is a sphere of action in which society, as distinguished from the individual, has, if any, only an indirect interest: comprehending all that portion of a person's life and conduct which affects only himself or, if it also affects others, only with their free, voluntary, and undeceived consent and participation. When I say only himself, I mean directly and in the first instance; for whatever affects himself may affect others through himself; and the objection which may be grounded on this contingency will receive consideration in the sequel. This, then, is the appropriate region of human liberty. It comprises, first, the inward domain of consciousness, demanding liberty of conscience in the most comprehensive sense, liberty of thought and feeling, absolute freedom of opinion and sentiment on all subjects, practical or speculative, scientific, moral, or theological. The liberty of expressing and publishing opinions may seem to fall under a different principle, since it belongs to that part of the conduct of an individual which concerns other people, but, being almost of as much importance as the liberty of thought itself and resting in great part on the same reasons, is practically inseparable from it. Secondly, the principle requires liberty of tastes and pursuits, of framing the plan of our life to suit our own character, of doing as we like, subject to such consequences as may follow, without impediment from our fellow creatures, so long as what we do does not harm them, even though they should think our

conduct foolish, perverse, or wrong. Thirdly, from this liberty of each individual follows the liberty within the same limits, of combination among individuals; freedom to unite for any purpose not involving harm to others: the persons combining being supposed to be of full age and not forced or deceived.

4   No society in which these liberties are not, on the whole, respected is free, whatever may be its form of government; and none is completely free in which they do not exist absolute and unqualified. The only freedom which deserves the name is that of pursuing our own good in our own way, so long as we do not attempt to deprive others of theirs or impede their efforts to obtain it. Each is the proper guardian of his own health, whether bodily or mental and spiritual. Mankind are greater gainers by suffering each other to live as seems good to themselves than by compelling each to live as seems good to the rest.

5   Though this doctrine is anything but new and, to some persons, may have the air of a truism, there is no doctrine which stands more directly opposed to the general tendency of existing opinion and practice. Society has expended fully as much effort in the attempt (according to its lights) to compel people to conform to its notions of personal as of social excellence. The ancient commonwealths thought themselves entitled to practice, and the ancient philosophers countenanced, the regulation of every part of private conduct by public authority, on the ground that the State had a deep interest in the whole bodily and mental discipline of every one of its citizens—a mode of thinking which may have been admissible in small republics surrounded by powerful enemies, in constant peril of being subverted by foreign attack or internal commotion, and to which even a short interval of relaxed energy and self-command might so easily be fatal that they could not afford to wait for the salutary permanent effects of freedom. In the modern world, the greater size of political communities and, above all, the separation between spiritual and temporal authority (which placed the direction of men's consciences in other hands than those which controlled their worldly affairs) prevented so great an interference by law in the details of private life; but the engines of moral repression have been wielded more strenuously against divergence from the reigning opinion in self-regarding than even in social matters; religion, the most powerful of the elements which have entered into the formation of moral feeling, having almost always been governed either by the ambition of a hierarchy seeking control over every department of human conduct, or by the spirit of Puritanism. . . .

6   The time, it is to be hoped, is gone by when any defense would be necessary of the "liberty of the press" as one of the securities against corrupt or tyrannical government. No argument, we may suppose, can now be needed against permitting a legislature or an executive, not identified in interest with the people, to prescribe opinions to them and determine what doctrines or

what arguments they shall be allowed to hear. This aspect of the question, besides, has been so often and so triumphantly enforced by preceding writers that it need not be specially insisted on in this place. Though the law of England, on the subject of the press, is as servile to this day as it was in the time of the Tudors, there is little danger of its being actually put in force against political discussion except during some temporary panic when fear of insurrection drives ministers and judges from their propriety; and, speaking generally, it is not, in constitutional countries, to be apprehended that the government, whether completely responsible to the people or not, will often attempt to control the expression of opinion, except when in doing so it makes itself the organ of the general intolerance of the public. Let us suppose, therefore, that the government is entirely at one with the people, and never thinks of exerting any power of coercion unless in agreement with what it conceives to be their voice. But I deny the right of the people to exercise such coercion, either by themselves or by their government. The power itself is illegitimate. The best government has no more title to it than the worst. It is as noxious, or more noxious, when exerted in accordance with the public opinion than when in opposition to it. If all mankind minus one were of one opinion, mankind would be no more justified in silencing that one person than he, if he had the power, would be justified in silencing mankind. Were an opinion a personal possession of no value except to the owner, if to be obstructed in the enjoyment of it were simply a private injury, it would make some difference whether the injury was inflicted only on a few persons or on many. But the peculiar evil of silencing the expression of an opinion is that it is robbing the human race, posterity as well as the existing generation—those who dissent from the opinion, still more than those who hold it. If the opinion is right, they are deprived of the opportunity of exchanging error for truth; if wrong, they lose, what is almost as great a benefit, the clearer perception and livelier impression of truth produced by its collision with error. . . .

7   I do not pretend that the most unlimited use of the freedom of enunciating all possible opinions would put an end to the evils of religious or philosophical sectarianism. Every truth which men of narrow capacity are in earnest about is sure to be asserted, inculcated, and in many ways even acted on, as if no other truth existed in the world, or at all events none that could limit or qualify the first. I acknowledge that the tendency of all opinions to become sectarian is not cured by the freest discussion, but is often heightened and exacerbated thereby; the truth which ought to have been, but was not, seen, being rejected all the more violently because proclaimed by persons regarded as opponents. But it is not on the impassioned partisan, it is on the calmer and more disinterested bystander, that this collision of opinions works its salutary effect. Not the violent conflict between parts of the truth, but the quiet suppression of half of it, is the formidable evil, there is always hope when people are forced to listen to both sides; it is when they attend

only to one that errors harden into prejudices, and truth itself ceases to have the effect of truth, by being exaggerated into falsehood. And since there are few mental attributes more rare than that judicial faculty which can sit in intelligent judgment between two sides of a question, of which only one is represented by an advocate before it, truth has no chance but in proportion as every side of it, every opinion which embodies any fraction of the truth, not only finds advocates, but is so advocated as to be listened to.

8   We have now recognized the necessity to the mental well-being of mankind (on which all their other well-being depends) of freedom of opinion, and freedom of the expression of opinion, on four distinct grounds, which we will now briefly recapitulate:

9   First, if any opinion is compelled to silence, that opinion may, for aught we can certainly know, be true. To deny this is to assume our own infallibility.

10   Secondly, though the silenced opinion be an error, it may, and very commonly does, contain a portion of truth; and since the general or prevailing opinion on any subject is rarely or never the whole truth, it is only by the collision of adverse opinions that the remainder of the truth has any chance of being supplied.

11   Thirdly, even if the received opinion be not only true, but the whole truth, unless it is suffered to be, and actually is, vigorously and earnestly contested, it will, by most of those who receive it, be held in the manner of a prejudice, with little comprehension or feeling of its rational grounds. And not only this, but, fourthly, the meaning of the doctrine itself will be in danger of being lost or enfeebled, and deprived of its vital effect on the character and conduct: the dogma becoming a mere formal profession, inefficacious for good, but cumbering the ground and preventing the growth of any real and heartfelt conviction from reason or personal experience.

12   Before quitting the subject of freedom of opinion, it is fit to take some notice of those who say that the free expression of all opinions should be permitted on condition that the manner be temperate, and do not pass the bounds of fair discussion. Much might be said on the impossibility of fixing where these supposed bounds are to be placed; for if the test be offense to those whose opinions are attacked, I think experience testifies that this offense is given whenever the attack is telling and powerful, and that every opponent who pushes them hard, and whom they find it difficult to answer, appears to them, if he shows any strong feeling on the subject, an intemperate opponent. But this, though an important consideration in a practical point of view, merges in a more fundamental objection. Undoubtedly, the manner of asserting an opinion, even though it be a true one, may be very objectionable and may justly incur severe censure. But the principal offenses of the kind are such as it is mostly impossible, unless by accidental self-betrayal, to bring home to conviction. The gravest of them is, to argue sophistically, to suppress facts or arguments, to misstate the elements of the case, or misrepresent the

opposite opinion. But all this, even to the most aggravated degree, is so continually done in perfect good faith by persons who are not considered, and in many other respects may not deserve to be considered, ignorant or incompetent, that it is rarely possible, on adequate grounds, conscientiously to stamp the misrepresentation as morally culpable, and still less could law presume to interfere with this kind of controversial misconduct. With regard to what is commonly meant by intemperate discussion, namely invective, sarcasm, personality, and the like, the denunciation of these weapons would deserve more sympathy if it were ever proposed to interdict them equally to both sides; but it is only desired to restrain the employment of them against the prevailing opinion; against the unprevailing they may not only be used without general disapproval, but will be likely to obtain for him who uses them the praise of honest zeal and righteous indignation. Yet whatever mischief arises from their use is greatest when they are employed against the comparatively defenseless; and whatever unfair advantage can be derived by any opinion from this mode of asserting it accrues almost exclusively to received opinions. The worst offense of this kind which can be committed by a polemic is to stigmatize those who hold the contrary opinion as bad and immoral men. To calumny of this sort, those who hold any unpopular opinion are peculiarly exposed, because they are in general few and uninfluential, and nobody but themselves feels much interested in seeing justice done them; but this weapon is, from the nature of the case, denied to those who attack a prevailing opinion: they can neither use it with safety to themselves, nor, if they could, would it do anything but recoil on their own cause. In general, opinions contrary to those commonly received can only obtain a hearing by studied moderation of language and the most cautious avoidance of unnecessary offense, from which they hardly ever deviate even in a slight degree without losing ground, while unmeasured vituperation employed on the side of the prevailing opinion really does deter people from professing contrary opinions and from listening to those who profess them. For the interest, therefore, of truth and justice it is far more important to restrain this employment of vituperative language than the other; and, for example, if it were necessary to choose, there would be much more need to discourage offensive attacks on infidelity than on religion. It is, however, obvious that law and authority have no business with restraining either, while opinion ought, in every instance, to determine its verdict by the circumstances of the individual case—condemning everyone, on whichever side of the argument he places himself, in whose mode of advocacy either want of candor, or malignity, bigotry, or intolerance of feeling manifest themselves; but not inferring these vices from the side which a person takes, though it be the contrary side of the question to our own; and giving merited honor to everyone, whatever opinion he may hold, who has calmness to see and honesty to state what his opponents and their opinions really are, exaggerating nothing to their discredit, keeping nothing back which tells, or can be supposed to tell, in their favor. This is the real morality of public discussion; and if often violated, I am happy to think that there are many controversialists who to a great extent observe it, and a still greater number who conscientiously strive toward it.

13   What, then, is the rightful limit to the sovereignty of the individual over himself? Where does the authority of society begin? How much of human life should be assigned to individuality, and how much to society?

14   Each will receive its proper share if each has that which more particularly concerns it. To individuality should belong the part of life in which it is chiefly the individual that is interested; to society, the part which chiefly interests society.

15   Though society is not founded on a contract, and though no good purpose is answered by inventing a contract in order to deduce social obligations from it, everyone who receives the protection of society owes a return for the benefit, and the fact of living in society renders it indispensable that each should be bound to observe a certain line of conduct toward the rest. This conduct consists, first, in not injuring the interests of one another, or rather certain interests, either by express legal provision or by tacit understanding, ought to be considered as rights; and secondly, in each person's bearing his share (to be fixed on some equitable principle) of the labors and sacrifices incurred for defending the society or its members from injury and molestation. These conditions society is justified in enforcing at all costs to those who endeavor to withhold fulfillment. Nor is this all that society may do. The acts of an individual may be hurtful to others or wanting in due consideration for their welfare, without going to the length of violating any of their constituted rights. The offender may then be justly punished by opinion, though not by law. As soon as any part of a person's conduct affects prejudicially the interests of others, society has jurisdiction over it, and the question whether the general welfare will or will not be promoted by interfering with it becomes open to discussion. But there is no room for entertaining any such question when a person's conduct affects the interests of no persons besides himself, or needs not affect them unless they like (all the persons concerned being of full age and the ordinary amount of understanding). In all such cases, there should be perfect freedom, legal and social, to do the action and stand the consequences. . . .

16   The distinction here pointed out between the part of a person's life which concerns only himself and that which concerns others, many persons will refuse to admit. How (it may be asked) can any part of the conduct of a member of society be a matter of indifference to the other members? No person is an entirely isolated being; it is impossible for a person to do anything seriously or permanently hurtful to himself without mischief reaching at least to his near connections, and often far beyond them. If he injures his property, he does harm to those who directly or indirectly derived support from it, and

usually diminishes, by a greater or less amount, the general resources of the community. If he deteriorates his bodily or mental faculties, he not only brings evil upon all who depended on him for any portion of their happiness, but disqualifies himself for rendering the services which he owes to his fellow creatures generally, perhaps becomes a burden on their affection or benevolence; and if such conduct were very frequent hardly any offense that is committed would detract more from the general sum of good. Finally, if by his vices or follies a person does no direct harm to others, he is nevertheless (it may be said) injurious by his example, and ought to be compelled to control himself for the sake of those whom the sight or knowledge of his conduct might corrupt or mislead.

[17]   And even (it will be added) if the consequences of misconduct could be confined to the vicious or thoughtless individual, ought society to abandon to their own guidance those who are manifestly unfit for it? If protection against themselves is confessedly due to children and persons under age, is not society equally bound to afford it to persons of mature years who are equally incapable of self-government? If gambling, or drunkenness, or incontinence, or idleness, or uncleanliness are as injurious to happiness, and as great a hindrance to improvement, as many or most of the acts prohibited by law, why (it may be asked) should not law, so far as is consistent with practicability and social convenience, endeavor to repress these also? And as a supplement to the unavoidable imperfections of law, ought not opinion at least to organize a powerful police against these vices and visit rigidly with social penalties those who are known to practice them? There is no question here (it may be said) about restricting individuality, or impeding the trial of new and original experiments in living. The only things it is sought to prevent are things which have been tried and condemned from the beginning of the world until now—things which experience has shown not to be useful or suitable to any person's individuality. There must be some length of time and amount of experience after which a moral or prudential truth may be regarded as established; and it is merely desired to prevent generation after generation from falling over the same precipice which has been fatal to their predecessors.

[18]   I fully admit that the mischief which a person does to himself may seriously affect, both through their sympathies and their interests, those nearly connected with him and, in a minor degree, society at large. When, by conduct of this sort, a person is led to violate a distinct and assignable obligation to any other person or persons, the case is taken out of the self-regarding class and becomes amenable to moral disapprobation in the proper sense of the term. If, for example, a man, through intemperance or extravagance, becomes unable to pay his debts, or, having undertaken the moral responsibility of a family, becomes from the same cause incapable of supporting or educating them, he is deservedly reprobated and might be justly punished; but it is for the breach of duty to his family or creditors, not for the extravagance....

Whenever, in short, there is a definite damage, or a definite risk of damage, either to an individual or to the public, the case is taken out of the province of liberty and placed in that of morality or law. . . .

[19]   But the strongest of all the arguments against the interference of the public with purely personal conduct is that, when it does interfere, the odds are that it interferes wrongly and in the wrong place. On questions of social morality, of duty to others, the opinion of the public, that is, of an overruling majority, though often wrong, is likely to be still oftener right, because on such questions they are only required to judge of their own interests, of the manner in which some mode of conduct, if allowed to be practiced, would affect themselves. But the opinion of a similar majority, imposed as a law on the minority, on questions of self-regarding conduct is quite as likely to be wrong as right, for in these cases public opinion means, at the best, some people's opinion of what is good or bad for other people, while very often it does not even mean that—the public, with the most perfect indifference, passing over the pleasure or convenience of those whose conduct they censure and considering only their own preference. There are many who consider as an injury to themselves any conduct which they have a distaste for, and resent it as an outrage to their feelings; as a religious bigot, when charged with disregarding the religious feelings of others, has been known to retort that they disregard his feelings by persisting in their abominable worship or creed. But there is no parity between the feeling of a person for his own opinion and the feeling of another who is offended at his holding it, no more than between the desire of a thief to take a purse and the desire of the right owner to keep it. And a person's taste is as much his own peculiar concern as his opinion or his purse. It is easy for anyone to imagine an ideal public which leaves the freedom and choice of individuals in all uncertain matters undisturbed and only requires them to abstain from modes of conduct which universal experience has condemned. But where has there been seen a public which set any such limit to its censorship? . . .

1859

U.S. Supreme Court

THE FLAG-BURNING CASE

A 1989 Supreme Court decision startled some people by asserting that the Constitution protects the rights of Americans to burn the flag. As you will see, the decision rests on the portion of the First Amendment that reads, "Congress

shall make no law ... abridging the freedom of speech, or of the press." A cen-
tral issue is whether a nonverbal act like flag-burning is protected by an amend-
ment designed to protect free speech. This record of the court's decision and of
the dissenting opinions illustrates again how alive the questions surrounding
censorship and freedom of expression remain. Once the judges who concur in
the majority opinion decide that flag burning is speech, then it seems clear to
them that the government cannot prohibit the message communicated by burn-
ing an American flag while condoning the message communicated by flying
one. The justices also worry about the slippery slope that prohibiting flag burn-
ing could create: "Could the government, on this theory, prohibit the burning
of state flags? Of copies of the Presidential seal? Of the Constitution?" (para-
graph 19). They stop short of the example we like to use: Could the government
by this logic prohibit the burning of photographs of the President?

The dissenting opinions of Justices Rehnquist and Stevens make this selec-
tion into another dialogue. Both dissenters take issue with the majority decision
that "there is ... no indication ... that a separate judicial category exists for the
American flag alone" (paragraph 20). Can you think of dissenting opinions that
would not turn on the question of the flag's special status? Is flag burning
speech? Are there any limits on freedom of expression that might apply in this
case, setting aside the special value that Rehnquist and Stevens attribute to the
flag? (We have eliminated the legal citations from the following opinions.)

JUSTICE BRENNAN delivered the opinion of the Court.

[1] After publicly burning an American flag as a means of political protest, Gregory Lee Johnson was convicted of desecrating a flag in violation of Texas law. This case presents the question whether his conviction is consistent with the First Amendment. We hold that it is not.

[2] While the Republican National Convention was taking place in Dallas in 1984, respondent Johnson participated in a political demonstration dubbed the "Republican War Chest Tour." As explained in literature distributed by the demonstrators and in speeches made by them, the purpose of this event was to protest the policies of the Reagan administration and of certain Dallas-based corporations. The demonstrators marched through the Dallas streets, chanting political slogans and stopping at several corporate locations to stage "die-ins" intended to dramatize the consequences of nuclear war. On several occasions they spray-painted the walls of buildings and overturned potted plants, but Johnson himself took no part in such activities. He did, however, accept an American flag handed to him by a fellow protestor who had taken it from a flag pole outside one of the targeted buildings.

[3] The demonstration ended in front of Dallas City Hall, where Johnson unfurled the American flag, doused it with kerosene, and set it on fire. While the flag burned, the protestors chanted, "America, the red, white, and blue,

we spit on you." After the demonstrators dispersed, a witness to the flag burning collected the flag's remains and buried them in his backyard. No one was physically injured or threatened with injury, though several witnesses testified that they had been seriously offended by the flag burning.

4   Of the approximately 100 demonstrators, Johnson alone was charged with a crime. The only criminal offense with which he was charged was the desecration of a venerated object in violation of Tex. Penal Code Ann. §42.09 (a)(3) (1989). After a trial, he was convicted, sentenced to one year in prison and fined $2,000. . . .

5   Texas claims that its interest in preventing breaches of the peace justifies Johnson's conviction for flag desecration. However, no disturbance of the peace actually occurred or threatened to occur because of Johnson's burning of the flag. Although the State stresses the disruptive behavior of the protestors during their march toward City Hall, it admits that "no actual breach of the peace occurred at the time of the flag burning or in response to the flag burning." The State's emphasis on the protestors' disorderly actions prior to arriving at City Hall is not only somewhat surprising given that no charges were brought on the basis of this conduct, but it also fails to show that a disturbance of the peace was a likely reaction to *Johnson*'s conduct. The only evidence offered by the State at trial to show the reaction to Johnson's actions was the testimony of several persons who had been seriously offended by the flag burning.

6   The State's position, therefore, amounts to a claim that an audience that takes serious offense at particular expression is necessarily likely to disturb the peace and that the expression may be prohibited on this basis. Our precedents do not countenance such a presumption. On the contrary, they recognize that a principal "function of free speech under our system of government is to invite dispute. It may indeed best serve its high purpose when it induces a condition of unrest, creates dissatisfaction with conditions as they are, or even stirs people to anger." It would be odd indeed to conclude *both* that "if it is the speaker's opinion that gives offense, that consequence is a reason for according it constitutional protection," *and* that the Government may ban the expression of certain disagreeable ideas on the unsupported presumption that their very disagreeableness will provoke violence.

7   Thus, we have not permitted the Government to assume that every expression of a provocative idea will incite a riot, but have instead required careful consideration of the actual circumstances surrounding such expression, asking whether the expression "is directed to inciting or producing imminent lawless action and is likely to incite or produce such action." To accept Texas' arguments that it need only demonstrate "the potential for a breach of the peace," and that every flag burning necessarily possesses that potential, would be to eviscerate our holding in *Brandenburg*. This we decline to do.

8   Nor does Johnson's expressive conduct fall within that small class of "fighting words" that are "likely to provoke the average person to retaliation, and thereby cause a breach of the peace." No reasonable onlooker would have regarded Johnson's generalized expression of dissatisfaction with the policies of the Federal Government as a direct personal insult or an invitation to exchange fisticuffs.

9   We thus conclude that the State's interest in maintaining order is not implicated on these facts. The State need not worry that our holding will disable it from preserving the peace. We do not suggest that the First Amendment forbids a State to prevent "imminent lawless action." And, in fact, Texas already has a statute specifically prohibiting breaches of the peace, Tex. Penal Code Ann. §42.01 (1989), which tends to confirm that Texas need not punish this flag desecration in order to keep the peace.

10   The State also asserts an interest in preserving the flag as a symbol of nationhood and national unity. In *Spence*, we acknowledged that the Government's interest in preserving the flag's special symbolic value "is directly related to expression in the context of activity" such as affixing a peace symbol to a flag. We are equally persuaded that this interest is related to expression in the case of Johnson's burning of the flag. The State, apparently, is concerned that such conduct will lead people to believe either that the flag does not stand for nationhood and national unity, but instead reflects other, less positive concepts, or that the concepts reflected in the flag do not in fact exist, that is, we do not enjoy unity as a Nation. These concerns blossom only when a person's treatment of the flag communicates some message, and thus are related "to the suppression of free expression" within the meaning of *O'Brien*. We are thus outside of *O'Brien*'s test altogether.

11   It remains to consider whether the State's interest in preserving the flag as a symbol of nationhood and national unity justifies Johnson's conviction.

12   As in *Spence*, "[w]e are confronted with a case of prosecution for the expression of an idea through activity," and "[a]ccordingly, we must examine with particular care the interests advanced by [petitioner] to support its prosecution." Johnson was not, we add, prosecuted for the expression of just any idea; he was prosecuted for his expression of dissatisfaction with the policies of this country, expression situated at the core of our First Amendment values.

13   Moreover, Johnson was prosecuted because he knew that his politically charged expression would cause "serious offense." If he had burned the flag as a means of disposing of it because it was dirty or torn, he would not have been convicted of flag desecration under this Texas law: federal law designates burning as the preferred means of disposing of a flag "when it is in such condition that it is no longer a fitting emblem for display," and Texas has no quarrel with this means of disposal. The Texas law is thus not aimed at pro-

tecting the physical integrity of the flag in all circumstances, but is designed instead to protect it only against impairments that would cause serious offense to others. Texas concedes as much: "Section 42.09(b) reaches only those severe acts of physical abuse of the flag carried out in a way likely to be offensive. The statute mandates intentional or knowing abuse, that is, the kind of mistreatment that is not innocent, but rather is intentionally designed to seriously offend other individuals."

[14]   Whether Johnson's treatment of the flag violated Texas law thus depended on the likely communicative impact of his expressive conduct. Our decision in *Boos* v. *Barry* tells us that this restriction on Johnson's expression is content-based. In *Boos*, we considered the constitutionality of a law prohibiting "the display of any sign within 50 feet of a foreign embassy if that sign tends to bring that foreign government into 'public odium' or 'public disrepute.'" Rejecting the argument that the law was content-neutral because it was justified by "our international law obligation to shield diplomats from speech that offends their dignity," we held that "[t]he emotive impact of speech on its audience is not a 'secondary effect'" unrelated to the content of the expression itself.

[15]   According to the principles announced in *Boos*, Johnson's political expression was restricted because of the content of the message he conveyed. We must therefore subject the State's asserted interest in preserving the special symbolic character of the flag to "the most exacting scrutiny."

[16]   Texas argues that its interest in preserving the flag as a symbol of nationhood and national unity survives this close analysis. Quoting extensively from the writings of this Court chronicling the flag's historic and symbolic role in our society, the State emphasizes the "'special place'" reserved for the flag in our Nation....

[17]   Texas' focus on the precise nature of Johnson's expression, moreover, misses the point of our prior decisions: their enduring lesson, that the Government may not prohibit expression simply because it disagrees with its message, is not dependent on the particular mode in which one chooses to express an idea. If we were to hold that a State may forbid flag burning wherever it is likely to endanger the flag's symbolic role, but allow it wherever burning a flag promotes that role—as where, for example, a person ceremoniously burns a dirty flag—we would be saying that when it comes to impairing the flag's physical integrity, the flag itself may be used as a symbol—as a substitute for the written or spoken word or a "short cut from mind to mind"— only in one direction. We would be permitting a State to "prescribe what shall be orthodox" by saying that one may burn the flag to convey one's attitude toward it and its referents only if one does not endanger the flag's representation of nationhood and national unity.

[18]   We never before have held that the Government may ensure that a symbol be used to express only one view of that symbol or its referents. Indeed,

in *Schacht* v. *United States*, we invalidated a federal statute permitting an actor portraying a member of one of our armed forces to "'wear the uniform of that armed force if the portrayal does not tend to discredit that armed force.'" This proviso, we held, "which leaves Americans free to praise the war in Vietnam but can send persons like Schacht to prison for opposing it, cannot survive in a country which has the First Amendment."

[19]   We perceive no basis on which to hold that the principle underlying our decision in *Schacht* does not apply to this case. To conclude that the Government may permit designated symbols to be used to communicate only a limited set of messages would be to enter territory having no discernible or defensible boundaries. Could the Government, on this theory, prohibit the burning of state flags? Of copies of the Presidential seal? Of the Constitution? In evaluating these choices under the First Amendment, how would we decide which symbols were sufficiently special to warrant this unique status? To do so, we would be forced to consult our own political preferences, and impose them on the citizenry, in the very way that the First Amendment forbids us to do.

[20]   There is, moreover, no indication—either in the text of the Constitution or in our cases interpreting it—that a separate juridical category exists for the American flag alone. Indeed, we would not be surprised to learn that the persons who framed our Constitution and wrote the Amendment that we now construe were not known for their reverence for the Union Jack. The First Amendment does not guarantee that other concepts virtually sacred to our Nation as a whole—such as the principle that discrimination on the basis of race is odious and destructive—will go unquestioned in the marketplace of ideas. We decline, therefore, to create for the flag an exception to the joust of principles protected by the First Amendment.

[21]   It is not the State's ends, but its means, to which we object. It cannot be gainsaid that there is a special place reserved for the flag in this Nation, and thus we do not doubt that the Government has a legitimate interest in making efforts to "preserv[e] the national flag as an unalloyed symbol of our country." We reject the suggestion, urged at oral argument by counsel for Johnson, that the Government lacks "any state interest whatsoever" in regulating the manner in which the flag may be displayed. Congress has, for example, enacted precatory regulations describing the proper treatment of the flag, and we cast no doubt on the legitimacy of its interest in making such recommendations. To say that the Government has an interest in encouraging proper treatment of the flag, however, is not to say that it may criminally punish a person for burning a flag as a means of political protest. "National unity as an end which officials may foster by persuasion and example is not in question. The problem is whether under our Constitution compulsion as here employed is a permissible means for its achievement."

22   We are fortified in today's conclusion by our conviction that forbidding criminal punishment for conduct such as Johnson's will not endanger the special role played by our flag or the feelings it inspires. To paraphrase Justice Holmes, we submit that nobody can suppose that this one gesture of an unknown man will change our Nation's attitude towards its flag. Indeed, Texas' argument that the burning of an American flag "'is an act having a high likelihood to cause a breach of the peace,'" and its statute's implicit assumption that physical mistreatment of the flag will lead to "serious offense," tend to confirm that the flag's special role is not in danger; if it were, no one would riot or take offense because a flag had been burned.

23   We are tempted to say, in fact, that the flag's deservedly cherished place in our community will be strengthened, not weakened, by our holding today. Our decision is a reaffirmation of the principles of freedom and inclusiveness that the flag best reflects, and of the conviction that our toleration of criticism such as Johnson's is a sign and source of our strength. Indeed, one of the proudest images of our flag, the one immortalized in our own national anthem, is of the bombardment it survived at Fort McHenry. It is the Nation's resilience not its rigidity, that Texas sees reflected in the flag—and it is that resilience that we reassert today.

24   The way to preserve the flag's special role is not to punish those who feel differently about these matters. It is to persuade them that they are wrong. "To courageous, self-reliant men, with confidence in the power of free and fearless reasoning applied through the processes of popular government, no danger flowing from speech can be deemed clear and present, unless the incidence of the evil apprehended is so imminent that it may befall before there is opportunity for full discussion. If there be time to expose through discussion the falsehood and fallacies, to avert the evil by the processes of education, the remedy to be applied is more speech, not enforced silence." And, precisely because it is our flag that is involved, one's response to the flag-burner may exploit the uniquely persuasive power of the flag itself. We can imagine no more appropriate response to burning a flag than waving one's own, no better way to counter a flag-burner's message than by saluting the flag that burns, no surer means of preserving the dignity even of the flag that burned than by— as one witness here did—according its remains a respectful burial. We do not consecrate the flag by punishing its desecration, for in doing so we dilute the freedom that this cherished emblem represents.

25   Johnson was convicted for engaging in expressive conduct. The State's interest in preventing breaches of the peace does not support his conviction because Johnson's conduct did not threaten to disturb the peace. Nor does the State's interest in preserving the flag as a symbol of nationhood and national unity justify his criminal conviction for engaging in political expression. The judgment of the Texas Court of Criminal Appeals is therefore *affirmed.*

JUSTICE KENNEDY, concurring.

26   I write not to qualify the words Justice Brennan chooses so well, for he says with power all that is necessary to explain our ruling. I join his opinion without reservation, but with a keen sense that this case, like others before us from time to time, exacts its personal toll. This prompts me to add to our pages these few remarks.

27   The case before us illustrates better than most that the judicial power is often difficult in its exercise. We cannot here ask another branch to share responsibility, as when the argument is made that a statute is flawed or incomplete. For we are presented with a clear and simple statute to be judged against a pure command of the Constitution. The outcome can be laid at no door but ours.

28   The hard fact is that sometimes we must make decisions we do not like. We make them because they are right, right in the sense that the law and the Constitution, as we see them, compel the result. And so great is our commitment to the process that, except in the rare case, we do not pause to express distaste for the result, perhaps for fear of undermining a valued principle that dictates the decision. This is one of those rare cases.

29   Our colleagues in dissent advance powerful arguments why respondent may be convicted for his expression, reminding us that among those who will be dismayed by our holding will be some who have had the singular honor of carrying the flag in battle. And I agree that the flag holds a lonely place of honor in an age when absolutes are distrusted and simple truths are burdened by unneeded apologetics.

30   With all respect to those views, I do not believe the Constitution gives us the right to rule as the dissenting members of the Court urge, however painful this judgment is to announce. Though symbols often are what we ourselves make of them, the flag is constant in expressing beliefs Americans share, beliefs in law and peace and that freedom which sustains the human spirit. The case here today forces recognition of the costs to which those beliefs commit us. It is poignant but fundamental that the flag protects those who hold it in contempt.

31   For all the record shows, this respondent was not a philosopher and perhaps did not even possess the ability to comprehend how repellent his statements must be to the Republic itself. But whether or not he could appreciate the enormity of the offense he gave, the fact remains that his acts were speech, in both the technical and the fundamental meaning of the Constitution. So I agree with the Court that he must go free.

CHIEF JUSTICE REHNQUIST, with whom JUSTICE WHITE and JUSTICE O'CONNOR join, dissenting.

32   In holding this Texas statute unconstitutional, the Court ignores Justice Holmes' familiar aphorism that "a page of history is worth a volume of logic."

For more than 200 years, the American flag has occupied a unique position as the symbol of our Nation, a uniqueness that justifies a governmental prohibition against flag burning in the way respondent Johnson did here.

33   At the time of the American Revolution, the flag served to unify the Thirteen Colonies at home, while obtaining recognition of national sovereignty abroad. Ralph Waldo Emerson's Concord Hymn describes the first skirmishes of the Revolutionary War in these lines:

> By the rude bridge that arched the flood
>   Their flag to April's breeze unfurled,
> Here once the embattled farmers stood
>   And fired the shot heard round the world.

During that time, there were many colonial and regimental flags, adorned with such symbols as pine trees, beavers, anchors, and rattle snakes, bearing slogans such as "Liberty or Death," "Hope," "An Appeal to Heaven," and "Don't Tread on Me." The first distinctive flag of the Colonies was the "Grand Union Flag"—with 13 stripes and a British flag in the left corner—which was flown for the first time on January 2, 1776, by troops of the Continental Army around Boston. By June 14, 1777, after we declared our independence from England, the Continental Congress resolved:

> That the flag of the thirteen United States be thirteen stripes, alternate red and white: that the union be thirteen stars, white in a blue field, representing a new constellation.

One immediate result of the flag's adoption was that American vessels harassing British shipping sailed under an authorized national flag. Without such a flag, the British could treat captured seamen as pirates and hang them summarily; with a national flag, such seamen were treated as prisoners of war.

34   During the War of 1812, British naval forces sailed up Chesapeake Bay and marched overland to sack and burn the city of Washington. They then sailed up the Patapsco River to invest the city of Baltimore, but to do so it was first necessary to reduce Fort McHenry in Baltimore Harbor. Francis Scott Key, a Washington lawyer, had been granted permission by the British to board one of their warships to negotiate the release of an American who had been taken prisoner. That night, waiting anxiously on the British ship, Key watched the British fleet firing on Fort McHenry. Finally, at daybreak, he saw the fort's American flag still flying; the British attack had failed. Intensely moved, he began to scribble on the back of an envelope the poem that became our national anthem:

> Oh! say you can see by the dawn's early light,
> What so proudly we hailed at the twilight's last gleaming?
> Whose broad stripes and bright stars, thro' the perilous fight,

O'er the ramparts we watched were so gallantly streaming?
And the rockets' red glare, the bombs bursting in air,
Gave proof thro' the night that our flag was still there.
Oh! say does that star-spangled banner yet wave
O'er the land of the free and the home of the brave?

35   The American flag played a central role in our Nation's most tragic conflict, when the North fought against the South. The lowering of the American flag at Fort Sumter was viewed as the start of the war. The Southern States, to formalize their separation from the Union, adopted the "Stars and Bars" of the Confederacy. The Union troops marched to the sound of "Yes We'll Rally Round The Flag Boys, We'll Rally Once Again." President Abraham Lincoln refused proposals to remove from the American flag the stars representing the rebel States, because he considered the conflict not a war between two nations but an attack by 11 States against the National Government. By war's end, the American flag again flew over "an indestructible union, composed of indestructible states."

36   One of the great stories of the Civil War is told in John Greenleaf Whittier's poem, "Barbara Frietchie":

Up from the meadows rich with corn,
Clear in the cool September morn,
The clustered spires of Frederick stand
Green-walled by the hills of Maryland.
Round about them orchards sweep,
Apple and pear tree fruited deep,
Fair as the garden of the Lord
To the eyes of the famished rebel horde,
On that pleasant morn of the early fall
When Lee marched over the mountain wall;
Over the mountains winding down,
Horse and foot, into Frederick town.
Forty flags with their silver stars,
Forty flags with their crimson bars,
Flapped in the morning wind: the sun
Of noon looked down, and saw not one.
Up rose old Barbara Frietchie then,
Bowed with her fourscore years and ten;
Bravest of all in Frederick town,
She took up the flag the men hauled down,
In her attic-window the staff she set,
To show that one heart was loyal yet.
Up the street came the rebel tread,
Stonewall Jackson riding ahead.
Under his slouched hat left and right
He glanced; the old flag met his sight.
"Halt!"—the dust-brown ranks stood fast.

"Fire!"—out blazed the rifle-blast.
It shivered the window, pane and sash;
It rent the banner with seam and gash.
Quick, as it fell, from the broken staff
Dame Barbara snatched the silken scarf.
She leaned far out on the window-sill,
And shook it forth with a royal will.
"Shoot if you must, this old grey head,
But spare your country's flag," she said.
A shade of sadness, a blush of shame,
Over the face of the leader came;
The nobler nature within him stirred
To life at that woman's deed and word;
"Who touches a hair of yon grey head
Dies like a dog! March on!" he said.
All day long through Frederick street
Sounded the tread of marching feet:
All day long that free flag tost
Over the heads of the rebel host.
Ever its torn folds rose and fell
On the loyal winds that loved it well;
And through the hill-gaps sunset light
Shone over it with a warm good-night.
Barbara Frietchie's work is o'er,
And the rebel rides on his raids no more.
Honor to her! and let a tear
Fall, for her sake, on Stonewall's bier.
Over Barbara Frietchie's grave,
Flag of Freedom and Union, wave!
Peace and order and beauty draw
Round thy symbol of light and law;
And ever the stars above look down
On thy stars below in Frederick town!

37   In the First and Second World Wars, thousands of our countrymen died on foreign soil fighting for the American cause. At Iwo Jima in the Second World War, United States Marines fought hand-to-hand against thousands of Japanese. By the time the Marines reached the top of Mount Suribachi, they raised a piece of pipe upright and from one end fluttered a flag. That ascent had cost nearly 6,000 American lives. The Iwo Jima Memorial in Arlington National Cemetery memorializes that event. President Franklin Roosevelt authorized the use of the flag on labels, packages, cartons, and containers intended for export as lend-lease aid, in order to inform people in other countries of the United States' assistance.

38   During the Korean War, the successful amphibious landing of American troops at Inchon was marked by the raising of an American flag within an

hour of the event. Impetus for the enactment of the Federal Flag Desecration Statute in 1967 came from the impact of flag burnings in the United States on troop morale in Vietnam. Representative L. Mendel Rivers, then chairman of the House Armed Services Committee, testified that, "The burning of the flag . . . has caused my mail to increase 100 percent from the boys in Vietnam, writing me and asking me what is going on in America." Representative Charles Wiggins stated: "The public act of desecration of our flag tends to undermine the morale of American troops. That this finding is true can be attested by many Members who have received correspondence from servicemen expressing their shock and disgust of such conduct."

[39]   The flag symbolizes the Nation in peace as well as in war. It signifies our national presence on battleships, airplanes, military installations, and public buildings from the United States Capitol to the thousands of county courthouses and city halls throughout the country. Two flags are prominently placed in our courtroom. Countless flags are placed by the graves of loved ones each year on what was first called Decoration Day, and is now called Memorial Day. The flag is traditionally placed on the casket of deceased members of the Armed Forces, and it is later given to the deceased's family. Congress has provided that the flag be flown at half-staff upon the death of the President, Vice President, and other government officials "as a mark of respect to their memory." The flag identifies United States merchant ships, and "[t]he laws of the Union protect our commerce wherever the flag of the country may float."

[40]   No other American symbol has been as universally honored as the flag. In 1931, Congress declared "The Star Spangled Banner" to be our national anthem. In 1949, Congress declared June 14th to be Flag Day. In 1987, John Philip Sousa's "The Stars and Stripes Forever" was designated as the national march. Congress has also established "The Pledge of Allegiance to the Flag" and the manner of its deliverance. The flag has appeared as the principal symbol on approximately 33 United States postal stamps and in the design of at least 43 more, more times than any other symbol.

[41]   Both Congress and the States have enacted numerous laws regulating misuse of the American flag. Until 1967, Congress left the regulation of misuse of the flag up to the States. Now, however, Title 18 U. S. C. §700(a), provides that:

> Whoever knowingly casts contempt upon any flag of the United States by publicly mutilating, defacing, defiling, burning, or trampling upon it shall be fined not more than $1,000 or imprisoned for not more than one year, or both.

Congress has also prescribed, *inter alia*, detailed rules for the design of the flag, the time and occasion of flag's display, the position and manner of its display, respect for the flag, and conduct during hoisting, lowering and passing of the flag. With the exception of Alaska and Wyoming, all of the States now have statutes prohibiting the burning of the flag. Most of the state statutes are patterned after the Uniform Flag Act of 1917, which in §3 provides: "No person shall publicly mutilate, deface, defile, defy, trample upon, or by word or act cast contempt upon any such flag, standard, color, ensign or shield." Most were passed by the States at about the time of World War I.

42   The American flag, then, throughout more than 200 years of our history, has come to be the visible symbol embodying our Nation. It does not represent the views of any particular political party, and it does not represent any particular political philosophy. The flag is not simply another "idea" or "point of view" competing for recognition in the marketplace of ideas. Millions and millions of Americans regard it with an almost mystical reverence regardless of what sort of social, political, or philosophical beliefs they may have. I cannot agree that the First Amendment invalidates the Act of Congress, and the laws of 48 of the 50 States, which make criminal the public burning of the flag.

43   More than 80 years ago in *Halter* v. *Nebraska*, this Court upheld the constitutionality of a Nebraska statute that forbade the use of representations of the American flag for advertising purposes upon articles of merchandise. The Court there said:

> For that flag that every true American has not simply an appreciation but a deep affection.... Hence, it has often occurred that insults to a flag have been the cause of war, and indignities put upon it, in the presence of those who revere it, have often been resented and sometimes punished on the spot.

44   The result of the Texas statute is obviously to deny one in Johnson's frame of mind one of many means of "symbolic speech." Far from being a case of "one picture being worth a thousand words," flag burning is the equivalent of an inarticulate grunt or roar that, it seems fair to say, is most likely to be indulged in not to express any particular idea, but to antagonize others. Only five years ago we said in *Los Angeles City Council* v. *Taxpayers for Vincent*, that "the First Amendment does not guarantee the right to employ every conceivable method of communication at all times and in all places." The Texas statute deprived Johnson of only one rather inarticulate symbolic form of protest—a form of protest that was profoundly offensive to many—and left him with a full panoply of other symbols and every conceivable form of verbal expression to express his deep disapproval of national policy. Thus, in no way can it be said that Texas is punishing him because his hearers—or any other group of people—were profoundly opposed to the message that he sought to convey. Such opposition is no proper basis for restricting speech or expression under the First Amendment. It was Johnson's use of this particular symbol, and not the idea that he sought to convey by it or by his many other expressions, for which he was punished.

45   But the Court today will have none of this. The uniquely deep awe and respect for our flag felt by virtually all of us are bundled off under the rubric

of "designated symbols," that the First Amendment prohibits the government from "establishing." But the government has not "established" this feeling; 200 years of history have done that. The government is simply recognizing as a fact the profound regard for the American flag created by that history when it enacts statutes prohibiting the disrespectful public burning of the flag.

46 The Court concludes its opinion with a regrettably patronizing civics lecture, presumably addressed to the Members of both Houses of Congress, the members of the 48 state legislatures that enacted prohibitions against flag burning, and the troops fighting under that flag in Vietnam who objected to its being burned: "The way to preserve the flag's special role is not to punish those who feel differently about these matters. It is to persuade them that they are wrong." The Court's role as the final expositor of the Constitution is well established, but its role as a platonic guardian admonishing those responsible to public opinion as if they were truant school children has no similar place in our system of government. The cry of "no taxation without representation" animated those who revolted against the English Crown to found our Nation—the idea that those who submitted to government should have some say as to what kind of laws would be passed. Surely one of the high purposes of a democratic society is to legislate against conduct that is regarded as evil and profoundly offensive to the majority of people—whether it be murder, embezzlement, pollution, or flag burning.

47 Our Constitution wisely places limits on powers of legislative majorities to act, but the declaration of such limits by this Court "is, at all times, a question of much delicacy, which ought seldom, if ever, to be decided in the affirmative, in a doubtful case." Uncritical extension of constitutional protection to the burning of the flag risks the frustration of the very purpose for which organized governments are instituted. The Court decides that the American flag is just another symbol, about which not only must opinions pro and con be tolerated, but for which the most minimal public respect may not be enjoined. The government may conscript men into the Armed Forces where they must fight and perhaps die for the flag, but the government may not prohibit the public burning of the banner under which they fight. I would uphold the Texas statute as applied in this case.

JUSTICE STEVENS, dissenting.

48 As the Court analyzes this case, it presents the question whether the State of Texas, or indeed the Federal Government, has the power to prohibit the public desecration of the American flag. The question is unique. In my judgment rules that apply to a host of other symbols, such as state flags, armbands, or various privately promoted emblems of political or commercial identity, are not necessarily controlling. Even if flag burning could be considered just another species of symbolic speech under the logical application of the rules that the Court has developed in its interpretation of the First

Amendment in other contexts, this case has an intangible dimension that makes those rules inapplicable.

[49]   A country's flag is a symbol of more than "nationhood and national unity." It also signifies the ideas that characterize the society that has chosen that emblem as well as the special history that has animated the growth and power of those ideas. The fleurs-de-lis and the tricolor both symbolized "nationhood and national unity," but they had vastly different meanings. The message conveyed by some flags—the swastika, for example—may survive long after it has outlived its usefulness as a symbol of regimented unity in a particular nation.

[50]   So it is with the American flag. It is more than a proud symbol of the courage, the determination, and the gifts of nature that transformed 13 fledgling Colonies into a world power. It is a symbol of freedom, of equal opportunity, of religious tolerance, and of goodwill for other peoples who share our aspirations. The symbol carries its message to dissidents both at home and abroad who may have no interest at all in our national unity or survival.

[51]   The value of the flag as a symbol cannot be measured. Even so, I have no doubt that the interest in preserving that value for the future is both significant and legitimate. Conceivably that value will be enhanced by the Court's conclusion that our national commitment to free expression is so strong that even the United States as ultimate guarantor of that freedom is without power to prohibit the desecration of its unique symbol. But I am unpersuaded. The creation of a federal right to post bulletin boards and graffiti on the Washington Monument might enlarge the market for free expression, but at a cost I would not pay. Similarly, in my considered judgment, sanctioning the public desecration of the flag will tarnish its value—both for those who cherish the ideas for which it waves and for those who desire to don the robes of martyrdom by burning it. That tarnish is not justified by the trivial burden on free expression occasioned by requiring that an available, alternative mode of expression—including uttering words critical of the flag—be employed.

[52]   It is appropriate to emphasize certain propositions that are not implicated by this case. The statutory prohibition of flag desecration does not "prescribe what shall be orthodox in politics, nationalism, religion, or other matters of opinion or force citizens to confess by word or act their faith therein." The statute does not compel any conduct or any profession of respect for any idea or any symbol.

[53]   Nor does the statute violate "the government's paramount obligation of neutrality in its regulation of protected communication." The content of respondent's message has no relevance whatsoever to the case. The concept of "desecration" does not turn on the substance of the message the actor intends to convey, but rather on whether those who view the *act* will take serious offense. Accordingly, one intending to convey a message of respect for the flag by burning it in a public square might nonetheless be guilty of desecration if he knows that others—perhaps simply because they misperceive

the intended message—will be seriously offended. Indeed, even if the actor knows that all possible witnesses will understand that he intends to send a message of respect, he might still be guilty of desecration if he also knows that this understanding does not lessen the offense taken by some of those witnesses. Thus, this is not a case in which the fact that "it is the speaker's opinion that gives offense" provides a special "reason for according it constitutional protection." The case has nothing to do with "disagreeable ideas." It involves disagreeable conduct that, in my opinion, diminishes the value of an important national asset.

[54]   The Court is therefore quite wrong in blandly asserting that respondent "was prosecuted for his expression of dissatisfaction with the policies of this country, expression situated at the core of our First Amendment values." Respondent was prosecuted because of the method be chose to express his dissatisfaction with those policies. Had he chosen to spray paint—or perhaps convey with a motion picture projector—his message of dissatisfaction on the facade of the Lincoln Memorial, there would be no question about the power of the Government to prohibit his means of expression. The prohibition would be supported by the legitimate interest in preserving the quality of an important national asset. Though the asset at stake in this case is intangible, given its unique value, the same interest supports a prohibition on the desecration of the American flag.

[55]   The ideas of liberty and equality have been an irresistible force in motivating leaders like Patrick Henry, Susan B. Anthony, and Abraham Lincoln, schoolteachers like Nathan Hale and Booker T. Washington, the Philippine Scouts who fought at Bataan, and the soldiers who scaled the bluff at Omaha Beach. If those ideas are worth fighting for—and our history demonstrates that they are—it cannot be true that the flag that uniquely symbolizes their power is not itself worthy of protection from unnecessary desecration.

[56]   I respectfully dissent.

1989

Charles R. Lawrence III

ON RACIST SPEECH

As anyone on an American college or university campus knows, an important current issue is how to deal with speech and behavior designed to make the members of a particular group feel unwelcome, inferior, or threatened. The First Amendment guarantees our right to speak freely, even when our views are unpopular or offensive. But, as Lawrence points out, the Supreme Court has found that the First Amendment does not protect "fighting words," that is, words that "inflict injury" or provoke the hearer to violence. Drawing the line between "offending," which is protected, and verbally "inflicting injury," which is not, is extraordinarily difficult. College campuses cannot function without the free exchange of ideas, nor are they likely to function well if racist, sexist, or homophobic behavior produces an atmosphere of hostility and fear. Many campuses have adopted codes prohibiting "hate speech," but such a code is extremely difficult to formulate without encroaching on constitutional rights to freedom of expression. As Derek Bok, former president of Harvard University, puts it, "I have difficulty understanding why a university such as Harvard should have less free speech than the surrounding society." Lawrence's essay appeared in The Chronicle of Higher Education, *read by university administrators and faculty. How would you describe his intention in relation to such an audience? Do you agree with his goals? His means?*

1　　I have spent the better part of my life as a dissenter. As a high school student, I was threatened with suspension for my refusal to participate in a civil defense drill, and I have been a conspicuous consumer of my First Amendment liberties ever since. There are very strong reasons for protecting even racist speech. Perhaps the most important of these is that such protection reinforces our society's commitment to tolerance as a value, and that by protecting bad speech from government regulation, we will be forced to combat it as a community.

2　　But I also have a deeply felt apprehension about the resurgence of racial violence and the corresponding rise in the incidence of verbal and symbolic assault and harassment to which blacks and other traditionally subjugated and excluded groups are subjected. I am troubled by the way the debate has been framed in response to the recent surge of racist incidents on college and university campuses and in response to some universities' attempts to regulate harassing speech. The problem has been framed as one in which the liberty of free speech is in conflict with the elimination of racism. I believe this has placed the bigot on the moral high ground and fanned the rising flames of racism.

3　　Above all, I am troubled that we have not listened to the real victims, that we have shown so little understanding of their injury, and that we have abandoned those whose race, gender, or sexual preference continue to make them second-class citizens. It seems to me a very sad irony that the first instinct of civil libertarians has been to challenge even the smallest, most narrowly framed efforts by universities to provide black and other minority students with the protection the Constitution guarantees them.

4　　The landmark case of *Brown v. Board of Education* is not a case that we normally think of as a case about speech. But *Brown* can be broadly read as articulating the principle of equal citizenship. *Brown* held that segregated schools were inherently unequal because of the *message* that segregation conveyed— that black children were an untouchable caste unfit to go to school with white children. If we understand the necessity of eliminating the system of signs and symbols that signal the inferiority of blacks, then we should hesitate before proclaiming that all racist speech that stops short of physical violence must be defended.

5   University officials who have formulated policies to respond to incidents of racial harassment have been characterized in the press as "thought police," but such policies generally do nothing more than impose sanctions against intentional face-to-face insults. When racist speech takes the form of face-to-face insults, catcalls, or other assaultive speech aimed at an individual or small group of persons, it falls directly within the "fighting words" exception to First Amendment protection. The Supreme Court has held that words which "by their very utterance inflict injury or tend to incite an immediate breach of the peace" are not protected by the First Amendment.

6   If the purpose of the First Amendment is to foster the greatest amount of speech, racial insults disserve that purpose. Assaultive racist speech functions as a preemptive strike. The invective is experienced as a blow, not as a proffered idea, and once the blow is struck, it is unlikely that a dialogue will follow. Racial insults are particularly undeserving of First Amendment protection because the perpetrator's intention is not to discover truth or initiate dialogue but to injure the victim. In most situations, members of minority groups realize that they are likely to lose if they respond to epithets by fighting and are forced to remain silent and submissive.

7   Courts have held that offensive speech may not be regulated in public forums such as streets where the listener may avoid the speech by moving on, but the regulation of otherwise protected speech has been permitted when the speech invades the privacy of the unwilling listener's home or when the unwilling listener cannot avoid the speech. Racist posters, fliers, and graffiti in dormitories, bathrooms, and other common living spaces would seem to clearly fall within the reasoning of these cases. Minority students should not be required to remain in their rooms in order to avoid racial assault. Minimally, they should find a safe haven in their dorms and in all other common rooms that are a part of their daily routine.

8   I would also argue that the university's responsibility for ensuring that these students receive an equal educational opportunity provides a compelling justification for regulations that ensure them safe passage in all common areas. A minority student should not have to risk becoming the target of racially assaulting speech every time he or she chooses to walk across campus. Regulating vilifying speech that cannot be anticipated or avoided would

not preclude announced speeches and rallies—situations that would give minority-group members and their allies the chance to organize counter-demonstrations or avoid the speech altogether.

9   The most commonly advanced argument against the regulation of racist speech proceeds something like this: We recognize that minority groups suffer pain and injury as the result of racist speech, but we must allow this hate mongering for the benefit of society as a whole. Freedom of speech is the lifeblood of our democratic system. It is especially important for minorities because often it is their only vehicle for rallying support for the redress of their grievances. It will be impossible to formulate a prohibition so precise that it will prevent the racist speech you want to suppress without catching in the same net all kinds of speech that it would be unconscionable for a democratic society to suppress.

10   Whenever we make such arguments, we are striking a balance on the one hand between our concern for the continued free flow of ideas and the democratic process dependent on that flow, and, on the other, our desire to further the cause of equality. There can be no meaningful discussion of how we should reconcile our commitment to equality and our commitment to free speech until it is acknowledged that there is real harm inflicted by racist speech and that this harm is far from trivial.

11   To engage in a debate about the First Amendment and racist speech without a full understanding of the nature and extent of that harm is to risk making the First Amendment an instrument of domination rather than a vehicle of liberation. We have not known the experience of victimization by racist, misogynist, and homophobic speech, nor do we equally share the burden of the societal harm it inflicts. We are often quick to say that we have heard the cry of the victims when we have not.

12   The *Brown* case is again instructive because it speaks directly to the psychic injury inflicted by racist speech by noting that the symbolic message of segregation affected "the hearts and minds" of Negro children "in a way unlikely ever to be undone." Racial epithets and harassment often cause deep emotional scarring and feelings of anxiety and fear that pervade every aspect of a victim's life.

13   *Brown* also recognized that black children did not have an equal opportunity to learn and participate in the school community if they bore the additional burden of being subjected to the humiliation and psychic assault contained in the message of segregation. University students bear an analogous burden when they are forced to live and work in an environment where at any moment they may be subjected to denigrating verbal harassment and assault. The same injury was addressed by the Supreme Court when it held that sexual harassment that creates a hostile or abusive work environment violates the ban on sex discrimination in employment of Title VII of the Civil Rights Act of 1964.

[14]   Carefully drafted university regulations would bar the use of words as assault weapons and leave unregulated even the most heinous of ideas when those ideas are presented at times and places and in manners that provide an opportunity for reasoned rebuttal or escape from immediate injury. The history of the development of the right to free speech has been one of carefully evaluating the importance of free expression and its effects on other important societal interests. We have drawn the line between protected and unprotected speech before without dire results. (Courts have, for example, exempted from the protection of the First Amendment obscene speech and speech that disseminates official secrets, that defames or libels another person, or that is used to form a conspiracy or monopoly.)

[15]   Blacks and other people of color are skeptical about the argument that even the most injurious speech must remain unregulated because, in an unregulated marketplace of ideas, the best ones will rise to the top and gain acceptance. Our experience tells us quite the opposite. We have seen too many good liberal politicians shy away from the issues that might brand them as being too closely allied with us.

[16]   Whenever we decide that racist speech must be tolerated because of the importance of maintaining societal tolerance for all unpopular speech, we are asking blacks and other subordinated groups to bear the burden for the good of all. We must be careful that the ease with which we strike the balance against the regulation of racist speech is in no way influenced by the fact that the cost will be borne by others. We must be certain that those who will pay that price are fairly represented in our deliberations and that they are heard.

[17]   At the core of the argument that we should resist all government regulation of speech is the ideal that the best cure for bad speech is good, that ideas that affirm equality and the worth of all individuals will ultimately prevail. This is an empty ideal unless those of us who would fight racism are vigilant and unequivocal in that fight. We must look for ways to offer assistance and support to students whose speech and political participation are chilled in a climate of racial harassment.

[18]   Civil rights lawyers might consider suing on behalf of blacks whose right to an equal education is denied by a university's failure to ensure a nondiscriminatory educational climate or conditions of employment. We must embark upon the development of a First Amendment jurisprudence grounded in the reality of our history and our contemporary experience. We must think hard about how best to launch legal attacks against the most indefensible forms of hate speech. Good lawyers can create exceptions and narrow interpretations that limit the harm of hate speech without opening the floodgates of censorship.

[19]   Everyone concerned with these issues must find ways to engage actively in actions that resist and counter the racist ideas that we would have the First

Amendment protect. If we fail in this, the victims of hate speech must rightly assume that we are on the oppressors' side.

1989

Nat Hentoff

"SPEECH CODES" ON THE CAMPUS AND PROBLEMS OF FREE SPEECH

Nat Hentoff is a prolific journalist and vigorous advocate of free speech. As his essay indicates, he frequently lectures at colleges and universities. He disagrees strongly with Lawrence's view of how best to ensure respectful treatment for all members of an academic community. How would Hentoff respond to Lawrence's argument that "Carefully drafted university regulations would bar the use of words as assault weapons and leave unregulated even the most heinous of ideas when those ideas are presented at times and places and in manners that provide an opportunity for reasoned rebuttal or escape from immediate injury" (paragraph 14)? How would you describe the differences in ethos between Lawrence and Hentoff? Although their positions clearly oppose one another, would you say that their argumentative techniques are similar or different?

1   During three years of reporting on anti–free-speech tendencies in higher education, I've been at more than twenty colleges and universities—from Washington and Lee and Columbia to Mesa State in Colorado and Stanford.

2   On this voyage of initially reverse expectations—with liberals fiercely advocating censorship of "offensive" speech and conservatives merrily taking the moral high ground as champions of free expression—the most dismaying moment of revelation took place at Stanford.

3   In the course of a two-year debate on whether Stanford, like many other universities, should have a speech code punishing language that might wound minorities, women, and gays, a letter appeared in the *Stanford Daily.* Signed by the African-American Law Students Association, the Asian-American Law Student Association, and the Jewish Law Students Association, the letter called for a harsh code. It reflected the letter and the spirit of an earlier declaration by Canetta Ivy, a black leader of student government at Stanford during the period of the grand debate. "We don't put as many restrictions on freedom of speech," she said, "as we should."

4   Reading the letter by this rare ecumenical body of law students (so press-ing was the situation that even Jews were allowed in), I thought of twenty, thirty years from now. From so bright a cadre of graduates, from so presti-gious a law school would come some of the law professors, civic leaders, col-lege presidents, and even maybe a Supreme Court justice of the future. And many of them would have learned—like so many other university students in the land—that censorship is okay provided your motives are okay.

5   The debate at Stanford ended when the president, Donald Kennedy, fol-lowing the prevailing winds, surrendered his previous position that once you start telling people what they can't say, you will end up telling them what they can't think. Stanford now has a speech code.

6   This is not to say that these gags on speech—every one of them so over-board and vague that a student can violate a code without knowing he or she has done so—are invariably imposed by student demand. At most colleges, it is the administration that sets up the code. Because there have been racist or sexist or homophobic taunts, anonymous notes or graffiti, the administra-tion feels it must *do something*. The cheapest, quickest way to demonstrate that it cares is to appear to suppress racist, sexist, homophobic speech.

7   Usually, the leading opposition among the faculty consists of conserva-tives—when there is opposition. An exception at Stanford was law professor Gerald Gunther, arguably the nation's leading authority on constitutional law. But Gunther did not have much support among other faculty members, conservative or liberal.

8   At the University of Buffalo Law School, which has a code restricting speech, I could find just one faculty member who was against it. A liberal, he spoke only on condition that I not use his name. He did not want to be cate-gorized as a racist.

9   On another campus, a political science professor for whom I had great respect after meeting and talking with him years ago, has been silent—stu-dents told me—on what Justice William Brennan once called "the pall of orthodoxy" that has fallen on his campus.

10   When I talked to him, the professor said, "It doesn't happen in my class. There's no 'politically correct' orthodoxy here. It may happen in other places at this university, but I don't know about that." He said no more.

11   One of the myths about the rise of P. C. (politically correct) is that, coming from the left, it is primarily intimidating conservatives on campus. Quite the contrary. At almost every college I've been, conservative students have their own newspaper, usually quite lively and fired by a muckraking glee at expos-ing "politically correct" follies on campus.

12   By and large, those most intimidated—not so much by the speech codes themselves but by the Madame Defarge-like spirit behind them—are liberal students and those who can be called politically moderate.

13   I've talked to many of them, and they no longer get involved in class discussions where their views would go against the grain of P. C. righteousness. Many, for instance, have questions about certain kinds of affirmative action. They are not partisans of Jesse Helms or David Duke, but they wonder whether progeny of middle-class black families should get scholarship preference. Others have a question about abortion. Most are not pro-life, but they believe that fathers should have a say in whether the fetus should be sent off into eternity.

14   Jeff Shesol, a recent graduate of Brown and now a Rhodes scholar at Oxford, became nationally known while at Brown because of his comic strip, "Thatch," which, not too kindly, parodied P. C. students. At a forum on free speech at Brown before he left, Shesol said he wished he could tell the new students at Brown to have no fear of speaking freely. But he couldn't tell them that, he said, advising the new students to stay clear of talking critically about affirmative action or abortion, among other things, in public.

15   At that forum, Shesol told me, he said that those members of the left who regard dissent from their views as racist and sexist should realize that they are discrediting their goals. "They're honorable goals," said Shesol, "and I agree with them. I'm against racism and sexism. But these people's tactics are obscuring the goals. And they've resulted in Brown no longer being an open-minded place." There were hisses from the audience.

16   Students at New York University Law School have also told me that they censor themselves in class. The kind of chilling atmosphere they describe was exemplified last year as a case assigned for a moot court competition became subject to denunciation when a sizable number of law students said it was too "offensive" and would hurt the feelings of gay and lesbian students. The case concerned a divorced father's attempt to gain custody of his children on the grounds that their mother had become a lesbian. It was against P. C. to represent the father.

17   Although some of the faculty responded by insisting that you learn to be a lawyer by dealing with all kinds of cases, including those you personally find offensive, other faculty members supported the rebellious students, praising them for their sensitivity. There was little public opposition from the other students to the attempt to suppress the case. A leading dissenter was a member of the conservative Federalist Society.

18   What is P. C. to white students is not necessarily P. C. to black students. Most of the latter did not get involved in the N. Y. U. protest, but throughout the country many black students do support speech codes. A vigorous exception was a black Harvard law school student during a debate on whether the law school should start punishing speech. A white student got up and said that the codes are necessary because without them, black students would be driven away from colleges and thereby deprived of the equal opportunity to get an education.

19   A black student rose and said that the white student had a hell of a nerve to assume that he—in the face of racist speech—would pack up his books and go home. He's been familiar with that kind of speech all his life, and he had never felt the need to run away from it. He'd handled it before and he could again.

20   The black student then looked at his white colleague and said that it was condescending to say that blacks have to be "protected" from racist speech. "It is more racist and insulting," he emphasized, "to say that to me than to call me a nigger."

21   But that would appear to be a minority view among black students. Most are convinced they do need to be protected from wounding language. On the other hand, a good many black student organizations on campus do not feel that Jews have to be protected from wounding language. Though it's not much written about in reports of the language wars on campuses, there is a strong strain of anti-Semitism among some—not all, by any means—black students. They invite such speakers as Louis Farrakhan, the former Stokely Carmichael (now Kwame Touré), and such lesser but still burning bushes as Steve Cokely, the Chicago commentator who has declared that Jewish doctors inject the AIDS virus into black babies. That distinguished leader was invited to speak at the University of Michigan.

22   The black student organization at Columbia University brought to the campus Dr. Khallid Abdul Muhammad. He began his address by saying: "My leader, my teacher, my guide is the honorable Louis Farrakhan. I thought that should be said at Columbia Jewniversity."

23   Many Jewish students have not censored themselves in reacting to this form of political correctness among some blacks. A Columbia student, Rachel Stoll, wrote a letter to the *Columbia Spectator*: "I have an idea. As a white Jewish American, I'll just stand in the middle of a circle comprising.... Khallid Abdul Muhammad and assorted members of the Black Students Organization and let them all hurl large stones at me. From recent events and statements made on this campus, I gather this will be a good cheap method of making these people feel good."

24   At UCLA, a black student magazine printed an article indicating there is considerable truth to the *Protocols of the Elders of Zion*. For months, the black faculty, when asked their reactions, preferred not to comment. One of them did say that the black students already considered the black faculty to be insufficiently militant, and the professors didn't want to make the gap any wider. Like white liberal faculty members on other campuses, they want to be liked—or at least not too disliked.

25   Along with quiet white liberal faculty members, most black professors have not opposed the speech codes. But unlike the white liberals, many honestly do believe that minority students have to be insulated from barbed language. They do not believe—as I have found out in a number of conver-

sations—that an essential part of an education is to learn to demystify language, to strip it of its ability to demonize and stigmatize you. They do not believe that the way to deal with bigoted language is to answer it with more and better language of your own. This seems very elementary to me, but not to the defenders, black and white, of the speech codes.

26 Consider University of California president David Gardner. He has imposed a speech code on all the campuses in his university system. Students are to be punished—and this is characteristic of the other codes around the country—if they use "fighting words"—derogatory references to "race, sex, sexual orientation, or disability."

27 The term "fighting words" comes from a 1942 Supreme Court decision, *Chaplinsky* v. *New Hampshire*, which ruled that "fighting words" are not protected by the First Amendment. That decision, however, has been in disuse at the High Court for many years. But it is thriving on college campuses.

28 In the California code, a word becomes "fighting" if it is directly addressed to "any ordinary person" (presumably, extraordinary people are above all this). These are the kinds of words that are "inherently likely to provoke a violent reaction, *whether or not they actually do.*" (Emphasis added).

29 Moreover, he or she who fires a fighting word at any ordinary person can be reprimanded or dismissed from the university because the perpetrator should "reasonably know" that what he or she has said will interfere with the "victim's ability to pursue effectively his or her education or otherwise participate fully in university programs and activities."

30 Asked Gary Murikami, chairman of the Gay and Lesbian Association at the University of California, Berkeley: "What does it mean?"

31 Among those—faculty, law professors, college administrators—who insist such codes are essential to the university's purpose of making *all* students feel at home and thereby able to concentrate on their work, there has been a celebratory resort to the Fourteenth Amendment.

32 That amendment guarantees "equal protection of the laws" to all, and that means to all students on campus. Accordingly, when the First Amendment rights of those engaging in offensive speech clash with the equality rights of their targets under the Fourteenth Amendment, the First Amendment must give way.

33 This is the thesis, by the way, of John Powell, legal director of the American Civil Liberties Union, even though that organization has now formally opposed all college speech codes—after a considerable civil war among and within its affiliates.

34 The battle of the amendments continues, and when harsher codes are called for at some campuses, you can expect the Fourteenth Amendment—which was not intended to censor *speech*—will rise again.

35 A precedent has been set at, of all places, colleges and universities, that the principle of free speech is merely situational. As college administrators

change, so will the extent of free speech on campus. And invariably, permissible speech will become more and more narrowly defined. Once speech can be limited in such subjective ways, more and more expression will be included in what is forbidden.

36   One of the exceedingly few college presidents who speaks out on the consequences of the anti–free-speech movement is Yale University's Benno Schmidt:

> Freedom of thought must be Yale's central commitment. It is not easy to embrace. It is, indeed, the effort of a lifetime. . . . Much expression that is free may deserve our contempt. We may well be moved to exercise our own freedom to counter it or to ignore it. But universities cannot censor or suppress speech, no matter how obnoxious in content, without violating their justification for existence. . . .
>
> On some other campuses in this country, values of civility and community have been offered by some as paramount values of the university, even to the extent of superseding freedom of expression.
>
> Such a view is wrong in principle and, if extended, is disastrous to freedom of thought. . . .The chilling effects on speech of the vagueness and open-ended nature of many universities' prohibitions . . . are compounded by the fact that these codes are typically enforced by faculty and students who commonly assert that vague notions of community are more important to the academy than freedom of thought and expression. . . .
>
> This is a flabby and uncertain time for freedom in the United States.

37   On the Public Broadcasting System in June, I was part of a Fred Friendly panel at Stanford University in a debate on speech codes versus freedom of expression. The three black panelists strongly supported the codes. So did the one Asian-American on the panel. But then so did Stanford law professor, Thomas Grey, who wrote the Stanford code, and Stanford president Donald Kennedy, who first opposed and then embraced the code. We have a new ecumenicism of those who would control speech for the greater good. It is hardly a new idea, but the mix of advocates is rather new.

38   But there are other voices. In the national board debate at the ACLU on college speech codes, the first speaker—and I think she had a lot to do with making the final vote against codes unanimous—was Gwen Thomas.

39   A black community college administrator from Colorado, she is a fiercely persistent exposer of racial discrimination.

40   She started by saying, "I have always felt as a minority person that we have to protect the rights of all because if we infringe on the rights of any persons, we'll be next."

41   "As for providing a nonintimidating educational environment, our young people have to learn to grow up on college campuses. We have to teach them how to deal with adversarial situations. They have to learn how to survive offensive speech they find wounding and hurtful."

42   Gwen Thomas is an educator—an endangered species in higher education.

1991

Nell Irvin Painter

IT'S TIME TO ACKNOWLEDGE THE DAMAGE INFLICTED BY INTOLERANCE

The two preceding essays by Lawrence and Hentoff disagree over the desirability of campus speech codes. Painter, a history professor at Princeton University, says in her final paragraph that she is "not advocating hate-speech codes," which might suggest that her position is closer to Hentoff's, and yet, like Lawrence, she suggests that something must be done to counter the effect of hate speech on the members of targeted groups. What exactly is her solution? What does she mean when, in paragraph 19, she says "Let us protest against all speech that insults our fellow citizens" and then says in paragraph 20 that she is not calling for protests? Do you agree with her that criticizing a person or position as "politically correct" is a way of excusing or minimizing the "damage inflicted by intolerance"? How would you characterize her intention?

1   During the last several years I've been watching and sometimes reluctantly entering the ruckus over political correctness, better known as "PC." I've been called a "queen of political correctness" for defending affirmative action. I've been ridiculed and have even received some ugly hate mail for supporting multiculturalism and questioning the ways in which universities were run before faculties and student bodies became more diverse. The definition of "PC" always seems one-sided to me, though: people who decry hate speech, cartoons, or other actions directed against members of minority groups are accused of being oversensitive and are denigrated as being PC, while the people who characterized the groups in derogatory ways in the first place become heroes of free speech or otherwise get off the hook.

2   Various kinds of bigotry exist: homophobia, sexism, racism, anti-Semitism, to name the most salient. In the last few years, when some of us tried to explore ways to combat the first three types, we heard a lot about the First Amendment and were warned against limiting free expression in the service of political correctness. Freedom of speech, we were told, is a fundamental American value, more precious than the sensitivities of those who might be bruised by the speech.

3   Yet consider the current situation, in the wake of wide publicity about the deeply anti-Semitic statements of some black activists in speeches at college campuses. Although many scholars and college administrators grudgingly admit that such activists must be allowed to speak in public forums, their position is subject to tremendous opposition. What I am hearing now are demands that hate speech be condemned immediately. Two questions come to my mind: Why are those who decry the anti-Jewish statements not also labeled politically correct? Is speech directed against Jews somehow different or more serious than speech directed against people of color or gays?

4   Within the current lexicon, PC has been used to characterize objections to many kinds of speech and behavior, ranging from anger over jokes and banter, to insistence that speech considered offensive cease, to a broad attempt to censor speech that is deemed incorrect because it might, through some stretch of imagination, offend a tiny, marginal group.

5   Last year, the news media highlighted one memorable example of what critics labeled PC in action—the suppression of free speech by some African American students at the University of Pennsylvania. The students carried off and destroyed a portion of the press run of the *Daily Pennsylvanian,* the undergraduate student newspaper. The students contended that the newspaper had repeatedly published racist material.

6   After national news reports about the incident, Sheldon Hackney, then president of the university, was questioned closely about the incident during a hearing on his nomination to be chairman of the National Endowment for the Humanities. Mr. Hackney, his opponents charged, had caved in to the demands of political correctness by failing to discipline vigorously the students who had suppressed speech that should have been protected under the First Amendment. As this story was cast in the media, emphasis fell squarely on the black students' bad conduct; virtually no attention was paid to the material that originally sparked the students' anger—for example, a photograph of a black man drinking cheap wine under the caption "West Philadelphian," which students saw as a racist generalization about the area around the university.

7   Time and again, charges of politically correct behavior have played out the same way. Members of minority groups and feminists and homosexuals are cast as villains who infringe on freedom of speech and clamor for censorship for reasons that are, finally, illegitimate.

8   A completely separate discussion is going on now about anti-Semitic utterances by black (not white) anti-Semites. The recent history of this phenomenon, which has received sustained media coverage, goes back to the Reverend Jesse Jackson's 1984 presidential campaign and his small-minded remarks about Jews in New York City. Demands that Mr. Jackson apologize arose immediately and continued for years, despite several mea culpas on his

part. Prominent black New Yorkers also came under pressure to condemn and recondemn Mr. Jackson's statements.

9   Ten years later, Mr. Jackson's "Hymie-town" slur seems relatively innocuous, since the talk has gotten much worse. Two leading figures in the Nation of Islam, its head, Louis Farrakhan, and his former top aid, Khalid Abdul Muhammad, have become emblems of public anti-Semitism. Mr. Farrakhan has delivered enough ugly speeches to make his name a symbol of hatred, and, in a speech late last year at Kean College, Mr. Muhammad vociferously attacked Jews and practically everyone else, including black people who disagree with him. Other African Americans have received prominent coverage for their nasty and senseless verbal assaults against Jews—the City College of New York professor Leonard Jeffries and the pan-Africanist Kwame Toure (known in the 1960s and 1970s as Stokely Carmichael). The air has crackled with calls for their condemnation, from the editorial page of my local newspaper in New Jersey to the halls of Congress.

10   Today's anti-Semitism is indeed disturbing for many reasons, not the least of which is its atavism. However, rather than replaying the coarse ethnic and racial humor that has been a staple of American life since the early nineteenth century (as exemplified in Jesse Jackson's 1984 remark), Mr. Farrakhan and Mr. Muhammad have resuscitated the terms of nineteenth- and early-twentieth-century European anti-Semitism. They seem to have been mining that fraudulent source of European bigotry, the *Protocols of the Learned Elders of Zion*, a 1905 document claiming that Jews wanted to take over the world. They are using it as a means to replay the accusations made by the leaders of Nazi Germany: Jews control all the power in society; they have joined in a conspiracy against us (defined as whoever is making the charges); Jews, though a numerically small minority, are our most potent enemies.

11   This kind of demagoguery has evoked a tide of denunciation, for not only does it spew gratuitous hatred against millions of Americans, it also belongs to a deadly tradition. It should come as no surprise that a people who have lost so many to the Holocaust are now deeply alarmed by hearing again some of the phrases that preceded it.

12   But this reaction applies to other people, as well. Any people whose history is full of oppression is understandably sensitive to the lexicon of hate, and other people besides Jews have been subjected to such hate and have been targets of violence and discrimination. Today, the other languages of bigotry—such as racism and homophobia—are not being taken with the same seriousness as is anti-Semitism.

13   Let me return to those black students at the University of Pennsylvania. The news reports that circulated nationally never revealed what had been published in the *Daily Pennsylvanian* that had upset the black students who were so roundly damned as agents of PC. As the words that had hurt the University of Pennsylvania students disappeared beneath a pile of outrage over

threats to freedom of speech, those young black people became assailants without a cause. According to media coverage, only they were in the wrong—not whatever had appeared in the newspaper's columns.

14   Comparing the lack of public concern about the nature and details of the black students' grievances against the newspaper with the publicity accorded their action is, indeed, quite revealing. And it fits into a long tradition of ignoring or trivializing the terrible things that happen to African Americans—black life, for instance, seems always to have counted for rather little, when compared with the value of the lives of whites.

15   The silence surrounding what appeared in the *Daily Pennsylvanian* speaks all the louder when set against the coverage of Mr. Muhammad's and Mr. Farrakhan's speeches, which have been quoted directly, again and again. Every editorial, every news story, contains some of the specific offending quotations.

16   The clamor provoked by Mr. Muhammad and Mr. Farrakhan seldom includes ringing demands for protection of their freedom of speech. These days, in fact, the cry of freedom of speech is seldom heard. A New Jersey assemblyman is sponsoring a bill to ban incendiary speakers and deprive colleges of state funds if they let rabble-rousers use their facilities.

17   As disturbing as the disparity is between the response to the Penn students and to spokesmen for the Nation of Islam, this gap suggests a means of dealing with both PC and anti-Semitism. In our current public life, where bigotry against many kinds of people is flourishing, we can combine our concerns for freedom of speech and our antipathy to anti-Semitism.

18   Why not, in a spirit of reconciliation, deal with all hate speech in the same way, no matter whom it hurts? Let everyone talk—yes, even bigots. But at the same time that we uphold freedom of speech, let us denounce *all* words that denigrate members of groups that have suffered discrimination. Let us denounce anti-Semitism vigorously and indefatigably. But let our denunciations not stop with anti-Semitism.

19   Let us protest against all speech that insults our fellow citizens, be they black, female, gay, lesbian, fat, disabled, or Jewish. Let us set aside the PC narrative that turns the targets of hate speech into the targets of ridicule: no more jokes about "differently abled, visually challenged, lesbian, Jewish, Native Americans"; no more automatic rejection—without even looking at the material in question—when students of color or women protest that what they are assigned to read is insulting. When students or colleagues, particularly those who have not preciously been numerous in academe, complain of discrimination, their complaints should be taken as seriously as we take anti-Semitism, not ridiculed as representing PC.

20   I'm not advocating hate-speech codes or calling for protests. I am suggesting that various kinds of insult be taken with the same gravity. It is time

that we reaffirmed the values of fellowship and decency by admitting that intolerance—whether anti-Semitism, racism, or homophobia—intimidates and injures others. Better to reach out to one another and acknowledge that *any* hateful invective hurts its intended targets—and should be subject to quick condemnation. It's time to bury accusations of political correctness.

1994

Reacting and Writing

The pieces by Plato and Mill that begin this symposium are basic texts that have continued to shape discussions of First Amendment issues. You may wish to begin your writing for this sequence by assessing their arguments. Notice that Plato works from the notion that one must shape the citizens to better the commonwealth, while Mill thinks about how to shape the commonwealth to suit its citizens. Which of Plato's and Mill's arguments do we still hear today, and which seem to you to belong to the past?

The essays by Charles R. Lawrence III, Nat Hentoff, and Nell Irvin Painter take positions on the desirability of the codes being formulated on many college campuses to try to curb verbal harrassment or hate speech. If your campus is debating such a code, you could put into writing your position on the issue. Or you could take a particular example of hate speech and write a focused argument upholding or denying the speaker's right to make such a statement. For example, a student at the University of Connecticut was expelled for posting a sign on her door listing types of people unwelcome in her room, mostly along the lines of "nerds" and "dweebs," but one of which was allegedly "homos." She was found to be in violation of the campus' code prohibiting "slurs or epithets based on race, sex, ethnic origin, disability, religion, or sexual orientation." Although the student denied including that term, she brought a suit arguing that, even assuming she had used it, her free speech was protected by the First Amendment. What do you think? Using a hypothetical case, a case from Lawrence, Hentoff, or Painter, or one that you know about, make an argument upholding or challenging the need for speech codes.

II. OUR RELATIONSHIP TO OUR NATURAL ENVIRONMENT

At least since the Industrial Revolution, and probably long before, human beings have had a problematic relationship to their natural environment. Most people, if asked, will say that they favor clean water over dirty, fresh air over polluted air, and pristine countryside over the ravages of industry. But most of us are unwilling to give up the high standard of living and the many creature comforts that produce pollution as a by-product. As you know, those committed to conservation of resources don't agree where the biggest threat lies. Many environmentalists stress that we are fast running out of places to dispose of our convenient disposables; others emphasize the destructive effects that air pollution is having on our forests and on the ozone layer. Some people claim that nuclear energy is our only hope, and others regard it as the final instrument of death and destruction by technology.

Do we have a need for extensive wilderness areas? Are they a luxury for overzealous back-to-nature types, or are they a mainstay of life and sanity? The readings in this section begin with a prophetic letter written in 1855 by a Native American. It provides an overview of nearly every issue raised in the later pieces. Next we present the two sides of a major environmental debate of the early twentieth century. The other readings then broaden to consider ways of looking at ourselves in relation to the natural world.

Seattle

THE EARTH IS NOT THE WHITE MAN'S BROTHER

Seattle, a stirring rhetor whose words also appear in Chapter 2, wrote this letter to President Franklin Pierce in 1855. If you read it carefully and think about the meaning of each assertion, you will find that Seattle predicts a large number of the environmental issues that most concern us today. Urban blight, noise pollution, air and water pollution, waste disposal, endangered and extinct species, the throwaway attitude of consumerism—all are touched on in this brief letter. The modern science of ecology might be said to be founded on Seattle's observation that "All things are connected." Why do you think that he engages in self-deprecation in this letter? What do you think is his intention in regard to the American president he addresses?

1   We know that the white man does not understand our ways. One portion of the land is the same to him as the next, for he is a stranger who comes in the night and takes from the land whatever he needs. The earth is not his brother, but his enemy, and when he has conquered it, he moves on. He leaves his fathers' graves, and his children's birthright is forgotten. The sight of your cities pains the eyes of the red man. But perhaps it is because the red man is a savage and does not understand.

2   There is no quiet place in the white man's cities. No place to hear the leaves of spring or the rustle of insect's wings. But perhaps because I am a savage and do not understand, the clatter only seems to insult the ears. The Indian prefers the soft sound of the wind darting over the face of the pond, the smell of the wind itself cleansed by a mid-day rain, or scented with the

piñon pine. The air is precious to the red man. For all things share the same breath—the beasts, the trees, the man. Like a man dying for many days, he is numb to the stench.

3   What is man without the beasts? If all the beasts were gone, men would die from great loneliness of spirit, for whatever happens to the beasts also happens to man. All things are connected. Whatever befalls the earth befalls the sons of the earth.

4   It matters little where we pass the rest of our days; they are not many. A few more hours, a few more winters, and none of the children of the great tribes that once lived on this earth, or that roamed in small bands in the woods, will be left to mourn the graves of a people once as powerful and hopeful as yours.

5   The whites, too, shall pass—perhaps sooner than other tribes. Continue to contaminate your bed, and you will one night suffocate in your own waste. When the buffalo are all slaughtered, the wild horses all tamed, the secret corners of the forest heavy with the scent of many men, and the view of the ripe hills blotted by talking wires, where is the thicket? Gone. Where is the eagle? Gone. And what is it to say goodby to the swift and the hunt, the end of living and the beginning of survival? We might understand if we knew what it was that the white man dreams, what he describes to his children on the long winter nights, what visions he burns into their minds, so they will wish for tomorrow. But we are savages. The white man's dreams are hidden from us.

1855

John Muir

THE HETCH-HETCHY VALLEY

The debate over building a dam on the Hetch-Hetchy River in a beautiful wilderness area of northern California is commonly regarded as the classic debate on environmental matters. On the one side was John Muir, the founder of the Sierra Club and the leading advocate of the wilderness. On the other side was Marsden Manson, a conservationist but also San Francisco's City Engineer and a supporter of the building of the dam. The following essay by John Muir appeared in a publication sent to members of the Sierra Club, a group dedicated to wilderness preservation. How does his essay reflect the nature of his audience?

1   It is impossible to overestimate the value of wild mountains and mountain temples as places for people to grow in, recreation grounds for soul and

body. They are the greatest of our natural resources, God's best gifts, but none, however high and holy, is beyond reach of the spoiler. In these ravaging money-mad days monopolizing San Francisco capitalists are now doing their best to destroy the Yosemite Park, the most wonderful of all our great mountain national parks. Beginning on the Tuolumne side, they are trying with a lot of sinful ingenuity to get the Government's permission to dam and destroy the Hetch-Hetchy Valley for a reservoir, simply that comparatively private gain may be made out of universal public loss, while of course the Sierra Club is doing all it can to save the valley. The Honorable Secretary of the Interior has not yet announced his decision in the case, but in all that has come and gone nothing discouraging is yet in sight on our side of the fight.

2   As long as the busy public in general knew little or nothing about the Hetch-Hetchy Valley, the few cunning drivers of the damming scheme, working in darkness like moles in a low-lying meadow, seemed confident of success; but when light was turned on and the truth became manifest that next to Yosemite, Hetch-Hetchy is the most wonderful and most important feature of the great park, that damming it would destroy it, render it inaccessible, and block the way through the wonderful Tuolumne Cañon to the grand central campground in the upper Tuolumne Valley, thousands from near and far came to our help—mountaineers, nature-lovers, naturalists. Most of our thousand club members wrote to the President or Secretary protesting against the destructive reservoir scheme while other sources of city water as pure or purer than the Hetch-Hetchy were available; so also did the Oregon and Washington mountaineering clubs and the Appalachian of Boston and public-spirited citizens everywhere. And the President, recognizing the need of beauty as well as bread and water in the life of the nation, far from favoring the destruction of any of our country's natural wonder parks and temples, is trying amid a host of other cares to save them all. Within a very short time he has saved the petrified forests of Arizona and the Grand Cañon, and in our own State the jagged peaks of San Benito county known as "The Pinnacles," making them national monuments or parks to be preserved for the people forever. None, therefore, need doubt that everything possible will be done to save Hetch-Hetchy.

3   After my first visit, in the autumn of 1871, I have always called it the Tuolumne Yosemite, for it is a wonderfully exact counterpart of the great Yosemite, not only in its crystal river and sublime rocks and waterfalls, but in the gardens, groves, and meadows of its flowery park-like floor. The floor of Yosemite is about 4,000 feet above the sea, the Hetch-Hetchy floor about 3,700; the walls of both are of gray granite, rise abruptly out of the flowery grass and groves, are sculptured in the same style, and in both every rock is a glacial monument.

4   Standing boldly out from the south wall is a strikingly picturesque rock called "Kolana" by the Indians, the outermost of a group 2,300 feet high corresponding with the Cathedral Rocks of Yosemite both in relative position

and form. On the opposite side of the valley facing Kolana there is a counterpart of the El Capitan of Yosemite rising sheer and plain to a height of 1,800 feet, and over its massive brow flows a stream which makes the most graceful fall I have ever seen. From the edge of the cliff it is perfectly free in the air for a thousand feet, then breaks up into a ragged sheet of cascades among the boulders of an earthquake talus. It is in all its glory in June, when the snow is melting fast, but fades and vanishes toward the end of summer. The only fall I know with which it may fairly be compared is the Yosemite Bridal Veil; but it excels even that favorite fall both in height and fineness of fairy airy beauty and behavior. Lowlanders are apt to suppose that mountain streams in their wild career over cliffs lose control of themselves and tumble in a noisy chaos of mist and spray. On the contrary, on no part of their travels are they more harmonious and self-controlled. Imagine yourself in Hetch-Hetchy on a sunny day in June, standing waist-deep in grass and flowers (as I have oftentimes stood), while the great pines sway dreamily with scarce perceptible motion. Looking northward across the valley you see a plain gray granite cliff rising abruptly out of the gardens and groves to a height of 1,800 feet, and in front of it Tueeulala's silvery scarf burning with irised sunfire in every fiber. In the first white outburst of the stream at the head of the fall there is abundance of visible energy, but it is speedily hushed and concealed in divine repose; and its tranquil progress to the base of the cliff is like that of downy feathers in a still room. Now observe the fineness and marvelous distinctness of the various sun-illumined fabrics into which the water is woven: they sift and float from form to form down the face of that grand gray rock in so leisurely and unconfused a manner that you can examine their texture, and patterns, and tones of color as you would a piece of embroidery held in the hand. Near the head of the fall you see groups of booming comet-like masses, their solid white heads separate, their tails like combed silk interlacing among delicate shadows, ever forming and dissolving, worn out by friction in their rush through the air. Most of these vanish a few hundred feet below the summit, changing to the varied forms of cloudlike drapery. Near the bottom the width of the fall has increased from about twenty-five to a hundred feet. Here it is composed of yet finer tissues, and is still without a trace of disorder—air, water, and sunlight woven into stuff that spirits might wear.

5   So fine a fall might well seem sufficient to glorify any valley; but here as in Yosemite Nature seems in no wise moderate, for a short distance to the eastward of Tueeulala booms and thunders the great Hetch-Hetchy fall, Wapama, so near that you have both of them in full view from the same standpoint. It is the counterpart of the Yosemite Fall, but has a much greater volume of water, is about 1,700 feet in height, and appears to be nearly vertical though considerably inclined, and is dashed into huge outbounding bosses of foam on the projecting shelves and knobs of its jagged gorge. No two falls could be more unlike—Tueeulala out in the open sunshine descend-

ing like thistledown; Wapama in a jagged shadowy gorge roaring and thundering, pounding its way with the weight and energy of an avalanche. Besides this glorious pair there is a broad massive fall on the main river a short distance above the head of the valley. Its position is something like that of the Vernal in Yosemite, and its roar as it plunges into a surging trout-pool may be heard a long way, though it is only about twenty feet high. There is also a chain of magnificent cascades at the head of the valley on a stream that comes in from the northeast, mostly silvery plumes, like the one between the Vernal and Nevada falls of Yosemite, half-sliding, half-leaping on bare glacier-polished granite, covered with crisp clashing spray into which the sunbeams pour with glorious effect. And besides all these a few small streams come over the walls here and there, leaping from ledge to ledge with birdlike song and watering many a hidden cliff-garden and fernery, but they are too unshowy to be noticed in so grand a place.

6   The correspondence between the Hetch-Hetchy walls in their trends, sculpture, physical structure, and general arrangement of the main rockmasses has excited the wondering admiration of every observer. We have seen that the El Capitan and Cathedral Rocks occupy the same relative position in both valleys, so also do their Yosemite Points and North Domes. Again that part of Yosemite Falls has two horizontal benches timbered with the Yosemite north wall immediately to the east of the gold-cup oak at about 500 and 1,500 feet above the floor. Two benches similarly situated and timbered occur on the same relative portion of the Hetch-Hetchy north wall, to the east of Wapama Fall, and on no other. The Yosemite is bounded at the head by the great Half Dome. Hetch-Hetchy is bounded in the same way, though its head rock is far less wonderful and sublime in form.

7   The floor of the valley is about three and a half miles long and from a fourth to half a mile wide. The lower portion is mostly a level meadow about a mile long with the trees restricted to the sides, and partially separated from the upper forested portion by a low bar of glacier-polished granite, across which the river breaks in rapids.

8   The principal trees are the yellow and sugar pines, Sabine pine, incense cedar, Douglas spruce, silver fir, the California and gold-cup oaks, Balm of Gilead poplar, Nuttall's flowering dogwood, alder, maple, laurel, tumion, etc. The most abundant and influential are the great yellow pines, the tallest over 200 feet in height, and the oaks with massive rugged trunks four to six or seven feet in diameter, and broad arching heads, assembled in magnificent groves. The shrubs forming conspicuous flowery clumps and tangles are manzanita, azalea, spiræa, brier-rose, ceanothus, calycanthus, philadelphus, wild cherry, etc.; with abundance of showy and fragrant herbaceous plants growing about them, or out in the open in beds by themselves—lilies, Mariposa tulips, brodiæas, orchids—several species of each,—iris, spraguea, draperia, collomia, collinsia, castilleia, nemophila, larkspur, columbine, gold-

enrods, sunflowers, and mints of many species, honeysuckle, etc., etc. Many fine ferns dwell here, also; especially the beautiful and interesting rock-ferns,—pellæa, and cheilanthes of several species,—fringing and resetting dry rock-piles and ledges; woodwardia and asplenium on damp spots with fronds six or seven feet high, the delicate maidenhair in mossy nooks by the falls, and the sturdy broad-shouldered pteris beneath the oaks and pines.

9   It appears therefore that Hetch-Hetchy Valley, far from being a plain common rockbound meadow, as many who have not seen it seem to suppose, is a grand landscape garden, one of Nature's rarest and most precious mountain mansions. As in Yosemite, the sublime rocks of its walls seem to the nature-lover to glow with life, whether leaning back in repose or standing erect in thoughtful attitudes giving welcome to storms and calms alike. And how softly these mountain rocks are adorned, and how fine and reassuring the company they keep—their brows in the sky, their feet set in groves and gay emerald meadows, a thousand flowers leaning confidingly against their adamantine bosses, while birds, bees, and butterflies help the river and waterfalls to stir all the air into music—things frail and fleeting and types of permanence meeting here and blending, as if into this glorious mountain temple Nature had gathered her choicest treasures, whether great or small, to draw her lovers into close confiding communion with her.

10   Strange to say, this is the mountain temple that is now in danger of being dammed and made into a reservoir to help supply San Francisco with water and light. This use of the valley, so destructive and foreign to its proper park use, has long been planned and prayed for, and is still being prayed for by the San Francisco board of supervisors, not because water as pure and abundant cannot be got from adjacent sources outside the park,—for it can,—but seemingly only because of the comparative cheapness of the dam required.

11   Garden- and park-making goes on everywhere with civilization, for everybody needs beauty as well as bread, places to play in and pray in, where Nature may heal and cheer and give strength to body and soul. This natural beauty-hunger is displayed in poor folks' window-gardens made up of a few geranium slips in broken cups, as well as in the costly lily gardens of the rich, the thousands of spacious city parks and botanical gardens, and in our magnificent National Parks,—the Yellowstone, Yosemite, Sequoia, etc.,—Nature's own wonderlands, the admiration and joy of the world. Nevertheless, like everything else worth while, however sacred and precious and well-guarded, they have always been subject to attack, mostly by despoiling gain-seekers,—mischief-makers of every degree from Satan to supervisors, lumbermen, cattlemen, farmers, etc., eagerly trying to make everything dollarable, often thinly disguised in smiling philanthropy, calling pocket-filling plunder "Utilization of beneficent natural resources, that man and beast may be fed and the dear Nation grow great." Thus long ago a lot of enterprising merchants made part of the Jerusalem temple into a place of business instead of a place of

prayer, changing money, buying and selling cattle and sheep and doves. And earlier still the Lord's garden in Eden, and the first forest reservation, including only one tree, was spoiled. And so to some extent have all our reservations and parks. Ever since the establishment of the Yosemite National Park by act of Congress, October 8, 1890, constant strife has been going on around its borders, and I suppose will go on as part of the universal battle between right and wrong, however its boundaries may be shorn or wild beauty destroyed. The first application to the Government by the San Francisco supervisors for the use of Lake Eleanor and the Hetch-Hetchy Valley was made in 1903, and denied December 22d of that year by the Secretary of the Interior. In his report on this case he well says: "Presumably the Yosemite National Park was created such by law because of the natural objects, of varying degrees of scenic importance, located within its boundaries, inclusive alike of its beautiful small lakes, like Eleanor, and its majestic wonders, like Hetch-Hetchy and Yosemite Valley. It is the aggregation of such natural scenic features that makes the Yosemite Park a wonderland which the Congress of the United States sought by law to preserve for all coming time as nearly as practicable in the condition fashioned by the hand of the Creator—a worthy object of national pride and a source of healthful pleasure and rest for the thousands of people who may annually sojourn there during the heated months."

12   The most delightful and wonderful campgrounds in the park are the three great valleys—Yosemite, Hetch-Hetchy, and Upper Tuolumne; and they are also the most important places with reference to their positions relative to the other great features—the Merced and Tuolumne Cañons, and the High Sierra peaks and glaciers, etc., at the head of the rivers. The main part of the Tuolumne Valley is a beautiful spacious flowery lawn four or five miles long, surrounded by magnificent snowy mountains. It is about 8,500 feet above the sea, and forms the grand central High Sierra campground from which excursions are made to the noble mountains, domes, glaciers, etc.; across the range to the Mono Lake and volcanoes; and down the Tuolumne Cañon to Hetch-Hetchy. But should Hetch-Hetchy be submerged, as proposed, not only would it be made utterly inaccessible, but the sublime cañon way to the heart of the High Sierra would be hopelessly blocked. None, as far as I have learned, of all the thousands who have seen the park is in favor of this destructive water scheme.

13   My last visit to the valley was made in the autumn of last year, with William Keith, the artist. The leaf-colors were then ripe, and the great god-like rocks in repose seemed to glow with life. The artist, under their spell, wandered day after day along the beautiful river and through the groves and gardens, studying the wonderful scenery; and, after making about forty sketches, declared with enthusiasm that in picturesque beauty and charm Hetch-Hetchy surpassed even Yosemite.

¹⁴   That any one would try to destroy such a place seemed impossible, but sad experience shows that there are people good enough and bad enough for anything. The proponents of the dam scheme bring forward a lot of bad arguments to prove that the only righteous thing for Hetch-Hetchy is its destruction. These arguments are curiously like those of the devil devised for the destruction of the first garden—so much of the very best Eden fruit going to waste, so much of the best Tuolumne water. Very few of their statements are even partly true, and all are misleading. Thus, Hetch-Hetchy, they say, is "a low-lying meadow."

¹⁵   On the contrary, it is a high-lying natural landscape garden.

¹⁶   "It is a common minor feature, like thousands of others."

¹⁷   On the contrary, it is a very uncommon feature, after Yosemite, the rarest and in many ways the most important in the park.

¹⁸   "Damming and submerging it 175 feet deep would enhance its beauty by forming a crystal-clear lake."

¹⁹   Landscape gardens, places of recreation and worship, are never made beautiful by destroying and burying them. The beautiful lake forsooth would be only an eyesore, a dismal blot on the landscape, like many others to be seen in the Sierra. For, instead of keeping it at the same level all the year, allowing Nature to make new shores, it would of course be full only a month or two in the spring, when the snow is melting fast; then it would be gradually drained, exposing the slimy sides of the basin and shallower parts of the bottom, with the gathered drift and waste, death and decay, of the upper basins, caught here instead of being swept on to decent natural burial along the banks of the river or in the sea. Thus the Hetch-Hetchy dam-lake would be only a rough imitation of a natural lake for a few of the spring months; an open mountain sepulcher the others.

²⁰   "Hetch-Hetchy water is the purest, wholly unpolluted, and forever unpollutable."

²¹   On the contrary, excepting that of the Merced below Yosemite, it is less pure than that of most of the other Sierra streams, because of the sewerage of campgrounds draining into it, especially of the Big Tuolumne Meadows campgrounds, where hundreds of tourists and mountaineers, with their animals, are encamped for months every summer, soon to be followed by thousands of travelers from all the world.

²²   These temple destroyers, devotees of ravaging commercialism, seem to have a perfect contempt for Nature, and instead of lifting their eyes to the mountains, lift them to dams and town skyscrapers.

²³   Dam Hetch-Hetchy! As well dam for water-tanks the people's cathedrals and churches, for no holier temple has ever been consecrated by the heart of man.

1908

Marsden Manson

A STATEMENT OF SAN FRANCISCO'S SIDE OF THE HETCH-HETCHY RESERVOIR MATTER

Marsden Manson's piece is a direct response: he knows that his audience has heard John Muir's side of the argument. How does this affect Manson's argument? What does the fact that Muir lost (the dam was built) tell you about the attitudes and beliefs of the day? The Secretary of the Interior suggested in 1986 that the Hetch-Hetchy debate be reopened; he thought perhaps the dam should be destroyed and the valley returned to its natural state. The mayor of San Francisco, generally a liberal-minded supporter of environmental issues, objected that San Francisco needed the power supplied by the dam. How would you adapt the arguments of Muir and Manson to appeal to a modern audience?

To the Members of the Sierra Club:

1   There has been sent out a ballot for an election on the Hetch-Hetchy question, to be held on Saturday, January 29, 1910. This ballot presents two questions apparently worded to draw out a vote for or against the use of the Hetch-Hetchy Valley as a reservoir. Both of these propositions are speciously arranged, and neither presents the question in its true light.

> *Proposition 1:* "I desire that the Hetch-Hetchy Valley shall remain intact and unaltered as a part of the Yosemite National Park and oppose its use as a reservoir for a water supply for San Francisco, unless an impartial federal commission shall determine that it is absolutely necessary for such use."

2   The facts regarding this proposition are that San Francisco made an application under the law of February 15, 1901, for the use of this reservoir space for the storage of water for domestic purposes. Such use is pointed out by the U. S. Geological Survey in the 21st Annual Report, Part IV, pages 450–453. This survey was conducted during the years 1897–99, specifically making an estimate of the volumes of water possible to store in this reservoir and of the character of the dam and work necessary for its utilization as such. Congress, acting upon the results of this work, formally made it possible to file upon this and other reservoirs in Yosemite National Park, and other parks and reservations; and *under this formal dedication to public uses of the reservoir spaces within the Yosemite National Park, and other parks and reservations* named in the law of February, 1901, made it possible for individuals, corporations and municipalities to utilize the natural resources originating in these

parks, which resources had been previously prohibited by the provisions of the law of October 1, 1890, defining the limits and setting aside the Yosemite Reservation.

3   Lying within the floor of this reservoir are comparatively level lands, some 800 to 900 acres, of which *San Francisco owns in fee simple 720 acres under patent issued prior to the Act of October 1, 1890.* The area of the water surface when raised to about 150 feet above the level of the lower end of the Valley is about 1200 acres, which embraces quite a considerable area of gravelly and rocky soil at the upper end of the valley and the sloping sides thereof up to the level above named. The application made by San Francisco in 1901 for this permit was denied by the then Secretary of the Interior, and again denied upon a rehearing, the denial being based upon the ground that he was not authorized to make such grant. He used as the basis of his action the prior law of October, 1890, and refused to recognize the modifying effects of the subsequent law of February 15, 1901. Upon the reference of this question to the Attorney-General of the United States, the Acting Attorney-General, Judge Purdy, decided that full authority rested in the Secretary of the Interior under the law of February 15, 1901, and the then Secretary, Mr. Garfield, ultimately made the grant for the use of the remaining lands in the Hetch-Hetchy Reservoir site on May 11, 1908.

4   The question submitted under Proposition 1 on the ballot is therefore misleading in the extreme, and is not one that under any plea of either law or equity that can be referred to a so-called "impartial federal commission." It is misleading again in the fact that this commission is to determine that the use as a reservoir "is absolutely necessary."

5   By reference to the grant of May, 1908, under Stipulation No. 3, it will be observed that Lake Eleanor must first be developed to its full capacity before the development of Hetch-Hetchy shall be begun, which shall be undertaken only when the City and County of San Francisco, and adjacent cities, may require such further development. It is manifest, therefore, that the calling into effect of an "impartial federal commission" to determine what has already been determined is not making a just and equitable presentation to the members of the Sierra Club of the question at issue.

> *Proposition 2:* "I favor the use of Hetch-Hetchy Valley as a reservoir for a future water supply for San Francisco and I favor a present dedication by Congress of the right to such use without further investigation."

6   From the preceding discussion and statement of the facts, it will be seen that San Francisco already holds the right, under the laws of Congress as interpreted by the Attorney-General of the United States and administered by its executive officers, to use that portion of the floor of this valley which remains in the park for a reservoir after having developed Lake Eleanor to its full capacity and upon finding *that the additional supply is necessary.* So far

as the laws of Congress can make this dedication, and so far as a conservative and just administrative officer of the government can guard public interests, this dedication has already been made by Congress, accepted by the people of the city under the terms imposed by the executive branch of the government, and no dedication of Congress whatever is needed, nor is asked for.

7   It is manifest from the above simple recital of the facts with reference to the laws and the actions taken thereunder, that neither of the propositions submitted on the ballot for the election of January 29, 1910, are fairly and equitably stated. This is made still more manifest by the re-issuance by Mr. John Muir, under date of November, 1909, of a pamphlet of some twenty odd pages of garbled quotations and specious statements protesting against the "unnecessary destruction of Hetch-Hetchy Valley." In this it is made to appear on page 3 that the Sierra Club of California formally joins in the protest against the alleged "unnecessary destruction of Hetch-Hetchy Valley." It is claimed by the undersigned that no destruction of the Valley is contemplated even in the remote future, when the use of this valley as a water supply for the homes of the cities about the bay shall become imperative. A reference to the pictures upon the latter pages of this pamphlet will make this perfectly manifest. There are nine of these pictures, and they will be referred to in order of their occurrence in the pamphlet, the pages on which they are printed not being numbered.

8   The first picture presents a very beautiful view of a portion of the valley opposite the falls known as Wapama. The highest level of the proposed reservoir will not reach the base of these falls. Therefore but little of the base of the granite sides of the valley will be flooded. The floor to be covered is owned in fee simple by San Francisco to the extent heretofore named, or about 720 acres. All of the floor of the valley within the limits of this picture is so owned.

9   In picture No. 2 the same remarks are true. Neither of the falls will be affected in any way.

10   Picture No. 3, the same is true.

11   In picture No. 4 it may be observed that San Francisco again owns the greater portion or all of the floor of the valley within sight, and that the great granite mass of Kolana will be flooded at its base by the highest dam about 10 per cent of its height.

12   Of pictures Nos. 5 and 6, no features will be affected except the floor of the valley, which again in these pictures embraces areas owned by San Francisco. The falls shown in these two pictures will not be affected in the least.

13   Pictures 7 and 8 represent landscapes in that portion of the valley owned by San Francisco. The general view given in No. 9 will be covered up to a point some fifty feet below the lowest portion of the ledge on the left side of the picture.

14   This pamphlet is devoted principally to three arguments: First, *that the flooding of the valley floor will destroy the scenic beauty of the Hetch-Hetchy.* The most striking natural features about the valley are all above the highest level to which it is proposed a quarter of a century or more hence to raise the level of the water. The cliffs rise to a height of more than 2500 feet above the valley floor, and as the reservoir will not in any case be more than 275 to 300 feet deep the apparent decrease in the height of the walls will not be perceptible to the eye of the ordinary observer. All of these peaks and cliffs, with their varied markings and color, will remain as now, and will be reflected in the waters of the lake, as are the cliffs surrounding the other lakes in the Sierras. Both of the falls strike the slopes of the bluffs above the level of the highest reservoir surface, and will therefore be in no way altered. The lake which will be formed in the valley by the construction of the dam will be as beautiful as the other lakes which add charm to the landscapes of the Sierras. The floor of the valley owned by San Francisco in its greater portion and for the highest purposes for which it can be used, will be flooded, and this substitution of a lake for the trees and meadows is the measure of the alleged "unnecessary destruction of the Hetch-Hetchy Valley."

15   It is also true that for about two months in the year the floor of this valley is a "paradise for campers," but it must be remembered that the greater portion of this paradise is owned by San Francisco for the exclusive purpose of making the homes of tens of thousands of families that will never have the opportunity of visiting this "paradise for campers" a source of health and happiness, by introducing into those homes the greatest element of health, namely, the purest water from the most available source.

16   Secondly: *That the use of the reservoir will make it necessary to exclude the public from the 480 square miles of watershed above it.*

17   It is not true that the flooding of the valley will shut out visitors from the watershed tributary thereto, for this region is not reasonably accessible for only about three and a half months, during which time the same precautions now taken in Yosemite Valley itself will be ample for many decades, and probably centuries, to keep Tuolumne Meadows clean. Even when these simple precautions shall prove inadequate, no such drastic steps as are proposed in this pamphlet, namely, the shutting out of the public from the watershed, will be necessary, as may be seen by referring to the views of an eminent authority in sanitary engineering, Prof. C. D. Marx, who, on page 341 of the Transactions of the Commonwealth Club, of November 1909, reviews and gives definite proof that there will be absolutely no necessity for in any way restricting the use of the drainage area, and that the simple precautionary measures which are deemed sufficient to protect the supplies of Boston and other cities would be sufficient, and that if the supply shall be suspected of contamination modern methods will remedy this at very small cost and without the drastic measures urged by the opponents to the use of this reservoir.

[18] The character of the watershed above the Hetch-Hetchy is such that it is absurd to suppose that it will be necessary to shut out travel from it. This travel reaches it only in the late summer and early autumn, when dangerous germs are exposed, if upon the surface, to the glaring sun of California skies, one hour of which is fatal to any known pathogenic germ; later to the severe frosts of October, and then to the snows from November to June, and finally to the oxidizing influences in the twenty miles of foaming torrents between the meadows and Hetch-Hetchy, and to the further influences of long storage in the reservoir. When even these great natural safeguards have been overcome as pointed out by Prof. Marx, very simple remedial measures can then be applied.

[19] Thirdly: *That there are many other sources from which San Francisco can draw its water supply, thirteen of them being named.*

[20] The statements that other sources of supply are open to the city as alleged on pages 4, 5 and 6 of Mr. Muir's pamphlet do not present the facts as they stand at present. None of the supplies named on these pages is comparable in availability, abundance, nor purity. Moreover, the pleadings that San Francisco be turned over to the tender mercies of the individuals and corporations owning all of the other Sierra supplies are specious and misleading in the extreme and serve only as a screen behind which the avariciousness and selfishness of corporate greed can be used against the interests of San Francisco and the Bay municipalities. All of these sources have been fully considered, and rejected, by the engineers employed by San Francisco, and this rejection concurred in by Secretary Garfield, who points out in his very able review of the matter that it is not for him, for Congress, nor other authority to determine for San Francisco what source she should select, and it ill becomes the members of the Sierra Club to put themselves in a position in which, whether intending it or not, they are the mere screen for the selfishness of corporations and those who hold "rights to water and power" which have been secured without opposition from those who so earnestly and persistently opposed San Francisco's rights. It is suggested that the city take water from one of these companies after it has been used in their power stations. It is well known that at this elevation it cannot flow by gravity to San Francisco, and will require pumping, and that to pump this to the elevations required for delivery in San Francisco will ultimately require a yearly expenditure of $1,000,000, or a capital investment of about $25,000,000, and the plea that San Francisco accept or acquire these supplies without the necessary power to pump it over the Coast Range and to the higher elevations of the city will play into the hands of the great electrical power monopoly to the extent above named. No wonder, therefore, that if the existing monopoly of these water and power companies be appealed to to furnish funds to oppose San Francisco in the acquisition of rights, which will furnish the water as well as pump it to the homes of the city, that they would be inclined to generously contribute.

21   Mr. John D. Galloway, an able engineer and member of the American Society of Civil Engineers, with a thorough acquaintance with the entire field, and after going into detail over the various possible sources, says, in the Transactions of the Commonwealth Club above referred to, "As a matter of fact, the development of long distance transmission of electric power started first in California, and there is not now a single large river within two hundred miles of San Francisco except the Tuolumne and the Merced which has not one or more electric power plants upon it. Without the Hetch-Hetchy supply the city will indeed be at a loss as to where to go."

22   The Commonwealth Club of California, an organization formed of broad-minded citizens who take up and have presented to them both sides of the great civic problems which are brought before them, took up the question of this Hetch-Hetchy supply at its meetings of September and November, 1909. At the meeting of the latter month the "Society for the Preservation of National Parks" put the following question: "If you decide that a National Park shall be the last resort, then you must require a complete and thorough showing that no other like utility is reasonably available." To which the Club replied that it was not necessarily the first or the last resort in a municipality in need of water, and "In such a case as that of Hetch-Hetchy it should be shown that no other like utility is available under reasonable conditions of engineering, extinguishment of adverse claims, cost, etc. The city of San Francisco has fulfilled this requirement to the satisfaction of eminent engineers in and out of the city's employment, and to that of Secretary Garfield. Your committee is unwilling to pass upon the statements of those who believe that the city's investigations of other sources have not been sufficiently exhaustive. But, as the Federal authorities have, after examining the data presented by the city's engineers, approved the conclusions of the San Francisco authorities, it would seem only just that those who assert that other sources are available under reasonable conditions should set forth with equal detail the facts on which they base their opinions."

23   It is manifest, therefore, that the statements made in this pamphlet are only apparently substantiated by the garbled quotations presented therein, and are not in reality based upon true and correct facts, but upon a partisan presentation of selected and misleading quotations to which the city's representative is forced to take this means of refuting. These garbled quotations are grossly misleading, in that they are separated out and arranged to masquerade as the unqualified opinions of those from whom they are quoted, when in many instances the opinions are the exact opposite of the impression which this pamphlet undertakes to scatter broadcast.

24   As showing the trend of the best minds in San Francisco, for which we think the Commonwealth Club can fairly be said to stand, it may be noted that the Club, after sending a committee to visit the Hetch-Hetchy and make its report (the report was a most elaborate and careful document), and after

devoting two evenings to a discussion of the subject, at which Mr. George Edwards, of the Society for the Preservation of National Parks, and Mr. E. T. Parsons, one of the Directors of the Sierra Club, addressed the Club, by a vote of eight to one endorsed the proposition of the immediate development of the Hetch-Hetchy water supply for San Francisco.

25   The City and County of San Francisco must provide for a supply in the future of at least two hundred million gallons a day. Its present plans include the acquisition of the local supply, which can economically be developed to forty million gallons a day; the building of a reservoir at Lake Eleanor, which can develop a supply of sixty million gallons a day, possibly a supply of one hundred and twenty million gallons a day, which will carry the city along for a period of thirty or forty years' development. When these sources have reached their ultimate development, it is then planned to develop the Hetch-Hetchy supply. By this development it will be a generation or longer before the Hetch-Hetchy supply will be touched. The beauties of this Valley will therefore, under this arrangement, be preserved to the present generation and perhaps to the one that follows it. Should the privileges be taken away from the city, we may well doubt whether such a source of water and power as is presented by the Hetch-Hetchy proposition can be saved for an equal length of time from acquisition by private corporations, which would use them for their own instead of the public use.

26   We therefore urge that the efforts of San Francisco to acquire and use this source of water for the highest purpose to which water can be devoted should receive the support of the members of the Sierra Club.

27   The actual reservoir areas to which this grant by Secretary Garfield applies are by no means the entire areas of the reservoirs: In the first one to be developed, Lake Eleanor, all the very desirable meadow lands are privately owned, and San Francisco is acquiring these. The remainder, *less than a square mile at the highest development, is in the Park, and constitutes less than one twelve-hundredth (1/1200) part of the Park area.*

28   In the second one to be developed, Hetch-Hetchy, San Francisco owns 720 acres, and the *grant of reservoir rights of way again applies to less than a square mile, or to another one twelve-hundredth (1/1200) part of the Park.*

29   THE GRANT THEREFORE ONLY APPLIES TO LESS THAN ONE SIX-HUNDREDTH (1/600) PART OF THE PARK area, and to the use of this small fraction in conjunction with the greater areas owned by the city, for the highest purpose for which they can ever be used, the Sierra Club is asked to protest in the face of a use made available and possible by Congress in the law of February 15, 1901, granted in accordance with this law and accepted by San Francisco by a vote of over six to one.

30   You are therefore respectfully requested and urged to vote in favor of Proposition No. 2, with the mental reservation that you do not advocate a dedication by Congress of the right to such use without further investigation, for the reason that so far as Congressional action is concerned, such dedication was made by the Act of February 15, 1901, after due and careful consid-

eration of all the facts by a Scientific Bureau of our country, and that this supply was open to San Francisco, and if denied must inevitably be put to use for some of the great necessities of the human race, and probably through the instrumentality of some selfish corporation.

1909

Edward Abbey

THE DAMNATION OF A CANYON

John Muir's pamphlet on the Hetch-Hetchy was made before the damming, and his intention was clearly to move his audience to prevent it from being built. This argument by Edward Abbey also concerns the damage to the environment that occurs when a natural river is altered by a dam. But in this case the dam has already been built. How then would you describe Abbey's intention toward his audience? Does Abbey respond to any of the points raised by Manson about the needs of city dwellers? (Abbey's Glen Canyon was dammed to create water power.) How does Abbey's use of the three appeals compare to Muir's? The difference in Abbey's ethos is striking: imagine Muir announcing early on that, yes, he is a "butterfly chaser, googly eyed bleeding heart and wild conservative," as Abbey does in paragraph 5. Is Abbey more honest or just angrier?

1   There was a time when, in my search for essences, I concluded that the canyonland country has no heart. I was wrong. The canyonland did have a heart, a living heart, and that heart was Glen Canyon and the golden, flowing Colorado River.

2   In the summer of 1959 a friend and I made a float trip in little rubber rafts down through the length of Glen Canyon, starting at Hite and getting off the river near Gunsight Butte—The Crossing of the Fathers. In this voyage of some 150 miles and ten days our only motive power, and all that we needed, was the current of the Colorado River.

3   In the summer and fall of 1967 I worked as a seasonal park ranger at the new Glen Canyon National Recreation Area. During my five-month tour of duty I worked at the main marina and headquarters area called Wahweap, at Bullfrog Basin toward the upper end of the reservoir, and finally at Lee's Ferry downriver from Glen Canyon Dam. In a number of powerboat tours I was privileged to see almost all of our nation's newest, biggest and most impressive "recreational facility."

4   Having thus seen Glen Canyon both before and after what we may fairly call its damnation, I feel that I am in a position to evaluate the transformation

of the region caused by construction of the dam. I have had the unique opportunity to observe firsthand some of the differences between the environment of a free river and a power-plant reservoir.

5   One should admit at the outset to a certain bias. Indeed I am a "butterfly chaser, googly eyed bleeding heart and wild conservative." I take a dim view of dams; I find it hard to learn to love cement; I am poorly impressed by concrete aggregates and statistics in the cubic tons. But in this weakness I am not alone, for I belong to that ever-growing number of Americans, probably a good majority now, who have become aware that a fully industrialized, thoroughly urbanized, elegantly computerized social system is not suitable for human habitation. Great for machines, yes. But unfit for people.

6   Lake Powell, formed by Glen Canyon Dam, is not a lake. It is a reservoir, with a constantly fluctuating water level—more like a bathtub that is never drained than a true lake. As at Hoover (or Boulder) Dam, the sole practical function of this impounded water is to drive the turbines that generate electricity in the powerhouse at the base of the dam. Recreational benefits were of secondary importance in the minds of those who conceived and built this dam. As a result the volume of water in the reservoir is continually being increased or decreased according to the requirements of the Basin States Compact and the power-grid system of which Glen Canyon Dam is a component.

7   The rising and falling water level entails various consequences. One of the most obvious, well known to all who have seen Lake Mead, is the "bathtub ring" left on the canyon walls after each drawdown of water, or what rangers at Glen Canyon call the Bathtub Formation. This phenomenon is perhaps of no more than aesthetic importance; yet it is sufficient to dispel any illusion one might have, in contemplating the scene, that you are looking upon a natural lake.

8   Of much more significance is the fact that plant life, because of the unstable water line, cannot establish itself on the shores of the reservoir. When the water is low, plant life dies of thirst; when high, it is drowned. Much of the shoreline of the reservoir consists of near-perpendicular sandstone bluffs, where very little flora ever did or ever could subsist, but the remainder includes bays, coves, sloping hills and the many side canyons, where the original plant life has been drowned and new plant life cannot get a foothold. And of course where there is little or no plant life there is little or no animal life.

9   The utter barrenness of the reservoir shoreline recalls by contrast the aspect of things before the dam, when Glen Canyon formed the course of the untamed Colorado. Then we had a wild and flowing river lined by boulder-strewn shores, sandy beaches, thickets of tamarisk and willow, and glades of cottonwoods.

10   The thickets teemed with songbirds: vireos, warblers, mockingbirds and thrushes. On the open beaches were killdeer, sandpipers, herons, ibises, egrets. Living in grottoes in the canyon walls were swallows, swifts, hawks,

wrens and owls. Beaver were common if not abundant: not an evening would pass, in drifting down the river, that we did not see them or at least hear the whack of their flat tails on the water. Above the river shores were the great recessed alcoves where water seeped from the sandstone, nourishing the semitropical hanging gardens of orchid, ivy and columbine, with their associated swarms of insects and birdlife.

11   Up most of the side canyons, before damnation, there were springs, sometimes flowing streams, waterfalls and plunge pools—the kind of marvels you can now find only in such small-scale remnants of Glen Canyon as the Escalante area. In the rich flora of these laterals the larger mammals—mule deer, coyote, bobcat, ring-tailed cat, gray fox, kit fox, skunk, badger and others—found a home. When the river was damned almost all of these things were lost. Crowded out—or drowned and buried under mud.

12   The difference between the present reservoir, with its silent sterile shores and debris-choked side canyons, and the original Glen Canyon, is the difference between death and life. Glen Canyon was alive. Lake Powell is a graveyard.

13   For those who may think I exaggerate the contrast between the former river canyon and the present man-made impoundment, I suggest a trip on Lake Powell followed immediately by another boat trip on the river below the dam. Take a boat from Lee's Ferry up the river to within sight of the dam, then shut off the motor and allow yourself the rare delight of a quiet, effortless, drifting down the stream. In that twelve-mile stretch of living green, singing birds, flowing water and untarnished canyon walls—sights and sounds a million years older and infinitely lovelier than the roar of motorboats—you will rediscover a small and imperfect sampling of the kind of experience that was taken away from everybody when the oligarchs and politicians condemned our river for purposes of their own.

14   The effects of Glen Canyon Dam also extend downstream, causing changes in the character and ecology of Marble Gorge and Grand Canyon. Because the annual spring floods are now a thing of the past, the shores are becoming overgrown with brush, the rapids are getting worse where the river no longer has enough force to carry away the boulders washed down from the lateral canyons, and the beaches are disappearing, losing sand that is not replaced.

15   Lake Powell, though not a lake, may well be as its defenders assert the most beautiful reservoir in the world. Certainly it has a photogenic backdrop of buttes and mesas projecting above the expansive surface of stagnant waters where the speedboats, houseboats and cabin cruisers ply: But it is no longer a wilderness. It is no longer a place of natural life. It is no longer Glen Canyon.

16   The defenders of the dam argue that the recreational benefits available on the surface of the reservoir outweigh the loss of Indian ruins, historical sites, wildlife and wilderness adventure. Relying on the familiar quantitative logic

of business and bureaucracy, they assert that whereas only a few thousand citizens ever ventured down the river through Glen Canyon, now millions can—or will—enjoy the motorized boating and hatchery fishing available on the reservoir. They will also argue that the rising waters behind the dam have made such places as Rainbow Bridge accessible by powerboat. Formerly you could get there only by walking (six miles).

[17]   This argument appeals to the wheelchair ethos of the wealthy, upper-middle-class American slob. If Rainbow Bridge is worth seeing at all, then by God it should be easily, readily, immediately available to everybody with the money to buy a big powerboat. Why should a trip to such a place be the privilege only of those who are willing to walk six miles? Or if Pikes Peak is worth getting to, then why not build a highway to the top of it so that anyone can get there? Anytime? Without effort? Or as my old man would say, "By Christ, one man's just as good as another—if not a damn sight better."

[18]   Or as ex-Commissioner Floyd Dominy of the U. S. Bureau of Reclamation pointed out poetically in his handsomely engraved and illustrated brochure *Lake Powell: Jewel of the Colorado* (produced by the U. S. Government Printing Office at our expense): "There's something about a lake which brings us a little closer to God." In this case, Lake Powell, about five hundred feet closer. Eh, Floyd?

[19]   It is quite true that the flooding of Glen Canyon has opened up to the motorboat explorer parts of side canyons that formerly could be reached only by people able to walk. But the sum total of terrain visible to the eye and touchable by hand and foot has been greatly diminished, not increased. Because of the dam the river is gone, the inner canyon is gone, the best parts of the numerous side canyons are gone—all hidden beneath hundreds of feet of polluted water, accumulating silt, and mounting tons of trash. This portion of Glen Canyon—and who can estimate how many cubic miles were lost?—*is no longer accessible to anybody.* (Except scuba divers.) And this, do not forget, was the most valuable part of Glen Canyon, richest in scenery, archaeology, history, flora and fauna.

[20]   Not only has the heart of Glen Canyon been buried, but many of the side canyons above the fluctuating waterline are now rendered more difficult, not easier, to get into. This because the debris brought down into them by desert storms, no longer carried away by the river, must unavoidably build up in the area where flood meets reservoir. Narrow Canyon, for example, at the head of the impounded waters, is already beginning to silt up and to amass huge quantities of driftwood, some of it floating on the surface, some of it half afloat beneath the surface. Anyone who has tried to pilot a motorboat through a raft of half-sunken logs and bloated dead cows will have his own thoughts on the accessibility of these waters.

[21]   Hite Marina, at the mouth of Narrow Canyon, will probably have to be abandoned within twenty or thirty years. After that it will be the turn of Bull-

frog Marina. And then Rainbow Bridge Marina. And eventually, inevitably, whether it takes ten centuries or only one, Wahweap. Lake Powell, like Lake Mead, is foredoomed sooner or later to become a solid mass of mud, and its dam a waterfall. Assuming, of course, that either one stands that long.

22   Second, the question of costs. It is often stated that the dam and its reservoir have opened up to the many what was formerly restricted to the few, implying in this case that what was once expensive has now been made cheap. Exactly the opposite is true.

23   Before the dam, a float trip down the river through Glen Canyon would cost you a minimum of seven days' time, well within anyone's vacation allotment, and a capital outlay of about forty dollars—the prevailing price of a two-man rubber boat with oars, available at any army-navy surplus store. A life jacket might be useful but not required, for there were no dangerous rapids in the 150 miles of Glen Canyon. As the name implies, this stretch of the river was in fact so easy and gentle that the trip could be and was made by all sorts of amateurs: by Boy Scouts, Camp Fire Girls, stenographers, schoolteachers, students, little old ladies in inner tubes. Guides, professional boatmen, giant pontoons, outboard motors, radios, rescue equipment were not needed. The Glen Canyon float trip was an adventure anyone could enjoy, on his own, for a cost less than that of spending two days and nights in a Page motel. Even food was there, in the water: the channel catfish were easier to catch and a lot better eating than the striped bass and rainbow trout dumped by the ton into the reservoir these days. And one other thing: at the end of the float trip you still owned your boat, usable for many more such casual and carefree expeditions.

24   What is the situation now? Float trips are no longer possible. The only way left for the exploration of the reservoir and what remains of Glen Canyon demands the use of a powerboat. Here you have three options: (1) buy your own boat and engine, the necessary auxiliary equipment, the fuel to keep it moving, the parts and repairs to keep it running, the permits and licenses required for legal operation, the trailer to transport it; (2) rent a boat; or (3) go on a commercial excursion boat, packed in with other sightseers, following a preplanned itinerary. This kind of play is only for the affluent.

25   The inescapable conclusion is that no matter how one attempts to calculate the cost in dollars and cents, a float trip down Glen Canyon was much cheaper than a powerboat tour of the reservoir. Being less expensive, as well as safer and easier, the float trip was an adventure open to far more people than will ever be able to afford motorboat excursions in the area now.

26   What about the "human impact" of motorized use of the Glen Canyon impoundment? We can visualize the floor of the reservoir gradually accumulating not only silt, mud, waterlogged trees and drowned cattle but also the usual debris that is left behind when the urban, industrial style of recreation is carried into the open country. There is also the problem of human wastes. The waters of the wild river were good to drink, but nobody in his senses

would drink from Lake Powell. Eventually, as is already sometimes the case at Lake Mead, the stagnant waters will become too foul even for swimming. The trouble is that while some boats have what are called "self-contained" heads, the majority do not; most sewage is disposed of by simply pumping it into the water. It will take a while, but long before it becomes a solid mass of mud Lake Powell ("Jewel of the Colorado") will enjoy a passing fame as the biggest sewage lagoon in the American Southwest. Most tourists will never be able to afford a boat trip on this reservoir but everybody within fifty miles will be able to smell it.

27   All of the foregoing would be nothing but a futile exercise in nostalgia (so much water over the dam) if I had nothing constructive and concrete to offer. But I do. As alternate methods of power generation are developed, such as solar, and as the nation establishes a way of life adapted to actual resources and basic needs, so that the demand for electrical power begins to diminish, we can shut down the Glen Canyon power plant, open the diversion tunnels, and drain the reservoir.

28   This will no doubt expose a drear and hideous scene: immense mud flats and whole plateaus of sodden garbage strewn with dead trees, sunken boats, the skeletons of long-forgotten, decomposing water-skiers. But to those who find the prospect too appalling, I say give nature a little time. In five years, at most in ten, the sun and wind and storms will cleanse and sterilize the repellent mess. The inevitable floods will soon remove all that does not belong within the canyons. Fresh green willow, box elder and redbud will reappear, and the ancient drowned cottonwoods (noble monuments to themselves) will be replaced by young of their own kind. With the renewal of plant life will come the insects, the birds, the lizards and snakes, the mammals. Within a generation—thirty years—I predict the river and canyons will bear a decent resemblance to their former selves. Within the lifetime of our children Glen Canyon and the living river, heart of the Canyonlands, will be restored to us. The wilderness will again belong to God, the people and the wild things that call it home.

1984

Henry David Thoreau

WHERE I LIVED, AND WHAT I LIVED FOR

This essay from Walden *chronicles Thoreau's famous experiment, his decision to leave the society of his town, Concord, Massachusetts, to live very sim-*

ply in a rustic cabin on Walden Pond. Thoreau's essay is now well over a century and a half old. Does it still have something to contribute to our modern debate on environmental issues? What, in Thoreau's opinion, does the natural world have to offer us, in addition to beauty? What do you think of Thoreau's ethos? Would you say that you are in the audience for his argument? If so, is it persuasive? If not, how would it have to change to include you? Where is Thoreau's audience when his essay begins, and where does he hope to move them? A discussion of Thoreau's audience might focus on his statement that his intention is "to brag as lustily as chanticleer in the morning, standing on his roost, if only to wake my neighbors up." What does he mean? What parts of the essay best illustrate that intention?

1   At a certain season of our life we are accustomed to consider every spot as the possible site of a house. I have thus surveyed the country on every side within a dozen miles of where I live. In imagination I have bought all the farms in succession, for all were to be bought, and I knew their price. I walked over each farmer's premises, tasted his wild apples, discoursed on husbandry with him, took his farm at his price, at any price, mortgaging it to him in my mind; even put a higher price on it,—took every thing but a deed of it,—took his word for his deed, for I dearly love to talk,—cultivated it, and him too to some extent, I trust, and withdrew when I had enjoyed it long enough, leaving him to carry it on. This experience entitled me to be regarded as a sort of real-estate broker by my friends. Wherever I sat, there I might live, and the landscape radiated from me accordingly. What is a house but a *sedes*, a seat?—better if a country seat. I discovered many a site for a house not likely to be soon improved, which some might have thought too far from the village, but to my eyes the village was too far from it. Well, there I might live, I said; and there I did live, for an hour, a summer and a winter life; saw how I could let the years run off, buffet the winter through, and see the spring come in. The future inhabitants of this region, wherever they may place their houses, may be sure that they have been anticipated. An afternoon sufficed to lay out the land into orchard, woodlot, and pasture, and to decide what fine oaks or pines should be left to stand before the door, and whence each blasted tree could be seen to the best advantage; and then I let it lie, fallow perchance, for a man is rich in proportion to the number of things which he can afford to let alone.

2   My imagination carried me so far that I even had the refusal of several farms,—the refusal was all I wanted,—but I never got my fingers burned by actual possession. The nearest that I came to actual possession was when I bought the Hollowell place, and had begun to sort my seeds, and collected materials with which to make a wheelbarrow to carry it on or off with; but before the owner gave me a deed of it, his wife—every man has such a wife— changed her mind and wished to keep it, and he offered me ten dollars to

release him. Now, to speak the truth, I had but ten cents in the world, and it surpassed my arithmetic to tell, if I was that man who had ten cents, or who had a farm, or ten dollars, or all together. However, I let him keep the ten dollars and the farm too, for I had carried it far enough; or rather, to be generous, I sold him the farm for just what I gave for it, and, as he was not a rich man, made him a present of ten dollars, and still had my ten cents, and seeds, and materials for a wheelbarrow left. I found thus that I had been a rich man without any damage to my poverty. But I retained the landscape, and I have since annually carried off what it yielded without a wheelbarrow. With respect to landscapes,—

> I am monarch of all I *survey,*
> My right there is none to dispute.

3   I have frequently seen a poet withdraw, having enjoyed the most valuable part of a farm, while the crusty farmer supposed that he had got a few wild apples only. Why, the owner does not know it for many years when a poet has put his farm in rhyme, the most admirable kind of invisible fence, has fairly impounded it, milked it, skimmed it, and got all the cream, and left the farmer only the skimmed milk.

4   The real attractions of the Hollowell farm, to me, were; its complete retirement, being about two miles from the village, half a mile from the nearest neighbor, and separated from the highway by a broad field; its bounding on the river, which the owner said protected it by its fogs from frosts in the spring, though that was nothing to me; the gray color and ruinous state of the house and barn, and the dilapidated fences, which put such an interval between me and the last occupant; the hollow and lichen-covered apple trees, gnawed by rabbits, showing what kind of neighbors I should have; but above all, the recollection I had of it from my earliest voyages up the river, when the house was concealed behind a dense grove of red maples, through which I heard the house-dog bark. I was in haste to buy it, before the proprietor finished getting out some rocks, cutting down the hollow apple trees, and grubbing up some young birches which had all sprung up in the pasture, or, in short, had made any more of his improvements. To enjoy these advantages I was ready to carry it on; like Atlas, to take the world on my shoulders,—I never heard what compensation he received for that,—and do all those things which had no other motive or excuse but that I might pay for it and be unmolested in my possession of it; for I knew all the while that it would yield the most abundant crop of the kind I wanted if I could only afford to let it alone. But it turned out as I have said.

5   All that I could say, then, with respect to farming on a large scale (I have always cultivated a garden), was, that I had had my seeds ready. Many think that seeds improve with age. I have no doubt that time discriminates between the good and the bad; and when at last I shall plant, I shall be less likely to be

disappointed. But I would say to my fellows, once for all, as long as possible live free and uncommitted. It makes but little difference whether you are committed to a farm or the county jail.

6   Old Cato, whose "De Re Rusticâ" is my "Cultivator," says, and the only translation I have seen makes sheer nonsense of the passage, "When you think of getting a farm, turn it thus in your mind, not to buy greedily; nor spare your pains to look at it, and do not think it enough to go round it once. The oftener you go there the more it will please you, if it is good." I think I shall not buy greedily, but go round and round it as long as I live, and be buried in it first, that it may please me the more at last.

7   The present was my next experiment of this kind, which I purpose to describe more at length; for convenience, putting the experience of two years into one. As I have said, I do not propose to write an ode to dejection, but to brag as lustily as chanticleer in the morning, standing on his roost, if only to wake my neighbors up.

8   When first I took up my abode in the woods, that is, began to spend my nights as well as days there, which, by accident, was on Independence day, or the fourth of July, 1845, my house was not finished for winter, but was merely a defence against the rain, without plastering or chimney, the walls being of rough weather-stained boards, with wide chinks, which made it cool at night. The upright white hewn studs and freshly planed door and window castings gave it a clean and airy look, especially in the morning, when its timbers were saturated with dew, so that I fancied that by noon some sweet gum would exude from them. To my imagination it retained throughout the day more or less of this auroral character, reminding me of a certain house on a mountain which I had visited the year before. This was an airy and unplastered cabin, fit to entertain a travelling god, and where a goddess might trail her garments. The winds which passed over my dwelling were such as sweep over the ridges of mountains, bearing the broken strains, or celestial parts only, of terrestrial music. The morning wind forever blows, the poem of creation is uninterrupted; but few are the ears that hear it. Olympus is but the outside of the earth every where.

9   The only house I had been the owner of before, if I except a boat, was a tent, which I used occasionally when making excursions in the summer, and this is still rolled up in my garret; but the boat, after passing from hand to hand, has gone down the stream of time. With this more substantial shelter about me, I had made some progress toward settling in the world. This frame, so slightly clad, was a sort of crystallization around me, and reacted on the builder. It was suggestive somewhat as a picture in outlines. I did not need to go out doors to take the air, for the atmosphere within had lost none of its freshness. It was not so much within doors as behind a door where I sat, even in the rainiest weather. The Harivansa says, "An abode without birds is like

a meat without seasoning." Such was not my abode, for I found myself suddenly neighbor to the birds; not by having imprisoned one, but having caged myself near them. I was not only nearer to some of those which commonly frequent the garden and the orchard, but to those wilder and more thrilling songsters of the forest which never, or rarely, serenade a villager,—the woodthrush, the veery, the scarlet tanager, the field-sparrow, the whippoor-will, and many others.

10   I was seated by the shore of a small pond, about a mile and a half south of the village of Concord and somewhat higher than it, in the midst of an extensive wood between that town and Lincoln, and about two miles south of that our only field known to fame, Concord Battle Ground; but I was so low in the woods that the opposite shore, half a mile off, like the rest, covered with wood, was my most distant horizon. For the first week, whenever I looked out on the pond it impressed me like a tarn high up on the side of a mountain, its bottom far above the surface of other lakes, and, as the sun arose, I saw it throwing off its nightly clothing of mist, and here and there, by degrees, its soft ripples or its smooth reflecting surface was revealed, while the mists, like ghosts, were stealthily withdrawing in every direction into the woods, as at the breaking up of some nocturnal conventicle. The very dew seemed to hang upon the trees later into the day than usual, as on the sides of mountains.

11   This small lake was of most value as a neighbor in the intervals of a gentle rain storm in August, when, both air and water being perfectly still, but the sky overcast, mid-afternoon had all the serenity of evening, and the woodthrush sang around, and was heard from shore to shore. A lake like this is never smoother than at such a time; and the clear portion of the air above it being shallow and darkened by clouds, the water, full of light and reflections, becomes a lower heaven itself so much the more important. From a hill top near by, where the wood had been recently cut off, there was a pleasing vista southward across the pond, through a wide indentation in the hills which form the shore there, where their opposite sides sloping toward each other suggested a stream flowing out in that direction through a wooded valley, but stream there was none. That way I looked between and over the near green hills to some distant and higher ones in the horizon, tinged with blue. Indeed, by standing on tiptoe I could catch a glimpse of some of the peaks of the still bluer and more distant mountain ranges in the north-west, those true-blue coins from heaven's own mint, and also of some portion of the village. But in other directions, even from this point, I could not see over or beyond the woods which surrounded me. It is well to have some water in your neighborhood, to give buoyancy to and float the earth. One value even of the smallest well is, that when you look into it you see that earth is not continent but insular. This is as important as that it keeps butter cool. When I looked across the pond from this peak toward the Sudbury meadows, which

in time of flood I distinguished elevated perhaps by a mirage in their seething valley, like a coin in a basin, all the earth beyond the pond appeared like a thin crust insulated and floated even by this small sheet of intervening water, and I was reminded that this on which I dwelt was but *dry land.*

12   Though the view from my door was still more contracted, I did not feel crowded or confined in the least. There was pasture enough for my imagination. The low shrub-oak plateau to which the opposite shore arose, stretched away toward the prairies of the West and the steppes of Tartary, affording ample room for all the roving families of men. "There are none happy in the world but beings who enjoy freely a vast horizon,"—said Damodara, when his herds required new and larger pastures.

13   Both place and time were changed, and I dwelt nearer to those parts of the universe and to those eras in history which had most attracted me. Where I lived was as far off as many a region viewed nightly by astronomers. We are wont to imagine rare and delectable places in some remote and more celestial corner of the system, behind the constellation of Cassiopeia's Chair, far from noise and disturbance. I discovered that my house actually had its site in such a withdrawn, but forever new and unprofaned, part of the universe. If it were worth the while to settle in those parts near to the Pleiades or the Hyades, to Aldebaran or Altair, then I was really there, or at an equal remoteness from the life which I had left behind, dwindled and twinkling with as fine a ray to my nearest neighbor, and to be seen only in moonless nights by him. Such was that part of creation where I had squatted;—

> There was a shepherd that did live
>   And held his thoughts as high
> As were the mounts whereon his flocks
>   Did hourly feed him by.

What should we think of the shepherd's life if his flocks always wandered to higher pastures than his thoughts?

14   Every morning was a cheerful invitation to make my life of equal simplicity, and I may say innocence, with Nature herself. I have been as sincere a worshipper of Aurora as the Greeks. I got up early and bathed in the pond; that was a religious exercise, and one of the best things which I did. They say that characters were engraven on the bathing tub of king Tching-thang to this effect: "Renew thyself completely each day; do it again, and again, and forever again." I can understand that. Morning brings back the heroic ages. I was as much affected by the faint hum of a mosquito making its invisible and unimaginable tour through my apartment at earliest dawn, when I was sitting with door and windows open, as I could be by any trumpet that ever sang of fame. It was Homer's requiem; itself an Iliad and Odyssey in the air, singing its own wrath and wanderings. There was something cosmical about it; a standing advertisement, till forbidden, of the everlasting vigor and fer-

tility of the world. The morning, which is the most memorable season of the day, is the awakening hour. Then there is least somnolence in us; and for an hour, at least, some part of us awakes which slumbers all the rest of the day and night. Little is to be expected of that day, if it can be called a day, to which we are not awakened by our Genius, but by the mechanical nudgings of some servitor, are not awakened by our own newly-acquired force and aspirations from within, accompanied by the undulations of celestial music, instead of factory bells, and a fragrance filling the air—to a higher life than we fell asleep from; and thus the darkness bear its fruit, and prove itself to be good, no less than the light. That man who does not believe that each day contains an earlier, more sacred, and auroral hour than he has yet profaned, has despaired of life, and is pursuing a descending and darkening way. After a partial cessation of his sensuous life, the soul of man, or its organs rather, are reinvigorated each day, and his Genius tries again what noble life it can make. All memorable events, I should say, transpire in morning time and in a morning atmosphere. The Vedas say, "All intelligences awake with the morning." Poetry and art, and the fairest and most memorable of the actions of men, date from such an hour. All poets and heroes, like Memnon, are the children of Aurora, and emit their music at sunrise. To him whose elastic and vigorous thought keeps pace with the sun, the day is a perpetual morning. It matters not what the clocks say or the attitudes and labors of men. Morning is when I am awake and there is a dawn in me. Moral reform is the effort to throw off sleep. Why is it that men give so poor an account of their day if they have not been slumbering? They are not such poor calculators. If they had not been overcome with drowsiness they would have performed something. The millions are awake enough for physical labor; but only one in a million is awake enough for effective intellectual exertion, only one in a hundred millions to a poetic or divine life. To be awake is to be alive. I have never yet met a man who was quite awake. How could I have looked him in the face?

15   We must learn to reawaken and keep ourselves awake, not by mechanical aids, but by an infinite expectation of the dawn, which does not forsake us in our soundest sleep. I know of no more encouraging fact than the unquestionable ability of man to elevate his life by a conscious endeavor. It is something to be able to paint a particular picture, or to carve a statue, and so to make a few objects beautiful; but it is far more glorious to carve and paint the very atmosphere and medium through which we look, which morally we can do. To affect the quality of the day, that is the highest of arts. Every man is tasked to make his life, even in its details, worthy of the contemplation of his most elevated and critical hour. If we refused, or rather used up, such paltry information as we get, the oracles would distinctly inform us how this might be done.

16   I went to the woods because I wished to live deliberately, to front only the essential facts of life, and see if I could not learn what it had to teach, and not,

when I came to die, discover that I had not lived. I did not wish to live what was not life, living is so dear; nor did I wish to practice resignation, unless it was quite necessary. I wanted to live deep and suck out all the marrow of life, to live so sturdily and Spartan-like as to put to rout all that was not life, to cut a broad swath and shave close, to drive life into a corner, and reduce it to its lowest terms, and, if it proved to be mean, why then to get the whole and genuine meanness of it, and publish its meanness to the world; or if it were sublime, to know it by experience, and be able to give a true account of it in my next excursion. For most men, it appears to me, are in a strange uncertainty about it, whether it is of the devil or of God, and have *somewhat hastily* concluded that it is the chief end of man here to "glorify God and enjoy him forever."

17   Still we live meanly, like ants; though the fable tells us that we were long ago changed into men; like pygmies we fight with cranes; it is error upon error, and clout upon clout, and our best virtue has for its occasion a superfluous and evitable wretchedness. Our life is frittered away by detail. An honest man has hardly need to count more than his ten fingers, or in extreme cases he may add his ten toes, and lump the rest. Simplicity, simplicity, simplicity! I say, let your affairs be as two or three, and not a hundred or a thousand; instead of a million count half a dozen, and keep your accounts on your thumb nail. In the midst of this chopping sea of civilized life, such are the clouds and storms and quicksands and thousand-and-one items to be allowed for, that a man has to live, if he would not founder and go to the bottom and not make his port at all, by dead reckoning, and he must be a great calculator indeed who succeeds. Simplify, simplify. Instead of three meals a day, if it be necessary eat but one; instead of a hundred dishes, five; and reduce other things in proportion. Our life is like a German Confederacy, made up of petty states, with its boundary forever fluctuating, so that even a German cannot tell you how it is bounded at any moment. The nation itself, with all its so called internal improvements, which, by the way, are all external and superficial, is just such an unwieldy and overgrown establishment, cluttered with furniture and tripped up by its own traps, ruined by luxury and heedless expense, by want of calculation and a worthy aim, as the million households in the land; and the only cure for it as for them is in a rigid economy, a stern and more than Spartan simplicity of life and elevation of purpose. It lives too fast. Men think that it is essential that the *Nation* have commerce, and export ice, and talk through a telegraph, and ride thirty miles an hour, without a doubt, whether *they* do or not; but whether we should live like baboons or like men, is a little uncertain. If we do not get out sleepers, and forge rails, and devote days and nights to the work, but go to tinkering upon our *lives* to improve *them*, who will build railroads? And if railroads are not built, how shall we get to heaven in season? But if we stay at home and mind our business, who will want railroads? We do not ride on the railroad;

it rides upon us. Did you ever think what those sleepers are that underlie the railroad? Each one is a man, an Irishman, or a Yankee man. The rails are laid on them, and they are covered with sand, and the cars run smoothly over them. They are sound sleepers, I assure you. And every few years a new lot is laid down and run over; so that, if some have the pleasure of riding on a rail, others have the misfortune to be ridden upon. And when they run over a man that is walking in his sleep, a supernumerary sleeper in the wrong position, and wake him up, they suddenly stop the cars, and make a hue and cry about it, as if this were an exception. I am glad to know that it takes a gang of men for every five miles to keep the sleepers down and level in their beds as it is, for this is a sign that they may sometime get up again.

18   Why should we live with such hurry and waste of life? We are determined to be starved before we are hungry. Men say that a stitch in time saves nine, and so they take a thousand stitches today to save nine to-morrow. As for *work*, we haven't any of any consequence. We have the Saint Vitus' dance, and cannot possibly keep our heads still. If I should only give a few pulls at the parish bellrope, as for a fire, that is, without setting the bell, there is hardly a man on his farm in the outskirts of Concord, notwithstanding that press of engagements which was his excuse so many times this morning, nor a boy, nor a woman, I might almost say, but would forsake all and follow that sound, not mainly to save property from the flames, but, if we will confess the truth, much more to see it burn, since burn it must, and we, be it known, did not set it on fire,—or to see it put out, and have a hand in it, if that is done as handsomely; yes, even if it were the parish church itself. Hardly a man takes a half hour's nap after dinner, but when he wakes he holds up his head and asks, "What's the news?" as if the rest of mankind had stood his sentinels. Some give directions to be waked every half hour, doubtless for no other purpose; and then, to pay for it, they tell what they have dreamed. After a night's sleep the news is as indispensable as the breakfast. "Pray tell me any thing new that has happened to a man any where on this globe,"—and he reads it over his coffee and rolls, that a man has had his eyes gouged out this morning on the Wachito River; never dreaming the while that he lives in the dark unfathomed mammoth cave of this world, and has but the rudiment of an eye himself.

19   For my part, I could easily do without the post-office. I think that there are very few important communications made through it. To speak critically, I never received more than one or two letters in my life—I wrote this some years ago—that were worth the postage. The penny-post is, commonly, an institution through which you seriously offer a man that penny for his thoughts which is so often safely offered in jest. And I am sure that I never read any memorable news in a newspaper. If we read of one man robbed, or murdered, or killed by accident, or one house burned, or one vessel wrecked, or one steamboat blown up, or one cow run over on the Western Railroad, or

one mad dog killed, or one lot of grasshoppers in the winter,—we never need read of another. One is enough. If you are acquainted with the principle, what do you care for a myriad instances and applications? To a philosopher all *news*, as it is called, is gossip, and they who edit and read it are old women over their tea. Yet not a few are greedy after this gossip. There was such a rush, as I hear, the other day at one of the offices to learn the foreign news by the last arrival, that several large squares of plate glass belonging to the establishment were broken by the pressure,—news which I seriously think a ready wit might write a twelvemonth or twelve years beforehand with sufficient accuracy. As for Spain, for instance, if you know how to throw in Don Carlos and the Infanta, and Don Pedro and Seville and Granada, from time to time in the right proportions,—they may have changed the names a little since I saw the papers,—and serve up a bull-fight when other entertainments fail, it will be true to the letter, and give us as good an idea of the exact state or ruin of things in Spain as the most succinct and lucid reports under this head in the newspapers: and as for England, almost the last significant scrap of news from that quarter was the revolution of 1649; and if you have learned the history of her crops for an average year, you never need attend to that thing again, unless your speculations are of a merely pecuniary character. If one may judge who rarely looks into the newspapers, nothing new does ever happen in foreign parts, a French revolution not excepted.

20   What news! how much more important to know what that is which was never old! "Kieou-he-yu (great dignitary of the state of Wei) sent a man to Khoung-tseu to know his news. Khoung-tseu caused the messenger to be seated near him, and questioned him in these terms: What is your master doing? The messenger answered with respect: My master desires to diminish the number of his faults, but he cannot accomplish it. The messenger being gone, the philosopher remarked: What a worthy messenger! What a worthy messenger!" The preacher, instead of vexing the ears of drowsy farmers on their day of rest at the end of the week,—for Sunday is the fit conclusion of an ill-spent week, and not the fresh and brave beginning of a new one,—with this one other draggletail of a sermon, should shout with thundering voice, "Pause! Avast! Why so seeming fast, but deadly slow?"

21   Shams and delusions are esteemed for soundest truths, while reality is fabulous. If men would steadily observe realities only, and not allow themselves to be deluded, life, to compare it with such things as we know, would be like a fairy tale and the Arabian Nights' Entertainments. If we respected only what is inevitable and has a right to be, music and poetry would resound along the streets. When we are unhurried and wise, we perceive that only great and worthy things have any permanent and absolute existence,—that petty fears and petty pleasures are but the shadow of the reality. This is always exhilarating and sublime. By closing the eyes and slumbering, and consenting to be deceived by shows, men establish and confirm their daily

life of routine and habit every where, which still is built on purely illusory foundations. Children, who play life, discern its true law and relations more clearly than men, who fail to live it worthily, but who think that they are wiser by experience, that is, by failure. I have read in a Hindoo book, that "there was a king's son, who, being expelled in infancy from his native city, was brought up by a forester, and, growing up to maturity in that state, imagined himself to belong to the barbarous race with which he lived. One of his father's ministers having discovered him, revealed to him what he was, and the misconception of his character was removed, and he knew himself to be a prince. So soul," continues the Hindoo philosopher, "from the circumstances in which it is placed, mistakes its own character, until the truth is revealed to it by some holy teacher, and then it knows itself to be *Brahme*." I perceive that we inhabitants of New England live this mean life that we do because our vision does not penetrate the surface of things. We think that that *is* which *appears* to be. If a man should walk through this town and see only the reality, where, think you, would the "Milldam" go to? If he should give us an account of the realities he beheld there, we should not recognize the place in his description. Look at a meeting-house, or a court-house, or a jail, or a shop, or a dwelling-house, and say what that thing really is before a true gaze, and they would all go to pieces in your account of them. Men esteem truth remote, in the outskirts of the system, behind the farthest star, before Adam and after the last man. In eternity there is indeed something true and sublime. But all these times and places and occasions are now and here. God himself culminates in the present moment, and will never be more divine in the lapse of all the ages. And we are enabled to apprehend at all what is sublime and noble only by the perpetual instilling and drenching of the reality that surrounds us. The universe constantly and obediently answers to our conceptions; whether we travel fast or slow, the track is laid for us. Let us spend our lives in conceiving then. The poet or the artist never yet had so fair and noble a design but some of his posterity at least could accomplish it.

[22]   Let us spend one day as deliberately as Nature, and not be thrown off the track by every nutshell and mosquito's wing that falls on the rails. Let us rise early and fast, or break fast, gently and without perturbation; let company come and let company go, let the bells ring and the children cry,—determined to make a day of it. Why should we knock under and go with the stream? Let us not be upset and overwhelmed in that terrible rapid and whirlpool called a dinner, situated in the meridian shallows. Weather this danger and you are safe, for the rest of the way is down hill. With unrelaxed nerves, with morning vigor, sail by it, looking another way, tied to the mast like Ulysses. If the engine whistles, let it whistle till it is hoarse for its pains. If the bell rings, why should we run? We will consider what kind of music they are like. Let us settle ourselves, and work and wedge our feet downward through the mud and

slush of opinion, and prejudice, and tradition, and delusion, and appearance, that alluvion which covers the globe, through Paris and London, through New York and Boston and Concord, through church and state, through poetry and philosophy and religion, till we come to a hard bottom and rocks in place, which we can call *reality*, and say, This is, and no mistake; and then begin, having a *point d'appui*, below freshet and frost and fire, a place where you might found a wall or a state, or set a lamppost safely, or perhaps a gauge, not a Nilometer, but a Realometer, that future ages might know how deep a freshet of shams and appearances had gathered from time to time. If you stand right fronting and face to face to a fact, you will see the sun glimmer on both its surfaces, as if it were a cimeter, and feel its sweet edge dividing you through the heart and marrow, and so you will happily conclude your mortal career. Be it life or death, we crave only reality. If we are really dying, let us hear the rattle in our throats and feel cold in the extremities; if we are alive, let us go about our business.

23   Time is but the stream I go a-fishing in. I drink at it; but while I drink I see the sandy bottom and detect how shallow it is. Its thin current slides away, but eternity remains. I would drink deeper; fish in the sky, whose bottom is pebbly with stars. I cannot count one. I know not the first letter of the alphabet. I have always been regretting that I was not as wise as the day I was born. The intellect is a cleaver; it discerns and rifts its way into the secret of things. I do not wish to be any more busy with my hands than is necessary. My head is hands and feet. I feel all my best faculties concentrated in it. My instinct tells me that my head is an organ for burrowing, as some creatures use their snout and fore-paws, and with it I would mine and burrow my way through these hills. I think that the richest vein is somewhere hereabouts; so by the divining rod and thin rising vapors I judge; and here I will begin to mine.

1854

Brigid Brophy

THE MENACE OF NATURE

Brophy wrote this essay in the mid-1960s, when the environmentalist movement was attracting a great deal of attention. As you will see, she challenges the beliefs held by Muir, Thoreau, and Abbey. What does her method of approach tell you about her audience? Her intention? Are you within her audience? Is her essay persuasive? How might Muir, Thoreau, or Abbey respond?

1   So? Are you just back? Or are you, perhaps, staying on there for the extra week? By "there" I mean, of course, one of the few spots left where the machine has not yet gained the upper hand; some place as yet unstrangled by motorways and unfouled by concrete mixers; a place where the human spirit can still—but for how much longer?—steep itself in natural beauty and recuperate after the nervous tension, the sheer stress, of modern living.

2   Well (I assume you're *enough* recuperated to stand this information?): I think you've been piously subscribing to a heresy. It's a heresy I incline off-hand to trace, with an almost personally piqued sense of vendetta, to the old heresiarch himself, the sometimes great, often bathetic but never cogently thoughtful poet, William Wordsworth. Since the day he let the seeds of heresy fall (on, no doubt, the Braes of the Yarrow or the Banks of Nith), the thing has spread and enlarged itself into one of the great parroted, meaningless (but slightly paranoid) untruths of our age.

3   *I am not trying to abolish the countryside.* (I *state* this because it is true; I emphasise it because I don't want the lynch mob outside my window.) I'm not such a pig as to want the country built on or littered up with bottles and plastic bags merely because it doesn't appeal to *me.* As it happens, my own taste for countryside, though small, is existent. I've found the country very pleasant to be driven through in a tolerably fast car by someone whose driving I trust and whose company I like. But I admit that landscape as such bores me—to the extent that I have noticed myself in picture galleries automatically pausing to look at "Landscape with Ruins" or "Bandits in a Landscape" but walking straight past the pure landscapes at a speed which is obviously trying to simulate the effect of being driven past in a car.

4   I'm not, however, out to dissuade *you* from spending your holiday as a sort of legalised bandit in the landscape. Neither am I antiholiday. Holidays have been sniped at lately as things everyone feels an obligation to enjoy but no one really does. Yet I suspect there would be fewer dissatisfied holiday-makers if social pressure didn't try to limit our choice to "Landscape" or "Landscape with Seascape." You can be made to feel quite guiltily antisocial in the summer months if you are, like me, constitutionally unable either to relax or to take a suntan. Indeed, relaxation is becoming this decade's social *sine qua non,* like Bridge in the 'thirties. They'll scarcely let you have a *baby* these days if you can't satisfy them beforehand you're adept at relaxing. But on the in some ways more private question of having a holiday, constitutional urbanites are still free, if only they can resist being shamed onto the beaches, to opt out of a rest and settle for the change which even the proverb allows to be as good as it. By simply exchanging their own for a foreign city, they are released from the routine of earning their daily bread and washing up after it, but don't suffer the disorientation, the uncorseted discomfort, which over-takes an urbanite cast up on a beach with no timetable to live by except the tides.

5   Still, it isn't in the holidays but during the rest of the year that the great rural heresy does its damage. How many, for example, of the middle-class parents who bring up their children in London do so with unease or even apology, with a feeling that they are selfishly depriving the children of some "natural heritage" and sullying their childhood with urban impurities? Some parents even let this guilt drive them out to the suburbs or further, where they believe they cancel the egocentricity of their own need or desire for the town by undergoing the martyrdom of commuting. This parental masochism may secure the child a rural heritage (though parents should enquire, before moving, whether their child has the rural temperament and *wants* the rural heritage) but it deprives him of the cultural one; he gains the tennis club but is condemned to the tennis club light-opera society's amateur production of *No, No, Nanette* because the trains don't run late enough to bring him home after Sadler's Wells.

6   The notion that "nature" and "nature study" are somehow "nice" for children, regardless of the children's own temperament, is a sentimental piety—and often a hypocritical one, like the piety which thinks Sunday School nice for *them* though we don't go to church ourselves. (In fact, it is we middle-aged who may need fresh air and exercise; the young are cat-like enough to remain lithe without.) Historically, it is not inept to trace the supposed affinity between children and "nature" to Wordsworth's time. It was about that time that there settled on England, like a drizzle, the belief that sex is *not* "nice" for children. Children's sexual curiosity was diverted to "the birds and the bees" and gooseberry bushes; and birds, bees and bushes—in other words, "nature"—have remained "suitable" for children ever since.

7   If the romantic belief in children's innocence is now exploded, its numinous energy has only gone to strengthen the even more absurd romantic belief in the innocence of landscape's, as opposed to man-created, beauty. But I reject utterly the imputation that a brook is purer than Bach or a breeze more innocent than *As You Like It*. I warn you I shall be suspicious of this aesthetic faculty of yours that renders you so susceptible to the beauty of Snowdon if it leaves you unable to see anything in All Souls', Langham Place; and I shall be downright sceptical of it if (I am making allowance for your sensibility to run exclusively in that landscape groove which mine leaves out) you doat on the Constable country but feel it vaguely impure to take a 74 to the V. & A. to see a Constable.

8   You'll protest you feel no such impurity. Yet didn't you read the first paragraph of this article without taking so much as a raised eyebrow's worth of exception? Didn't you let the assumption pass that the city is corrupt? Weren't you prepared to accept from me, as you have from a hundred august authorities—sociologists, physicians, psychologists—that *idée reçue* about the nervous tension and stress of modern urban life? But what in heaven's name is this stressful modern urban life being compared with? Life in a medieval

hamlet? Will no one take into account the symptoms into which the stress of *that* erupted—the epidemics of dancing madness and flagellation frenzy? Or life in a neolithic cave—whose stress one can only imagine and flinch at?

9   The truth is that the city is a device for *reducing* stress—by giving humans a freer choice of escapes from the pressure (along with the weather) of their environment. The device doesn't always work perfectly: traffic jams *are* annoying; the motor car does maim and must be prevented from doing so: but the ambulance which arrives so mercifully quick is also powered by a motor. The city is one of the great indispensable devices of civilisation (itself only a device for centralising beauty and transmitting it as a heritage). It is one of the cardinal simple brilliant inventions, like currency. Like currency, it is a medium of exchange and thereby of choice—whereas the country is a place where one is under the thumb of chance, constrained to love one's neighbour not out of philanthropy but because there's no other company.

10   What's more, in the eighteenth century the city was suddenly upgraded from a device of civilisation to a manifestation of it. The city became an art form. (The form had been discovered, but not very consciously remarked, earlier. It was discovered, like many art forms, by accident—often, as at Venice and Bruges, an accident of water.) We are in dire danger now of clogging up our cities as devices and at the same time despoiling them as works of art; and one of the biggest villains in this process is our rural heresy.

11   Most western European beings have to live in cities, and all but the tiny portion of them who are temperamental rustics would do so contentedly, without wasting energy in guilt, and with an appreciative eye for the architecturescapes round them, had they not been told that liking the country is purer and more spiritual. Our cities run to squalor and our machines run amok because our citizens' minds are not on the job of mastering the machines and using them to make the cities efficient and beautiful. Their eyes are blind to the Chirico-esque handsomeness of the M1, because their hearts are set on a rustic Never-Never Land. Rustic sentimentality makes us build our suburban villas to mimic cottages, and then pebble-dash their outside walls in pious memory of the holiday we spent sitting agonised on the shingle. The lovely terraced facades of London are being undermined, as by subsidence, by our yearning, our sickly nostalgia, for a communal country childhood that never existed. We neglect our towns for a fantasy of going "back" to the land, back to our "natural" state. But there isn't and never was a natural man. We are a species that doesn't occur wild. No pattern in his genes instructs man on what pattern to build his nest. Instead, if he's fortunate, the Muses whisper to him the ground-plan of an architectural folly. Even in his cave, he frescoed the walls. All that is infallibly natural to our species is to make things that are artificial. We are *homo artifex, homo faber, homo Fabergé.* Yet we are so ignorant of our own human nature that our cities are falling into disrepair and all we worry about is their encroachment on "nature."

12 For, as I said at the start, the rural fantasy is paranoid. A glance at history shows that it is human life which is frail, and civilisation which flickers in constant danger of being blown out. But the rural fantasy insists that every plant is a delicate plant. The true paranoid situation is on the other foot. I wouldn't wish to do (and if we live at sensibly high densities there's no need to do) either, but were I forced either to pull down a Nash terrace or to build over a meadow, I'd choose the latter. If you don't like what you've put up on the meadow, you can take it away again and the meadow will re-seed itself in a year or two; but human semen is lucky if it engenders an architectural genius a century. The whole Wordsworthian fallacy consists in gravely underestimating the toughness of plants. In fact, no sooner does civilisation admit a crack—no sooner does a temple of Apollo lapse into disuse—than a weed forces its wiry stem through the crack and urges the blocks of stone further apart. During the last war, the bomber engines were hardly out of earshot before the loosestrife leapt up on the bombed site. Whether we demolish our cities in a third world war or just let them tumble into decay, the seeds of the vegetable kingdom are no doubt waiting to seize on the rubble or sprout through the cracks. *Aux armes, citoyens.* To your trowels and mortar. Man the concrete mixers. The deep mindless silence of the countryside is massing in the Green Belt, ready to move in.

1965

Annie Dillard

TOTAL ECLIPSE

Dillard included this piece in her 1982 collection, Teaching a Stone to Talk: Expeditions and Encounters. *She has compared her interests as a writer to Thoreau's: like him, she wrote in* Pilgrim at Tinker Creek, *she wishes to offer "a meteorological journal of the mind." And like Thoreau, she suggests that there are truths in nature that, if we would heed them, would make us far more discerning about what we value and how we spend our energies. What does she find so deeply terrifying about the eclipse? What does she want us to see about our relation to the natural world?*

I

1 It had been like dying, the sliding down the mountain pass. It had been like the death of someone, irrational, that sliding down the mountain pass

and into the region of dread. It was like slipping into fever, or falling down that hole in sleep from which you wake yourself whimpering. We had crossed the mountains that day, and now we were in a strange place—a hotel in central Washington, in a town near Yakima. The eclipse we had traveled here to see would occur early in the next morning.

2   I lay in bed. My husband, Gary, was reading beside me. I lay in bed and looked at the painting on the hotel room wall. It was a print of a detailed and lifelike painting of a smiling clown's head, made out of vegetables. It was a painting of the sort which you do not intend to look at, and which, alas, you never forget. Some tasteless fate presses it upon you; it becomes part of the complex interior junk you carry with you wherever you go. Two years have passed since the total eclipse of which I write. During those years I have forgotten, I assume, a great many things I wanted to remember—but I have not forgotten that clown painting or its lunatic setting in the old hotel.

3   The clown was bald. Actually, he wore a clown's tight rubber wig, painted white; this stretched over the top of his skull, which was a cabbage. His hair was bunches of baby carrots. Inset in his white clown makeup, and in his cabbage skull, were his small and laughing human eyes. The clown's glance was like the glance of Rembrandt in some of the self-portraits: lively, knowing, deep, and loving. The crinkled shadows around his eyes were string beans. His eyebrows were parsley. Each of his ears was a broad bean. His thin, joyful lips were red chili peppers; between his lips were wet rows of human teeth and a suggestion of a real tongue. The clown print was framed in gilt and glassed.

4   To put ourselves in the path of the total eclipse, that day we had driven five hours inland from the Washington coast, where we lived. When we tried to cross the Cascades range, an avalanche had blocked the pass.

5   A slope's worth of snow blocked the road; traffic backed up. Had the avalanche buried any cars that morning? We could not learn. This highway was the only winter road over the mountains. We waited as highway crews bulldozed a passage through the avalanche. With two-by-fours and walls of plywood, they erected a one-way, roofed tunnel through the avalanche. We drove through the avalanche tunnel, crossed the pass, and descended several thousand feet into central Washington and the broad Yakima valley, about which we knew only that it was orchard country. As we lost altitude, the snows disappeared; our ears popped; the trees changed, and in the trees were strange birds. I watched the landscape innocently, like a fool, like a diver in the rapture of the deep who plays on the bottom while his air runs out.

6   The hotel lobby was a dark, derelict room, narrow as a corridor, and seemingly without air. We waited on a couch while the manager vanished

upstairs to do something unknown to our room. Beside us on an overstuffed chair, absolutely motionless, was a platinum-blond woman in her forties wearing a black silk dress and a strand of pearls. Her long legs were crossed; she supported her head on her fist. At the dim far end of the room, their backs toward us, sat six bald old men in their shirtsleeves, around a loud television. Two of them seemed asleep. They were drunks. "Number six!" cried the man on television. "Number six!"

7   On the broad lobby desk, lighted and bubbling, was a ten-gallon aquarium containing one large fish; the fish tilted up and down in its water. Against the long opposite wall sang a live canary in its cage. Beneath the cage, among spilled millet seeds on the carpet, were a decorated child's sand bucket and matching sand shovel.

8   Now the alarm was set for six. I lay awake remembering an article I had read downstairs in the lobby, in an engineering magazine. The article was about gold mining.

9   In South Africa, in India, and in South Dakota, the gold mines extend so deeply into the earth's crust that they are hot. The rock walls burn the miners' hands. The companies have to air-condition the mines; if the air conditioners break, the miners die. The elevators in the mine shafts run very slowly, down, and up, so the miners' ears will not pop in their skulls. When the miners return to the surface, their faces are deathly pale.

10   Early the next morning we checked out. It was February 26, 1979, a Monday morning. We would drive out of town, find a hilltop, watch the eclipse, and then drive back over the mountains and home to the coast. How familiar things are here; how adept we are; how smoothly and professionally we check out! I had forgotten the clown's smiling head and the hotel lobby as if they had never existed. Gary put the car in gear and off we went, as off we have gone to a hundred other adventures.

11   It was dawn when we found a highway out of town and drove into the unfamiliar countryside. By the growing light we could see a band of cirrostratus clouds in the sky. Later the rising sun would clear these clouds before the eclipse began. We drove at random until we came to a range of unfenced hills. We pulled off the highway, bundled up, and climbed one of these hills.

II

12   The hill was five hundred feet high. Long winter-killed grass covered it, as high as our knees. We climbed and rested, sweating in the cold; we passed clumps of bundled people on the hillside who were setting up telescopes and fiddling with cameras. The top of the hill stuck up in the middle of the sky. We tightened our scarves and looked around.

13   East of us rose another hill like ours. Between the hills, far below, was the highway which threaded south into the valley. This was the Yakima valley; I had never seen it before. It is justly famous for its beauty, like every planted valley. It extended south into the horizon, a distant dream of a valley, a Shangri-la. All its hundreds of low, golden slopes bore orchards. Among the orchards were towns, and roads, and plowed and fallow fields. Through the valley wandered a thin shining river; from the river extended fine, frozen irrigation ditches. Distance blurred and blued the sight, so that the whole valley looked like a thickness or sediment at the bottom of the sky. Directly behind us was more sky, and empty lowlands blued by distance, and Mount Adams. Mount Adams was an enormous, snow-covered volcanic cone rising flat, like so much scenery.

14   Now the sun was up. We could not see it; but the sky behind the band of clouds was yellow, and, far down the valley, some hillside orchards had lighted up. More people were parking near the highway and climbing the hills. It was the West. All of us rugged individuals were wearing knit caps and blue nylon parkas. People were climbing the nearby hills and setting up shop in clumps among the dead grasses. It looked as though we had gathered on hilltops to pray for the world on its last day. It looked as though we had all crawled out of spaceships and were preparing to assault the valley below. It looked as though we were scattered on hilltops at dawn to sacrifice virgins, make rain, set stone stelae in a ring. There was no place out of the wind. The straw grasses banged our legs.

15   Up in the sky where we stood the air was lusterless yellow. To the west the sky was blue. Now the sun cleared the clouds. We cast rough shadows on the blowing grass; freezing, we waved our arms. Near the sun, the sky was bright and colorless. There was nothing to see.

16   It began with no ado. It was odd that such a well-advertised public event should have no starting gun, no overture, no introductory speaker. I should have known right then that I was out of my depth. Without pause or preamble, silent as orbits, a piece of the sun went away. We looked at it through welders' goggles. A piece of the sun was missing; in its place we saw empty sky.

17   I had seen a partial eclipse in 1970. A partial eclipse is very interesting. It bears almost no relation to a total eclipse. Seeing a partial eclipse bears the same relation to seeing a total eclipse as kissing a man does to marrying him, or as flying in an airplane does to falling out of an airplane. Although the one experience precedes the other, it in no way prepares you for it. During a partial eclipse the sky does not darken—not even when 94 percent of the sun is hidden. Nor does the sun, seen colorless through protective devices, seem terribly strange. We have all seen a sliver of light in the sky; we have all seen the crescent moon by day. However, during a partial eclipse the air does indeed get cold, precisely as if someone were standing between you and the fire. And blackbirds do fly back to their roosts. I had seen a partial eclipse before, and here was another.

18   What you see in an eclipse is entirely different from what you know. It is especially different for those of us whose grasp of astronomy is so frail that, given a flashlight, a grapefruit, two oranges, and fifteen years, we still could not figure out which way to set the clocks for Daylight Saving Time. Usually it is a bit of a trick to keep your knowledge from blinding you. But during an eclipse it is easy. What you see is much more convincing than any wild-eyed theory you may know.

19   You may read that the moon has something to do with eclipses. I have never seen the moon yet. You do not see the moon. So near the sun, it is as completely invisible as the stars are by day. What you see before your eyes is the sun going through phases. It gets narrower and narrower, as the waning moon does, and, like the ordinary moon, it travels alone in the simple sky. The sky is of course background. It does not appear to eat the sun; it is far behind the sun. The sun simply shaves away; gradually, you see less sun and more sky.

20   The sky's blue was deepening, but there was no darkness. The sun was a wide crescent, like a segment of tangerine. The wind freshened and blew steadily over the hill. The eastern hill across the highway grew dusky and sharp. The towns and orchards in the valley to the south were dissolving into the blue light. Only the thin river held a trickle of sun.

21   Now the sky to the west deepened to indigo, a color never seen. A dark sky usually loses color. This was a saturated, deep indigo, up in the air. Stuck up into that unworldly sky was the cone of Mount Adams, and the alpenglow was upon it. The alpenglow is that red light of sunset which holds out on snowy mountaintops long after the valleys and tablelands are dimmed. "Look at Mount Adams," I said, and that was the last sane moment I remember.

22   I turned back to the sun. It was going. The sun was going, and the world was wrong. The grasses were wrong; they were platinum. Their every detail of stem, head, and blade shone lightless and artificially distinct as an art photographer's platinum print. This color has never been seen on earth. The hues were metallic; their finish was matte. The hillside was a nineteenth-century tinted photograph from which the tints had faded. All the people you see in the photograph, distinct and detailed as their faces look, are now dead. The sky was navy blue. My hands were silver. All the distant hills' grasses were finespun metal which the wind laid down. I was watching a faded color print of a movie filmed in the Middle Ages; I was standing in it, by some mistake. I was standing in a movie of hillside grasses filmed in the Middle Ages. I missed my own century, the people I knew, and the real light of day.

23   I looked at Gary. He was in the film. Everything was lost. He was a platinum print, a dead artist's version of life. I saw on his skull the darkness of night mixed with the colors of day. My mind was going out; my eyes were receding the way galaxies recede to the rim of space. Gary was light-years away, gesturing inside a circle of darkness, down the wrong end of a telescope. He smiled as if he saw me; the stringy crinkles around his eyes moved.

The sight of him, familiar and wrong, was something I was remembering from centuries hence, from the other side of death: yes, *that* is the way he used to look, when we were living. When it was our generation's turn to be alive. I could not hear him; the wind was too loud. Behind him the sun was going. We had all started down a chute of time. At first it was pleasant; now there was no stopping it. Gary was chuting away across space, moving and talking and catching my eye, chuting down the long corridor of separation. The skin on his face moved like thin bronze plating that would peel.

24   The grass at our feet was wild barley. It was the wild einkorn wheat which grew on the hilly flanks of the Zagros Mountains, above the Euphrates valley, above the valley of the river we called *River*. We harvested the grass with stone sickles, I remember. We found the grasses on the hillsides; we built our shelter beside them and cut them down. That is how he used to look then, that one, moving and living and catching my eye, with the sky so dark behind him, and the wind blowing. God save our life.

25   From all the hills came screams. A piece of sky beside the crescent sun was detaching. It was a loosened circle of evening sky, suddenly lighted from the back. It was an abrupt black body out of nowhere; it was a flat disk; it was almost over the sun. That is when there were screams. At once this disk of sky slid over the sun like a lid. The sky snapped over the sun like a lens cover. The hatch in the brain slammed. Abruptly it was dark night, on the land and in the sky. In the night sky was a tiny ring of light. The hole where the sun belongs is very small. A thin ring of light marked its place. There was no sound. The eyes dried, the arteries drained, the lungs hushed. There was no world. We were the world's dead people rotating and orbiting around and around, embedded in the planet's crust, while the earth rolled down. Our minds were light-years distant, forgetful of almost everything, only an extraordinary act of will could recall to us our former, living selves and our contexts in matter and time. We had, it seems, loved the planet and loved our lives, but could no longer remember the way of them. We got the light wrong. In the sky was something that should not be there. In the black sky was a ring of light. It was a thin ring, an old, thin silver wedding band, an old, worn ring. It was an old wedding band in the sky, or a morsel of bone. There were stars. It was all over.

III

26   It is now that the temptation is strongest to leave these regions. We have seen enough; let's go. Why burn our hands any more than we have to? But two years have passed; the price of gold has risen. I return to the same buried alluvial beds and pick through the strata again.

27   I saw, early in the morning, the sun diminish against a backdrop of sky. I saw a circular piece of that sky appear, suddenly detached, blackened, and backlighted; from nowhere it came and overlapped the sun. It did not look like the moon, it was enormous and black. If I had not read that it was the moon, I could have seen the sight a hundred times and never thought of the moon once. (If, however, I had not read that it was the moon—if, like most of the world's people throughout time, had simply glanced up and seen this thing—then I doubtless would not have speculated much, but would have, like Emperor Louis of Bavaria in 840, simply died of fright on the spot.) It did not look like a dragon, although it looked more like a dragon than the moon. It looked like a lens cover, or the lid of a pot. It materialized out of thin air— black, and flat, and sliding, outlined in flame.

28   Seeing this black body was like seeing a mushroom cloud. The heart screeched. The meaning of the sight overwhelmed its fascination. It obliterated meaning itself. If you were to glance out one day and see a row of mushroom clouds rising on the horizon, you would know at once that what you were seeing, remarkable as it was, was intrinsically not worth remarking. No use running to tell anyone. Significant as it was, it did not matter a whit. For what is significance? It is significance for people. No people, no significance. This is all I have to tell you.

29   In the deeps are the violence and terror of which psychology has warned us. But if you ride these monsters deeper down, if you drop with them farther over the world's rim, you find what our sciences cannot locate or name, the substrate, the ocean or matrix or ether which buoys the rest, which gives goodness its power for good, and evil its power for evil, the unified field: our complex and inexplicable caring for each other, and for our life together here. This is given. It is not earned.

30   The world which lay under darkness and stillness following the closing of the lid was not the world we know. The event was over. Its devastation lay around about us. The clamoring mind and heart stilled, almost indifferent, certainly disembodied, frail, and exhausted. The hills were hushed, obliterated. Up in the sky, like a crater from some distant cataclysm, was a hollow ring.

31   You have seen photographs of the sun taken during a total eclipse. The corona fills the print. All of those photographs were taken through telescopes. The lenses of telescopes and cameras can no more cover the breadth and scale of the visual array than language can cover the breadth and simultaneity of internal experience. Lenses enlarge the sight, omit its context, and make of it a pretty and sensible picture, like something on a Christmas card. I assure you, if you send any shepherds a Christmas card on which is printed a three-by-three photograph of the angel of the Lord, the glory of the Lord, and a multitude of the heavenly host, they will not be sore afraid. More fearsome things can come in envelopes. More moving photographs than those of

the sun's corona can appear in magazines. But I pray you will never see anything more awful in the sky.

32   You see the wide world swaddled in darkness; you see a vast breadth of hilly land, and an enormous, distant, blackened valley; you see towns' lights, a river's path, and blurred portions of your hat and scarf; you see your husband's face looking like an early black-and-white film; and you see a sprawl of black sky and blue sky together, with unfamiliar stars in it, some barely visible bands of cloud, and over there, a small white ring. The ring is as small as one goose in a flock of migrating geese—if you happen to notice a flock of migrating geese. It is one 360th part of the visible sky. The sun we see is less than half the diameter of a dime held at arm's length.

33   The Crab Nebula, in the constellation Taurus, looks, through binoculars, like a smoke ring. It is a star in the process of exploding. Light from its explosion first reached the earth in 1054; it was a supernova then, and so bright it shone in the daytime. Now it is not so bright, but it is still exploding. It expands at the rate of seventy million miles a day. It is interesting to look through binoculars at something expanding seventy million miles a day. It does not budge. Its apparent size does not increase. Photographs of the Crab Nebula taken fifteen years ago seem identical to photographs of it taken yesterday. Some lichens are similar. Botanists have measured some ordinary lichens twice, at fifty-year intervals, without detecting any growth at all. And yet their cells divide; they live.

34   The small ring of light was like these things—like a ridiculous lichen up in the sky, like a perfectly still explosion 4,200 light-years away: it was interesting, and lovely, and in witless motion, and it had nothing to do with anything.

35   It had nothing to do with anything. The sun was too small, and too cold, and too far away, to keep the world alive. The white ring was not enough. It was feeble and worthless. It was as useless as a memory; it was as off kilter and hollow and wretched as a memory.

36   When you try your hardest to recall someone's face, or the look of a place, you see in your mind's eye some vague and terrible sight such as this. It is dark; it is insubstantial; it is all wrong.

37   The white ring and the saturated darkness made the earth and the sky look as they must look in the memories of the careless dead. What I saw, what I seemed to be standing in, was all the wrecked light that the memories of the dead could shed upon the living world. We had all died in our boots on the hilltops of Yakima, and were alone in eternity. Empty space stoppered our eyes and mouths; we cared for nothing. We remembered our living days wrong. With great effort we had remembered some sort of circular light in the sky—but only the outline. Oh, and then the orchard trees withered, the ground froze, the glaciers slid down the valleys and overlapped the towns. If

there had ever been people on earth, nobody knew it. The dead had forgotten those they had loved. The dead were parted one from the other and could no longer remember the faces and lands they had loved in the light. They seemed to stand on darkened hilltops, looking down.

IV

38   We teach our children one thing only, as we were taught: to wake up. We teach our children to look alive there, to join by words and activities the life of human culture on the planet's crust. As adults we are almost all adept at waking up. We have so mastered the transition we have forgotten we ever learned it. Yet it is a transition we make a hundred times a day, as, like so many will-less dolphins, we plunge and surface, lapse and emerge. We live half our waking lives and all of our sleeping lives in some private, useless, and insensible waters we never mention or recall. Useless, I say. Valueless, I might add—until someone hauls their wealth up to the surface and into the wide-awake city, in a form that people can use.

39   I do not know how we got to the restaurant. Like Roethke, "I take my waking slow." Gradually I seemed more or less alive and already forgetful. It was now almost nine in the morning. It was the day of a solar eclipse in central Washington, and a fine adventure for everyone. The sky was clear; there was a fresh breeze out of the north.

40   The restaurant was a roadside place with tables and booths. The other eclipse-watchers were there. From our booth we could see their cars' California license plates, their University of Washington parking stickers. Inside the restaurant we were all eating eggs or waffles; people were fairly shouting and exchanging enthusiasms, like fans after a World Series game. Did you see...? Did you see...? Then somebody said something which knocked me for a loop.

41   A college student, a boy in a blue parka who carried a Hasselblad, said to us, "Did you see that little white ring? It looked like a Life Saver. It looked like a Life Saver up in the sky."

42   And so it did. The boy spoke well. He was a walking alarm clock. I myself had at that time no access to such a word. He could write a sentence, and I could not. I grabbed that Life Saver and rode it to the surface. And I had to laugh. I had been dumbstruck on the Euphrates River, I had been dead and gone and grieving, all over the sight of something which, if you could claw your way up to that level, you would grant looked very much like a Life Saver. It was good to be back among people so clever; it was good to have all the world's words at the mind's disposal, so the mind could begin its task. All those things for which we have no words are lost. The mind—the culture— has two little tools, grammar and lexicon: a decorated sand bucket and a

matching shovel. With these we bluster about the continents and do all the world's work. With these we try to save our very lives.

43   There are a few more things to tell from this level, the level of the restaurant. One is the old joke about breakfast. "It can never be satisfied, the mind, never." Wallace Stevens wrote that, and in the long run he was right. The mind wants to live forever, or to learn a very good reason why not. The mind wants the world to return its love, or its awareness; the mind wants to know all the world, and all eternity, and God. The mind's sidekick, however, will settle for two eggs over easy.

44   The dear, stupid body is as easily satisfied as a spaniel. And, incredibly, the simple spaniel can lure the brawling mind to its dish. It is everlastingly funny that the proud, metaphysically ambitious, clamoring mind will hush if you give it an egg.

45   Further: while the mind reels in deep space, while the mind grieves or fears or exults the workaday senses, in ignorance or idiocy, like so many computer terminals printing out market prices while the world blows up, still transcribe their little data and transmit them to the warehouse in the skull. Later, under the tranquilizing influence of fried eggs, the mind can sort through this data. The restaurant was a halfway house, a decompression chamber. There I remembered a few things more.

46   The deepest, and most terrifying, was this: I have said that I heard screams. (I have since read that screaming, with hysteria, is a common reaction even to expected total eclipses.) People on all the hillsides, including, I think, myself, screamed when the black body of the moon detached from the sky and rolled over the sun. But something else was happening at that same instant, and it was this, I believe, which made us scream.

47   The second before the sun went out we saw a wall of dark shadow come speeding at us. We no sooner saw it than it was upon us, like thunder. It roared up the valley. It slammed our hill and knocked us out. It was the monstrous swift shadow cone of the moon. I have since read that this wave shadow moves 1,800 miles an hour. It was 195 miles wide. No end was in sight—you saw only the edge. It rolled at you across the land at 1,800 miles an hour, hauling darkness like plague behind it. Seeing it, and knowing it was coming straight for you, was like feeling a slug of anesthetic shoot up your arm. If you think very fast, you may have time to think, "Soon it will hit my brain." You can feel the deadness race up your arm; you can feel the appalling, inhuman speed of your own blood. We saw the wall of shadow coming, and screamed before it hit.

48   This was the universe about which we have read so much and never before felt: the universe as a clockwork of loose spheres flung at stupefying,

unauthorized speeds. How could anything moving so fast not crash, not veer from its orbit amok like a car out of control on a turn?

49 Less than two minutes later, when the sun emerged, the trailing edge of the shadow cone sped away. It coursed down our hill and raced eastward over the plain, faster than the eye could believe; it swept over the plain and dropped over the planet's rim in a twinkling. It had clobbered us, and now it roared away. We blinked in the light. It was as though an enormous, loping god in the sky had reached down and slapped the earth's face.

50 Something else, something more ordinary, came back to me along about the third cup of coffee. During the moments of totality, it was so dark that drivers on the highway below turned on their cars' headlights. We could see the highway's route as a strand of lights. It was bumper-to-bumper down there. It was eight-fifteen in the morning, Monday morning, and people were driving into Yakima to work. That it was as dark as night, and eerie as hell, an hour after dawn, apparently meant that in order to *see* to drive to work, people had to use their headlights. Four or five cars pulled off the road. The rest, in a line at least five miles long, drove to town. The highway ran between hills; the people could not have seen any of the eclipsed sun at all. Yakima will have another total eclipse in 2086. Perhaps, in 2086, businesses will give their employees an hour off.

51 From the restaurant we drove back to the coast. The highway crossing the Cascades range was open. We drove over the mountain like old pros. We joined our places on the planet's thin crust; it held. For the time being, we were home free.

52 Early that morning at six, when we had checked out, the six bald men were sitting on folding chairs in the dim hotel lobby. The television was on. Most of them were awake. You might drown in your own spittle, God knows, at any time; you might wake up dead in a small hotel, a cabbage head watching TV while snows pile up in the passes, watching TV while the chili peppers smile and the moon passes over the sun and nothing changes and nothing is learned because you have lost your bucket and shovel and no longer care. What if you regain the surface and open your sack and find, instead of treasure, a beast which jumps at you? Or you may not come back at all. The winches may jam, the scaffolding buckle, the air conditioning collapse. You may glance up one day and see by your headlamp the canary keeled over in its cage. You may reach into a cranny for pearls and touch a moray eel. You yank on your rope; it is too late.

53 Apparently people share a sense of these hazards, for when the total eclipse ended, an odd thing happened.

54   When the sun appeared as a blinding bead on the ring's side, the eclipse was over. The black lens cover appeared again, backlighted, and slid away. At once the yellow light made the sky blue again; the black lid dissolved and vanished. The real world began there. I remember now: we all hurried away. We were born and bored at a stroke. We rushed down the hill. We found our car; we saw the other people streaming down the hillsides; we joined the highway traffic and drove away.

55   We never looked back. It was a general vamoose, and an odd one, for when we left the hill, the sun was still partially eclipsed—a sight rare enough, and one which, in itself, we would probably have driven five hours to see. But enough is enough. One turns at last even from glory itself with a sigh of relief. From the depths of mystery, and even from the heights of splendor, we bounce back and hurry for the latitudes of home.

1982

Renée Askins

RELEASING WOLVES FROM SYMBOLISM

In January of 1995, the U.S. Fish and Wildlife Service began a program of capturing gray wolves in Canada and releasing them in Wyoming, Montana, and Idaho, in order to reestablish the species in the American West. Two legislators from affected states asked for a hearing before the House Committee on Resources to air the concerns of residents. One of those who testified was Renée Askins, the executive director of the Wolf Fund, an organization working for the return of wolves to Yellowstone National Park. Think about her argument that it is not the wolves themselves that present the problem so much as what wolves have been made to mean or to symbolize for each side. As she observes in her final paragraph, "Our attitudes toward wolves and our treatment of them cut to the very marrow of how we view our relationship to the natural world."

1   If I were a rancher I probably would not want wolves returned to the West. If I faced the conditions that ranchers face in the West—falling stock prices, rising taxes, prolonged drought, and a nation that is eating less beef and wearing more synthetics—I would not want to add wolves to my woes. If I were a rancher in Montana, Idaho, or Wyoming in 1995, watching my neighbors give up and my way of life fade away, I would be afraid and I

would be angry. I would want to blame something, to fight something, even kill something.

2   The wolf is an ideal target: it is tangible, it is blamable, and it is real. Or is it? When ranchers talk about wolves they say, "You know, it's not the wolves we're worried about, it's what the wolves represent; it's not what they'll do, it's what they mean." Wolves mean changes. Wolves mean challenges to the old ways of doing things. Wolves mean loss of control. Wolves aren't the cause of the changes occurring in the West any more than the rooster's crow is the cause of the sun's rising, but they have become the means by which ranchers can voice their concern about what's happening around them.

3   Ranchers deserve our compassion and our concern. Whether the threat of wolves is imagined or actual, the ranchers' fear and anger are real. I honor that. However, it is my job, as a scientist and an advocate, to distinguish fact from fiction and purpose from perception.

4   Ranchers claim that wolves will devastate the livestock industry in the West. Yet all the science, the studies, the experts, and the facts show that wolves kill far less than 1 percent of the livestock available to them. According to the *Bozeman Chronicle,* even if federal specialists have wildly underestimated the number of cows and sheep that wolves would kill in the Yellowstone and central Idaho areas, the actual total would be much smaller than the number that die each year in the state of Montana alone because of storms, dogs, and ovine ineptitude. In fact, the number of wolf-caused sheep deaths would have to be almost thirty times higher than predicted before it matched the number of Montana sheep that starved to death in 1993 because they rolled over onto their backs and were unable to get up.

5   In effect, the livestock industry has successfully transferred to the general public one of its most basic operational costs: prevention of predator losses. If you raise Christmas trees, part of the cost and risk of doing business is losing a few trees to gypsy moths and ice storms; inherent in the cost of ranching, particularly on public lands, should be the cost and risk of losing livestock to predators. Instead, every year 36 million tax dollars go to kill native predators on our public lands so that private industry can make a profit.

6   It is important to remember that wolves are missing from the Yellowstone region only because we eliminated them. They did not vanish from the area in response to loss of prey or lack of habitat; they did not die out as a result of disease or natural catastrophe. We systematically, intentionally, consciously killed every wolf we could find (and we found all of them). And we didn't just remove wolves that killed livestock. The wars against predators at the turn of the century weren't about ridding ourselves of a nuisance; they were about the principle of dominance, and the wolf, the symbol of wild, untamable nature, was the object of conquest. We didn't just want to control

wolves, we wanted to conquer them. So we didn't just kill wolves, we tortured them. We lassoed them and tore them apart by their limbs; we wired their jaws shut and left them to starve; we doused them with gasoline and ignited them.

7   Opponents of wolf reintroduction assume that because there are no wolves, there should be no wolves, and over the last two decades they have effectively framed the reintroduction debate around that assumption. They have promoted the idea that the return of wolves is somehow radical or extreme, some sort of environmental luxury, some romantic nonsense that only urbanites and rich Easterners advocate at the expense of the poor, beleaguered Western livestock industry. (In fact, surveys of the residents of Wyoming, Montana, and Idaho show that Westerners support the reintroduction.) The industry's cry of economic loss has eclipsed the costs to the general public of not having wolves. In the West we now live in a "wolf-free" environment. Or is it "wolf-deprived"? Who has gained and who has lost? How do we assign a value to the importance of a predator in the ecosystem? How do we determine the cost of removing one note from a Mozart symphony, one sentence from a Tolstoy novel, or one brush stroke from a Rembrandt? Having wolves in Yellowstone is not a luxury but a right. We should not have to pay for clean air or water, nor should we believe that they are somehow a luxury. Similarly, we have a right to a full complement of wildlife on our public lands.

8   Because of the passion and politics involved, it is easy to oversimplify this debate. Just as unrealistic as the ranchers' scare tactics are the claims by certain environmentalists that wolves are sweet and docile animals; that the wolf is the ultimate symbol of harmony; and that everything noble, wise, and courageous is somehow embodied in this one creature. According to this view, ranchers, hunters, and industry are the bane of the environment, and saving the wolf, no matter what the cost, will be our redemption. Both environmentalists and ranchers have used exaggerated rhetoric to alarm constituents. Both advocates and opponents of reintroduction have tried to use wolves as the "line in the sand" that divides the old West from the new. Both sides want us to see this issue as a distillation of all endangered-species conflicts, as a simple question of either/or: don't touch a tree vs. clear-cut all trees; no wolves vs. fully protected, untouchable wolves; unrestricted grazing vs. no grazing. The tragedy is that while the armies fight their wars, the rest of America stands by, confused, uncertain, and unaware that something they care about might be at stake.

9   The truth, as always, lies somewhere in the middle. Wolves are not killing machines that deserve hideous deaths; neither are they cuddly creatures needing tender, righteous protection. Wolves survive by killing; they have an extraordinary and complex social system, they are smart, strong, and, at the

core, consummate predators. Restoring wolves will not rescue us from our economic or ecological troubles, but neither will their presence contribute to them. Some ranchers may indeed lose sheep or cattle to wolves. Some outfitters may find fewer elk for their clients to shoot. Yet neither ranchers nor outfitters will face economic doom due to the presence of wolves.

10   Emotions, not facts, have controlled the wolf debate. Wolves have never been just wolves: the wolf is the devil's keeper, the slayer of innocent girls, the nurturer of abandoned children, the sacred hunter, the ghostly creature of myth and legend. In short, wolves are symbolic; Yellowstone is symbolic; restoring wolves to Yellowstone is a deeply and profoundly symbolic act.

11   We are a culture of symbols. It is not surprising that ranchers and environmentalists use the symbolic force of wolves to debate powerful changes. We distill ideologies into incidents, processes into people; we use symbols to help us order and make sense of an increasingly complex world. The Yellowstone wolf-recovery debate is fundamentally an expression of a culture in transition; it is the struggle that accompanies old assumptions clashing against the new. The story of this conflict is the story of how we view ourselves in relation to animals, whether we can replace the assumption of "dominion" that has been so destructive to us and the natural world with a worldview that recognizes that we live in a state of reciprocity with the birds and the beasts—that we are not only the product of nature but also part of it. Our attitudes toward wolves and our treatment of them cut to the very marrow of how we view our relationship to the natural world. Is wolf recovery loss or enrichment? Relinquishing or sharing? Wolves mean something to everyone. But in the end, wolves are only wolves. The real issue is one of making room, and there is still a little room in the West—room for hunters, for environmentalists, for ranchers, and for wolves.

1995

Alston Chase

WOLF REINTRODUCTION
AN ENVIRONMENTAL CRAPSHOOT

Chase's view of wolves is shared by many western ranchers and numerous other residents of the areas into which the U. S. Fish and Wildlife Service has reintroduced the species. A newspaper columnist from Montana, Chase, too, is aware of the symbolism that surrounds the wolf in the American imagination. By alluding, however facetiously, to the role of wolves as the villains of fairy tales, Chase reminds his readers that wolves have deep and long-standing meanings in our culture. How do his allusions to Little Red Riding Hood and the Three Little Pigs help to further his argument? What does he suggest about the relationship to nature sustained by the supporters of wolf reintroduction? By the ranchers and other opponents of the program?

1   As western ranchers and Interior Department officials snarl at each other over wolf reintroduction in Yellowstone National Park, the nation seems confronted with yet another environmental cliche. The $7 million federal scheme to plant 15 wolves in the park each of the next few years, say the media, pits a regional interest group against the environment—a theme we've heard a zillion times before.

2   The selfish interests in question this time supposedly belong to stockmen, who have sued to stop reintroduction and who doggedly insist that any canine that could eat Little Red Riding Hood's grandmother and then wear her clothes is perfectly capable of scarfing leg-of-lamb once in a while.

3   Environmentalists dismiss this as a fairy tale spread by rednecks who lack tolerance for cross-dressing mammals. Wolves are necessary for "ecological balance," they insist, and piggish people who fear fanged intruders huffing and puffing and blowing doors down shouldn't live in straw houses. Meanwhile, the feds insist they are merely enforcing the Endangered Species Act, which mysteriously requires wolf "recovery" in Yellowstone but not in, say, Scarsdale, N.Y. or Washington's Rock Creek Park.

4   But this fight isn't what it seems. It is not a local issue. It is not about welfare cowboys and has nothing to do with "ecological balance." Rather, it raises questions about the fairness of a policy that will ultimately affect everyone.

5   Wolf "recovery" is another step towards fulfilling the environmentalist agenda of "returning" the continent to "pre-settlement conditions." But, rather than resembling the past its effects will be unique and unpredictable. Federal "preservation" policy has already created unprecedented conditions that threaten the very values it seeks to enhance. Leaving wilderness alone ignores how Native Americans shaped the landscape through burning and produces forests that are older and less biologically diverse than when Columbus landed. Overly protected game populations have reached levels never seen before. These creatures damage vegetation and provide unlimited food sources for mountain lions, whose numbers in many regions are greater than any time in natural history.

6   These same misguided schemes transformed Yellowstone. Elk, surpassing original numbers by 50,000 or more, have consumed habitat important to other animals such as white-tail and mule deer, big horn sheep and beaver. Introducing wolves into this unusual mix will produce results no one can anticipate. Authorities hope the new arrivals will eat elk and won't bother

cattle. But that may not happen. In the last century, these canines revealed a decided taste for livestock. And in Minnesota (which has 2,000 "threatened" wolves of its own), predation on domestic animals is surging.

7   Rather, "reintroduction" is an ecological crap-shoot. Several scenarios are possible:

1. Wolves may prefer to eat deer. But deer, whose park habitat has been colonized by elk, stay mostly in surrounding farmland. Ergo, wolves will loiter in hay pastures and develop a fondness for hamburger.

2. Wolves may "key" on Yellowstone's big horn sheep. Since these creatures are already stressed by competition with elk, they will be wiped out quickly. Then, wolves may switch to the big horn's domestic cousins.

3. Wolves may take elk. Since this food is abundant, canine numbers skyrocket. Elk will decrease and wolves multiply until legions of hungry canines invade celebrity enclaves like Jackson and Aspen, taking occasional Labrador retrievers.

8   In any case, wolves will continue their march across the continent. Alaska has 6,000, and packs are multiplying in North Carolina and Arizona. A recovery program is underway in Idaho. Minnesota's wolves are increasing 3 percent to 5 percent a year and have reached Hinckley, not far from St. Paul. A southward migration from Canada is underway in the Rockies.

9   Over time, these carnivores may displace ranchers—which is what many environmentalists hope. Thus government is forcing rural landowners to subsidize the atavistic pleasures of others in the name of "ecology." The feds won't pay for damages done by its animals. And, although the Defenders of Wildlife, a conservation group, promises to compensate for losses to cattle (and not to sheep), its funds might not suffice. Minnesota, which disburses up to $40,000 a year for stock losses has found that amount insufficient. Most kills go unreimbursed, and pet owners never receive compensation.

10   The issue, therefore, is fairness. While wolves should indeed return to Yellowstone, they must not become Trojan horses for primitivists who wish to dismantle civilization. Justice requires the animals be confined to the park and that realistic control and compensation systems be established.

11   But this probably won't happen until wolves take up residence on the yuppie spreads proliferating around Yellowstone. When carnivores begin eating upscale dogs and scaring children, the politics of this species will get really interesting.

1995

Reacting and Writing

In talking about environmental issues, no one argues directly for the advantages of pollution or for the bulldozing of magnificent natural settings. Instead, the arguments have generally been made case by case: should *this* wild river be dammed? should *this* virgin forest be cut? One way to give focus to this symposium is to begin with a test case of local or national interest, informing yourself about the case and then examining it from the different perspectives provided by the readings.

For a more philosophical essay, you might try to work up a definition of your relationship to the natural world, profiting from the example of the writer who most appeals to you. Do you have a "natural beauty-hunger," as Muir claims in paragraph 11 of his argument? Interestingly, writers have traditionally associated the healing power of nature with pastoral landscapes—scenes of pasturing animals and traditional methods of farming—not with pristine wilderness, which frequently lacked charm for people who lived closer to it than most of us do. Why should the experience of "raw" nature be healing if nature (at least according to evolutionary theory) is essentially a blood bath? Can one's "natural beauty-hunger" be satisfied as well by a beautiful building as by a natural landscape, as Brigid Brophy suggests? Is it possible to release wolves from symbolism, as Askins asks us to do? Is it possible to release nature from symbolism?

Another writing possibility is to take a place of beauty that you are familiar with and write an essay explaining why it ought to be preserved. Decide in advance whether you are arguing to a sympathetic audience like Muir's or to the pro-development side with a monetary interest in developing the site. The challenge is to get beyond the argument that the spot should be preserved *because* it is beautiful. Apparently we can't preserve everything that is beautiful and still live in houses and drink clean water. Why should your spot in particular be set aside? What values for nature *other than beauty* are the writers in this symposium able to suggest?

A useful metaphor for analyzing arguments is to think of the writer's point of view as a lens through which his or her topic is viewed. The lens itself affects the perception of the sight by altering the color, the sharpness of focus, the size, and the boundaries. Thoreau looks at nature in various ways; perhaps most striking is the lens of his literary culture. His vision of a farm is influenced by his reading of Chaucer and Cato the Elder; his appreciation of the morning by his recollections of Homer and the Vedas. We might say that Dillard sees the eclipse through the lens of a lens: she describes herself and her husband as in a movie. Both Askins and Chase are very conscious of the difficulty most people have in seeing wolves as wolves because the wolf has played such a large role in fairy tales and has such strong symbolic associations. What lens or lenses affect your view of the natural world? A particular writer? A set of photographs or paintings? The imagination and aesthetic appreciation of a parent or other early companion? A set of early experiences?

If you are interested in writing a position paper, you could research the wolf reintroduction issue and make an argument for or against the project, or you could take another environmental issue currently under debate. What audience would you wish to reach with your arguments?

III. SEX, GENDER, FAMILY

No area generates more controversy in contemporary America than questions of sexuality. Calls for a return to "family values," demands for the establishment of gay rights, the bitter debates over abortion, or widespread accusations of sexual harassment—all are rooted in varying understandings of our sexuality as human beings. In what follows we begin with some classic treatments of sex, gender, and family, and then move to some contemporary issues.

The Book of Genesis

ADAM AND EVE

Many discussions of gender and family have begun with the enigmatic story of Adam and Eve from the Bible; we start with it as well. The first chapter of Genesis describes the creation of the world, including the creation of the first human beings. "God created man in his own image, in the image of God he created him; male and female he created them. And God blessed them and said to them, 'Be fruitful and multiply and fill the earth and subdue it.'" The second chapter then focuses on the story of the first two human beings and their disobedience to God.

1   In the day that the Lord God made the earth and the heavens, when no plant of the field was yet in the earth and no herb of the field had yet sprung up—for the Lord God had not caused it to rain upon the earth, and there was no man to till the ground; but a mist went up from the earth and watered the whole face of the ground—then the Lord God formed man of dust from the ground, and breathed into his nostrils the breath of life; and man became a living being. And the Lord God planted a garden in Eden, in the east; and there he put the man whom he had formed. And out of the ground the Lord God made to grow every tree that is pleasant to the sight and good for food, the tree of life also in the midst of the garden, and the tree of the knowledge of good and evil.

2   A river flowed out of Eden to water the garden, and there it divided and became four rivers. The name of the first is Pishon; it is the one which flows around the whole land of Havilah, where there is gold; and the gold of that land is good; bdellium and onyx stone are there. The name of the second river is Gihon; it is the one which flows around the whole land of Cush. And the name of the third river is Hiddekel, which flows east of Assyria. And the fourth river is the Euphrates.

3   The Lord God took the man and put him in the garden of Eden to till it and keep it. And the Lord God commanded the man, saying, "You may freely

eat of every tree of the garden; but of the tree of the knowledge of good and evil you shall not eat, for in the day that you eat of it you shall die."

4   Then the Lord God said, "It is not good that the man should be alone; I will make him a helper fit for him." So out of the ground the Lord God formed every beast of the field and every bird of the air, and brought them to the man to see what he would call them; and whatever the man called every living creature, that was its name. The man gave names to all cattle, and to the birds of the air, and to every beast of the field; but for the man there was not found a helper fit for him. So the Lord God caused a deep sleep to fall upon the man, and while he slept took one of his ribs and closed up its place with flesh; and the rib which the Lord God had taken from the man he made into a woman and brought her to the man. Then the man said,

"This at last is bone of my bones and flesh of my flesh;
she shall be called Woman, because she was taken out of Man."

5   Therefore a man leaves his father and his mother and cleaves to his wife, and they become one flesh. And the man and his wife were both naked, and were not ashamed.

6   Now the serpent was more subtle than any other wild creature that the Lord God had made. He said to the woman, "Did God say, 'You shall not eat of any tree of the garden'?" And the woman said to the serpent, "We may eat of the fruit of the trees of the garden; but God said, 'You shall not eat of the fruit of the tree which is in the midst of the garden, neither shall you touch it, lest you die.'" But the serpent said to the woman, "You will not die. For God knows that when you eat of it your eyes will be opened, and you will be like God, knowing good and evil." So when the woman saw that the tree was good for food, and that it was a delight to the eyes, and that the tree was to be desired to make one wise, she took of its fruit and ate; and she also gave some to her husband, and he ate. Then the eyes of both were opened, and they knew that they were naked; and they sewed fig leaves together and made themselves aprons.

7   And they heard the sound of the Lord God walking in the garden in the cool of the day, and the man and his wife hid themselves from the presence of the Lord God among the trees of the garden. But the Lord God called to the man, and said to him, "Where are you?" And he said, "I heard the sound of thee in the garden, and I was afraid, because I was naked; and I hid myself." He said, "Who told you that you were naked? Have you eaten of the tree of which I commanded you not to eat?" The man said, "The woman whom thou gavest to be with me, she gave me fruit of the tree, and I ate." Then the Lord God said to the woman, "What is this that you have done?" The woman said, "The serpent beguiled me, and I ate." The Lord God said to the serpent,

"Because you have done this,
cursed are you above all cattle,
and above all wild animals;

upon your belly you shall go,
    and dust you shall eat
    all the days of your life.
I will put enmity between you and
      the woman,
    and between your seed and her
      seed;
he shall bruise your head,
    and you shall bruise his heel."

To the woman he said,

"I will greatly multiply your pain in
      childbearing;
    in pain you shall bring forth
      children,
yet your desire shall be for your
      husband,
    and he shall rule over you."

And to Adam he said,

"Because you have listened to the
      voice of your wife,
    and have eaten of the tree
of which I commanded you,
    'You shall not eat of it,'
cursed is the ground because of you;
    in toil you shall eat of it all the
      days of your life;
thorns and thistles it shall bring
      forth to you;
    and you shall eat the plants of
      the field.
In the sweat of your face
    you shall eat bread
till you return to the ground,
    for out of it you were taken;
you are dust,
    and to dust you shall return."

8   The man called his wife's name Eve, because she was the mother of all living. And the Lord God made for Adam and for his wife garments of skins, and clothed them.

9   Then the Lord God said, "Behold, the man has become like one of us, knowing good and evil; and now, lest he put forth his hand and take also of the tree of life, and eat, and live for ever"—therefore the Lord God sent him forth from the garden of Eden, to till the ground from which he was taken. He

drove out the man; and at the east of the garden of Eden he placed the cherubim, and a flaming sword which turned every way, to guard the way to the tree of life.

10   Now Adam knew Eve his wife, and she conceived and bore Cain, saying "I have gotten a man with the help of the Lord."

ca. **950** B.C.

Augustine of Hippo

THE BLESSING OF FERTILITY AND THE INSTITUTION OF MARRIAGE*

The precise meaning of the story of Adam and Eve and its implications for our understanding of sexuality and marriage have been disputed as much as any part of Scripture. One of the most influential interpretations within Western Christianity was that offered by fourth-century North African bishop and saint Augustine of Hippo. In the following brief excerpt from his massive City of God, *Augustine ties the foundation of marriage to God's command, "Be fruitful and multiply."*

1   We must never allow ourselves to believe that God's blessing, 'Increase and multiply and fill the earth' would have been fulfilled through this lust by the pair who were set in paradise. It was, in fact, after the sin that this lust arose. It was after the sin that man's nature felt, noticed, blushed at, and concealed this lust; for man's nature retained a sense of decency, although it had lost the authority to which the body had been subordinate in every part. But the nuptial blessing, bidding the married couple to increase and multiply and fill the earth, still stood, although they were offenders; yet it had been given before the offence, so that it might be realized that the procreation of children belonged to the glory of marriage and not to the punishment of sin.

2   There are, however, men at the present time who are evidently unaware of the bliss that existed in paradise. They suppose that children could not have been begotten except by the means with which they are familiar, namely, by means of lust, which, as we observe, brings a sense of shame even in the honourable state of matrimony. Some of them utterly reject the holy Scriptures, and even scoff at them in their unbelief, in the passage where we are told that after their sin our first parents were ashamed of their nakedness and that they covered their parts of shame—their pudenda. Others of them,

*Translated by Henry Bettenson.

in contrast, accept and honour the Scriptures; but while so doing they maintain that the words 'increase and multiply' should not be interpreted as referring to carnal fertility, on the grounds that a somewhat similar remark is made with reference to the soul, 'You will multiply me with strength (*or* virtue) in my soul.' And so they interpret the words that follow in Genesis, 'Fill the earth and hold sway over it', in this way: 'earth' they take to mean the flesh, which the soul 'fills' with its own presence and over which it 'holds sway' when it is 'multiplied in strength (virtue)'. Carnal offspring, in their opinion, could not then have been born, any more than they can be born now, without the lust which arose after sin, the lust which was noticed, caused embarrassment, and was concealed. They assert that children would not have been born in paradise, but outside it, which is what in fact happened. For it was after the pair had been sent away from paradise that they came together to beget children, and did beget them.

3   For myself, however, I have no shadow of doubt that to increase and multiply and fill the earth in accordance with God's blessing is a gift of marriage, and that God instituted marriage from the beginning, before man's Fall, in creating male and female: the difference in sex is quite evident in the physical structure. And the actual blessing was obviously attached to this work of God, for the words, 'he created them male and female', are immediately followed, in the scriptural account, by this statement: 'And God blessed them, saying, "Increase and multiply, and fill the earth and hold sway over it"', and so on.

4   Now it is true that we can quite properly give this a spiritual meaning; however, we cannot interpret 'male' and 'female' allegorically, by finding an analogy in the individual, namely a distinction between the ruling element and the ruled. There is no denying the obvious evidence of bodies of different sex, which shows that it would be a manifest absurdity to deny the fact that male and female were created for the purpose of begetting children, so as to increase and multiply and fill the earth. And when the Lord was asked whether it was allowed to dismiss a wife for any cause whatever (since Moses allowed the giving of a bill of divorce because of the hardness of heart of the Israelites) his reply had nothing to do with the spirit which commands and flesh which obeys, or the rational mind which rules and the irrational desire which submits to rule, or the contemplative virtue which is pre-eminent and the active virtue which is subject to it, or the intellectual power of the mind and the body's perception. The Lord's answer explicitly concerned the marriage bond which binds the two sexes to one another. He said,

> Have you not read that the Creator made the male and female from the start? And that he said: 'This is why a man will say goodbye to his father and mother, and will be joined to his wife, and they will be two in one flesh'? So they are no longer two, but one flesh. Therefore, what God joined together, man must not separate.

5   It is certain then that at the beginning male and female were constituted just as two human beings of different sex are now, in our observation and knowledge, and that they are said to be 'one' either on account of their being joined together in marriage, or because of woman's origin, since she was created from the man's side. For the Apostle appeals to this latter fact as an illustration, a precedent instituted by God, when he admonishes husbands, telling them that each one of them should love his wife.[1]

426 A.D.

Geoffrey Chaucer

THE WIFE OF BATH'S PROLOGUE AND TALE[*]

A great early work in English is Chaucer's The Canterbury Tales. *Its General Prologue describes a group of medieval pilgrims who assemble in an inn just south of London. They are about to set out on a pilgrimage to a shrine in Canterbury, and the Host or innkeeper finds them so merry that he decides to join them. He suggests that to pass the time pleasurably, they take part in a storytelling contest: whoever tells the most meaningful and most pleasing tale will be treated to a dinner by the other pilgrims when they return. Chaucer's narrator describes each pilgrim, including the Wife of Bath, a prosperous widow with a ruddy, bold face and elaborate garments. We are told that she has been married five times, an issue that comes up in her Prologue, that she has traveled extensively on pilgrimages, and that she knows a great deal about the "old dance"—about love and war between the sexes.*

The Wife's Prologue combines autobiography and argument. In fact, as her opening words about lived experience and written authority indicate, her autobiography is argument. What is most striking about her words for the purposes of this symposium is the way in which she argues back against the long, strong

---

[1]The Apostle mentioned by Augustine is Paul. Augustine is alluding to two passages from Paul's letters with which he presumed his audience would be familiar. In the first, Paul writes simply, "Wives, be subject to your husbands. Husbands, love your wives." In the second, he is more expansive:

Be subject to one another out of reverence for Christ. Wives, be subject to your husbands, as to the Lord. For the husband is the head of the wife as Christ is the head of the church, his body, and is himself its Savior. As the church is subject to Christ, so let wives also be subject in everything to their husbands. Husbands, love your wives, as Christ loved the church and gave himself up for her, that he might sanctify her, having cleansed her by the washing of water with the word, that the church might be presented before him in splendor, without spot or wrinkle or any such thing, that she might be holy and without blemish. Even so husbands should love their wives as their own bodies. He who loves his wife loves himself.

[*]Translated by John K. Bollard.

tradition of masculine authority represented in the selections from Genesis and Augustine, with its deep reservations about women and sexuality. Many of her traits, such as gossiping, henpecking, and sexual blackmail, come from anti-feminist stereotypes of the day. Yet many readers find that Chaucer has endowed his fictional character with so much humor, life, and plausibility that instead of affirming the audience's belief in the ability of such stereotypes to account for the otherness of women, he reveals the stereotypes' narrowness and inadequacy. You can judge for yourself the overall effect of her Prologue and tale. Notice the parallels between the Wife's own marital experiences, especially with her fifth husband, Jenkin, and those of the old woman in the tale. Does the tale seem to further or to contradict the points about marriage and sexuality made in the Prologue?

The Prologue of the Wife of Bath's Tale

"Experience, though no authority
Had yet been written, is enough for me
To speak of the misery of marriage;
For, my lords, since I was twelve years of age,
Thanks be to God, eternally on high,
Of husbands at the church door I've had five,
(If so oft I be allowed to marry),
And all were worthy men in their degree.
But I was told, not long ago it was,
That since our lord Christ never went but once   10
To a wedding, in Cana in Galilee,
That by the same example He taught me
That I should not be wedded except once.
Hearken, too, to the sharp word, for the nonce,
That, by a well, Jesus, both God and man,
Spoke in reproof of the Samaritan:
'You have thus far had five husbands,' said He,
'And that same man who has you presently
Is not your husband,' He said, 'certainly.'
But what He meant by that I cannot say;   20
Therefore I ask, Why is it the fifth man
Was not husband to the Samaritan?
How many men *can* she have in marriage?
I never yet heard tell in all my age
Anyone give a number specifically.
Men may ponder and interpret as they wish,
But I know well, clearly, without a lie,
God said that we should wax and multiply;

That gracious text I can well understand.
Also, I know well, He said my husband
Should leave father and mother and come to me.
But no mention of number made He,
Not of bigamy or octogamy.
Why then should men call it a villainy?
Lo, there is the wise king, lord Solomon;
I believe he had, of wives, more than one.
I wish to God it were lawful for me
To be refreshed half as often as he!
What a gift of God he had of all his wives!
No man alive in this world has the like.
God knows, this noble king, as I see it,
The first night had many a merry fit
With each of them, so happy was his life.
Blessèd be God that I have wedded five!
From all of them I have picked out the best,
Both for their nether purses and their chests.
Just as diverse schools can produce good clerks,
And diverse practices in all sorts of work
Can certainly produce skilful workmen,
So have I learned from five different husbands.
Welcome the sixth, whenever he shall come,
For truly I won't stay chaste forever.
When my husband from this world is gone,
Some Christian man shall wed with me anon,
For then the apostle says that I am free
To wed, by God, wherever it pleases me.
He says that to be wedded is no sin;
It is better to be married than to burn.
What do I care if folk say villainy
Of cursèd Lamech and his bigamy?
I know well Abraham was a holy man,
And Jacob too, as far as I know,
And each of them had more wives than two,
And many another holy man also.
Where can you say, in any time or age,
That God on high has forbidden marriage
By express word? I pray, tell it to me.
Or where did He command virginity?
I know as well as you, there is no doubt,
When the apostle speaks of maidenhood,

He said that he had no precept for it.
Men may counsel women to be alone,
But counselling is not a commandment.
Thus he left it up to our own judgement;
For if God had commanded maidenhood,
Then He would have damned marriage with that deed.
And certainly, if there were no seed sown,
Then whereof should such virginity grow?
Saint Paul did not dare to command, at least,
80   A thing for which his Master gave no hest.
The prize is set up for virginity,
Catch it who may; who runs best we shall see.

But this does not apply to everyone;
Only where God pleases to bestow it.
I know the apostle was a virgin,
But nevertheless, though he wrote and said
He wished that everyone were such as he,
This is but to counsel virginity.
He gave me permission to be a wife
90   By his leave, and so it is no reproof
For me to marry, if my mate should die,
Without the objection of bigamy.
Although it were good no woman to touch,
He meant in his own bed or in his couch,
For there's danger in bringing fire near flax—
You know what is meant by this example.
This is the whole: he held virginity
More perfect than marrying in frailty.
Frailty I call it, unless he and she
100   Would lead all their lives in chastity.

I grant it well, I do not resent it
If maidenhood is better than remarriage.
It pleases them to be pure, body and soul;
Of my estate I make no kind of boast,
For you know well, a lord in his household
Does not have every vessel of pure gold;
Some are wood and do their lord good service.
God calls people to him in sundry ways,
And everyone has a proper gift from God,
110   Some this and some that, just as He provides.

Virginity is a great perfection
And continence, also, with devotion,
But Christ, who of perfection is the well,
Did not bid every man he should go sell
All that he had, and give it to the poor,
And in such wise follow in His footsteps.
He spoke to those who would live perfectly.
And, my lords, by your leave, that is not I;
I will bestow the flower of all my age
120 In the acts and in the fruits of marriage.

Tell me also, just for what conclusion
Were the organs of generation made,
And by so perfectly wise a Maker wrought?
You can trust well they were not made for nought,
Gloss who will, and argue both up and down
That they were only made for purgation
Of urine, and that both our things so small
Were just to tell a female from a male
And for no other cause. Do you say no?
130 Experience knows well it is not so.
Just so the scholars be not vexed with me,
I will say this: that they were made for both,
That is, both for those functions and for ease
Of procreation, that God be not displeased.
Why else should men in their books set
Down that man should yield to his wife her debt?
Now with what else should he make his payment,
If he can't use his harmless instrument?
Thus these things were put upon a creature
140 To purge urine *and* for procreation.

But I don't say everyone is obliged,
Who has such harness as I have described,
To go and use it for procreation.
Then no one would take heed of chastity.
Christ was a virgin and shaped as a man,
And many a saint since the world began,
Yet did they live in perfect chastity.
But I will not envy virginity;
Let virgins be called bread of fine wheat seed,
150 And let us wives, then, be called barley bread.
And yet with barley bread, Saint Mark can tell,

Our Lord Jesus refreshed many people.
In such estate as God has called us to,
I will persevere; I am not fussy.
In wifehood I will use my instrument
As freely as my Maker has sent it;
If I be niggardly, God give me sorrow!
My husband shall have it evening and morrow,
When he wants to come forth and pay his debt.
160   A husband I shall have—I will not quit—
Who shall be both my debtor and my thrall
And have his tribulation, too, besides,
Upon his flesh, while I remain his wife.
I have the power during all my life
Over his own body, and not he.
Right thus the apostle told it unto me,
And bade our husbands they should love us well.
Of this argument I like the whole deal."

Just then the Pardoner[1] started up anon.
170   "Now, dame," said he, "by God and by Saint John,
You are a noble preacher in this case!
I was about to wed a wife, alas!
Why should I pay for it with my flesh so dear?
I'd rather not wed any wife this year!"

"Quiet," said she, "my tale has not begun.
No, you shall drink from another tun
Before I go; you'll savor worse than ale.
And when I have told forth to you my tale
Of trials and tribulation in marriage,
180   In which I am expert for all my age,
(That is to say, I've myself been the whip),
Then may you choose whether you want to sip
From that same tun that I shall shortly broach.
Beware of it, lest too near you approach,
For I shall give examples, more than ten.
'He that will not be warned by other men,
By his example others warned will be.'
These same words were written by Ptolemy;
Read in his *Almagest* and find it there."

---

[1] *Pardoner:* A travelling cleric who sold pardons for sins

190

"Dame, I do pray you, if it were your will,"
Said the pardoner, "just as you began,
Tell forth your tale and spare not any man,
And teach us young men some of your practice."

"Gladly," she replied, "since you may like this;
But yet I pray to all this company,
If I speak according to my fancy,
Do not be too annoyed by what I say,
For my intent is just to tease and play.

Now, sir, now will I tell forth my tale.

200

If ever I might drink good wine or ale,
I'll tell the truth; those husbands that I had,
Well, three of them were good, and two were bad.
The three were good men, and rich, and old;
Scarcely could they uphold the marriage law
By which they were bound in debt unto me;
You know well what I mean by this, surely!
So help me God, I laugh when I recall
How piteously at night I made them work!
And, by my faith, I thought it no great measure.

210

They had given me their land and their treasure;
I needed no more to be diligent
To win their love, nor show them reverence.
Those three loved me so well, by God above,
That I did not need to value their love!
A wise woman will keep busy always
To gain men's love, surely, where none she has;
But since I had them wholly in my hand,
And since they had given me all their land,
Why should I care at all how I please them,

220

Unless for my own profit and my ease?
I set them so to work, by God I say,
That many a night they sang 'Welaway!'
The bacon was not fetched for them, I know,
That men win for not quarreling at Dunmow.[2]
I governed them so well, by my firm reign,
That each of them was blissful and was fain
To bring me eagerly gifts from the fair.

[2]In the village of Dunmow in Essex, a side of bacon, known as the Dunmow flitch, was offered to any married couple who lived for a year and a day without quarreling or repenting of their marriage. This continued into the twentieth century.

They were glad when I spoke to them nicely,
For, God knows, I scolded them cruelly.

230   Now listen how I bore myself properly,
You wise wives, who ought well to understand.
When you speak, accuse them falsely at hand,
For not half so boldly can any man
Swear and lie as well as a woman can.
I say this not about wives who are wise,
Unless it be when they mistake their ways.
A wise wife, if she knows what's for her good,
Will convince him the tattling birds are mad,
And take for witness to it her own maid,
240   Who will agree.[3] But hearken what I said:

    'Sir, old dotard, is this all your array?
Why is my neighbor's wife always so gay?
She is honored wherever she may go;
I sit at home; I have no decent clothes.
What do you do there at my neighbor's house?
Is she *that* fair? Are you *that* amorous?
What do you whisper to our maid? Bless me!
Sir, you old lecher, let your joking be!
And if I have a companion or friend,
250   Without guilt, you scold me just like a fiend
If I should walk or go play at his house!
You can come home as drunken as a mouse,
And preach at me from your bench, bad luck to you!
You say to me it is a great mischief
To wed a poor woman, for the expense;
And if she should be rich and of high birth,
Then you say that it would be a torment
To suffer her pride and her sullenness.
And if she is fair, you absolute knave,
260   You say every lecher wants to have her.
She may not long in chastity abide
Who is assailed on each and every side.

    You say some men desire us for riches,
Some for our shape, and some for our fairness,
Some because we can either sing or dance,
And some for gentility and dalliance,

[3]A reference to the tale of the bird who tells a husband of his wife's adultery

Some for their hands and for their arms so small;
Thus all go to the devil, by your tale.
You say no men can hold a castle wall
270 So long it can't be taken after all.

And if she is ugly, you say that she
Must covet every man that she might see,
And on him, like a spaniel, she will leap,
Until she finds some man to pay her keep.
Nor is there so grey a goose in the lake,
So you say, that will be without a mate.
And you say it's a hard thing to control
Something that no man willingly will hold.
Thus say you, scoundrel, when you go to bed,
280 And that no wise man should need to be wed,
Nor any man who hopes to go to heaven.
With wild thunderclaps and fiery lightning
May your skinny withered neck be broken!

You say that leaky roofs and also smoke
And scolding wives all three cause men to flee
Out of their own houses. Ah, God bless me!
What causes such an old man thus to chide?
You say we wives try to hide our vices
Until we're secure, and then they will show.
290 That may well be the proverb of a shrew!

You say that oxen, asses, horse, and hounds
Are put to the test at various times,
Basins and wash bowls, before men buy them,
Spoons and stools, and all such household sundries,
And so are pots and clothes and such array,
But no one can make a trial of his wife
Until he is wed, you dotard old shrew,
And then, you say, all our vices will show.

You also say that it displeases me
300 Unless you're always praising my beauty,
And unless you always gaze on my face,
And call me "fair dame" in every place,
And unless you hold a feast on the day
That I was born, and make me fresh and gay,
And unless to my nurse you show honor,

And to my chambermaid in my boudoir,
And to my father's folk and his allies;
Thus say you, you old barrelful of lies.

And yet of our apprentice, young Jenkin,
With his curled hair, shining like gold so fine,
Because he attends me in every way,
You have developed a false suspicion.
I want him not, though you died tomorrow!

But tell me this: Why hide, to your sorrow,
The keys of your chest away from me?
They are my goods as well as yours, surely!
Do you think to make a fool of your dame?
Now, by the one who is known as Saint James,
You shall not both, even though you were mad,
Be master of my body *and* my goods;
One you shall forgo, in spite of your eyes!
What does it help me to ask or to spy?
I believe you would lock me in your chest!
You *should* say, "Wife, go wherever you wish.
Take your disport; I'll hear no tales with malice.
I know you are a true wife, Dame Alice."
We love no man who is concerned or cares
Where we go; we're free to go anywhere.

Among all men, blessèd he ought to be,
The wise astronomer, Lord Ptolemy,
Who says this proverb in his *Almagest,*
"Of all men his wisdom is the highest
Who worries not who has the world in hand."
By this proverb you should well understand
You have enough; why should you need to care
How merrily some other folk might fare?
For certainly, old dotard, by your leave,
You'll have enough of a quaint thing at eve!
He is too great a miser who'd decline
To light someone's candle with his lantern;
He would thus have no less light, certainly.
You have enough, so don't complain of me!

You say also, that if we make us gay
With fine clothing and with precious array,

That it's a danger to our chastity;
Yet, (to your sorrow!), you insist to me
And say these words in the apostle's name,
"'In a garment made of chastity and shame
You women should be appareled,' said he,
350   'And not with tressed up hair and jewelry
And pearls, nor with gold, nor with fine clothing.'"
Neither with your text nor with your rubric
Will I agree any more than a gnat.

And you said this, that I was like a cat,
Because whoever would singe a cat's skin,
Then well would the cat want to stay within.
But if the cat's fur should be sleek and gay,
She will not dwell in a house half a day,
But forth she will go before the day's dawning,
360   To show off her fur and go caterwauling.
That is to say, if I be gay, Sir Shrew,
I'll wear my own plain clothes for all to view.

Sir, old fool, what does it help you to spy?
Though you asked Argus with his hundred eyes
To be my bodyguard, as he knows best,
In faith, he'd only keep me if I wished;
I could still fool his beard, I bet my life!

You said to me also there are three things
That cause trouble over all of this earth,
370   And that no one might endure the fourth.
Oh, dear Sir Shrew, Jesus shorten your life!
Still do you preach and say a hateful wife
Is reckoned as one of those mischances.
Are there no other forms of resemblance
That you may liken your parables to,
Without a poor wife being one of those?

You also liken woman's love to hell,
To barren land where water may not dwell.
You liken it also to the wild fire;
380   The more it burns, the more does it desire
To consume everything that can be burned.
You say, just as worms can destroy a tree,

Just so a wife can destroy her husband;
They know this, those who are bound to their wives.'

My lords, right thus you may well understand
That to my husbands I swore by my hand
They spoke thus to me in their drunkenness;
All was false, except that I took witness
Against Jenkin and my kinswoman, too.
390 Oh Lord, the pain I caused them, and the woe,
Completely without guilt, by God's sweet pain!
For like a horse I could both bite and whine.
I could complain even if I were wrong,
Or else oftentimes I would have been ruined.
Whoever comes first to the mill, first grinds;
I complained first, thus would our conflict end.
They were glad to excuse themselves quickly
For a thing of which they'd not been guilty.
I would accuse them of wenching, at hand,
400 When out of illness they could barely stand.

Yet I tickled his heart, just because he
Thought that I had great affection for him.
I swore that all of my nightly walking
Was to spy the wenches he was enjoying;
Under that false pretense I had much mirth!
For all such wit is given us at birth;
Deceit, weeping, and spinning did God give
To women as their nature while they live.
And thus of one thing I boast of myself—
410 At last I got the best in all respects,
By sleight, or force, or by some kind of thing,
As by continual grumbling or griping.
Namely, in bed they had the misfortune
That I would chide and give them no pleasure.
I would no longer in the bed abide
If I felt his arm go over my side,
Until he paid his ransom unto me;
Then I would allow him his nicety!
Therefore this tale to every man I tell:
420 Win whoever may—for all is for sale;
With an empty hand no hawks will you lure.
For profit all his lust I would endure,
And pretend I had a good appetite;

Yet in old bacon I took no delight.
That made me so that I would always chide,
For, though the pope were sitting by their side,
I would not spare them even at their board,
For in truth I repaid them word for word.
So help me very God omnipotent,
Though right now I should make my testament,
There was not a word that was not repaid.
I brought it about thus, by my own wits,
That they must give it up, all for the best,
Or else we never would have had a rest;
For though he looked as fierce as a lion,
Yet would he fail before the conclusion.

Then would I say, 'My good sweet love, take heed
How meekly looks Wilkyn, my little sheep!
Come near, my spouse, and let me kiss your cheek!
You should have been more patient and more meek,
And have had a more sweetly spiced conscience,
Since you do preach so much of Job's patience.
Endure always, since so well you can preach;
And unless you do, certainly I will teach
You that it's good to have a wife in peace.
One of us must bow down, there is no doubt;
And since a man is more reasonable
Than woman is, you must be more patient.
What ails you that you gripe so much and groan?
Is it that you want my quaint thing alone?
Why, take it all. Lo, it's yours every bit!
But Peter curse you if you don't love it.
For if I wanted to sell my *belle chose*,[4]
I could go about as fresh as a rose,
But I will keep it just for your own use.
You are to blame; by God, I tell the truth!'

These were the kinds of words we had on hand,
Now I will speak about my fourth husband.

My fourth husband was quite a reveller,
(That is to say, he had a paramour[5]),
And I was young and full of lechery,

430

440

450

460

---

[4]*belle chose*: French for "pretty thing"
[5]*paramour*: mistress

Stubborn, strong, and jolly as a magpie.
Oh, how I could dance to the harp so small,
And sing, to be sure, like a nightingale,
When I had drunk a good draught of sweet wine!
Metellius, the foul villain, the swine,
That with a staff bereft his wife of her life
Because she drank wine—if I'd been his wife,
He would not have frightened me from my drink!
And after wine, of Venus do I think,
For as surely as cold engenders hail,
A gluttonous mouth must have a lecherous tail.
A woman full of wine has no defence,
And lechers know this by experience.

But, Lord Christ, when the memory comes to me
Of my youth and my former jollity,
It tickles me right down to my heart's root;
To this very day it does my heart good
That I've enjoyed the world in my own time!
But age, alas, that envenoms all things,
Has bereft me of beauty and vigor.
Let it go! Farewell! The devil with it!
The flour is gone; there is no more to tell;
The bran, as best I can, now must I sell.
But still I will try to be quite merry.

Now will I tell about my fourth husband.
I tell you, I had in my heart a great spite
That in any other he took delight.
But he was repaid, by God and Saint Josse!
From the same wood I made him a cross—
Not of my body in any foul manner,
But certainly I showed men such good cheer
That in his own grease I left him to fry,
Out of anger and out of jealousy.
By God, on earth I was his purgatory,
For which I hope his soul is in glory.
For God knows, often he'd sit and complain
When his shoe was causing his foot great pain.
Except God and he, no one else could say
How sorely I tortured him, many ways.
He died when I came from Jerusalem,
And lies in a grave under the rood beam,

Although his tomb is not so curious
As was the sepulcher of Darius
That Appelles constructed so subtly;
It's a waste to bury him elaborately.
May he fare well and God give his soul rest!
He is now in his grave and in his chest.

Now of my fifth husband I will tell;
May God never let his soul go to hell!
And yet to me he was the greatest shrew;
I feel it in my ribs, all in a row,
And ever shall, until my final day.
But in our bed he was so fresh and gay,
And there, oh, how skilfully he could coax
Whenever he wished to have my *belle chose,*
So that, had he beat me on every bone,
He could win my love back again anon.
I believe I loved him best because he
Was always aloof with his love to me.
We women have, if I shan't tell a lie,
In this matter a quaint inclination:
Whatever thing we may not easily have,
We'll cry all day, for that thing we will crave;
Forbid something and that we will desire;
Entreat us firmly and away we fly;
With great reluctance do we show our wares,
For great crowds raise the price at market-fairs;
Too cheap a bargain is not thought a prize.
A woman knows all this if she is wise.

My fifth husband, his soul be blessed by God,
Whom I took just for love and not riches,
At one time was a scholar at Oxford
And had left school and went back home to board
With my good friend, who lived there in our town.
God save her soul! Her name was Alison.
She knew my heart and secrets of my life
Better than our parish priest, upon my life.
I'd tell her the deepest secret of all.
For whether my husband pissed on a wall,
Or did something that should cost him his life,
To her, and to another worthy wife,
And to my niece, whom I loved quite dearly,

I loved to tell his secret completely.
And so I did, so much, I swear to God,
That it often made his face red and hot
For very shame, and blamed himself that he
Had told me something in such secrecy.

And so it happened that once during Lent,
(For oftentimes I went to my best friend,
Because all the time I loved to be gay,
And walk about in March, April, and May
From house to house to hear various tales),
That Jenkin the clerk, my good friend Alice,
And I myself, out to the fields we went.
My husband was in London all that Lent,
Thus I had more leisure in which to play,
And in which to see and also be seen
By gay folk. I did not know where my grace
Was destined to be found, nor in what place,
And therefore I made my visitations
To holy vigils and to processions,
To preaching, and to these pilgrimages,
To miracle plays, and to marriages,
And wore about myself gay scarlet clothes.
No worms, nor any mites, nor any moths,
I swear by my soul, devoured the least bit.
Why? Because I was always wearing it!

Now I will tell you what happened to me.
As I said, in the fields we walked, we three,
Till truly we had such a flirtation,
This clerk and I, that for my provision
I spoke to him and suggested that he,
If I were a widow, should marry me.
For, (I say this not out of presumption),
I never was without readymade plans
For marriage, nor of other things I seek.
I hold a mouse's heart not worth a leek
That has but one hole to which he can run,
And if that one should fail then he is done.
I convinced him he had enchanted me,
(My mother once taught me that subtlety),
And I said, too, I dreamed of him all night,
That he would slay me as I lay so straight,

And that all my bed was covered with blood,
'And yet I hope that you shall do me good,
For blood betokens gold, as I was taught.'
And this was false, because I dreamed of nought;
I was but following my mother's lore
In this matter, as well as many more.

But now, sir, let's see, what was I saying?
Aha! By God, I have my tale again.

When my fourth husband was laid on his bier,
I wept continuously, with sorry cheer,
As wives must do, for that is the usage,
And with my kerchief covered my visage.
But because I was ensured of a mate,
I wept only a bit, I can affirm that.

My husband was borne to church that morning;
With him went the neighbors who were mourning,
And Jenkin, our scholar, was one of those.
And so help me God, when I saw him go
After the bier, I thought he had a pair
Of legs and of feet so shapely and fair
That all my heart I gave him there to hold.
He was, I believe, just twenty years old,
And I was forty, to tell you the truth,
But I always did have a young colt's tooth.
Gap-toothed I was, and that became me well;
I had the print of Saint Venus's seal.
So help me God, I was a lusty one,
And fair, and rich, and young, and well set up,
And truly, as my husbands said to me,
I had the best *quoniam*⁶ there could be.
For certainly I am ruled by Venus
In my feelings, and in my heart by Mars.
Venus gave me lust and lecherousness,
And Mars gave me my sturdy hardiness.
My ascendant was Taurus, and Mars therein.
Alas, alas! that ever love was sin!
I always followed my inclination
By the virtue of my constellation,

590

600

610

620

---

⁶*quoniam*: Latin for "whereas . . .," used here as a euphemism which has, like *quaint* (lines 338 and 450), a suggestive sound

Which made me so that I could not withhold
My chamber of Venus from a good fellow.
I still have the mark of Mars on my face
And also in another private place.
As God may surely be my salvation,
I have never loved in moderation,
But always followed my own appetite,
630   Whether he was short or tall, black or white.
I didn't care, as long as he liked me,
How poor he was, or else of what degree.

What can I say, but by the same month's end,
This jolly clerk, Jenkin, this fine young gent,
Had married me with great solemnity,
And to him I gave all the land and fee
That ever was given to me before.
But afterward I repented sorely;
He would not allow anything I wished.
640   By God, he hit my ear once with his fist
Because out of his book I tore a leaf,
And since that stroke my ear has been quite deaf.

I was as stubborn as a lioness,
And with my mouth a constant chatterer,
And I would walk, as I had done before,
From house to house, although he forbade it.
Because of this he would oftentimes preach
And from old Roman stories he would teach
How Simplicius Gallus left his wife
650   And forsook her for the rest of his life,
Simply because he saw her bareheaded
While looking out of the front door one day.

Another Roman, he told me his name,
Just because she was at a summer's game
Without his permission, forsook his wife.
And then he would go get his Bible and look
For that proverb in Ecclesiasticus
Where he commands and firmly exhorts
That a man not let his wife wander out.
660   And then he would say to me, without doubt,
'Whoever builds his house out of willows,
Spurs his horse to go over the fallows,

Lets his wife be a pilgrim to hallowed
Places deserves to hang on the gallows.'
But all for nothing; I cared not two haws
For all of his proverbs and his old saws,
Nor would I ever let him correct me;
I hate him who tells my vices to me,
And so do more of us, God knows, than I.
670   This would make him mad with me utterly;
I would not put up with him in any case.

Now I'll tell you truly, by Saint Thomas,
Why right out of his book I tore a leaf,
For which he hit me so hard I was deaf.

He had a book that gladly, night and day,
For his enjoyment he would read always,
By Valerius and Theophrastus,
Which always, as he read, would make him laugh.
And also there was once a clerk in Rome,
680   A cardinal, who was called Saint Jerome,
Who wrote a book against Jovinian.
In this book also were Tertullian,
Crisippus, Trotula, and Heloïse,
Who was an abbess not far from Paris,
Also the Parables of Solomon,
Ovid's *Art of Love,* and many other ones.
All these were bound into that one volume,
And each night and day it was his custom,
When he had leisure or a vacation
690   From his other worldly occupation,
To read out of this book of wicked wives.
He knew of them more legends and more lives
Than there are of good wives in the Bible.
For, trust me well, it is impossible
That any scholar will speak well of wives,
Unless it be about holy saints lives,
But not of any other women, no!
For who painted the lion? Tell me, who?[7]
By God, if women had written stories,
700   As scholars have in their oratories,

---

[7]A reference to the fable of the lion who asks this question of a man who shows it a painting of
a man killing a lion

They'd have written of men more wickedness
Than all the men since Adam could redress.
The children of Venus and Mercury
Are in their actions completely contrary,
For Mercury loves wisdom and science,
And Venus loves wanton extravagance.
And from their opposing disposition,
One falls at the other's exaltation.
Thus Mercury is in desolation
In Pisces at Venus's exaltation,
And Venus falls when Mercury is raised.
Thus no woman by a scholar is praised.
The scholar, when he's old and cannot do
Venus's work better than his old shoe,
Then he sits down and writes in his dotage
That women can't stay faithful in marriage!

But back to my purpose, why I told you
That I was beaten for a book, indeed!
One certain night Jenkin, my lord and master,
Read in his book, as he sat by the fire,
First of Eve, because of whose wickedness
All of mankind was brought to wretchedness,
And for which Jesus Christ was slain,
Who redeemed us with his heart's blood again.
Lo, here of woman you may clearly find
That woman caused the fall of all mankind.

He read to me how Sampson lost his hair
Sleeping: his lover cut it with her shears,
Through which treason he lost both of his eyes.

Then he read to me, if I shall not lie,
Of Hercules and of Dianira,
Because of whom he set himself on fire.

Nor did he forget the care and the woe
That Socrates had with his wives, too;
How Xanthippe threw piss upon his head.
This innocent man sat still, as if dead;
He wiped his head and no more would he say
Than 'After the thunder ends, then comes the rain!'

For his perversity he thought how sweet
The tale of Pasiphae, the queen of Crete.
Fie! Speak no more (it is a grisly thing)
Of her horrible lust and her likings.
Of Clytemnestra, who for lechery
Deceitfully caused her husband to die,
He read out with complete dedication.

He told me, also, what was the reason
That at Thebes Amphiorax lost his life.
My husband had a legend of his wife,
Eriphyle, who for an ounce of gold
Went secretly unto the Greeks and told
How her husband was hid, and in what place,
For which at Thebes he suffered death's disgrace.

He told me of Livia and Lucia,
Who with poison caused their husbands to die,
One of them for love, the other for hate.
Livia, late on one evening, poisoned
Her husband, who had kept her from her beau.
Wanton Lucia loved her husband so
That, in order to make him only think
Of her, she gave him a potion to drink,
But it killed him before the morrow,
And thus do husbands always have sorrow.

Then he told me how one Latumius
Complained unto his good friend Arrius
That in his garden was growing a tree.
Upon this tree, as he told it, all three
Of his wives had hanged themselves out of spite.
'Oh, my dear brother,' said this Arrius,
'Give me a branch of that same blessèd tree,
And in my garden planted it shall be.'

Of some wives in later times he has read
That they have killed their husbands in their bed
And let their lovers lay with them all night,
While the corpse lay on the floor stretched out straight.
And some have driven nails into their brains
While they slept, and thus were their husbands slain.
Some have given them poison in their drink.

He spoke more harm than any heart might think,
And therewithal he knew of more proverbs
780 Than in this world are growing grass and herbs.
'Better,' said he, 'that your habitation
Be with a lion or a foul dragon
Than with any woman who loves to chide.
Better,' said he, 'in the attic for life
Than down in the house with an angry wife;
They are so wicked and so rebellious
That they hate whatever their husbands love.'
He said, 'A woman casts her shame away
When she casts off her smock,' and furthermore,
790 'A fair woman, unless she's chaste also,
Is like a gold ring set in a sow's nose.'
Who could imagine, or who would suppose,
How much woe was in my heart, how much pain?

And when I saw he would never refrain
From reading in this cursèd book all night,
All of a sudden three leaves I just plucked
Out of his book, right as he read, then quick
With my fist I hit him so on the cheek
That into the fire he fell back and down.
800 And he jumped up just like a mad lion,
And with his fist he hit me on the head.
I lay on the floor as if I were dead.
And then when he saw how still that I lay,
He was aghast and would have fled away,
Until at last out of my swoon I woke.
'Oh! Have you killed me, you false thief?' I spoke.
'And for my land have you thus murdered me?
But yet, before I die, let me kiss you.'

And nearer he came, and kneeling right down,
810 He answered, 'My own dear sweet Alison,
So help me God, I shall never hit you,
And what I have done is mostly your fault.
Forgive me for it; that is all I seek!'
And there and then I hit him on the cheek,
And said, 'You thief, that will help pay you back!
And now will I die; no more can I speak.'
But at last, with very much care and woe,
We reached an accord, each with the other.

He gave me all the bridle in my hand,
820 To have the governance of house and land,
And of his tongue, and of his hand also.
I made him burn his book straightway right then.
And then when I had gotten for myself,
By my mastery, all the sovereignty,
And when he said to me, 'My own true wife,
Do as you wish for the rest of your life;
Keep your honor, and keep, too, my estate,'
After that day we had not one debate.
God so help me, I was as kind to him
830 As any wife from Denmark to India,
And also true, and so was he to me.
I pray to God, who sits in majesty,
To bless his soul for his mercy dear.

Now will I tell my tale, if you will hear."

Here follow the words of the Summoner and the Friar.

The Friar laughed when he had heard all this.
"Now, Dame," he said, "may I have joy or bliss;
This is a long preamble to a tale!"
And when the Summoner[8] heard the Friar exclaim,
"Lo," said the Summoner, "by God's two arms!
840 A friar will interfere every time!
Lo, good men, a fly and also a friar
Will fall in every dish and each matter.
What do you speak of preambulation?
What! Amble, trot, or peace, or go sit down!
You hinder our good sport in this manner."
"Yes, say you so, Sir Summoner?" said the Friar.
"Now, by my faith, I shall, before I go,
Tell of a summoner such a tale or two
That everyone will laugh who's in this place."

850 "And another thing, Friar—I curse your face,"
Said this Summoner, "and a curse on me
Unless I tell tales, at least two or three,
About friars, before we reach Sittingbourne.
Then I'll be able to make your heart mourn,
For I know well that your patience is gone."

---

[8]*Summoner:* An official who delivered summonses to appear in ecclesiastical court

Our Host then cried out, "Peace! And that at once!"
And said, "Let the woman tell us her tale.
You act like folk that are drunken with ale.
Dame, do tell forth your tale; that would be best."

860 "All ready, sir," she said, "just as you wish,
If I have permission of this good Friar."

"Indeed, dame," he said, "speak, and I will hear."

Here ends the Wife of Bath's Prologue.

Here begins the Tale of the Wife of Bath.

"In the olden days when lived King Arthur,
Of whom the Britons speak with great honor,
All of this country was filled with fairies.
The elf queen, with her jolly company,
Danced quite often in many a green mead.
This was the old opinion, so I read;
I speak of many hundred years ago.
870 But now I know that men see elves no more
For now the great charity and the prayers
Of limiters[9] and other holy friars
Who go through every land and every stream,
As thick as motes are in a bright sunbeam,
Blessing halls, chambers, kitchens, and bowers,
Cities, boroughs, castles, and high towers,
Villages and barns, stables and dairies—
This is the reason there are no fairies.
For places where once might have walked an elf,
880 There walks these days the limiter himself,
Early in the day and in the mornings,
Saying his prayers and his holy things
As he goes about his limitation.
Women may go safely up and down;
In every bush or under every tree
There is no incubus[10] but he,
And he will bring them only dishonor.

And so it befell that this King Arthur
Had in his household a knight bachelor,

---

[9]*limiters:* friars, licensed to beg within certain limits
[10]*incubus:* a spirit believed to father children with sleeping women

890 That one day came riding from the river.
And it happened, alone as he was born,
That he saw a maiden walking before.
From this maid, in spite of all that she did,
By very force, he took her maidenhead.
For this oppression there was such clamor
And suing for justice from King Arthur
That this same knight was condemned to be dead;
According to law, should have lost his head
(As it happened that was the statute then),
900 Except that the queen and other ladies
So long entreated the king of his grace
That the king left him his life in that place
And gave him to the queen, all at her will,
To choose whether she wished him saved or killed.

The queen thanked the king with all of her might,
And after this she spoke thus to the knight,
When she saw the chance on a certain day:
'You stand yet,' she told him, 'in such array
That your life still has no security.
910 I grant you your life, if you can tell me
What thing it is that women most desire.
Beware, and keep your neck-bone from the iron!
And if you cannot tell it to me now,
I will still give you permission to go
For twelve months and a day to seek and learn
An answer sufficient in this matter.
Your promise I will have, before you ride,
To yield up your body here at that time.'

Woeful was this knight; sorrowfully he sighed.
920 Indeed! He may not do just as he liked.
At last he decided he would set out
And come back again right at the year's end,
With such answer as God would provide him.
He took his leave and set forth on his way.

He searched in every house and every place
In which he thought he might have such good grace
As to learn there what women loved most,
But he could not arrive at any coast
Or place where he might find in this matter

930   Any two creatures in close agreement.
Some folk said that women best loved riches,
Some said honor, and some said happiness,
Some fine clothing, and some said joy in bed
And many times to be widowed and wed.
Some said that women's hearts may best be eased
Whenever we are flattered and are pleased.
This comes quite near the truth, I will not lie;
A man shall win us best with flattery,
And with close attendance and attention
940   We are quite often caught, both great and small.

And some people say that women love best
To be free ourselves and do as we wish,
And that no man reprove us for any vice,
But say that we are wise and not foolish.
For truly there is not one of us all,
If anyone rubs us where we are sore,
That won't kick back, although he says the truth.
Try it, and he shall find it happens thus;
For, be we never so vicious within,
950   We'd like to be thought wise and free of sin.

And some say we take the greatest delight
In being held both stable and discreet,
And in one purpose steadfastly to dwell,
And not betray the secrets people tell.
But that idea is not worth a rake;
We women can't keep anything secret,
As in the case of Midas; here's the tale:

Ovid, among other trivial things,
Told how Midas, under his long hair, had
960   Two ass's ears growing on his head,
A defect which he hid as best he might,
Kept carefully out of everyone's sight,
So that, except for his wife, no one knew.
He loved her most, and he trusted her too.
He prayed to her that no living creature
Should learn from her of his shameful feature.

She promised, 'No!' For all this world to win,
She would not do such villainy or sin

To bring foul reputation to his name;
970   Nor would she reveal it for her own shame.
But nevertheless she thought she would die
If too long she must keep the secret hid.
It seemed to her it swelled up in her heart
And that surely some word from her would start,
And since she dared to tell it to no man
Down to a nearby marsh one day she ran.
By the time she got there her heart was afire,
And as a bittern rumbles in the mire,
Down into the water she laid her mouth,
980   'Betray me not, Oh water, with your sound,'
She said. 'This is only for you to hear:
My husband has two long ass's ears!
Ah, now my heart is whole, now it is out.
I could no longer keep it, there's no doubt!'
Here you may see, although we may abide,
Yet it must out; we can no secrets hide.
The rest of the tale, if you wish to hear,
Read in Ovid and you will learn it there.

This knight, whom my tale is about really,
990   When he saw he might not find a reply,
That is to say, what women love the most,
Within his breast his spirit was downcast.
But home he goes; the end of his sojourn
Had finally come, and he must homeward turn.
And on his way he just happened to ride,
With all his care, under a forest side,
And there he saw some ladies; twenty-four
Were moving in a dance, and maybe more.
And toward this dance eagerly he did go,
1000   In hopes he'd learn some wisdom they might know.
But suddenly, before he was quite there,
The dance just vanished, he did not know where.
He saw no living creature anywhere,
But on the green an old woman sat there;
A fouler creature no one could devise.
This old woman then rose to meet the knight
And said, 'Sir knight, beyond here is no path;
Tell me what you are seeking, by your faith.
Perhaps it may prove the better for you;
1010   These old folk may know many things,' said she.

'My dear mother,' said this knight then, 'surely
I'm as good as dead unless I can say
Just what it is that women most desire.
If you could tell me, I'd repay your hire.'

'Swear me your oath, here in my hand,' said she,
'That the next thing I ask of you, truly,
You shall do it, if it lies in your might,
And I will answer you before tonight.'

'I grant you here,' said the knight, 'my firm oath.'

1020 'Then,' said she, 'I dare say that I can boast
Your life is safe, for I will stand with you.
By my life, the queen will say what I do.
Let's see who is so proud among them all,
Of those who wear a kerchief or a shawl,
Who would dare say "Nay" to what I will teach.
Let us go forth now with no further speech.'
Then she whispered a message in his ear
And told him to be glad and have no fear.

When they had come unto the court, this knight
1030 Then said that he had lived up to his word
And had his answer ready, so he said.
Then many noble wives and many maids
And many widows, chosen for their wisdom,
And the queen herself, sitting as justice,
Were assembled there to hear his answer,
And the knight was commanded to appear.

To everyone was commanded silence
So that the knight could tell that audience
What thing that worldly women love the best.
1040 This knight did not delay, as would a beast,
But straightway to his question he answered
In a manly voice that all the court heard:

'My liege lady, generally,' said he,
'A woman desires most to have sovereignty
Over her husband as well as her love,
In mastery to be the one above.
This is your greatest desire, though you kill me.

Do as you wish; I am here at your will.'
In all the court there was no wife or maid
1050 Or widow who disputed what he said,
But he said he was worthy to have his life.
And with that word up jumped the old woman
Which the knight had seen sitting on the green.

'Mercy,' said she, 'my sovereign lady queen!
Before you depart from court, do me right.
It was I who told the answer to the knight,
For which he gave a promise to me there
That the first thing from him I would require,
He would do it, if it lay in his might.
1060 Before the court, then, I pray you, sir knight,'
Said she, 'that you take me as your own wife,
For well you know that I have saved your life.
If I speak falsely, say "No," by your faith.'

This knight answered, 'Alas and welaway!
I know full well that that's what I promised.
For the love of God, make a new request!
Take all my goods and let my body go!'
'Nay, then,' said she, 'I curse the two of us!
For although I am foul, and old, and poor,
1070 I wish nothing, for all the gold and ore
That is under the earth or lies above,
Except to be your wife and have your love.'

'My love?' said he, 'Not so; my damnation!
Alas that any of my relation
Should ever be degraded so foully!'
But all for nought. The end is this, that he
Was constrained, and now he had to be wed,
And take his aged wife, and go to bed.

And now some men might say, it seems to me,
1080 That out of negligence I do not care
To tell of the joy and all the array
Of the feast that was held on that same day.
To which I have here an answer withal:
I say there was no joy or feast at all.
There was only heaviness and sorrow,
For secretly he wed her on the morrow,

And hid himself all day just like an owl,
Such woe he had that his wife looked so foul.

Great was the woe the knight had in his thought
1090 When he was brought with his wife to his bed.
He twisted and turned himself to and fro,
And his old wife lay smiling evermore,
And said, 'Oh dear husband, may God bless you!
Does every knight act with his wife as you do?
Is this the custom of King Arthur's house?
Is every knight of his so hard to please?
I am your own love and your lawful wife,
And I am she who has just saved your life.
Certainly I have done you only right.
1100 Why do you treat me thus on this first night?
You act like a man who has lost his wits.
What is my guilt? For God's love, tell me it
And it shall be amended, if I may.'

'Amended?' said the knight, 'Alas, nay, nay!
It will not be amended evermore.
You are so loathly, and so old also,
And also you come from such a low line
That it's no wonder that I toss and turn.
I wish to God that my own heart would burst!'
1110 'Is this,' said she, 'the cause of your unrest?'

'Yes,' said he, 'and it's no wonder it is.'

'Now, sir,' said she, 'I could amend all this,
If I so desired, in two days or three,
So that you might behave better towards me.

'But since you speak of such gentility
As is descended out of old riches,
And that for wealth you should be noble men,
Such arrogance is not worth a hen.
Observe who is most virtuous always,
1120 In public and private, and strives each day
To do whatever noble deeds he can;
Take *him* for the greatest gentleman.
Christ desires that we claim our nobleness
From Him, and not from our elders' riches.

For though they gave us all their heritage,
For which we claim to be of high lineage,
Yet they may not bequeath, for anything,
To any of us the virtuous living
That raised them up to their gentility,
1130   And bade us follow in the same degree.

'Well can the famous poet of Florence,
Who is called Dante, speak with the same sense.
Lo, in this sort of rhyme is Dante's tale:
"Prowess seldom stems from the family tree,
And this is because God, of His goodness,
Desires we claim from Him our gentleness."
For from our elders nothing can we claim
But temporal things that may hurt and maim.

'And everyone knows this as well as I:
1140   If nobility were planted naturally
In a certain lineage down the line,
In public and private, never would end
The nobility of all their service;
They would do neither villainy nor vice.

'Carry a fire into the darkest house
Between here and Mount Caucasus
And let men shut tight the doors and go thence;
Just as fair will the fire still lie and burn
As if twenty-thousand men did behold;
1150   To its natural function it will hold,
I swear by my life, until it should die.

'Here you may see well how gentility
Is in no way annexed to possessions,
Since people don't carry out their functions
Always, as the fire does, lo, in its kind.
For, as God knows, well may men often find
A lord's son doing shame and villainy.
He who would be praised for nobility
Because he was born of a noble house,
1160   With his forebears noble and virtuous,
And yet himself will do no gentle deed,
Nor follow his ancestors who are dead,
He is not noble, though a duke or earl;

Villainous sinful deeds make him a churl.
For nobility is only renown
Of your forebears for their exalted deeds,
Which is not a part of your own person.
Your gentility comes from God alone.
Thence comes our true nobility by grace;
It was not bequeathed to us with our place.

'Think how noble, as says Valerius,
Was the king Tullius Hostilius
Who rose from poverty to nobility.
Read Seneca and read Boethius;
There is no doubt, you shall find if you read,
That he is noble who does noble deeds.
And therefore, dear husband, thus I conclude:
Although my ancestors were humble and rude,
Yet may the high God, as I hope and pray,
Grant me the grace to live virtuously.
Then I become noble, when I begin
To live virtuously and avoid sin.

'And though for poverty you reprove me,
Yet the high God, in whom we do believe,
In willing poverty He lived His life.
And surely every man, maiden, or wife
May understand that Jesus, Heaven's King,
Would not have chosen a vicious living.
Humble poverty is an honest thing;
Thus do Seneca and other writers say.
Whoever can accept his poverty,
I hold him rich, though he has not a shirt.
He that covets is a much poorer man,
For he wishes to have more than he can;
But he that has nought, and covets no more,
Is rich, though you may think he is a boor.
True poverty sings appropriately;
Juvenal speaks of poverty pleasantly:
"The poor man, when he travels on his way,
Before thieves is free to dance and to play."
Poverty is a hateful good and, I guess,
One that encourages much business,
A great improver, too, of sapience
In whoever accepts it in patience.

Poverty is thus, though it seems a shame,
A possession that no one else will claim.
Poverty often, when a man is low,
Makes that man know his God and himself, too.
Poverty is a glass, it seems to me,
Through which a man may see his faithful friends.
Therefore, sir, since I've done no injury,
Reprove me no more for my poverty.

'And, sir, for being old you reprove me,
And surely, sir, though no authority
Had been written, gentlemen of honor
Say that men should show an elder favor
And say "father," out of gentility;
And I'm sure I can find authorities.

'And since you say that I am foul and old,
You should not fear to become a cuckold,
For foulness and age, I admit freely,
Are mighty guardians of chastity.
But nonetheless, since I know your delight,
I shall fulfill your worldly appetite.

'Now choose either of these two things,' said she:
'To have me foul and old until I die,
And be to you a true and humble wife,
And never to displease you all my life,
Or else you may have me be young and fair,
And take your chances with the visitors
That shall come to your house because of me,
Or in some other place, it may well be.
Now choose yourself which of those you might like.'
The knight contemplated and sorely sighed,
But at last he spoke in this manner:

'My lady and my love and wife so dear,
I place myself in your wise governance.
Choose yourself which may be the most pleasant
And most honor to you and me also.
It matters not to me which of the two,
For as you like it, that suffices me.'

'Then do I have the mastery,' asked she,
'Since I may choose and govern as I wish?'

'Yes, surely, wife,' said he, 'I hold it best.'

1210

1220

1230

1240

'Kiss me,' said she, 'we'll be no longer wroth,
For, on my oath, I will be to you both.
That is to say, indeed, both fair and good.
I pray to God that I might die quite mad
Unless to you I am as good and true

1250　As ever wife was since the world was new.
If tomorrow I'm not as fair to see
As any lady, or empress, or queen
Anywhere between the east and the west,
Do with my life or death just as you wish.
Raise up the curtain and see how it is.'

And when the knight truly perceived all this,
That she was so fair, and also so young,
For joy he took hold of her in his arms.
His heart was bathed in a bath of true bliss.

1260　A thousand times in a row he kissed her,
And she obeyed him in everything
That would be for his pleasure or liking.

And thus they live unto their lives' end
In perfect joy; and may Jesus Christ send
Husbands both meek and young, and fresh abed,
And the grace to survive those that we wed.
And I pray Jesus to shorten their lives
If they will not be governed by their wives.
And old and angry misers in expence—

1270　God send them soon the very pestilence."

Here ends the Wife of Bath's Tale.

ca. **1396**

Plato

ARISTOPHANES ON LOVE*

Within the Greco-Roman tradition, there were moralists who treated sexuality as sternly as did Augustine. Other writers, however, took a lighter view, as did the bawdy Greek dramatist Aristophanes. In one Aristophanes play, the

*Translated by J. Warrington.

women decide to end all war by simply withholding their sexual favors until men stop killing each other. Plato captured well Aristophanes's irreverent attitude in a speech he attributed to him in his dialogue, The Symposium. *Here Aristophanes detaches sexuality from reproduction, and from marriage. You might try to reformulate Aristophanes's view without his pervasive humor (much of it at the expense of the Greek gods).*

1   I am convinced that mankind has never had any conception of the power of Love, for if we had known him as he really is, surely we should have raised the mightiest temples and altars, and offered the most splendid sacrifices, in his honor, and not—as in fact we do—have utterly neglected him. Yet he of all the gods has the best title to our service, for he, more than all the rest, is the friend of man; he is our great ally, and it is he that cures us of those ills whose relief opens the way to man's highest happiness. And so, gentlemen, I will do my best to acquaint you with the power of Love, and you in your turn shall pass the lesson on.

2   First of all I must explain the real nature of man, and the change which it has undergone—for in the beginning we were nothing like we are now. For one thing, the race was divided into three; that is to say, besides the two sexes, male and female, which we have at present, there was a third which partook of the nature of both, and for which we still have a name, though the creature itself is forgotten. For though 'hermaphrodite' is only used nowadays as a term of contempt, there really was a man-woman in those days, a being which was half male and half female.

3   And secondly, gentlemen, each of these beings was globular in shape, with rounded back and sides, four arms and four legs, and two faces, both the same, on a cylindrical neck, and one head, with one face one side and one the other, and four ears, and two lots of privates, and all the other parts to match. They walked erect, as we do ourselves, backward or forward, whichever they pleased, but when they broke into a run they simply stuck their legs straight out and went whirling round and round like a clown turning cartwheels. And since they had eight legs, if you count their arms as well, you can imagine that they went bowling along at a pretty good speed.

4   The three sexes, I may say, arose as follows. The males were descended from the Sun, the females from the Earth, and the hermaphrodites from the Moon, which partakes of either sex, and they were round and they *went* round, because they took after their parents. And such, gentlemen, were their strength and energy, and such their arrogance, that they actually tried—like Ephialtes and Otus in Homer—to scale the heights of heaven and set upon the gods.

5   At this Zeus took counsel with the other gods as to what was to be done. They found themselves in rather an awkward position; they didn't want to blast them out of existence with thunderbolts as they did the giants, because that would be saying good-by to all their offerings and devotions, but at the same time they couldn't let them get altogether out of hand. At last, however, after racking his brains, Zeus offered a solution.

6   I think I can see my way, he said, to put an end to this disturbance by weakening these people without destroying them. What I propose to do is to cut them all in half, thus killing two birds with one stone, for each one will be only half as strong, and there'll be twice as many of them, which will suit us very nicely. They can walk about, upright, on their two legs, and if, said Zeus, I have any more trouble with them, I shall split them up again, and they'll have to hop about on one.

7   So saying, he cut them all in half just as you or I might chop up sorb apples for pickling, or slice an egg with a hair. And as each half was ready he told Apollo to turn its face, with the half-neck that was left, toward the side that was cut away—thinking that the sight of such a gash might frighten it into keeping quiet—and then to heal the whole thing up. So Apollo turned their faces back to front, and, pulling in the skin all the way round, he stretched it over what we now call the belly—like those bags you pull together with a string—and tied up the one remaining opening so as to form what we call the navel. As for the creases that were left, he smoothed most of them away, finishing off the chest with the sort of tool a cobbler uses to smooth down the leather on the last, but he left a few puckers round about the belly and the navel, to remind us of what we suffered long ago.

8   Now, when the work of bisection was complete it left each half with a desperate yearning for the other, and they ran together and flung their arms around each other's necks, and asked for nothing better than to be rolled into one. So much so, that they began to die of hunger and general inertia, for neither would do anything without the other. And whenever one half was left alone by the death of its mate, it wandered about questing and clasping in the hope of finding a spare half-woman—or a whole woman, as we should call her nowadays—or half a man. And so the race was dying out.

9   Fortunately, however, Zeus felt so sorry for them that he devised another scheme. He moved their privates round to the front, for of course they had originally been on the outside—which was now the back—and they had begotten and conceived not upon each other, but, like the grasshoppers, upon the earth. So now, as I say, he moved their members round to the front and made them propagate among themselves, the male begetting upon the female—the idea being that if, in all these clippings and claspings, a man should chance upon a woman, conception would take place and the race would be continued, while if man should conjugate with man, he might at least obtain such satisfaction as would allow him to turn his attention and his energies to the everyday affairs of life. So you see, gentlemen, how far back we can trace our innate love for one another, and how this love is always trying to reintegrate our former nature, to make two into one, and to bridge the gulf between one human being and another.

10   And so, gentlemen, we are all like pieces of the coins that children break in half for keepsakes—making two out of one, like the flatfish—and each of us is forever seeking the half that will tally with himself. The man who is a slice of the hermaphrodite sex, as it was called, will naturally be attracted by

women—the adulterer, for instance—and women who run after men are of similar descent—as, for instance, the unfaithful wife. But the woman who is a slice of the original female is attracted by women rather than by men—in fact she is a Lesbian—while men who are slices of the male are followers of the male, and show their masculinity throughout their boyhood by the way they make friends with men, and the delight they take in lying beside them and being taken in their arms. And these are the most hopeful of the nation's youth, for theirs is the most virile constitution.

11 I know there are some people who call them shameless, but they are wrong. It is not immodesty that leads them to such pleasures, but daring, fortitude, and masculinity—the very virtues that they recognize and welcome in their lovers—which is proved by the fact that in after years they are the only men who show any real manliness in public life. And so, when they themselves have come to manhood, their love in turn is lavished upon boys. They have no natural inclination to marry and beget children. Indeed, they only do so in deference to the usage of society, for they would just as soon renounce marriage altogether and spend their lives with one another.

12 Such a man, then, gentlemen, is of an amorous disposition, and gives his love to boys, always clinging to his like. And so, when this boy lover—or any lover, for that matter—is fortunate enough to meet his other half, they are both so intoxicated with affection, with friendship, and with love, that they cannot bear to let each other out of sight for a single instant. It is such reunions as these that impel men to spend their lives together, although they may be hard put to it to say what they really want with one another, and indeed, the purely sexual pleasures of their friendship could hardly account for the huge delight they take in one another's company. The fact is that both their souls are longing for a something else—a something to which they can neither of them put a name, and which they can only give an inkling of in cryptic sayings and prophetic riddles.

13 Now, supposing Hephaestus were to come and stand over them with his tool bag as they lay there side by side, and suppose he were to ask, Tell me, my dear creatures, what do you really want with one another?

14 And suppose they didn't know what to say, and he went on, How would you like to be rolled into one, so that you could always be together, day and night, and never be parted again? Because if that's what you want, I can easily weld you together, and then you can live your two lives in one, and, when the time comes, you can die a common death and still be two-in-one in the lower world. Now, what do you say? Is that what you'd like me to do? And would you be happy if I did?

15 We may be sure, gentlemen, that no lover on earth would dream of refusing such an offer, for not one of them could imagine a happier fate. Indeed, they would be convinced that this was just what they'd been waiting for—to be merged, that is, into an utter oneness with the beloved.

16   And so all this to-do is a relic of that original state of ours, when we were whole, and now, when we are longing for and following after that primeval wholeness, we say we are in love. For there was a time, I repeat, when we were one, but now, for our sins, God has scattered us abroad, as the Spartans scattered the Arcadians. Moreover, gentlemen, there is every reason to fear that, if we neglect the worship of the gods, they will split us up again, and then we shall have to go about with our noses sawed asunder, part and counterpart, like the basso-relievos on the tombstones. And therefore it is our duty one and all to inspire our friends with reverence and piety, for so we may ensure our safety and attain that blessed union by enlisting in the army of Love and marching beneath his banners.

17   For Love must never be withstood—as we do, if we incur the displeasure of the gods. But if we cling to him in friendship and reconciliation, we shall be among the happy few to whom it is given in these latter days to meet their other halves. Now, I don't want any coarse remarks from Eryximachus. I don't mean Pausanias and Agathon, though for all I know they may be among the lucky ones, and both be sections of the male. But what I am trying to say is this—that the happiness of the whole human race, women no less than men, is to be found in the consummation of our love, and in the healing of our dissevered nature by finding each his proper mate. And if this be a counsel of perfection, then we must do what, in our present circumstances, is next best, and bestow our love upon the natures most congenial to our own.

18   And so I say that Love, the god who brings all this to pass, is worthy of our hymns, for his is the inestimable and present service of conducting us to our true affinities, and it is he that offers this great hope for the future—that, if we do not fail in reverence to the gods, he will one day heal us and restore us to our old estate, and establish us in joy and blessedness.

ca. **385 B.C.**

Sigmund Freud

CIVILIZATION AND ITS DISCONTENTS*

No writer has more influenced twentieth-century discussions of sexuality than the psychologist Sigmund Freud. What has remained a matter of rancorous disagreement from Freud's day to our own is whether this influence is a good thing. In the following selection, Freud makes what for him is a characteristic

*Translated by James Strachey.

move: he connects the desire for sexual gratification to a whole range of cul-
tural phenomena that superficially seem unrelated. In the process, he makes all
sorts of provocative assertions, including that for civilization—any civiliza-
tion—"sexuality as a source of enjoyment for its own sake is unacceptable."

[1] After primal man had discovered that it lay in his own hands, literally, to improve his lot on earth by working, it cannot have been a matter of indifference to him whether another man worked with or against him. The other man acquired the value for him of a fellow-worker, with whom it was useful to live together. Even earlier, in his ape-like prehistory, man had adopted the habit of forming families, and the members of his family were probably his first helpers. One may suppose that the founding of families was connected with the fact that a moment came when the need for genital satisfaction no longer made its appearance like a guest who drops in suddenly, and, after his departure, is heard of no more for a long time, but instead took up its quarters as a permanent lodger. When this happened, the male acquired a motive for keeping the female, or, speaking more generally, his sexual objects, near him; while the female, who did not want to be separated from her helpless young, was obliged, in their interests, to remain with the stronger male.[1] In this primitive family one essential feature of civilization is still lacking. The arbitrary

---

[1]The organic periodicity of the sexual process has persisted, it is true, but its effect on psychical sexual excitation has rather been reversed. This change seems most likely to be connected with the diminution of the olfactory stimuli by means of which the menstrual process produced an effect on the male psyche. Their role was taken over by visual excitations, which, in contrast to the intermittent olfactory stimuli, were able to maintain a permanent effect. The taboo on menstruation is derived from this 'organic repression', as a defence against a phase of development that has been surmounted. All other motives are probably of a secondary nature. (Cf. C. D. Daly, 1927.) This process is repeated on another level when the gods of a superseded period of civilization turn into demons. The diminution of the olfactory stimuli seems itself to be a consequence of man's raising himself from the ground, of his assumption of an upright gait; this made his genitals, which were previously concealed, visible and in need of protection, and so provoked feelings of shame in him.

The fateful process of civilization would thus have set in with man's adoption of an erect posture. From that point the chain of events would have proceeded through the devaluation of olfactory stimuli and the isolation of the menstrual period to the time when visual stimuli were paramount and the genitals became visible, and thence to the continuity of sexual excitation, the founding of the family and so to the threshold of human civilization. This is only a theoretical speculation, but it is important enough to deserve careful checking with reference to the conditions of life which obtain among animals closely related to man.

A social factor is also unmistakably present in the cultural trend towards cleanliness, which has received *ex post facto* justification in hygienic considerations but which manifested itself before their discovery. The incitement to cleanliness originates in an urge to get rid of the excreta, which have become disagreeable to the sense perceptions. We know that in the nursery things are different. The excreta arouse no disgust in children. They seem valuable to them as being a part of their own body which has come away from it. Here upbringing insists with special energy on hastening the course of development which lies ahead, and which should make the excreta worthless, disgusting, abhorrent and abominable. Such a reversal of values would scarcely be possible if the substances that are expelled from the body were not doomed by their strong smells to share the fate which overtook olfactory stimuli after man adopted the erect posture.

will of its head, the father, was unrestricted. In *Totem and Taboo* [1912–13] I have tried to show how the way led from this family to the succeeding stage of communal life in the form of bands of brothers. In overpowering their father, the sons had made the discovery that a combination can be stronger than a single individual. The totemic culture is based on the restrictions which the sons had to impose on one another in order to keep this new state of affairs in being. The taboo-observances were the first 'right' or 'law'.[2] The communal life of human beings had, therefore, a two-fold foundation: the compulsion to work, which was created by external necessity, and the power of love, which made the man unwilling to be deprived of his sexual object—the woman—, and made the woman unwilling to be deprived of the part of herself which had been separated off from her—her child. Eros and Ananke [Love and Necessity] have become the parents of human civilization too. The first result of civilization was that even a fairly large number of people were now able to live together in a community. And since these two great powers were co-operating in this, one might expect that the further development of civilization would proceed smoothly towards an even better control over the external world and towards a further extension of the number of people included in the community. Nor is it easy to understand how this civilization could act upon its participants otherwise than to make them happy.

2   Before we go on to enquire from what quarter an interference might arise, this recognition of love as one of the foundations of civilization may serve as an excuse for a digression which will enable us to fill in a gap which we left in an earlier discussion. We said there that man's discovery that sexual (genital) love afforded him the strongest experiences of satisfaction, and in fact provided him with the prototype of all happiness, must have suggested to him that he should continue to seek the satisfaction of happiness in his life along the path of sexual relations and that he should make genital erotism the central point of his life. We went on to say that in doing so he made himself dependent in a most dangerous way on a portion of the external world, namely, his chosen love-object, and exposed himself to extreme suffering if he should be rejected by that object or should lose it through unfaithfulness or

---

Anal erotism, therefore, succumbs in the first instance to the 'organic repression' which paved the way to civilization. The existence of the social factor which is responsible for the further transformation of anal erotism is attested by the circumstance that, in spite of all man's developmental advances, he scarcely finds the smell of *his own* excreta repulsive, but only that of other people's. Thus a person who is not clean—who does not hide his excreta—is offending other people; he is showing no consideration for them. And this is confirmed by our strongest and commonest terms of abuse. It would be incomprehensible, too, that man should use the name of his most faithful friend in the animal world—the dog—as a term of abuse if that creature had not incurred his contempt through two characteristics: that it is an animal whose dominant sense is that of smell and one which has no horror of excrement, and that it is not ashamed of its sexual functions.

[2][The German '*Recht*' means both 'right' and 'law'.]

death. For that reason the wise men of every age have warned us most emphatically against this way of life; but in spite of this it has not lost its attraction for a great number of people.

3   A small minority are enabled by their constitution to find happiness, in spite of everything, along the path of love. But far-reaching mental changes in the function of love are necessary before this can happen. These people make themselves independent of their object's acquiescence by displacing what they mainly value from being loved on to loving; they protect themselves against the loss of the object by directing their love, not to single objects but to all men alike; and they avoid the uncertainties and disappointments of genital love by turning away from its sexual aims and transforming the instinct into an impulse with an *inhibited aim.* What they bring about in themselves in this way is a state of evenly suspended, steadfast, affectionate feeling, which has little external resemblance any more to the stormy agitations of genital love, from which it is nevertheless derived. Perhaps St. Francis of Assisi went furthest in thus exploiting love for the benefit of an inner feeling of happiness. Moreover, what we have recognized as one of the techniques for fulfilling the pleasure principle has often been brought into connection with religion; this connection may lie in the remote regions where the distinction between the ego and objects or between objects themselves is neglected. According to one ethical view, whose deeper motivation will become clear to us presently, this readiness for a universal love of mankind and the world represents the highest standpoint which man can reach. Even at this early stage of the discussion I should like to bring forward my two main objections to this view. A love that does not discriminate seems to me to forfeit a part of its own value, by doing an injustice to its object; and secondly, not all men are worthy of love.

4   The love which founded the family continues to operate in civilization both in its original form, in which it does not renounce direct sexual satisfaction, and in its modified form as aim-inhibited affection. In each, it continues to carry on its function of binding together considerable numbers of people, and it does so in a more intensive fashion than can be effected through the interest of work in common. The careless way in which language uses the word 'love' has its genetic justification. People give the name 'love' to the relation between a man and a woman whose genital needs have led them to found a family; but they also give the name 'love' to the positive feelings between parents and children, and between the brothers and sisters of a family, although *we* are obliged to describe this as 'aim-inhibited love' or 'affection'. Love with an inhibited aim was in fact originally fully sensual love, and it is so still in man's unconscious. Both—fully sensual love and aim-inhibited love— extend outside the family and create new bonds with people who before were strangers. Genital love leads to the formation of new families, and aim-inhibited love to 'friendships' which become valuable from a cultural standpoint because they escape some of the limitations of genital love, as, for instance, its exclusiveness. But in the course of development the relation of love to civiliza-

tion loses its unambiguity. On the one hand love comes into opposition to the interests of civilization; on the other, civilization threatens love with substantial restrictions.

5   This rift between them seems unavoidable. The reason for it is not immediately recognizable. It expresses itself at first as a conflict between the family and the larger community to which the individual belongs. We have already perceived that one of the main endeavours of civilization is to bring people together into large unities. But the family will not give the individual up. The more closely the members of a family are attached to one another, the more often do they tend to cut themselves off from others, and the more difficult is it for them to enter into the wider circle of life. The mode of life in common which is phylogenetically the older, and which is the only one that exists in childhood, will not let itself be superseded by the cultural mode of life which has been acquired later. Detaching himself from his family becomes a task that faces every young person, and society often helps him in the solution of it by means of puberty and initiation rites. We get the impression that these are difficulties which are inherent in all psychical—and, indeed, at bottom, in all organic—development.

6   Furthermore, women soon come into opposition to civilization and display their retarding and restraining influence—those very women who, in the beginning, laid the foundations of civilization by the claims of their love. Women represent the interests of the family and of sexual life. The work of civilization has become increasingly the business of men, it confronts them with ever more difficult tasks and compels them to carry out instinctual sublimations of which women are little capable. Since a man does not have unlimited quantities of psychical energy at his disposal, he has to accomplish his tasks by making an expedient distribution of his libido. What he employs for cultural aims he to a great extent withdraws from women and sexual life. His constant association with men, and his dependence on his relations with them, even estrange him from his duties as a husband and father. Thus the woman finds herself forced into the background by the claims of civilization and she adopts a hostile attitude towards it.

7   The tendency on the part of civilization to restrict sexual life is no less clear than its other tendency to expand the cultural unit. Its first, totemic, phase already brings with it the prohibition against an incestuous choice of object, and this is perhaps the most drastic mutilation which man's erotic life has in all time experienced. Taboos, laws and customs impose further restrictions, which affect both men and women. Not all civilizations go equally far in this; and the economic structure of the society also influences the amount of sexual freedom that remains. Here, as we already know, civilization is obeying the laws of economic necessity, since a large amount of the psychical energy which it uses for its own purposes has to be withdrawn from sexuality. In this respect civilization behaves towards sexuality as a people or a stratum of its population does which has subjected another one to its exploitation.

Fear of a revolt by the suppressed elements drives it to stricter precautionary measures. A high-water mark in such a development has been reached in our Western European civilization. A cultural community is perfectly justified, psychologically, in starting by proscribing manifestations of the sexual life of children, for there would be no prospect of curbing the sexual lusts of adults if the ground had not been prepared for it in childhood. But such a community cannot in any way be justified in going to the length of actually *disavowing* such easily demonstrable, and, indeed, striking phenomena. As regards the sexually mature individual, the choice of an object is restricted to the opposite sex, and most extra-genital satisfactions are forbidden as perversions. The requirement, demonstrated in these prohibitions, that there shall be a single kind of sexual life for everyone, disregards the dissimilarities, whether innate or acquired, in the sexual constitution of human beings; it cuts off a fair number of them from sexual enjoyment, and so becomes the source of serious injustice. The result of such restrictive measures might be that in people who are normal—who are not prevented by their constitution—the whole of their sexual interests would flow without loss into the channels that are left open. But heterosexual genital love, which has remained exempt from outlawry, is itself restricted by further limitations, in the shape of insistence upon legitimacy and monogamy. Present-day civilization makes it plain that it will only permit sexual relationships on the basis of a solitary, indissoluble bond between one man and one woman, and that it does not like sexuality as a source of pleasure in its own right and is only prepared to tolerate it because there is so far no substitute for it as a means of propagating the human race.

8   This, of course, is an extreme picture. Everybody knows that it has proved impossible to put it into execution, even for quite short periods. Only the weaklings have submitted to such an extensive encroachment upon their sexual freedom, and stronger natures have only done so subject to a compensatory condition, which will be mentioned later. Civilized society has found itself obliged to pass over in silence many transgressions which, according to its own rescripts, it ought to have punished. But we must not err on the other side and assume that, because it does not achieve all its aims, such an attitude on the part of society is entirely innocuous. The sexual life of civilized man is notwithstanding severely impaired; it sometimes gives the impression of being in process of involution as a function, just as our teeth and hair seem to be as organs. One is probably justified in assuming that its importance as a source of feelings of happiness, and therefore in the fulfilment of our aim in life, has sensibly diminished.[3] Sometimes one seems to perceive that it is not only the pressure of civilization but something in the nature of the function

[3]Among the works of that sensitive English writer, John Galsworthy, who enjoys general recognition to-day, there is a short story of which I early formed a high opinion. It is called 'The Apple-Tree', and it brings home to us how the life of present-day civilized people leaves no room for the simple natural love of two human beings.

itself which denies us full satisfaction and urge us along other paths. This may be wrong; it is hard to decide.

1929

May Sarton

THE REWARDS OF LIVING A SOLITARY LIFE

May Sarton was an extremely productive poet, novelist, and essayist. This reflective essay voices a position often overlooked in discussions of the changing shape of American households: "the most interesting thing about a solitary life, and mine has been that for the last twenty years, is that it becomes increasingly rewarding." Her commitment to the self "till death do us part," as she puts it in the final paragraph, suggests that she thinks of her solitude as equivalent or preferable to the marital bond usually sealed with those words. Why do you think she includes her opening anecdote about the gregarious man surprised by solitude? What does it suggest about her intention?

1   The other day an acquaintance of mine, a gregarious and charming man, told me he had found himself unexpectedly alone in New York for an hour or two between appointments. He went to the Whitney and spent the "empty" time looking at things in solitary bliss. For him it proved to be a shock nearly as great as falling in love to discover that he could enjoy himself so much alone.

2   What had he been afraid of, I asked myself? That, suddenly alone, he would discover that he bored himself, or that there was, quite simply, no self there to meet? But having taken the plunge, he is now on the brink of adventure; he is about to be launched into his own inner space, space as immense, unexplored, and sometimes frightening as outer space to the astronaut. His every perception will come to him with a new freshness and, for a time, seem startlingly original. For anyone who can see things for himself with a naked eye becomes, for a moment or two, something of a genius. With another human being present vision becomes double vision, inevitably. We are busy wondering, what does my companion see or think of this, and what do I think of it? The original impact gets lost, or diffused.

3   "Music I heard with you was more than music." Exactly. And therefore music *itself* can only be heard alone. Solitude is the salt of personhood. It brings out the authentic flavor of every experience.

4   "Alone one is never lonely: the spirit adventures, walking/In a quiet garden, in a cool house, abiding single there."

5   Loneliness is most acutely felt with other people, for with others, even with a lover sometimes, we suffer from our differences of taste, temperament, mood. Human intercourse often demands that we soften the edge of perception, or withdraw at the very instant of personal truth for fear of hurting, or of being inappropriately present, which is to say naked, in a social situation. Alone we can afford to be wholly whatever we are, and to feel whatever we feel absolutely. That is a great luxury!

6   For me the most interesting thing about a solitary life, and mine has been that for the last twenty years, is that it becomes increasingly rewarding. When I can wake up and watch the sun rise over the ocean, as I do most days, and know that I have an entire day ahead, uninterrupted, in which to write a few pages, take a walk with my dog, lie down in the afternoon for a long think (why does one think better in a horizontal position?), read and listen to music, I am flooded with happiness.

7   I am lonely only when I am overtired, when I have worked too long without a break, when for the time being I feel empty and need filling up. And I am lonely sometimes when I come back home after a lecture trip, when I have seen a lot of people and talked a lot, and am full to the brim with experience that needs to be sorted out.

8   Then for a little while the house feels huge and empty, and I wonder where my self is hiding. It has to be recaptured slowly by watering the plants, perhaps, and looking again at each one as though it were a person, by feeding the two cats, by cooking a meal.

9   It takes a while, as I watch the surf blowing up in fountains at the end of the field, but the moment comes when the world falls away, and the self emerges again from the deep unconscious, bringing back all I have recently experienced to be explored and slowly understood, when I can converse again with my hidden powers, and so grow, and so be renewed, till death do us part.

1974

Brent Hartinger

A CASE FOR GAY MARRIAGE

Like May Sarton's, Hartinger's argument is for a broadening of options in thinking about the American family. While Sarton argues for more acceptance for those who choose to live alone, Hartinger asks for acceptance of a much more controversial change—that homosexuals be allowed to marry. This piece

and the one that follows by Dennis O'Brien appeared in the magazine Commonweal *as part of a symposium on the topic of same-sex marriage. What are
the main objections that Hartinger anticipates? Why should such marriages be
legal, according to him?*

1   In San Francisco this year, homosexuals won't just be registering for the
draft and to vote. In November 1990, voters approved legislation which
allowed unmarried live-in partners—heterosexual or homosexual—to register themselves as "domestic partners," publicly agreeing to be jointly responsible for basic living expenses. Like a few other cities, including New York
and Seattle, San Francisco had already allowed bereavement leave to the
domestic partners of municipal employees. But San Francisco lesbians and
gays had been trying for eight years to have some form of partnership regis-
tration—for symbolic reasons at least—ever since 1982 when then-mayor
Diane Feinstein vetoed a similar ordinance. A smattering of other cities provide health benefits to the domestic partners of city employees. In 1989, a
New York court ruled that a gay couple is a "family" in that state, at least in
regard to their rent-controlled housing (the decision was reaffirmed late last
year). And in October of 1989, Denmark became the first industrialized country to permit same-sex unions (since then, one-fifth of all marriages performed there have been homosexual ones).

2   However sporadic, these represent major victories for gay men and lesbians for whom legal marriage is not an option. Other challenges are coming
fast and furious. Two women, Sandra Rovira and Majorie Forlini, lived
together in a marriage-like relationship for twelve years—and now after her
partner's death, Rovira is suing AT&T, Forlini's employer, for refusing to pay
the death benefits the company usually provides surviving spouses. Craig
Dean and Patrick Gill, a Washington, D.C., couple, have filed a $1 million dis-
crimination suit against that city for denying them a marriage license and
allegedly violating its human rights acts which outlaw discrimination on the
basis of sexual orientation; the city's marriage laws explicitly prohibit polygamous and incestuous marriages, but not same-sex ones.

3   Legally and financially, much is at stake. Most employee benefit plans—
which include health insurance, parental leave, and bereavement leave—
extend only to legal spouses. Marriage also allows partners to file joint
income taxes, usually saving them money. Social Security can give extra payment to qualified spouses. And assets left from one legal spouse to the other
after death are not subject to estate taxes. If a couple splits up, there is the
issue of visitation rights for adopted children or offspring conceived by artificial insemination. And then there are issues of jurisprudence (a legal spouse
cannot be compelled to testify against his or her partner) and inheritance, tenancy, and conservatorship: pressing concerns for many gays as a result of
AIDS.

4   In terms of numbers alone, a need exists. An estimated 10 percent of the population—about 25 million Americans—is exclusively or predominantly homosexual in sexual orientation, and upwards of 50 percent of the men and about 70 percent of the women are in long-term, committed relationships. A 1990 survey of 1,266 lesbian and gay couples found that 82 percent of the male couples and 75 percent of the female ones share all or part of their incomes.

5   As a result, many lesbians and gays have fought for "domestic partnership" legislation to extend some marital and family benefits to unmarried couples—cohabitating partners either unwilling or, in the case of homosexuals, unable to marry. In New York City, for example, unmarried municipal workers who have lived with their partners at least a year may register their relationships with the personnel department, attesting to a "close and committed" relationship "involving shared responsibilities," and are then entitled to bereavement leave.

6   But such a prescription is inadequate; the protections and benefits are only a fraction of those resulting from marriage—and are available to only a small percentage of gays in a handful of cities (in the above-mentioned survey, considerably less than 10 percent of lesbian and gay couples were eligible for any form of shared job benefits). Even the concept of "domestic partnership" is seriously flawed. What constitutes a "domestic partner"? Could roommates qualify? A women and her live-in maid? It could take an array of judicial decision-making to find out.

7   Further, because the benefits of "domestic partnership" are allotted to couples without much legal responsibility—and because the advantages of domestic partnership are necessarily allowed for unmarried heterosexual partners as well as homosexual ones—domestic partnership has the unwanted consequence of weakening traditional marriage. Society has a vested interest in stable, committed relationships—especially, as in the case of most heterosexual couples, when children are concerned. But by eliminating the financial and legal advantages to marriage, domestic partnership dilutes that institution.

8   Society already has a measure of relational union—it's called marriage, and it's not at all difficult to ascertain: you're either married or you're not.

9   Yet for unmarried heterosexual couples, marriage is at least an option. Gay couples have no such choice—and society also has an interest in committed, long-lasting relationships even between homosexuals. An estimated 3 to 5 million homosexuals have parented children within heterosexual relationships, and at least 1,000 children were born to lesbian or gay couples in the San Francisco area alone in just the last five years. None of the recent thirty-five studies on homosexual parents has shown that parental sexual orientation has any adverse effect on children (and the children of gays are no more likely to be gay themselves). Surely increased stability in the relationships of

lesbians and gay men could only help the gays themselves and their many millions of children.

10   Some suggest that legal mechanisms already exist by which lesbian and gay couples could create some of the desired protections for their relationships: power-of-attorney agreements, proxies, wills, insurance policies, and joint tenancy arrangements. But even these can provide only a fraction of the benefits of marriage. And such an unwieldy checklist guarantees that many lesbian and gay couples will not employ even those available.

11   There is a simpler solution. Allow gay civil marriage. And throw the weight of our religious institutions behind such unions.

12   In 1959, Mildred Jeter and Richard Loving, a mixed-race Virginia couple married in Washington, D.C., pleaded guilty to violating Virginia's ban on interracial marriages. Jeter and Loving were given a suspended jail sentence on the condition that they leave the state. In passing the sentence, the judge said, "Almighty God created the races white, black, yellow, Malay, and red, and he placed them on separate continents. And but for the interference with his arrangements, there would be no cause for such marriages. The fact that he separated the races shows that he did not intend for the races to mix." A motion to overturn the decision was denied by two higher Virginia courts until the state's ban on interracial marriage was declared unconstitutional by the United States Supreme Court in 1967. At the time, fifteen other states also had such marital prohibitions.

13   Clearly, one's sexual orientation is different from one's race. While psychological consensus (and compelling identical and fraternal twin studies) force us to concede that the homosexual *orientation* is not a choice (nor is it subject to change), homosexual behavior definitely is a choice, very unlike race. Critics maintain that gays can marry—just not to members of their same sex.

14   But with regard to marriage, whether homosexual behavior is a choice or not is irrelevant, since one's marriage partner is *necessarily* a choice. In 1959, Richard Loving, a white man, could have chosen a different partner to marry other than Mildred Jeter, a black woman; the point is that he did not. The question is whether, in the absence of a compelling state interest, the state should be allowed to supersede the individual's choice.

15   Some maintain that there are compelling state interests to prohibiting same-sex marriages: that tolerance for gay marriages would open the door for any number of unconventional marital arrangements—group marriage, for example. In fact, most lesbian and gay relationships are probably far more conventional than most people think. In the vast majority of respects, gay relationships closely resemble heterosexual ones—or even actually improve upon them (gay relationships tend to be more egalitarian than heterosexual ones). And in a society where most cities have at least one openly gay bar and sizable gay communities—where lesbians and gays appear regularly on tele-

vision and in the movies—a committed relationship between two people of the same sex is not nearly the break from convention that a polygamous one is. More important, easing the ban on same-sex marriage would make lesbians and gays, the vast majority of whom have not chosen celibacy, even more likely to live within long-term, committed partnerships. The result would be more people living more conventional lifestyles, not more people living less conventional ones. It's actually a conservative move, not a liberal one.

16   Similarly, there is little danger that giving legitimacy to gay marriages would undermine the legitimacy of heterosexual ones—cause "the breakdown of the family." Since heterosexuality appears to be at least as immutable as homosexuality (and since there's no evidence that the prevalence of homosexuality increases following the decriminalization of it), there's no chance heterosexuals would opt for the "homosexual alternative." Heterosexual marriage would still be the ultimate social union for heterosexuals. Gay marriage would simply recognize a consistent crosscultural, transhistorical minority and allow that significant minority to also participate in an important social institution. And since marriage licenses are not rationed out, homosexual partnerships wouldn't deny anyone else the privilege.

17   Indeed, the compelling state interest lies in *permitting* gay unions. In the wake of AIDS, encouraging gay monogamy is simply rational public health policy. Just as important, gay marriage would reduce the number of closeted gays who marry heterosexual partners, as an estimated 20 percent of all gays do, in an effort to conform to social pressure—but at enormous cost to themselves, their children, and their opposite-sex spouses. It would reduce the atmosphere of ridicule and abuse in which the children of homosexual parents grow up. And it would reduce the number of shameful parents who disown their children or banish their gay teen-agers to lives of crime, prostitution, and drug abuse, or to suicide (psychologists estimate that gay youth comprise up to 30 percent of all teen suicides, and one Seattle study found that a whopping 40 percent of that city's street kids may be lesbian or gay, most having run away or been expelled from intolerant homes). Gay marriage wouldn't weaken the family; it would *strengthen* it.

18   The unprecedented social legitimacy given gay partnerships—and homosexuality in general—would have other societal benefits as well: it would dramatically reduce the widespread housing and job discrimination, and verbal and physical violence experienced by most lesbians and gays, clear moral and social evils.

19   Of course, legal and religious gay marriage wouldn't as some writers claim, "celebrate" or be "an endorsement" of homosexual sexual behavior—any more than heterosexual marriage celebrates heterosexual sex or endorses it; gay marriage would celebrate the loving, committed relationship between two individuals, a relationship in which sexual behavior is one small part.

Still, the legalization of gay marriage, while not making homosexual sexual behavior any more prevalent, would remove much of the stigma concerning such behavior, at least that which takes place within the confines of "marriage." And if the church sanctions such unions, a further, moral legitimacy will be granted. In short, regardless of the potential societal gains, should society and the church reserve a centuries-old moral stand that condemns homosexual sexual behavior?

20   We have no choice: the premises upon which the moral stand are based have changed. Science now acknowledges the existence of a homosexual sexual *orientation*, like heterosexuality, a fundamental affectional predisposition. Unlike specific behaviors of, say, rape or incest, a homosexual's sexual behavior is the logical expression of his or her most basic, unchangeable sexual make-up. And unlike rape and incest, necessarily manifestations of destruction and abuse, sexual behavior resulting from one's sexual orientation can be an expression of love and unity (it is the complete denial of this love—indeed, an unsettling preoccupation with genital activity—that make the inflammatory comparisons of homosexual sex to rape, incest, and alcoholism so frustrating for lesbians and gays).

21   Moral condemnation of homosexual sexual behavior is often founded on the belief that sex and marriage are—and should be—inexorably linked with child-rearing; because lesbians and gay men are physiologically incapable of creating children alone, all such sexual behavior is deemed immoral—and gays are considered unsuitable to the institution of marriage. But since moral sanction is not withheld from infertile couples or those who remain childless, this standard is clearly being inconsistently—and unfairly—applied.

22   Some cite the promiscuity of some male gays as if this is an indication that all homosexuals are incapable or undeserving of marriage. But this standard is also inconsistently applied; it has never been seriously suggested that the existence of promiscuous heterosexuals invalidate all heterosexuals from the privilege of marriage. And if homosexuals are more likely than heterosexuals to be promiscuous—and if continual, harsh condemnation hasn't altered that fact—the sensible solution would seem to be try to lure gays back to the monogamous fold by providing efforts in the direction with some measure of respect and social support: something gay marriage would definitely provide.

23   Human beings are sexual creatures. It is simply not logical to say, as the church does, that while one's basic sexual outlook is neither chosen nor sinful, any activity taken as a result of that orientation is. One must then ask exactly where does the sin of "activity" begin anyway? Hugging a person of the same sex? Kissing? Same-sex sexual fantasy? Even apart from the practical impossibilities, what about the ramifications of such an attempt? How does the homosexual adolescent formulate self-esteem while being told that

any expression of his or her sexuality *ever* is unacceptable—or downright evil? The priest chooses celibacy (asexuality isn't required), but this *is* a choice—one made well after adolescence.

24   Cultural condemnations and biblical prohibitions of (usually male) homosexual behavior were founded upon an incomplete understanding of human sexuality. To grant the existence of a homosexual orientation requires that there be some acceptable expression of it. Of course, there's no reason why lesbians and gays should be granted moral leniency over heterosexuals—which is why perhaps the most acceptable expression of same-sex sexuality should be within the context of a government sanctioned, religiously blessed marriage. But before we can talk about the proper way to get two brides or two grooms down a single church aisle, we have to first show there's an aisle wide enough to accommodate them.

1991

Dennis O'Brien

AGAINST GAY MARRIAGE

Dennis O'Brien, the president of the University of Rochester, argues that there are "distinct spiritual problems with homosexual 'marriage' in the Jewish and Christian traditions." Look at the way in which he moves the debate from the legal and financial to the social and religious implications of same-sex marriage. Does O'Brien's argument address Hartinger's claim that "Cultural condemnations and biblical prohibitions of (usually male) homosexual behavior were founded upon an incomplete understanding of human sexuality"? What do O'Brien's arguments suggest about the values and the religious beliefs of his audience?

1   My firmest conviction on this debate is that it will end with no conviction. To reach some common view would require an agreement on the meaning of *marriage*—no easy subject; an agreement on whether homosexuality has a meaning—or is it just a natural fact; finally, we would have to find a tone of "sexual wisdom" for the discussion—we are usually too passionate about our passions for wise dispassion.

2   The very day that *Commonweal* asked me to comment on the subject, I happened to read a personality squib in the local paper about the movie actors Kurt Russell and Goldie Hawn. It seems that they are "together" after previous unhappy marriages. They now have a four-year-old son and they would consider marriage if their current arrangement proved difficult to the youngster. Since Hollywood is usually the avant-garde of the culture, it may

be that marriage of any kind is a charming anachronism. I assume that the reluctance to enter marriage is that it destroys the honesty and commitment of "true love." Genuine commitment does not need the sanctions of judge or priest. In fact, it shows a weakening of ardor to rest fidelity on formality.

3   I have no doubt that there are deep and abiding homosexual commitments. What would formal marriage add? Legal marriages do help in divorce proceedings because there is a known system for dissolution and disposition of claims. If legal rights are an issue, they can, of course, be settled by (non-marriage) civil contracts. Should Kurt and Goldie break up this side of marriage, there are "palimony" settlements and similar suits have been brought for homosexual partnerships.

4   If the sole meaning of "marriage" is legal, then marriage of any sex may become a matter of "indifference." Perhaps truly loving couples should be as "indifferent" to marriage as our Hollywood pair. That there have been homosexual palimony cases would suggest that the law already brings homosexual partners into some sort of "coupled" network of legal restriction. It seems a short step from palimony to matrimony.

5   If there is an *issue* regarding homosexual marriage, it must rest on some deeper political or "religious" concerns. I do not mean what the newspapers think of as "political": who has the clout to carry the day. I am interested in the basic values of the American *polis*. What does our society express about itself and the human condition through its sanctioned institutions?

6   One might believe that the American *polis* avoids deep value issues; America is a debating society of opposing philosophies and life styles. Arguments are settled, if necessary or at all, by clout not cultural commitment. On the other hand, it is doubtful that any *polis* can exist at all without a cultural sense, however suppressed. American democracy rests on a powerful set of assumptions about human nature and society which legitimate the character of its institutions. Would homosexual marriage harmonize with our underlying values? I am not certain I can answer that question, but it is worth pointing out that "nonnormal" marriages have previously received constitutional scrutiny. The most famous are "the Mormon cases" which ruled on the legitimacy of polygamy (as a religiously protected right). The Supreme Court struck down polygamous marriage in part on *democratic* grounds. "Polygamy leads to the patriarchal principle ... which, when applied to large communities, fetters the people in stationary despotism, while that principle cannot long exist in connection with monogamy" *Reynolds* v. *United States* 98 US 145 (1879).

7   I am not overwhelmed by the sociology of the Court's opinion, but the justices were correct in attempting to connect marriage customs with the deeper values of the society. If homosexual marriage were to be seriously advanced, similar large concepts should be brought into play.

8   Are there potential problems for the *polis* if homosexual marriage becomes a legally sanctioned institution? There are some obvious social concerns. Heterosexual arrangements remain the mainstay for creating the next generation—which is not an incidental issue for any continuing social body.

Surrounding heterosexual arrangements with political blessing and legal structures could be judged to have special social utility on that ground alone. Giving heterosexual marriage a positive place in the legal structure does not, however, imply that homosexual relations need suffer from negative legal stricture. What consenting adults do, and so forth—but the state is not obliged to bless every bedroom. (The Athenian *polis,* while it practiced a form of sanctioned homosexuality, did not amalgamate that practice to marriage.)

9   A *religious* position on homosexual marriage would go beyond the merely legal and the larger political values. (I believe that homosexuality should not be discussed as a straightforward *moral* issue; *moral* issues generally deal with specific acts but the concern here is a life choice. The church has thought traditionally that a religiously celibate life choice was more exalted than marriage. For all that, marriage did not thus become "immoral.")

10   Is the *meaning of marriage* (as religious sacrament) consonant with *the meaning of homosexuality*? The latter meaning may be even less recoverable than the former. To the extent that superficial accounts of homosexuality treat it as a direct expression of a biologically determined appetite, they displace it from the web of cultural development that would assay the worth of homosexual life patterns. If all there is to homosexuality (or heterosexuality) is natural determinism, we could remove it from the human spiritual agenda.

11   I would like to believe that sex is a human artifact for all that it has a biological base. (Human eating habits are not just feeding behavior. The prevalence of fantasy in sex certainly suggests heavy human seasoning of an essential appetite.) Assuming that sex has a human meaning, it seems plausible that homosexual life patterns differ from heterosexual if for no other reason than that male bodies and female bodies are different. If we were only accidentally related to our bodies (angels in disguise, ghosts in a machine), then how these mechanisms got sexual kicks might not *fundamentally* invade our sense of person and human value. *Playboy* and Puritanism both assume the triviality of bodies; they are for playful/sinful distraction only. Catholics seem more stuck with incarnation—and somewhere along that line would be a Catholic answer to the question posed.

12   I am no fan at all of the "natural law" arguments about procreative sexuality as presented in *Humanae vitae.* These arguments assume that one can read the moral law off the book of nature. Social Darwinists argued that because humans are naturally aggressive, war was morally desirable. (The same mistake occurs when someone argues from a natural urge for hetero/ homosexuality to the moral obligation to carry forward the urge.) But for all that nature gives no dogmas, nature presents an ur-text for human meaning. Heterosexual marriage is a deep story developed from the ur-text of genital biology.

13   What difference could there possibly be in homosexual relations? Well, perhaps homosexual relations are better sex. After all, one knows one's own

sex's response better than the heterosexual response. "It takes one to know one!" (As Oscar Wilde said about masturbation: "cleaner, more efficient, and you meet a better class of people.") The sexiness of homosexuality may or may not be the case, but I believe that reflection on hetero/homosexual embodiments would reveal quite different erotic story lines. It seems eminently plausible that bedding with an other (strange?) sex is as different as travel abroad can be from staying at home.

14   One could conclude that the homosexual story line was valuable—perhaps more valuable than the heterosexual. But not all things are possible in either variation. There are distinct spiritual problems with homosexual "marriage" in the Jewish and Christian traditions. Franz Rosenzweig states a deep truth when he attempts to explicate Jewish "faith": "the belief of the Jew is not the content of a testimony, but rather the product of reproduction. The Jew, engendered a Jew, attests his belief by continuing to procreate the Jewish people."

15   Underneath all the heated argument about artificial contraception, abortion, population control, family planning and the lot, the traditional Jewish *mitzvah* for procreation expresses human solidarity with a Creator God. The Christian claim for an embodied God moves in the same spiritual territory. (I do not imply that family size scales one up in blessedness.)

16   Kierkegaard regarded marriage as spirit's proper synthesis of recollection and hope. Without getting into deep theological water, it is certainly the case that heterosexual marriage normally carries with it the meaning of recollection and hope. Normative heterosexual marriage recollects parents in the act of parenting and literally embodies hope in the bringing forth of children. Homosexuals may, of course, recall parents and be hopeful for the future but they do not, of course, embody a family history. In so far as these Judaic faiths are not finally enacted in the realm of attitudes, they seem destined to give a special place to embodiment. Procreative "marriage" seems to me to be a special and irreplaceable central symbol of the tradition.

1991

Deborah Fallows

WHY MOTHERS SHOULD STAY HOME

Even the title of Fallows's argument draws her directly into a major contemporary debate. Her point is that mothers should stay home, but the issue for some readers will be whether mothers should stay home. Look carefully at each of her arguments and ask whether the same benefit would occur if it were a father who stayed home. At a higher level of abstraction, are there physical and biological reasons that women have generally been responsible for the nurture of children, or is it that women are socially conditioned from an early age to develop the qualities important in caring for children? Like most men, many young women now intend to have children as well as demanding careers, and it is only when they reach that point that they face a painful dilemma of conflicting obligations. Even the happiest and most successful two-career couple will agree that paying for child care sounds much less problematic than it is. Fallows offers one solution; are there others?

1   About 18 months ago, when our first son was three years old and our second was about to be born, I decided to stop working and stay at home with our children. At the time, I wrote an article about the myth of the superwoman, saying that contrary to the prevailing notion of the day, it was not possible to be both a full-time career woman and a full-fledged mother. I said that while everyone recognizes the costs a stay-at-home mother pays in terms of power, prestige, money, and advancement in traditional careers, we are not always aware of or do not so readily admit what a full-time working woman loses and gives up in terms of mothering.

2   I've been at home with our children for almost a year and a half now, and I've learned a number of things about my choice. My convictions about the importance of mothering, which were based more on intuition than experience at the time, run even deeper and stronger. Nothing means more to me now than the hours I spend with my children, but I find myself coping with a problem I hadn't fully foreseen. It is the task of regearing my life, of learning to live as a full-time mother without a professional career but still with many of the interests and ambitions that I had before I had children. And this is the hard part. It means unraveling those long-held life plans for a certain kind of career and deciding which elements are possible to keep and which I must discard. Perhaps even more important, it means changing the way I've been taught to think about myself and value the progress of my life.

3   My mother became a mother in 1946; she had gone to college, studied music, and worked for a year at her father's office. Then she married and had my sister by the time she was 22. She wasn't expected to have a career outside the home, and she didn't. When I was growing up, the only mothers who worked were those who, as we whispered, "had to." Even the high school teachers, who we recognized probably weren't doing it just for the money, were slightly suspect.

4   But between my mother's time and our own, the climate of opportunity and expectations for women started to change. Betty Friedan and *The Feminine Mystique* came between all of those mothers and all of us daughters. The small town in northern Ohio where I grew up was not exactly a hotbed of

feminist activity, but even there the signals for young women were changing in the mid-sixties. We were raised with a curious mixture of hope of becoming homecoming queen and pressure to run for student council president. When I was 11, the mothers in our neighborhood bundled off their awkward, preadolescent daughters to Saturday morning charm classes, where we learned how to walk on a straight line, one foot directly in front of the other, and the proper way to don a coat. We all felt a little funny and humiliated, but we didn't say anything. By the time we were 17, we were May Queens, princesses, head drum majorettes, and cheerleaders, but we were also class valedictorians, editors of the school paper and yearbook, student directors of the school band, and candidates for six-year medical programs, Seven Sisters colleges, and honors programs at the Big Ten universities. I admit with some embarrassment that my two most thrilling moments in high school were being chosen for the homecoming court and being named first-chair trumpet in the concert band.

5   *This* was the way we were supposed to achieve—to be both beautiful and brilliant, charming and accomplished. It was one step beyond what our mothers did: we were aiming to be class presidents, not class secretaries; for medical school, not nursing school; we were building careers, not just jobs to tide us over before we landed husbands and started raising babies.

6   When I made my decision to stop working and stay home with our children, it was with a mixture of feelings. Part was defiance of the background I've just described—how could feminism dare tell me that I couldn't choose, with *pride,* motherhood alone? Part was anxiety—how could I keep some grasp on my extra-mothering self, on the things I had really enjoyed doing before I had children? I didn't want to become what the world kept telling me housewives are—ladies whose interests are confined to soap operas and the laundry. Certainly I knew from my own mother and from other women who had spent their middle years as full-time mothers that it was possible to be a thoughtful and sensitive person and still be a mother, But I didn't know how, and I didn't know where to turn to ask. Even my mother didn't have the answers. She was surprised when I told her I wanted to stop working and stay home with my kids. "You young women seem to handle everything so easily, so smoothly," she told me. "I never knew you were so torn between being a mother and being a professional."

7   The arrival of children in a woman's late twenties or early thirties can be handy, of course, because it means you can finish your education and start a career before taking "time out" to start your family. But it's also awkward.

8   At my tenth college reunion last June, I found that many of my friends had just become partner or vice-president of one thing or another, doctor-in-charge of some ward, tenured professor, editor-in-chief, and so forth. In these moments, I feel as if everyone is growing up around me. My reactions, though human, are not altogether pretty. I feel sorry for myself—there but for two

small children go I. I feel frustrated in being passed over for things I know I could handle as well as or better than the next person. I feel anxious, wondering if I am going to "lose my touch," get rusty, boring, old, trivial too quickly. And I am afraid that in putting aside my professional ambitions just now, I may be putting aside forever the chance to attain the levels I once set for myself.

9   All of us, I think, spend time once in a while pondering the "what ifs" of our lives, and we all experience momentary pangs of self-pity over the course we've taken. I know I'm not an exception to this, but I also know that when I add up the pluses and minuses my choice was right for me, and it might be right for other women.

The Importance of 'Quantity' Time

10   The first adjustment on that first morning that I dressed for motherhood rather than for success was to believe intellectually in what I felt emotionally: that it was as important, as worthy for me to spend my time with my small children as to study, do research, try cases, or invest a bank's money. Furthermore, I had to believe it was worth it to the children to have me—not someone else—there most of the time. There are a thousand small instances I have witnessed over the past year and a half that illustrate this feeling. One that stays in my mind happened last summer.

11   I had just dropped off our older son at the morning play camp at the neighborhood school. I was about to drive off when a little boy about eight years old burst out of the school and ran down the front steps in tears. His mother was on her way down the walk and of course she saw him. She led him over to the steps, took his hands in hers, looked him directly in the eyes, and talked with him softly but deliberately for a few minutes, calming him down so he could go back inside happily and she could go on her way. What I recognized in that instant was something I'd been trying to put my finger on for months. I'd witnessed dozens of similar events, when a child was simply overwhelmed by something, and I knew there was a differences—a distinct difference in the way parents respond at such moments from the way I had seen babysitters or maids act, however loving and competent they may have been. Parents seem to have some combination of self-assurance, completeness, deliberateness, and consistency. If that boy had been my son, I would have wanted to be with him, too.

12   Perhaps this one episode was no more important than the many reprimands or comforts I give my children during the day. But the more I'm around my children, the more such instances I happen to see and deal with. Perhaps a thousand of these episodes add up to the values and security I want to give my children.

13   I spend a lot of time with my children at playgrounds. We often go out on nice afternoons when our older son gets home from school, sampling new

ones or returning to old favorites. I particularly like playgrounds because of the balance they afford: they encourage the kids to strike out on their own but let me be there as a fallback. I've watched my older son in his share of small fistfights and scuffles, and I have been able to let him fight without intervening. He knows I'm there and runs back as often for protection as for nice things like a "Mom, see what I can do." Or our younger son toddles toward the big slide and needs me to follow him up and hold him as we slide down together. After so many hours, we've developed a style of play. I think my children know what to expect of me and I have learned their limits. I've watched the styles of many mothers and children, and you often can see, after a time, a microcosm of their lives together. I've also seen plenty of children there with full-time maids. The maids have their own styles, which usually are different from the mothers'. I've never seen a maid slide down a slide with her small charge, but I have seen plenty scold children for climbing too high on the jungle gym, and I've seen plenty step in to stop the sandfights before anyone gets dirty or hurt. There's a reason for this, of course: a maid has a lot to explain if a youngster arrives home with a bloody nose, but a mother doesn't. Sometimes, I think, the nose is worth the lesson learned from it, yet that is something only a parent—not a maid or babysitter—can take the responsibility to decide.

14   It has taken me a few years to realize I have very high standards for my role as a mother. I don't have to be a supermom who makes my children's clothes (I really can't sew), who does all the volunteer work at school (I do my share), or who cooks gourmet meals (we eat a lot of hamburgers). But I have to be around my children—a lot. I have to know them as well as I possibly can and see them in as many different environments and moods as possible in order to know best how to help them grow up—by comforting them, letting them alone, disciplining and enjoying them, being dependable but not stifling. What I need with them is time—in quantity, not quality.

15   I'm not talking about being with my children every minute of the day. From the time they were several months old, we sent them out for short periods to the favorite neighborhood babysitter's. By the time he was two and a half, our older son was in a co-op nursery school (my husband and I would take turns doing parent duty for the 17 kids); now he's in pre-kindergarten for a full school day. These periods away from me are clearly important for my sanity, as well as for my children's socialization, their development of trust in people, and their ability to experience other ways of living. But there is a big difference between using childcare from 8 to 6, Monday through Friday, and using a babysitter or a nursery school three mornings a week.

16   I realize that not everyone enjoys the luxury of choice. Some of my female friends work because it's the only way to make ends meet. But I think a lot of people pretend they have less room for choice than they really do. For some women, the reason may be the feeling—which is widespread among men—

that their dignity and success are related to how much money they earn. For others, there is a sense of independence that comes with earning money that is hard to give up. (I know that I felt freer to buy things, especially for myself, or spend money on babysitters when I was contributing to the family income.) And still others define "necessities" in an expensive way: I've heard more than one woman say she "has to work" to keep up payments on the second house. Such a woman is the parallel to the government appointee who "has to resign" from his post to return to his former profession because he "can no longer afford government service."

[17]   Even though some women do have a choice, I am not suggesting that all the responsibility for home and children should lie with the mother. While my husband and I are an example of a more traditional family, with a bread-winning father, a full-time mother, and two children, he shares with me many of the family responsibilities: night-tending, diapering, bathing, cooking, and playtime. A woman's decision to stay home or work is, at worst, a decision made by herself and, at best, a decision made with her spouse.

[18]   But with all these qualifications noted, I still know that my own choice is to stay with my children. Why does this seem to be at odds with the climate of the times, especially among certain feminists? I think it is because of a confused sense of ambition—based, in turn, on a mistaken understanding of what being a housewife or mother actually means.

[19]   While the world's idea of the comparative importance of career and motherhood may have changed a good deal since my mother's time, the general understanding of what motherhood means for those who choose it has not changed or advanced. And that may be the real problem for many women of my generation: who can blame them for shying away from a commitment to full-time motherhood if they're told, despite raising children, that motherhood is a vapid life of chores, routines, and TV? I couldn't stand motherhood myself if that were true. One of my many discoveries as a mother is that motherhood requires not the renunciation of my former ambitions but rather their refinement.

[20]   Even for those who intend to rush straight back to work, motherhood involves some interruption in the normal career plan. Separating people, even temporarily, from their professional identities, can help them see the difference between the ambition to *be*—to have an impressive job title to drop at cocktail parties—and the ambition to *do* specific things that seem satisfying and rewarding. The ambition to be is often a casualty of motherhood; the ambition to do need not be.

[21]   I see many of my friends intensely driven to keep doing things, to keep involved in their former interests, or to develop entirely new ones that they can learn from and grow with. In the free time they manage to set aside—thanks to babysitters, co-op babycare, naptimes, grandmothers' help, and husbands like mine who spend a lot of time with the children—they are thinking and doing.

[22]   Women I have talked to have described how, after some months or years of settling into motherhood, their sense of what work is worth, and what

they're looking for in work, has greatly changed. They are less tolerant, more selective, more demanding in what they do. One woman said that before she had children she would focus on a "cause," and was willing to do just about anything as her job toward that cause. Now she's still interested in advancing the cause, but she has no patience for busywork. In the limited time she can spare from her family, she wants to do things that really count, work in areas where her efforts make a difference. I'm not suggesting narcissism here but a clearer focus on a search for some long-range goal, some tangible accomplishment, a feeling so necessary during the season of child-raising when survival from one end of the day to the other is often the only achievement.

23   Each one's search is different, depending on factors like her husband's job (if she has a husband) and the extent of his role as a caretaker, her children's needs, her family's financial situation, and her personal lifestyle.

24   One of my friends had taught English in public high schools for the last ten years. She was the kind of teacher you remember fondly from your own childhood and hope your kids are lucky enough to have because she's dedicated, demanding, and creative. She expanded her subject to include other humanities, keeping herself several steps ahead of her students by reading and studying on her own, traveling to see museums and exhibits firsthand, collecting slides and books as she goes. She has a new baby daughter now and has stopped working to stay home with her child. She's decided to go back to school next fall, taking one or two courses at a time, to pursue a master's in fine arts—a chance to study formally what she's mostly taught herself and to return to her job someday with an even better background and more ideas for her teaching.

25   Going to school can be perfect for new mothers, as many in my own mother's generation found. It requires very little time away from home, which means cutting down on time away from the children as well as on child-care costs. It can be cheap, as with my friend, who can attend a virtually tuition-free state university. You can pace your work to suit demands at home by carefully choosing the number of courses you take and the type of work required. And it's physically easy but intellectually challenging—the complement to the other demands of the early years of mothering.

26   Other mothers I know do different things with their time. One friend, formerly a practicing lawyer and now a full-time mother, volunteers some of her time to advising the League of Women Voters on legal matters. Another, formerly a producer at a big radio station, now produces her own shows, albeit at a slower pace. A third quit her job to raise her daughter but spends a lot of time on artistic projects, which she sells.

27   But if there's no real blueprint for what a modern mother should be, you wouldn't know it from what comes through in the media. On the *Today Show* last summer, for instance, Jane Pauley interviewed Felice Schwartz, the president of Catalyst, an organization that promotes career development for women. They were discussing women's changing lifestyles. Ms. Schwartz said that now women are going back to work full-time four months after hav-

ing children, while 15 years ago they were taking 20 years off to have them. "Isn't that fantastic progress?" she said. Fantastic it certainly is; progress it is not, except toward the narrowest and least generous notion of what achievement means for women or for humanity. Progress such as this is a step not toward "liberation" but toward the enslavement to career that has been the least attractive aspect of masculine success.

28   What it is really like to be a mother today seems to be a secret that's kept from even my contemporaries who may be considering motherhood themselves. At a dinner recently, I sat near a young woman about my age, a New York television producer and recently anointed White House fellow. She and my husband and I were having a conversation about bureaucracy and what she found new or interesting or surprising about it in her new position. After several minutes, she turned away from my husband to me directly and said, "And how old are your children, Debbie?" It wasn't the question—not at all—but the tone that was revealing, the unattractive, condescending tone I've heard many older people use with youngsters, or doctors with patients. If I'd had her pegged as a fast-track super-achiever, she had me pegged as little mother and lady of the house.

29   Hurt and anger were the wrong feelings at a moment like that, although I felt them. Instead, I should have felt sorry for her, not because of her own choice but because she had no sense that a choice exists—waiting to be made by women like her and like me. The choice is *not* to be either a career woman or a dumb housewife. The issue is one that she, a woman at the age when careers take off and childbearing ability nears its eleventh hour, should be sensitive to and think about.

1982

Laurie Ouellette

BUILDING THE THIRD WAVE: REFLECTIONS OF A YOUNG FEMINIST

Written in 1992 by an author in her twenties, Laurie Ouellette's essay looks at sex, gender, and family from the perspective of the feminist movement. Her vision for a third wave of feminism sets goals and priorities different from those of her mother's generation, the 1970s feminists of the "second wave." Ouellette argues that issues of family and childrearing will be central to women of her generation: "In these hard economic times, young women can look forward to mandatory full-time jobs and second shifts of house care and child care in their

*homes. Where are the parental-leave policies, the flexible schedules, the ade-
quate health care, the subsidized day care, and the male cooperation that will
ease these situations? As yet, nowhere to be found. . . ." How does your own
understanding of the pressures on the contemporary American family accord
with hers?*

1   I am a member of the first generation of women to benefit from the gains
of the 1970s women's movement without having participated in its struggles.
I grew up on on the sidelines of feminism—too young to take part in the
moments, debates, and events that would define the women's movement
while at the same time experiencing firsthand the societal changes that feminism had demanded.

2   Ironically, it is due to the modest success of feminism that many young
women like myself were raised with an illusion of equality. I never really
thought much about feminism as I was growing up, but looking back, I believe
I've always had feminist inclinations. Having divorced parents and a father
who was ambivalent about his parental responsibilities probably has much to
do with this. I was only five when my parents separated in 1971, and I couldn't
possibly have imagined or understood the ERA marches, consciousness-
raising groups, or triumphal passing of *Roe* v. *Wade* that shortly would make
history. Certainly, I couldn't have defined the word "feminism." Still, watching my young mother struggle emotionally and financially as a single parent
made the concept of gender injustice painfully clear, teaching me a lesson that
would follow me always.

3   My first real introduction to feminism came secondhand. During the
height of the seventies' women's movement, I watched my mother become
"liberated" after the breakup of yet another marriage. It was she, not I, who
sought some answers from the counterculture of the time. It was confusing,
if not terrifying, to watch her dramatically change her life—and, by association, mine—during those years, transforming herself into a woman I barely
recognized. She quit her job and returned to college and then graduate
school, working odd jobs and devoting her time to books and meetings and
new-age therapy and talking it all out with her never-ending supply of free-
spirited divorced comrades. I was thirteen the year I found her copy of *The
Women's Room*, a book which so intrigued me that I read it cover to cover in
the course of only a few nights. Like the heroine of the book, my mother was
becoming "independent" and "hip," but I had never been so miserable.

4   Like most women my age, though, I never really considered feminism in
terms of my own life until I reached college. It was during those years that I
first took an interest in feminist classics such as *The Feminine Mystique, Sister-
hood Is Powerful,* and *Sexual Politics.* As powerful as these texts were, they
seemed to express the anger of an earlier generation, simultaneously capti-
vating and excluding me. Reading them so long after the excitement of their

publication made my own consciousness-raising seem anticlimactic. These books and countless others that I encountered seemed to speak more to my mother's generation than mine. They explained a great deal about the limited choices awaiting such women and attempted to guide them in ways to overcome patriarchal oppression. But I, like many of my white, middle-class friends, saw women's liberation from quite a different perspective. Many of us really believed that we wouldn't have to worry about issues like discrimination, oppression, and getting stuck in the housewife role. Indeed, many of my friends considered my interest in feminism "radical" and irrelevant to the times.

5   Although I participated in feminist activities sporadically in college, including prochoice demonstrations, it was really in my experiences outside of that environment where my feminist politics took root. Several events stand out as catalysts. First was an internship I held at a public television station while in college. Armed with an eager attitude and practical experience, I felt my enthusiasm wane when I was given mainly menial and secretarial tasks to perform while my male co-interns, who had less experience than I, were frequently asked to do editing assignments and were invited along on shoots. I had never before experienced sexual discrimination, and in fact honestly believed it was something I would never have to face. In retrospect, this experience marked my first realization that there was much work to be done in creating a world where women and men were treated with equal respect, on the job and off.

6   Living in an inner-city neighborhood and my involvement in community issues there were also important. I saw the dire need for drastic political change in the lives of the poor women, elderly women, and women of color who were my neighbors. Watching these women, many of them single parents, struggling daily to find shelter, child care, and food made me realize that they, unlike me, had not been touched at all by the gains of the seventies' women's movement. How could women's liberation possibly be perceived as won when these women had been so forgotten? I began to reconsider feminism in an attempt to find the answers.

7   Today I am among the minority of young women who have committed themselves to feminism in the hopes of achieving social and political goals for all women. While we are attempting to carve out a place for ourselves in a movement still heavily dominated by another generation, the majority of young women have been reluctant to do the same. Confused about their roles in relation to the media stereotypes about feminists or intimidated by the legacy of the women's movement past, many have become "no, but" feminists. That is, they approve of—indeed, demand—equal pay, economic independence, sexual freedom, and reproductive choice but are still reluctant to define themselves with the label "feminist." The results of a recent poll by *InView,* a magazine for college women, is typical of many surveys that report this contradiction. Of the 514 female undergraduates surveyed by *InView,* 90 percent agreed that men and women should earn equal pay for equal work;

93 percent said that women want equality with men; 84 percent agreed that women should have access to birth control, regardless of age or marital status; 90 percent believed that sexism still exists. Still, only 16 percent of the women said they were definitely feminists.

8   Yet the evidence clearly shows that young women's situations are dismal: *Roe* v. *Wade* is under fire, and if overturned, my generation and those to come will be affected most profoundly; parental consent laws, which require parental notification or permission for abortion, have been mandated in many states; date rape and violence against women have become epidemics on college campuses and everywhere; eating disorders, linked to the unreasonable societal standards for women's body sizes, have claimed the lives of thousands of us; and we still can expect to earn seventy cents for every dollar earned by men. Sure, our chances of having professional careers are greater. However, more of us than in any previous generation have grown up in single-parent families—we have seen the myth of the "supermom" professional "bringing home that bacon and frying it up in a pan" and can call it for what it is. In these hard economic times, young women can look forward to mandatory full-time jobs and second shifts of house care and child care in their homes. Where are the parental-leave policies, the flexible schedules, the adequate health care, the subsidized day care, and the male cooperation that will ease these situations? As yet, nowhere to be found, and considering the present political climate, there doesn't seem to be much hope for the near future.

9   Given all this, what can explain why so many young women have shunned feminism? In her survey of young women, *Feminist Fatale: Voices from the Twentysomething Generation Explore the Future of the Women's Movement*, Paula Kamen found that media-fueled stereotypes of feminists as "man-bashers" and "radical extremists" were behind the fact that many young women don't identify with the women's movement.

10   But these are not the only reasons. Kamen also points to the lack of young feminist role models as an important factor. The failure of a major feminist organization such as NOW to reach out to a wider spectrum of women, including young women, must be acknowledged as a part of this problem. While individual chapters do have young feminist committees and sometimes officers, they and the national office are led and staffed primarily by older women, and consequently often fail to reflect the interests and needs of a complex generation of young women.

11   Yet another reason young women have turned away from feminism may lie within its history. If the young women who have gained the most from feminism—that is, white, middle-class women who took advantage of increased accessibility to higher education and professional employment— have been reluctant to associate themselves with feminism, it is hardly surprising that most economically disadvantaged women and women of color, who have seen fewer of those gains, have not been eager to embrace feminism either. The women's movement of the seventies has been called an upper-middle-class white women's movement, and to a large degree I believe that

is true. More than a few young feminists—many influenced by feminists of color such as Flo Kennedy, Audre Lorde, and bell hooks—have realized that feminism must also acknowledge issues of race and class to reach out to those women whose concerns have been overlooked by the women's movement of the past. Indeed, numerous statistics, including a poll by the *New York Times,* have noted that young African American women are more likely than white women to acknowledge many of the concerns conducive to a feminist agenda, including a need for job training and equal earning power outside the professional sector. But for them, feminism has not provided the only answer. Only by making issues of class and race a priority can feminism hope to influence the lives of the millions of women for whom the daily struggle to survive, not feminist activism, is a priority. Will ours be the first generation of feminists to give priority to fighting cuts in Aid to Families with Dependent Children, establishing the right to national health care, day care, and parental leave, and bringing to the forefront other issues pertinent to the daily struggle of many women's lives? If there is to be a third wave of feminism, they must.

12 While the women's movement of the seventies focused primarily on the ERA, getting women into high-paying, powerful occupations, and combatting sexual discrimination in the workplace, these issues—though still critical—must not be the only goals of feminism. My sister is an example. We have taken very different paths indeed. I have focused on attending graduate school and writing about women's issues; she has chosen to forfeit similar plans, for now, in favor of marrying young and raising a family. Does she signify a regression into the homemaker role of the 1950s? On the contrary. In fact, she is among the feminists I most respect, even though she herself believes that the feminist movement may not have a place for her because of the choices she has made. For her, issues such as getting midwifery legalized and covered by insurance plans, providing information about the importance of breastfeeding to rural mothers, countering the male-dominated medical establishment by using and recommending natural and alternative healing methods, protecting the environment, and raising her own daughter with positive gender esteem are central to what she defines as a feminist agenda. Who am I to say that she—and other young women like her who are attempting to reclaim the power and importance of motherhood—aren't correct? If there is to be a third wave of feminism, it must acknowledge and support a wide range of choices for all women.

13 Surely the greatest challenge facing all young women is the frightening assault on reproductive rights, and if any issue can unite women from all backgrounds, it is this. While we have never known the horrors of coathanger abortions, we have seen our reproductive rights drastically shrink. If the legacy of the women's movement has left young women confused about their roles in a structure still heavily dominated by older white women, this is one issue on which the torch must be shared. If feminism is to succeed in

challenging this patriarchal assault on women's bodies, a coalition of women from all backgrounds will have to join forces to address the underlying assumptions of this attack. Young women have been among the first to organize on this fight, witnessed by the proliferation of prochoice activity on college campuses around the United States. Still, if this movement is to progress beyond a single-issue campaign, uniting women inside and outside the academy in the name of feminism, it will mean expanding the agenda: insisting upon birth control options for all women and giving equal energy to addressing the lack of educational opportunities, child care, day care, and health care options that are fundamental to the campaign for reproductive choice.

14   Only by recognizing and helping provide choices for all women, and supporting all women in their struggles to obtain those choices, will the women of my generation, the first raised in the shadow of the second wave and witness to its triumphs and failures, be able to build a successful third wave of the feminist movement. The initial step must be to reclaim the word "feminism" as an appealing, empowering term in women's lives by building a movement that commits to all women while recognizing their multiple concerns.

1992

Reacting and Writing

One way into this symposium is to isolate an aspect of the discussion in which you are particularly interested and look carefully at how your issue is addressed in different selections. The meaning and nature of marriage, the biological and the social factors influencing our understanding of it, the traditional roles of the sexes in marriage, the new challenges to these traditional understandings, the implications of changing gender roles for childrearing—any of these issues can be traced though a selected group of readings. How does the definition of the issue change as audience and intention vary? For example, how might Deborah Fallows adapt her argument about mothers staying home with children to suit the marriages between two men advocated by Brent Hartinger, some of which might involve the adopting of children? The Wife of Bath's argument is designed for those who believe in the teachings of Genesis and Augustine: How would she have to adapt it for an audience persuaded by Freud? Or you could compare the assumptions about the purpose of marriage found in Genesis, Augustine, Hartinger, and O'Brien.

If you are interested in working with the early pieces, try updating one of the arguments for a modern audience. What changes would there be in the attitudes and beliefs that you appeal to? Or you could press hard on the modern pieces, asking difficult questions. For example, opponents of Hartinger's argument for gay marriage often raise the slippery slope argument. If marriage is not defined as a union between one man and one woman, if two people of the same sex have the right to marry, then why not three people, for example? How might Hartinger respond to such an argument?

A major change in postwar America has been the movement of women into the workforce, a change that necessarily alters their traditional role as the partner with primary responsibility for childrearing and family life. Deborah Fallows speaks of the stay-at-home mother's unjustified sense of inferiority to the woman with a prestigious career. Women with no children and highly satisfying careers sometimes speak of feeling empty or incomplete because they have not given birth or raised children. Many women with children *and* admirable careers manage to feel inferior both to mothers who raise their children with all their energy and to co-workers who pour all their resources into their work. What sources can you identify for these feelings and what changes might help to alleviate them?

If you find that our selections omit or undervalue a particular kind of family arrangement, write an essay arguing for its importance or its merits. Sarton's essay on living alone might serve as a model or point of departure. Or you could refute one of the proposed models, explaining why you don't agree.

IV. POLITICS, PRINCIPLES, AND PRACTICALITIES

This last symposium presents varying opinions about political decisions, especially the tensions between moral ideals and the brutal realities of power.

Three Arguments About Leadership

We begin with three contrasting portraits of the leader. Cicero, the ancient Roman orator and writer, presents the example of Regulus as an ideal of civic virtue. Then Niccolò Machiavelli, the leading political theorist of the Italian Renaissance, describes his ideal prince with chilling realism. However much Cicero and Machiavelli differ, they both think that a leader can make a difference for good or ill. Quite a different perspective is offered by the nineteenth-century Russian novelist, Leo Tolstoy, in *War and Peace*. In our selection from that novel, Tolstoy argues that the power of the leader is only an illusion.

Marcus Tullius Cicero
THE EXAMPLE OF REGULUS*

The following selection is from Cicero's book On Duties, *perhaps the most influential work produced in the ancient world on the relationship between politics and morality. Throughout this work, Cicero argues that there is no fun-*

*Translated by Harry Edinger.

damental tension between the individual and society because individuals can only truly fulfill themselves through service to the common good. His whole work, therefore, is a sustained argument against individualism, against the view that we are most fulfilled by following our personal inclinations.

The example of Regulus is an extreme test of Cicero's philosophy. Regulus turned himself over to be tortured to death by the Carthaginians, the enemies of Rome; he did so in part because he thought that Rome's enemies should know that Romans always keep their word. In other words, he willingly sacrificed himself for the common good as he understood it.

Is Cicero right that this constitutes the proper test of a leader?—that when private advantage and public good conflict, a leader forgoes private advantage? The case of Regulus is particularly pointed not just because of the horrible death that awaited him. He also would not have been breaking Roman law by breaking his oath to the Carthaginians. Clearly, he was regarded as a fool by many; otherwise, Cicero would not have felt he needed to defend his action at such length.

1   Marcus Atilius Regulus, then consul for the second time, had been captured by a trick in Africa. His captor was the commander Xanthippus from Sparta, under the generalship of Hamilcar, the father of Hannibal. They sent Regulus to the Roman Senate under oath, the condition being that Regulus himself should return to Carthage unless the Romans agreed to return certain captive nobles to the Carthaginians. When he came to Rome, he saw how attractive his personal advantage would be, but he decided this advantage was false, as the result makes clear. The attraction was this: to remain in his fatherland, to live in his own home with his wife and his children, and to retain his rank of consular authority, adopting the opinion that the defeat he had sustained was nothing extraordinary in the fortunes of war. Who do you suppose denied that these things are advantageous? Regulus, with his nobility and courage, said they were not advantageous.

2   Do you require any more reliable authorities? It is the essence of nobility and courage not to fear anything, to hold in contempt anything merely mortal, and to assume that it is possible to endure anything that can happen to a man.

3   What did Regulus do? He came into the Senate and explained his commission, he refused to pronounce his opinion and said that, as long as he was bound by the oath given to the enemy, he was not a senator. He even said (someone or other will say, "What a foolish man! How he fights against his own advantage!") that it was not a good idea to return the Carthaginian prisoners. He explained that they were young men and good leaders, while he was already worn out by old age. His prestige prevailed, the prisoners were not released, Regulus himself went back to Carthage, and neither his affection for his fatherland nor for his own family held him back. Of course, at that

point he knew very well that he was returning to an extremely cruel enemy and refined tortures, but he maintained his belief that he must respect his oath. The Carthaginians murdered him by forced lack of sleep. Yet, I maintain that even so the reasoning for his decision was more valid than if he had stayed in Rome, an old man, a man who had once surrendered to the enemy, a man of consular rank who had broken his oath.

4   "But he acted foolishly," someone might reply. "Not only did he argue against sending back the prisoners, but he even dissuaded others who wanted to return them!" In what way did he act foolishly? Did he act foolishly even though he was helping the government? In fact, is it possible that an action that harms the state can be of advantage to an individual citizen?

5   Men distort truths that are the very basis of nature when they force a separation between advantageousness and right action. Granted, each one of us is seeking his own advantage. We are pulled along toward that end, and in no way can we act differently. Who would run away from advantages, or rather, who does not pursue them with the greatest eagerness? But I cannot discover any advantage anywhere except in honor, in glory, and in right action. Therefore I consider these goals to be primary and supreme over all others. Advantage should not be thought of as something separate and glorious in itself, but as something bound up with these higher goals.

6   Someone might say, "But what is there in an oath, anyway? Are we afraid of the anger of Jupiter? There is no reason for that fear. Let me cite an opinion common to all philosophers, both those who believe that a god himself has no worries and does not interfere with mortals and also those who think a god is always active and always working in the world: they both assert that God never grows angry and does not do any harm. What greater harm could an angry Jupiter have done than the harm Regulus willingly caused himself? There was no power in religion that could have upset the advantage Regulus could have enjoyed, had he remained in Rome."

7   Someone else might say, "Was he afraid of acting immorally? As the saying goes, his problem was to choose the lesser of two evils. After all, was the immorality really as full of evil as his torture? And then there is also that quotation from Accius:

> —Did you break your oath?
> —I did not give it, and I do not give it
> To anyone at all who is without trustworthiness.

Although an impious king said this, still it is brilliantly said."

8   Just as I might say that some things appear to be advantageous that really are not, these critics also say that some things appear to be right actions that really are not. "For example, the very act of returning to face torture in order to keep an oath seems to be a right action. But it should not have been considered right. He should not have honored an oath that he made because the

enemy applied force." They also assert that almost anything that is extremely advantageous might turn out to be right action, even if it did not seem so previously.

9   These are pretty much the points they raise against the conduct of Regulus. Let us examine the initial objections.

10   "There was no need to fear that Jupiter in his anger would do harm; he neither gets angry nor does harm." This argument has no more force against the oath of Regulus than against any oath in the world. Where an oath is involved, our attention should not be focused on fear of possible punishment but on the essence of taking the oath itself. An oath is a sacred and binding undertaking; and what you promise as an obligation, with God as witness, as it were, you must honor. At that point it does not involve the wrath of the gods, which does not exist, but it involves justice and trust. Ennius, you remember, wrote a famous line:

A nourishing Trust, fitted with wings, and the oath of Jupiter!

The man who violates an oath violates Trust, which our ancestors understood to be "the neighbor of Jupiter Optimus Maximus on the Capitoline," as a speech of Cato puts it.

11   "But still, even Jupiter in his wrath would not have done more harm to Regulus than he did to himself." Of course, if it were true that nothing is evil except suffering. However, philosophers with the strongest authority contend that suffering is by no means the worst evil, but in fact is not an evil at all. Please, I entreat you, do not slander the testimony of those philosophers, which is not slight, nor that of Regulus himself, who, I suspect, is the most impressive witness of all. Indeed, what more authoritative witness can we want than a leader of the Roman people who willingly underwent torture to remain true to his duty?

12   As for their third contention that "the lesser of two evils" should be chosen, that is, that one should act immorally rather than undergo destruction: is there any evil greater than immorality? If there is something not very agreeable in a deformity of the body, how great must seem the distortion and ugliness of a demoralized soul! That is why men who judge these matters very strictly go so far as to say that the *only* evil is immorality; and even those whose judgment is less strict do not hesitate to call that the greatest evil. As for the quotation about an oath cited above,

I did not give it, and I do not give it
To anyone at all who is without trustworthiness,

the poet was justified in writing it because he was dealing with Atreus and had to be consistent with the character. If anyone assumes that an oath sworn to an untrustworthy person is void, he should beware, because he might thereby be creating a loophole for perjury.

13   There is also the law of war. Your fidelity to an oath often has to be maintained with an enemy. An oath given in such a way that the mind intends to keep the oath must be observed. If the oath is not so sworn and is then not kept, there is no perjury. For example, if you do not give to some pirates the ransom you agreed upon for your life, there is no deceit, not even if you agreed under oath to pay a ransom. By definition a pirate is not on the list of fair enemies but rather is everyone's common enemy. No one should enter into an agreement or take an oath with him. Swearing to something false is not perjury by itself. Rather, perjury is failure to perform an action which you have sworn to do "upon your conscience," as the traditional phrase expresses it. Euripides wrote cleverly,

> I swear in words, my mind remains unsworn.

In fact, Regulus had no right to perjure himself and renounce the conditions and agreements of war between enemies to which he consented. The Romans were conducting hostilities with a legally and properly declared enemy, to whom the Fetial law applied and many treaty regulations.

14   If the Romans had not observed this code of laws, the Senate would never have put a number of famous men in chains and surrendered them to the enemy.

15   When Titus Veturius and Spurius Postumius were consuls for the second time, a disastrous battle took place near Caudium, and Roman legions were sent under the yoke. But the consuls were surrendered to the Samnites because they had made peace with them and had done so without the consent of the people and the Senate.

16   In the same era, Tiberius Numicius and Quintus Maelius, who were then tribunes of the people, were surrendered to the Samnites in order to repudiate their peace with them. The peace had been concluded only on their authority. In fact, the same Postumius who had been previously surrendered at the time of Caudium was among those who advocated and urged this surrender.

17   Many years later Gaius Mancinus met the same fate. He spoke in the Senate in favor of the motion to surrender himself to the Numantini, because he had concluded a treaty with them without authority from the Senate. Lucius Furius and Sextus Atilius introduced a *senatus consultum* to this effect, and when it passed, he was turned over to the enemy. Mancinus acted more correctly than Quintus Pompeius, who, in the same situation, refused to consent, and the law did not pass. Here, what seemed advantageous had more power than right action. In the previous cases, however, the false appearance of advantageousness was overcome by the authority of right action.

18   The critics of Regulus argue, "But an action performed under duress should not have been binding." As if duress could really be applied to a brave man!

19   "Then why did he set out for the Roman Senate, especially since he intended to dissuade it from returning the captives?" These people are criticizing the most impressive aspect of the case. Regulus did not act on his own decision, but he undertook the mission so that there could be a decision by the Senate. The Romans would certainly have returned the captives to the Carthaginians, except that Regulus himself advocated the opposite decision in the Senate. Had the captives been returned, Regulus would have remained safe in his fatherland; but he did not think their return was advantageous to his fatherland, and so he believed it was right action for himself both to declare that opinion and to suffer.

20   As to their assertion that an extremely advantageous action may prove to be right action, they should rather say that it is truly right, not that it may prove to be right. There is nothing advantageous that is not also right action. Nothing is right action because it is advantageous; but because something is morally right, it is advantageous. Because of this, one will not find it easy to select from among the many splendid stories in Roman history one more praiseworthy or more outstanding than that of Regulus.

21   Amidst all this praise of Regulus one fact remains most worthy of admiration: that Regulus himself advised that the captives should not be released. Nowadays it seems to us an amazing thing that he went back, but in those days he could not act differently. To praise that action, therefore, is not praise of Regulus, but of his age; for our ancestors believed that the binding force that would keep trust most securely in place must be a man's given word.

44 B.C.

Niccolò Machiavelli

OF THE THINGS FOR WHICH MEN, AND ESPECIALLY PRINCES, ARE PRAISED OR BLAMED*

Cicero's dutiful, even moralistic view of politics could not have a stronger contrast than Machiavelli's cold-blooded realism. Machiavelli grew up amidst the ruthless world of Italian politics in the Renaissance, when numerous small states divided Italy into continually feuding factions. During his own stunted career as a diplomat, he found moral principles to be a weakness in politicians and ruthlessness to be a prime strength. His study of Roman history convinced him that the Romans, despite what Cicero claimed, were no different.

*Translated by Luigi Ricci, revised by E. R. P. Vincent.

Some readers find Machiavelli's amoral view of politics so repugnant they cannot believe he was serious and conclude that his Prince (from which the following selection is taken) must be a satire, like Swift's "A Modest Proposal." Whatever their tone, Machiavelli's conclusions follow straightforwardly from his generalizations about human nature. As you read this, seek out these generalizations, such as that in paragraph 8 that men in general are "ungrateful, voluble, dissemblers, anxious to avoid danger, and covetous of gain." You might then ask if such views are accurate in describing, say, the contemporary American public. Is Machiavelli's description of human nature, for instance, much different from the implied audience of political advertisements? Is it inconsistent with the behavior of contemporary world leaders?

1   It now remains to be seen what are the methods and rules for a prince as regards his subjects and friends. And as I know that many have written of this, I fear that my writing about it may be deemed presumptuous, differing as I do, especially in this matter, from the opinions of others. But my intention being to write something of use to those who understand, it appears to me more proper to go to the real truth of the matter than to its imagination; and many have imagined republics and principalities which have never been seen or known to exist in reality; for how we live is so far removed from how we ought to live, that he who abandons what is done for what ought to be done, will rather learn to bring about his own ruin than his preservation. A man who wishes to make a profession of goodness in everything must necessarily come to grief among so many who are not good. Therefore it is necessary for a prince, who wishes to maintain himself, to learn how not to be good, and to use this knowledge and not use it, according to the necessity of the case.

2   Leaving on one side, then, those things which concern only an imaginary prince, and speaking of those that are real, I state that all men, and especially princes, who are placed at a greater height, are reputed for certain qualities which bring them either praise or blame. Thus one is considered liberal, another *misero* or miserly (using a Tuscan term, seeing that *avaro* with us still means one who is rapaciously acquisitive and *misero* one who makes grudging use of his own); one a free giver, another rapacious; one cruel, another merciful; one a breaker of his word, another trustworthy; one effeminate and pusillanimous, another fierce and high-spirited; one humane, another haughty; one lascivious, another chaste; one frank, another astute; one hard, another easy; one serious, another frivolous; one religious, another an unbeliever, and so on. I know that every one will admit that it would be highly praiseworthy in a prince to possess all the above-named qualities that are reputed good, but as they cannot all be possessed or observed, human conditions not permitting of it, it is necessary that he should be prudent enough to avoid the scandal of those vices which would lose him the state, and guard

himself if possible against those which will not lose it him, but if not able to, he can indulge them with less scruple. And yet he must not mind incurring the scandal of those vices, without which it would be difficult to save the state, for if one considers well, it will be found that some things which seem virtues would, if followed, lead to one's ruin, and some others which appear vices result in one's greater security and well-being.

Of Liberality and Niggardliness

3   Beginning now with the first qualities above named, I say that it would be well to be considered liberal; nevertheless liberality such as the world understands it will injure you, because if used virtuously and in the proper way, it will not be known, and you will incur the disgrace of the contrary vice. But one who wishes to obtain the reputation of liberality among men, must not omit every kind of sumptuous display, and to such an extent that a prince of this character will consume by such means all his resources, and will be at last compelled, if he wishes to maintain his name for liberality, to impose heavy taxes on his people, become extortionate, and do everything possible to obtain money. This will make his subjects begin to hate him, and he will be little esteemed being poor, so that having by this liberality injured many and benefited but few, he will feel the first little disturbance and be endangered by every peril. If he recognises this and wishes to change his system, he incurs at once the charge of niggardliness.

4   A prince, therefore, not being able to exercise this virtue of liberality without risk if it be known, must not, if he be prudent, object to be called miserly. In course of time he will be thought more liberal, when it is seen that by his parsimony his revenue is sufficient, that he can defend himself against those who make war on him, and undertake enterprises without burdening his people, so that he is really liberal to all those from whom he does not take, who are infinite in number, and niggardly to all to whom he does not give, who are few. In our times we have seen nothing great done except by those who have been esteemed niggardly; the others have all been ruined. Pope Julius II, although he had made use of a reputation for liberality in order to attain the papacy, did not seek to retain it afterwards, so that he might be able to wage war. The present King of France has carried on so many wars without imposing an extraordinary tax, because his extra expenses were covered by the parsimony he had so long practised. The present King of Spain, if he had been thought liberal, would not have engaged in and been successful in so many enterprises.

5   For these reasons a prince must care little for the reputation of being a miser, if he wishes to avoid robbing his subjects, if he wishes to be able to defend himself, to avoid becoming poor and contemptible, and not be forced to become rapacious; this niggardliness is one of those vices which enable

him to reign. If it is said that Caesar attained the empire through liberality, and that many others have reached the highest positions through being liberal or being thought so, I would reply that you are either a prince already or else on the way to become one. In the first case, this liberality is harmful; in the second, it is certainly necessary to be considered liberal. Caesar was one of those who wished to attain the mastery over Rome, but if after attaining it he had lived and had not moderated his expenses, he would have destroyed that empire. And should any one reply that there have been many princes, who have done great things with their armies, who have been thought extremely liberal, I would answer by saying that the prince may either spend his own wealth and that of his subjects or the wealth of others. In the first case he must be sparing, but for the rest he must not neglect to be very liberal. The liberality is very necessary to a prince who marches with his armies, and lives by plunder, sack and ransom, and is dealing with the wealth of others, for without it he would not be followed by his soldiers. And you may be very generous indeed with what is not the property of yourself or your subjects, as were Cyrus, Caesar, and Alexander; for spending the wealth of others will not diminish your reputation, but increase it, only spending your own resources will injure you. There is nothing which destroys itself so much as liberality, for by using it you lose the power of using it, and become either poor and despicable, or, to escape poverty, rapacious and hated. And of all things that a prince must guard against, the most important are being despicable or hated, and liberality will lead you to one or the other of these conditions. It is, therefore, wiser to have the name of a miser, which produces disgrace without hatred, than to incur of necessity the name of being rapacious, which produces both disgrace and hatred.

Of Cruelty and Clemency, and Whether It Is Better to Be Loved or Feared

6   Proceeding to the other qualities before named, I say that every prince must desire to be considered merciful and not cruel. He must, however, take care not to misuse this mercifulness. Cesare Borgia was considered cruel, but his cruelty had brought order to the Romagna, united it, and reduced it to peace and fealty. If this is considered well, it will be seen that he was really much more merciful than the Florentine people, who, to avoid the name of cruelty, allowed Pistoia to be destroyed. A prince, therefore, must not mind incurring the charge of cruelty for the purpose of keeping his subjects united and faithful; for, with a very few examples, he will be more merciful than those who, from excess of tenderness, allow disorders to arise, from whence spring bloodshed and rapine; for these as a rule injure the whole community, while the executions carried out by the prince injure only individuals. And of all princes, it is impossible for a new prince to escape the reputation of cru-

elty, new states being always full of dangers. Wherefore Virgil through the mouth of Dido says: "*Res dura, et regni novitas me talia cogunt Moliri, et late fines custode tueri.*" ["The harsh condition and my new position as ruler force me to take such stern measures and to guard my boundaries far and wide."]

7   Nevertheless, he must be cautious in believing and acting, and must not be afraid of his own shadow, and must proceed in a temperate manner with prudence and humanity, so that too much confidence does not render him incautious, and too much diffidence does not render him intolerant.

8   From this arises the question whether it is better to be loved more than feared, or feared more than loved. The reply is, that one ought to be both feared and loved, but as it is difficult for the two to go together, it is much safer to be feared than loved, if one of the two has to be wanting. For it may be said of men in general that they are ungrateful, voluble, dissemblers, anxious to avoid danger, and covetous of gain; as long as you benefit them, they are entirely yours; they offer you their blood, their goods, their life, and their children, as I have before said, when the necessity is remote; but when it approaches, they revolt. And the prince who has relied solely on their words, without making other preparations, is ruined; for the friendship which is gained by purchase and not through grandeur and nobility of spirit is bought but not secured, and at a pinch is not to be expended in your service. And men have less scruple in offending one who makes himself loved than one who makes himself feared; for love is held by a chain of obligation which, men being selfish, is broken whenever it serves their purpose; but fear is maintained by a dread of punishment which never fails.

9   Still, a prince should make himself feared in such a way that if he does not gain love, he at any rate avoids hatred; for fear and the absence of hatred may well go together, and will be always attained by one who abstains from interfering with the property of his citizens and subjects or with their women. And when he is obliged to take the life of any one, let him do so when there is a proper justification and manifest reason for it; but above all he must abstain from taking the property of others, for men forget more easily the death of their father than the loss of their patrimony. Then also pretexts for seizing property are never wanting, and one who begins to live by rapine will always find some reason for taking the goods of others, whereas causes for taking life are rarer and more fleeting.

10   But when the prince is with his army and has a large number of soldiers under his control, then it is extremely necessary that he should not mind being thought cruel; for without this reputation he could not keep an army united or disposed to any duty. Among the noteworthy actions of Hannibal is numbered this, that although he had an enormous army, composed of men of all nations and fighting in foreign countries, there never arose any dissension either among them or against the prince, either in good fortune or in bad. This could not be due to anything but his inhuman cruelty, which together

with his infinite other virtues, made him always venerated and terrible in the sight of his soldiers, and without it his other virtues would not have sufficed to produce that effect. Thoughtless writers admire on the one hand his actions, and on the other blame the principal cause of them.

11 And that it is true that his other virtues would not have sufficed may be seen from the case of Scipio (famous not only in regard to his own times, but all times of which memory remains), whose armies rebelled against him in Spain, which arose from nothing but his excessive kindness, which allowed more license to the soldiers than was consonant with military discipline. He was reproached with this in the senate by Fabius Maximus, who called him a corrupter of the Roman militia. Locri having been destroyed by one of Scipio's officers was not revenged by him, nor was the insolence of that officer punished, simply by reason of his easy nature; so much so, that some one wishing to excuse him in the senate, said that there were many men who knew rather how not to err, than how to correct the errors of others. This disposition would in time have tarnished the fame and glory of Scipio had he persevered in it under the empire, but living under the rule of the senate this harmful quality was not only concealed but became a glory to him.

12 I conclude, therefore, with regard to being feared and loved, that men love at their own free will, but fear at the will of the prince, and that a wise prince must rely on what is in his power and not on what is in the power of others, and he must only contrive to avoid incurring hatred, as has been explained.

In What Way Princes Must Keep Faith

13 How laudable it is for a prince to keep good faith and live with integrity, and not with astuteness, every one knows. Still the experience of our times shows those princes to have done great things who have had little regard for good faith, and have been able by astuteness to confuse men's brains, and who have ultimately overcome those who have made loyalty their foundation.

14 You must know, then, that there are two methods of fighting, the one by law, the other by force: the first method is that of men, the second of beasts; but as the first method is often insufficient, one must have recourse to the second. It is therefore necessary for a prince to know well how to use both the beast and the man. This was covertly taught to rulers by ancient writers, who relate how Achilles and many others of those ancient princes were given to Chiron the centaur to be brought up and educated under his discipline. The parable of this semi-animal, semi-human teacher is meant to indicate that a prince must know how to use both natures, and that the one without the other is not durable.

15   A prince being thus obliged to know well how to act as a beast must imitate the fox and the lion, for the lion cannot protect himself from traps, and
the fox cannot defend himself from wolves. One must therefore be a fox to
recognise traps, and a lion to frighten wolves. Those that wish to be only lions
do not understand this. Therefore, a prudent ruler ought not to keep faith
when by so doing it would be against his interest, and when the reasons
which made him bind himself no longer exist. If men were all good, this precept would not be a good one; but as they are bad, and would not observe
their faith with you, so you are not bound to keep faith with them. Nor have
legitimate grounds ever failed a prince who wished to show colourable
excuse for the non-fulfillment of his promise. Of this one could furnish an
infinite number of modern examples, and show how many times peace has
been broken, and how many promises rendered worthless, by the faithless-
ness of princes, and those that have been best able to imitate the fox have succeeded best. But it is necessary to be able to disguise this character well, and
to be a great feigner and dissembler; and men are so simple and so ready to
obey present necessities, that one who deceives will always find those who
allow themselves to be deceived.

16   I will only mention one modern instance. Alexander VI did nothing else
but deceive men, he thought of nothing else, and found the occasion for it; no
man was ever more able to give assurances, or affirmed things with stronger
oaths, and no man observed them less; however, he always succeeded in his
deceptions, as he well knew this aspect of things.

17   It is not, therefore, necessary for a prince to have all the above-named
qualities, but it is very necessary to seem to have them. I would even be bold
to say that to possess them and always to observe them is dangerous, but to
appear to possess them is useful. Thus it is well to seem merciful, faithful,
humane, sincere, religious, and also to be so; but you must have the mind so
disposed that when it is needful to be otherwise you may be able to change
to the opposite qualities. And it must be understood that a prince, and especially a new prince, cannot observe all those things which are considered
good in men, being often obliged, in order to maintain the state, to act against
faith, against charity, against humanity, and against religion. And, therefore,
he must have a mind disposed to adapt itself according to the wind, and as
the variations of fortune dictate, and, as I said before, not deviate from what
is good, if possible, but be able to do evil if constrained.

18   A prince must take great care that nothing goes out of his mouth which
is not full of the above-named five qualities, and, to see and hear him, he
should seem to be all mercy, faith, integrity, humanity, and religion. And
nothing is more necessary than to seem to have this last quality, for men in
general judge more by the eyes than by the hands, for every one can see, but
very few have to feel. Everybody sees what you appear to be, few feel what
you are, and those few will not dare to oppose themselves to the many, who

have the majesty of the state to defend them; and in the actions of men, and especially of princes, from which there is no appeal, the end justifies the means. Let a prince therefore aim at conquering and maintaining the state, and the means will always be judged honourable and praised by everyone, for the vulgar is always taken by appearances and the issue of the event; and the world consists only of the vulgar, and the few who are not vulgar are isolated when the many have a rallying point in the prince. A certain prince of the present time, whom it is well not to name, never does anything but preach peace and good faith, but he is really a great enemy to both, and either of them, had he observed them, would have lost him state or reputation on many occasions.

1513

Leo Tolstoy

THE ILLUSION OF THE LEADER'S FREEDOM*

Cicero and Machiavelli, however much they disagree, do agree on one simple point: leaders are important because their choices have consequences. Cicero wished his leaders to make principled choices in the manner of Regulus. Machiavelli advised his to make shrewd choices, lest they end up like Regulus. The nineteenth-century Russian novelist, Leo Tolstoy, thinks Cicero and Machiavelli are both deluded.

In his massive novel, War and Peace, *Tolstoy portrayed the freedom he believed us to have in our immediate relations with family and friends and in our private choices. But he also showed how this freedom is illusory when extrapolated into the public realm—into the vast panorama of history and the struggle for power. So his novel continually contrasts the potentially delightful world of peace with the titanically impersonal world of war.*

The implication of Tolstoy's novel seems to be that we should withdraw from public life. Who wants to be a slave, even to history? Who wants to sacrifice oneself as Regulus does, only to end up as a label, or as a statue that serves as a pigeon perch? On the other hand, what of the great moral causes that impinge on politics? Should we withdraw from these too, if we agree with Tolstoy? Is Tolstoy telling us a humbling truth, or is he providing rationalization for complete selfishness?

---

*Translated by Constance Garnett.

1   Towards the end of the year 1811, there began to be greater activity in levying troops and in concentrating the forces of Western Europe, and in 1812 these forces—millions of men, reckoning those engaged in the transport and feeding of the army—moved from the west eastward, towards the frontiers of Russia, where, since 1811, the Russian forces were being in like manner concentrated.

2   On the 12th of June the forces of Western Europe crossed the frontier, and the war began, that is, an event took place opposed to human reason and all human nature. Millions of men perpetrated against one another so great a mass of crime—fraud, swindling, robbery, forgery, issue of counterfeit money, plunder, incendiarism, and murder—that the annals of all the criminal courts of the world could not muster such a sum of wickedness in whole centuries, though the men who committed those deeds did not at that time look on them as crimes.

3   What led to this extraordinary event? What were its causes? Historians, with simple-hearted conviction, tell us that the causes of this event were the insult offered to the Duke of Oldenburg, the failure to maintain the continental system, the ambition of Napoleon, the firmness of Alexander, the mistakes of the diplomatists, and so on.

4   According to them, if only Metternich, Rumyantsev, or Talleyrand had, in the interval between a levée and a court ball, really taken pains and written a more judicious diplomatic note, or if only Napoleon had written to Alexander, 'I consent to restore the duchy to the Duke of Oldenburg,' there would have been no war.

5   We can readily understand that being the conception of the war that presented itself to contemporaries. We can understand Napoleon's supposing the cause of the war to be the intrigues of England (as, he said, indeed, in St. Helena); we can understand how to the members of the English House of Commons the cause of the war seemed to be Napoleon's ambition; how to the Duke of Oldenburg the war seemed due to the outrage done him; how to the trading class the war seemed due to the continental system that was ruining Europe; to the old soldiers and generals the chief reason for it seemed their need of active service; to the regiments of the period, the necessity of re-establishing correct principles; while the diplomatists of the time set it down to the alliance of Russia with Austria in 1809 not having been with sufficient care concealed from Napoleon, and the memorandum, No. 178 having been awkwardly worded. We may well understand contemporaries believing in those causes, and in a countless, endless number more, the multiplicity of which is due to the infinite variety of men's points of view. But to us of a later generation, contemplating in all its vastness the immensity of the accomplished fact, and seeking to penetrate its simple and fearful significance, those explanations must appear insufficient. To us it is inconceivable that millions of Christian men should have killed and tortured each other, because Napoleon was ambitious, Alexander firm, English policy crafty, and the

Duke of Oldenburg hardly treated. We cannot grasp the connection between these circumstances and the bare fact of murder and violence, nor why the duke's wrongs should induce thousands of men from the other side of Europe to pillage and murder the inhabitants of the Smolensk and Moscow provinces and to be slaughtered by them.

6   For us of a later generation, who are not historians led away by the process of research, and so can look at the facts with common-sense unobscured, the causes of this war appear innumerable in their multiplicity. The more deeply we search out the causes the more of them we discover; and every cause, and even a whole class of causes taken separately, strikes us as being equally true in itself, and equally deceptive through its insignificance in comparison with the immensity of the result, and its inability to produce (without all the other causes that concurred with it) the effect that followed. Such a cause, for instance, occurs to us as Napoleon's refusal to withdraw his troops beyond the Vistula, and to restore the duchy of Oldenburg; and then again we remember the readiness or the reluctance of the first chance French corporal to serve on a second campaign; for had he been unwilling to serve, and a second and a third and thousands of corporals and soldiers had shared that reluctance, Napoleon's army would have been short of so many men, and the war could not have taken place.

7   If Napoleon had not taken offence at the request to withdraw beyond the Vistula, and had not commanded his troops to advance, there would have been no war. But if all the sergeants had been unwilling to serve on another campaign, there could have been no war either.

8   And the war would not have been had there been no intrigues on the part of England, no Duke of Oldenburg, no resentment on the part of Alexander; nor had there been no autocracy in Russia, no French Revolution and consequent dictatorship and empire, nor all that led to the French Revolution, and so on further back: without any one of those causes, nothing could have happened. And so all those causes—myriads of causes—coincided to bring about what happened. And consequently nothing was exclusively the cause of the war, and the war was bound to happen, simply because it was bound to happen. Millions of men, repudiating their common-sense and their human feelings, were bound to move from west to east, and to slaughter their fellows, just as some centuries before hordes of men had moved from east to west to slaughter their fellows.

9   The acts of Napoleon and Alexander, on whose words it seemed to depend whether this should be done or not, were as little voluntary as the act of each soldier, forced to march out by the drawing of a lot or by conscription. This could not be otherwise, for in order that the will of Napoleon and Alexander (on whom the whole decision appeared to rest) should be effective, a combination of innumerable circumstances was essential, without any one of which the effect could not have followed. It was essential that the millions of men in whose hands the real power lay—the soldiers who fired guns and

transported provisions and cannons—should consent to carry out the will of those feeble and isolated persons, and that they should have been brought to this acquiescence by an infinite number of varied and complicated causes.

10 We are forced to fall back upon fatalism in history to explain irrational events (that is those of which we cannot comprehend the reason). The more we try to explain those events in history rationally, the more irrational and incomprehensible they seem to us. Every man lives for himself, making use of his free-will for attainment of his own objects, and feels in his whole being that he can do or not do any action. But as soon as he does anything, that act, committed at a certain moment in time, becomes irrevocable and is the property of history, in which it has a significance, predestined and not subject to free choice.

11 There are two aspects to the life of every man: the personal life, which is free in proportion as its interests are abstract, and the elemental life of the swarm, in which a man must inevitably follow the laws laid down for him.

12 Consciously a man lives on his own account in freedom of will, but he serves as an unconscious instrument in bringing about the historical ends of humanity. An act he has once committed is irrevocable, and that act of his, coinciding in time with millions of acts of others, has an historical value. The higher a man's place in the social scale, the more connections he has with others, and the more power he has over them, the more conspicuous is the inevitability and predestination of every act he commits. 'The hearts of kings are in the hand of God.' The king is the slave of history.

13 History—that is the unconscious life of humanity in the swarm, in the community—makes every minute of the life of kings its own, as an instrument for attaining its ends.

14 Although in that year, 1812, Napoleon believed more than ever that to shed or not to shed the blood of his peoples depended entirely on his will (as Alexander said in his letter to him), yet then, and more than at any time, he was in bondage to those laws which forced him, while to himself he seemed to be acting freely, to do what was bound to be his share in the common edifice of humanity, in history.

15 The people of the west moved to the east for men to kill one another. And by the law of the coincidence of causes, thousands of petty causes backed one another up and coincided with that event to bring about that movement and that war: resentment at the non-observance of the continental system, and the Duke of Oldenburg, and the massing of troops in Prussia—a measure undertaken, as Napoleon supposed, with the object of securing armed peace—and the French Emperor's love of war, to which he had grown accustomed, in conjunction with the inclinations of his people, who were carried away by the grandiose scale of the preparations, and the expenditure on those preparations, and the necessity of recouping that expenditure. Then there was the intoxicating effect of the honours paid to the French Emperor in Dresden, and the negotiations too of the diplomatists, who were supposed by contempo-

raries to be guided by a genuine desire to secure peace, though they only inflamed the pride of both sides; and millions upon millions of other causes, chiming in with the fated event and coincident with it.

16   When the apple is ripe and falls—why does it fall? Is it because it is drawn by gravitation to the earth; because its stalk is withered, because it is dried by the sun, because it grows heavier, because the wind shakes it, or because the boy standing under the tree wants to eat it?

17   Not one of those is the cause. All that simply makes up the conjunction of conditions under which every living, organic, elemental event takes place. And the botanist who says that the apple has fallen because the cells are decomposing, and so on, will be just as right as the boy standing under the tree who says the apple has fallen because he wanted to eat it and prayed for it to fall. The historian, who says that Napoleon went to Moscow because he wanted to, and was ruined because Alexander desired his ruin, will be just as right and as wrong as the man who says that the mountain of millions of tons, tottering and undermined, has been felled by the last stroke of the last workingman's pickaxe. In historical events great men—so called—are but the labels that serve to give a name to an event, and like labels, they have the least possible connection with the event itself.

18   Every action of theirs, that seems to them an act of their own free-will, is in an historical sense not free at all, but in bondage to the whole course of previous history, and predestined from all eternity.

1869

Two Ancient Political Debates

When reading the two debates recorded by Thucydides, try to decide where you would stand and what course of action you would recommend. However, before you do so, think how Cicero, Machiavelli, and Tolstoy might have responded to the issues under discussion.

Thucydides

THE MYTILENIAN DEBATE*

This first debate was recreated by the ancient Greek historian Thucydides in Book 3 of his history, The Peloponnesian War. *At the time of the debate, the*

---

*Adapted from the translation by Benjamin Jowett.

Athenians had gained control of the rebellious city of Mytilene. They had the population at their mercy. The debate was over what to do with the inhabitants. It was a question of life or death for hundreds of people. As the selection indicates, in the heat of anger the majority had decided to put the Mytilenian men to death and to enslave the women and children. Now the Athenians are to reconsider their vote. Thus Cleon's task is to hold his majority position; Diodotus's job is to win new votes.

1   When the captives arrived at Athens, the Athenians instantly put Sala-ethus to death, although he made various offers, and among other things promised to procure the withdrawal of the Peloponnesians from Plataea, which was still blockaded. Concerning the other captives, a discussion was held, and, in their indignation, the Athenians determined to put to death not only the men then at Athens, but all the grown-up citizens of Mytilene, and to enslave the women and children; the act of the Mytilenians appeared inexcusable, because they were not subjects like the other states which had revolted, but free. That Peloponnesian ships should have had the audacity to find their way to Ionia and assist the rebels contributed to increase the fury of the Athenians; and the action showed that the revolt was a long premeditated affair. So they sent a ship to Paches announcing their determination, and bidding him to put the Mytilenians to death at once. But on the following day a kind of remorse seized them; they began to reflect that a decree which doomed to destruction not only the guilty, but a whole city, was cruel and monstrous. The Mytilenian envoys who were at Athens perceived the change of feeling, and they and the Athenians who were sympathetic prevailed on the magistrates to bring the question again before the people; this they were willing to do because they saw themselves that the majority of the citizens were anxious to have an opportunity to reconsider their decision. An assembly was again summoned, and different opinions were expressed by different speakers. In the former assembly, Cleon, the son of Cleaenetus, had carried the decree condemning the Mytilenians to death. He was the most violent of the citizens, and at that time exercised by far the greatest influence over the people. And now he came forward a second time and spoke as follows.

2   "I have remarked again and again that a democracy cannot manage an empire, but never more than now, when I see you regretting your condemnation of the Mytilenians. Having no fear or suspicion of one another in daily life, you deal with your allies upon the same principle, and you do not consider that whenever you yield to them out of pity or are misled by their specious tales, you are guilty of a weakness dangerous to yourselves, and receive no thanks from them. You should remember that your empire is a dictatorship exercised over unwilling subjects, who are always conspiring against you; they do not obey in return for any kindness which you do them to your own injury, but only because you are their masters; they have no loyalty to

you, but they are held down by force. Besides, what can be more detestable than to be perpetually changing our minds? We forget that a state in which the laws, though imperfect, are inviolable, is better off than one in which the laws are good but ineffective. Dullness and common sense are a more useful combination than intelligence and lawlessness; and the simpler sort of people generally make better citizens than the more astute. For the latter desire to be thought wiser than the laws; they want to be always getting their own way in public discussions; they think that they can nowhere have a finer opportunity for displaying their intelligence, and their folly generally ends in the ruin of their country. Whereas the others, mistrusting their own capacity, admit that the laws are wiser than themselves. They do not pretend to criticize the arguments of a great speaker; and being impartial judges, not ambitious rivals, they hit the mark. That is the spirit in which we should act; not suffering ourselves to be so excited by our own cleverness in a war of wits as to advise the Athenian people contrary to our own better judgment.

3   "I myself think as I did before, and I wonder at those who have brought forward the case of the Mytilenians again, thus imposing a delay which is in the interest of the evil-doer. For, after a time, the anger of the victim dulls, and he pursues the criminal with less keenness, but the vengeance which follows closest upon the wrong is most adequate to it and exacts the fullest retribution. And again I wonder who will answer me, and whether he will attempt to show that the crimes of the Mytilenians are a benefit to us, or that when we suffer, our allies suffer with us. Clearly he must be someone who has such confidence in his powers of speech as to contend that you never adopted what was most certainly your resolution; or else he must be someone who, under the inspiration of a bribe, elaborates a sophistical speech in the hope of diverting you from the point. In such rhetorical contests the city gives away prizes, while she takes the risk upon herself. And you are to blame for instituting these harmful contests. When speeches are to be heard, you are too fond of using your eyes, but, where actions are concerned, you trust your ears. You estimate the value of future enterprises from the eloquence of an orator; but when it comes to accomplished facts, you believe not your own eyes but only what ingenious critics tell you. No men are better dupes, sooner deceived by novel notions, or slower to follow approved advice. You despise what is familiar, while you are worshipers of every new extravagance. Every one of you would be an orator if he could. When he cannot, he will not yield to a more successful rival; he would rather show that he does not let his wits come limping after, but that he can praise a sharp remark before it is well out of another's mouth. He would like to be as quick in anticipating what is said, as he is slow in foreseeing its consequences. You are always hankering after an ideal state, but you do not put your minds even to what is right before you. In a word, you are at the mercy of your own ears, and sit like spectators attending a performance of sophists, not like counsellors of a state.

4   "I want you to put aside this trifling matter and therefore I say to you that no single city has ever injured us so deeply as Mytilene. I can excuse those who find our rule too heavy to bear, or who have revolted because the enemy has compelled them. But islanders who had walls, and were unassailable by our enemies, except at sea, and there were sufficiently protected by a fleet of their own, islanders who were independent and treated by us with the highest regard, when they act thus, have not revolted (that word would imply that they were oppressed), but have betrayed us, and, entering the ranks of our bitterest enemies, have conspired with them to seek our ruin. And surely this is far more atrocious than if they had been led by motives of ambition to take up arms against us on their own account. They learned nothing from the misfortunes of their neighbours who had already revolted and been subdued by us, nor did the happiness which they were enjoying make them hesitate to court destruction. They trusted recklessly to the future. Cherishing hopes which, if less than their wishes, were greater than their powers, they went to war, preferring might to right. No sooner did they seem likely to win than they set upon us, although we were doing them no wrong. Too swift and sudden a rise is apt to make cities insolent; and, in general, ordinary good-fortune is safer than extraordinary. Human beings apparently find it easier to drive away adversity than to retain prosperity. We should from the first have made no difference between the Mytilenians and the rest of our allies, and then their insolence would never have risen to such a height; for men naturally despise those who court them, but respect those who do not give way to them. Yet it is not too late to punish them as their crimes deserve. And do not absolve the people while you throw the blame upon their leaders. For they were all of one mind when we were to be attacked. Had the people deserted the leaders and come over to us, they might at this moment have been reinstated in their city; but they considered that their safety lay in sharing the dangers of the oligarchy, and therefore they joined in the revolt. Reflect: If you impose the same penalty upon those of your allies who willfully rebel and upon those who are constrained by the enemy, which of them will not revolt upon any pretext however trivial, seeing that, if successful, he will be free, and, if unsuccessful, no irreparable evil will follow? We in the meantime shall have to risk our lives and our fortunes against every one in turn. When conquerors, we shall recover only a ruined city, and, for the future, the revenues which are our strength will be lost to us. But if we fail, the number of our adversaries will be increased. And when we ought to be employed in repelling our enemies, we shall be wasting time in fighting our own allies.

5   "Do not then hold out a hope to the Mytilenians that because of eloquence or bribes they are to be excused and their error is to be deemed only a human mistake. Their attack was not unpremeditated. That might have been an excuse for them, but they knew what they were doing. This was my

original contention, and I still maintain that you should abide by your former decision, and not be misled either by pity, or by the charm of words, or by a too forgiving nature. There are no three things more prejudicial to your power. Mercy should be reserved for the merciful, and not thrown away upon those who will have no compassion on us, and who must by the force of circumstances always be our enemies. And our charming orators will still have an arena, but one in which the questions at stake will not be so grave, and the city will not pay so dearly for her brief pleasure in listening to them, while they will continue to get a good fee for a good speech. Lastly, forgiveness is naturally shown to those who, being reconciled, will continue friends, and not to those who will always remain what they were, an enemy. In one word, if you do as I say, you will do what is just to the Mytilenians, and also what is expedient for yourselves; but, if you take the opposite course, they will not be grateful to you, and you will be self-condemned. For, if they were right in revolting, you must be wrong in maintaining your empire. But if, right or wrong, you are resolved to rule, then rightly or wrongly they must be chastised for your own good. Otherwise you must give up your empire; and then, when virtue is no longer dangerous, you may be as virtuous as you please. Punish them as they would have punished you; let not those who have escaped appear to have less feeling than those who conspired against them. Consider this. What might not they have been expected to do if they had conquered, especially since they were the aggressors? For those who wantonly attack others always rush into extremes, and sometimes, like these Mytilenians, to their own destruction. They know the fate which is reserved for them by an enemy who is spared: When a man is injured wantonly, he is more dangerous if he escapes than the enemy who has only suffered what he has inflicted. Be true then to yourselves, and recall as vividly as you can what you felt at the time; think how you would have given the world to crush your enemies, and now take your revenge. Do not be soft-hearted at the sight of their distress, but remember the danger which was once hanging over your heads. Chastise them as they deserve, and prove by an example to your other allies that rebellion will be punished with death. If this is made quite clear to them, your attention will no longer be diverted from your enemies by wars against your own allies."

6   Such were the words of Cleon; and after him Diodotus, the son of Eucrates, who in the previous assembly had been the chief opponent of the decree which condemned the Mytilenians, came forward again and spoke as follows.

7   "I am far from blaming those who invite us to reconsider our sentence upon the Mytilenians, nor do I approve of the censure which has been cast on the practice of deliberating more than once about matters so critical. In my opinion the two things most adverse to good counsel are haste and passion; the former is generally a mark of folly, the latter of crudity and narrow-

mindedness. When a man insists that words ought not to be our guides in action, he is either wanting in sense or wanting in honesty. He is wanting in sense if he does not see that there is no other way in which we can throw light on the unknown future; and he is not honest if, seeking to carry a discreditable measure, and knowing that he cannot speak well in a bad cause, he reflects that he can slander well and terrify his opponent and his audience by the audacity of his slanders. Worst of all are those who, besides other topics of abuse, declare that their opponent is hired to make an eloquent speech. If they accused him of stupidity only when he failed to make his case, he might go his way having lost his reputation for sense but not for honesty; whereas he who is accused of dishonesty, even if he succeeds, is viewed with suspicion, and, if he fails, is thought to be both stupid and dishonest. And so the city suffers, for she is robbed of her counsellors by fear. Happy would she be if such citizens could not speak at all, for then the people would not be misled. The good citizen should prove his superiority as a speaker, not by trying to intimidate those who are to follow him in debate, but by fair argument; and the wise city ought not to give increased honour to her best counsellor, any more than she will deprive him of that which he has; while he whose proposal is rejected not only ought to receive no punishment, but should be free from all reproach. Then he who succeeds will not say pleasant things contrary to his better judgment in order to gain a still higher place in popular favour, and he who fails will not be striving to attract the multitude to himself by similar flatteries.

8 "But we take an opposite course and still worse. Even when we know a man to be giving the wisest counsel, a suspicion of corruption is released; and, from a jealousy which is perhaps groundless, we allow the state to lose an undeniable advantage. It has come to this, that the best advice when offered in plain terms is as much distrusted as the worst. Not only he who wishes to lead the multitude into the most dangerous courses must deceive them, but he who speaks in the cause of right must make himself believed by lying. In this city, and in this city only, to do good openly and without deception is impossible because you, its citizens, are too clever. When a man confers an unmistakable benefit on you, he is rewarded by a suspicion that, in some underhanded manner, he gets more than he gives. But, whatever you may suspect, when great interests are at stake, we who advise ought to look further and weigh our words more carefully than you whose vision is limited. And you should remember that we are accountable for our advice to you, but you who listen are accountable to nobody. If he who gave and he who followed evil counsel suffered equally, you would be more reasonable in your ideas; but now, whenever you meet with a reverse, you are led away by the passion of the moment and punish the individual who is your adviser for his error of judgment. But your own errors you condone, if the judgments of many concurred in them.

9   "I do not come forward either as an advocate of the Mytilenians or as their accuser. The question for us, rightly considered, is not, 'What are their crimes?' but, 'What is best for us?' If I prove them ever so guilty, I will not on that account bid you put them to death, unless it is expedient. Neither, if there happened to be some degree of excuse for them, would I have you spare them, unless it be clearly for the good of the state. For I conceive that we are now concerned, not with the present, but with the future. When Cleon insists that the infliction of death will be expedient and will secure you against revolt in time to come, I, as concerned as he is about the future, strongly maintain the contrary position; and I would not have you be misled by the apparent attractiveness of his proposal, and reject the real advantages of mine. You are angry with the Mytilenians, and his argument appeals to that anger; but we are not a court of law, and do not want to be told what is just; we are considering a question of policy, and desire to know how we can use the Mytilenians to our best advantage.

10   "Societies have punished lesser offences than theirs with death; nevertheless, excited by hope, men still risk their lives. No one has ever yet committed a crime thinking he was certain to get caught. And what city when entering on a revolt ever imagined that the power which she had, whether her own or obtained from her allies, did not justify the attempt? All are by nature prone to err both in public and in private life, and no law will prevent them. Men have gone through the whole catalog of penalties in the hope that, by increasing their severity, they may suffer less at the hands of evil-doers. In early ages punishments, even of the worst offences, would naturally be milder; but as time went on and mankind continued to transgress, they seldom stopped short of death. And still there are transgressors. Some greater terror is needed; certainly death is no deterrent. For poverty infuses necessity with daring; and wealth engenders avarice with pride and ambition; and the various conditions of human life that put men under the sway of some mighty and fatal power, lure men through their passions to destruction. Desire and hope are never wanting, the one leading, the other following, the one devising the enterprise, the other suggesting that fortune will be kind; and they are the most ruinous, for, being unseen, they far outweigh the dangers which are seen. Luck too assists the illusion, for she often presents herself unexpectedly, and induces states as well as individuals to run into peril, however inadequate their means; and states even more than individuals, because they are throwing the dice for a higher stake, freedom or empire, and because, when a man has a whole people acting with him, he magnifies himself out of all reason. In a word then, it is impossible and simply absurd to suppose that human nature when bent upon some favorite project, can be restrained either by the strength of law or by any other terror.

11   "We ought not therefore to act hastily out of a mistaken reliance on the security which the penalty of death affords. Nor should we drive our rebel-

lious subjects to despair; they must not think that there is no place for repentance, or that they may not at any moment give up their mistaken policy. Consider this: At present, although a city may actually have revolted, when she becomes conscious of her weakness she will capitulate while still able to defray the cost of the war and to pay tribute for the future. However, if we are too severe, will not the citizens make better preparations, and, when besieged, resist to the last, knowing that it is all the same whether they come to terms early or late? Shall not we ourselves suffer? For we shall waste our money by a lengthy siege of a city which refuses to surrender; when the place is taken it will be a mere wreck, and we shall in future lose the revenues derived from it; and in these revenues lies our military strength. Do not then weigh offences with the severity of a judge, when you will only be injuring yourselves. Rather, have an eye to the future; let the penalties which you impose on rebellious cities be moderate, and then their wealth will be undiminished and at your service. Do not hope to find a safeguard in the severity of your laws, but only in the vigilance of your administration. At present we do just the opposite. A free people under a strong government will always revolt in the hope of independence; and when we have put them down we think that they cannot be punished too severely. But instead of inflicting extreme penalties on free men who revolt, we should practice extreme vigilance before they revolt, and never allow such a thought to enter their minds. When however they have been once put down, we ought to extenuate their crimes as much as possible.

12   "Think of another great error into which you would fall if you listened to Cleon. At present the members of the popular party are everywhere our friends; either they do not join with the oligarchs, or, if compelled to do so, they are always ready to turn against the authors of the revolt; and so, in going to war with a rebellious state, you have the multitude on your side. But, if you destroy the people of Mytilene who took no part in the revolt, and who voluntarily surrendered the city as soon as they got arms into their hands, think of the consequences. In the first place they were your benefactors, and to slay them would be a crime; in the second place you will play into the hands of oligarchic parties, who henceforward, in inciting a revolt, will at once have the people on their side, for you will have proclaimed to all that the innocent and the guilty will share the same fate. Even if they were guilty, you should wink at their conduct, and not allow the only friends whom you have left to be converted into enemies. It would be far more conducive to the maintenance of our empire to suffer wrong willingly than for the sake of justice to put to death those whom we had better spare. Cleon may speak of a punishment which is just and also expedient, but you will find that in any proposal like his the two cannot be combined.

13   "Be assured then that what I advise is for the best, and yield neither to pity nor to leniency, for I am as unwilling as Cleon can be that you should be

influenced by any such motives. Simply weigh the arguments which I have urged, and accept my proposal. Pass sentence at your leisure on the Mytilenians, whom Paches judged guilty and has sent here. But leave the rest of the inhabitants where they are. This will be good policy for the future, and will right now strike terror into your enemies. For wise counsel is really more formidable to an enemy than the severity of unreasoning violence."

14   Thus spoke Diodotus, and such were the proposals on either side which most nearly represented the opposing parties. In spite of the reaction, there was a struggle between the two opinions; the show of hands was very close, but the motion of Diodotus prevailed. The Athenians instantly dispatched another boat, hoping that, if the second could overtake the first, which had a start of about 24 hours, it might be in time to save the city. The Mytilenian envoys provided wine and barley for the crew and promised them great rewards if they arrived first. And such was their energy that they continued rowing while they ate their barley, kneaded with wine and oil, and slept and rowed by turns. Fortunately no adverse wind sprang up, and, the first of the two ships sailing in no great hurry on her unhappy errand and the second hastening as I have described, the first did indeed arrive sooner than the other, but not much sooner. Paches had read the decree and was about to put it into execution, when the second appeared and saved the city.

15   So near was Mytilene to destruction.

ca. **431–403** B.C.

Thucydides
THE MELIAN DIALOGUE*

The "Melian Dialogue," from Book 5 of Thucydides's great history of the Peloponnesian War, represents a discussion between the powerful and imperialistic ancient Athenians and the Melians, the residents of a small Greek island. Although the Melians are a colony of the Spartans, the rivals to the Athenians for control of the Mediterranean, they have refrained from taking sides in the struggle between these two great powers. The selection opens with the arrival of the Athenian generals who are to take over the tiny, weakly defended island.

1   The Athenians next made an expedition against the island of Melos with 30 ships of their own and eight others furnished by their allies in the islands. The Melians are colonists of the Lacedaemonians who would not submit to

*Adapted from the translation by Benjamin Jowett.

Athens like the other islanders. At first they were neutral and took no part. But when the Athenians tried to coerce them by ravaging their lands, they were driven into open hostilities. The generals, Cleomedes the son of Lycomedes and Tisias the son of Tisimachus, encamped with the Athenian forces on the island. But before they did the country any harm, they sent envoys to negotiate with the Melians. Instead of bringing these envoys before the people, the Melians desired them to explain their errand to the magistrates and to the dominant class. They spoke as follows.

2 ATHENIANS: So we are not allowed to speak to the people, lest they should be deceived by persuasive and unanswerable arguments which they would hear set forth in a single uninterrupted speech. We are perfectly aware that this is why you bring us before only a select few. You who are sitting here may as well make assurance yet surer. Let us have no set speeches at all. Instead reply to each statement with which you disagree and criticise it at once. Do you approve of this procedure?

3   The Melian representatives answered: The quiet interchange of explanations is a reasonable thing, and we do not object to that. But your warlike movements, which are present not only to our fears but to our eyes, seem to belie your words. We see that, although you may reason with us, you mean to be our judges; and that at the end of the discussion, if the justice of our cause prevail and we therefore refuse to yield, we may expect war; if we are convinced by you, we may expect slavery.

4 ATHENIANS: No, but if you are only going to argue concerning your suspicions about the future, or if you meet us with any other intention than that of looking your circumstances in the face and saving your city, then this discussion is finished. However, if this is your intention, we will proceed.

5 MELIANS: It is an excusable and natural thing that men in our position should neglect no argument and no view which may avail. But we admit that this conference has met to consider the question of our preservation; and therefore let the discussion proceed in the manner which you propose.

6 ATHENIANS: Well, then, we Athenians will use no fine words. We will not go out of our way to prove at length that we have a right to rule because we overthrew the Persians; or that we attack you now because we are suffering any injury at your hands. We would not convince you if we did; nor must you expect to convince us by arguing that, although a colony of the Lacedaemonians, you have taken no part in their expeditions, or that you have never done us any wrong. But you and we should say what we really think, and aim only at what is possible, for we both alike know that into the discussion of human affairs the question of justice only enters where there is equal power to enforce it. Otherwise, the strong do what they will, the weak what they must.

7   MELIANS: Well, since you set aside justice and invite us to speak of expediency, in our judgment it is certainly expedient that you should respect a principle which is for the common good: To every man when in peril a reasonable claim should be accounted a claim of right, and any plea which he is disposed to urge, even if failing of the point a little, should help his cause. Your interest in this principle is quite as great as ours, inasmuch as you, if you fall, will incur the heaviest vengeance, and will be the most terrible example to mankind.

8   ATHENIANS: The fall of our empire, if it should fall, is not an event to which we look forward with dismay; for ruling states such as Lacedaemon are not cruel to their vanquished enemies. With the Lacedaemonians, however, we are not now contending; the real danger is from our many subject states, who may of their own initiative rise up and overcome their masters. But this is a danger which you may leave to us. And we will now endeavour to show that we have come in the interests of our empire, and that in what we are about to say we are only seeking the preservation of your city. For we want to make you ours with the least trouble to ourselves, and it is for the interests of us both that you should not be destroyed.

9   MELIANS: It may be in your interest to be our masters, but how can it be in ours to be your slaves?

10 ATHENIANS: To you the gain will be that by submission you will avert the worst; and we shall be all the richer for your preservation.

11 MELIANS: But must we be your enemies? Will you not receive us as friends if we are neutral and remain at peace with you?

12 ATHENIANS: No, your enmity is not half so mischievous to us as your friendship; for the one is in the eyes of our subjects an argument of our power, the other of our weakness.

13 MELIANS: But are your subjects really unable to distinguish between states in which you have no concern, and those which are chiefly your own colonies, and in some cases have revolted and been subdued by you?

14 ATHENIANS: Why, they do not doubt that both of them have a good deal to say for themselves on the score of justice, but they think that states like yours are left free because they are able to defend themselves, and that we do not attack them because we dare not. So your subjection will give us an increase of security, as well as an extension of empire. For we are masters of the sea, and you who are islanders, and insignificant islanders at that, must not be allowed to escape us.

15 MELIANS: But do you not recognize another danger? For, once more, since you drive us from the pleas of justice and press upon us your doctrine of expediency, we must show you what is in our interest; and, if it be in yours too, then we may hope to convince you. Will you not be making enemies of all who are now neutrals? When they see how you are treating

us, they will expect you some day to turn against them. If so, are you not strengthening the enemies whom you already have, and bringing upon you others who, if they could help it, would never dream of being your enemies at all?

16 ATHENIANS: We do not consider our really dangerous enemies to be any of the peoples inhabiting the mainland who, secure in their freedom, may defer indefinitely any measures of precaution which they take against us. Really dangerous are islanders who, like you, happen to be under no control, and all who may be already irritated by the necessity of submission to our empire—these are our real enemies, for they are the most reckless and most likely to bring themselves as well as us into a danger which they cannot but foresee.

17 MELIANS: Surely then, if you and your subjects will brave all this risk, you in order to preserve your empire and they to be free of it, how base and cowardly would it be in us, who retain our freedom, not to do and suffer anything rather than be your slaves.

18 ATHENIANS: Not so, if you calmly reflect. For you are not fighting against equals to whom you cannot yield without disgrace, but you are taking counsel whether you will resist an overwhelming force. The question is not one of honour but of prudence.

19 MELIANS: But we know that the fortunes of war are sometimes capricious, and not always on the side of numbers. If we yield now, all is over; but if we fight, there is yet a hope that we may prevail.

20 ATHENIANS: Hope is a good comforter in the hour of danger; and when men have something else to depend upon, although hurtful, she is not ruinous. But when her spendthrift nature has induced them to stake their all, they see her as she really is at the moment of their fall when it is too late to be wary. You are weak and a single turn of the scale might be your ruin. Do not be deluded; avoid the error of which so many are guilty, who, although they might still be saved if they would take the natural means, have recourse to the invisible, to prophecies and oracles and the like, which ruin men by the hopes which they inspire in them.

21 MELIANS: We know only too well how hard the struggle must be against your power, and against fortune, if she does not mean to be impartial. Nevertheless we do not despair of fortune; for we hope to stand as high as you in the favor of heaven, because we are just and you against whom we contend are unjust. And we are satisfied that our deficiency in power will be compensated by the aid of our allies the Lacedaemonians. They cannot refuse to help us, if only because we are their kinsmen, and for the sake of their own honor. And therefore our confidence is not so utterly blind as you suppose.

22 ATHENIANS: As for the gods, we expect to have quite as much of their favor as you; for we are not doing or claiming anything which goes beyond

common opinion concerning divine or human desires about human things. For of the gods we believe, and of men we know, a law of their nature: Wherever they can rule, they will. This law was not made by us, and we are not the first who have acted upon it; we did but inherit it, and shall bequeath it to all time, and we know that you and all mankind, if you were as strong as we are, would do as we do. So much for the gods; we have told you why we expect to stand as high in their good opinion as you. And then as to the Lacedaemonians—when you imagine that out of every shame they will assist you, we admire the innocence of your idea, but we do not envy you the folly of it. The Lacedaemonians are exceedingly virtuous among themselves, according to their national standard of morality. But, in respect to their dealings with others, although many things might be said, they can be described in few words: Of all men whom we know, they are the most notorious for identifying what is pleasant with what is honorable, and what is expedient with what is just. But how inconsistent is such a character with your present blind hope of deliverance!

23 MELIANS: That is the very reason why we trust them; they will look to their own interest, and therefore will not be willing to betray the Melians, who are their own colonists, lest they should be distrusted by their friends in Greece and play into the hands of their enemies.

24 ATHENIANS: But do you not see that the path of expediency is safe, whereas justice and honor involve danger in practice, and such dangers the Lacedaemonians seldom care to face?

25 MELIANS: On the other hand, we think that whatever perils there may be, they will be ready to face them for our sakes, and will consider danger less dangerous where we are concerned. For if they need our aid, we are close at hand, and they can better trust our loyal feeling because we are their kinsmen.

26 ATHENIANS: Yes, but what encourages men who are invited to join in a conflict is clearly not the good-will of those who summon them to their side, but a decided superiority in real power. To this no men look more keenly than the Lacedaemonians; so little confidence have they in their own resources that they only attack their neighbors when they have numerous allies, and therefore they are not likely to find their way by themselves to an island, when we are masters of the sea.

27 MELIANS: But they may send their allies. The Cretan sea is a large place; and the masters of the sea will have more difficulty in overtaking vessels that want to escape than the pursued will have in escaping. If the attempt should fail, they may invade Attica itself, and find their way to allies of yours. Then you will have to fight, not for the conquest of a land in which you have no concern, but nearer home, for the preservation of your confederacy and of your own territory.

28 ATHENIANS: Help may come from Lacedaemon to you as it has come to others, and should you ever have actual experience of it, then you will know that never once have the Athenians retired from a siege through fear of a foe elsewhere. You told us that the safety of your city would be your first care, but we remark that, in this long discussion, not a word has been uttered by you which would give a reasonable man expectation of deliverance. Your strongest grounds are hopes deferred, and what power you have is not to be compared with that which is already arrayed against you. Unless after we have withdrawn you mean to come, as even now you may, to a wiser conclusion, you are showing a great want of sense. For surely you cannot dream of flying to that false sense of honor which has been the ruin of so many when danger and dishonor were staring them in the face. Many men with their eyes still open to the consequences have found the word "honor" too much for them, and have allowed a mere name to lure them on, until it has drawn down upon them real and irretrievable calamities. Through their own folly they have incurred a worse dishonor than fortune would have inflicted upon them. If you are wise you will not run this risk. You ought to see that there can be no disgrace in yielding to a great city which invites you to become her ally on reasonable terms, keeping your own land, and merely paying tribute. You will certainly gain no honor if, having to choose between two alternatives, safety and war, you obstinately prefer the worse. To maintain our rights against equals, to be politic with superiors, and to be moderate toward inferiors is the path of safety. Reflect once more when we have withdrawn, and say to yourselves over and over again that you are deliberating about your one and only country, which may be saved or may be destroyed by a single decision.

29   The Athenians left the conference; the Melians, after consulting among themselves, resolved to persevere in their refusal, and made the following as a final response. "Men of Athens, our resolution is unchanged; and we will not in a moment surrender that liberty which our city, founded 700 years ago, still enjoys. We will trust to the good fortune which, by the favor of the gods, has hitherto preserved us, and for human help to the Lacedaemonians, and endeavor to save ourselves. We are ready, however, to be your friends, and the enemies neither of you nor of the Lacedaemonians, and we ask you to leave our country when you have made such a peace as may appear to be in the interest of both parties."

30   Such was the answer of the Melians; the Athenians, as they left the conference, spoke as follows. "Well, we must say, judging from the decision at which you have arrived, that you are the only men who deem the future to be more certain than the present, and regard things unseen as already realized in your fond expectation, and that the more you cast yourselves upon

the Lacedaemonians and fortune and hope, and trust them, the more complete will be your ruin."

31   The Athenian envoys returned to the army; and the generals, when they found that the Melians would not yield, immediately commenced hostilities. They surrounded the town of Melos with a wall, dividing the work among the several contingents. They then left troops of their own and of their allies to keep guard both by land and by sea, and retired with the greater part of their army; the remainder carried on the blockade....

32   The Melians took that part of the Athenian wall which looked toward the agora by a night assault, killed a few men, and brought in as much corn and other necessities as they could; they then retreated and remained inactive. After this the Athenians set a better watch. So the summer ended.

33   In the following winter... the Melians took another part of the Athenian wall; for the fortifications were insufficiently guarded. Whereupon the Athenians sent fresh troops, under the command of Philocrates the son of Demeas. The place was now under a vigorous siege and there was treachery among the citizens themselves. So the Melians were induced to surrender unconditionally. The Athenians thereupon put to death all who were of military age, and made slaves of the women and children. They then colonized the island, sending to Melos 500 settlers of their own.

ca. **431–403** B.C.

Intervention or Isolation: An Enduring Issue in American Politics

Our last debate centers on another perennial issue of American politics: how involved should the American republic be in the affairs of the world at large? First George Washington, the nation's first president, warns against the young republic getting involved in European disputes. Yet American efforts to remain neutral in the Napoleonic wars of the early nineteenth century (the very subject of Tolstoy's *War and Peace,* by the way) led to war with Britain in 1812. Moreover, as early as 1823, President James Monroe announced his famous Monroe Doctrine: "The American continents, by the free and independent condition which they have assumed and maintain, are henceforth not to be considered as subjects for future colonization by any European powers." He added that the United States would enforce this doctrine because its own "rights and interests... are involved."

Proponents of the Monroe Doctrine regard it as a natural extension of our Declaration of Independence—as we demanded our own sovereignty, naturally we respect that of other nations. Others, however, have taken a different view. For instance, the Mexican diplomat Carlos Pereya wrote in the early years of this century that the Monroe Doctrine is "a myth which serves as a wrapper concealing the actual fact, namely the ambitions of a strong people who claim to exercise hegemony over a group of weak peoples, giving to their domination over them the hypocritical appearances of disinterest and benevolence." For some-one like Pereya, the United States was behaving like the Athens of Thucydides, preserving its own freedom while suppressing that of others less powerful.

This debate continues in our own time, and not just with respect to Central and South America. With the collapse of the Soviet Union and the apparent end of the Cold War, the debate has, in fact, taken on new urgency. Following Washington's address are three recent occasional pieces designed to have an immediate impact on public opinion. The first is an essay by Patrick Buchanan that argues what has come to be called the neo-isolationist position: the United States has performed heroically for the past half-century as the world's policeman but now should withdraw and attend more narrowly to its national interests.

The last two pieces take positions on U.S. involvement in Bosnia. Warren Christopher gave a speech before the House Committee on International Relations in November of 1995 explaining the Clinton administration's decision to "join our NATO Allies to help peace take hold in Bosnia-Herzegovina." George Kenney's piece appeared in *The Nation* in January of 1996; he takes the opposing position, that "putting 20,000 American troops in Bosnia is a mistake." What differences do you notice between Washington's, Buchanan's, and Kenney's arguments for avoiding entanglements in foreign wars? How have subsequent events supported or contradicted these arguments?

George Washington
FAREWELL ADDRESS

1 ...Observe good faith and justice towards all nations; cultivate peace and harmony with all; religion and morality enjoin this conduct; and can it be that good policy does not equally enjoin it? It will be worthy of a free, enlightened, and, at no distant period, a great nation, to give to mankind the magnanimous and too novel example of a people always guided by an exalted justice and benevolence. Who can doubt that, in the course of time and things, the fruits of such a plan would richly repay any temporary advantages that might be lost by a steady adherence to it? Can it be, that Providence has not connected the permanent felicity of a nation with its virtue? The experiment, at least, is recommended by every sentiment which ennobles human nature. Alas! is it rendered impossible by its vices?

2 In the execution of such a plan, nothing is more essential than that permanent, inveterate antipathies against particular nations, and passionate attachments for others, should be excluded; and that in place of them, just

and amicable feelings towards all should be cultivated. The nation, which indulges towards another an habitual hatred, or an habitual fondness, is in some degree a slave. It is a slave to its animosity or to its affection, either of which is sufficient to lead it astray from its duty and its interest. Antipathy in one nation against another, disposes each more readily to offer insult and injury, to lay hold of slight causes of umbrage, and to be haughty and intractable, when accidental or trifling occasions of dispute occur.

3   Hence frequent collisions, obstinate, envenomed, and bloody contests. The nation, prompted by ill-will and resentment, sometimes impels to war the government, contrary to the best calculations of policy. The government sometimes participates in the national propensity, and adopts through passion what reason would reject; at other times, it makes the animosity of the nation subservient to projects of hostility instigated by pride, ambition and other sinister and pernicious motives. The peace often, and sometimes, perhaps, the liberty of nations, has been the victim.

4   So, likewise, a passionate attachment of one nation for another produces a variety of evils. Sympathy for the favorite nation facilitating the illusion of an imaginary common interest in cases where no real common interest exists, and infusing into one the enmities of the other, betrays the former into a participation in the quarrels and wars of the latter, without adequate inducement or justification. It leads also to concessions to the favorite nation of privileges denied to others, which is apt doubly to injure the nation making the concessions; by unnecessarily parting with what ought to have been retained; and by exciting jealousy, ill-will, and a disposition to retaliate, in the parties from whom equal privileges are withheld; and it gives to ambitious, corrupted, or deluded citizens (who devote themselves to the favorite nation) facility to betray, or sacrifice the interests of their own country, without odium, sometimes even with popularity; gilding, with the appearances of a virtuous sense of obligation, a commendable deference for public opinion, or laudable zeal for public good, the base or foolish compliances of ambition, corruption, or infatuation.

5   As avenues to foreign influence, in innumerable ways, such attachments are particularly alarming to the truly enlightened and independent patriot. How many opportunities do they afford to tamper with domestic factions; to practise the arts of seduction; to mislead public opinion; to influence or awe the public councils! Such an attachment of a small or weak nation, toward a great and powerful one, dooms the former to be the satellite of the latter.

6   Against the insidious wiles of foreign influence (I conjure you to believe me, fellow-citizens), the jealousy of a free people ought to be constantly awake; since history and experience prove, that foreign influence is one of the most baneful foes of republican government. But that jealousy, to be useful, must be impartial; else it becomes the instrument of the very influence to be avoided, instead of a defence against it. Excessive partiality for one foreign

nation, and excessive dislike of another, cause those whom they actuate, to see danger only on one side; and serve to veil and even second the arts of influence on the other. Real patriots, who may resist the intrigues of the favorite, are liable to become suspected and odious; while its tools and dupes usurp the applause and confidence of the people, to surrender their interests.

7   The great rule of conduct for us, in regard to foreign nations is, in extending our commercial relations, to have with them as little political connection as possible. So far as we have already formed engagements, let them be fulfilled with perfect good faith. Here let us stop.

8   Europe has a set of primary interests, which to us have none, or a very remote relation. Hence she must be engaged in frequent controversies, the causes of which are essentially foreign to our concerns. Hence, therefore, it must be unwise in us to implicate ourselves, by artificial ties, in the ordinary vicissitudes of her politics, or the ordinary combinations and collisions of her friendships and enmities.

9   Our detached and distant situation invites and enables us to pursue a different course. If we remain one people, under an efficient government, the period is not far off when we may defy material injury from external annoyance; when we may take such an attitude as will cause the neutrality we may at any time resolve upon, to be scrupulously respected; when belligerent nations, under the impossibility of making acquisitions upon us, will not lightly hazard the giving us provocation; when we may choose peace or war, as our interest, guided by justice, shall counsel.

10   Why forego the advantages of so peculiar a situation? Why quit our own, to stand upon foreign ground? Why, by interweaving our destiny with that of any part of Europe, entangle our peace and prosperity in the toils of European ambition, rivalship, interest, humor, or caprice?

11   'Tis our true policy to steer clear of permanent alliances with any portion of the foreign world; so far, I mean, as we are now at liberty to do it; for let me not be understood as capable of patronizing infidelity to existing engagements. I hold the maxim no less applicable to public than to private affairs, that honesty is always the best policy. I repeat it, therefore, let those engagements be observed in their genuine sense. But, in my opinion, it is unnecessary, and would be unwise, to extend them.

12   Taking care always to keep ourselves, by suitable establishments, in a respectable defensive posture, we may safely trust to temporary alliances for extraordinary emergencies.

13   Harmony, and a liberal intercourse with all nations, are recommended by policy, humanity, and interest. But even our commercial policy should hold an equal and impartial hand; neither seeking nor granting exclusive favors or preferences; consulting the natural course of things; diffusing and diversifying, by gentle means, the streams of commerce, but forcing nothing; establishing, with powers so disposed, in order to give trade a stable course, to define the

rights of our merchants, and to enable the government to support them, conventional rules of intercourse, the best that present circumstances and mutual opinion will permit, but temporary, and liable to be, from time to time, abandoned or varied, as experience and circumstances shall dictate; constantly keeping in view, that it is folly in one nation to look for disinterested favors from another; that it must pay, with a portion of its independence, for whatever it may accept under that character; that, by such acceptance, it may place itself in the condition of having given equivalents for nominal favors, and yet of being reproached with ingratitude for not giving more. There can be no greater error than to expect or calculate upon real favors from nation to nation. It is an illusion, which experience must cure, which a just pride ought to discard.

[14] In offering to you, my countrymen, these counsels of an old and affectionate friend, I dare not hope they will make the strong and lasting impression I could wish; that they will control the usual current of the passions, or prevent our nation from running the course which has hitherto marked the destiny of nations! But, if I may even flatter myself, that they may be productive of some partial benefit, some occasional good; that they may now and then recur to moderate the fury of party spirit; to warn against the mischiefs of foreign intrigues; to guard against the impostures of pretended patriotism; this hope will be a full recompense for the solicitude for your welfare, by which they have been dictated.

[15] How far, in the discharge of my official duties, I have been guided by the principles which have been delineated, the public records and other evidences of my conduct must witness to you and to the world. To myself the assurance of my own conscience is, that I have at least believed myself to be guided by them.

[16] In relation to the still subsisting war in Europe, my proclamation of April 22, 1793, is the index to my plan. Sanctioned by your approving voice, and by that of your representatives in both Houses of Congress, the spirit of that measure has continually governed me, uninfluenced by any attempts to deter or divert me from it.

[17] After deliberate examination, with the aid of the best lights I could obtain, I was well satisfied that our country, under all the circumstances of the case, had a right to take, and was bound in duty and interest to take, a neutral position. Having taken it, I determined, as far as should depend upon me, to maintain it with moderation, perseverance, and firmness.

[18] The considerations which respect the right to hold this conduct, it is not necessary, on this occasion, to detail. I will only observe, that, according to my understanding of the matter, that right, so far from being denied by any of the belligerent powers, has been virtually admitted by all.

[19] The duty of holding a neutral conduct may be inferred, without anything more, from the obligation which justice and humanity impose on every

nation, in cases in which it is free to act, to maintain inviolate the relations of peace and amity towards other nations.

20 The inducements of interest for observing that conduct will best be referred to your own reflection and experience. With me, a predominant motive has been to endeavor to gain time to our country to settle and mature its yet recent institutions, and to progress, without interruption, to that degree of strength and consistency which is necessary to give it, humanly speaking, the command of its own fortunes.

21 Though, in reviewing the incidents of my administration, I am unconscious of intentional error, I am, nevertheless, too sensible of my defects, not to think it probable that I may have committed many errors. Whatever they may be, I fervently beseech the Almighty to avert or mitigate the evils to which they may tend. I shall also carry with me the hope that my country will never cease to view them with indulgence, and that after forty-five years of my life dedicated to its service, with an upright zeal, the faults of incompetent abilities will be consigned to oblivion, as myself must soon be to the mansions of rest.

22 Relying on its kindness in this, as in other things, and actuated by that fervent love towards it, which is so natural to a man who views in it the native soil of himself and his progenitors for several generations, I anticipate, with pleasing expectations, that retreat in which I promise myself to realize, without alloy, the sweet enjoyment of partaking, in the midst of my fellow-citizens, the benign influence of good laws under a free government—the ever favorite object of my heart, and the happy reward, as I trust, of our mutual cares, labors, and dangers.

1796

Patrick Buchanan

A NEW NATIONALISM

1 On the birthday of Thomas Jefferson, dead half a decade, the President of the United States raised his glass, and gave us, in a six-word toast, our national purpose: "The Union," Old Hickory said, "it must be preserved."

2 It was to "create a more perfect Union" that the great men came to Philadelphia; it was to permit the Republic to grow to its natural size that James K. Polk seized Texas and California; it was to preserve the Union—not end slavery—that Lincoln invaded and subjugated the Confederate states.

³ "A republic if you can keep it," Franklin told the lady in Philadelphia. Surely, preservation of the Republic, defense of its Constitution, living up to its ideals, that is our national purpose.

⁴ "America does not go abroad in search of monsters to destroy," John Quincy Adams said. "She is the well-wisher of the freedom and independence of all. She is the champion and vindicator only of her own."

⁵ Yet, when the question is posed, "What is America's national purpose?," answers vary as widely as those who take it. To Randall Robinson of Trans-Africa, it is overthrow of South Africa; to Jesse Jackson, it is to advance "justice" by restoring the wealth the white race has robbed from the colored peoples of the earth; to AIPAC [American Israel Public Affairs Committee], it is to keep Israel secure and inviolate; to Ben Wattenberg, America's "mission" is a crusade to "wage democracy" around the world.

⁶ Each substitutes an extra-national ideal for the national interest; each sees our national purpose in another continent or country; each treats our Republic as a means to some larger end.

⁷ "National purpose" has become a vessel, emptied of original content, into which ideologues of all shades and hues are invited to pour their own causes, their own visions.

⁸ In Charles Krauthammer's "vision," the "wish and work" of our nation should be to "integrate" with Europe and Japan inside a "super-sovereign" entity that is "economically, culturally, and politically hegemonic in the world." This "new universalism," he writes, "would require the conscious depreciation not only of American sovereignty but of the notion of sovereignty in general. This is not as outrageous as it sounds."

⁹ While Krauthammer's superstate may set off onanistic rejoicing inside the Trilateral Commission, it should set off alarm bells in more precincts than Belmont, Mass. As national purpose, or national interest, like all of the above, it fails the fundamental test: Americans will not fight for it.

¹⁰ Long ago, Lord McCauley wrote:

> And how can man die better
> Than facing fearful odds
> For the ashes of his fathers,
> And the temples of his Gods.

¹¹ A nation's purpose is discovered not by consulting ideologies, but by reviewing its history, by searching the hearts of its people. What is it for which Americans have always been willing to fight?

¹² Well, let us go back to a time when the Establishment wanted war, but the American people did not want to fight.

¹³ In the fall of 1941, Europe from the Pyrenees to Moscow, from the Arctic to North Africa, was ruled by Hitler's Third Reich; east of Moscow, Stalin's Gulag extended across Asia to Manchuria, where it met the belligerent

Empire of the Rising Sun, whose domain ran to mid-Pacific. England was in her darkest hour. Yet, still, America wanted to stay out; we saw, in the world's bloody conflict, no cause why our soldiers should be sent overseas to spill a single drop of American blood. Pearl Harbor, not FDR [Franklin Delano Roosevelt], convinced America to go to war.

14   The isolationism of our fathers is today condemned, and FDR is adjudged a great visionary, because he sought early involvement in Britain's war with Hitler. But, even the interventionists' arguments were, and are, couched in terms of American national interest.

15   Perhaps we did not see it, we are told, but our freedom, our security, our homes, our way of life, our Republic were at risk. Thus do even the acolytes of interventionism pay tribute to the true national interest of the United States, which are not to be found in some hegemonic and utopian world order.

16   When Adams spoke, he was echoing Washington's farewell address that warned his fickle countrymen against "inveterate antipathies against particular nations, and passionate attachments for others.... The nation which indulges toward another a habitual hatred, or a habitual fondness, is in some degree a slave. It is a slave to its animosities or to its affections, either of which is sufficient to lead it astray from its duty and its interest."

17   After V-E [Victory in Europe] Day and V-J [Victory in Japan] Day, all America wanted to "bring the boys home," and we did. Then, they were sent back, back to Europe, back to Asia, because Americans were persuaded—by Joseph Stalin—that the Cold War must be waged, because Lenin's Party had made the United States the "main enemy" in its war against the West. As the old saw goes, you can refuse almost any invitation, but when the man wants to fight, you've got to oblige him.

18   If the Cold War is ending, what are the terms of honorable peace that will permit us to go home? Are they not withdrawal of the Red Army back within its own frontiers, liberation of Central Europe and the Baltic republics, reunification of Germany, and de-Leninization of Moscow, i.e., overthrow of the imperialist party that has prosecuted the 70 Years' War against the West?

19   Once Russia is rescued from Leninism, its distant colonies, Cuba and Nicaragua, must eventually fall, just as the outposts of Japan's empire, cut off from the home islands, fell like ripe apples into the lap of General Mac-Arthur. Withdrawal of the Red Army from Europe would remove from the hand of Mikhail Gorbachev's successor the military instrument of Marxist restoration.

20   The compensating concession we should offer: total withdrawal of U.S. troops from Europe. If Moscow will get out, we will get out. Once the Red Army goes home, the reason for keeping a U.S. army in Europe vanishes. Forty years after the Marshall Plan, it is time Europe conscripted the soldiers for its own defense.

21   As the Austrian peace treaty demonstrates, troop withdrawals are the most enduring and easily verifiable form of arms control. If we negotiate the 600,000 troops of the Red Army out of Central Europe, they cannot return, short of launching a new European war.

22   There is another argument for disengagement. When the cheering stops, there is going to be a calling to account for the crimes of Teheran, Yalta, and Potsdam, where the Great Men acceded to Stalin's demand that he be made cartographer of Europe. In the coming conflicts, over Poland's frontiers east and west, over Transylvania, Karelia, Moldavia, the breakup of Yugoslavia, our role is diplomatic and moral, not military.

23   In 1956, at the high-water mark of American power, the U. S. stood aside as Soviet tanks crushed the Hungarian revolution. With that decision, Dwight Eisenhower and John Foster Dulles told the world that, while we support freedom in Central Europe, America will not go to war with Russia over it. The year of revolution, 1989, revealed the logical corollary: from Berlin to Bucharest to Beijing, as Lord Byron observed, "Who would be free, themselves must strike the blow."

24   Would America be leaving our NATO [North Atlantic Treaty Organization] allies in the lurch? Hardly. NATO Europe contains 14 states, which, together, are more populous and three times as wealthy as a Soviet Union deep in an economic, social, and political crisis. Moreover, NATO would have a new buffer zone of free, neutral, anti-Communist nations between the Soviet and German frontiers. Our job will have been done.

25   To conquer Germany, the Red Army would have to cross a free Poland of 500 miles and 40 million, before reaching the frontier of a united Reich of 80 million, whose tradition is not wholly pacifist. In the first hours of invasion, Moscow would see her economic ties to the West severed, and a global coalition forming up against her, including Germany, France, Britain, China, Japan, and the United States. As the Red Army advanced, it would risk atomic attack. To what end? So the Kremlin can recapture what the Kremlin is giving up as an unwanted and unmanageable empire?

26   The day of the *realpoliticians,* with their Metternichian "new architectures," and balance-of-power stratagems, and hidden fear of a world where their op-ed articles and televised advice are about as relevant as white papers from Her Majesty's colonial office, is over.

27   But disengagement does not mean disarmament.

28   Still the greatest trading nation on earth, the U.S. depends on freedom of the seas for its prosperity. The strength of the U.S. Navy should be nonnegotiable; and when the President is invited to enter naval arms control negotiations, the answer should be no, even if it means Moscow walks out.

29   With the acquisition of ballistic missiles by China, Iran, Iraq, Syria, and Libya, with atomic weapons work being done in half a dozen countries of the Third World, the United States needs nay, requires, a crash research and

development program for missile defense, to protect our homeland, our warships, our bases. No arms control agreement is worth trading away SDI.

30   An island continent, America should use her economic and technological
superiority to keep herself permanent mistress of the seas, first in air power,
first in space. Nor is the cost beyond our capacity. For, it is not warships and
weapons that consume half our defense budget; it is manpower and benefits.
When defense cuts are made, they should come in army bases, no longer
needed for homeland defense, and ground troops no longer needed on foreign soil.

31   As U.S. bases close down in Europe, we should inform Moscow we want
all Soviet bases closed in the Caribbean and Central America, all Soviet
troops out of the Western hemisphere. They have no business here. This is our
hemisphere; and the Monroe Doctrine should be made again the cornerstone
of U.S. foreign policy.

32   As the U.S. moves off the mainland of Europe, we should move our
troops as well off the mainland of Asia. South Korea has twice the population, five times the economic might of North Korea. She can be sold the
planes, guns, missiles, and ships to give her decisive superiority; then, U. S.
troops should be taken out of the front line.

33   We are not going to fight another land war in Asia; no vital interest justifies it; our people will not permit it. Why, then, keep 30,000 ground troops on
the DMZ [demilitarized zone]? If Kim Il Sung attacks, why should Americans
be first to die? If we must intervene, we can do so with air and sea power,
without thousands of Army and Marine dead. It is time we began uprooting
the global network of "trip wires," planted on foreign soil, to ensnare the
United States in the wars of other nations, to back commitments made and
treaties signed before this generation of American soldiers was even born.

34   The late Barbara Tuchman wrote of the Kaiser that he could not stand it
if, somewhere in the world, a quarrel was going on and he was not a party to
it. Blessed by Providence with pacific neighbors, north and south, and vast
oceans, east and west, to protect us, why seek permanent entanglement in
other people's quarrels?

35   As we ascend the staircase to the 21st century, America is uniquely situated to lead the world.

36   Japan has a population older and not half so large as ours; her land and
resources cannot match California's. Even united, the two Germanies have
but a third of our population, a fifth of our gross national product, and a land
area smaller than Oregon and Washington. Neither Japan nor Germany is a
nuclear power; neither has a Navy or Air Force to rival ours; even their combined GNP is dwarfed by ours. While the Soviet Union has the size,
resources, and population to challenge us as a world power, she is a prison
house of nations whose ethnic hatreds and unworkable system mean a
decade of turmoil. Who is left? The corrupt, bankrupt China of Deng Xaio-

ping? It will not survive the decade. [Yasuhiro] Nakasone was right: The 20th century was the American Century. The 21st century will be the American Century as well.

37 But America can lead the world into the 21st century only if she is not saddled down by all the baggage piled up in the 20th.

38 For 50 years, the United States has been drained of wealth and power by wars, cold and hot. Much of that expenditure of blood and treasure was a necessary investment. Much was not.

39 We cannot forever defend wealthy nations that refuse to defend themselves; we cannot permit endless transfusions of the lifeblood of American capitalism into the mendicant countries and economic corpses of socialism, without bleeding ourselves to death. Foreign aid is an idea whose time has passed. The Communist and socialist world now owe the West a thousand billion dollars and more, exclusive of hundreds of billions we simply gave away. Our going-away gift to the globalist ideologues should be to tell the Third World we are not sending the gunboats to collect our debts, neither are we sending more money. The children are on their own....

40 With the Cold War ending, we should look, too, with a cold eye on the internationalist set, never at a loss for new ideas to divert U. S. wealth and power into crusades and causes having little or nothing to do with the true national interest of the United States.

41 High among these is the democratist temptation, the worship of democracy as a form of government and the concomitant ambition to see all mankind embrace it, or explain why not. Like all idolatries, democratism substitutes a false god for the real, a love of process for a love of country.

42 When we call a country "democratic," we say nothing about whether its rulers are wise or good, or friendly or hostile; we only describe how they were chosen, a process that produced Olaf Palme, Lopez Portillo, Pierre Trudeau, Sam Nujoma, Kurt Waldheim, and the Papandreous [father and sons], as well as Ronald Reagan.

43 Raul Alfonsin, elected president, led Argentina to ruin; while General Augusto Pinochet, who seized power in a coup, rescued Chile from Castroism, and leaves her secure, prosperous, and on the road to freedom. Why, then, celebrate Alfonsin, and subvert Pinochet?

44 As cultural traditions leave many countries unsuited to U.S.-style democracy, any globalist crusade to bring its blessings to the natives everywhere must end in frustration, and surely will be marked by hypocrisy. While the National Endowment for Democracy (NED) meddles in the affairs of South Africa, the State Department props up General Mobutu. Where is the consistency?...

45 How other people rule themselves is their own business. To call it a vital interest of the United States is to contradict history and common sense. And

for the Republic to seek to dictate to 160 nations, what kind of regime each should have, is a formula for interminable meddling and endless conflict; it is a textbook example of that "messianic globaloney" against which Dean Acheson warned; it is, in scholar Clyde Wilson's phrase, a globalization of that degenerate form of Protestantism known as the Social Gospel.

46   "We must consider first and last," Walter Lippmann wrote in 1943, "the American national interest. If we do not, if we construct our foreign policy on some kind of abstract theory of rights and duties, we shall build castles in the air. We shall formulate policies which in fact the nation will not support with its blood, its sweat, and its tears." Exactly.

47   What do Tibetans, Mujahedeen, UNITA [National Union for the Total Independence of Angola] rebels, and *contras* have in common? Not belief in a bicameral legislature, or in separation of church and state, but love of liberty and a hatred of Communism. Is it not that spirit of patriotism that brought down the vassal regimes of Central Europe, that today threatens to tear apart the Soviet Empire?

48   "Enlightened nationalism," was Lippmann's idea of a foreign policy to protect America's true national interest. What we need is a new nationalism, a new patriotism, a new foreign policy that puts America first, and not only first, but second and third as well.

1990

Warren Christopher

BOSNIA: WE MUST BE THE LEADERS OF PEACE

1   Thank you, Mr. Chairman. On Monday night, President Clinton addressed the nation to explain why American troops should join our NATO Allies to help peace take hold in Bosnia-Herzegovina. Secretary Perry, General Shalikashvili, and I are here to further explain our purpose and our plans, to answer your questions, and to seek your support.

2   We have a fundamental choice. As the President made clear, if the United States does not participate, there will be no NATO force. If there is no NATO force, there will be no peace in Bosnia, and the war will reignite.

3   We do not have to imagine the consequences. We know what would happen. There would be more massacres, more concentration camps, more hunger, a real threat of a wider war, and immense damage to our leadership in

NATO, in Europe, and the world. That is the alternative we can and must avoid. We must continue to secure the peace.

4   The war in the former Yugoslavia has been a threat to our nation's interests and an affront to our nation's values. We have been witness to horrors and cruelties that my generation—the generation that fought World War II—once thought were consigned to a dark and distant past. We have faced the constant threat of a wider, even more terrible war in an unstable part of Europe. We have had to contemplate the possibility that our troops would be called upon to rescue our allies from Bosnia under fire.

5   This summer, the conflict in Bosnia reached a crisis point. The President launched a carefully conceived initiative that took us step by step from the most horrifying events of the war—the fall of Srebrencia and Zepa—to this hopeful point.

6   At the July London Conference, we persuaded our Allies to take decisive measures to protect Bosnia's remaining safe areas. We led a NATO bombing campaign to convince the Bosnian Serbs that nothing more could be gained by continuing the war. Our diplomacy produced a cease-fire and a set of constitutional principles for a single Bosnian state. And last week, we led the parties to a comprehensive settlement in Dayton. That settlement will be formally signed in Paris on December 14.

7   As a result of the President's initiative, the fighting has stopped. We now have an opportunity to secure an enduring peace because of American strength and American diplomacy. We will achieve our goal only if America continues to lead. The parties have taken risks for peace and we must continue to support them.

8   Our national interest in implementing the Dayton settlement is clear.

9   We have a strong interest in ending the worst atrocities in Europe since World War II—atrocities that are all the more pernicious because they have been directed at specific groups of people because of their faith. By helping peace take hold, we can make sure that the people of Bosnia see no more days of dodging bullets, no more winters of freshly dug graves, no more years of isolation from the outside world.

10   We have a strong interest in making sure that this conflict does not spread. Bosnia lies on a faultline in a volatile region of Europe. To the south are Kosovo, Albania, and the Former Yugoslav Republic of Macedonia, the likeliest flashpoints of a wider war, as well as Greece and Turkey, two NATO allies. To the north and east lie Hungary, Romania and Bulgaria, fragile new democracies deeply threatened by the prospect of ethnic conflict in the Balkans. To the north also lies the Eastern Slavonia region of Croatia, which could yet spark a regional war if the Dayton accords are not implemented.

11   Peace in this part of Europe matters to the United States because Europe matters to the United States. Twice this century, we have sent millions of American soldiers to war across the Atlantic. The first of this century's great

wars began with violence in Sarajevo. The second began with aggression in Central Europe and with horrors that the world ignored until it was too late. Ever since, our leaders, Republican and Democrat alike, have acted to protect our vital interest in European stability. If we do not take this opportunity for peace, we could be faced with the prospect of action far costlier and more dangerous than anything being contemplated now.

12   The United States also has a vital interest in maintaining our leadership in the world. Taking action in Bosnia now is an acid test of American leadership. After creating this opportunity for peace, we cannot afford to walk away. I can tell you from my personal experience as Secretary of State that if we are seen as a country that does not follow through on its initiatives, no nation will follow us—not in Europe, not in the Middle East, not in Asia, not anywhere.

13   Mr. Chairman, the agreement we initialed in Dayton advances our national interests and gives us every reason to believe that peace can take hold in Bosnia. The settlement was negotiated in 21 long days against the backdrop of four bloody years of war. It includes many hard-fought compromises. But on every important issue, it meets the principled and practical standards on which my negotiating team and I insisted. It is an agreement not just of goals, but of means.

14   It preserves Bosnia as a single state with federal institutions that represent its Croat, Muslim, and Serb communities alike.

15   It reunifies Sarajevo within the Federation of Bosnia and Herzegovina, and connects Gorazde to the Federation by a secure land corridor.

16   It gives the people of Bosnia the right to move freely throughout the country. It gives refugees the right to return to their homes. And it creates a mechanism for settling claims to property.

17   It makes it possible for democratic, internationally-run elections to be held next year. I spent hours in Dayton convincing the parties that refugees should have a choice between voting where they currently live or in their original homes.

18   The agreement excludes war criminals from office. And it explicitly obligates all the parties to cooperate with the investigation and prosecution of war crimes.

19   It protects human rights and creates new institutions to investigate and punish violations.

20   Most fundamentally, it ends the war, and requires the parties to move their armed forces behind agreed lines.

21   Sometimes in a negotiation like this, there is a temptation to take short cuts, to deal with the hardest issues in an ambiguous way. But in Dayton, we insisted on concrete and detailed commitments on the most critical issues that divided the parties. Because the agreement is comprehensive, it is far more likely to endure.

22   In the long run, restoring the fabric of Bosnia's society will still require an immense effort. But at least that effort can now begin. After all, only with peace does Bosnia have a chance to exist as a single state. Only with peace does it have a chance to build a multi-ethnic democracy. Only with peace will we have a chance to bring war criminals to justice, and to ensure that no more war crimes are committed.

23   The Dayton accord does require the parties to take extremely difficult steps on the road to peace. I believe that each is prepared to carry out its commitments, but only if each is confident that the other parties will carry out theirs. Each party made it clear that they would reach settlement only if NATO agreed to lead a peace implementation force.

24   Secretary Perry and General Shalikashvili will speak in greater detail about our participation in IFOR. But let me address some of the questions I know are on your mind.

25   I know many Americans have wondered why Europe cannot provide all of the ground troops in this NATO force. NATO is built on the sharing of effort and risk. We are NATO's largest member, the core of its strength and resolve. The Alliance cannot undertake what will be the largest mission in its history if we decline to do our share. At the same time, we should remember that other nations, including nearly all our NATO allies, Russia, and many of our new partners in Central Europe, will contribute 2/3 of the troops in IFOR.

26   Others have asked whether, after four years of bloodshed, the parties are willing to carry through with this agreement. We must remember that we secured the agreement because peace is the key to what all the parties want: from reconstruction, to justice, to rejoining the international community. We constructed the agreement to ensure that it will be carried out. We have made certain that sanctions against Serbia, our main source of leverage with that country, will be reimposed if the agreement is not implemented. Sanctions against the Bosnian Serbs will remain in place until their forces withdraw behind the agreed boundary of the Serb Republic. Moreover, our troops will have the strength and authority to enforce key military provisions of the agreement.

27   In addition, let me emphasize that it was not enough for me that President Milosevic was specifically authorized to negotiate the accord on behalf of the Bosnian Serbs. I insisted that the Bosnian Serbs initial it as well. In Dayton, President Milosevic promised to obtain their agreement within 10 days: as it turned out, he did so in just two days. This kind of response increases my confidence that this accord will be carried out.

28   Mr. Chairman, as we negotiated in Dayton, we constantly insisted on an agreement that our military could implement and enforce. Each part of the agreement was carefully constructed to take into account the needs of our armed forces and the advice of the military members of our team. As a result,

the military annex to the agreement contains the kind of detailed provisions our military considered essential to their task.

29   Let me assure you that IFOR's mission is well-defined and limited. Our troops will enforce the military aspects of the agreement—enforcing the cease-fire, supervising the withdrawal of forces, and establishing a zone of separation between them. But it will not be asked to guarantee the success of democracy or reconstruction, or to act as a police force. One of the lessons we have learned in the last few years is that our military should not be a permanent guarantor of peace. It should create opportunities that others must then seize.

30   Because IFOR's mission is well defined, we have a clear end point, which Secretary Perry will describe in detail. In this respect, I want to stress that we are committed to achieving stable military balance within Bosnia and among the states of the former Yugoslavia, so that peace will endure. This should be achieved, to the extent possible, through arms limitations and reductions.

31   It is not likely, however, that arms control measures alone will be sufficient to achieve military stabilization. The armed forces of the Federation, which have been most severely constrained by the arms embargo, will likely need to obtain some equipment and training in order to establish an effective self-defense capability. For our part, the United States will ensure that Federation armed forces receive the necessary assistance. Neither IFOR nor the U.S. military will directly participate in this effort. The best approach—and the one we will pursue—is for the United States to coordinate an international effort to provide the necessary assistance.

32   Civilian agencies from around the world will carry out a separate program to help the people of Bosnia rebuild. Our European allies will pay for most of this vital civilian effort. International organizations will also play an important role. The OSCE will supervise elections. The UNHCR will coordinate the return of refugees. The World Bank and IMF will help Bosnia's economy recover, with the EU also playing a leading role. The UN will help monitor and train local police.

33   But none of these important tasks will be carried out unless the peace agreement endures. There is no middle ground between peace and war in Bosnia. And in the choice between peace and war, as the President so plainly put it Monday night, "America must choose peace."

34   Many years from now, I have no doubt that people will look back on this month in history as a critical turning point for the United States and Europe. Let it be remembered as the moment when our country grasped the chance we created for peace, not as the moment when we hesitated to act.

35   The President has made his choice. The United States must act as the great nation that we are. We must protect our interests. We must uphold our ideals. We must keep our commitments. And we must lead.

[36] In the coming days, Mr. Chairman, the Administration will continue to consult fully with you and with the Congress. We will continue to work hard to gain the bipartisan support of the Congress, just as we work to gain the support and understanding of the American people. We are confident that the case for moving forward is clear and strong. We are prepared to answer your questions and to hear your concerns today. Thank you.

1995

George Kenney

STEERING CLEAR OF THE BALKAN SHOALS

[1] In my bones, I feel that putting 20,000 American troops in Bosnia is a mistake. It's an invitation to a shipwreck because our maps aren't any good, and imagination and pluck aren't enough to carry us through Balkan shoals. Insofar as U.S. policy toward Bosnia has more to do with idealistic American illusions than with genuine concern for parochial Balkan interests, this is our Vietnam experience all over again.

[2] I became a Yugoslav desk officer at the State Department's headquarters in Washington in February 1992, where I worked until I resigned over policy that August, calling for American intervention. I had no background in the Balkans or Eastern Europe; I hadn't been to Yugoslavia, I didn't even speak Serbo-Croatian. I was on the desk long enough to convince myself I knew what was going on and become certain that missteps, delay and denial would produce a debacle for U.S. foreign policy, but not quite long enough to see the bigger picture. I've been on a learning curve ever since.

[3] When I resigned I hoped to have more influence for intervention outside government, but over time I've changed my mind substantially on the issues. Because of that, I've been attacked in *The New Republic* and vilified by American interventionists who now see me as a traitor to the cause, though both evolving conditions and additional information left me no recourse but to alter my initial conclusions.

[4] I was one of the original authors of "lift and strike" (lifting the United Nations arms embargo against the Bosnian government and backing it with NATO airstrikes), arguing for it until early 1993; then, until late 1993, I argued for forcibly disarming all combatants; and after that for a variety of diplomatic plans backed by limited force.

[5] My resignation brought immediate media attention and invitations to speak, all of which I took to like a duck to water. The first college I visited,

William and Mary, turned out an S.R.O. crowd of several hundred for my two-hour extemporaneous address, and the crowd broke into a standing ovation when I finished. I quickly realized that the call for intervention in Bosnia was dynamite. That potency frightened me because it implied a huge responsibility not to distort the truth for the sake of setting an audience on fire. But I worry that many interventionists have felt the same power and been carried away.

6　　When prominent intellectuals consistently level charges of "genocide," comparing events in Bosnia to the Holocaust, we must demand evidence. While any killing is to be condemned, circumstantial evidence isn't enough, and while it's unreasonable to expect absolute proof, there can be no disdain for facts. There has never been evidence presented for the widely accepted claim that 250,000 people were butchered in Bosnia. Throughout the war, we haven't known exactly what's happened, exactly how many have been killed, who they were or how they died. Mass graves on all sides could contain civilians killed in cold blood or soldiers killed in battle who needed a rapid burial or, most likely, both. No doubt thousands were slaughtered in cold blood. This doesn't mean, however, that Bosnia was a killing field on the order of Cambodia or Nazi Germany.

7　　From contacts in the U.S. intelligence community, I am positive the U.S. government doesn't have proof of any genocide. And anyone reading the press critically can see the paucity of evidence, despite interminably repeated claims and bloodcurdling speculation. Last April 23 I published some of my research on fatalities in *The New York Times Magazine,* in which I challenged allegations of 250,000 dead; my estimate was 25,000 to 60,000 deaths, for civilian and military on all sides in Bosnia, from the start of the war to the date of the article. One Pulitzer Prize–winning correspondent harangued me for not giving up my sources but never bothered retracing my steps, which he could have easily done. I have yet to see a written rebuttal, and I don't expect to, because a careful search through press reports shows unambiguously that estimates for huge numbers of fatalities came originally from the Bosnian government without documentation; journalists repeated them without corroboration, or even attribution, until the charges stuck. Reporters covering the Yugoslav war, as NPR's Sylvia Poggioli put it (*Nieman Reports,* Fall 1993), "have been better at pulling emotional strings than at analyzing facts."

8　　Much of the early war was fought not on the battlefield but through high-powered (and high-priced) lobbying firms. Since late 1992 there has also been a splendidly effective volunteer army of journalists, think-tank analysts, Capitol Hill staff and administration hawks pushing the Bosnian, and secondarily Croatian, causes. The mainstream establishment couldn't bring itself to say "We don't know." To question Washington's bias is taboo, as William Maynes, the editor of *Foreign Policy,* found out when he published such a critique. The Serbs, unlike the Croats and Muslims, had little understanding of the propaganda war and, without patrons to guide them, quickly lost it without firing a shot.

9   The result is that everywhere that counts in America, it is almost impossible to be too anti-Serb. And if you accept the premise that the Serbs are wholly evil, two patently false corollaries emerge: There can be no moral equivalence between Serb-perpetrated atrocities and others, and it's all right to give superficial attention to Croat and Muslim crimes. While "ethnic cleansing," deaths and atrocities are not equally distributed among the three sides, each group rightly feels it has suffered enormously. Although the Serbs started as the bloodier side and were responsible for the most atrocities, they make up the largest share of recent victims and may be the most vulnerable potential victims. The Croats and Muslims have perpetrated equally horrific, albeit fewer and less systematic, atrocities.

10   But if the United States gives the Croats and Muslims the wherewithal to exact further tribal justice, they will. For proof, look at the Croats' scorched-earth practices regarding land they're supposed to hand over to the Serbs under the Dayton agreement, or their refusal to deliver indicted war criminals to the International War Crimes Tribunal in The Hague. And the top echelon of Muslim leaders, deeply penetrated by radical Islamist elements from Iran, continues to talk to its domestic constituency of prolonged warfare.

11   Since leaving government I've worked as a writer and consultant, focusing on Balkan issues. I got to know the senior leadership of Croatia and Bosnia fairly well, and as time went by I found many were neither honest nor competent; and many others were driven by pathological nationalism (Croatian Defense Minister Gojko Susak, for example, a former Canadian pizza king).

12   In December 1992 in Zagreb, I spoke at length with Bosnian President Alija Izetbegovic, who had minutes earlier come out of a meeting with Croatian President Franjo Tudjman, Lord Owen and Cyrus Vance (then the European Community and U.N. mediators, respectively). He told me he had just been forced to make the most difficult decision of his life: to negotiate directly for the first time with the Bosnian Serb leader Radovan Karadzic. Izetbegovic was clearly exhausted and anguished over his decision; as we talked he kept wondering aloud whether he'd done the right thing. I said that by agreeing to negotiate he had inexorably set the logic for a compromise that satisfied the Bosnian Serbs' most important claims. Izetbegovic replied he wasn't interested in compromise, he merely wanted to get out from under Western pressure.

13   I saw this attitude more starkly the last time we talked, in December 1993 in Sarajevo. Izetbegovic kept going over the pros and cons of his options, but ruled out taking a strong stand against Western mediators because he "didn't want to be seen by history as the spoiler" of an agreement. His intention seemed to be to pretend to go along with negotiations while continuing the

war. Never, in the course of those conversations or several others we had in Washington, did he voice doubts about the cost of the war to the Bosnian people. In this one certainty amid his otherwise incessant vacillation he has been consistent. Confirming this aspect of the man, *The New York Times,* reporting on the Dayton talks, noted American negotiators' amazement that Izetbegovic seemed to think war was more important than peace and reconstruction.

[14]   From the beginning, the United States should have engaged seriously in diplomacy; in particular, U.S. support for European efforts in the spring of 1992 might have prevented war. That March, the three factions had agreed to a plan similar to the Dayton agreement. Unfortunately, Izetbegovic reneged on his word after encouragement from U.S. Ambassador Warren Zimmermann, and the deal fell apart. Two weeks later U.S. and European recognition of Bosnia triggered the war.

[15]   I've often been asked at what point I changed my mind. But it wasn't ever so simple—I had no conversion. Rather, it was a cumulative process. As mistrustful as I was of the Serbs generally, and aware of their culpability for the war, nevertheless I began to feel some sympathy for the political dilemma they faced in the former Yugoslavia. Their search for elemental justice, however criminal their tactics, should have been considered. To be evenhanded, Washington should have treated in a procedurally equal way all the factions' claims to self-determination. It goes beyond a consideration of power balances. American interests, as I understand them, flow from our philosophical support for local political legitimacy; we should not be in the business of imposing arbitrary solutions from above.

[16]   "Slippery slope" and "tar baby" arguments blinded George Bush's team to the harm done by America in not exercising diplomatic leadership. They failed to admit, until the spring of 1992, that Europe couldn't pick up the slack; even so, the United States didn't directly participate in international mediation efforts until the first London Conference that August. By then, however, Bush and his Secretary of State, James Baker, had used such heated rhetoric about the principles at stake (rhetoric I helped write) that it wasn't possible to seize pragmatic solutions and throw the rhetoric overboard without damaging American prestige. But it wasn't possible to act on the rhetoric unless the United States was prepared to use force and escalate to whatever level was necessary to achieve our stated goals. Whether the American public was more prepared then than it is now to become engaged is not so clear, but leadership by the Bush Administration could have galvanized support. Its willingness to drift was the heart of the problem.

[17]   President Bush thus anchored the United States in a totally irresponsible position, which President Clinton uncritically adopted. Indeed, the legacy of rhetorical excess has carried over to undermine the Dayton agreement. By

granting U.S. forces authority (without requiring its use) to conduct an expansive mission covering everything under the sun, the Clinton Administration cannot then define in precise terms what the mission is—the yardstick for success or failure—and instead speaks vaguely of a one-year time limit. The U.S. army of occupation has an exit date, but no exit strategy. Instead of overdetermining the outcome of negotiations by promising too much, the United States should have continued negotiations until the parties themselves agreed to a settlement that was largely self-enforcing.

18   When I started on the Balkan desk I quickly became convinced by the strong consensus among intelligence analysts that recognition would worsen problems in Croatia and bring war in Bosnia. I went so far as to explore, with a senior C.I.A. Balkan analyst, possible land and population swaps in Bosnia that might reduce conflict before recognition. Once the United States recognized Bosnia, however, I wrongly thought the commitment implied by that decision—the most basic commitment the conservative state system can make—superseded objections because it required the people of the former Yugoslavia to play by our rules.

19   Reflecting on my mistaken judgment, I've often thought of the *Iliad's* deities, who knew better, when tipping the scales of the Trojan war, than to try to change the behavior of human warriors. It's arrogant to assume Americans can resolve all others' conflicts with a result that is guaranteed to be democratic. If we tip the scales enough to make them stop fighting—and we can—they'll continue with their own political evolution.

20   Recognition of Yugoslavia's successor states was the taproot of European and American policy failure. We had not thought through principles of self-determination; instead, Western governments recognized Bosnia as a way to punish the Serbs because we believed they were guilty of aggression. In a vicious circle, recognition then put off-limits the issues that caused the war in the first place because it automatically defined one side as an international aggressor, subject to further punishment. It also violated centuries of international legal tradition not to recognize separatist bodies in a civil war until the dust clears. (Actually, there may be fewer reasons to worry about the consequences of admitting a mistake than there are principled reasons to avoid such a mangled precedent for the next case of international intervention in a major civil war.)

21   The Clinton team correctly realized in mid-1995 that unless recognition was amended somehow, the problems of self-determination in the former Yugoslavia couldn't be fully addressed. Since withdrawing recognition was too politically costly, the Administration accepted de facto partition. Officials erred, though, in believing that the implications of Bosnia's sovereign status still make a good justification for beating up on the Serbs. I believe, to the contrary, that ephemeral larger interests allegedly associated with recognition pale in importance beside the real suffering in the region and the useless

deaths we will incur as we try to impose an unwelcome settlement. American objectives should be limited simply to ending the war, using minimal force as required. We have missed the opportunity to negotiate an inherently more stable agreement. Ideally, a European ground force of 20,000–30,000, backed by American air power and having robust rules of engagement but without a hidden nation-building mission, could police the confrontation lines of a genuine cease-fire, which the parties could agree to without international coercion. Intervention on other grounds predisposes us to take sides and (unintentionally) subsidize the very same horrors we condemn.

22   Tom Gjelten of NPR once remarked to me that it's hard to make sense of the Yugoslav war because everyone is seen as having vested interest, or is accused of having one. For intellectuals who believe they influence policy, those vested interests have until now been affected less by events in the former Yugoslavia than by wanting to stand on the right side—for truth, justice and so forth. The American intellectual establishment, indeed, has lost its collective head over imperialistic panaceas, putting itself squarely at odds with the vast majority of public opinion. When there are questions about that kind of vested interest, people don't really respond in the sophisticated way Gjelten meant, but instead turn Bosnia into a foreign policy Rorschach test. I think—and I hate to admit this—the real story as far as the public debate is concerned has been mainly about popular illusions and ordinary human incompetence at learning foreign politics, a far cry from the notion that Bosnia is the moral proving ground of my generation. Government officials must now think clearly for American troops to have the best chance of getting out of the Balkans safely.

1996

Reacting and Writing

Which of the theoretical positions taken by Cicero, Machiavelli, and Tolstoy seems most convincing? Which seems most relevant to the debate about the United States and its involvement in world affairs? Can you use one of the historical debates to illustrate the points made by Cicero, Machiavelli, or Tolstoy? What connections do you see among these applications of general political principles?

Decide which side you take in one of the debates raised here and write an argument trying to convince your audience that your side is preferable. Be clear about whether you see the issue as moral, practical, or both.

Are pieces like the last three in this symposium of interest only as the events they describe are taking place, or can their positions and techniques be generalized to transcend their immediate context? Why is it that some arguments can and some can't? That is, the Peloponnesian Wars are ancient history, and the Napoleonic Wars are long since over, but modern writers still refer to the arguments made by Thucydides and Tolstoy? Why? Do events subsequent to the publication of this book seem to bear out the arguments made here? How do these events affect your assessment of the lasting value of these contemporary pieces?

Suggestions for Further Reading

The books on this list are readily available either as paperbacks or in academic libraries. You can find full references in *Books in Print* or in the catalogue of your library. Our principle of selection was simply to recommend a variety of works that we have found useful for teaching and learning about how arguments work.

I. SOME WORKS FROM WHICH WE HAVE TAKEN SELECTIONS

Arendt, Hannah. *Eichmann in Jerusalem*
Austen, Jane. *Pride and Prejudice*
Chaucer, Geoffrey. *The Canterbury Tales*
Cicero, Marcus Tullius. *Political Speeches*
Darwin, Charles. *Origin of Species*
Dillard, Annie. *Teaching a Stone to Talk*
Fisher, M. F. K. *The Art of Eating*
Homer. *The Iliad*
Ibsen, Henrick. *Enemy of the People*
Kingston, Maxine Hong. *The Woman Warrior*
Laclos, Choderlos de. *Les Liaisons Dangereuses*
Mill, John Stuart. *On Liberty*
Plato. *The Republic*
Rich, Adrienne. *On Lies, Secrets, and Silence*
Sandburg, Carl. *Abraham Lincoln*
Shakespeare, William. *Julius Caesar*
Soto, Gary. *A Summer Life*
Sarton, May. *Journal of a Solitude*
Thucydides. *The Peloponnesian War*
Virgil. *The Aeneid*

Wilbur, Richard. *New and Collected Poems*
Woolf, Virginia. *A Room of One's Own*

II. FURTHER READING

Abbey, Edward. *The Monkey Wrench Gang*
Atwood, Margaret. *The Handmaid's Tale*
Augustine of Hippo. *Confessions*
de Beauvoir, Simone. *The Second Sex*
Booth, Wayne. *Modern Dogma and the Rhetoric of Assent*
Burke, Edmund. *Reflections on the Revolution in France*
Carlyle, Thomas. *Heroes and Hero Worship*
Ehrenreich, Barbara. *The Worst Years of Our Lives*
Frith, Simon. *Sound Effects: Youth, Leisure and the Politics of Rock 'n' Roll*
Harvey, William. *On the Motion of the Heart*
Heilbroner, Robert. *An Inquiry into the Human Prospect*
Hume, David. *Enquiry Concerning Human Understanding*
Keller, Evelyn Fox. *Reflections on Science and Gender*
Kozol, Jonathan. *Savage Inequalities*
Lewis, C. S. *The Problem of Pain*
Marx, Karl. *The Communist Manifesto*
Milosz, Czeslaw. *Visions from San Francisco Bay*
Momaday, Scott. *The Way to Rainy Mountain*
Naipaul, V. S. *Among the Believers*
Newman, John Henry. *The Idea of a University*
Rodriguez, Richard. *Hunger of Memory*
Rousseau, Jean Jacques. *Discourses*
Solzhenitsyn, Aleksandr. *Warning to the West*
Sontag, Susan. *AIDS and Its Metaphors*
Steele, Shelby. *The Content of Our Characters*
Veblen, Thorstein. *Theory of the Leisure Class*
Warren, Robert Penn. *All the King's Men*
Wideman, John Edgar. *Brothers and Keepers*

CREDITS *(continued from page ii)*

HANNAH ARENDT, "Epilogue," from *Eichmann in Jerusalem* by Hannah Arendt. Copyright © 1963, 1964 by Hannah Arendt. Used by permission of Viking Penguin, a division of Penguin Books USA Inc.

SAINT AUGUSTINE, from *City of God,* translated by Henry Bettenson (Penguin Classics, 1972). Translation copyright © Henry Bettenson, 1972.

MARGARET CULKIN BANNING, "Letters I and II" from *Letters to Susan.* Copyright 1934 by Margaret Culkin Banning. Copyright renewed © 1961 by Margaret Culkin Banning. Reprinted by permission of Brandt & Brandt Literary Agents, Inc.

IMAMU AMIRI BARAKA (Leroi Jones), "Young Soul," from *Black Magic.* Reprinted by permission of Sterling Lord Literistic, Inc. Copyright © 1975 Amiri Baraka.

BRIGID BROPHY, "The Menace of Nature." Reprinted by permission of Sir Michael Levey.

PAT BUCHANAN, "A New Nationalism," from *The Wanderer,* March 15, 1990. Reprinted with permission of Tribune Media Services.

ALSTON CHASE, "Wolf Reintroduction an Ecological Crap-shoot," *Bozeman Daily Chronicle,* January 25, 1995. By permission of Alston Chase and Creators Syndicate.

GEOFFREY CHAUCER, "The Wife of Bath's Prologue and Tale," translated by John K. Bollard. Reprinted by permission of the translator.

MARCUS TULLIUS CICERO, "The Example of Regulus," from *Cicero: De Officiis/On Duties,* translated by Edinger, Harry D., © 1974. Reprinted by permission of Prentice-Hall, Inc., Upper Saddle River, NJ.

DAVID DENBY, "How the West Was Lost." Copyright © 1990 K-III Magazine Corporation. All rights reserved. Reprinted with the permission of *New York* Magazine.

JOAN DIDION, "Georgia O'Keeffe," from *The White Album* by Joan Didion. Copyright © 1979 by Joan Didion. Reprinted by permission of Farrar, Straus & Giroux, Inc.

ANNIE DILLARD, "Total Eclipse," from *Teaching a Stone to Talk* by Annie Dillard. Copyright © 1982 by Annie Dillard. Reprinted by permission of HarperCollins Publishers, Inc.

MICHAEL DORRIS, "Indians in Aspic," *The New York Times,* February 24, 1991. Copyright © 1991 by The New York Times Co. Reprinted by permission.

LARS EIGHNER, "On Dumpster Diving," from *Travels with Lizbeth* by Lars Eighner. Copyright © 1993 by Lars Eighner. Reprinted with permission of St. Martin's Press, Incorporated.

EURIPIDES, "Jason Explains," excerpt from *Medea,* from *The Complete Greek Tragedies,* eds. David Grene and Richmond Lattimore. Translated by Rex Warner. Reprinted courtesy of the Estate of Rex Warner and the Bodley Head (London: Random Century Group).

DEBORAH FALLOWS, "Why Mothers Should Stay Home," from *The Washington Monthly,* January 1982. Reprinted with permission from *The Washington Monthly.* Copyright by The Washington Monthly Company, 1611 Connecticut Ave., N. W., Washington, D.C. 20009 (202) 462–0128.

M. F. K. FISHER, "Foreword" and "The Measure of My Powers" from *The Gastronomical Me.* Reprinted with permission of Macmillan General Reference USA, a Division of Simon & Schuster, from *The Art of Eating* by M. F. K. Fisher. Copyright 1943, and renewed © 1971, by M. F. K. Fisher.

F. SCOTT FITZGERALD, "Letter to Scottie," and SCOTTIE FITZGERALD LANAHAN, "My Father's Letters." Reprinted with permission of Scribner, a Division of Simon & Schuster, from *F. Scott Fitzgerald: Letters to His Daughter,* edited by Andrew Turnbull. Copyright © 1963, 1965 by Frances Scott Fitzgerald Lanahan. Copyright renewed 1991 by Joanne J. Turnbull, Joanne T. Turnbull, Frances L. Turnbull, and Eleanor Lanahan, Matthew J. Bruccoli, Samuel J. Lanahan, Sr., Trustees u/a dated 7/3/75, created by Frances Scott Fitzgerald Smith.

E. M. FORSTER, "Not Listening to Music," from *Two Cheers for Democracy,* copyright 1939 and renewed 1967 by E. M. Forster, reprinted by permission of Harcourt Brace & Company.

SIGMUND FREUD, from *Civilization and Its Discontents,* translated by James Strachey. Translation copyright © 1961 by James Strachey, renewed 1989 by Alix Strachey. Reprinted by permission of W. W. Norton & Company, Inc.

CARLOS FUENTES, "High Noon in Latin America." First published in *Vanity Fair.* Copyright © 1983 by Carlos Fuentes. All rights reserved. Reprinted by permission of Brandt & Brandt Literary Agents, Inc.

600

GENESIS 2:1–10, from the Revised Standard Version of the Bible, copyright 1946, 1952, 1971 by the Division of Christian Education of the National Council of the Churches of Christ in the USA. Used by permission.

MICHAEL GORRA, "Learning to Hear the Small, Soft Voices," *The New York Times Magazine,* May 1, 1988. Copyright © 1988 The New York Times Co. Reprinted by permission.

STEPHEN J. GOULD, "Genesis vs. Geology," from *The Atlantic Monthly,* September 1982. Reprinted by permission of the author.

BRENT HARTINGER, "A Case for Gay Marriage," *Commonweal,* November 22, 1991. © 1991 Commonweal Foundation.

NAT HENTOFF, "'Speech Codes' on the Campus and Problems of Free Speech," from *Dissent,* Fall 1991. Reprinted by permission of the author.

ADOLF HITLER, "On Propaganda." Excerpt from *Mein Kampf* by Adolf Hitler, translated by Ralph Manheim. Copyright © 1943, renewed 1971 by Houghton Mifflin Company. Reprinted by permission of Houghton Mifflin Company. All rights reserved.

HOMER, "The Embassy to Achilles," from *The Iliad,* translated by Richmond Lattimore. Chicago: University of Chicago Press, 1951. Copyright 1951 by the University of Chicago. Reprinted by permission of the publisher.

ZORA NEALE HURSTON, "How It Feels to Be Colored Me," from *I Love Myself When I Am Laughing.* Copyright 1979 by the Estate of Zora Neale Hurston. Reprinted by permission of Lucy Ann Hurston.

PAULINE KAEL, "Dances With Wolves," from *For Keeps* by Pauline Kael. Copyright © 1994 by Pauline Kael. Used by permission of Dutton Signet, a division of Penguin Books USA Inc.

GEORGE KENNEY, "Steering Clear of the Balkan Shoals," *The Nation,* January 8/15, 1996. Reprinted with permission from *The Nation* magazine. © The Nation Company, L. P.

WILLIAM KILPATRICK, "Why Johnnny Can't Tell Right from Wrong." Reprinted with the permission of Simon & Schuster from *Why Johnny Can't Tell Right from Wrong* by William Kilpatrick. Copyright © 1992 by William Kilpatrick.

MARTIN LUTHER KING, JR., "Letter from Birmingham Jail," from *Why We Can't Wait* by Martin Luther King, Jr. Reprinted by arrangement with The Heirs to the Estate of Martin Luther King, Jr., c/o Writers House, Inc. as agent for the proprietor. Copyright 1963 by Martin Luther King, Jr., copyright renewed 1991 by Coretta Scott King.

MAXINE HONG KINGSTON, "No Name Woman." From *The Woman Warrior* by Maxine Hong Kingston. Copyright © 1975, 1976 by Maxine Hong Kingston. Reprinted by permission of Alfred A. Knopf, Inc.

ROBIN LAKOFF, "Tag Questions," from *You Are What You Say.* Reprinted by permission of the author.

CHARLES F. LAWRENCE III, "On Racist Speech," from *The Chronicle of Higher Education,* October 25, 1989. Reprinted by permission of the author.

A. J. LIEBLING, "Ahab and Nemesis," from *The Sweet Science* by A. J. Liebling. Copyright 1951, 1952, 1953, 1954, 1955, 1956 by A. J. Liebling. Copyright renewed © 1981, 1982, 1983, 1984 by Norma Stonehill. Used by permission of Viking Penguin, a division of Penguin Books USA Inc. First published in *The New Yorker,* October 8, 1955.

ENRIQUE "HANK" LÓPEZ, "Back to Bachimba." Reprinted by permission of *American Heritage* Magazine, a division of Forbes, Inc. © Forbes, Inc., 1967.

MARK, Gospel of Mark 411–20 from the Revised Standard Version of the Bible, copyright 1946, 1952, 1971 by the Division of Christian Education of the National Council of the Churches of Christ in the USA. Used by permission.

PAULE MARSHALL, "From the Poets in the Kitchen." Reprinted, by permission, from Paule Marshall, "The Making of the Writer: From the Poets in the Kitchen, *Reena and Other Stories* (New York: The Feminist Press at The City University of New York, 1983), pp. 3–12. © 1983 Paule Marshall. All rights reserved.

DENNIS O'BRIEN, "Against Gay Marriage," *Commonweal,* November 22, 1991. © 1991 Commonweal Foundation.

GEORGE ORWELL, "The Case for the Pigs." Excerpt from *Animal Farm* by George Orwell, copyright 1946 by Harcourt Brace & Company and renewed 1974 by Sonia Orwell, reprinted by permission of the publisher.

Author and Title Index